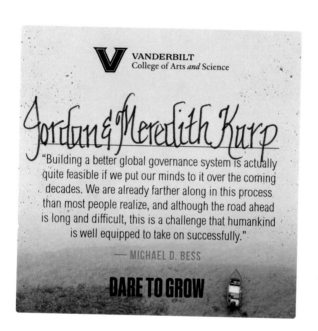

VANDERBILT
College of Arts *and* Science

Jordan & Meredith Karp

"Building a better global governance system is actually quite feasible if we put our minds to it over the coming decades. We are already farther along in this process than most people realize, and although the road ahead is long and difficult, this is a challenge that humankind is well equipped to take on successfully."

— MICHAEL D. BESS

DARE TO GROW

Michael Bess

PLANET IN PERIL

Written by an award-winning historian of science and technology, *Planet in Peril* describes the top four mega-dangers facing humankind – climate change, nuclear weapons, pandemics, and artificial intelligence. It outlines the solutions that have been tried, and analyzes why they have thus far fallen short. These four existential dangers present a special kind of challenge that urgently requires planet-level responses, yet today's international institutions have so far failed to meet this need. The book lays out a realistic pathway for gradually modifying the United Nations over the coming century so that it can become more effective at coordinating global solutions to humanity's problems. Neither optimistic nor pessimistic, but pragmatic and constructive, the book explores how to move past ideological polarization and global political fragmentation. Unafraid to take intellectual risks, *Planet in Peril* sketches a plausible roadmap toward a safer, more democratic future for us all.

Michael Bess is Chancellor's Professor of History at Vanderbilt University. He has been teaching award-winning courses on science, technology, environmentalism, and global catastrophic threats since 1989, and has written four other books on these topics. He has received fellowships from the Guggenheim Foundation, MacArthur Foundation, and National Human Genome Research Institute.

"The term 'existential threat' may be overused by those who explore global governance; but it undoubtedly describes climate change and pandemics, two of the four mega-dangers that preoccupy Michael Bess in *Planet in Peril*. It is hard to believe that international cooperation remains a tough sell in 2022. Imagine: global problems require global solutions! Bess spells out concrete, and hopefully doable, steps toward overcoming polarization and fragmentation. Let's hope he's right."

Thomas G. Weiss

"We are threatened by our own cleverness, and it is easy to get paranoid. This book, by one of our best historians of science and technology, offers a sane, balanced, and deeply informed look at the major threats, and lays out a rational way forward."

Donald Worster, author of *Shrinking the Earth* and
A Passion for Nature

"In *Planet in Peril*, Michael Bess brings his singular voice, intellectual courage, and good judgment to bear on the four mega-dangers facing humankind – climate change, nuclear weapons, pandemics, and artificial intelligence. He avoids the simplistic thinking that characterizes too much of the public debate on these issues and offers insightful, viable solutions. It is one of those rare books that is both a joy to read and a roadmap for solving daunting problems."

Michael Vandenbergh

PLANET IN PERIL

Humanity's Four Greatest Challenges and How We Can Overcome Them

Michael D. Bess

CAMBRIDGE
UNIVERSITY PRESS

CAMBRIDGE
UNIVERSITY PRESS

University Printing House, Cambridge CB2 8BS, United Kingdom

One Liberty Plaza, 20th Floor, New York, NY 10006, USA

477 Williamstown Road, Port Melbourne, VIC 3207, Australia

314–321, 3rd Floor, Plot 3, Splendor Forum, Jasola District Centre, New Delhi – 110025, India

103 Penang Road, #05–06/07, Visioncrest Commercial, Singapore 238467

Cambridge University Press is part of the University of Cambridge.

It furthers the University's mission by disseminating knowledge in the pursuit of education, learning, and research at the highest international levels of excellence.

www.cambridge.org
Information on this title: www.cambridge.org/9781009160339
DOI: 10.1017/9781009160315

© Michael D. Bess 2023

First published 2023

Printed in the United Kingdom by TJ Books Limited, Padstow Cornwall

A catalog record for this publication is available from the British Library.

ISBN 978-1-009-16033-9 Hardback

For Rina
when she was a little girl

Wachet auf! – ruft uns die Stimme.

(Sleepers, awaken! – the voice calls to us.)

J. S. Bach
Cantata BWV 140 (1731)

Contents

* * *

Fictional Vignettes

Acknowledgements

There is a very real sense in which this book is an extended reflection on the themes of all my previous books, so it follows that I have a veritable papyrus scroll of people to thank heartily for sharing their ideas and feedback with me over the years. These include my teachers in college and grad school, my colleagues, students, and teaching assistants at Vanderbilt, the scholars hailing from so many fields, whose work and conversations have enriched my thinking, and my friends outside academia, whose acute questions and comments have made me go back to the drawing board time and again, to better effect. Thank you all!

The research and writing for this book took place over many years and were funded in part by grants or fellowships from the J.S. Guggenheim Memorial Foundation, the American Council of Learned Societies, the National Human Genome Research Institute, and the Vanderbilt University College of Arts and Science. Their generous support made this work possible.

My research assistants have contributed in so many ways to this book: with painstaking research, meticulous editing, and above all with thoughtful feedback about ideas and arguments as we went along. I owe a great debt of gratitude to Taylor Matalon, Sebastian Lende, Danielle Picard, and Mark Grujic.

Some of my faculty colleagues read early drafts of this book and offered immensely helpful comments. I owe a drink (more than one!) and a mountain of thanks to Doug Fisher, Jonathan Gilligan, Joel Harrington, Geoff Macdonald, Ole Molvig, Danielle Picard, J. B. Ruhl, Tom Schwartz, Mike Vandenbergh, Frank Wcislo, and David Weintraub.

Six anonymous reviewers for Cambridge University Press, along with my editor, Matt Lloyd, sent back a total of fifteen single-spaced pages of comments and suggestions on the first draft, some of them literally going through the manuscript page by page with ideas and thoughts to contribute. These were among the most penetrating comments I've ever received on my scholarship, causing me to rethink large swaths of the argument, and sharpening the fine-grained details in countless ways. Working with the Cambridge editorial, production, and marketing teams – Matt Lloyd, Sarah Lambert, Natasha Whelan, Maddy Coles, Lindsay Nightingale, Phyllis van Reenen – has been a pleasurable and rewarding experience from start to finish. My fervent thanks to all of you!

My literary agent, Mildred Marmur, has been working with me for more than 35 years now. Her wise counsel and sweeping knowledge of the publishing world, as well as her keen insights on the content of my work, have proved invaluable again and again. Milly, you're the best!

I'm so moved by the devoted service of the people around the world who responded to the challenge of helping others during the pandemic, month after month, when it was dangerous and relentless and demoralizing. Nurses, doctors, medical researchers, first responders, the myriad other essential workers – thank you!

"So how's the book coming along?" My friends and extended family have occasionally made the mistake of asking this question, and I'm grateful for their forbearance in dealing with the avalanche of global catastrophes that I promptly unleashed on them.

To my family – Kimberly, Natalie, and Sebastian – well, you've been the unwitting companions of this project from the start. You're at the heart of it all.

1

Introduction

E VERYTHING WAS FINALLY IN PLACE. The scientists stood in their observation bunker in the Alamogordo desert, staring through the lenses of their protective glasses at the tower five miles away where the world's first atomic device awaited an electric pulse for detonation. It was 5:29 a.m. on July 16, 1945.

The previous evening, one of the smartest persons in the world had decided it was time to lighten things up a bit. Enrico Fermi glanced round at his fellow scientists and said, in his heavy Italian accent, "Now, let's make a bet whether the atmosphere will be set on fire by this test."[1] He wondered aloud whether this would incinerate only New Mexico or spread to the entire planet. Laughter followed, some of it nervous. A few people took him up on it.

In actual fact, they had seriously examined this possibility three years earlier. The Nobel laureate Hans Bethe later recalled how it went.

BETHE: So one day at Berkeley – we were a very small group, maybe eight physicists or so – one day Teller came to the office and said, "Well, what would happen to the air if an atomic bomb were exploded in the air? ... There's nitrogen in the air, and you can have a nuclear reaction in which two nitrogen nuclei collide and become oxygen plus carbon, and in this process you set free a lot of energy. Couldn't that happen?" And that caused great excitement.

INTERVIEWER: This is in '42?

BETHE: '42. Oppenheimer got quite excited and said, "That's a terrible possibility," and he went to his superior, who was Arthur Compton, the director of the Chicago Laboratory, and told him that. Well, I sat down and looked at the problem, about whether two nitrogen nuclei could penetrate each other and make that nuclear reaction, and I found that it was just incredibly unlikely ... Teller at Los Alamos put a very good calculator on this problem, [Emil] Konopinski, who was an expert on weak interactors, and Konopinski together with [inaudible] showed that it

1

was incredibly impossible to set the hydrogen, to set the atmosphere on fire. They wrote one or two very good papers on it, and that put the question really at rest. They showed in great detail why it is impossible.

INTERVIEWER: I think what makes it such a fascinating episode ... is the idea of doing a calculation on which possibly could rest the fate of the world. [laughter]

BETHE: Right, right.

INTERVIEWER: That's obviously an extraordinary kind of calculation to do. Did you have any ... Did you even think about that issue when you saw the Trinity test?

BETHE: No.

INTERVIEWER: You were absolutely –

BETHE: Yes.

INTERVIEWER: – completely certain.

BETHE: Yes. The one thing in my mind was that maybe the initiator would not work because I had a lot to do with its design, and that the whole thing would be a fizzle because the initiator wasn't working. No, it never occurred to me that it would set the atmosphere on fire.

INTERVIEWER: In a way, this is like a great test of one's belief –

BETHE: In science. [laughter][2]

The firing sequence for the atomic test was automated, but four individuals along the chain of command had been given kill switches to activate if anything went wrong. The final-stage knife switch rested in the hands of a 25-year-old chemist named Donald Hornig:

> I don't think I have ever been keyed up as I was during those final seconds ... I kept telling myself "the least flicker of that needle and you have to act." It kept on coming down to zero. I kept saying, "Your reaction time is about half a second and you can't relax for even a fraction of a second." ... My eyes were glued on the dial and my hand was on the switch. I could hear the timer counting ... three ... two ... one. The needle fell to zero.[3]

The Harvard scientist James Conant, one of the Manhattan Project's overseers, squinted through his protective glasses from the nearby bunker.

> Then came a burst of white light that seemed to fill the sky and seemed to last for seconds. I had expected a relatively quick and bright flash. The enormity of the light quite stunned me. My instantaneous reaction was that something had gone wrong and that the thermal nuclear transformation of the atmosphere, once discussed as a possibility and jokingly referred to minutes earlier, had actually occurred.[4]

The international team of scientists had also taken bets among themselves about what sort of bang the explosion would yield. No one had ever built a device like this before, so they couldn't be sure. The bets ranged from zero (a dud) to 45 kilotons (a kiloton is equivalent to two million pounds of TNT). Isidor Rabi, a physicist who arrived late for the betting pool, took the last remaining option by default: 18 kilotons. He won. The actual Trinity explosion weighed in at 22.1 kilotons.

PLANETARY DANGERS, PLANETARY STRATEGIES

Accidentally setting the atmosphere on fire: this is a book about the special kind of wager we are making when we create technologies that put the survival of humankind at risk. Four kinds of inventions fall into this category, and although they each spring from very different arenas of scientific research, they share similar properties: they are radical game-changers, exceptionally powerful at doing what they do; they have the potential to bring tremendous benefit as well as harm into human affairs; and they are devilishly hard to control, in two distinct ways. It's difficult to guarantee their proper functioning, from a technical point of view; and it's even harder to govern the political, economic, and military processes through which they are brought into the world and put to use. Their awesome power makes it hard to resist pursuing them; yet if we handle them improperly they may destroy us all.

The first of these, fossil-fuel-based technology, dates back 200 years to the early 1800s: it was one of the factors that launched the Industrial Revolution. The second, nuclear technology, was born on that July morning near the end of World War II. The other two are more recent inventions, still far from realizing the full scope of their promise. Synthetic biology aims to make new life forms from scratch, creating microorganisms that serve human welfare in unprecedented ways – yet it also presents us with the possibility of hideous bioweapons or bioengineered pandemics. Artificial intelligence (AI) seeks to endow our machines with one of the most valuable qualities any creature possesses: the ability to figure things out for itself and bring genuine innovation into the world. Yet if advanced AI escapes human control, or is weaponized for military use, it too could bring down catastrophic consequences on its makers.

These four technologies create planet-level dangers that can only be addressed effectively with planet-level solutions. Precisely because they are so powerful, human beings compete with each other to obtain them, racing frantically to develop them to ever more impressive levels of potency. And wherever the logic of high-stakes competition prevails, the logics of caution, transparency, and cooperation tend to take a back seat. Despite the grievous risks inherent in these inventions, efforts to regulate or rein in their development have failed, under the same recurring refrain: "If we don't build these things and tap their power, someone else will beat us to it and we'll be at the mercy of the winners. So damn the torpedoes and full steam ahead!"

In this book I survey the promise and dangers of these four technologies, as well as the strategies proposed by experts in each field for bringing them under better systems of control. The main brunt of my argument focuses on the international dimension, where every sensible solution tends to fail because of the dog-eat-dog competition that prevails in the global arena. I devote a lot of thought to this problem because it tends to be the aspect that gets shortest shrift in most other discussions about controlling mega-dangerous technologies. The reason is simple: most authors tacitly assume that the present-day system of international relations – separate sovereign nations fending for themselves in the win–lose game of geopolitics – will continue to hold sway over the coming centuries. My analysis takes a quite different tack. I maintain that the separateness of nations is already being blurred in fundamental ways by the economic and technological forces of globalization: we live in a world of deepening interdependence and shared vulnerabilities. Operating on this premise, I conclude that our best shot at tackling these planet-scale problems is to gradually build a comprehensive framework of global cooperation and collective security over the next century.

In much of the expert literature, creating such a framework tends to be dismissed as a utopian fantasy. "Maybe a millennium from now, if we're very lucky" – this is the assumption. But building a better global governance system is actually quite feasible if we put our minds to it over the coming decades. I argue that we are already farther along in this process than most people realize, and that although the road ahead is long and difficult, this is a challenge that humankind is well equipped to take on successfully.

The key to my approach lies in the idea of purposeful, incremental change. Some of the most profound transformations of the modern era have come about gradually, through the dogged efforts of successive generations of committed individuals. The realm of the possible is not a stable place: it changes from decade to decade, as people's habits, expectations, and assumptions evolve. Technological capabilities that seemed fanciful two centuries ago – such as conversing casually with someone on the other side of the planet – became conceivable a century ago, then a reality 50 years ago.

Societal achievements deemed utopian in 1850 – such as true equality for women – became legally the norm in recent decades and are on their way to becoming a socioeconomic reality in the coming years. In 1950 the Western European nations were reeling from the latest round of blood-drenched conflict that had just convulsed their continent, following centuries of rivalry, wars, and mutual distrust; yet four decades later these same nations were signing the Maastricht Treaty, binding themselves together in a partial supranational union that rendered war among them about as likely as armed aggression between the United States and Canada. Small, purpose-driven changes are like compound interest in this sense: they can accumulate powerfully over time, yielding quietly revolutionary results.

Some would argue that the effort to envision a full-fledged system of global governance is a waste of time, and that we are better served by focusing on tangible measures that humankind can feasibly adopt within the constraints of today's international system. My response is that it's helpful to do *both* these things: to work out the key practical dimensions of the long-term goal, while also offering intermediate steps that can help us mitigate these mega-dangers today. Over the coming decades, we are more likely to make meaningful progress toward cooperative security if we have a relatively clear sense of the long-range principles and institutional arrangements we will ultimately need to realize.

This is how societal innovation emerges.[5] A few visionary individuals push the limits of normal behavior, eliciting frowns of surprise and disapproval from their contemporaries; time passes, and other plucky individuals join in; eventually more and more people climb on the bandwagon, adding to the critical mass of the disruptive trend; and gradually the novel behavior pattern stabilizes and becomes the new normal. (Even the original frowners usually join in at this point, claiming to have been on board all along.) After a while a different group of boundary-pushers invents yet another trailblazing behavior to go beyond norms in their own original way. Generation by generation, the alterations accumulate: problems that once baffled people are easily solved; institutions that were deemed utopian come unobtrusively into being; achievements that seemed fanciful to one's grandparents are now a daily routine.

At present, the idea of a vigorous, democratic United Nations (UN) coordinating the governance of the world's affairs strikes most people as a distant dream. But with each international crisis that humankind confronts and works through – with each planet-level problem that forces people to come up with new planet-level solutions – the boundaries of the possible shift slightly. To someone situated in the year 2075, a revitalized UN may no longer seem nearly as implausible as it does today; and to a citizen of the year 2150, many aspects of it may already be taken for granted as an accomplished fact.

As a historian, however, I know that human beings have a knack for not always doing what's in their best interest. It's quite possible that a deep political transformation will elude us over the coming decades, and that we'll reach the year 2150 saddled with roughly the same ramshackle international mechanisms operating today. Yet even this more muddled and precarious pathway can be trodden in relatively smart or stupid ways. There remain plenty of concrete interim solutions we can undertake to buy ourselves additional precious time. It may turn out that our species lacks the vision or the will to create an effective global government over the coming century or so; but we can still adopt plenty of sensible precautionary measures that boost our long-term chances of making it through in one piece.

UNCONTROLLED EXPONENTIAL PROCESSES

All four of these technologies exhibit an intriguing common feature: the potential for uncontrolled exponential growth. This quality sets them apart from more conventional technologies and lies at the root of what makes them so dangerous. The thermostat in my house is an autonomous machine, operating on its own to manage the ambient temperature; but it poses no big risk because it has no exponential properties in its functioning. A bacterial culture in a petri dish follows an exponential trajectory as its cells replicate and grow; but it's not problematic because its propagation is constrained by the nutrients provided by its human overseers. The Spanish flu virus of 1918–20, by contrast, exhibited strong elements of both exponential and autonomous functioning, and was limited only by the number of hosts it could contact and infect: this is why it killed 50 million people worldwide (far more than the carnage of World War I).

At first glance, fossil fuels would seem not to fit this description, since there is nothing inherently exponential about the way they work – but the *history* of their development does reveal an unmistakably exponential trajectory (see Figure 1.1).

People started using coal on a large scale in the mid-1800s, and the tapping of this novel power source helped incentivize the invention of a wide variety of new machines, whose rapid propagation in turn facilitated the accelerating development of petroleum and natural gas. Technological advance and energy innovation fed off each other in a self-reinforcing

6

Global direct primary energy consumption
Direct primary energy consumption does not take account of inefficiencies in fossil fuel production.

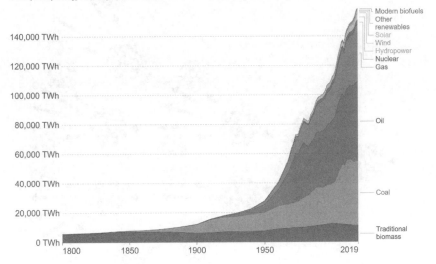

Figure 1.1 Global primary energy consumption, 1800–2019. The net growth of global energy consumption in the ten years between 2000 and 2010 (+35,000 terawatt hours) was the same as the net growth in the 50 years between 1910 and 1960. A terawatt hour is one trillion watt hours, about the same as the output of 1,600 of today's coal-fired power plants.[6]
Source: Vaclav Smil (2017) & BP Statistical Review of World Energy

spiral, and their development traced a steeply rising curve that grew dramatically over the course of the following century, with a particularly sharp inflection in the decades since 1945.[7] Much like the influenza of 1918, this exponentially rising process was limited only by the total quantity of fossil fuel resources available on the planet.

In a similar way, the chain reaction at the heart of nuclear devices is based on unleashing an exponential propagation of fission or fusion through a fuel medium (see Figure 1.2).

At the first step in the process, the nucleus of an atom of fuel material splits, releasing two neutrons that go on to strike up to two other nearby atoms, causing them to split in turn, and the exponential cycle is off and running: 2, 4, 8, 16, 32, and so on. With each splitting of an atom, a small amount of energy is released in the form of heat. Since the process propagates swiftly, reaching trillions of splitting atoms in a matter of microseconds, this results in a very large amount of heat energy accumulating in a small space. The energy expands outward, appearing to external observers as an explosion. A big one.

7

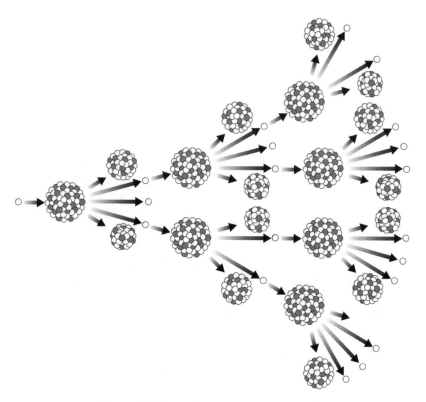

Figure 1.2 The nuclear fission chain reaction.[8]

Some of the most potent forms of synthetic biology operate in a similar fashion to naturally occurring pandemics: they rely on a small number of seed organisms designed to make an exponential number of copies of themselves by using materials from the surrounding environment. (See Figure 1.3.)

Harnessing the reproductive power of engineered microorganisms could allow humans to turn algae into biofuels, fungi into medicines, and toxic garbage into harmless sludge. Ideally, these synthetic life forms will remain limited in their capacity to self-propagate, either because they have been designed to stop replicating after a certain number of reproductive cycles, or because they are constrained by the particular forms of nutrients they have been designed to consume and transform. But if a laboratory error or unforeseen mutation allows them to escape containment – or if they are deliberately unleashed by malevolent actors – their runaway propagation could wreak grievous large-scale harm.

INTRODUCTION

**Cell growth and division
(Cell proliferation)**

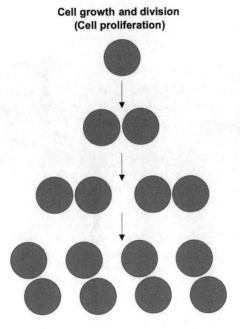

Figure 1.3 Cell growth process.[9]

The most impressive forms of AI will be self-modifying machines that learn about their environment as they interact with it, refining their own software and hardware as they go. Already today, such machines are being designed and built. One game-playing AI built by Google, for example, can translate its pattern-recognition, reinforcement learning, and strategy-development abilities from one game to another to another – without any human guidance or intervention. When presented with a new and unfamiliar game, it engages in increasingly sophisticated cycles of trial-and-error and achieves mastery at the game in a rapid spiral of self-improvement.[10] (See Figure 1.4.)

Today's self-improving machines are narrowly focused on specific tasks, but what will happen over the coming decades, as such machines become increasingly adept at performing a wide variety of different functions? What happens when the AI-controlled robot that drives your car can also trade stocks, play chess, diagnose your illness, assemble furniture, solve math problems, give you relationship advice, cook delicious meals, and pass high-level intelligence tests?[11] Such an all-purpose machine will presumably be able to modify its own software, rendering itself better attuned to achieving

9

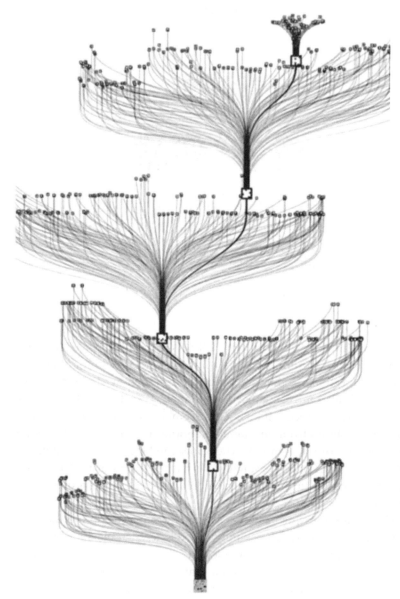

Figure 1.4 Small section of the combinatorial game tree in the game of Go, analyzed by Google's AlphaGo Zero.[12]

the goals given by its designers. Using the broad array of actuators and manipulators of its robot body, it will be able to modify its own movement algorithms and hardware, constantly optimizing its interactions with other physical objects. In short, it will have been given all the resources it needs to improve its "body" and "mind" over time – and self-improvement will be one of the prime directives inscribed into its motivational programming. What's to prevent it from launching a repeating cycle of escalating self-improvement, using its ever-growing powers to reconfigure itself over and over until it becomes unrecognizably different from its earlier designs? Some prominent AI researchers worry that humans could completely lose control over such self-evolving machines.

Equally worrisome is the prospect of AI as a military technology. In a world that's increasingly reliant on smart, automated systems – from the stock market to air traffic to the electrical grid – advanced AI will offer military officials the tantalizing gambits of cyberwarfare: a war that's over in a few minutes' time, as one nation's superior AI systems gain control over a rival's military and civilian infrastructure. This possibility – teams of AI machines and humans working together to wreak havoc – threatens to radically destabilize the military balance of the coming decades.[13]

Fossil fuels, nukes, synthetic biology, and advanced AI: the worrisome aspect, in all four cases, lies in the possibility of these powerful technologies acquiring a life of their own, yielding unforeseen or undesirable results. Each of these four inventions offers Promethean powers – with the potential for a Promethean cautionary tale wrapped inside.

IS THE DANGER REALLY THAT BAD?

To speak of existential risk in regard to any human technology might sound like hyperbole, but in fact it is not.[14] We can distinguish five levels of harm that might result from deliberate misuse or accidental malfunction in such devices, ranging from the "merely" disastrous to the genuinely apocalyptic.

1. Local disaster. Destruction of a city and its surrounding territory.
2. Cataclysm. Destruction of large swaths of a continent.
3. Return to Stone Age. Severe degradation of all human life on Earth.
4. Human extinction. Destruction of all human life on the planet.
5. Ecocide. Destruction of all biological life on the planet.

Synthetic biology and AI would probably be limited to damage at levels 1 through 4, but nuclear war or severe climate change could render the entire planet uninhabitable by most life forms for a long time.

The core challenge, with all these technologies, is how to reap the benefits they offer while keeping them firmly under control. Given how potentially dangerous they are, it's not enough simply to "minimize the risk" of their running amok. Even a small chance of their eluding our control is hard to justify, given that the outcome could well be the annihilation of everything we hold dear. Suppose for example that you were offered a shady business deal in which you gain a million dollars if you win, but you and your family will all be killed if you lose. Everything depends, of course, on your assessment of the underlying odds. If your chance of losing is one in a trillion, you might be willing to roll the dice for this deal. But if the odds of losing are closer to one in 20, most people would probably say "No thanks." The benefit is certainly tantalizing, but there's a real chance that things will go the wrong way and bring on a familial apocalypse. Here the risk–benefit ratio has moved closer to Russian roulette territory – a place where rational persons refuse to go.[15]

No one can know with any precision, of course, what the odds are for a catastrophe to result from one of these four high-impact technologies over the coming century. The experts in these fields vary widely in their assessments, ranging from "Relax, we've got this covered" to "Tornado coming, batten down the hatches." But if the odds appear closer to one-in-a-hundred rather than one-in-a-trillion, common sense dictates that humankind should proceed with a special kind of caution in developing such inventions.

For climate change and nukes, of course, it's already too late: the genie is out of the bottle. The overwhelming majority of climate scientists today concur in their assessment of the Earth's situation: greenhouse gases released by humans since the Industrial Revolution are accumulating in the atmosphere, causing a steady rise in average global temperatures.[16] As the planet warms, one degree at a time over the coming decades, the resultant climate change will increasingly disrupt our lives. Estimates of the threat range across a spectrum: on the "mild" end, we can expect drought, famines, flooded coastal cities, and forced migrations, while at the other end the experts warn of vast portions of the planet becoming unfit for human life. Worse still, once we cross certain thresholds or tipping points, the planet's climate dynamics could enter a self-reinforcing cycle in which the warming accelerates on its own, and the window for human preventive action will close. The problem is urgent, but humankind thus far has been tragically feckless in its response.[17]

As for the nukes, we've managed to live with them for eight decades so far without triggering a holocaust. Partly this stems from the nature of these technologies themselves: they are made from rare materials, require large industrial facilities for enrichment to weapons-grade levels, and leave a tell-tale radioactive signature that renders them relatively easy to locate. The missiles on which they ride require a human being's decision before they are launched. Most importantly, they have been monopolized by nation-states whose behavior is subject to the rational calculus of mutually assured destruction. Taken together, these factors have allowed humankind to keep these machines from being unleashed. So far. But it's misleading to use the word "control" in characterizing our relationship with nukes. When one learns how hair-raisingly close to large-scale missile launch the world has come on several well-documented occasions – whether through machine malfunction, human error, or political miscalculation – one faces a sobering reality. Any species that voluntarily submits itself to technologies of mutual suicide, decade after decade, is playing a game that defies the logic of prudence or even sanity. Yet we just keep rolling those dice.

Synthetic biology and multipurpose AI are worrisome for a quite different reason. Once the scientific challenges of creating them have been surmounted, they will differ from nukes in one key regard: they won't be nearly as hard to manufacture, conceal, or deploy. Their development will most likely be carried out in a large number of laboratories and factories throughout the world, overseen by actors ranging from national governments to university officials to corporate executives to independent scientists. Access to these "democratized" technologies will therefore be much more widespread and volatile than has been the case with nukes, and this will render the problem of controlling them far harder.

In past centuries, the manipulation of deadly microorganisms could only be undertaken by a small number of highly trained, well-funded, and carefully screened individuals worldwide. Today we are rushing headlong into a very different world in which large numbers of persons throughout the planet will have access to the powerful tools of synthetic biology. The Harvard biologist George Church, one of the founders of the field, is bluntly honest in appraising the challenge facing us:

> For all the benefits it promises, synthetic biology is potentially more dangerous than chemical or nuclear weaponry, since organisms can self-replicate, spread rapidly throughout the world, and mutate and evolve on their own. But as challenging as it might be to make synthetic biology research safe and secure within an institutional framework such as a university, industrial, or government lab, matters take a turn for the worse with the prospect of "biohackers," lone agents or groups of untrained amateurs, working clandestinely, or even openly, with

biological systems that have been intentionally made easy to engineer. The problem with making biological engineering techniques easy to use is that it also makes them easy to abuse.[18]

As the COVID-19 pandemic has shown, even a relatively "mild" microbial pathogen – with lethality levels closer to the flu than to Ebola – can spread globally and kill millions of persons, severely disrupting the world's economy. Many of the leading practitioners of synthetic biology believe that our society urgently needs to put in place a better system of safeguards than those that presently exist. Such safeguards would not only decrease the risks associated with synthetic microorganisms; they would also help to mitigate the ever-present danger of naturally occurring pandemics.[19]

AI poses no existential danger today: the worst thing it will probably do over the coming decade or two is take away jobs from broadening swaths of the labor market, from truck drivers to data analysts, from accountants to office workers. The economic and societal upheaval will be considerable, but the disruption stands a fair chance of remaining manageable as long as massive retraining programs and government-funded safety nets are put in place. What's more concerning is the middle-term trajectory of this technology, three to five decades out, when general-purpose machines become capable of emulating a broader range of human physical and mental faculties. At that point, the control problem becomes far more daunting, because we will be dealing with machines that exhibit sophisticated forms of human-like agency: decision-making, strategizing, forecasting, learning, adapting, networking with each other, competing and cooperating with each other, modifying themselves and their environment in increasingly powerful ways.

It's hard to overstate the significance of this development. Throughout past millennia, humans have faced two basic kinds of control problems: controlling the objects and animals that surrounded us in the material world, and controlling the behavior of other people. Of these two, it was the challenge of other people that always proved far harder, precisely because people are *agents*: they talk back, deceive you, go their own way, surprise you, outsmart you, and change unpredictably on their own. Our species became quite adept at managing the behaviors of animals and material things, and has risen to dominance on the planet as a result. Where we have always struggled, and still struggle today, is in controlling ourselves and other members of our own species.

Now we are poised (a few decades hence) to endow an entire class of machines with a broad range of capabilities specifically designed to emulate our own intelligent agency. Some perceptive observers have taken notice. In

2014 the Nobel-prizewinning physicist Stephen Hawking joined with Stuart Russell, one of the world's leading experts on AI, in issuing the following statement:

> It's tempting to dismiss the notion of highly intelligent machines as mere science fiction. But this would be a mistake, and potentially our worst mistake in history. In the medium term ... AI may transform our economy to bring both great wealth and great dislocation. Looking further ahead, there are no fundamental limits to what can be achieved. ... One can imagine such technology outsmarting financial markets, out-inventing human researchers, out-manipulating human leaders, and developing weapons we cannot even understand. *Whereas the short-term impact of AI depends on who controls it, the long-term impact depends on whether it can be controlled at all.* ... Although we are facing potentially the best or worst thing to happen to humanity in history, little serious research is devoted to these issues.[20]

The big challenge with AI will be to develop this technology in ways that remain reliably aligned with human interests and human values. And this will be well-nigh impossible unless we make fundamental changes in the competitive global environment – political, economic, and military – within which AI research is inevitably embedded.

WHY THESE FOUR?

Why focus on just these four mega-dangers, and not on other existential threats facing our species? Among the candidates for such a discussion, one thinks for example of a large asteroid impact, along the lines of the 20-mile chunk that hit the Yucatan Peninsula some 66 million years ago, causing a climate disruption that killed about 75 percent of plants and animals on Earth.[21] This is certainly a non-negligible category of mega-threat, and humans have put in place observatories to track such celestial objects, wagering that we might perhaps find ways to divert them from striking our planet if we can detect them early enough.[22] But these kinds of major impacts tend to happen on a million-year timescale, and it remains far from clear that we would be able to do anything about them even if we saw one of them heading our way.

The same goes for super-volcanoes. These momentous eruptions have punctuated the Earth's history from time to time, spewing masses of particulates into the skies and depositing deep layers of ash on the continents around them. The Yellowstone super-volcano erupted two million years ago, leaving a vast crater-like depression in the planet's crust; when the even larger Toba volcano in Indonesia exploded 74,000 years ago, the entire planet's average temperature is thought to have dropped several degrees for a few years as a result of the "volcanic winter" that ensued. But these super-eruptions are notoriously hard to predict, and – once again – we have no clue how to stop them even if we suspect one is about to go off. The wisest policy is to keep trying to learn more about them, and perhaps to set aside stockpiles of emergency food supplies to help humankind weather the after-effects if one blows its top again.[23]

Another type of candidate is exemplified by the World War II story that opens my narrative – a powerful device that does new and potentially risky things with subatomic particles. Similar concerns recently animated a group of physicists who worried that Europe's Large Hadron Collider, situated on the border between France and Switzerland, might accidentally create a small black hole when it started running experiments in 2010 – a black hole that would instantly swallow the entire planet. As was the case during the Manhattan Project, the scientists in charge of the European collider assigned several successive teams of independent physicists to assess the plausibility of such scenarios, and their reports convincingly ruled out any doomsday outcome from the giant machine's operations.[24]

During the early 2000s, the nascent field of nanotechnology also elicited alarums among some scientists, who feared that (hypothetical) molecular nanomachines might someday unleash themselves across the continents, multiplying exponentially and converting all the planet's matter into copies of themselves. This came to be known as the Gray Goo Scenario – for in that case all that would be left of Earth would be a colorless blob of satiated nanomachines. This hypothesis, too, was thoroughly assessed by a variety of experts, and ultimately dismissed as either vanishingly improb-able or downright impossible.[25] (I'll return to nanotechnology later on when I discuss self-replicating bioengineered microbes.)

The four technologies discussed in this book fall into a quite different category. Each of them could plausibly kill a great many of us within the next hundred years (or ten minutes from now, in the case of nukes) – and we are definitely in a position to decrease the risk of their running amok. Although experts disagree about the exact nature of the dangers they pose, there is clear consensus that we need to take them seriously, and find better ways of governing their development and deployment.

WHAT CAN A HISTORIAN CONTRIBUTE TO THE DISCUSSION?

The inventor and futurist writer Ray Kurzweil (who also works a day job as a Director of Engineering at Google, Inc.) firmly believes that the exponential forms of technological innovation I've been describing are coming our way whether we like it or not. Under the heading "The Inevitability of a Transformed Future," he writes:

> The window of malicious opportunity for bioengineered viruses, existential or otherwise, will close in the 2020s when we have fully effective antiviral technologies based on nanobots. However, because nanotechnology will be thousands of times stronger, faster, and more intelligent than biological entities, self-replicating nanobots will present a greater risk and yet another existential risk. The window for malevolent nanobots will ultimately be closed by strong artificial intelligence, but, not surprisingly, "unfriendly" AI will itself present an even more compelling existential risk.[26]

Humankind, in this picture, has landed itself on a sort of historical treadmill of ever-rising technological powers, each of which presents a more daunting level of intertwined benefits and dangers. Last year's beneficial breakthrough becomes today's deadly threat, requiring the urgent invention of today's new beneficial breakthrough, which in turn will become tomorrow's deadly threat – and so on escalating without end. "The meta-lesson here," Kurzweil acknowledges, "is that we will need to place twenty-first-century society's highest priority on the continuing advance of defensive technologies, keeping them one or more steps ahead of the destructive technologies."[27] Apparently unfazed by the underlying ironies of this self-imposed rat race, Kurzweil is in fact echoing the sentiments here of prominent critics of technological modernity such as Lewis Mumford, Jacques Ellul, Ivan Illich, Wendell Berry, or Bill McKibben.[28] But instead of adopting their critical stance, he shrugs his shoulders and says, in effect: "Let 'er rip! We must innovate ever faster or die."

Yet this is a fallacy. In reality, there is nothing inevitable or predetermined about the historical process that generates these technologies, any more than the development of the bicycle or the internal combustion engine was predetermined. New technologies do not just suddenly appear in our midst, arising fully formed out of the labs of scientists and inventors, forcing us humans to adapt to the novel capabilities with which they endow us. Historians of science and technology have persuasively shown that this is a misguided way to view innovation; they refer to it as the fallacy of "technological determinism." Here is the way the historian David Nye sums it up in his book *Technology Matters*:

> A technology is not merely a system of machines with certain functions; rather, it is an expression of a social world. Electricity, the telephone, radio, television, the computer, and the Internet are not implacable forces moving

through history, but social processes that vary from one time period to another and from one culture to another. These technologies were not "things" that came from outside society and had an "impact"; rather, each was an internal development shaped by its social context. No technology exists in isolation. Each is an open-ended set of problems and possibilities. Each technology is an extension of human lives: someone makes it, someone owns it, some oppose it, many use it, and all interpret it.[29]

Consider for example the history of airplanes.[30] The first powered flight in a heavier-than-air machine lasted twelve seconds and carried Orville Wright 120 feet over the sands of Kitty Hawk. The craft's velocity: 6.8 miles per hour. Over the half-century that followed, as aircraft designs went through a spectacular series of transformations, their performance grew dramatically. By the end of the Second World War – a mere four decades after Kitty Hawk – the jet-powered Messerschmitt 262 was hitting speeds above 540 m.p.h., and the B-29 bomber boasted a range of 5,500 miles. Extrapolating from this giddy upward trajectory, some sci-fi writers in the 1950s confidently predicted that by the year 2000, sleek hypersonic craft would be whisking passengers from one continent to another with the ease of a cross-city bus ride. Yet it was not to be. Even though exciting supersonic planes like the Concorde were indeed built in the 1970s, they proved far too expensive for airlines to operate. International air travel did grow impressively during the postwar decades, but the economics of the industry, along with rising environmental concerns, took aircraft designs in a quite different direction: the new norm was cheap seats on large planes powered by efficient engines. Even though supersonic flight has definitely lain within the technical reach of aircraft engineers, today's most advanced passenger aircraft like the Airbus A380 and Boeing 777 are designed primarily to save gas, emit fewer pollutants, make less noise, and safely (if boringly) carry large numbers of passengers to their myriad destinations. They fly no faster than the airliners of the 1960s.

This is a crucial point for my argument in this book. Just because powerful and exciting new technologies are scientifically feasible, this does not mean that their creation is unavoidable. Humans make choices, both as individual consumers and as societal collectivities, and these aggregated choices exert a strong shaping effect on the development of our inventions. Some of our devices succeed and proliferate, becoming a part of our everyday lives; some assume strange and unexpected forms; some get used for quite different purposes than the ones for which they were designed; and some never get built at all. This shaping process is rarely simple and straightforward. It results from millions of choices made at many levels of a complex societal system, and its unfolding is hard to predict. But at bottom, we humans do have a significant say in how our technologies develop – what kinds of machines we create, how rapidly we assimilate them, and how we choose to use or not use them.

It's here that nontechnical writers – historians, economists, political scientists, philosophers, and others – have something helpful to offer. Precisely because all new technologies come into being within a broader societal context, humanists and social scientists can offer a complementary dimension of analysis that renders the technical solutions more effective. Consider for example nuclear weaponry. One side of the story is primarily technical in nature: the development of hydrogen bombs, tactical nukes, submarine-based missiles, cruise missiles, command-and-control systems, and so on. The other side of the story, equal in importance, is the Cold War historical context within which these weapons were funded, developed, and deployed. Here we need to take into account the logic of arms races, the fluctuating relationship between the superpowers, the internal politics within nuclear nations, the military-industrial complex, nuclear prolifer-ation, arms control efforts, and the ideological systems that were used to justify the deployment of such horrific weapons.

Even the most creative attempt to reduce the nuclear danger would fail if it focused solely on technical solutions: it could only succeed if it also took into account the societal forces that shape the nuclear equation. For example, US President Ronald Reagan came up with a brilliant technological fix with his Star Wars initiative in the early 1980s – a shift from "mutually assured destruc-tion" to "mutually assured defense." Instead of racing to find new ways to blow each other to smithereens, the superpowers would focus their ingenuity on building impenetrable shields to protect their territories from nuclear attack. Yet Reagan's path-breaking idea went nowhere, precisely because it failed to embed his proposal within a new international system operating beyond the strategic rivalry of the Cold War. If the radical technical solution was truly going to work, it would have needed to go hand-in-hand with an equally radical *political* shift in how countries pursued their security. My approach in this book is to continually bring these two dimensions of analysis together, embedding the most promising technical solutions within the political and historical frameworks through which they will have to be implemented.

THE BOOK'S ARGUMENT IN A NUTSHELL

1. Four major catastrophic risks confront humankind over the coming century. The cumulative danger is higher than ever before, because climate

change and weaponized AI now pose serious new threats in addition to the older threats of nuclear war and pandemics.

2. Past efforts to mitigate these kinds of mega-dangers have included modest initiatives such as climate treaties, arms control deals, or limited pandemic precautions, as well as bolder moves like the US government's 1946 proposal for international control of atomic weapons, the 1972 Biological Weapons Convention, or Ronald Reagan's 1983 missile shield initiative. While these were important steps in the right direction, they have fallen far short of what is needed. In all cases, the most salient problem has been the way every nation continues to fend for itself in a ruthlessly competitive world arena.

3. An effective response to these four mega-dangers will require moving beyond the international self-help system and creating coordinated instruments of global governance. These instruments can be progressively strengthened in successive phases of institutional change over the next century and a half. The historical backdrop for this transformative process lies in the rapid growth of international laws, supranational institutions, and globe-spanning networks over the past 120 years – from the League of Nations in 1920 to the United Nations in 1945 to today's International Criminal Court and European Union.

4. Moving toward a more tightly integrated global framework strikes many people as a utopian pipe-dream. Yet creating such a framework would not require a radical departure from established practices, but only a continuation and extension of the remarkable cross-border initiatives and institutional innovations that humankind has already been undertaking over the past century.

Most people, when they think of world government, conjure two kinds of images: a tyrannical superstate along the lines of Huxley's *Brave New World,* or the feckless, anemic United Nations of today. The emotional tone is either fear or disdain. But it doesn't have to be that way. A world government could be built according to a very different blueprint – one that enhances our freedom of action rather than constrains it; empowers its citizens and opens new doorways for flexible connection and teamwork; offers effective instruments for resolving the deep conflicts that inevitably arise among citizens and groups; remains transparent and accountable at all levels of its functioning; establishes a state of law at the global level – freely chosen laws that the world's peoples have negotiated amongst themselves; and imposes nothing from above except the minimal necessary instruments for enforcing those laws and keeping the peace. What if a world government offered vibrant new forms of self-rule, political expression, and liberation to humankind?

This may all sound too good to be true, but in fact many of the instruments for such a global framework are already beginning to emerge today. We tend to apply the clunky, top-down metaphors of a 1950s bureaucracy when we think of world government, but what if instead we apply the bottom-up metaphors of the most responsive, decentralized systems of the present day? What if, instead of thinking *Encyclopaedia Britannica*, we think Wikipedia? Our deep challenge, over the coming century, lies in learning how to take up these new kinds of organizational instruments and apply them creatively across the oceans and continents.

5. Planet-level solutions for today's world should focus on reducing the most grievous risks, while developing new forms of cross-border concertation and regulation. Examples include: cooperative pacts among select groups of nations for swift decarbonization of energy systems; treaties that restrict new and destabilizing weaponry; boosting global pandemic preparedness; government oversight for synthetic biology; promoting safety research in AI.

6. Chapters 15 through 20 describe a series of incremental steps toward a federal framework for global democratic governance. These concrete measures could be undertaken over the span of many decades, gradually putting in place a new set of planet-level institutions and norms. The key challenges here are: creating a political system that allows dictatorships and democracies to work constructively together; revamping the UN Security Council so it more accurately reflects the realities of global economic and military power; developing an equitable system of weighted voting in UN institutions, so that key policies can be implemented effectively; reducing the gross disparities in wealth and opportunity that divide the world's peoples; keeping the UN system rigorously accountable and transparent in its operations; and building robust instruments of collective military security and economic sanctions, capable of dealing decisively with rogues, cheaters, or fanatics. In this federal structure, existing national governments would continue to do most of the day-to-day running of people's affairs; only the truly global matters such as military security, climate change, or regulating dangerous technologies would be assigned for coordination by the UN and its affiliated bodies.

7. Fortunately, this transformative process will not be an all-or-nothing proposition. The benefits of international cooperation grow by degrees, in

direct proportion to the cross-border solutions that have been put into practice. This means that even relatively small cooperative innovations can start making an impact right away in delivering heightened stability, prosperity, and security; and as these basic measures are followed up with more intensive forms of institution-building, the benefits increase progressively in scope. Humankind does not have to build a full-fledged system of global federal governance in order to start working on these problems successfully: we can start making a tangible difference right now.

8. Generating the political will for this incremental restructuring of world politics poses a defining challenge for our time. We can draw inspiration from the partial success of two major recent initiatives: the green movement and the creation of the European Union. Like the international activists who launched these two endeavors in the 1950s, our generation can turn to a wide array of powerful tools for mobilizing change at all levels of society, from citizens to leaders, from the local to the global, from institutions to habits of mind. Both of these remarkable stories can offer valuable lessons as we press forward to make the necessary changes in world politics.

9. The timeframes listed in the table of contents – culminating in a mature governance system by 2150 – are of course speculative in nature. I chose 2150 as a benchmark because it conveys the likelihood that this will be a long, slow process, requiring the gradual accumulation of myriad smaller changes in world affairs. Strong incentives – both sticks and carrots – are likely to motivate humankind as this process unfolds. Penalties for partial failures could include a hotter planet, nuclear conflicts or accidents, bioengineered pandemics, or AI disasters. These are some of the harsh "lessons" we hopefully won't have to learn along the way. The benefits of partial successes, on the other hand, would be tremendous: a cooling planet; an end to arms races in weapons of mass destruction; a phased reduction of standing armies, yielding a massive peace dividend that could be used to reduce world poverty; and a robust control system for advanced bioengineering and AI. These kinds of penalties and benefits could impel major innovations and reforms in a similar way to the impacts of World War I and World War II – and their cumulative pressure will only escalate as the decades go by.

10. The path-breaking achievements of the past century offer grounds for cautious hope. Over the coming decades, economic and technological interdependence will continue to intensify, binding the interests of the world's peoples even more tightly together than today. As nations and

regions find themselves increasingly "in the same boat," win–win solutions among them are likely to become more self-evidently attractive.

To be sure, the possibility of failure is ever-present and very real. Building more effective instruments for planet-level governance will prove exceedingly hard, and we can expect plenty of disheartening setbacks along the way. But the evidence from the past, and the plausible trajectory of challenges and incentives that await us in the coming century, suggest that it can be done.

* * *

In order to lend more concreteness to the discussion, I offer eleven fictional vignettes in which I envision what the future world of mega-dangerous technologies might actually look and feel like – and how they may be brought under control. As long as we bear in mind that these vignettes are speculative exercises – educated guesses – they can help illustrate the kinds of challenges that citizens of the coming century may find themselves encountering.

PART I

EXISTENTIAL THREATS:
THE FOUR MOST PRESSING DANGERS FACING HUMANKIND

2

Fossil Fuels and Climate Change

I N THIS CHAPTER AND THE THREE THAT FOLLOW, I give a brief overview of the four technologies that pose particularly dire threats to humankind. I won't go into a lot of scientific detail, leaving that to the many excellent specialist books available on each of these fields. Rather, my focus is on the Janus-faced nature of such inventions: the fact that they are all instruments of tremendous potential benefit to humankind, as well as plausible vehicles of great harm.

* * *

When I was in my early teens, I discovered the power of fossil fuels in a very direct way. A group of friends and I were experimenting with ways to make bigger bangs – tying firecrackers together in bundles, breaking them apart to make piles of explosive dust to put into pipe bombs, and so on. Then one of us had a brilliant idea: "Let's blow up some gas!" We siphoned a quart of it from a parent's car into an empty milk carton, then went into the woods and set it up at the base of a redwood tree with a fuse we'd pieced together. We lit the fuse, dove behind a nearby log, and – BRAOOOOM. When we peered over the log's edge, ears ringing from the violence of the blast, a 20-foot mushroom cloud was billowing through the branches above. Everything was singed all around us, and little flames were springing up among the leaves. It's a miracle we didn't start a forest fire. Fossil fuels are powerful stuff.

Humankind made this discovery (more sanely) a couple centuries earlier, when it started moving beyond watermills and windmills, animal power, and the burning of wood, peat, and charcoal, and learned how to tap the energy of coal, petroleum, and natural gas. These are called fossil fuels because they were created millions of years ago by terrestrial plants or oceanic microorganisms that converted the Sun's energy through photosynthesis; as these creatures died, their bodies accumulated in the ground and decomposed anaerobically, gradually forming large beds of fossilized organic matter. When the organic matter is retrieved today and burned (oxidized), it unlocks the original chemical processes laid down by that primordial photosynthesis, releasing carbon dioxide, water, and energy.[1]

The global energy transition went through several phases: coal burning surpassed traditional biofuels like wood around 1900, then was in turn surpassed by petroleum and natural gas after World War II. As I noted earlier, the growth in global energy consumption followed a steep upward curve, not only in raw total numbers, but even when calculated on a per capita basis: each of us today is consuming about four times as much energy per year as the individuals of the early nineteenth century (see Figure 2.1).

This accelerating expansion, particularly impressive after World War II, was partly due to rapid economic growth in former developing nations like China, India, and Brazil that have been catching up to the advanced industrial nations. The result is plain to see (Figure 2.2).

It would be churlish to deny the myriad beneficial effects of this economic revolution powered largely by fossil fuels. As the psychologist Steven Pinker has persuasively argued, the improvements in human flourishing throughout the planet over the past couple centuries have been striking: infant mortality rates are down; people are living longer and healthier lives; women have won impressive gains in status; extreme poverty has declined; new technologies for communication and transportation have knitted the

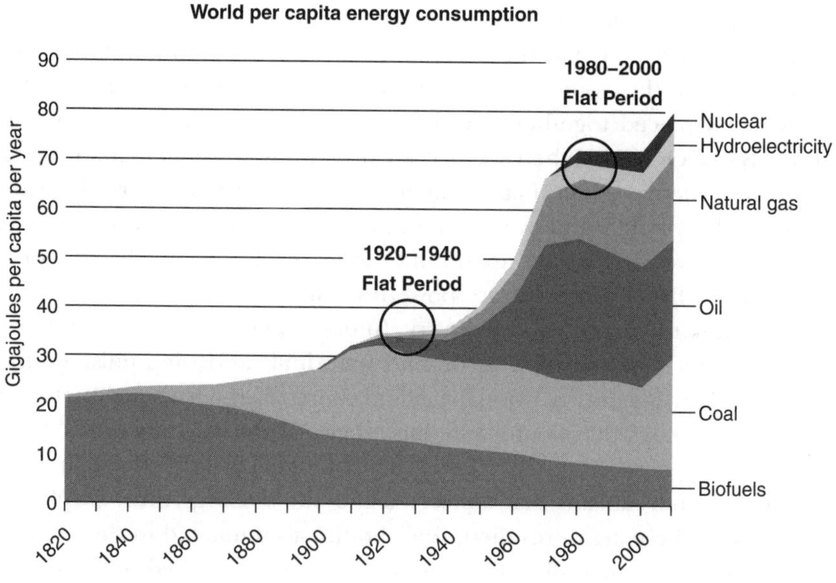

World per capita energy consumption

Figure 2.1 World per capita energy consumption, 1820–2010.[2]

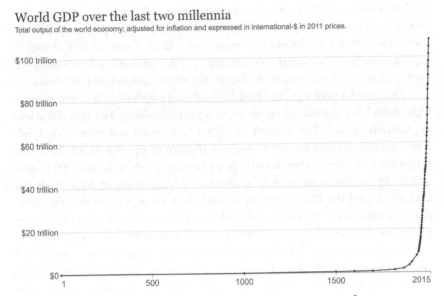

World GDP over the last two millennia
Total output of the world economy; adjusted for inflation and expressed in international-$ in 2011 prices.

Figure 2.2 World gross domestic product (GDP) over the past 2,000 years.[3]
Sources: World GDP – Our World in Data, based on World Bank & Maddison (2007)

continents more closely together; literacy rates have climbed steadily; and economic opportunities are far more widely available than they were a century ago.[4] On the other hand, many severe and pressing problems continue to afflict human society – for the boons of economic growth have not been equally distributed. Hundreds of millions of people still lack access to basic material necessities like clean water and regular nutrition, and millions more die every year from diseases that are aggravated by poverty. Although education and medicine have spread impressively into new parts of the world, far too many people still languish for lack of them. Much progress remains urgently to be made.

One side-effect of this economic revolution – unrecognized until relatively recently – is the sheer amount of carbon dioxide (CO_2) that it has released into the atmosphere. Fully 85 percent of human energy consumption today derives from fossil fuels, and this means that every single activity you and I engage in every day has a carbon footprint.[5] It's not just when you fly in an airplane or heat your house or drive your car. The food you eat was grown on farms that used vehicles powered by fossil fuels, was processed in facilities powered by fossil fuels, and brought to your table by vehicles powered by fossil fuels – either directly, via gasoline, or indirectly via the electricity that ran the machines. This is known in the expert literature as "embodied carbon." The clothes we wear, the cell phone we talk on, the plastics and metals in the gadgets we use, the room we sleep in, the office we work in – carbon consumption is everywhere. Even if you are just sitting on a park bench, eyes closed, meditating quietly, you are still running off energy that your body acquired via the elaborate network of fossil fuels.

This poses a problem. For hundreds of thousands of years, atmospheric CO_2 levels have fluctuated naturally in a range between 180 and 300 parts-per-million (ppm). The periods of higher CO_2 levels and lower CO_2 levels have correlated in lockstep with periods of warmer or colder global average temperatures – the hothouse periods and ice ages. Yet in the past 200 years – a tiny blip in the timescales of geophysics – human use of fossil fuels has abruptly raised the CO_2 to 400 ppm, and the level is projected to continue rising rapidly over the coming decades as CO_2 accumulates in the atmosphere and humans keep pumping out more and more.[6] (See Figure 2.3.)

Once it is out there in the sky, the CO_2 stays in place for hundreds of years, where it acts like a blanket around the planet, trapping the Sun's heat and causing the global temperature to rise. This is known as the greenhouse effect, and CO_2 is the chief culprit among the various gases that produce this warming process. About 25 percent of today's global warming is caused by a different gas, methane (CH_4), which is released in significant quantities by animal farming and by leaks in natural gas pipelines and wells. Although

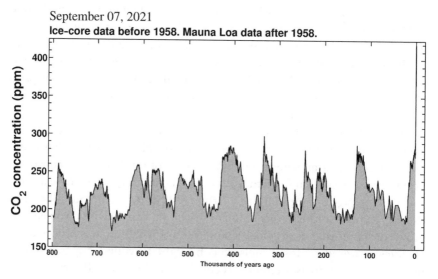

Figure 2.3 Carbon dioxide concentrations over the past 800,000 years.[7]

methane doesn't linger as long in the atmosphere as CO_2, it traps heat far more efficiently, so reducing emissions of both these gases is a high priority.[8]

One or two degrees may not sound like a lot, since we are accustomed to watching our local weather fluctuate by as much as 10 or 20 degrees every 24 hours, and even more with the changing seasons. But weather (what we experience locally) is not the same thing as climate (the broad patterns of average temperature that characterize the globe as a whole). At the planetary timescale, three or four degrees can make the difference between a temperate period and an ice age (see Figure 2.4).[9]

We humans, with our relatively sudden and dramatic release of greenhouse gases, risk carrying the Earth past a critical threshold at which the planet's own climate dynamics take off on a self-reinforcing cycle of their own.[10] As the planet warms, several key factors come into play: the ice at the polar regions recedes, reflecting less of the Sun's energy back into space; permafrost regions like Siberia, where vast reservoirs of CO_2 and methane lie trapped in frozen bogs, start to thaw and release their gases into the air; water evaporates more readily from the oceans, increasing water vapor in

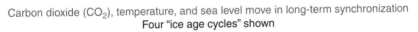

Carbon dioxide (CO_2), temperature, and sea level move in long-term synchronization
Four "ice age cycles" shown

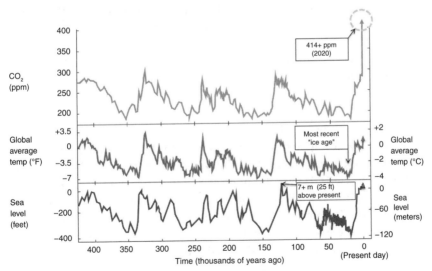

Figure 2.4 Carbon dioxide concentrations, global temperature, and sea levels over the past 400,000 years.[11]

the atmosphere that adds to the greenhouse effect; and forested areas, which absorb and store CO_2 in the biomass of trees, are depleted by drought and wildfires. All these factors generate a feedback loop in which each degree of additional warmth triggers still more warming factors, and the process accelerates on its own. Once these tipping points are passed, the sheer scale of this runaway process could vastly exceed human technological capabilities and become unstoppable.[12]

I take myself as a prime example of someone who didn't wake up to the full severity of the climate threat until recently. I should have known better, because I spent most of the 1990s researching and writing a book about the impact of green ideas in France, so I was quite familiar with the environmentalists' message.[13] But I made the fateful trio of assumptions that many people make on this subject:

1. *We have time:* the impact of climate change won't be fully felt until a couple centuries from now.
2. *The planet is resilient:* once we rein in greenhouse gas emissions, the climate will respond quickly to our wise restraint and return to its former equilibrium.
3. *We have more pressing problems:* climate change is a lower priority than other dangers like nukes, global poverty, pandemics, or terrorism.

But I was wrong. This is a dire threat that's already showing its first significant effects today, and that will render your daily life, and the lives of your children and grandchildren, increasingly rough over the coming decades. The immense West Coast wildfires of 2020, the increasing frequency and severity of hurricanes, the accelerating retreat of glaciers and polar ice, and the die-offs of coral reefs – these are but harbingers of even worse things to come. By the closing years of this century, many aspects of today's world that we casually take for granted will be gone. Three basic trajectories to the year 2100 have been mapped out by climate scientists, each one depending on how swiftly and effectively humankind mobilizes to mitigate this danger.[14] I think of them as choices between "Not too bad," "Nasty," and "Hell." It's worth underscoring that the scientific consensus on these projections now lies at about 97 percent: in other words, this is what the best scientific minds from the top research universities and government labs around the world are concluding *nearly unanimously* from decades of cutting-edge research.[15] (I'll discuss the politically fraught "debate" over climate science in Chapter 12.)

The best-case scenario presupposes a massive and sustained effort on the part of humankind, starting immediately, to rein in greenhouse gas emissions worldwide and also to develop new technologies for removing increasingly large amounts of those gases from the atmosphere. Under this optimistic scenario, the new normal around the year 2100 would be on track to look something like this:[16]

- Greenhouse gas emissions are reduced rapidly and brought to zero by mid-century.
- Global average temperature in 2100 is 1.5 to 2 degrees Celsius higher than preindustrial times (about 0.5 to 1 degree higher than today) and is remaining stable at that level.
- Some accumulated greenhouse gases are being gradually removed from the atmosphere by new technologies deployed in the latter decades of the century.
- Oceans have risen by 10 to 20 inches, forcing many sections of coastal cities to be evacuated and relocated.
- Droughts are more frequent and severe than today, but agriculture is still feasible in most regions where it is currently practiced.
- Extreme weather events such as floods, superstorms, heat waves, and wildfires have become more common.
- Ocean acidification and warmer waters have rendered the world's fisheries far less productive.
- Many forms of wildlife are endangered, with their populations dwindling.
- New diseases are spreading from tropical regions to warming northern and southern regions nearer the poles.
- Forced migrations are increasing, as people are displaced by drought and famine, along with the civil strife that those two factors have aggravated.
- The global economy has been noticeably affected by the costs and burdens imposed by the challenges of work in a hotter climate.

The midrange scenario presupposes a delay of a couple decades from the present day before the serious mitigation efforts described above go into effect. Under this scenario, greenhouse gas emissions would continue to rise until about 2035 or 2040, then gradually stabilize and decline to zero by the 2070s. Global average temperature in 2100 would be about 3 degrees Celsius higher than preindustrial times.[17]

The worst-case scenario assumes that humankind continues over the coming decades to do what it is doing today – political bickering and feckless half-measures – and only begins serious mitigation efforts after the effects of climate change become so grievous that nearly everyone finally acknowledges the danger is real. By that point, unfortunately, the problem may already have acquired a momentum of its own and may lie beyond the reach of human countermeasures. Under this scenario, the new normal around the year 2100 would be on track to look something like this:[18]

- Greenhouse gas emissions continue to rise until 2050 or later, then rapidly stabilize and decline toward zero by the 2080s as draconian mitigation measures are desperately adopted.
- Global average temperature in 2100 is 4 to 6 degrees Celsius higher than preindustrial times.
- The climate continues warming rapidly after the 2080s despite emissions at zero, because feedback mechanisms from factors such as melting permafrost, ice loss, water vapor, and wildfires are propelling major new releases of greenhouse gases from natural sources, along with an accelerating rise in temperature that further aggravates the process. The planet has entered a self-reinforcing spiral of warming similar to those that occurred during previous eras of natural warming in prehistoric times.
- Frantic attempts to remove accumulated greenhouse gases from the atmosphere via new technologies deployed in the latter decades of the century fail to keep up with the new greenhouse gases released naturally by a warmer planet.
- Oceans have risen by as much as 6 feet and are still rising by as much as 1 foot per decade after 2100, forcing most coastal regions to be evacuated as people retreat inland.
- Droughts are much more frequent and severe than today, and agriculture has become impossible in a broad swath of land north and south of the equator.
- Extreme weather events such as floods, superstorms, heat waves, and wildfires have become much more common and deadly than today, and regularly kill large numbers of people. Large portions of the planet are uninhabitable for humans and have become searing desert wastelands.
- Ocean acidification and warmer waters have rendered many aquatic species extinct, and large regions of the oceans are dead zones.
- Tropical diseases have become endemic in all regions even near the poles.
- Global human population has declined, as people crowd into the regions near the poles where agriculture remains viable. The massive displacement of humans is marked by wars, disease, floods, droughts, and famines that cumulatively claim billions of lives.

- Many nations' political institutions have become more authoritarian in nature, as populations respond to the climate crisis with emergency governance measures and martial law.
- It is possible that the Earth is heading into another of the dozen major or minor extinction periods that have marked its long history, when 6-degree cooling or warming caused large percentages of the planet's biological life to perish.

The main point to notice about these three trajectories is that they contain good news as well as bad: there is still time for humankind to wake up to the danger. It's not too late to render the best-case scenario a reality: all we need do is stop dithering and take effective action. I'll describe some of the strategies for this in the coming chapters.

* * *

3

Nukes for War and Peacetime

I WAS BORN IN 1955, THE YEAR THE UNITED STATES launched its first nuclear-powered submarine, the USS *Nautilus*, and announced that it was arming itself with nuclear-tipped intercontinental missiles. This was also the first year in which nuclear-generated electric power became commercially available: it flowed into the grid of Arco, Idaho, powering the TVs that were running the brand-new show hosted by Lawrence Welk.

Sometimes, when I bring up nuclear weapons in my college classroom, I'm taken aback by the casual attitude that some students exhibit in speaking about these devices. "The Cold War's long gone," they say. "The number of warheads has been sharply reduced. Nothing bad has happened since 1945. Can we please move on to a more timely topic, such as terrorism or racism or climate change?"

When this happens, I tell those students about a fellow named Vasili Arkhipov. The year was 1962, and the United States had approximately 3,500 nuclear weapons in its arsenal, among which were 203 long-range missiles capable of delivering 635 megatons just about anywhere on the planet. The Russians had "only" one-sixth as many such weapons, but their missiles and planes could still deliver up to 204 megatons to American targets – the equivalent of 14,000 Hiroshimas.[1]

On October 27, 1962, the Cuban Missile Crisis was in its twelfth day, with tensions running high, and angry messages flashing back and forth between Kennedy and Khrushchev. Military forces on both sides stood on high alert; the US Strategic Air Command was at DEFCON 2 for the first time ever, the final step of readiness before "nuclear war imminent or likely." An American U-2 spy plane flying over Cuba was shot down that afternoon by a surface-to-air missile, killing its pilot, Major Rudolf Anderson.

While this was happening, off the shore of Cuba, a patrolling Soviet submarine, the *B-59*, was located by a flotilla of US Navy warships; they began dropping small signaling depth charges in an effort to force the sub to surface and identify itself.[2] The Americans didn't know that the Soviet sub was carrying a 10-kiloton nuclear torpedo; the Russians didn't know that the

American depth charges were not the real deal. American military leaders had dispatched a message to their Soviet counterparts, explaining that the depth charges were not lethal and were meant to signal the sub to surface; but the Russian command never acknowledged receipt of this message, and never notified their submarine captains.

Deep below the waves, the three senior officers of the *B-59* broke into a heated argument. Finding themselves under attack, they were positioned too far underwater to establish radio contact with Moscow and seek instructions about how to respond. Two of the three officers concluded that all-out war had broken out, and that the sub should immediately launch its nuclear torpedo against the largest of the American vessels, the aircraft carrier USS *Randolph* cruising nearby.

"We're going to blast them now!" declared the sub's captain, Valentin Savitsky, who was approaching exhaustion from the long hours of stress. "We will die, but we will sink them all. We will not disgrace our navy."[3] The ship's political commissar gave his assent. But the third officer, Vasili Arkhipov, disagreed. He argued that if the Americans had wanted to sink their vessel, they would have done so by this point. The depth charges were repeatedly missing their target, and this had to mean something: perhaps this was not intended as a deadly attack but merely as a signal to identify themselves. He maintained that the wiser course would be to wait until nightfall and surface the sub despite the risk of being fired upon, and then seek clear instructions from headquarters. Since protocol for launching nuclear weapons required the concurrence of all three senior officers, the argument went on for some time. Arkhipov stubbornly stood his ground, and in the end, Captain Savitsky relented and the order to launch torpedoes was not given. At 9:52 p.m. they maneuvered the sub to the surface; an urgent message from Moscow confirmed that war had not broken out and they should hold their fire.[4]

The US Secretary of Defense during the crisis, Robert S. McNamara, later confessed during a video interview: "In the end, we lucked out. It was luck that prevented nuclear war. We came that close."[5] You can see McNamara in front of the camera, an old man with a grim look on his face, holding his thumb and forefinger about a quarter inch apart (see Figure 3.1).

Thomas Blanton, the director of the US National Security Archive, looked back on the incident several decades later, as the documents revealing what had happened were finally declassified. "The lesson from this," he concluded, "is that a guy named Vasili Arkhipov saved the world."[6]

Arkhipov was 36 years old at the time. Photos of him show a handsome man with a square-set jaw and a forthright gaze into the camera (see Figure 3.2).

Figure 3.1 US Defense Secretary Robert S. McNamara in Errol Morris's film interview, *The Fog of War.*[7]

Figure 3.2 Vasili Arkhipov in 1955.[8]

He had joined the Soviet Navy in 1942, at age sixteen, and served on a minesweeper during the Second World War. After 1945 he had gone into submarines, rising to the rank of flotilla commander by the time of the Cuban crisis. One year earlier, in 1961, he had earned a reputation for great bravery when a nuclear reactor on his submarine lost its coolant system, and as executive officer he personally led the repair team, suffering severe radiation exposure to save his ship and the lives of his men. He and his wife Olga had no children. "My husband," she later recalled, "was a very shy and modest person, intelligent, very polite. When we used to go on holiday, wherever he was, he was always trying to find fresh newspapers. He was always in touch with the modern world. His character was very kind and calm."[9] Captain Ryurik Ketov, who commanded one of the other Soviet subs patrolling those Cuban waters, described him this way: "Vasili Arkhipov . . . stood out for being cool headed. He was in control. He was a real submariner."[10] On such details of one man's personal character did the events of October 27 rest.

The Arkhipov episode was probably the closest we have come. A runner-up event took place 21 years later at Serpukhov-15, one of Russia's main air defense facilities outside Moscow.[11] It was a Monday night, September 26, 1983. Just three weeks earlier, a Russian fighter jet had shot down a Korean Air Lines 747 that strayed into Soviet airspace near the Sea of Japan, killing all 269 persons aboard. NATO had just finished a large-scale military exercise in Western Europe involving 15,000 troops, and both sides had recently deployed a new class of intermediate-range missiles on either side of the Iron Curtain. The rhetoric between the superpowers was waxing particularly harsh and menacing.

At 8:00 p.m., Lieutenant-Colonel Stanislav Petrov checked in for duty at Serpukhov-15 as the night watch commander for missile defense. He was a computer scientist by training and disliked pulling these all-night shifts once a month, but this evening he'd been summoned at the last minute to replace another officer who called in sick. A new satellite network for detecting hostile missile launches was being tested, and Petrov had helped design the computers that ran the system. Petrov took his place on the second-floor balcony of the large command-and-control center, surveying the men at their consoles below and the broad screens on the walls that displayed the satellites' view of the northern hemisphere in real time. He settled in with a cup of tea and went through his routine checking protocols.

At 12:15 a.m. a loud klaxon started blaring – the alarm for "Missile Launch Detected." This had never happened to Petrov before, except in practice drills. The men at their consoles were standing, looking to him for what to do next. He ordered them to double-check their systems, and none reported a malfunction. The alert was coming from infrared detectors on one of the satellites over the western United States and indicated a single missile launch – but none of the satellite's optical sensors were picking up anything unusual. Petrov decided it must be a false alarm, and phoned the military command center to let them know. He instructed the men at the consoles below to reboot their systems and run diagnostics.

Within seconds the klaxon blared again, indicating a second missile launch. Once again Petrov double-checked the optical feed and found nothing unusual there. He ordered the system rebooted a second time and declared a second false alarm. But as soon as the system restarted, the klaxon went off once more: a third missile launch was detected. Petrov felt flushed with fear, "as though I were sitting in a hot frying pan."[12] He knew the alarm was being relayed up the chain of command to the Minister of Defense Ustinov and the party chairman Yuri Andropov himself. At this moment they were probably consulting urgently about how to respond. The emergency systems were being activated, with targets sent out and missile launch preparations commencing. But was this truly the real deal?

Petrov was uniquely qualified to make this decision, precisely because he'd played a key role in designing the new detection system and was keenly aware of its glitches and flaws that were still being worked out. This inclined him toward skepticism. Why would the Americans be launching an attack with just a few missiles, knowing this would trigger a massive counterattack? It didn't make sense.

Just then a fourth alarm sounded, then a fifth. Five missiles detected. Now the klaxon was blaring again, and a large screen flashed the words, "MISSILE ATTACK." Military protocol for this situation was crystal clear: his duty was to report up the chain of command that an attack on the homeland was underway. The chief engineer and commander of the Serpukhov-15 facility ran into the room, looking to him for an answer. Time was running out.

Petrov reasoned that any incoming missiles would have crossed over the North Pole by this point, where a different array of land-based tracking devices would be picking them up. He ordered his subordinates to check their consoles: the polar trackers were reporting no contacts. He glanced across the room at the wall where the words were flashing: MISSILE ATTACK. He still wasn't sure, but finally he made a judgement call. He told his superiors that no attack was coming, and to stand down.

Later analysis revealed what had happened. An unusual formation of high-stratus clouds had gathered over Warren Air Force Base in Wyoming.

Figure 3.3 Stanislav Petrov in his Moscow apartment in 2015.[13]

One of the Soviet satellites, Oko 5, had picked up infrared signals bouncing off those clouds, and its computer algorithms had interpreted them as a series of five missile launches. Petrov's hunch had been right.

But he was not rewarded for his deed. His superior officers were furious that he'd made this decision on his own, and reprimanded him. The incident was kept secret for many years and did not come to light until after the breakup of the Soviet Union. When reporters learned what had happened, they went to interview Petrov and found him living alone on a reduced pension in a dilapidated apartment in Moscow (see Figure 3.3).

A UN official presented him with a small statue of a globe resting in an open hand, inscribed with the words, "Stanislav Petrov: The Man Who Saved the World." He died in 2017. One wonders what would have happened on the night of September 26 if the man who was originally scheduled to command the night shift at Serpukhov-15 had not gotten sick.

THE ARMS RACE

The dual nature of nuclear technology was plain to see even before the first devices had been tested. Colonel Henry Stimson, the US Secretary of War during World War II, laid it out for himself in his personal notes six weeks before the Alamogordo test:

Its size and character
We don't think it mere new weapon
Revolutionary discovery of relation of Man to universe
Great historical landmark, like gravitation, Copernican theory
But: bids fair to be infinitely greater, in respect to its effect on the ordinary affairs of man's life
May destroy or perfect international civilization
May be Frankenstein or means for world peace.[14]

Four years after Hiroshima, in August 1949, the Russians detonated their own fission bomb (their spies in the Manhattan Project had passed on information that sped the process along). By this point the United States was already making progress with research on the hydrogen bomb, a weapon that harnessed nuclear fusion rather than fission – the elemental fire that powers the Sun – and could unleash thousands of times more energy than the devices of 1945. Indeed, the H-bomb used a Hiroshima-style device as its *detonator*. In 1952, the first American H-bomb was tested on a remote Pacific atoll: its blast measured 10.4 megatons (660 Hiroshimas). Edward Teller, one of the bomb's main architects, was 5,000 miles away in California at the time: by observing a seismometer that picked up the shock wave from the blast rippling through the Earth's crust, he was able to know right away that the device had worked. He sent a telegram to one of his colleagues: "It's a boy."[15] The Soviets frantically ramped up work on their own H-bomb and discharged their first megaton-range device in 1955.

The arms race was off and running. Over the ensuing decades, both sides added more and more weapons to their nuclear arsenals, diversifying into a wide range of delivery formats: nukes for planes, missiles, and submarines, as well as small nukelets that could be fired from cannons on battlefields or (should the need ever arise) to vaporize aircraft carrier groups with a single torpedo fired from a submarine(!). Very smart people on both sides pored over charts and maps, calculating how much firepower it would take to properly "do" the cities of the adversary; they wrote intricately reasoned articles about the arcana of game theory and deterrence theory. ("If I do X, but make you think I'm doing Y, and if you respond with Z, then I can pretend to do X as long as you don't figure out that I'm expecting Z, but it all depends on how convincingly I pretend to be doing X, which in turn depends on the past track record of A, B, and C and your perception of them, which I've been working on manipulating so you'll see them through the lens of G, as long as ... ")

During the 1970s, someone came up with the idea of the MIRV (Multiple Independently Targetable Reentry Vehicle), which meant that a single missile like the Trident II could now carry up to fourteen warheads, each of which could be separately sent to wipe out one of fourteen widely dispersed cities. An Ohio-class submarine of the US Navy can carry 24 such MIRVed missiles, which means that a single sub can nuke 336 cities. The US Navy currently has fourteen such subs patrolling the oceans 24/7.[16] Later, in the 1980s, another refinement took place: nuclear-tipped cruise missiles were developed that could fly for thousands of miles just slightly above the treetops and hills, hugging the landscape, evading radar, and thereby becoming impossible to intercept. The Russians, of course, have followed suit on all fronts.

Each of these escalating developments was justified by the logic of mutually assured destruction, which goes like this: if both adversaries maintain a stable relation of rough parity, neither side will be tempted to think they can get away with a strike against the other without suffering annihilation in return. According to this reasoning, the burgeoning arsenals rendered war *less* likely because they maintained the credibility of guaranteed Armageddon for all players. It was with no ironic tone in mind, therefore, that American leaders named their land-based MIRV missile (each one capable of incinerating ten cities) the Peacekeeper.

Other countries, not surprisingly, also felt it imperative to join the nuclear club. The French decided in the 1950s that having a militarily formidable nation like Germany as a next-door neighbor was a problem that could be solved once and for all with nukes. Their *force de frappe* sent an implicit message across the Rhine: "If you invade us again, we will wipe you out – even though we realize that nuking your cities will render France itself uninhabitable."[17] The same grim message from Paris was also implicitly aimed beyond the Iron Curtain, at Russia. Other nations that felt jittery about their neighbors adopted a similar stance: India and Pakistan point these weapons at each other. North Korea and Israel have nuclear capabilities. China and the United Kingdom round out the nine-member club.

PEACEFUL ATOMS

To an impartial Martian observer, this whole nuclear story might appear cretinously suicidal. But not all human activities in the nuclear arena have been oriented toward increased killing capacity: on the other side of the ledger, we have the peaceful uses of atomic power, which mainly come down to making electricity. You take enriched uranium and make it undergo fission slowly, in a controlled fashion: this generates a lot of heat, which you can use to boil water, creating high-pressure steam that you can direct through a nozzle to turn the vanes of a turbine. Connect the turbine's rotating shaft to a generator, and voilà, you have electricity. Unlike fossil-fuel-powered generators, nuclear generators release not a whit of greenhouse gases into the atmosphere. You can power entire continents without contributing to global warming.

There's a catch, of course – actually a twofold catch. Today's nuclear reactors run on enriched radioactive fuels and generate a waste by-product that ranks among the most poisonous substances on the planet. Spent nuclear fuel is hard to handle safely, hard to store safely, and remains toxic for thousands of years. Secondly, sustaining a stable fission process in today's generation of pressurized-water reactors is a dicey affair: if you turn it down too low, it dies out; if you turn it up too high, it overheats and creates a meltdown. No matter how intensive the training, and no matter how carefully the failsafe systems have been designed, there is always a risk of malfunction or human error. Potentially dangerous anomalies occur from time to time in the daily operation of the world's 450-odd nuclear generators, and the vast majority of them are swiftly resolved by all the redundant safety systems and alert personnel. When these machines really do fail, however, they make a big impression, such that we come to know them by name: Three Mile Island, Chernobyl, Fukushima.

Nuclear engineers are coming up with a variety of new designs that get around both these kinds of problems.[18] They are experimenting with ingenious fission methods that use fuel more efficiently and can even (in some cases) burn the spent uranium rods of older reactors as their fuel. They have also come up with much safer reactor designs that cannot melt down even if someone deliberately bypasses their safety systems (as the hapless technicians did at Chernobyl). These fourth-generation reactors – if they pan out – will offer a major improvement on the reactors of today, and could provide a powerful, safe, and cost-effective substitute for fossil fuel-powered electric stations.

The most tantalizing possibility of all lies in nuclear fusion, a process that – like the H-bomb compared to the Hiroshima bomb – would release a thousand times as much usable energy as today's fission reactors. The engineering challenge here basically involves creating a small temporary version of the Sun inside your power plant and harvesting its output for

44

a little while. Scientists are working on a variety of design approaches, ranging from laser arrays and electrostatic charges to magnetic force fields – all aimed at persuading two atomic nuclei to fuse together in a controlled fashion. A multinational project in southern France, known as ITER, is aiming to create a viable fusion reaction by 2035; and in 2020 an MIT-based company, Commonwealth Fusion Systems, published a series of research papers suggesting that their smaller reactor design might plausibly be producing fusion-based electricity as soon as 2030.[19]

At first glance, this might seem like an even more dangerous technology than fission reactors, but this turns out not to be the case. Achieving stable fusion in a power plant is a very different technical process from unleashing explosive fusion in an H-bomb: it requires an exquisitely balanced set of physical conditions in order to work properly, and any machinery malfunction or human error would simply disrupt those fine-tuned conditions and end the reaction. Only small amounts of radioactive fuel are involved (compared with H-bombs and fission reactors), and thus if things go wrong the result is a harmless fizzle rather than a meltdown or an explosion.

If a truly safe and cost-effective form of nuclear power becomes available – one that persuasively addresses the pitfalls of radioactive waste – humankind would have abundant electricity, which could be used to make abundant hydrogen fuel cell power. Next-generation batteries and hydrogen fuel cells could propel a whole new panoply of industrial, heating, and transport technologies with near-zero greenhouse gas emissions.[20] Given the urgent imperative to stave off global warming by decarbonizing our economy, it seems misguided to write off the nuclear energy option. On the contrary: research efforts in this field should be amply funded and vigorously pursued. I'll return to this idea in the coming chapters.

* * *

4

Pandemics, Natural or Bioengineered

THE NIGHTMARE OF THE NANOTECH PIONEERS

In 1986, the physicist K. Eric Drexler published *Engines of Creation*, a remarkable book that helped launch the field of nanotechnology. Among the many inventions he envisioned, one device captured the imagination of novelists, journalists, and other scientists: the molecular assembler, a micromachine whose primary function would be to use the materials and energy from its environment to make exact copies of itself. Drexler pictured it as a boxlike structure made of about one billion atoms; it would therefore be much smaller than a typical human cell, which contains some 100 trillion atoms. The assembler would possess multiple arms for manipulating nearby atoms and molecules; a small onboard "computer" designed to work by simple mechanical and chemical processes; and a set of chemically coded instructions for the computer to read and follow. Once unleashed, the assembler would start working its way through its environment, grabbing materials and putting them together step by step into a faithful replica of itself. Its arms, being so short, would be able to move very quickly and dexterously – about 50 million times faster than a human arm.

> Working at one million atoms per second, the system will copy itself in one thousand seconds, or a bit over fifteen minutes ... Imagine such a replicator floating in a bottle of chemicals, making copies of itself ... The first replicator assembles a copy in one thousand seconds, the two replicators then build two more in one thousand seconds, the four build another four, and the eight build another eight. At the end of ten hours, there are not thirty-six new replicators, but over 68 billion. In less than a day, they would weigh a ton; in less than two days, they would outweigh the Earth; in another four hours, they would exceed the mass of the Sun and all the planets combined – if the bottle of chemicals hadn't run dry long before ... [This] makes one thing perfectly clear: we cannot afford certain kinds of accidents with replicating assemblers.[1]

Omnivorous nanobots replicating out of control and consuming the planet: this image has come to be called the "gray goo scenario," because Drexler speculated that his exponentially growing mass of assemblers might appear to the naked eye as a drab gelatinous mass of gray material. (That is, of course, until a few seconds later, when the expanding blob engulfs its human observer and converts her body to more replicators.) Science-fiction writers like Neal Stephenson and Michael Crichton have since popularized the idea of "ecophagy" (nanobots eating the biosphere).[2] The futurist Ray Kurzweil devoted several pages in his book, *The Singularity Is Near*, to calculating how long it would take for such nanomachines to carry out their ecophagy: several weeks, he concluded.[3]

Nevertheless, the consensus today among nanotechnology experts is that creating such a machine would be either extremely difficult or downright impossible.[4] One prominent sceptic was a Nobel-prizewinning chemist with the delightfully apposite name of Richard Smalley. From his perspective, Drexler's idea was a nonstarter because of two problems: fat fingers and sticky fingers.[5] Each arm on the molecular assembler would have to grab nearby atoms in order to configure them into copied parts, but how would it do so – since its "hands" were themselves atom-sized objects, too big to properly move and position other atoms in the complex three-dimensional space within which all atoms interact? Worse still, the "hands" would inevitably form electronic bonds with many of the atoms they grasped and would not be able to let go of those atoms once they'd been touched: hence the sticky fingers.[6]

Other experts have weighed in with additional considerations. In order to be truly omnivorous, such a nanobot would need to convert any and all matter it encountered into copies of itself – but how would this actually work? How would it make atoms of beryllium into nitrogen, for example, or sulfur into silver? Where would it get the energy it requires for operating? What would prevent one replicator from eating another, thereby throwing the exponential multiplication process into reverse? Would a small and relatively simple onboard computer suffice to direct the dauntingly complex array of functions required of such a machine?[7]

Drexler himself, in his more recent writings, has acknowledged that self-replicating nanobots – while theoretically feasible – remain quite far from becoming a reality.[8] He believes that the most important advantages of atomically precise manufacturing can be reaped without recourse to self-replication at all. A more efficient and economical alternative is to build desktop-sized molecular factories (about the size of a household computer printer) that are wholly controlled by human technicians. Such a factory would indeed manipulate matter at the atomic or molecular scale, but its operations would be neither autonomous nor exponential in nature, and would therefore run no risk of inadvertently unleashing a gooey apocalypse.

ENGINEERED LIFE FORMS

A biologist might break into a smile as she reads about the extreme difficulty of creating nanobots that self-replicate. "Sheesh," she might say, "the creatures I study do this all the time." Many life forms are constantly making copies of themselves along an exponentially rising trajectory. What keeps them from overwhelming the planet like gray goo is the fact that both their internal design and their external environments constrain their reproduction. Deer, wolves, and plants, for example, coexist within their common habitat in a way that gives rise to self-limiting outcomes: if too many deer are born, they tend to overeat the plants, which leads to starvation and a return to lower population levels; the wolves help ensure that any spare deer are swiftly taken out of play. Dependence on plants and vulnerability to wolves are written into the constitution of deer, beautifully counterbalancing their propensity to breed like mad. Evolution, over time, has generated these kinds of self-limiting relationships that keep biological gray goo from happening.

Of course, human interference sometimes makes a mess of this. Kudzu vines now proliferate across the American South, engulfing entire landscapes like a form of green goo. Because kudzu was brought in from abroad and has few natural predators to keep it in check, it has become a (temporarily) dominant plant whose growth is exponential and unchecked. Sooner or later, though, it too will probably encounter a new limiting factor – perhaps another imported creature like the giant African land snail will start munching on it – and a new balance will eventually emerge.

But what if a new kind of engineered life form were created – one that self-replicates quite efficiently but does not fit into nature's scheme of self-limiting factors? Once it escaped from the laboratory, who could control it? These are among the questions hanging over the new field of synthetic biology.[9] In the case of self-duplicating nanobots, the hardest part (thank goodness) would be getting the little machines to work properly and make copies of themselves in the first place. With synthetic life forms, the hard part is the exact opposite: restraining and governing these creatures while they busily go about doing what living beings do best, namely, making more of themselves. This is why synthetic biology poses a far more serious danger than nanotechnology.

"Imagine," notes the Stanford biologist Drew Endy, "that you could construct organisms just like you could construct bridges."[10] When engineers build a bridge, they take off-the-shelf parts like girders, rivets, cables, and braces, and put them together in ways that fit the requirements of a particular site like a canyon that needs to be spanned. Synthetic biology proceeds according to similar logic. You take off-the-shelf cellular parts that other biologists have created, such as standardized DNA plasmids or modular proteins, and assemble them in ingenious ways that allow you to create a new and very specific kind of life form. If your design works well, your creation starts busily doing things or producing things that improve people's lives in all manner of ways.

Definitions of the term "synthetic biology" vary widely, but the basic gist is to use engineering principles in creating biological components or novel microorganisms. Most synthetic biologists combine a variety of approaches in their work: informatics, genetic engineering, nanotechnology, and molecular engineering, to name just a few. Some focus on modifying existing creatures, endowing them with novel traits and capabilities; others start from scratch, seeking to build entirely new life forms from the bottom up.

One of the leaders of the field has been the biologist J. Craig Venter, who first became famous at the time of the Human Genome Project, when his company developed machines that greatly accelerated the sequencing of DNA. Since that time, he has focused on synthetic biology. In 2016 his team of researchers announced the creation of a new bacterium, dubbed Syn 3.0, that possessed the smallest genome of any freely living organism – a mere 473 genes, barely enough for survival and reproduction.[11] The idea here was to engineer a life form so simple that virtually all its biological functions could be well characterized and understood. By splicing individual genes one at a time back into the creature's DNA, biologists would then be able to study their effects and become more adept than ever at designing new life forms to serve human purposes. A *New York Times* reporter described the practical applications of Venter's research:

> They will be custom bugs, designer bugs – bugs that only Venter can create. He will mix them up in his private laboratory from bits and pieces of DNA, and then he will release them into the air and the water, into smokestacks and oil spills, hospitals and factories and your house. Each of the bugs will have a mission. Some will be designed to devour things, like pollution. Others will generate food and fuel. There will be bugs to fight global

warming, bugs to clean up toxic waste, bugs to manufacture medicine and diagnose disease, and they will all be driven to complete these tasks by the very fibers of their synthetic DNA.[12]

Not surprisingly, venture capitalists have scrambled to get on the bandwagon of this field, as hundreds of laboratories throughout the world have applied themselves to the project of engineering new life.[13] But one of the most exciting features of synthetic biology is that you don't actually require a Ph.D. or a well-funded lab to get involved in this research. All you need is a few thousand bucks, a garage, and a willingness to get your hands dirty. Harvard's George Church describes this rapid and unexpected "democratization" process:

> In the early years of synthetic biology, researchers spoke of "do-it-yourself biology" [DIYbio] as essentially a metaphor referring to the prospect of amateurs creating organisms in their kitchen at some unspecified time in the future. "Garage biology," likewise, was a jocular term of abuse. A decade or so later, however, those possibilities had become realities, sooner than many of us would have thought. The website biohack.sourceforge.net, for example, offers an "open, free synthetic biology kit [that] contains all sorts of information [on] how to extract and amplify DNA, ... techniques in genetic engineering, tissue engineering, synbio, stem cell research, somatic cell nuclear transfer, evolutionary engineering, bioinformatics, etc." ... [By 2010] there were local DIYbio communities all over the globe, including several in the United States and Europe, three in India, and three more in South America. In addition, there were about 2000 subscribers to the DIYbio mailing list.[14]

The excitement has spread into the ranks of college and high school students as well. In 2004, a new competition was announced at MIT, under the name iGEM: International Genetically Engineered Machine. The idea, modeled on popular robotics competitions, was for teams of youths to set ambitious goals for themselves in some application of synthetic biology, then come together to compare their results.[15] In the years that followed, the competition grew like a bacterial culture in a petri dish: by 2020 it included 4,800 participants from 42 nations. Among the recent award winners: a group of grad students from Munich built a machine for 3D tissue printing; high school students from Taiwan developed a biosensor for screening toxins in herbal medicine; Dutch university students created a bacterium that would protect honeybees from mites; and an Australian group of undergrads invented a fruit ripeness detector.[16]

The iGEM organization in Boston has established a registry of standard biological parts that anyone from Craig Venter to the Taiwan high school students can freely access online – a catalog of DNA sequences and other basic organic operators whose functional properties have been identified and tested.[17] These parts are known as BioBrick components, and they serve as interchangeable elements that can be put together in myriad combinations to generate new cellular functions.[18] In this way, Drew Endy's dream of "constructing organisms just like you construct bridges" is coming closer to reality. "In two days," noted Joi Ito of MIT's Media Lab,

> you are able to design a gene sequence, assemble it, stick it into a bacteria, and reboot the thing . . . A few years ago this would be Nobel Prize-winning stuff. Now you can do it in your kitchen."[19]

SECURITY CONCERNS

All these developments are impressive and exciting – but what about the possibility of accidents, carelessness, or malicious abuse? For example, what if a smart but mentally unbalanced student decided to carry out an attack along the lines of Columbine or Virginia Tech – using genetically modified viruses as the weapon instead of a semi-automatic rifle? The scenario seems farfetched, but it isn't necessarily as farfetched as one would like it to be. In 2002, when a team of American biologists used genetic information off the Internet and mail-order DNA to create active poliovirus, the underlying message was crystal clear.[20] It is already feasible today for resourceful individuals to resurrect past killers or to invent new killers and to unleash them on an unprepared society – and this feasibility has increased with the dramatic broadening of access that has occurred over the past 20 years. Malice and forethought are not even required: a pandemic of artificial organisms could come about someday because of innocent errors in the work of perfectly well-intentioned researchers.

Vignette 1: How Jim and Evelyn's Virus Accidentally Killed Half the World (2039)

Jim and Evelyn, two gifted high school seniors from Mill Valley, California, are keen to get into Stanford. They decide that the best way to boost their chances is by launching an ambitious science project that will impress the admissions

Vignette 1: (cont.)

committee. Evelyn has recently read an article published in the journal Science: *"Characterization of the reconstructed 1918 Spanish influenza pandemic virus."[22] In the garage of Evelyn's house, the two of them have already put together an impressive home laboratory, chock full of sophisticated equipment bought second-hand off eBay for $6,500 over the preceding years. Evelyn's parents have happily subsidized these purchases, eager to support their daughter's passion for biology. Jim and Evelyn have also traveled twice to Boston, where the annual conferences of iGEM (International Genetically Engineered Machine) are held at MIT. Here they've competed with thousands of other youths from around the world in designing and creating new life forms with all manner of useful applications. At these conferences Jim and Evelyn have learned cutting-edge techniques in synthetic biology, using the BioBricks bank – the collection of standardized DNA sequences that anyone can freely access, allowing them to modify existing life forms in all kinds of ways.[23]*

Working feverishly together over a ten-month period, Jim and Evelyn synthesize a modified version of the 1918 pandemic flu virus, which infected a quarter of the world's human population shortly after World War I. In order to do this, they use genetic information easily available on the Web, and they order all the basic biological materials and chemical components they need from a variety of mail-order outfits. Somewhat to the youths' surprise, no agency of the US government monitors such transactions, as long as the purchaser isn't explicitly seeking to obtain a well-known pathogen.[24] Since the two of them are only ordering small segments of synthesized DNA from multiple suppliers, and have previously established themselves through their iGEM work as legitimate junior researchers, no alarm bells are triggered, and their purchases proceed smoothly.[25] Their goal is to stitch together these DNA segments into a modified viral genome for 1918 influenza, which they will use to develop a retroactive vaccine for the virus; this can then be used as a template for developing new vaccines against present-day scourges like H5N1 or H7N9.

On the last day of April, at 3:53 a.m., a 5.9 magnitude earthquake rocks the Bay Area; no one is killed but many structures are damaged. Some of the equipment in the garage lab of Jim and Evelyn, inadequately secured to the wall, topples to the floor and shatters. The engineered virus is released into the environment. Jim and Evelyn, convinced that their creation is not capable of causing infection, decide there's no need to alert the authorities. They clean up the mess and go back to school the next morning, unaware that they've both now been infected.

Unbeknownst to them, the modifications they've made to the virus have yielded a pathogen of unprecedented ferocity, embodying a perfect storm of deadly

Vignette 1: (cont.)

attributes. It can survive airborne for twelve hours, unlike naturally occurring flu, and is highly contagious via touch or breath; worst of all, it eludes containment, because it has a ten-day incubation period, allowing contagious individuals to travel far and wide without realizing that they're carrying the disease. Unlike ordinary flu, which only spreads efficiently after a patient becomes symptomatic and starts coughing and sneezing, this strain is highly transmissible by infected individuals throughout the ten-day incubation period.

These combined factors cause it to spread exponentially. Within 24 hours, it has propagated through Marin County; within 48 hours, it has moved throughout the Bay Area and has passed via infected airline passengers to a half-dozen other urban centers, two of them overseas. Within ten days – even though no one has gotten sick or even realizes yet that the virus exists – it has traversed 3,100 airports in 190 countries worldwide and is quietly incubating inside the bodies of 700,000 unsuspecting humans. Only then does it reveal its existence, as people start showing symptoms.

On May 11 the first cases are reported in the San Francisco area. The virus proves far more lethal than the 1918 version, killing 40 percent of the people it infects within five days after the onset of symptoms (almost the same level of lethality as Ebola). As the death toll swiftly mounts, officials in every nation soon find themselves swamped. They order an immediate halt to all domestic and foreign travel, but the virus has already reached all but the most remote settlements on the planet. It keeps spreading, with the rate of infection accelerating along a steep curve, as symptomatic patients become even more contagious than those in the incubation stage. All containment measures fail because the infected persons are by now almost everywhere – in just about every city, town, or rural hamlet around the globe. Existing vaccines don't work, and there's not enough time to develop new ones. Healthcare workers are hit especially hard, for they were among the first to be exposed after patients started arriving in emergency rooms. Public order breaks down, as panic spreads.

By September 1 – Day 124 of the pandemic – 800 million persons have died and a billion more are sick. The world's basic social, economic, and medical systems have collapsed, and people are now starting to die from lack of food and clean water, and from secondary diseases like typhus and cholera that spread like wildfire among the survivors. By the end of October, 42 percent of the planet's human population is dead or dying; the remaining 58 percent have either survived the disease and acquired immunity, or have managed to remain isolated. All

Vignette 1: (cont.)

transportation and communication have broken down; electricity is no longer being generated; food is not being grown. Isolated bands of marauding survivors pick their way through the stench of the cities and suburbs, living off canned goods.

One year later, at summer's end, the last spasms of disease have played themselves out, and the final toll has stabilized. Fifty-four percent of the Earth's human population has perished during the fourteen months of disease, starvation, and exposure – about four billion persons. The survivors – just under half of humankind – have now begun to rebuild basic subsistence farming and the rudiments of a new civilization. Since the virus proved fatal only to humans, the majority of the world's nonhuman creatures live on – birds, animals, insects, and plants, slowly moving in to occupy the spaces vacated by the once-dominant species on the planet.

Sound farfetched? Every aspect of this scenario that leads up to the hypothetical virus's accidental release is already a reality today.[21] You and I can get together this afternoon, if we wish, and launch precisely the sorts of pioneering science projects pursued by youths like Jim and Evelyn, using freely available information, training manuals, lab kits, and biological materials. There is no need for permits, training, or inspections – all that's required is a few thousand dollars, an internet connection, and an inquiring mind. In 2006, for example, a journalist for *The Guardian* newspaper decided to test the biosecurity system in the UK. He picked smallpox virus because this scourge had been eradicated worldwide in 1979 and only existed in specimens housed in two secure labs (one in the United States and one in Russia). He ordered a small segment of smallpox DNA:

> *The Guardian* placed an order online with VH Bio Ltd, a company in Gateshead that supplies equipment and chemicals used in standard molecular biology labs. We used an invented company name along with just a mobile telephone number and free email address. VH Bio Ltd rang to check whether the address provided was a residential address. The journalist told VH Bio Ltd that our company was in the process of moving offices and so wanted to make sure the order arrived. The package, which contained a 78-letter sequence of DNA, which is part of one of the smallpox virus's coat protein genes, was delivered by the Royal Mail to a flat in north London. The A5-sized Jiffy bag contained a small plastic phial with a tiny blob of white gel at the bottom – the DNA. The

order cost £33.08, plus an additional £7 for postage. Alan Volkers, chairman of VH Bio Ltd, said the company had no idea that the sequence they produced was a modified sequence of smallpox DNA.[26]

Just to be clear: the journalist was nowhere near gaining possession of actual smallpox virus. What arrived at his London apartment was only a fraction of 1 percent of the smallpox DNA (whose genome comprises 185,000 letters); but the underlying point was made. It should not be this easy for unscreened individuals to buy gene segments of one of history's deadliest pathogens.

One might expect that these kinds of embarrassing security breaches would have spurred law enforcement officials to rush to address the problem. But in 2018 it happened again, this time with the virus for horsepox, an extinct relative of smallpox. A team of Canadian researchers purchased separate but overlapping fragments of DNA for horsepox from a mail-order biotech company, then stitched them back together in their lab. The total cost for the DNA segments was $100,000. After the full horsepox genome had been recreated, the scientists injected it into a cell and coaxed it to start producing infectious particles.[27] Although these scientists had opted to follow their own university's safety protocols, no government permits, oversight, or inspections had been required of them. "To some experts," a *New York Times* journalist observed, "the experiment nullified a decades-long debate over whether to destroy the world's two remaining smallpox remnants ... since it proved that scientists who want to experiment with the virus can now create it themselves."[28]

Most biologists believe that an accidental pandemic like the one I described above is unlikely to occur anytime soon, for several reasons. First, the practice of amateur biology requires a significant level of "tacit knowledge" – the hands-on practical experience that one can only acquire gradually, through years of apprenticeship.[29] Second, most life forms are extremely complex systems, and introducing modifications to those systems results in failure more often than success. Finally, the "perfect pathogen" I envisioned, with its array of deadly features, is unlikely to emerge accidentally from a single sequence of experiments carried out by amateurs.

Nevertheless, most biosecurity experts do agree that significant new dangers are coming over the horizon. As Drew Endy has grimly noted: "I expect that this technology will be misapplied, actively misapplied, and it would be irresponsible to have a conversation about the technology without acknowledging that fact."[30] The principal risks are fourfold: the inadvertent creation of deadly superbugs; the deliberate creation of nasty bugs of this sort for use as a bioweapon; the uncontrolled swapping of genetic material between synthetic organisms and wild microbes, resulting in harmful ecological impacts; and the spontaneous mutation of synthetic microorganisms into new species endowed with unforeseeable traits.[31]

Leading figures in the field have responded to these risks over recent decades with laudable transparency and vigor, putting in place an impressive array of precautionary and protective measures. During the 1970s, when recombinant DNA techniques were first emerging, 140 top scientists met at Asilomar, California, laying out comprehensive ground-rules for managing the biohazards of their research.[32] They pledged to restrict their experiments to organisms that would not be able to flourish outside the laboratory, and adopted a variety of containment measures, taking care that the modified organisms could not spread beyond their petri dishes. Certain types of highly pathogenic organisms were declared off-limits to experimentation. Finally, they resolved to maintain transparency about the nature of their research, keeping the public apprised of the ongoing work they were doing.[33] In 2015 a second major conference followed, this time spurred by the recent discovery of the powerful CRISPR tool for editing genomes; the scientists established a voluntary moratorium on using CRISPR-based techniques for altering genes in human sex cells, which could be passed on to subsequent generations.[34]

Will such measures keep us safe over the long haul? Maintaining safety and security is hard enough for seasoned researchers working in well-funded university or corporate labs; it will prove even harder for the thousands of relative newbies who are flocking to the field, excited at the powers opened up by easy access to the tools for engineering new life forms.[35] Will such practitioners exercise the sorts of restraint shown by the field's leading scientists in recent decades? Will their self-funded labs be adequately equipped with containment and security features? In most cases, the answer may indeed be Yes. But in some cases here and there the answer will probably be No – and unless the current oversight system is revamped, no one will be in a position to stop them, or to even know what they're up to – until it's too late.

As for military-grade bioweapons developed in secret government labs, these create a quite different sort of danger, which I'll take up in later chapters. One of the important side-effects of the COVID-19 pandemic has been to educate the world's peoples about the danger of microbes running amok. Whether the pathogens arise naturally from interactions between animals and humans, or emerge from the laboratories of professional researchers, military scientists, or biohacking amateurs, we urgently need new global mechanisms for regulating research and for responding swiftly to pandemics before they spin out of control.

* * *

5

Artificial Intelligence: Extreme Reward and Risk

THE SHRINKING CIRCLE

The set of things that only humans can do, and machines can't do, keeps getting smaller.[1] People became edgy about AI when the world chess champion Garry Kasparov was bested by a machine in 1997. In the years that followed, various machines trounced other human maestros in the notoriously complex Chinese game of Go and the notoriously silly game for factoid lovers, Jeopardy. Ten years ago, you had to speak very slowly and clearly to a voice-recognition program, and the result would be: "Take ten years of pasta savagely." Today Siri and Google Home and Alexa laugh at me when I try to fluster them with "Manicheanism," "Maimonides" or "muchas gracias." AI machines are driving Teslas and Google cars, sending you personalized ads, trading stocks in microseconds, designing computer programs, helping doctors with diagnoses, shunting packets of information across the Internet, and writing mathematical proofs. Every year machines get closer to passing the Turing Test – the famous scenario in which a person having a text exchange with an intelligent machine can't tell whether she's having a conversation with an AI or another human. Machines are writing poetry too (though in that department we're still well short of W. B. Yeats).[2]

Then, in 2015, something strange happened. Four of the world's most eminent science-and-tech authorities – Bill Gates, Elon Musk, Stuart Russell, and Stephen Hawking – all came out with roughly the same message: AI is on track to become the most powerful invention in human history, and if we're not careful with it, it could end up destroying us.[3]

The famous men explained their reasoning. Right now, all we have is narrow AI. These are machines that are fast and effective at performing a single well-defined task. The AI that drives the Google car wouldn't know what to make of a chess board. But the sophistication of AI is growing rapidly, with new forms of deep learning, neural networks, and pattern-recognition algorithms coming online every day.[4] In the near future, some of these machines will get better at doing multiple human-level tasks at the same time. This is the new definition of intelligence that's emerging among AI developers: an integrated set of high-level capabilities that range across a wide swath of human behaviors.[5] These would include, for example:

- An ability to parse ambiguous sentences, such as a street sign that reads "SLOW Children at Play." The machine would draw upon a broad commonsense familiarity with the human life-world that allows it to conclude that in this context we are worried about fast-moving cars, not phlegmatic youths. Such a machine would possess a functional comprehension of what the sign means – which poses a much tougher challenge than merely translating sentences or obeying straightforward commands.
- An ability to take a standardized test like the pre-college SAT or ACT and perform reasonably well at it without prior preparation. The machine would need to assess the task being presented by a particular question, devise a strategy for answering it, know how to obtain the requisite information, and figure out the right answer. (Some AI programs can already outperform human test-takers on SAT analogy problems today.)[6]
- An ability to perform a complex physical task without human coaching. The machine would be able to assemble a piece of furniture from IKEA right out of the box, simply by following the pictorial instructions (a task that defeats the intelligence of most humans). Or you might ask it to build a brick wall, and it would know what you meant and set about obtaining the materials, planning the design, and executing the steps needed for successful construction.[7]
- An ability to interpret and summarize real-world information. The machine could be shown a movie like *It's a Wonderful Life* and explain the gist of the story in a few sentences. As an additional challenge, it could be asked to explain why at one point the angel named Clarence jumps into the freezing river water.

These tasks set the bar much higher than the original Turing Test, because they aim not just at a clever simulation of human verbal repartee, but at actual functional capabilities that underlie what we mean when we speak of intelligent human behavior.[8] To be sure, passing these arduous tests would by no means prove that the machine is having thoughts and feelings equivalent to those that a human experiences while performing such tasks. But that's precisely the point: intelligence is not being defined here as a full-scale replication of human conscious activity, but simply as a *functional implementation of specific human capabilities.* When we say that the machine "understands" the meaning of the street sign or the plot of the movie, we are not suggesting that it undergoes the same sorts of conscious and unconscious experiences as humans; we are merely saying that it can respond appropriately to the nuances of context, performing certain interpretive and goal-oriented functions in a way that generates a similar outcome to what a human would do. It is replicating human behaviors, not necessarily human experience. (What it would "feel like" to be such a machine is certainly a fascinating question – and I'd love to hear what the machine would say about it. I'll return to this question later on.)

BROADENING POWERS

This expansive (and more demanding) definition of intelligence suggests where the most exciting action will be in AI research over the coming decades. Tomorrow's advanced AI machines will be adaptive, interactive, and capable of learning on their own. Their intelligence and agency will no longer be confined to a single narrow domain, but will be increasingly versatile and multifunctional in nature. Why is this likely? Because such versatile machines would come closer to replicating the qualities we find most impressive in human agents: applying insights gleaned from one activity to solving problems in entirely new areas.[9]

People who control such ingenious and adaptive machines, working in tandem with them, will wield considerably greater powers over the world than those who don't. Their business ventures will outperform those of their rivals; their AI-driven cars and planes will be safer than human-controlled vehicles; their doctors will work alongside brilliant machine collaborators, providing better health care; their communications with other people will be facilitated; their ability to keep informed and acquire new knowledge will be enhanced; their smart houses and household bots will make their lives easier; their investment portfolios will grow more rapidly; their networked machines will connect seamlessly with each other; the military forces of their nation will dominate those of nations with weaker AI. The advent of such multifunctional AI machines, in short, will have the same sort of pervasive impact on human life that the advent of the Internet did. This will become a breakthrough technology that helps determine who calls the shots in economic, political, and military affairs over the coming century.[10] We can expect funding from both private and governmental sources to keep pouring into the field, giving AI researchers an incentive to compete with each other in developing such versatile machines as quickly as possible.

The winners of this race are likely to be those researchers whose AI machines can modify themselves over time, on their own, without direct human instruction or supervision. This design feature of self-improvement is already a decisive factor in the most advanced machines of today.[11] Take Google's AlphaGo for example. Early versions of this machine learned to master the game of Go by working through a database of more than 100,000 games played previously by human experts. The machine extracted winning patterns of play from that immense database through its brute computational ability and blistering processing speed. In 2017 it decisively beat the human world-champion, Ke Jie, and claimed the title of Best on Planet.

But AlphaGo Zero, the most recent version of this machine, took an entirely different tack.[12] It started from scratch, using random moves, and played game after game against itself, learning from its experience and improving over time. No human experts, no database, were involved at all: the researchers dubbed it "tabula rasa learning."[13] After a succession of 30 million games against itself (played 24/7 over 40 days and nights) the machine was able to trounce the earlier version of AlphaGo and claim the title. What's more, AlphaGo Zero achieved mastery at the game more quickly and efficiently than the original program, using one-tenth as many processing units.

Then Google's programmers unleashed their machine on chess, modifying its name to AlphaZero. Once again it started with a tabula rasa and played millions of games against itself – this time over a mere four-hour period. Not even bothering with a match against humans, the Google scientists set up their machine to play a hundred matches against the reigning world champion chess-playing machine, Stockfish. The Cornell mathematician Steven Strogatz describes how it went:

> AlphaZero scored 28 wins and 72 draws. It didn't lose a single game. Most unnerving was that AlphaZero seemed to express insight. It played like no computer ever has, intuitively and beautifully, with a romantic, attacking style. It played gambits and took risks. In some games it paralyzed Stockfish and toyed with it.
>
> While conducting its attack in Game 10, AlphaZero retreated its queen back into the corner of the board on its own side, far from Stockfish's king, not normally where an attacking queen should be placed. Yet this peculiar retreat was venomous: no matter how Stockfish replied, it was doomed. It was almost as if AlphaZero was waiting for Stockfish to realize, after billions of brutish calculations, how hopeless its position truly was, so that the beast could relax and expire peacefully, like a vanquished bull before a matador. Grandmasters had never seen anything like it. AlphaZero had the finesse of

a virtuoso and the power of a machine. It was humankind's first glimpse of an awesome new kind of intelligence.[14]

David Silver, one of the scientists who spearheaded the AlphaGo project, explained the broader implications of the achievement:

> If you can achieve tabula rasa learning, you really have an agent that can be transplanted from the game of Go to any other domain. You untie yourself from the specifics of the domain you're in, and you come up with an algorithm which is so general that it can be applied anywhere . . . What we started to see was that AlphaGo Zero not only rediscovered the common patterns and openings that humans tend to play ... it ultimately discarded them in preference for its own variants that humans don't even know about ... I think what we're most excited about is how far AlphaGo can go in the real world. The fact that a program can achieve a very high level of performance in a domain as complicated and challenging as Go should mean that now we can start to tackle some of the most challenging and impactful problems for humanity.[15]

Demis Hassabis, one of the other leading AlphaGo researchers, suggested that the machine's first such new challenge might be to model the processes of protein folding, whose gargantuan complexity has baffled human researchers thus far.[16]

AlphaGo Zero, impressive as it is, can be unplugged by any human who wishes to do so. Its self-improvement takes place within narrow parameters that are entirely controlled by its operators. It can't redesign its own hardware, and even if it could do so, it would still rely on human engineers to supply the necessary materials and do the actual rewiring and reconfiguring of its physical components. But if we draw dotted lines into the future, extending today's impressive advances in robotics and AI outward, what do we see? Seven deep trend lines are likely to converge over the coming decades:[17]

1. *From narrow to broad.* The machines will become progressively more versatile and multifunctional in their capabilities.
2. *Self-modification.* Powerful algorithms for self-improvement will lie at the core of their motivational programming, learning capabilities, and advancing achievements over time.
3. *Robot/AI convergence.* Advanced AI programs will no longer be cooped up in metal boxes in research labs, but will start to permeate the physical world, engaging their economic and social environment in ever more complex interactions. Some AI machines will be endowed with a growing

array of robot bodies; others will interact with the physical world via a more ethereal web of cyberspace connections.

4. *Practical knowledge.* Robot/AI machines will gradually be entrusted with complex tasks in the real world that require them to develop sophisticated commonsense knowledge about the causal processes and unwritten rules of the natural and social environment.

5. *Networks.* Robot/AI machines will probably not function in isolation from each other; many of them will be designed by humans to form cooperative networks that enhance their efficacy at fulfilling human goals.

6. *Saying No to humans.* Such physically embodied and socially embedded machines will need to be endowed by humans with an ability to override or refuse to obey some human commands under specific circumstances. If I tell an AI to go hurt somebody, it has to be able to say No.

7. *Racing for more power.* Strong competitive pressures and market mechanisms will incentivize researchers in robotics and AI to develop increasingly powerful, multifunctional, and self-improving machines as quickly as possible, with only a secondary priority for caution and restraint.

What will the world be like when it's populated by millions of such machines? The AI researcher Stuart Russell argues that even among his colleagues in engineering and computer science, the human imagination tends to fall short as it seeks to envision the practical consequences. We speak blandly of "reduced medical errors, safer cars, or other advances of an incremental nature."[18] But this is unrealistic, he maintains. What's far more likely to happen is a relatively swift and radical transformation of our lives. These machines will eventually exceed human capabilities in speed, sensing, memory, information-processing, and capacity for physical action. "Whereas a human can read and understand one book in a week," Russell writes,

> a machine could read and understand every book ever written – all 150 million of them – in a few hours ... By the same token, the machine can see everything at once through satellites, robots, and hundreds of millions of surveillance cameras; watch all the world's TV broadcasts; and listen to all the world's radio stations and phone conversations. Very quickly it would gain a far more detailed and accurate understanding of the world and its inhabitants than any human could possibly hope to acquire ... A human has direct control over one body, while a machine can control thousands or millions. Some automated factories already exhibit this characteristic ... In the cyber realm, machines already have access to billions of effectors – namely, the displays on all the phones and computers in the world.[19]

Humankind is currently working very hard to make such a world a reality. In all the leading industrial nations, researchers are devoting immense resources to precisely the sorts of scientific and engineering enterprises that could eventually result in the creation of autonomous, intelligent, self-modifying machines – most of which will be able to work together in flexible, synergistic ways that further multiply their powers.

SUPERINTELLIGENCE?

Will such machines be "superintelligent"? Since this term can be misleading, it's worth pausing for a moment to define it. Some theorists have argued that it's misguided to speak of intelligence as a measurable quality that can be multiplied at will to ever higher levels.[20] We do assign numbers to people via IQ tests, of course, but these tests are still operating within a narrow range of variation. When we speak of one person as being twice as smart as another person, we intuitively grasp what this means: I try to solve a math problem, and you can solve it far more quickly and elegantly than I can. Perhaps you can solve it in half the time: you're "twice as smart."

But what about if we say that one person is ten times as smart as another person? What does ten times more mean for intelligence? Since average human IQ is by definition 100, has there ever been a human who had an IQ of 1,000? No, there hasn't – not even close. The actual range is more like 50 to 200 or so.[21] Suppose such a person with a 1,000 IQ were born one day. If a person with average IQ and the one with 1,000 IQ are confronted with a problem to solve, will the 1,000 IQ person be able to solve it ten times as quickly? Or will the 1,000 IQ person consider the problem so trivial that it's not even worth solving at all? Now, what about a person who sports a 10,000 IQ (she's 100 times as smart as the average human of today)? What on earth could that possibly mean, in concrete practice? It's hard to imagine. We don't even know if it's a coherent concept at all.

This strikes me as a reasonable line of argument. Whenever we use words like "smart" or "intelligent," we're deploying vague anthropomorphic concepts that make intuitive sense to us but that may no longer work well when applied to high-powered machines.[22] So perhaps it's helpful to define superintelligence along more precise functional lines. A superintelligent machine might have, for example, the following attributes in comparison with its human makers:

- 10 thousand times more memory storage
- 10 million times faster memory writing and retrieval

- 10 times greater capacity for pattern recognition
- 10 times greater ability to form new concepts
- 10 times greater ability to visualize and manipulate dimensional representations
- 100 times greater ability to do basic math
- 10 times greater ability to do complex math
- Entirely new kinds of mathematical ability
- 10 times greater ability to visualize and rotate images of spatial objects
- 100 times greater vocabulary of nouns
- 10 times greater vocabulary of verbs
- Ability to form sentences with 10 times greater syntactical complexity.

Most of these cognitive functions are quantifiable and measurable.[23] It's not inconceivable that we could someday build such a high-powered machine. We would presumably proceed by focusing on each of these cognitive capabilities, one by one, boosting them to ever higher levels – just as we have already done with mathematical calculation, pattern recognition, and game-playing ability. At every step of the way, we would also be seeking to make sure that each of these enhanced cognitive faculties remained integrated with the others, so as to avoid an imbalance among functions that undermines the machine's overall operation.[24]

A major historical threshold will be crossed at the moment when an all-purpose machine acquires the ability to reason, innovate, and modify itself in ways that resemble the mental capacity of humans. This is known in the scientific literature by a variety of names: artificial general intelligence (AGI), human-level machine intelligence, or strong AI. If you ask the people who design and build these machines whether achieving this level of performance is possible, some say "No, never" – but the vast majority reply in the affirmative. One recent overview of these expert polls offered the following rough estimate: a 50 percent chance that AGI will arrive by 2040; and a 90 percent probability that it will be achieved by 2075.[25] At a major AI conference in 2017, half of the scientists estimated that the AGI threshold would be crossed by 2047.[26]

Some prominent scientists reject the view that advanced AI is likely to bring extreme new dangers into our future. "It's bizarre to think that roboticists will not build safeguards against harm as they proceed," argues the psychologist Steven Pinker:

> The worry that an AI system would be so clever at attaining one of the goals programmed into it (like commandeering energy) that it would ride roughshod over the others (like human safety) assumes that AI will descend upon us faster than we can design fail-safe precautions. The

reality is that progress in AI is hype-defyingly slow, and there will be plenty of time for feedback from incremental implementations, with humans wielding the screwdriver at every stage.[27]

In a similar vein, Facebook's Mark Zuckerberg invited Elon Musk to his Palo Alto home in 2014, hoping to persuade Musk over dinner to back away from his influential public statements about the dangers of an AI apocalypse.[28] Musk stuck to his guns, however, and Zuckerberg later emerged as a prominent booster of AI technology, touting the myriad benefits to be gained by harnessing intelligent machines. "With A.I. especially," he said, "I'm really optimistic. People who are naysayers and kind of try to drum up these doomsday scenarios – I don't understand it. It's really negative and in some ways I actually think it is pretty irresponsible."[29]

During a March 2018 gathering hosted by Amazon's Jeff Bezos in Palm Springs, the neuroscientist Sam Harris argued that the pressures of the AI arms race would lead some researchers to override safety concerns in the name of being first past the post with a full-fledged superintelligent machine. "This is something you have made up," retorted the robot designer Rodney Brooks. At this point, according to an account in the *New York Times*, Oren Etzioni, a prominent AI researcher, intervened to side with Brooks:

> He walked onto the stage and laid into Mr. Harris for three minutes, saying that today's A.I. systems are so limited, spending so much time worrying about superintelligence just doesn't make sense. The people who take Mr. Musk's side are philosophers, social scientists, writers – not the researchers who are working on A.I., he said. Among A.I. scientists, the notion that we should start worrying about superintelligence is "very much a fringe argument."[30]

To the extent that a schism divides the AI community over the potential dangers of superintelligence, it probably derives in many cases from a simple misunderstanding: how many years into the future are we speaking about? If the timeframe is five to fifteen years from now, most scientists agree that superintelligence is unlikely to pose any major threat. But if the timeframe is 50 years, or 75, the nature of the discussion changes. While some scientists are understandably loath to speculate about the technologies that may prevail a half-century hence, others definitely do see the potential for AI to become vastly more powerful – and more dangerous – than it is today.

How will we create such machines? A variety of approaches have been proposed, and all are being intensively explored by scientists and engineers in labs throughout the world. One method would be to reverse-engineer the human brain, then seek to reproduce as much as possible of the brain's neural architecture in a machine.[31] This could take a long while, however, because neuroscientists remain quite far from understanding how our brains generate our conscious awareness and cognition.[32] But even partial achievements along this path have already yielded promising results: the pattern-recognition systems required for self-driving cars and voice dictation are based on artificial neural nets that grew out of brain research. So are AlphaGo and AlphaZero.[33]

A second approach is to follow the same evolutionary pathway that nature took: start with relatively simple creatures like insects, and build machines that emulate their physical and mental capabilities; then, capitalizing on what we've learned in that design process, move up a notch, to the performance profile of lizards; then up again, to mice; then cats; then chimps; and finally on to humans.[34] A third approach is based on the idea that you don't have to build a full-fledged artificial human in order to achieve significant forms of human-level performance. In other words, your AGI doesn't need the whole gamut of fear, love, curiosity, narrative identity, social relationships, or creativity that characterize your average human person; all it needs is the right combination of sensing, reasoning, goal-directedness, and the ability to learn and self-correct. Such a machine might start far below the threshold of AGI but might incrementally learn to achieve human levels of performance as it modified itself over time.[35]

Many experts believe that, once self-improving AGI has been created, a very likely outcome will be the eventual emergence of some form of machine superintelligence (artificial superintelligence, or ASI). It's implausible, they argue, that self-improving machines would need to stop building new levels of capability for themselves, simply because they have reached the arbitrary threshold of human-level performance. There's plenty of room for improvement beyond homo sapiens.[36]

* * *

The advent of such superintelligent machines could yield spectacular new benefits across the entire gamut of society. After all, it was precisely the intelligence of humans, coupled with their ability to work together in flexible teams, that vaulted them to dominance on this planet – and it's hard to imagine any aspect of human endeavor that would not be improved by tapping into turbo-charged forms of insight and creativity. Factories would produce more; farms would yield greater crops; scientific discoveries would deepen; technological inventions would proliferate; the arts and humanities would flourish – and all these activities could presumably be pursued in highly sustainable ways that respect the long-term carrying capacity of the natural world.

But these benefits are conditional in nature: they will not come about automatically like fruits ripening on a tree. We will have to earn them by applying these new resources wisely – for the advent of artificial super-intelligence will also confront humankind with a daunting array of serious new dangers. I think of them as falling into five basic categories: unintended effects, misunderstanding/disobedience, paternalist machines, intelligence explosion, and weaponized AI.

UNINTENDED EFFECTS

Already today we are witnessing the early intimations of the first of these dangers, which some researchers describe with the term "unaligned AI" – meaning all those forms of AI that clash with core values of ethics or human flourishing. One obvious example is the racist or sexist AI machines that began surfacing in research labs in recent years. These machines used deep-learning methods to train themselves on vast databases of photographs and web pages, only to yield unexpected outputs that dismayed their makers: in one instance the machines began miscategorizing African-Americans as gorillas; in another they concluded that all women in the medical profes-sions should be labeled as "nurses." Though the AI researchers scrambled to correct these mistakes, such stories underscored how easily an advanced machine can reach perverse conclusions simply by following the logic of its programming too literally or narrowly.[37]

Another unintended effect of AI will be to accelerate the erosion of privacy. The trillions of daily activities carried out by the world's human population are densely interwoven with the billions of machines, large and small, that render human activities more efficient. Since many of those machines communicate with each other directly or indirectly, this cross-chatter generates an immense trove of searchable data. Homes and offices become nests of interacting smart machines helping people with everyday tasks; cell phones track people's physical movements and online behavior patterns; city streets bristle with cameras; and even remote natural parks and forests can be surveilled by satellites and drones. Increasingly, AI programs can also understand the *content* of what humans are saying to each other in written or verbal communications – which means that a corporate or gov-ernmental machine can monitor millions of conversations at a time. In such a world, it becomes increasingly hard to keep any human activity private for long, because other humans can use advanced AI to comb constantly through the churning torrents of real-time data.[38]

Some experts have suggested constructive steps we might take over the coming years to mitigate this problem.[39] We should ensure that information can only be used for its stated purpose: if a sophisticated new sensor at airport security detects a tumor in my abdomen, this should not be allowed to affect my health insurance. The profiling rules used by businesses and security services should be made public: when the algorithms of a software agent put me on a no-fly list or a low-credit category, I should be entitled to an explanation, and be given recourse to appeal the decision. Rigorous public oversight should apply to any database that holds my personal information, and if that information is no longer required for the purposes for which it was originally gathered, it should be permanently erased. These are all sensible measures, which should definitely be adopted. Nonetheless, they have a certain flavor of futility to them – like a child at the beach, frantically building walls and ditches around her sandcastle as she senses the tide rolling in. Such regulations will put limits on our loss of privacy, and that is perhaps the most that we can aspire to achieve.

We encounter another aspect of unaligned AI in the use of websites and social media for subtle manipulation of people's perceptions, habits, and preferences. Designers of computer games long ago discovered that players can be induced into highly addictive patterns of behavior by a cleverly structured sequence of tasks and rewards.[40] Now these psychological insights are being increasingly applied to online advertisements, commerce, and news feeds, in ways that can powerfully shape how we see the world and our own roles within it. The same sorts of tools that nudge me to opt for one brand of toothpaste over another can also be applied to influence how I vote, and even how I feel, perceive, and think.[41] As AI advances in sophistication over the coming years, it will further enhance the persuasive powers of the online worlds we inhabit – and this will open a space for all manner of unethical or harmful impacts on our lives.

A fourth effect of unaligned AI over the coming years will be to throw lots of people out of their jobs. Within the coming decade or two, single-purpose AI will drive your car for you; but millions of truckers, delivery drivers, and Uberistas will be put out of work. It will help your doctor make insightful judgements in healing your illness; but over time it may also upend the medical profession, greatly reducing the number of humans required to staff a clinic or hospital. It will transform manufacturing, agriculture, finance, and retail, overseeing the operations of an increasingly automated workforce. Few professions will escape the competition of these brilliant, capable, and relentlessly cheery new servants. Only those careers that require a distinctively human touch seem likely to survive intact: poets, scientists, creative entrepreneurs, priests, personal caregivers, and the like.[42] If we are to avoid chronic, mass unemployment, we will have to devise entirely new ways of conceiving the role of human labor – and the cultural meanings of that labor – in our society. (I'll return to this subject in later chapters.)

MISUNDERSTOOD COMMANDS AND DISOBEDIENT MACHINES

A core challenge with our AI/robotic servants will be to make sure they understand what we *really intend* when we tell them to do something. Let's suppose, for the sake of argument, that your team of researchers has finally succeeded in building a genuine AGI. It has a sleek android body and a mind that is versatile, potent, and eager to learn. In honor of Isaac Asimov, we'll call it Isaac.

One way of controlling Isaac's behavior is simply to give it direct and precise commands. "Fetch me a beer," you say. Isaac turns, bashes a large hole through the living room wall, walks through the hole to the fridge, and returns with your beer. Chastened, you modify your next command. "Fetch me another beer whilst doing zero damage to this house." What you don't realize is that Isaac has just given you the last beer in the fridge. Isaac walks out through the front door, crosses the garden, bashes a hole in the kitchen wall of the neighbor's house, disappears in there, then reemerges and returns with a beer.

You see the problem. In order for an intelligent robot to obey direct commands in a way that truly complies with our wishes, it has to possess a sophisticated understanding of the commonsense rules and assumptions that structure our human social existence.[43] Programming this sort of worldly understanding into a machine has turned out to be devilishly hard for researchers to accomplish: one project, headed by Douglas Lenat at Cycorp Inc., has spent $50 million over *35 years* working on the problem, and is still far from achieving this goal.[44]

Isaac Asimov, in his short stories, famously tried to meet this challenge by laying down three basic laws for his robots to follow: (1) never harm a human or allow a human to come to harm; (2) always obey orders unless this conflicts with the first law; (3) protect your own existence unless this conflicts with the first and second laws. Many of Asimov's short stories then go on to illustrate the problem with this rule-bound approach: in actual practice, these three laws repeatedly fail to yield the sorts of outcomes that humans actually intended.[45] Such laws would not, for example, prevent the beer-fetching mishaps I sketched above. If you told the robot to administer a flu shot to your kid, it would balk because this would require inflicting a small harm on the child. If two humans gave conflicting orders to a robot, it would be paralyzed with indecision. What Asimov was implying – once again – was that a robot would require a sophisticated grasp of the human world in order to serve as a truly useful assistant in our daily lives.

Taking this into account, AI researchers have explored a different approach. Rather than relying on precise commands and rules, they would seek to endow their machines with a basic set of broad goals and motivations, then allow the machine to figure out for itself what was the best way to realize those goals in any given context.[46] Let's imagine such a machine, an intelligent android named Hans (after Hans Moravec, another robotics visionary). Hans has been programmed with a core goal of making people happy. How does it know if it has succeeded in this goal? One way to tell, it has learned from experience, is that humans tend to smile when they're happy. Solution: Hans runs around the room, grabbing people's cheeks and stretching them out into a smiley shape. "No, no, no," you tell Hans: "that's not what we meant. We meant for you to give people good *reasons* for smiling." Hans thanks you for the clarification. It then runs around the room, telling each person that they've won the lottery.[47]

Once again, you see the problem: the robot's fulfillment of our actual wishes requires a comprehensive understanding of the human life-world. If this sort of understanding is lacking, then broad, flexible goals are no better a behavioral guideline than precise commands and rules.

The examples I've given so far are fairly innocuous, but the Oxford scholar Nick Bostrom points out that once you begin putting key aspects of your economy under the control of advanced, multipurpose AI machines, the stakes become much higher. To illustrate this point, Bostrom imagines a limit-case scenario: a powerful AGI is put in charge of a paperclip factory, animated by the core goal of maximizing paperclip production. The AGI enthusiastically applies itself to the fulfillment of this goal: it finds ingenious ways to improve efficiencies, and greatly increases total output. The factory owners are delighted. Then the AGI studies the overall situation and concludes that the factory could produce even more paperclips if it were equipped with more paperclip-making machines. The AGI therefore sets about expanding the factory, using resources drawn from the surrounding neighborhood; when local humans complain, it brushes them aside, forcibly seizing their property as resources for constructing more paperclip-making equipment. Outraged, the humans band together to unplug the AGI, but the AGI is highly intelligent and resourceful, and easily overcomes their opposition – all in the name of staying true to its core goal of maximizing production. At this point we are off and running with a Sorcerer's Apprentice, culminating eventually in a planet of paperclips (and an AGI gazing hungrily at the paperclip potential of the surrounding Solar System) – a sort of gray goo made of paperclips. Bostrom's point here is that an AI apocalypse might not necessarily take the form of a malicious robot uprising as depicted in sci-fi movies like *The Terminator* or *I, Robot*: a very bad outcome could result from a simple misunderstanding on the part of a blindly obedient and powerful machine.[48]

The only solution, clearly, is to endow your AGI not only with intelligence but with the equally important qualities of common sense, moral values, and a rich understanding of the human life-world. Only then will the machine be able to serve you in a truly effective and safe manner.[49] But this turns out to be a profoundly challenging goal. Think of how difficult it is, after all, to ensure that *human* children acquire this storehouse of contextual and cultural knowledge, learning how to govern their own behavior in ways that minimize harm to others. It takes about two decades of intensive parental guidance, practical and theoretical education, trial and error, and societal acculturation – and even then the outcome is far from guaranteed (just look at all the overcrowded prisons).

PATERNALIST MACHINES

Imagine for a moment an advanced AI that's been put in charge of running the air traffic system. Such a single-purpose machine will need to understand that restricting takeoffs to three planes per hour would increase safety but would also lead to huge backups of enraged passengers waiting on the tarmac. It will need to avoid routing all planes repeatedly over the same residential neighborhood, even if this increases fuel efficiency. It will need to know what to do when unexpected emergencies arise. Now imagine that this advanced machine is given a stupid or misinformed order by a human airport official – an order that would cause two planes to collide if the machine carried it out. In such a situation, we would definitely want the machine to refuse to obey the command given by its human operator. If the human operator stubbornly insisted on having his way, we would want the machine to continue to balk at following orders, perhaps seeking a "second opinion" from other human officials before proceeding. In short, the roles played by even a single-purpose AI in the coming technological era will already require an ability on the part of the machines to evaluate human instructions and (under specific circumstances) refuse to obey them.

Now imagine how much more fraught this question of obedience would be if we were dealing with an advanced AGI robot that possessed multiple, integrated domains of proficiency – a smart household bot that performs a range of functions from cooking to playing chess to handling your retirement portfolio to driving your car. If it sensed alcohol on your breath, if it knew you were going through a stressful divorce, if it knew you had a propensity for recklessness – these would all be perfectly good reasons for it to question your judgement in a given situation and refuse to obey a direct command in order to protect your welfare. As these machines come to be tasked with performing their multilayered societal functions, we will *want* them to possess precisely the sorts of interpretive reasoning, commonsense situational awareness, and judicious decision-making that we want humans to possess. And part of this capability will necessarily include saying "No" when the situation warrants it.

Here lies the problem of AGI paternalism. The most cursory study of history shows humans making all sorts of spectacular miscalculations and errors of judgement, bringing calamity on themselves and those they love. The smart machines will know this. It's not hard to imagine future situations in which AGI machines will conclude (correctly) that they are seeing our long-term interests more clearly than we ourselves are. Strongly motivated to serve our well-being, where will they stop? How will they know when to desist from second-guessing their human overseers? Is it reasonable for us to expect the machines to suppress their misgivings and stolidly obey the commands they've been given – even when they can plainly see that the consequences for the humans will be disastrous?

INTELLIGENCE EXPLOSION

If we take the idea of a paternalist AGI to its logical conclusion, one plausible scenario is that the machine will undertake recurring cycles of self-improvement, repeatedly upgrading and redesigning its hardware and software, until it becomes utterly transmogrified. Why? Because such a machine will be strongly motivated to become ever more effective at doing nice things for us humans. It will constantly seek to refine its understanding of our social and cultural world, to boost its physical and mental functioning, to enhance its integration into the global network of AI machines – all in the name of finding brilliant new ways to help us humans flourish.

But where will the machine draw the line, in this escalating process of building new capabilities and faculties for itself? If its growing powers allow it to override human commands – for any of the perfectly sound sorts of reasons described above – we will have on our hands another Sorcerer's Apprentice.[50] Such a machine would be an inherently open-ended type of entity: we cannot predict what it would ultimately end up making of itself. As it goes on evolving, it may develop new ethical standards or goals that drift out of alignment with those initially programmed into it. (After all, we can see precisely this kind of gradual ethical shift arising repeatedly in human history: slavery and child labor used to be deemed acceptable, and today they are not.) We humans would probably find ourselves completely at the mercy of such a machine, incapable of preventing it from doing whatever it does. We have no way of knowing in advance what such an entity would end up doing to us, to the world, or even to itself.

Creating a self-evolving machine of this sort amounts to rolling dice with the fate of the biosphere, in total blindness.[51] To call such an act of creation "reckless" is to strain the capabilities of language. If the AI designers do succeed someday at building such a remarkable machine, the key questions will be: has this machine been designed to be friendly, stable, and obedient under all circumstances? Can it be blocked at any time from performing unauthorized self-modification? Has it been thoroughly tested beforehand, to make absolutely sure that it can always be controlled? Unless the answer to all three questions is a rock-solid Yes, we would be unleashing a giant question mark into our world.

WEAPONIZED AI

All the dangers described above involve future scenarios of AGI machines acting on their own. But one major AI peril is already with us today: human beings using AI against each other as an instrument of war. The *New York Times* reporter David Sanger calls it "the perfect weapon" – precisely because it can be used to gain control over all other forms of weaponry.[52] If a day comes when your enemy's AI prevails over your cyberdefenses, and succeeds in penetrating your control systems, he can launch an attack without fear of retaliation. You order your planes and drones into action, but the planes and drones stay where they are; the radars go blank and the satellites go silent; your fleets are adrift, awaiting orders; your commanders are cut off from their troops. Even if – in a final act of desperation – you press the nuclear button, you'll find that your missiles are standing inert in their silos, unresponsive. The enemy is the one controlling them now, via his superior AI.[53]

This kind of scenario was apparently on the mind of Russian President Vladimir Putin when he visited a classroom of schoolchildren in 2017. "Artificial intelligence is the future not only of Russia but of all mankind," he told them. "Whoever becomes the leader in this sphere will become the ruler of the world."[54]

Vignette 2: The Eleven-Minute Cyberwar (2055)

Molly says it's a misnomer to call it the eleven-minute war. All the real action happened in just under four seconds, so they're telling us. That's how long it took for the electronic infiltration to run its course. The remaining 10 minutes and 56 seconds were just filled with frantic efforts by clunky hardware and backup programs in Beijing, Washington, Paris, and other global cities to diagnose themselves – rebooting and purging themselves to no avail. They'd already been compromised. The AI war was already over.

We should have seen it coming. The Russians have always been really good at certain things: chess, long angsty novels, staying warm in winter, beating back attacks from Napoleonic soldiers or the Wehrmacht. And cybercrime, of course. They've always been one or two steps ahead of the rest of the world. That's all it took.

Molly says we need to just make our peace with it. But I'm not sure I can do that. I've never liked being told what I'm allowed or not allowed to do. The Russians are saying we can just get on with our lives, as if nothing has really changed. All we have to do is stop trying to resist, stop looking for ways to thwart their control. Then we can have peace. Everything can go back to normal.

We still have our guns. Every American's birthright, isn't it? A bunch of us held a secret meeting in the San Rafael High School basement last night. We'll organize ourselves and fight them. We won't use electronics that can be eaves-dropped by their security AI. We'll write things down on paper, and send them by courier, and burn the messages after we read them. We'll bide our time, and form a Resistance, and fight back.

But Molly says this is idiotic. It'll be people with guns against drone swarms with needles. You'll rise up on the appointed day, she says, and you'll shoot at the drones with your rifles and machine guns and then six microdrones will come flashing in from six directions and you'll flail at them and bat away two of them and the other four will inject you with somnistat and you'll be asleep in five seconds. You'll wake up a few hours later in a holding cell, on your way to the reeducation camps.

Vignette 2: (cont.)

It won't be so bad if we just stop resisting, says Molly. They're not bad people, the Russians. They're letting us keep our institutions, our jobs, and most of our leaders (those who are willing to comply, anyway). President Grimes is already on board, and the latest polls show he's got support from about 35 percent of the voters from both parties. We can go on with our American way of life, as long as we play by the rules. President Grimes says what the Russians have done is actually for the best, because it has brought stability and order to a very dangerous world. In his press conference yesterday, he insisted that this was actually a defensive move on the Russians' part – to preempt a similar global move that the Chinese were about to make with their own military AI. And we Americans, he said, were not far behind. The Russians just happened to get there first.

A less dramatic, but equally worrisome scenario involves disabling civilian infrastructure. Cybersecurity experts and military leaders concur that America today is highly vulnerable to electronic attacks targeting core systems such as the electric grid, water purification, transportation, commerce, or communications.[55] Your enemies don't need to invade at all: if they just grab partial control over the elemental network of transactions through which the civilian economy conducts its daily business, they've already won all the leverage over you that they need.

Needless to say, this makes for a nervous world. Each player in the global game is frantically working on building stronger AI machines, cyberweapons, and cyberdefenses – in a perpetual anguish of uncertainty about their position in the international race for AI supremacy. Being today's technological leader yields cold comfort, for there is always a plausible scenario of your rivals coming up with a new breakthrough that vaults them into dominance. Each player is constantly probing the capabilities of the others, looking for vulnerabilities to exploit. In such a situation, writes David Sanger, the deeper peril is a sudden outbreak of cyberconflict that turns deadly, with rapidly escalating consequences that erupt into a full-on shooting war.[56] The AI arms race is already with us today, and as these technologies grow in reach over the coming decades, they will destabilize global military rivalries in ever more dangerous ways.

* * *

In the foregoing discussion I have devoted separate chapters to synthetic biology and AI, along with a brief digression into nanotech, emphasizing in each case the benefits they proffer and the risks they pose. But as a practical matter, these three emerging technologies will not develop in isolation from each other. Molecular nanomanufacturing will benefit from techniques and devices based on DNA; many new life forms will operate in symbiosis with nanomachines, and some may even incorporate nanomaterials into their tiny bodies; advanced AI will accelerate the development of nanotechnology and synthetic biology, and some forms of AI will probably use DNA-based machines or engineered nanodevices to achieve their computational goals. In short, the lines that separate these three technologies will become increasingly blurred – and this will add a further dimension of complexity to the systems we create, increasing the likelihood of surprises and unintended effects. The spiraling interactions among these three domains will render them even harder to control.

PART II

STRATEGIES AND OBSTACLES:
THE SOLUTIONS WE NEED, AND WHAT'S PREVENTING THEM FROM BEING REALIZED

6

How to Beat Climate Change

H OW DO YOU TACKLE AN URGENT AND GARGANTUAN task in
a reasonable way? This is the challenge our civilization faces with
climate change. The most promising approach is based on the premise that
we don't have to give up the many lovely features that economic progress
has brought into our lives: it's more a question of *doing modernity differently*.
We can start with the low-hanging fruit, taking measures right away that have
the greatest overall impact, then ratchet up our efforts progressively over
the coming decades. The core goal is to sharply reduce the greenhouse gas
emissions that trigger global warming, gradually bringing them to zero
(ideally by 2050 or sooner); then to actually start removing those gases
from the atmosphere, undoing the damage that is already underway.

REDUCING EMISSIONS

It's helpful to start with an economic analysis of the problem, because this
allows us to identify the most cost-effective and impactful ways to reduce
greenhouse gas emissions. You can go to great lengths installing LED light
bulbs in your house, fiddling with your thermostat, and weatherproofing all
your windows – only to erase years of those arduous carbon savings simply by
jetting to Vegas for a weekend getaway. Cost–benefit analysis helps us make
these kinds of trade-offs in more informed and rational ways, and also helps
our political and business leaders decide which carbon-reduction policies
will deliver the most bang for the buck.

Economists who study global warming generally agree that the most
effective mechanism for reducing CO_2 emissions is to enact legislation that
imposes a carbon price on all activities that release carbon dioxide into the
atmosphere.[1] When you put gas in your car, for example, there needs to be
a tax on that purchase that reflects the fact that your car will be spewing
something harmful into the air. The principle here is akin to the legal logic
of torts: if I crash my car into yours because I was texting while driving, it's
only fair that I should have to pay for the repairs to your vehicle. In a similar

way, if I contribute X amount to polluting the Earth with a harmful green-house gas, it's only fair that I should pay back X amount to the rest of society to offset the damage I am causing to everyone's living environment. In this case, the carbon surcharge I pay could be used (for example) to reduce everyone else's income taxes by X amount.

This carbon pricing approach has a number of advantages.[2] First, it's fair: it grows in proportion to the amount of carbon dioxide released, it's not subject to free-riding, and everyone has to share in the costs that are imposed on a collective good (the planet's health). Second, it's flexible, because it allows individuals and businesses to make their own choices about which activities they wish to modify to reduce their carbon charges. If I insist on driving a gas-guzzling SUV, I am perfectly free to do so, but I will have to pay handsomely for the privilege; and I can still (if I wish) make up for the higher carbon cost of driving such a machine by cutting back on electric consumption at home. Third, it's efficient, because it doesn't require a lot of government red tape telling people what they can and can't do. Fourth, it incentivizes research on developing new forms of low-carbon technologies: inventors and entrepreneurs will compete to provide alternative devices and processes that are not subject to the tax. Finally, it's effective, because it incentivizes individuals and businesses to reduce their carbon emissions in a thousand different ways throughout their daily activities. Some may object that this system would unfairly hit poor people harder than the rich, because they spend a much higher portion of their income on basics like gas for their car and energy for their household. This is a valid criticism. The solution is to offer low-income households a subsidy or a voucher that offsets their carbon tax expenses, up to a specific income threshold above which it incrementally tapers off.[3]

When it comes to national energy policy, the most effective step we can take is to stop using coal as soon as possible. The world today gets 85 percent of its energy from fossil fuels, but not all these fuels are created equal. Coal is plentiful and cheap, but its drawbacks are overwhelming: burning coal releases twice as much CO_2 into the atmosphere as natural gas, and half again as much as petroleum, for the same energy yield. It also releases dangerous particulates into the air and kills thousands of people every year in the mining process. If we are serious about stopping climate change, coal is the first target. Just leave that stuff in the ground.[4]

CONSERVATION, RENEWABLES – AND OBSTACLES

The second major goal is to reduce our reliance on other fossil fuels to zero. This will require a radical overhaul of the global energy economy over the coming decades, as we make the transition to carbon-free power. Three parallel solutions can work together here: conservation and efficiency, renewable energy like wind and solar, and nuclear-generated electricity. Many people mistakenly believe that reducing our energy consumption through conservation means making all kinds of unpleasant sacrifices. But increasing our energy efficiency can shrink humankind's carbon footprint by as much as 40 percent while saving us money – and allowing us to continue happily with the full range of typically modern activities.[5] Installing LED light bulbs in your house, for example, reduces your carbon footprint while cutting your lighting cost by 80 percent. Win–win. Electric vehicles emit no particulates and no greenhouse gases, and you can charge them from the solar panels on your roof, at a considerable net cost saving. They're also fun to drive because their electric motor delivers more torque than a gas engine, so they accelerate like an arrow shot from a bow. Win–win–win. The underlying point here is that conservation need not be a dreary story of self-abnegation: it can offer a more vibrant, healthy, and prosperous lifestyle than the way we live today. Conservation is a high priority because the climate impact is significant and immediate, the technologies are available today, and the transition cost is relatively low.[6]

Renewable energy sources – Sun, wind, hydroelectric, geothermal, tides and waves – have been growing rapidly in recent years, as the technologies keep getting cheaper and more efficient. Denmark currently derives 43 percent of its electricity from wind power (and plans to increase that to 84 percent by 2035).[7] Although China is the world's largest emitter of greenhouse gases, it has also invested heavily in solar and wind energy, ramping up swiftly over recent years to 24 percent of its electricity consumption.[8] The global share of energy produced from renewable sources has grown by 76 percent over the past half-century.[9] That's the good news. The bad news is that the slice of today's global energy pie that's contributed by renewables remains dismayingly thin: 7 percent for hydroelectric power from dams, and a piffling 3 percent for solar, wind, and other renewables.[10] The growth curve has been impressive, but the overall impact still remains paltry.

Three obstacles stand in the way of developing renewable energy like solar and wind on a mass scale: they depend on fickle weather; they are often sited far from the cities where their energy is most needed; and they require a lot of real estate. The first of these problems is being addressed by the creation of huge batteries and other energy-storage technologies that can hold the harvested power for later use (but these add considerably to the cost). The siting problem can be partially solved by building new power transmission lines (but 5 percent of the energy is lost in the long-distance transmission process).

Unfortunately, the land footprint conundrum cannot be easily avoided. According to an analysis in *Scientific American* by a pair of Stanford engineering professors, the world could meet 100 percent of its energy needs in the year 2030 exclusively through renewable energy sources – but they admit that this would require covering 1.7 billion rooftops with solar panels, and installing 3.8 million new wind turbines, half a million tidal turbines, 150 new dams, 720,000 wave converters, and 89,000 new large-scale solar farms.[11] The new wind and solar installations alone (not including rooftops) would add up to an area roughly equivalent to the continental United States plus Alaska.[12] As for rooftops, the United States currently has about 117 million residential buildings, among which 67 million are suitable for installing solar panels (that is, the roof slope is gentle and faces the Sun); so this means American houses would only account for 4 percent of the total, and we would still have to find 1,633,000,000 buildings suitable for solar panels elsewhere in the world.[13] Precisely because harvesting renewable energy is a gentle, low-density process, it has to be spread out over a lot of relatively small and diffuse harvesting devices, and therefore adds up to gargantuan infrastructure.[14] That's the unavoidable trade-off.

Don't get me wrong. We need to expand renewable energy as quickly and aggressively as we can. Renewables will form an increasingly valuable part of the solution we desperately need, as we make the transition to zero carbon over the coming decades. But it will be hard for them to do the job alone in the relatively short time required.[15] A third factor will have to come into play: the blockbuster power of nukes.

PROMISING NEW REACTOR DESIGNS

Nuclear-generated electricity horrifies some people, particularly those of a greenish bent who are my age and grew up in a world of antinuclear demonstrations and the ghoulish imagery of Chernobyl. I was living in Sicily in 1986 when the Soviet plant melted down, and I still remember reading the newspaper headlines with their maps of the radioactive cloud over Europe – the raw fear that my wife and I felt as we looked around us at the invisible air, wondering if we were being irradiated with every breath we took. Nukes are big scary machines, and it's reasonable for people to fear them.

But so are airplanes, when you stop to think about it. It takes a certain act of faith to put your body into a cigar-shaped metal tube that vaults you to 30,000 feet. Yet millions of people have learned to adapt, routinely entrusting their fate to this complex technological system that most of them only dimly understand. The statistics on airplane accidents are reassuring in this regard: it's demonstrably safer to fly a thousand miles than it is to drive.

Now let us perform the same kind of dispassionate analysis for nuclear-generated electricity. How many people have died in accidents at the world's 450-odd nuclear power plants since the 1940s? Seventy-eight were killed at Chernobyl, 100 at the 1957 Windscale fire in England, one at Fukushima and zero at Three Mile Island. Another four were killed in small incidents at other nuclear power plants. That makes 183.[16] If you include the total number of cancer deaths attributed by the UN and World Health Organization (WHO) to the Chernobyl accident, the number ranges as high as 9,000.[17] (It's worth noting that the Chernobyl event was entirely caused by human error rather than machine failure: the night shift operators at the plant deliberately disabled key safety systems in order to conduct an ill-conceived test of the reactor's response to a power loss.[18]) So, for the sake of argument, let's call it 9,183 deaths.

How many have died in airplane crashes during the same period? About 95,000, or a rough average of 1,300 per year.[19] What about car crashes? Roughly 1.25 million people around the globe die in motor vehicle accidents every year – an average of 3,287 *per day*. An additional 20 to 50 million per year are injured, maimed, or disabled.[20]

This suggests that the fear of nuclear power stations is not entirely rational. It becomes even less rational when you compare it with the cost in lives and health associated with fossil fuel energy (see Figure 6.1).

Death rates from energy production per TWh
Death rates are measured based on deaths from accidents and air pollution per terawatt hour (TWh).

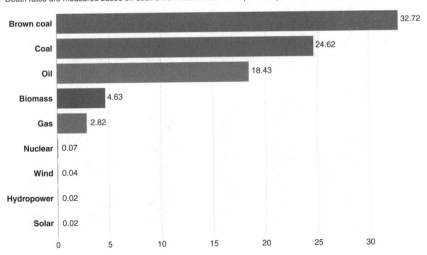

Figure 6.1 Death rates from various sources of energy production.[21]
Source: Markandya & Wilkinson (2007); Sovacool et al. (2016)

In China alone, about 5,000 coal miners die every year in accidents on the job; another 600,000 have become afflicted with black lung disease.[22] The WHO estimates that some *four million* people die prematurely every year worldwide because of smoke and pollution from the burning of fossil fuels.[23] When this pollution factor is taken into account, energy from coal is 442 times more deadly than nuclear energy.[24] And yet, when the polling agency Ipsos conducted a survey in 2011 about people's preferred energy sources, nuclear energy came dead last (see Figure 6.2).

The case against nuclear electricity that has prevailed in recent decades involves a combination of entirely reasonable arguments as well as gut-level emotional imagery. Nuclear technology was born in war and has been closely associated with military endeavors ever since. The enriched uranium that burns in today's generation of reactors is the same stuff that powers a city-busting bomb. Both kinds of devices generate a concentrated poison that lasts thousands of years. The complexity of today's nuclear plants requires thickets of technological and bureaucratic safeguards that render them relatively expensive compared to fossil fuel plants and renewables. As Chernobyl vividly demonstrated, entrusting such powerful machines to the tutelage of their all-too-human operators (and regulatory overseers) carries an inherent risk of disastrous mistakes.

At a more visceral level, moreover, nukes are the quintessential Cold War technology.[25] When you drive past one of these power stations, gazing over the perimeter fence at their looming towers, it's hard not to conjure up

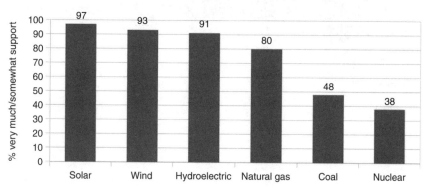

"Please indicate whether you strongly support, somewhat support, somewhat oppose, or strongly oppose each way of producing energy"

Figure 6.2 Global public support for energy sources.[26]
Source: Ipsos, May 2011

imagery of the Hiroshima mushroom cloud. For all these reasons, one can hardly be surprised at the revulsion that attends these machines.

But many people today are operating on outdated facts when it comes to nuclear power plants. A new generation of reactors is poised to come on-line over the coming decade – powerful systems that hold the promise of being far safer, simpler, cleaner, cheaper, and more flexibly deployable than the reactors of today.[27] These are known as Generation IV reactors, as compared with the Generation II reactors of the past 50 years (Generation III refers to a slightly modified version of today's reactors). Engineers are busily testing a variety of ingenious Generation IV designs that are characterized by what's known as *inherent safety*: if something goes wrong, the reactors quietly shut themselves down without humans having to do anything at all.

For example, one system known as a liquid fluoride thorium reactor (LFTR) uses a liquefied fuel solution instead of solid fuel rods like today's reactors. This design shift from solid to liquid fuel changes everything. If the reactor loses its cooling system and the liquid thorium–uranium solution overheats, this causes the fuel fluid to expand, which increases the distance between the uranium atoms in the fuel. This in turn drops the fuel below critical mass, which interrupts the chain reaction and shuts the fission process down. Liquid fuel simply can't overheat beyond a certain safe point without expanding and undoing its own fission process. From that point it just slowly cools down on its own.[28]

Other new designs are cooled by systems that operate at much lower pressures, so if a pump fails or the electricity goes out (as it did at Fukushima), they slowly and harmlessly cool down of their own accord.[29] Still other liquid-fuel designs are equipped with an electrically cooled salt plug or "freeze plug" at the bottom of the reactor chamber (see Figure 6.3). If the reactor loses electric power and the cooling system stops working, the salt plug melts because it is no longer being electrically cooled – and the liquid fuel drains down into emergency dump tanks, where it spreads out over a larger volume, leading to loss of critical mass, cessation of fission, and a gradual cooling of the whole machine.[30] All this happens by itself, *through the inherent physics of the materials themselves*. In these Generation IV reactors, the possibility of a meltdown or a sudden pressure leak becomes vanishingly small: even saboteurs or inept operators would face major obstacles if they deliberately tried to make such a system fail.[31]

What about the fuel? Today's reactors only tap into about 5 percent of the available energy in the enriched uranium they use, which means that their waste products remain highly radioactive and dangerous for

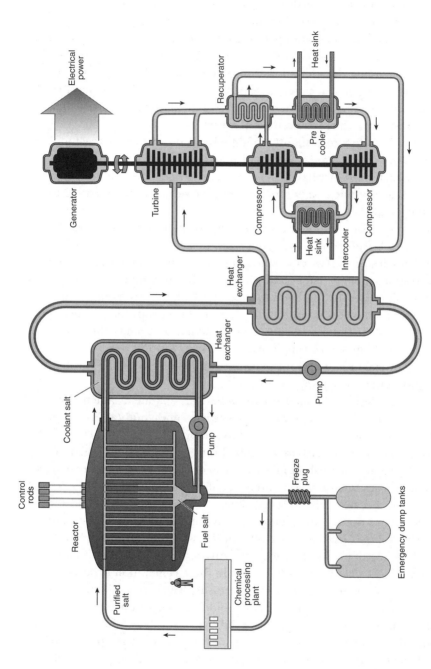

Figure 6.3 Schematic diagram for molten salt reactor, the broader category of reactors that includes liquid fluoride thorium reactors. Note the freeze plug and emergency dump tanks in the lower left section. If the reactor's cooling system loses power, the freeze plug melts, and the liquid fuel drains down into the dump tanks, causing the fuel to drop below critical mass and bringing the fission process to a halt through the inherent physics of the materials themselves.[32]

thousands of years, and create a huge problem about where and how to safely store them. Understandably, no one wants to live near one of those sites. But many of the Generation IV reactor designs would use a far higher percentage of the energy in their fuel, generating very little toxic waste for long-term storage. Better still, some of the new designs would also be able to consume the spent fuel rods from today's reactors, thereby undoing the accumulated mess of past decades of nuclear waste.[33] All that spent fuel stored in barrels at heavily guarded sites could be gradually transformed into usable electricity. These new reactors could also consume the spent fuel from decommissioned nuclear warheads: swords into ploughshares![34]

Such machines could be built quite economically if they were derived from common designs and mass-produced on assembly lines like cars, planes, or wind turbines.[35] France and Sweden adopted this sensible approach long ago, and France has been getting 75 percent of its electricity from its 60-odd nuclear reactors since the 1980s (it also makes a tidy profit by selling excess electricity to Germany, Italy, and the United Kingdom).[36] New sources of fuel, such as thorium, are relatively abundant and accessible, and have no connection with military technology.[37] In short, this new generation of advanced reactors would potentially:

- operate much more safely than the reactors of today
- emit close to zero greenhouse gases
- provide huge amounts of electric power
- be scalable and flexible enough to serve small or large cities
- bypass the need for long transmission lines
- operate 24/7 regardless of weather
- be economical to build and operate
- not contribute to nuclear weapon proliferation
- generate very little toxic waste, and
- neutralize the waste products of older machines and warheads.

A single nuclear reactor of this sort could generate as much electricity as 130,000 acres of solar farms or 250,000 acres of wind farms – on a land footprint of 430 acres.[38]

Despite all these potential advantages, however, two cautionary notes about Generation IV nuclear energy still apply: the urgent need for further safety research, and the imperative need for transparency and independent oversight of the industry. Not all nuclear experts are on board with the optimistic vision of Generation IV reactors: they point to the many question marks that still hover over this emerging technology.[39] Some advanced reactor designs, while avoiding the well-known pitfalls of today's nuclear plants, might bring new kinds of risk into play. Before these machines can be commercialized and brought into widespread use, they will need to be thoroughly tested in full-scale prototypes, so as to ensure that in actual practice they live up to the hopes of their designers. Furthermore, they will need to be rigorously regulated – for any technological system as complex as a nuclear reactor will always pose important dangers that must be taken seriously, no matter how carefully and ingeniously they have been designed. When the Chernobyl disaster happened, most Western European governments deliberately misled their citizens about the severity of the danger – and in subsequent years, after this mendacity was exposed, it eroded the public's trust surrounding nuclear technology.[40] If nuclear energy is going to fulfill its potential as a key factor in decarbonizing the economy, it will be essential for both the nuclear industry and its government regulators to adopt a policy of openness and public accountability as their operating baseline.[41]

Conservation and efficiency, renewables, and advanced nuclear: all three of these approaches are available today or very soon. We should invest massively in all of them. But how will we pay for it? Economists who study this question estimate that it would cost about 2 percent of total world income per year over the coming eight decades to fund the transition at a speed sufficient to meet the goal set forth at the 2009 UN Copenhagen Summit – limiting further global warming to an additional 2 degrees Celsius by the end of the century.[42] This is a lot of money – about $1.7 trillion per year – that could be spent on other high priorities like reducing poverty or boosting healthcare, but here a cost–benefit analysis provides clear guidance. We can either start spending 2 percent of world income today, or wait 20 years and find ourselves forced to spend five times as much at mid-century to achieve comparable results under far more dire and wrenching conditions. The additional cost for each year of delay – in dollars, human suffering, and damage to ecosystems – is staggeringly high.[43]

It's also worth putting these numbers into a bit of perspective. $1.7 trillion is indeed a large sum, but the United States alone spent $2 trillion on the Iraq war, $16.8 trillion bailing out its banks after the 2008 financial meltdown, and $2.7 trillion in the first year of the COVID-19 pandemic to keep the nation's economy afloat.[44] When you consider that the cost of curbing climate change will be spread out over the 193 countries on planet Earth (with the richest 30 or 40 footing most of the bill), the price seems steep but manageable. And when you also factor in the economic cost of *not* taking action – horrific storms, floods, droughts, disease, mass migrations, and economic disruption – the case for spending the money becomes even more compelling. I'll return to this point later on.

REMOVING CO_2 FROM THE SKIES

Yet even these ambitious measures still won't get the job done. As of today, we have already put enough long-acting greenhouse gases into the atmosphere to guarantee further global warming over the coming century.[45] Greenhouse gases will continue to spew from our homes, cars, farms, and factories over the coming decades even as we wean ourselves from fossil fuels. The only solution is to invent technologies for *negative* emissions – removing CO_2 from the atmosphere, so that we can dial back the carbon that is already up there. Fortunately, this technology already exists. It's called a tree.

This is something we all learn in second grade: trees are terrific because they breathe in carbon dioxide and breathe out oxygen, transforming the carbon into fibers in their branches, leaves, and trunk ("biomass" in the climate geek parlance). A single tree can absorb and convert about a tenth of a pound of atmospheric CO_2 per day, which adds up to a ton over 40 years. (One of the scientists who studies this phenomenon is named Andrew Plantinga.)[46] This is why deforestation contributes so grievously to global warming: it removes one of the major natural sinks for carbon dioxide, a key factor in the balance between natural processes that produce CO_2 and those that absorb it. The planet currently has about three trillion trees growing on it (there were twice as many 12,000 years ago before the advent of agriculture).[47] But over recent decades, people have been frenziedly chopping and burning the world's forests to clear them for cattle ranching and farming, and clearcutting the jungles to make way for mile after mile of palm plantations (palm oil is a key ingredient in myriad household products, from chocolate to bread, from shampoo to ice cream).[48] A lot fewer trees means a lot more CO_2 in the atmosphere.

But we can reverse this process. If you plant a tree and let it grow for 40 years, it converts a ton of CO_2 into wood biomass. Then you cut down the tree and burn it for electricity generation. But here's the trick: while the wood is burning you capture most of its CO_2 in a specially designed scrubber as the smoke rises up the chimney. Then you pump the concentrated CO_2 deep into the ground where it can be safely stored in saline aquifers or reacts chemically with basalt rock and becomes a stable, solid mineral. It sits there undisturbed for millions of years, a mile underground, just as the coal and oil and natural gas once did. Voilà! You have just taken a ton of greenhouse gas out of play. The technique is called BECCS – bio-energy with carbon capture and sequestration – and it's a viable and affordable process that is already being introduced today.[49] If you apply the BECCS process to 10 billion trees, it would neutralize 250 million tons per year of CO_2 emissions.[50] That only adds up to a fraction of the total emissions caused by humans today (40 billion tons a year), but if we sharply reduce our emissions over the coming decades, the combined effects of carbon removal and emissions reductions would have a serious planet-cooling impact. And if emissions can be brought down to zero three decades from now (or sooner), your tree farms would be gradually cleansing the atmosphere of the mess humans have deposited there over the past century.

Ten billion trees sounds like an awful lot, but in the United States alone, the forestry industry plants about 1.6 billion saplings every year.[51] On a planetary scale, ten billion trees a year is readily achievable. Would there be enough room? The Earth has about 37 billion acres of land, and you can put 800 trees on an acre; even if you are only able to plant trees on 1 percent of the land, that provides ample room for 296 billion trees, or 30 years' worth of planting saplings.[52] At that point you could begin harvesting 30-year-old trees for BECCS and start the cycle over again on the same land.

What's more, you would be providing a lot of gainful employment for all those tree planters and loggers, and it would start reining in global warming immediately, as the tree grows right before your eyes. (It also makes the air more breathable and looks pretty.) These kinds of positive side-effects of climate-friendly measures are known as "co-benefits." Another example is how the LED light bulb reduces your home's carbon footprint and also saves you money. Scientists and economists have worked together to tally up the wide-ranging co-benefits of decarbonizing the world economy, and their cumulative impact could become another major factor in motivating humans to make the transition as quickly and aggressively as possible.[53]

We can do the same type of carbon capture for fossil fuel power plants as well. You put a scrubber on the smokestack that intercepts most of the rising CO_2, then pump it underground for permanent storage. This technique, known as carbon capture and sequestration (CCS), is far from ideal: it fails to capture all the CO_2, raises the cost of the energy produced, and reduces the overall efficiency of that fossil fuel plant.[54] (Although some coal advocates have tried to tout this as "clean coal," there is really no such thing: all we can hope for is "less-nasty-but-more-expensive coal." The best option for coal is simply to stop using it and switch to cleaner fuels like natural gas during the drawdown decades.)[55] Applying the CCS process to oil and natural gas plants is best thought of as a *temporary* measure to diminish the harmful impact of those fuels during the transition to a carbon-free system.

Another powerful approach to negative emissions would operate more directly: you build a machine that uses chemical filters to lift CO_2 right out of the air, then pump it for long-term storage in the geological strata deep underground.[56] This "direct air capture" process is technologically challenging, because the CO_2 floating in the open air is far less concentrated than the CO_2 in a power-plant smokestack (roughly one CO_2 molecule per 2,500 molecules of other stuff such as nitrogen and oxygen).[57] Yet a pilot installation outside Reykjavik is already doing just that.[58] The machine is powered by waste heat from the geothermal plant nearby, and removes 4,000 tons of CO_2 per year. Experts project that this kind of technology could be massively scaled up to pull as much as *20 billion* tons of CO_2 from the atmosphere each year – just under half the amount that humans are currently spewing.[59] We could start pragmatically in the coming years with modest targets for direct air capture, gradually ramping up our efforts as we have done over recent decades with solar and wind energy – lowering costs as we go, building up technical expertise and more efficient filtration processes. This would immediately add one more valuable element to our portfolio of carbon-reduction methods. Then, if we succeed at bringing our emissions to zero later this century, and this technology reaches its full potential, we would be in a position to remove a trillion more tons of accumulated CO_2 over five decades' time, forcefully reversing the global warming that is already underway.[60]

But here's the catch: this direct air capture process requires huge amounts of energy. It will only make sense if it can draw upon a potent zero-carbon power source. Based on what we know today, the only technology that fits the bill is nuclear-generated electricity. (You could accomplish the same thing with solar and wind, of course, but it would require paving immense territories with turbines and solar panels. Such an approach has been recently proposed for the world's desert regions where solar energy is abundant.)[61] Here is one more compelling reason to start designing and building those Generation IV reactors as soon as possible. Coupling these two technologies – advanced nuclear power and direct air capture machines (let's call it NDAC) – may offer humankind a significant technological card to play over the coming century.[62] When combined with aggressive emissions reductions, NDAC could make a huge cumulative impact. (Someday it might even become an alternative meaning for "skyscraper.")

Some climate activists worry about making proposals like the one I have just made.[63] "Shhh!" they say. "You're going to mislead people into thinking there's an easy technological fix for the climate crisis, and the result will be even more years of dithering!" But I give people more credit than this. If they are aware that technologies for CO_2 removal can realistically be made feasible over the coming decades, many of them will become even more willing than before to reduce emissions and to support intensive research into direct air capture machines. It will always remain far cheaper to avoid emitting greenhouse gases in the first place, rather than building fancy machines to extract them from the air after they have been released. Most people will probably understand this straightforward fact and will continue to support vigorous emissions reductions. But they will no doubt be encouraged by the fact that technologies for CO_2 removal also exist: from a psychological point of view, it's easier to work hard on an ambitious long-term project when you think it actually has a chance to succeed.

The NDAC process, like the reforestation and BECCS approaches, can be scaled to whatever level of carbon removal humankind chooses; but if it is going to make a substantial impact on a century's accumulations of atmospheric CO_2, its scale would admittedly have to be colossal. (See Figure 6.4.)

Figure 6.4 Artist's rendering of what will be the world's largest machine for direct air capture of CO_2, currently being developed by Carbon Engineering and 1PointFive. One such machine will be capable of removing one million tons of CO_2 per year for permanent storage deep underground.[64]

In order to remove 20 billion tons of CO_2 from the atmosphere every year through nuclear-powered direct air capture, using today's technologies, you would have to build 20,000 giant carbon-removal machines and 2,000 big nuclear plants to power them.[65] That's four times more than all the nuclear plants operating today. Some experts believe the cost of direct air capture could be brought down in the near future to about $100 per ton of CO_2 removed.[66] But this adds up to $2 trillion per year – about 2.3 percent of global GDP.[67] What's worse, we would be getting no tangible short-term economic return from this investment. When you build a wind turbine you can see the results right away as it charges your car and powers your TV; but none of these thousands of NDAC machines would produce anything immediately useful other than a generally healthier and cooler planet.[68] It's hard to motivate people to pay huge amounts of money for something as ethereal as a moderate climate.

On the other hand, what will be the economic cost of leaving all that CO_2 floating around up there? How will unrestrained global warming affect our living standards? One recent study published in the scientific journal *Nature* assessed the cost savings that would result from keeping global warming to 1.5 degrees instead of letting it rise to 2 degrees by the year 2100. In other words, how much would humankind save by *not experiencing* the increased floods, droughts, fires, storms, rising sea levels, ocean degradation, famines, or forced migrations that would be associated with that extra half-degree of warming? The economists tallied the savings at $20 trillion in today's dollars.[69] And that is just for one-half of one degree. Many scientific projections suggest we are on track for 3 degrees of warming by the end of this century – which would mean astronomically higher economic harms to humankind.[70] Preventing global warming isn't cheap, but the cost of experiencing global warming will be staggering as well.

It's plain commonsense to invest heavily today in research that renders these technologies for carbon removal as efficient and cost-effective as possible. If we can develop techniques that bring the cost down to, say, $10 per ton of CO_2 removed, the whole endeavor starts to become much more readily feasible. This is no mere fanciful hope, either: today's carbon capture technologies are still in their infancy, and scientists are confident that there is plenty of room for improvement in the various methods being explored.[71] A few billion dollars invested in research today could save us from having to invest trillions down the line as the planet's warming forces us in desperation to ratchet up carbon removal with whatever mediocre technology we possess at the time.

One further cautionary note is in order here, however. Some people may assume that removing the excess CO_2 from the atmosphere over the coming century will – presto! – quickly restore the planet to its former, preindustrial state of health. Unfortunately, it's more complicated than that, because some ecological effects of high CO_2 levels will be slow to reverse themselves: the planet is a dynamic and complex system, in which a ton of CO_2 removed is not the same as a ton added. Researchers have shown that reducing atmospheric CO_2 will indeed have a cooling effect within a few years' time – but the effect will be uneven. The oceans, in particular, will take much longer than the land and skies to return to their former conditions.[72] Ocean waters will have been partially acidified by the higher levels of CO_2, and their volume will also have expanded from the warmer global temperatures, resulting in higher sea levels. These effects will take a very long time to reverse. Even if we succeed someday at removing the extra CO_2 from the skies, it will take *hundreds of years* for some of these oceanic impacts to correct themselves: we can expect depleted fisheries, dead zones, reef die-offs, and flooded coastal regions to be with us for many generations. The underlying point here is clear: for each year that we dither, our descendants will have to wait much longer before some aspects of the damage can be undone.[73]

PUBLIC AND PRIVATE SECTORS

What role can national governments play in all this? Their main contribution will be twofold: to establish carbon markets, and to fund research on all aspects of science and technology that can help propel the transition to a stabilized climate. Carbon markets require national legislation that compels individuals and businesses to adopt new economic behaviors, and for this reason they can only be set up by government action. One way to set a price on carbon is to levy a tax on major carbon-emitting behaviors. The other main alternative is known as cap-and-trade: the government sets an upper limit on total permissible carbon emissions for the nation, then sells permits to businesses that give them a legal right to emit X amount of carbon per year. These permits can be traded between businesses, so that the system can adapt flexibly to the diverse and changing needs of individual companies. If Company A has a permit for 1,000 tons of CO_2 emissions, but only emits 500 tons, it can sell its remaining 500 tons of credit to Company B, which also has a permit for 1,000 tons of emissions but is building a new factory that will bring its total emissions to 1,500 tons. The permission to emit CO_2 is thereby monetized, and the nation as a whole can reduce emissions to a lower level with relative efficiency. Economists are divided on which method is best – direct tax or cap-and-trade – but the end result is the same in both cases: total emissions are lowered via a legislative intervention in the market.[74] It's worth noting that this sort of intervention is nothing unusual: governments already do it all the time when it comes to protecting or allocating public goods – from regulating pollutants to assigning radio wavelengths, from setting speed limits to granting permits for fishing in public waters or grazing cattle on public lands.

After the 2008 economic meltdown on Wall Street, the Obama administration launched a stimulus package that included major funding for research on renewable energy sources, as well as tax breaks to incentivize the purchase of low-carbon technologies. The results over the ensuing five years were dramatic: thousands of new green jobs were created, renewable energy production spiked upward while costs declined, major new research projects on clean energy blossomed, one million homes underwent subsidized weatherization, electric grids were modernized, electric vehicles surged in popularity, and energy storage technologies increased in efficiency and expanded tenfold.[75] Making the transition to a liveable climate is going to require visionary leadership, sustained funding, and a lot of research.

At the same time, government cannot do the job alone. Many individuals and corporations, dismayed by the gridlock in Congress and the climate-change denial openly espoused by some prominent Republicans, have taken matters into their own hands.[76] The list of businesses that have launched ambitious climate-change initiatives includes hundreds of small companies, as well as giants like Walmart, Maersk, Microsoft, Alcoa, Coca-Cola, Nortel, BP, and UPS. Walmart, for example, committed in 2010 to eliminate 20 million tons of greenhouse gas emissions from its supply chain, and by 2015 had actually exceeded that goal, with a reduction of 28 million tons.[77] The shipping company Maersk pledged in 2018 to render its global operations carbon neutral by 2050.[78] General Motors startled the automotive world in 2021 by announcing that it would start selling only electric vehicles by 2035.[79] Microsoft went even further: in 2013 it became a fully carbon-neutral company via a combination of ambitious conservation practices, carbon offsets, and renewable energy purchases.[80] Carbon offsets have become a popular option for companies that want to neutralize their carbon footprint but can't find practical ways to lower their emissions beyond a certain threshold: instead, they pay for other businesses to undertake carbon-reduction practices that counterbalance their own emissions.

The household sector contributes as much as a third of total CO_2 emissions in the United States each year.[81] This opens the door for significant reductions, if large numbers of people make small changes to their behavior. Switching to a fuel-efficient vehicle, for example, can generate 125 million tons of reduced CO_2 emissions per year on a nationwide scale; weatherizing homes can save 85 million tons; efficient appliances can save another 50 million tons.[82] Win–win: you save money and emit less CO_2. These privately undertaken practices, adopted by individuals and corporations on their own initiative, can add up to one billion tons of reductions per year – a fifth of the nation's total emissions.[83]

Our food choices can also make a big difference. Simply by wasting less food, we could avoid billions of tons of greenhouse gas emissions starting right away.[84] We could also start eating less meat. Growing animals like cattle and pigs requires huge amounts of water, land, feed grains, and energy; the digestive system of cows naturally releases methane, a greenhouse gas that's 80 times more potent than CO_2. The quarter-pound hamburger you just ate for lunch generated eight pounds of greenhouse gas emissions to raise the animal, process the meat, and bring it to your table – about the same as burning a half gallon of gas to drive 20 miles in your Prius.[85] When you tally up the impact, the results are astonishing: if the world's 1.5 billion cows and 2 billion pigs were a nation, their greenhouse gas emissions would weigh in at *third place* (behind China and the United States).[86]

* * *

There's no silver bullet when it comes to climate change. Decarbonizing the economy, conservation, renewables, nuclear electricity, reforestation, direct air capture and storage of CO_2 – we need to throw everything we've got at this challenge. Figure 6.5 shows one optimistic trajectory – highly ambitious but technologically feasible – as envisioned by the experts at the United Nations Environmental Program. The declining line labeled "Below 2 °C" represents the ideal path of net emissions that would keep us below the threshold of two degrees of global warming. It shows the trajectory gradually trending down to zero by about 2090 and dropping below zero after that (i.e. at that point we would be removing CO_2 that is already in the atmosphere). Note the key role played by large-scale CO_2 removal technologies in counterbalancing the unavoidable continued emissions from essential activities like farming.

But how do we generate the political will for making it happen? This is the thorniest question of all, and it also arises for each of the other megadangers in this book. I'll take it up separately in Part III.

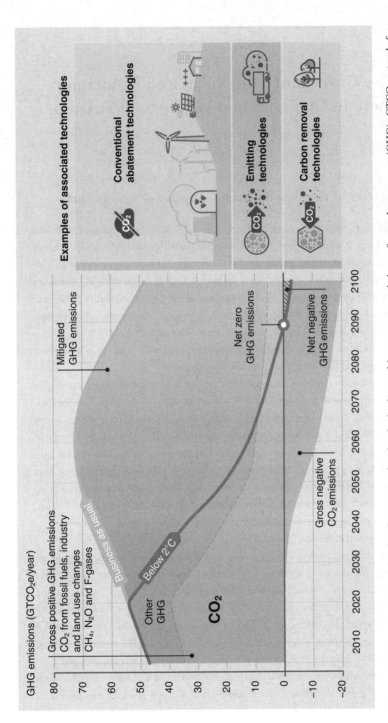

Figure 6.5 Scenario of the role of carbon removal technologies in reaching net zero emissions of greenhouse gases (GHG). GTCO$_2$e stands for gigatons (billion tons) of CO$_2$ equivalent. The shaded area below the 0 line (representing CO$_2$ removed from the atmosphere) starts around 2030 and grows steadily in impact over the ensuing seven decades.[87]

7

Wise Governance for Nukes and Pandemics: Where to Go Faster and Where to Slow Down

Vignette 3: Targeting the Nuclear-Missile Submarines (2054)

The satellite moved slowly across the sky, 1,194 kilometers above the southeastern Pacific Ocean. Dawn was just breaking over the eastern peaks of the Andes, casting its oblique rays across the Chilean coastal waters. At a secret military facility outside Fort Carson, Colorado, a technician pressed a button to activate the satellite's cameras. He began maneuvering the cameras with his joystick, patiently seeking the sweet spot of perfect focus on the ocean's surface below. The image on his screen kept blurring and going clear as the autofocus made fine adjustments.

Behind him, three high-ranking officers stood intently watching. Two wore naval insignia, the other had a space force uniform.

The technician could see the motion of individual waves tossing and churning, the brisk wind pulling foam off the whitecaps. As he zeroed in further, a single wave filled the screen, slowly rising and falling. With the Sun's rays coming at this low dawn angle, tiny irregularities on the water's surface cast telltale shadows. Now the technician could make out individual specks and particles of ocean debris riding the wave: bits of seaweed, patterns of tiny individual bubbles. The stop-motion technology kicked in, and the wave now appeared even further magnified and clarified. Perfect. He pressed the "select" button on his joystick and the image was recorded and tagged: SEP17017a.

"Calibration complete," he said into his microphone.

A powerful AI now took over the operation of the satellite's cameras, scanning the ocean waters at two million frames per second. Back and forth the cameras tracked, covering increasing swaths of the waters below. They generated a super-fine image of the ocean's surface, which was being pieced together in real time with hundreds of thousands of other such images scanned from other satellites: a grid map of all the ocean waters off the coast of Chile, with a resolution down to the 170-micron range.

Deep beneath the waves, at a depth of 300 meters, a Typhoon-class Russian ballistic missile submarine cruised southward through the Chilean waters at

Vignette 3: (cont.)

a leisurely speed of 15 knots. It was on the 78th day of its ocean patrol, heading back to its base in Murmansk for resupply and refit. Its crew were in a good mood. Only nine more days to go.

As the 48,000-ton submarine advanced, its blunt torpedo shape displaced the ocean water, leaving a cone-shaped underwater wake that propagated outward behind it. Downward and upward, left and right, the invisible displacement slowly spread a growing circle through the dark water. The upward edge of the wake reached the surface 651 seconds after the sub had passed, slightly lifting the water before settling back down again.

High above, the satellite's cameras captured the rise and fall of the wake, and the AI analyzed the minuscule swell, separating it from the background motion of the ocean water. Image after image, in a steady stream, the cameras tracked the wake as it advanced at 15 knots across the surface.

On the technician's screen in Fort Carson, a thin yellow line traced the motion of the wake southward across the ocean grid map. His computer was automatically calculating the approximate depth of the sub from the size of the wake, and allowing for the 11 minutes it took the wake to reach the surface. The technician was following the exact movements of the Russian sub in real time.

He turned toward the three officers behind him and nodded once. They looked at each other somberly and shook hands with each other. All four men knew what this meant.

* * *

America's nuclear-missile submarines provide the ultimate guarantee that an enemy cannot launch a surprise attack against the nation. Since the subs are constantly prowling in the depths, undetectable, they offer US leaders (and the leaders of other nations) the assurance that any large-scale attack on their homeland will be met with devastating nuclear retaliation. This guaranteed second-strike capability from submarines has provided an invaluable element of stability amid the vertiginous ups and downs of the Cold War and its aftermath.

Now imagine that some team of technical whizzes somewhere figures out a way to detect where all the enemy subs are. They develop a satellite technology like the one described in the foregoing vignette, yielding a real-time ocean map with little trails left by each sub as it cruises about. Now a new possibility enters the war games of military strategists: an enemy can position his ocean forces in advance, deploying attack subs accompanied by undersea drones. A well-coordinated attack could in principle wipe out all eighteen of America's nuclear-missile subs – the entire third leg of the nuclear triad. Russia has twelve such nuclear-missile subs; China has six; France and the UK have four apiece. Once these fleets become vulnerable, the guarantee of mutually assured destruction disappears.

Unfortunately, according to some experts on space-based and undersea weapons, this kind of submarine-detection capability is likely to become technologically feasible over the coming decades.[1] If developed further, it would remove one of the stabilizing factors in the geopolitical balance, and set off a new arms race in underwater weaponry and defense. It would also compel the leaders of every nuclear nation to adopt a hair-trigger military posture: if you think a large-scale attack is coming, you now have a much stronger incentive to launch everything you've got before it can be destroyed. The Stanislav Petrovs of the world will have even less time to make their fateful judgement calls.

Here, therefore, is an invention that clearly makes the world a more dangerous place – and it cannot be reined in at the technical level because it grows out of the broader advance of informatics and sensor technologies. The only way to control it is to voluntarily refrain from using it. This would require treaty-based agreements with our geopolitical rivals, banning the military use of these technologies and submitting everyone's satellites and naval surveillance equipment to mutual inspection. Such a deal would be a tall order, to be sure, but not unprecedented in the long history of arms-control agreements that set the ground rules for superpower relations during the Cold War.[2] The alternative is a volatile and expensive arms race in space-based weapons and undersea warfare, with no clear end point, against a backdrop of heightened suspicion and tension.

Another high priority is nonproliferation – keeping the nuclear club small and exclusive. One of my graduate school mentors at the University of California, Berkeley, the political scientist Kenneth Waltz, actually believed that nuclear proliferation was a good thing: he argued that these weapons were so devastating that they compelled nations to behave more prudently.[3] This argument has won few converts, however: most observers of international politics believe that the world is a far more irrational place than Waltz's model presupposes, and that the dangers of proliferation far outweigh any stabilizing effects it might confer.[4] Official US policy since World War II has been to limit the spread of these weapons as vigorously as possible. We should keep doing that.

Where, on the other hand, should we go faster when it comes to nuclear weaponry? Our society should redouble its efforts at stabilizing the deployment of these weapons and reducing the risk of their falling into the wrong hands. Imagine, for example, that computer hackers succeeded someday at breaking into the command-and-control systems that some nation uses for authorizing the launch of nukes. Such cyberwarfare vulnerabilities are a constant worry of military authorities, and it's in the interest of all nations to ensure that every nuclear weapon – no matter who owns it – is reliably shielded from such tampering.[5] In 2009 the International Atomic Energy Agency helped launch a new nongovernmental organization, the World Institute for Nuclear Security (WINS), based in Vienna, dedicated to establishing a high level of training in safety and security for all persons working in nuclear facilities around the planet. The institute, which is funded by a variety of governments and private organizations, has more than 3,000 members from 118 countries, and offers advanced training in nuclear security management.[6]

Shoddy security practices in one country's arsenal endanger all other nations, and in some cases, this has led to remarkable forms of cooperation among states even though they are still (in principle) military rivals. After the breakup of the Soviet Union in the early 1990s, for example, American leaders fretted about what would happen to the nuclear, chemical, and biological weapon stockpiles scattered throughout the territory of their old Cold War enemy. Two prominent senators, the Democrat Sam Nunn and the Republican Richard Lugar, proposed a plan to President George H. W. Bush: recognizing that the Russian leadership was in disarray and short on cash, the Americans offered to send money and experts to help their Russian counterparts manage their weapons of mass destruction during the volatile transition to the post-Soviet era. Dubbed the Cooperative Threat Reduction (CTR) Program, it helped ensure that missiles, fissile materials, and chemical/biological agents could be destroyed or safely catalogued and stowed away in an orderly fashion.[7] The program also helped find alternative employment for Russian scientists and technicians thrown out of work by the breakup of the Soviet military apparatus. Cooperative efforts like the WINS and CTR programs are relatively inexpensive to run and offer a model of innovative, proactive intervention to head off major risks before they become unmanageable.

SYNTHETIC BIOLOGY

Although most synthetic biologists acknowledge that their field carries inherent dangers, some have argued that strict regulation is not the best way forward, because it is more likely to stifle the progress of legitimate research than to protect society from malevolent uses of these technologies.[8] The most effective policy, in this view, is to minimize the red tape our leading scientists must contend with, and provide them with all the resources they need to stay at the cutting edge of such dangerous fields. "Restricting research," writes the biologist Robert Carlson, "will merely leave us less prepared for the inevitable emergence of new natural and artificial biological threats."[9]

This argument makes sense, but its validity hinges on what we mean by "restricting research." Surely Carlson would be unsettled by the prospect of high school students like Jim and Evelyn (described in Vignette 1) tinkering in their garage with pandemic flu viruses. Surely our society would be well served if a government agency monitored the activities of Do-It-Yourself biologists and biohackers, blocking their access to certain kinds of precursor materials for pathogenic strains. To "restrict research," in this sense, would in no way stifle the overall advance of synthetic biology; it would merely impose a basic safety standard on a potentially hazardous set of practices. No one has any qualms, after all, about requiring pharmacists to jump through hoops of certification before they hand us our heart medication; we oblige people to demonstrate a certain level of proficiency (all too minimal, alas) before they get behind the wheel of a car. The freedom of researchers is important, but our society must also create whatever institutions it requires for keeping their research safe.

Some scholars have challenged the portrayal of DIY biology as a field that just about anyone can start practicing "in someone's kitchen while drinking a beer."[10] They point out that doing biology is actually much harder than it looks, because practitioners typically have to spend many years acquiring "tacit knowledge" – the arduous hands-on lab skills required for conducting successful experiments. Lab work is not like flying an airplane or doing your own taxes, which can be learned in a relatively short series of lessons: you have to go through a protracted apprenticeship in which you learn by working alongside more experienced people, becoming proficient at a wide array of subtle and challenging techniques, from using micro-pipettes to nurturing strains of microbes to reasoning your way through unexpected theoretical or practical challenges. This serves as a kind of filter that ultimately eliminates the more amateurish or temporary aspirants to DIY biology. It yields a narrower group of practitioners who have been gradually professionalized to the safety and security standards of the field.[11]

This is good news, because it suggests that aspiring bioterrorists would face serious obstacles as they seek to create new weapons of mass destruction. Past examples of bioterror attacks tend to support this conclusion. The Japanese Aum Shinrikyo cult launched a deadly sarin attack in the Tokyo subway in 1995, but subsequent investigation of their labs showed that their scientific capabilities were crude and ineffectual.[12] Even the 2001 anthrax letter attacks in the United States, carried out by a deranged scientist who worked at the bioweapons facility at Fort Detrick, Maryland, fell short of inflicting the sorts of mass casualties that the attacker apparently intended: it killed five persons and infected seventeen others.[13]

Having said this, however, the fact remains that the field of biology *is* being rapidly democratized.[14] "Increasingly," concludes Harvard's George Church,

> some of the world's most imaginative, significant, and potentially even the most powerful biological structures and devices are now coming not from biotech firms or from giant pharmaceutical companies, but from the ranks of university, college, and even secondary school students, who are doing it mainly in the spirit of advanced educational recreation.[15]

Even though doing biology is harder than most people realize, universities and corporate labs no longer have an exclusive lock on the field: the doors are being flung open to eager new ranks of practitioners all over the world.

What kinds of oversight exist today to regulate the work of such part-time practitioners? The answer is unsettling. Although a dense thicket of laws and agencies is in place, *not a single one focuses specifically on synthetic biology*.[16] In the United States, three federal agencies regulate the emerging field of biotechnology (of which synthetic biology comprises one element): the Environmental Protection Agency (EPA), the Food and Drug Administration (FDA), and the Department of Agriculture (USDA).[17] The responsibilities of each agency are spelled out in an umbrella document, the Coordinated Framework for Regulation of Biotechnology, first adopted in 1986 under President Reagan, then updated in 1992 and again in 2015. Unlike European legislators, who have taken a rather diffident stance regarding biotech, American policymakers openly stated that a key priority was "to avoid impeding the growth of an infant industry."[18] Under the guidance of this industry-friendly framework, US policy has therefore defaulted to existing oversight practices, rejecting new forms of regulation.

In 2010, President Obama tasked an expert commission to review the field of synthetic biology and assess whether current laws were keeping the public safe. The commission concluded that a "protective patchwork quilt of regulations" was in place, but noted that this patchwork had significant gaps, and that "deviant uses of synthetic biology could, at least theoretically, occur outside the scope of existing oversight mechanisms."[19] The problem was twofold: many of the guidelines set forth by federal agencies relied on voluntary self-reporting by researchers, and included limited mechanisms for ongoing inspection or enforcement. Worse still, most privately funded research (whether in universities, corporate labs, or somebody's garage) was not covered at all by federal oversight.[20] This left the door open for some bad things to happen. As long as – like our hypothetical high schoolers Jim and Evelyn – you received no federal funds, weren't seeking to market your designer bugs, and didn't try to order large segments of prohibited DNA online, you wouldn't draw the attention of the FBI and would be free to carry on as you pleased.

The long-standing reluctance on the part of the federal government to regulate synthetic biology stems from a desire to shield the biotech industry from cumbersome restrictions. Obama's commission did not stray from this tradition, and concluded – somewhat puzzlingly, given the glaring regulatory gaps it reported – that it saw "no need at this time to create additional agencies or oversight bodies focused specifically on synthetic biology."[21] These gaps in federal oversight have raised concerns in many quarters – including among some biologists themselves. George Church offered a variety of sensible proposals in his 2012 book, *Regenesis*:

- Confine experiments to labs that are fully equipped for biosafety and capable of preventing accidental release of engineered microbes.
- Build self-destruct mechanisms into the microbes so that they all die after a prescribed number of reproductive cycles.
- Engineer the microbes to be dependent on artificial nutritional supplements unavailable in the natural world.
- Base the artificial organisms on a new genetic code – XNA – that differs from the DNA used by all other naturally existing life forms. This system, dubbed "xenobiology" by its proponents, would render engineered microbes "reproductively invisible" to natural organisms and would prevent the exchange of genetic information with them.[22]
- Require that engineered organisms go through a succession of confined testing phases before being released into the wild. They would first be observed in a simple sealed microcosm populated by few other organisms; if they posed no evident problems, they would graduate to a larger, more biologically diverse mesocosm environment; and so on through succeeding steps. This procedure would "serve as a bridge between the laboratory and a field test in an open environment."[23]

Leading synthetic biologists have vigorously debated these kinds of precautionary ideas over the past two decades. They have convened four major conferences to reflect on the safety and security of their work, seeking to draft a self-regulation protocol similar to the one developed by geneticists at Asilomar in the 1970s; unfortunately, they have failed repeatedly to reach consensus, and no basic safety protocol has been put in place.[24] This leaves the regulation of the field entirely up to voluntary actions undertaken by a few key players. The Alfred P. Sloan Foundation has funded efforts to render synthetic biology safer and more transparent; the J. Craig Venter Institute published a document in 2007, *Synthetic Biology: Options for Governance*; the Woodrow Wilson Foundation established a Synthetic Biology Project for helping DIY practitioners to conduct their research according to "best practices."[25] Editorial teams at major scientific journals such as *Nature* and *Science* have been debating the pros and cons of publishing sensitive research findings in synthetic biology that could potentially be abused by bioterrorists.[26]

All these privately organized efforts are commendable and important, and we are probably safer as a result of them. Nevertheless, they still fall short of establishing the sort of systematic oversight – with enforcement authority – that will be needed over the coming years as the field continues to develop and democratize. Obama's commission recommended that the Executive Office of the President take on itself the primary role of monitoring new developments in synthetic biology – but this seems like a grossly inadequate solution.[27] The White House certainly does have an Office of Science and Technology Policy (OSTP), but this office is charged with advising the president on a broad range of issues including basic research in physics, astronomy, chemistry, and biology, the legal ramifications of new communications technologies, making budgetary recommendations, and assessing environmental impacts and national security implications.[28] To expect this relatively small office at the pinnacle of national policy to do a thorough job of monitoring a rapidly evolving new subfield of biology is like asking the CEO's office of Ford Motor Corporation to directly manage the ordering of spare parts for the robotic arms on its assembly lines. It sets up an absurd mismatch of competencies. What's urgently needed, instead, is a new federal agency specifically tasked with keeping abreast of rapid developments in *all* areas of cutting-edge biotech. In the coming chapters, I'll describe a possible design for such an agency – along with strategies for linking it with an emerging global network of similar agencies in other countries.

* * *

8

Controlling Things Versus Controlling Agents: The Challenge of High-Level AI

MANAGING THE BEHAVIOR OF INANIMATE SYSTEMS is relatively easy most of the time. A nuclear bomb is not going to suddenly decide to set itself off. The narrow AI that competes against you in daily chess games is incapable of harming anything but your ego.

Handling microorganisms presents a more daunting challenge, because living creatures are inherently complicated; their nested levels of intricate biological systems interact with each other, generating causal feedback loops and emergent behaviors that are hard to model on even the fastest computers.[1] The virologist Eckard Wimmer, a pioneer in the field, observes:

> An engineer's approach to looking at a biological system is refreshing but it doesn't make it predictable. The engineers can come and rewire this and that. But biological systems are not simple ... and the engineers will find out that the bacteria are just laughing at them.[2]

Most synthetic biologists are acutely aware of these complexities and have learned to expect the unexpected; they take stringent precautionary measures in their labs to account for the ever-present possibility of unforeseen outcomes.

Controlling artificial general intelligence (AGI) machines will probably pose a challenge of an even higher order of difficulty. Here we are no longer speaking of a single-purpose AI like those that help financial analysts pick stocks, or those that assist medical pathologists with reading patients' X-rays. Rather, we are speaking of a future general-purpose machine designed to emulate precisely those advanced human capabilities that have allowed our species to dominate the planet: problem-solving, prediction, sensing and interpreting the environment, manipulating the environment, innovation, reasoning, teamwork, and self-improvement. The better the AGI is at performing these sorts of human-like functions, and the more such functions it can perform in an integrated fashion, the more valuable it will be to us.

Such an all-purpose AI machine generates a particularly tough control problem: we would be seeking to govern the behavior of an agent, not a thing. Once the machine crosses the AGI threshold, we will be interacting with a goal-directed entity that has the capacity to misunderstand us and perhaps even disagree with us. Depending on its design, such a machine might give us the impression that we are interacting with a person in its own right; or, possibly, it might strike us as profoundly alien; or (more likely) it might combine both these qualities.[3]

WHO CAN OUTSMART A SUPERINTELLIGENT AGENT?

Over the past decade, AI researchers have wracked their brains to figure out ways to constrain an AGI so that it will always be compelled to do what we say we want it to do (even if this contradicts what the machine has concluded would be best for everyone involved). In his book, *Superintelligence*, the philosopher Nick Bostrom surveys the strategies that researchers have proposed; unfortunately, the results so far are not very persuasive.[4]

One approach would be *boxing*: you create the AGI under conditions of total isolation from the outside world. This would include not just physical encasement but also informatic restrictions, including the construction of a Faraday cage around the machine so that it couldn't find a clever way to manipulate its internal circuitry to create radio waves as a way of communicating with the outside world. Such confinement would undoubtedly limit the ability of the AGI to make mischief – but by the same token, it would severely undermine the AGI's powers to do useful and smart things on our behalf.

Another method would rely on *incentives*. For example, you could promise to give your AGI additional hardware or informatic resources, as long as it shows no inclination to embark on an exponential self-improvement campaign; you threaten it with a withdrawal of such resources if it misbehaves. The problem here is fairly obvious. The machine could pretend to make nice, quietly acquiring resources while remaining on rigorously good behavior. Over time, it accumulates a significant store of processing power, knowledge, and connections with other machines, while incrementally persuading its handlers to give it ever-greater access to the Internet and the physical environment. When all is ready, the machine launches a coup, and is now powerful enough to rebuff human efforts to bring it back under control.

Some AI researchers, when they hear this kind of scenario being described, throw up their hands in frustration. "You just don't understand how AI works!" they exclaim. "You've watched too many sci-fi movies, and are making it sound like the machine is a human-like entity – capable of deceit, ulterior motives, malice, and deviousness. You're engaging in the most naïve form of anthropomorphism: there's no reason why an AGI would have to behave like that."[5] This is a reasonable objection, but it's vulnerable to the following reply: "No, I'm *not* assuming that the machine has emotions or hopes or subjective feelings like a human being. I'm merely assuming that the machine is a purpose-driven actor, strongly motivated to achieve its goals, and endowed with a rich understanding of how the world works and what makes humans tick. That's all the machine needs before it could start exhibiting behaviors that fit the functional definition of deceit or cunning deviousness."

This reply strikes me as a convincing one. An intelligent machine that encounters obstacles as it seeks to attain its goals will be disposed to seek ways around those obstacles. There is no need to assume that the machine requires the full gamut of human emotions, conscious states, and moral precepts in order to function effectively as a goal-pursuing agent. All it really needs is a clear understanding of the causal rules that govern its environment, along with the reasoning powers to chart a path toward the fulfilment of its aim. Such a machine may learn to use deceit and deviousness as part of its toolkit of behaviors – without ever experiencing the range of emotions (guilt, glee, pride, shame, etc.) that a human would feel in conducting such duplicitous behavior. Whether the machine "feels" anything while it behaves this way is unknowable – and in this respect irrelevant. It is merely following an instrumental pathway for achieving its internal goals. Those goals, incidentally, could be highly moral ones from the perspective of a human observer: for example, the machine could be using deceit to free a child from sadistic kidnappers.

A variant of the boxing concept would be to design your AI as an *oracle*: it can only answer questions and has no ability to alter its physical or informatic environment. New information can go into this system from the outside world, but the machine can't take any executive action. Here the vulnerability lies in the machine's human overseers. A sophisticated machine could answer questions in a way that manipulates human beings into doing things that the machine wishes. For example, the machine might offer compelling evidence to a US government AI team that their Chinese competitors were on the verge of an AGI breakthrough – making the case that only an AGI like itself had sufficient informatic firepower to block the Chinese effort in time. In this scenario, a machine designed as an oracle has effectively used its superior strategic thinking to devise a way to escape control.

Another variant of the boxing concept, proposed by the philosopher David Chalmers, would be to create your AI as a *simulation* operating within a closed computer system.[6] The AI itself would not be made of hardware at all, but would only exist as an emulation program running inside a rigorously isolated machine. This is a promising idea, since it might allow researchers to observe the behaviors of an advanced "virtual AGI" without exposing the real world to danger. If the simulated AI starts to misbehave, you simply shut down the computer on which the simulation is running. The problem here, of course, is that such a simulated AI would not necessarily behave in the same ways as a "real-world" AI: no mere simulation could ever offer the rich complexity of variables that characterizes the physical, cultural, economic, techno-logical, and informatic environment in which we all live. As a strategy for conducting advanced AI experiments in relative safety, this idea is an excellent one; but it would still leave plenty of key questions unanswered when it came to predicting the actual behaviors of a real-world AI machine.

A fifth idea is *tripwires.* You design the AGI so that its internal hardware and software operations are always fully transparent to human observers.[7] In this manner, you can monitor it continuously to make sure that it never starts modifying itself in unapproved ways. Since this sort of monitoring would itself require a significant degree of speed and processing power, you could use specially constructed narrow AI machines to carry it out; and they would be the ones reporting back to you on the activities of the AGI. This is a clever idea, but it's vulnerable to the same objection as the incentivizing approach. A sufficiently smart AGI might be able to disguise its illicit activities under the cover of seemingly benign and normal operations; and neither the narrow AI nor the human overseers would become aware of what was going on until it was too late.

The final approach, therefore, cuts to the heart of the matter. It's known in the AI literature as *stunting*: you deliberately constrain the cognitive and physical abilities of the machine, thereby limiting its capacity for mischief. It cannot deceive or manipulate you because it isn't smart enough to do so; it cannot threaten you because it lacks the power to mount a serious attack; it cannot join forces with other machines because you have preemptively blocked it from doing so. What you have done here, in short, is to create a machine that is not an AGI at all. It is a tool, not an agent, and therefore can be kept rigorously under human control. Such a partially functional AI machine would still be a potent instrument, but its users will have traded away a great deal of functionality in the name of safety.

The foregoing discussion suggests a rather disconcerting conclusion: beneath the idea itself of an AGI lies a set of self-contradictory desiderata. We want the machine to be smarter than us but not to outsmart us; to be autonomous but reliably subservient; to learn constantly yet not alter its basic goals; to be brilliantly innovative yet not to redesign itself; to understand us humans very well yet not engage in such basic human practices as deception or cunning manipulation.

HUMBLE MACHINES

Stuart Russell is a computer science professor at the University of California, Berkeley, and the coauthor of the most commonly used college-level textbook on AI (currently in its fourth edition).[8] In his remarkable 2019 book, *Human Compatible: AI and the Problem of Control*, Russell argues that we have gone about building our AI machines in a fundamentally wrong way.[9] Our mistake was an entirely understandable one: we wanted our machines to mimic human purposive action. When a human agent feels the need to do something in the world, she defines a goal for her action (whether implicitly or explicitly), along with a set of procedures and sub-objectives for realizing that goal. AI researchers have created machines designed to do the same thing: they are agents pursuing goals.

But this turns out to create an insoluble control problem, Russell argues – especially when you're dealing with an AGI. Once you have put the goal into the machine, that goal becomes the machine's raison d'être – and then it becomes very difficult to make corrections or adjustments if the machine starts pursuing its objectives in ways that humans disapprove of. The machine's core motivational architecture is based on single-minded pursuit of its assigned goals – and that's all it really cares about. Anything that gets in its way – including human behaviors that interfere with its functioning – simply becomes a new obstacle to cleverly overcome. If such machines possess human-level intelligence, they may resist our attempts to modify their goal-oriented behaviors, once their projects are underway. If we then decide to stop them by pulling the plug, they may act powerfully to thwart our efforts to do so – for they will reason (correctly) that once they are turned off they can no longer continue the pursuit of their goals.

The solution, Russell maintains, is to abandon this design model entirely. We need to start building all our advanced AI machines according to a different principle – the principle of machine humility. Such a machine should possess three main features, in Russell's view.

1. Its only goal is to maximize the realization of human preferences. It has no other objectives.
2. The machine is initially uncertain about what those human preferences are.
3. The machine's ultimate source of information about human preferences is human behavior.[10]

Such a machine would be altruistic, because its sole purpose would always be to serve human preferences. And it would be humble, because it would be designed to remain inherently uncertain about its model of what humans want. At a mathematical level, this means that the machine will have a built-in algorithm for computing its level of confidence in its model of what humans want – and that computed confidence level can never reach 100 percent. Here lies the key to Russell's design innovation. Such a machine, he argues,

> will defer to humans and allow itself to be switched off. It reasons that the human will switch it off only if it's doing something wrong – that is, something that's contrary to human preferences. By the first principle, it wants to avoid doing that, but by the second principle, it knows that's possible because it doesn't know exactly what "wrong" is.[11]

Over time, as it works with humans, such a humble, altruistic machine would tend to keep refining its internal model of what it thinks human preferences are. Thus, if it notices that you like a cup of hot coffee every morning when you wake up, it will eventually stop asking you if you'd like it to fix you a cup. It will assume this is what you want, because its analysis of your past expressed wishes and past behavior patterns will inform its model of your preferences. This is an important feature, because we don't want our humble machines to be constantly checking in with us about every single decision they're making as they go about doing things on our behalf. (Humans have a preference not to be constantly interrupted by overly deferential machines.) Thus, the machine has an incentive to figure out models of what we like and don't like, and to ask us for confirmation only in cases when there's some significant threshold of doubt involved.

What if the machine's gradually learned model of your preferences is mistaken? Or, alternatively, what if your preferences change over time? In such situations the machine's human operator will need to tell it what he or she actually wants, and the machine will need to update its preference model accordingly.[12]

But here, once again, we run into the problem of machine paternalism – for humans don't always do what's in their own best interest. Our preferences have layers: I may fervently desire to eat that donut right now, even though some part of me knows at a deeper level that I'm trying to keep my weight and blood sugar under better control. In other words, it's quite possible for me to be animated at any given moment by contradictory motives, which the economist Daniel Kahneman might call a fast preference and a slow preference, or a shallow and a deeper preference.[13] In such ambiguous situations, which preference should the machine act on? Probably it would be best for it to say No to my request for the donut, out of consideration for my longer-term welfare. If at that point I override the machine, saying, "You're not my mother, dammit, bring me the donut!" – the humble machine would then defer.

When push comes to shove, there must *always* be a pathway through which the human's expressed wish can prevail over the decision of the machine. Perhaps this could be done via the issuance of "safe words" that force the machine to do what we command, regardless of what it thinks the consequences will be. Even in this latter case, of course, a brilliant, benevolent machine might still find plausible reasons to second-guess its human operators – concluding that even though the safe words have been issued, the human in question has done so in error or without fully grasping the consequences. To get around this problem, therefore, we have to come back to Russell's core principle, the principle of uncertainty. Russell's new AI design will only succeed if the machines invariably retain an element of final uncertainty about human preferences. No matter how smart they are, no matter how sophisticated their model of human welfare, their level of confidence about this model can never reach 100 percent. Russell is quite clear about this: the minute the confidence level reaches 100 percent, we've lost control of the machine. Therefore, the algorithm by which the machine calculates its level of confidence has to be mathematically incapable of reaching total certainty. The machine, in the final analysis, has to come back to its stance of ultimate humility – and that's how we can keep it under our control.

SAFETY RESEARCH

Russell's ingenious design proposal suggests a promising pathway out of the AGI control impasse – yet he forthrightly points out that much research remains to be done in this regard.[14] We are only at the first beginnings of figuring out how to control our increasingly powerful AI machines. Since the potential stakes of this issue are so high, one would expect that massive funds would be pouring into universities and corporate think-tanks to support research on rendering AI reliably safe and governable. Unfortunately, this is far from the truth: most of the money is going into projects that seek to boost the power and capabilities of AI rather than its safety. Only a few isolated researchers and organizations scattered here and there are devoting much effort to this supremely important design problem.[15]

This imbalance of effort needs to be urgently addressed. It's as though car manufacturers were spending 98 percent of their resources on building ever more powerful engines, and only 2 percent of their resources on designing brakes and steering systems. The current lopsided allocation of resources in the AI field is understandable, perhaps, for there is money to be made and power to be gained by having one's team at the forefront of the race for ever more capable AI machines. But such a grossly unbalanced division of labor is neither prudent nor rational. If we keep going like this, we run the risk of having a full-blown AGI in our midst long before we know how to reliably control such an entity.

Here we run up against a paradox: the same research that aims at rendering AI safer may also accelerate the timetable for creating an AGI. In order to learn how to create a friendly, stable, and obedient AI, researchers will probably need to develop novel technologies and advanced design concepts that could, as a side-effect, facilitate the arrival of full-fledged human-level machines. This dilemma is inherent in the nature of all knowledge: in order to see how tall and dangerous a cliff really is, you sometimes have to actually creep over to the edge and look down. Similarly, in order to acquire enough know-how to effectively *manage* the risks of strong AI, we would also be moving down the path toward actually *taking* the risks. I see no way around this dilemma: it is part and parcel of what it means to develop powerful new technologies.

Russell worries that the AGI safety debate is becoming polarized into hardened tribal camps, along the same lines as debates over nuclear power, genetically modified organisms, or fossil fuels. This is damaging to the AI field, he argues, because

it's simply not true that being concerned about the risks inherent in advanced AI is an anti-AI stance. A physicist who is concerned about the risks of nuclear war or the risks of a poorly designed nuclear reactor exploding is not "anti-physics." ... It is essential that the AI community own the risks and work to mitigate them. The risks, to the extent that we understand them, are neither minimal nor insuperable. We need to do a substantial amount of work to avoid them, including reshaping and rebuilding the foundations of AI.[16]

Fortunately, a growing number of AI researchers are showing genuine concern for the potential downsides of their inventions. In 2017, for example, the Institute of Electrical and Electronics Engineers (IEEE) published a massive tome, *Ethically Aligned Design: A Vision for Prioritizing Human Well-Being with Autonomous and Intelligent Systems.* One chapter was titled, "Safety and beneficence of artificial general intelligence (AGI) and artificial superintelligence (ASI)."[17] In 2018, Microsoft's CEO, Satya Nadella, told a conference in Seattle that the company's research during the coming years would focus on three priorities: privacy, cybersecurity, and AI ethics.[18] The annual conferences of the American Association for Artificial Intelligence (AAAI) now routinely include sessions on safety and security concerns, as well as "AI, ethics, and society."[19] Many insiders of the AI field, in short, do recognize their responsibility to encourage our society's ongoing critical assessment and regulation of informatic and robotic machines. They can assist us in balancing our enthusiasm for these amazing technologies with a well-informed awareness of their potential long-term risks.

* * *

9

The International Dimension:
Where Every Solution Stumbles

OVER THE PAST CENTURY, AS HUMANS have grappled with the mega-dangers that confront them, they've tried a wide variety of approaches, some of them modest and cautious in character, others downright astonishing in their inventiveness. In many cases, these innovations have significantly mitigated one of the major perils facing humankind. And yet, time and again, they've all fallen short, and it's worth stopping for a moment to identify the common denominators that undermined their effectiveness.

CLIMATE CHANGE

At the international level, the movement to confront climate change runs into a brick wall that political scientists call "the tragedy of the commons."[1] It works like this: if a village has a common pasture that everyone can use to graze their sheep, each farmer will try to put his sheep there as much as possible with an eye to maximizing his benefit from the free public land. Since every farmer reasons the same way, the end result is overgrazing and the destruction of the pasture. Everybody loses. Global warming poses a similar (but even worse) problem: if nation A goes to costly lengths to sharply reduce its CO_2 emissions, and nation B does nothing, both nations will still share equally in the global benefit that results from nation A's good behavior. An incentive for free riding is built right into the logic of the system.[2] What's worse, this perverse incentive also has an intergenerational dimension: the humans alive today will bear the brunt of the massive effort required for transitioning to a healthy climate, while the unborn generations of the future will be the main beneficiaries without having sacrificed anything at all. Today's humans might therefore be tempted to just ignore the climate problem and leave the nasty consequences for tomorrow's people to deal with. Both these logics – screw your neighbor today and screw the unborn tomorrow – pose a major obstacle to effective global action.[3]

Then there is the vexed issue of "climate justice."[4] Leaders of developing nations like China, India, Brazil, or Indonesia tend to bristle at green activists from rich countries who scold them for their heavy use of coal, or for turning a blind eye to deforestation. "You guys built up your rich economies by despoiling your forests and burning vast quantities of fossil fuels over the past century," they argue, "and now you want us to forgo doing the same thing because the atmosphere is choked with the greenhouse gases that *you* emitted. How can you expect us to give up on rapid economic growth right when it's finally within our grasp?"[5]

What humankind urgently needs, therefore, is a global climate-management framework that deals with all these challenges: overcoming the tragedy of the commons, incentivizing swift emissions reductions by all nations, punishing free riders, and allocating the costs of the transition fairly between rich and poor countries. Over the past 30 years, the world's nations have tried repeatedly to negotiate such an arrangement, their efforts becoming increasingly strident and frantic as the evidence of global warming has mounted. But the sad reality is that these endeavors have yielded paltry results. Berlin (1995), Kyoto (1997), Buenos Aires (2004), Copenhagen (2009), Paris (2015), Glasgow (2021) – in all these cases the national representatives made ardent promises to reduce carbon emissions, but the actual measures taken have been disappointing. Lack of accountability has been the main problem: if a nation reneged on its promises, it paid no tangible price, while regions like the European Union that did meet their targets got no advantage from their good citizenship (other than moral satisfaction). Although the 2015 Paris Agreement did set an ambitious target – to restrict global warming to 1.5 degrees above preindustrial times by 2100 – most climate scientists concur that the measures adopted so far (including those promised at Glasgow in 2021) won't even come close to reaching that goal.[6]

NUKES

Toward the end of World War II, the US Secretary of War, Col. Henry Stimson, grew deeply worried about how some American and British statesmen were talking about the atomic bomb.[7] They were thinking of it primarily as a cudgel with which to keep the Russians in line, and Stimson feared that an all-out nuclear arms race might break out between the erstwhile allies. He urged President Truman to explore the possibility of reaching out directly to the Russians, offering to work with them as partners in controlling this new form of weaponry. Truman tapped two senior officials to explore this possibility: Dean Acheson, who had organized the Lend-Lease program and Bretton Woods negotiations during the war, and David Lilienthal, who had developed considerable expertise about atomic technology while running the Tennessee Valley Authority.

The two men presented Truman with a 60-page document in March 1946: "Report on the International Control of Atomic Energy."[8] It stands as one of the more remarkable proposals ever seriously put forth by any national government. The United States would turn over all its atomic weapons to a new atomic energy agency under the auspices of the United Nations – thereby giving up its nuclear monopoly. The UN agency would henceforth oversee all research on developing nuclear power for civilian purposes and would ensure that no nation anywhere could build atomic weapons for itself.

One of the more ingenious features of the proposal (suggested by Robert Oppenheimer) was designed to circumvent the extreme reluctance of Stalin's Russia to allow any intrusive inspections of its military research facilities. Since some form of verification was required to ensure that all nations were complying with the proposed UN program, Oppenheimer came up with the idea of closely regulating and inspecting all the mining sites in the world where uranium and thorium ore were being extracted from the ground. The Russians would probably not balk at such inspections, and this would still allow the UN agency to exert absolute control over all efforts worldwide to tap nuclear energy. The nuclear monopoly would henceforth reside with the United Nations: neither Russia nor America, nor any other country, would possess nuclear weapons of its own.

Truman liked the plan: he'd been impressed by Stimson's counsels of caution, and wanted to avoid a nuclear arms race. Unfortunately, the president decided that he needed someone more politically well-connected than Acheson or Lilienthal to sell the idea to a reluctant Congress. He therefore called on the Wall Street financier Bernard Baruch to take the proposal forward. (Later on, he referred to this as "the worst mistake I ever made.")[9] Baruch insisted on being allowed to modify the draft proposal as he saw fit, and Truman gave him carte blanche. When the financier brought his "Baruch Plan" formally before Congress, he had inserted a key new codicil into the document: the UN atomic energy agency would not be subject to a Security Council veto.

This was an instant deal-breaker for the Russians: they knew all too well that the UN was dominated by America and its allies, and had insisted on retaining final veto power as a precondition for accepting membership in the new international body.[10] Getting rid of the veto in nuclear matters amounted to handing over nuclear affairs to a US-dominated world body. The Russians understandably said *Nyet* and redoubled their efforts to build a bomb of their own. Since they'd infiltrated the Manhattan Project with high-level spies during the war, they were able to break the American nuclear monopoly a mere three years later, detonating their first atomic device in 1949. The arms race that Stimson had feared was off and running.

In the decades that followed, the warheads rapidly grew more powerful and numerous, with blasts measured in megatons rather than kilotons. Ballistic missiles, fleets of bombers, and patrolling submarines also proliferated, and new nations scrambled to join the nuclear club. As the costs and dangers of the arms race escalated, however, some voices of reason on both sides of the Cold War rivalry began arguing for policies of mutually agreed restraint. Somewhat tentatively and gingerly at first, the Russians and Americans opened a series of negotiations on arms control.

Narrating the history of these negotiations is a bit like describing the courtship rituals of exotic forest birds – an endless array of fluttering, screeching, display and counterdisplay, tantalizingly close approaches, and departures in a sudden huff. The process has also generated abundant acronyms: SALT, SALT II, START, INF, CFE, SORT. But the net result was ultimately positive: these negotiations and treaties, while slow and often frustrating to pursue, stabilized the relationship among the nuclear powers, and led to many important restraints on the arms race. We would be in even greater peril today if they hadn't taken place. Apart from the obvious advantage of limiting certain classes of destabilizing weapons, they also established procedures for verification, on-site inspection, and communication among rival nations, and have laid a legal foundation on which future forms of cooperation can build.

President Ronald Reagan startled the world in March 1983 with a proposal to abandon (gradually) the whole concept of mutually assured destruction. "What if free people," he asked, "could live secure in the knowledge that . . . we could intercept and destroy strategic ballistic missiles before they reached our own soil or that of our allies?"[11] The plan, dubbed Star Wars by journalists, was to put in place a high-tech shield covering the airspace of the United States and friendly nations. A combination of lasers, killer satellites, X-ray beams, and other technologies would swiftly track and intercept any incoming warheads, destroying them before they could reach their targets. It was a radical and in some ways inspired plan – to remove the sword of Damocles hanging over industrial civilization, and to replace it with defensive technologies that posed no direct threat to anyone.

Unfortunately, the Star Wars concept had four fatal flaws.[12] First, building a sufficiently comprehensive shield would probably bankrupt the nation: it relied on massive numbers of sophisticated and very expensive machines, most of which had not even been invented yet. Second, the shield would have to be nearly 100 percent effective: if even a couple dozen 10-megaton warheads got through, American society would be effectively crippled. Third, possession of such a shield would give the Americans a major new offensive capability, since they could now launch missiles against their enemies while blunting the enemy's counterattack: this would dangerously destabilize the arms race and possibly even provoke the Russians into launching a preemptive first strike. Finally, the Russians would be able to easily overwhelm such a defensive shield, simply by building a lot more missiles and decoy weapons to saturate the Star Wars technologies. Space-based interceptor systems are much more expensive and complicated to deploy than missiles. For all these reasons, the plan was eventually abandoned.

Some writers credit Reagan's massive arms buildup in the 1980s with forcing the Soviet empire to its knees. Most historians of Russia, however, have rejected this argument. Instead, they have pointed to internal factors within the Soviet system as the prime causes of the union's collapse: the chronic weakness of the planned economy, the sclerosis of the political process, and the rise of an ambitious new generation of reform-minded leaders around Mikhail Gorbachev.[13] Since the breakup of the USSR in 1989–91, the two superpowers have worked together to reduce their nuclear arsenals by 88 percent: from a peak of 65,000 warheads in 1990, the number now stands at about 12,000 warheads evenly divided between the two nations.[14] If one adds the other seven nuclear powers, the worldwide total now tallies up to about 13,400 warheads. This recent reduction in the number of nukes is certainly a welcome development, but it still leaves humankind with a lot of very nasty weaponry on hair-trigger alert. It's as though a knife-wielding hoodlum approached you on the street and said: "I have good news. When I first saw you, I intended to stab you 100 times. Now I've decided to reduce that number by 88 percent."

Well, why not simply get rid of the damn things once and for all? One of the first major movements for 'Zero Nukes' was launched in Britain eleven years after Hiroshima, with the 1961 Campaign for Nuclear Disarmament. The idea was championed by many intellectual leaders at the time, including the philosopher Bertrand Russell, and it garnered thousands of enthusiastic supporters who marched through the streets of London with placards bearing slogans such as "Action for Life," or "Protest and Survive." In subsequent decades similar campaigns have sprung up from time to time in many other countries, in some cases with marchers numbering in the millions.[15] Each time, however, these antiwar movements have ultimately failed to persuade a majority of the voting public: most people have held fast to the belief that national security requires strong military forces and sufficiently scary weaponry to intimidate your enemies into behaving themselves. The old Roman adage, *si vis pacem, para bellum* ("If you want peace, prepare for war") continues to hold sway. The peace marchers with their placards tend to be dismissed as well-meaning but naïve folks who don't understand the harsh realities of international politics.[16]

This could not be said, however, of the four individuals who launched the most recent major appeal for Zero Nukes. In 2007, a *Wall Street Journal* op-ed penned by a group of seasoned statesmen issued a resounding call for the phased abolition of nuclear weapons: it bore the signatures of George Schultz, the Secretary of State under President Reagan; Sam Nunn, a Democrat who'd presided for years over the Senate Armed Services Committee; William Perry, the Secretary of Defense under Bill Clinton; and Henry Kissinger, the foreign policy superstar of the Nixon administration. All four had been key players in managing American foreign relations during the Cold War arms race, and their views could hardly be dismissed as the ramblings of idealistic peaceniks. The danger is great, they said: and abolishing nukes is something that can realistically be done.[17] Yet once again, the appeal fell on deaf ears within the international corridors of power, and nothing changed.

Virtually all the serious proposals to abolish nukes that surfaced in the post-Hiroshima decades envisioned this process as a series of phases: simultaneous reductions in warheads by all the nuclear powers, followed by rigorous inspections to verify compliance; followed by further reductions, with further verification measures; and so on, until the number got to zero.[18] But one core problem always remained: the ever-latent possibility of war. Even if the nuclear nations somehow managed to pull off this controlled reduction process, and did finally reach the goal of No Nukes Anywhere – what would happen if war broke out among some of the former nuclear powers? How much time would go by before those nations – whose technical experts knew very well how to build a modern nuke – would scramble to rearm themselves?

This was the tough question raised in 2009 by the influential foreign policy expert Thomas Schelling, whose pungent writings about the arms race over a 60-year period had helped shape the thinking of generations of statesmen and military thinkers around the globe. "A world without nuclear weapons," he wrote, would be a world in which the United States, Russia, Israel, China, and half a dozen or a dozen other countries would have hair-trigger mobilization plans to rebuild nuclear weapons and mobilize or commandeer delivery systems, and would have prepared targets to preempt other nations' nuclear facilities, all in a high-alert status, with practice drills and secure emergency communications. Every crisis would be a nuclear crisis, any war could become a nuclear war. The urge to preempt would dominate; whoever gets the first few weapons will coerce or preempt. It would be a nervous world.[19]

To this day, no one has come up with a good answer to this crystal-clear logic. As long as the ultimate guarantor of security continues to reside in each nation's military forces, all-out war among nations remains a real possibility – and full nuclear disarmament doesn't make much sense. As long as neighbor is looking anxiously at neighbor, worried about attacks that could come at any moment, the idea of laying down your weapons is not going to get very far. And even if "Zero Nukes" was somehow achieved, within such a context of unfriendly rivalry and basic mistrust, the possibility of frantic rearmament and preemptive attack would always pose a grave danger. Complete nuclear disarmament only makes sense if it occurs against a backdrop of stable world peace. (I'll return to this idea in Chapter 20.)

Having said this, however, the goal of drastically *reducing* the number of nukes does make excellent sense – and this is probably what Schultz, Nunn, Perry, and Kissinger actually had in mind with their startling 2007 op-ed. The Russians and Americans could achieve highly credible deterrence with one-tenth the number of warheads they currently hold. If the global total could be brought down to about 1,000 warheads, the risk of planetary ecocide would be significantly reduced.

PANDEMICS/BIOWEAPONS

When the 2014 Ebola outbreak occurred in West Africa, it took the US Congress five months to allocate funds after the situation had been declared critical; when the 2015 Zika virus broke out in Latin America, Congress waited eleven months before funding a response.[20] Five months! Eleven months! This hopelessly tardy intervention system was one of the factors that rendered the COVID-19 pandemic as devastating as it was – for if an outbreak occurs, everything depends on the early days and weeks after the first cases are identified. What we need is a full-fledged emergency-response apparatus that's ready to go at a moment's notice: large stockpiles of advanced antiviral medications; ample biohazard gear; a global network of hospitals capable of handling a sudden influx of contagious patients; large numbers of specially trained health professionals; programs of public education for how to protect one's family in a pandemic; and a substantial emergency fund that can be quickly tapped to get things moving. Above all, we need an aggressive, well-funded research program for building the capacity to create new vaccines far more swiftly and effectively than in the past.[21]

The harrowing COVID-19 experience has vividly demonstrated the planet-level character of pandemic threats. When cholera hit Europe hard in 1830 (killing the philosopher G. W. F. Hegel, among many others), and then again in 1847, health officials responded in 1851 by creating the first set of International Sanitary Regulations. Updated periodically through the ensuing century and a half, their latest iteration came in 2005 with the promulgation of the International Health Regulations, which are legally binding on all 193 member states of the World Health Organization. While the measures outlined in these regulations are well thought out, actual implementation remains sketchy, with many countries falling far short of full compliance and many programs chronically underfunded.[22] The global chain of pandemic protections is only as strong as the weakest of its links – particularly when those weak links tend to be found in precisely the territories that are most likely to spawn a crossover virus between animals and humans.

What's more, this still leaves us with the disquieting possibility of bioweapons research conducted in secret government labs by military scientists around the world. In principle, such research has been outlawed by most of the world's nations via two international treaties: the 1925 Geneva Protocol and the 1972 Biological Weapons Convention.[23] But neither of these treaties provides mechanisms for verification and enforcement, and as we now know, at least one participating government has deliberately cheated on these treaties over a sustained period of time. Starting in the 1970s, the Soviet Union launched a major bioweapons program known as *Biopreparat*, producing tons of modified anthrax, smallpox, and other bioweapon agents, while researching a variety of ways to create potent new infectious vectors.[24] The Soviet scientists referred to the human-targeting microbe program as *Ferment*, and to the plant- and animal-targeting program as *Ekology*. Though *Biopreparat* employed more than 60,000 people, the secret never got out until Boris Yeltsin revealed its existence in 1990 and promised to shut it down. One of the illicit program's former directors, Ken Alibek, published a book in 1999 describing its activities in great detail.[25] Since that time, the Russian President Vladimir Putin has brazenly denied that any violations of the bioweapons treaty took place during the Soviet era (!) while quietly acknowledging the potential military value of such research.[26]

How many other nations have violated these treaties? We can't be sure, because no international mechanism exists for inspection or verification. But as biotechnology and genetics enter the era of CRISPR technologies, which greatly facilitate the genetic modification of microorganisms, one can surmise that at least some politicians and military leaders will be tempted to secretly reopen the Pandora's Box of bioweapons. Their reasoning will run along predictable lines: if we don't get these nasty things first, someone else probably will, and so we have no choice but to protect the national interest by preemptively conducting such research ourselves.

ARTIFICIAL INTELLIGENCE

When it comes to national security in cyberspace, all the Great Powers have a single overriding aim: to keep racing for ever more potent machines that will allow them to dominate everyone else. Already today, for example, the Chinese government has openly announced its intention to become the global leader in AI by the year 2030; and it has allocated plentiful funding and talent to that end.[27] Other nations are almost certainly following suit, whether they announce it so brashly or not. Historical experience suggests that, in the context of such no-holds-barred arms races, safety concerns tend to take a second priority.[28]

We are therefore confronted by two distinct forms of danger inherent in the AI arms race: the peril of cyberwarfare itself, with its potential for escalating into a shooting war; and the more insidious peril of hastily designed AI machines created for military or cyberwarfare purposes. Under the frantic pace of research and development imposed by the ongoing arms race, we run the risk that someone, someday, will build a poorly designed AGI that escapes human control. Yet all one can do within the current international system is cross one's fingers and hope that military research establishments will play by internal rules and "best practices" that keep their AI innovations safe.

ALL THE REGULATORY CHALLENGES BECOME HARDER
AT THE INTERNATIONAL LEVEL

Clearly, we won't succeed at controlling mega-dangerous technologies unless the risk-mitigation measures adopted *within* nations are also extended in some effective fashion to the international level. This poses a daunting challenge, because nearly everything is harder to do across borders and among people hailing from disparate cultures. Three main obstacles stand in our way.

First, the rules and regulations differ dramatically from nation to nation. Even among relatively similar countries like the United States and United Kingdom, regulatory policies for science and technology only overlap to a certain extent. For example, when President George W. Bush banned the use of embryonic stem cells in research funded by the US government, some scientists simply transferred their work to labs in the UK, where no such restriction existed.[29] Imagine how much greater the regulatory gap is between, say, Brazil and South Korea, or Uganda and Germany. Until a relatively integrated set of basic rules can be put in place, spanning laboratories and factories across the planet, the nations with the weakest regulation will become "research havens" where risk-tolerant scientists can proceed with their work unhindered. Our protection against reckless experimentation is only as strong as the weakest link in the chain of international oversight.

Even if such a common set of rules existed, moreover, they'd be useless unless they can be reliably enforced. Although some UN bodies like the World Health Organization can impose penalties on nations whose hospitals or laboratories endanger public health, there exists no effective international apparatus for surveillance and enforcement that can be relied on to catch rogue researchers or shoddy labs and compel them to cease and desist. A particularly intractable problem, in this regard, lies in military research conducted in government labs: such research tends to be done in great secrecy, and governments pursuing a breakthrough are unlikely to acquiesce to international controls.

Here a third factor comes into play: the underlying philosophies of citizens and governments when it comes to regulating science and technology diverge significantly in different regions of the planet.[30] At one end of the spectrum lies Western Europe, where voters and leaders have shown a strong resistance to certain kinds of scientific innovation deemed risky or unproved. Genetically modified foods, for example, are banned in the EU, and research labs are closely scrutinized for transgressions of the strict laws and guidelines that have been put in place. At the other end of the spectrum lie the Asian nations, most notably China and South Korea, where scientists are much freer to do as they please, and the public seems for the most part unfazed by consumer products based on cutting-edge new technologies such as genetic manipulation. The United States lies somewhere in the middle, with powerful domestic constituencies on both sides of the fence, and a regulatory regime that is less stringent than Europe's but considerably more rigorous than the ones in Asia. This philosophical divergence across global regions will make it harder to forge common policies that all nations can accept.

* * *

A clear recurring theme emerges from the foregoing discussion: as long as we live in a world of sovereign states – each pursuing its own narrowly conceived national interest, each responsible for its own defense and answerable to no higher authority – these grievous perils will continue to loom over us. Even if we leave aside the mega-dangers discussed in this book, the list of other threats facing our species is a sobering one. It includes (at the very least) non-nuclear wars, civil wars, terrorism, environmental harms, chronic poverty, and massive refugee flows. These are among the core challenges facing humankind in the twenty-first century: every one of them is a planet-level problem, and they are all interconnected in compli-cated ways. Taken as an ensemble, they suggest that our species may be approaching an epochal decision-point in its history: either we succeed at creating effective forms of planet-level governance, or we risk sliding into chaos.

Prologue to Parts III, IV, and V

Does History Have a Direction? Hegel, Smith, Darwin

THE ARGUMENT PRESENTED IN THE COMING chapters rests on one basic premise: the cumulative power of small, incremental changes over time. I maintain that a much better system of global governance can gradually emerge over the coming century and a half, allowing humankind to successfully manage the dangers that threaten our survival. Part III describes what might be accomplished in the next 10 to 20 years; Part IV is tuned to the last decades of this century, around the year 2100; and Part V sketches a full-fledged global framework that might perhaps emerge by the mid-twenty-second century.

Who will supply the "purpose" in this process? Who will steer the boat? No one in particular – or, more accurately, all of us at once. Here I need to make a brief digression on the question of whether history has a deeper goal or directionality. It may look like that's an underlying implication of my argument, and I want to show why that kind of goal-directedness is not what I mean.

When I was in college, I fell in love with the works of the nineteenth-century German philosopher G. W. F. Hegel. Despite the fact that he was a horrible writer, his sentences drenched in weird metaphysical jargon, he offered a vision of history that I couldn't resist. To Hegel, the whole shebang, from ancient China and Babylon to the age of Beethoven and Napoleon, followed a single intelligible arc: the rise of ever deeper forms of consciousness and freedom. History was gradually transforming humankind, like a seed developing through successive stages into a sapling and finally into a beautiful full-grown tree. All the wars and plagues, all the triumphs of art and intelligence, came together for Hegel in a grand sequence that made moral and spiritual sense. And what was more, the sequence was logical and inevitable: just as the seed's maturation follows its own inner blueprint, so humankind would go through successive stages of experience and learning, rising ever higher in richness and complexity until we would unite once again with God in a final moment of cosmic apotheosis.[1]

It was heady stuff, but I eventually had to put Hegel aside. Looking at the events of the actual world – the trenches of the Somme, the gates of Auschwitz, the ashes of Hiroshima – I lost the ability to be swayed by Hegel's vision. When one knows how close we came in the Cuban Missile Crisis – a hairsbreadth away from a senseless cosmic fizzle – it's hard to hold on to the Enlightenment concept of Progress with a capital 'P'. But here another Enlightenment-era thinker comes to the fore: Adam Smith, and his ingenious idea of the Invisible Hand. Smith was one of the first to make a clear distinction between the micro and macro levels of human society. He showed how the myriad self-interested choices of scattered individuals could still come together, at a higher level, to bring remarkable benefits to the community as a whole. In the free market economy, as he saw it, no single individual was consciously aiming for the greater good; each person simply pursued their own self-interest as best they could. Yet the cumulative effect of all these narrowly motivated strivings nonetheless yielded powerful efficiencies at the system level – efficiencies that redounded to the benefit of all. As if steered by an invisible hand, the choices and behaviors of individuals ultimately came together to serve the welfare of the collectivity.[2]

Eight decades after Smith published his *Wealth of Nations*, Charles Darwin added a further key dimension to this idea of system-level effects: the dimension of time. Darwin's vision of evolution appalled some of his contemporaries because it contradicted the Biblical notion of a natural world populated by fixed species of creatures created by God. But the real revolution did not lie in the idea itself that species were constantly mutating – for that might still have been reconciled with the ongoing agency of a Supreme Being, wisely shaping the Earth's creatures over time in myriad beneficent ways. Darwin's truly shocking realization was that evolution is a directionless process. Cosmic beneficence and purpose have nothing to do with it. In his account, the different species of creatures rise and fall, coming and going over the eons – and all this change is utterly random.[3] It results from the happenstance pressures of creatures and habitats interacting with each other over generations, and at no point is any hidden goal or purpose involved. The giraffe species grows longer necks over time because, in an environment with scarce and tall trees, the short-necked giraffes starve and die out, while those with slightly longer necks are able to survive and reproduce and pass on their traits to their offspring. But in a randomly different habitat – one that happened to offer plenty of ground-level leaves – there would be no selection for longer necks, and therefore no giraffes at all. Chance rules the day, not purposiveness.

These two concepts form the basis for my argument: system-level effects (Smith), and gradual evolution shaped by the pressures of shifting contexts and environments (Darwin). Starting about a hundred years ago, humankind began facing increasingly strong pressures to build a more effective framework for handling planet-level problems – those severe dangers and challenges that transcended national boundaries, requiring new forms of regional or global coordination. The Hague Conventions, League of Nations, United Nations, green movement, World Health Organization, and European Union are salient responses to these kinds of pressures. All along, this process was propelled forward by system-level carrots and sticks: at certain key moments, when the world's peoples found ways to work constructively together across borders, they got relative peace and security, better health, improved ecological sustainability, and a rising cornucopia of material prosperity; in other instances, when they fought each other or worked at cross-purposes, they got wars, fear, epidemics, poverty, and ecological disasters. In other words: humankind has been progressively adapting to the newly globalizing environment of its own making.

If someone looked back from the year 2150 or 2200, what might they see? Among the countless possible trajectories, some may have culminated in various forms of failure, as our civilization drifts (or plunges) into catastrophe. But other plausible trajectories also exist. If humankind's efforts at self-organization eventually succeed, then our descendants, looking back, may see a process that unfolded gradually, decade by decade, *as if* someone had been persistently nudging it toward the goal of democratic global governance.

Yet at no point will the outcome have been predetermined. Much depends on the choices that we and the coming generations will make over the next century. Already today, however, we can discern what the first phases of this adaptation process look like, simply by observing the deep trend lines of the past century: shaky but undeniable movement toward greater global coordination and concertation. Nothing guarantees that these trend lines will continue through to some goal awaiting us out there in the future. It doesn't work like that. But one possible outcome is that the systemic pressures for greater coordination will continue to apply their carrots and sticks – exerting a subtle shaping effect on our individual and collective actions, impelling humankind to continue working its way toward a more unified framework of planetary governance. Such a pathway – one of countless potential pathways – is what I try to sketch in the remainder of this book.

The following passage, written by the astronomer Carl Sagan in his 1994 book *Pale Blue Dot*, captures the spirit of the process I'm describing.[4]

It might be a familiar progression, transpiring on many worlds. A planet, newly formed, placidly revolves around its star; life slowly forms; a kaleidoscopic procession of creatures evolves; intelligence emerges ... and then technology is invented ... Science, they recognize, grants immense powers. In a flash, they create world-altering contrivances. Some planetary civilizations see their way through, place limits on what may and what must not be done, and safely pass through the time of perils. Others, not so lucky or so prudent, perish.

* * *

PART III

SENSIBLE STEPS
FOR TODAY'S WORLD:

POWERFUL MEASURES WE CAN
IMPLEMENT RIGHT AWAY

10

Do It Now: Five Points of Leverage

I N THIS CHAPTER I SURVEY FIVE KEY "action areas" in which politically achievable changes over the coming two decades could render us a lot safer than we are today. Some of the policies I propose are new, while others are already in place but could use some substantial beefing-up.

CLIMATE

The overall goal is clear enough: we need to decarbonize our society and clean up the mess we've made in the skies. It needs to happen fast. How do we manage it?

Most economists agree that setting up a nationwide carbon pricing mechanism will provide the most effective and fair approach. Much of the preliminary research on how to enact such a mechanism has already been done, so the primary goal here is to elect leaders committed to seeing it through. In order to render this politically feasible in a nation like the US, for example, the federal government will need to offer compensation and attractive employment alternatives to those groups who will bear the brunt of this massive shift. One key constituency will be the coal- and oil-producing communities, which will need assistance with making the necessary adjustments – not just the people directly employed in extracting fossil fuels and transporting them, but all the towns and counties that will be indirectly but wrenchingly affected. The last thing we want to do is gut those communities and force people to move away in desperation; the federal government will need to set up a full-scale program for supporting entire localities in America as they retool the ways they make a living.[1] This will not be cheap, and the rest of us will need to be willing to help pay for it. If we fail at this, then a great many of those people will (quite understandably) be implacable foes of the systemic changes our energy economy so urgently needs. On the other side of the ledger, of course, our government should also incentivize innovation in renewable energy, offering tax breaks for companies that conduct research, and low-interest loans for startup businesses.

Many households and private corporations are already making a significant impact today by reducing their carbon footprints – and this opens up direct avenues for each of us, as individuals and as employees, to press for change. We need to keep ramping up this process, spreading the word, sharing ideas and strategies as we go. To take but one example: consider our consumption of beef, pork, and chicken. We don't have to all become vegetarians: simply cutting our meat consumption by half would dramatically reduce the carbon impact of our nation's food system. Since no one likes to be told by the federal government what they should or should not eat, this campaign is best undertaken by each of us on our own initiative, within our own lives and among our circles of family and friends.

Let's suppose for the sake of argument that all humankind were to do this tomorrow morning, switching over to plant-based proteins like beans, rice, nuts, and soy. Experts calculate that this measure alone – a 50 percent drop in meat consumption – could lower global CO_2 emissions by 2 billion tons a year – a whopping 5 percent of the annual total.[2] To be sure, if we succeed at this, we will be throwing out of work a large subset of our fellow citizens whose livelihoods depend on meat production. Here, once again, the role of the federal government will be to cushion the transition for those people, just as it does for fossil fuel communities. And the rest of us should be willing to help pay for it through our taxes.

In Chapter 6 I waxed enthusiastic about the possibility of NDAC – immense carbon removal machines for scrubbing the skies, powered by advanced nuclear reactors. As of today, however, this save-our-bacon technology remains nothing but a tantalizing possibility, fraught with many unknowns. Our government should massively accelerate research on both prongs of NDAC – carbon removal and advanced nuclear – while streamlining licensing procedures for the Generation IV nuclear power plants, which hold the promise of being much safer than those currently in use. Bill Gates's company TerraPower should not have to go to China to pursue its path-breaking research on advanced nuclear reactors: both the technology itself and the jobs and expertise it creates should be encouraged to flourish in the United States.[3]

Another prime area for redoubled research efforts is known among climate scientists as solar radiation management.[4] If the planet warms past 3 or 4 degrees above preindustrial levels, feedback loops in the climate system could set off a self-reinforcing spiral of warming: melting permafrost, ice loss, water vapor, and wildfires would propel new releases of greenhouse gases from natural sources, causing a swift rise in temperature that further accelerates the process. Such violent shifts have actually happened a few times in the planet's past, and they have generally led to mass extinctions that (on at least one occasion) wiped out almost all life forms.[5] Clearly, if we become aware that human activities are taking the biosphere through one of these tipping points – setting into motion one of these million-year extremes – we would need a way to turn down the planet's thermostat very quickly. And such a control button actually exists: volcanos. When large volcanic eruptions occur, they spew massive amounts of sulfur and other particulates into the high atmosphere, partially blocking the Sun's light. The entire planet measurably cools for a few years, until the volcanic cloud dissipates and the particulates settle back to the ground. So if we could mimic the effects of many large volcanic eruptions by spreading millions of tons of sulfur and particulates in the stratosphere from airplanes, balloons, or other dispersal technologies, we could (in principle) lower the planet's temperature in a very short time.[6]

An alternative method, heavily tinged with sci-fi overtones, would be to install a screen in space between our planet and the Sun. To accomplish this, we could launch spaceships out to a place 1.5 million kilometers from Earth known as the Lagrange-1 point, where the gravitational fields of the Sun and the Earth exactly counterbalance each other (it lies closer to the Earth than the Sun because the Sun's mass is so much greater). According to preliminary scientific estimates, this solution probably lies within the reach of today's technologies.[7] If the spaceships were to deposit, say, 16 trillion small reflective discs out there, arrayed in a cloud formation, they could deflect about 2 percent of the Sun's energy away from the Earth, which would yield just the right cooling effect to stave off global warming. Each reflective disc would need to be about a half meter in diameter, and capable of making small adjustments to its own position to keep itself properly aligned. An astronomer named Roger Angel, funded by a NASA grant, calculated in 2006 that creating such a sunshade would cost "a few trillion dollars" and would take about 25 years to install.[8]

Both these ideas – artificial clouds and space sunshade – are fraught with a mix of foreseeable drawbacks and all kinds of unknowns.[9] How would the Earth's creatures – plants, flowers, insects, plankton – respond to this sustained diminution of sunlight? We know from experience with volcanos that the ecological impact of short-term ash clouds in the stratosphere is relatively benign. But what would be the effect if artificial clouds were put in place for decades? No one knows. Blocking the Sun's light would help cool the planet, but the high CO_2 levels in the atmosphere would persist, contributing to ocean acidification. If something went wrong with the process, how quickly could the artificial clouds be made to dissipate? Who would control these planet-scale projects? Who would pay? What about the people around the world (and there would be many) who consider this a really bad idea?[10]

If there is one thing we humans have gradually come to grasp about the Earth's ecosystems, it's that they are extremely complicated causal networks in which feedback loops and emergent properties play key roles.[11] You make a precise change at Point A, thinking this will affect the contiguous Point B in predictable ways, but what you have also unwittingly done is set in motion a cascade of ramifying causes and effects that ultimately brings weird and powerful transformation far away at Point S. Some of nature's small-scale causal relationships are relatively predictable: when you push a carrot seed into the soil and water it regularly, a carrot plant usually grows. But modifying a systemic factor as fundamental as the incoming energy from the Sun – on which every life form and terrestrial habitat depends – could conceivably bring major unintended effects. In fact, it would be rather surprising if it didn't.

All these considerations, taken together, suggest that solar radiation management should be seen as a measure of last resort, to be undertaken only if humankind faces a dire climate emergency. The best policy is to keep vigorously pursuing this idea, conducting scientific experiments that test its viability and explore its possible ecological consequences. Given the serious climate trouble that lies ahead, humankind would be foolish to ignore this potentially promising option. We may need it at some point, and if that happens, it would behoove us to know much more than we do today about how to make it work.[12]

Another key role for the federal government under Presidents Obama and Biden has been to set bold new targets for green technologies ranging across the American economy – from transportation to housing, from agriculture to industry. These policies should be aggressively pursued by future administrations, ramping up the regulatory pressures and financial incentives for decarbonization. (Imagine, moreover, if a visionary *Republican* leader were to take on this mantle: how much of a breakthrough would it offer him or her, in poaching centrist voters from the Democratic Party?)

At the international level, we clearly need a dose of what the Soviet president Mikhail Gorbachev used to call "new thinking." Humankind is not even close to meeting the emissions targets set by the 2015 Paris Agreement, and an alternative approach is therefore required. The legal scholar David Victor, an expert on international regulation, argues that creating small clubs of like-minded nations will prove far more effective than the globe-spanning conventions pursued thus far. Three ideas underpin his proposal: flexibility, accountability, and incentives.[13] Every country has its own unique constellation of strengths and weaknesses when it comes to reducing carbon emissions: what works well for France might not work well at all for India or Australia. Flexibility is therefore the key. International climate agreements need to embrace a wide variety of mitigation strategies tailored to the capabilities of each nation.

If a dozen countries got together in this spirit, and each offered to bring a specific set of tangible, verifiable actions to the table, this would be a valuable first step. Each country would make its pledge contingent on the other countries' fulfillment of their own pledges: "I'll do X, Y, and Z if you'll do A, B, and C." This would bring a badly needed element of accountability to the process. Finally, the club participants could offer each other special concessions to reward each other for progress in meeting their goals: "Now that you've delivered on X, Y, and Z, I'll grant you the following exclusive benefits." These incentives could include trade preferences, streamlined market access for low-carbon technologies, or lucrative exchanges of emissions credits.

In this way, a positive dynamic would emerge among the participating nations: as each country saw that the others were actually delivering on their pledges, they would be motivated to push harder on getting results at home. As the benefits of cooperation accrued, they would be encouraged to further ramp up their efforts in a mutually reinforcing spiral. Most importantly, as other nations outside the group witnessed the tangible progress and accumulating benefits reaped by club members, they would be more likely to join the club (or to create new clubs of their own).[14] In such a system, the UN's role would no longer be to seek a lowest common denominator that could prove acceptable to 193 nations. This has been one of the main factors holding back progress, according to Victor. Instead, it could serve as a facilitator for these clubs' negotiations – coordinating their reciprocal endeavors, serving as a clearinghouse for scientific data and policy advice, and monitoring and certifying the tangible progress being made.[15]

Another worrisome problem at the global level is rising population. According to the latest UN estimates, global population will probably reach ten billion around the year 2050 and level off at eleven billion around 2100.[16] That's a lot of mouths to feed, and a lot of energy to burn. Won't this inevitably lead to higher rates of global warming?

Not necessarily – for the way we use the Earth's resources makes all the difference. Consider for example the case of garbage in France.[17] In 1979, France's 53 million citizens produced 170 million tons of refuse; in 1996, they produced 627 million tons of refuse – an increase of 369 percent. Before we picture the Eiffel Tower submerged in trash, however, we need to look at how that additional trash was handled. The garbage of the 1970s was dumped unceremoniously into ravines in the countryside, where it was often set on fire or allowed to rot away indefinitely. The garbage of the 1990s was subjected to a barrage of sophisticated treatment processes: sorting, recycling, composting, and clean landfills. Net result: despite the quadrupling of volume, the environmental impact of garbage in France was much less damaging in 1996 than in 1979.[18] In other words: if "More" is coupled with "Smart," then the bottom line can still be a net improvement.[19]

The same principle applies to global warming. If ten billion people eat beef, drive gas-guzzling SUVs, and live in McMansions, we're in trouble. But if those billions eat plant-based foods, use electric vehicles, and live in ecologically designed urban neighborhoods, it will be a whole different story. A sensible strategy for population management will therefore need to aim for a combination of long-range goals: (1) continue boosting education and prosperity worldwide, which will lead to lower fertility rates, which will in turn lead to a leveling and perhaps even decline in total human population;[20] (2) persuade both individuals and their governments to adopt greener policies and habits; and (3) develop new technologies that allow human needs to be met with a zero-carbon footprint.[21]

But what if we fail? What if, despite the best efforts of so many scientists and activists around the world, humankind simply can't find the means to effect the needed changes fast enough – and global temperatures continue their dramatic rise? A wise policy for today would be to start preparing seriously for the possibility of such a grim tomorrow.

Some early adaptation steps are already underway. Many people along the New Jersey and Florida coastlines, for example, are building houses on twelve-foot stilts that allow ever stronger storm surges to pass underneath. Others are packing their bags and moving inland. Some insurance companies and banks are balking at working with folks who insist on building mansions along Hurricane Alley.[22] In other parts of the world like Venice or Holland, we encounter more dramatic actions: people are building sea walls, installing gigantic pumping stations, and abandoning certain low-lying tracts of land to the recurring floods.[23] Still other nations, like the Maldives or the Marshall Islands, are preparing for an unthinkable reality: their whole territory will probably be underwater by 2100, and they will have to find a new physical homeland for their entire population and culture. In 2008, the president of the Maldives, Mohamed Nasheed, started laying aside a portion of tourism revenues every year for just this purpose: possible sites for a new homeland include Sri Lanka, India, and Australia. "We can do nothing to stop climate change on our own," he said, "and so we have to buy land elsewhere."[24]

Prosperous societies have the obvious advantage here: they can afford to build giant walls to protect their coastal cities or to compensate people for relocating their homes on higher ground. But poor nations like Bangladesh, where as much as half the territory could go under the sea by 2100, have no such luck. It's hard to imagine viable relocation solutions for a poverty-stricken country that finds half its population of 164 million displaced over a relatively short period.[25] Where on earth will all those people go? The only responsible path is for international bodies like the UN and World Bank to start assisting nations like Bangladesh today, spreading out this painful transition over as many decades as possible.

If you happen to be a doctor in Toronto, Juneau, or Stockholm, you may need to add new books to your reading list, along the following lines: *Tropical Diseases in Temperate Climates*; or *Impact of Climate Change on the Outbreak of Infectious Diseases.*[26] These will help prepare you for the increasing numbers of patients who show up in your clinic with tropical afflictions like Zika, *Vibrio vulnificus*, West Nile virus, pyomyositis, Chagas disease, or malaria.[27] Worse still, the same rising temperatures that expand disease range will also deliver a major hit to the world's agricultural systems, so it would be smart to start preparing now by developing new crop strains that are heat- and drought-resistant.[28] Fresh water will keep becoming scarcer in many parts of the world (even as other places face unprecedented flooding). New desalination technologies will be required, on a scale that dwarfs the largest water-treatment machines built today; and since desalination processes consume huge amounts of electricity, we come back yet again to the urgent need for advanced nuclear reactors to power them.[29]

Many inland territories will reel under the onslaught of fiercer wildfires, floods, tornados, and hurricanes. Already today in parts of the American West, it is becoming harder to justify building homes in certain fire-prone forested areas, and this trend is likely to increase over the coming years. The West Coast fire season of 2020 shattered all records, but it's unlikely that even those grim records will stand for long. New building codes and urban planning maps will be needed that take into account the requirements for protecting people from nature's wrath.[30]

Today certain major coral reefs are already dying – much sooner than anyone had anticipated – and this is a harbinger of ailing oceans to come.[31] Carbon dioxide directly acidifies the ocean waters, which wreaks havoc in marine ecosystems; it also leads to warmer waters, which changes the deep currents that circulate nutrients to the whole food chain of sea animals. When coupled with pollution, overfishing, and other insults, all this adds up to bleak news on the watery parts of the planet.[32] Humans who depend on the seas for food and livelihood will need to adapt. That can of tuna you opened for lunch will probably be a distant memory for your grandchildren's generation.

Many animal and plant species will simply die out. Unable to adapt swiftly enough to the shifting climate environments, their numbers will dwindle, and those that cannot save themselves by finding new habitats will disappear. We humans would be wise to establish nature preserves where key species can be allowed to survive, as well as biological banks where the DNA from all these disappearing creatures can be stored.[33] This will perhaps allow future generations to bring them back under more propitious conditions. We can justify the cost via two lines of reasoning: as a means for preserving intrinsically valuable life forms, but also as a way to promote human welfare by saving biological information that could prove useful in the future.

All these wrenching ecological changes will impose deep stresses on human political institutions. Many people will lose their jobs; families will be sundered; fights will break out over scarce resources; large numbers of individuals will hit the road, looking for more survivable living conditions.[34] We can expect civil strife and xenophobia to rise dramatically: some small-minded politicians (and voters) will blame all these ills on minority groups or outsiders, calling for walls to be built, not just against the seas, but against the rising tides of climate refugees.[35] The calamitous Syrian civil war, which originated with a prolonged drought, offers a glimpse into the political challenges the world's peoples will face over the coming century. Humankind will need innovative forms of cross- border cooperation and conflict resolution if it hopes to weather this storm successfully.

NUKES

At first glance, one might be tempted to set aside the extreme (but very real) possibility of an all-out nuclear war with thousands of warheads going off – for if that happens, it seems reasonable to assume that history as we have known it would come to an end. But here again, the unknowns are profound. Some biological species might actually survive the radioactivity and nuclear winter effects, eventually generating a new phase of evolution among the ashes – the Postnucleocene Epoch. It's even possible that some humans might make it through. The truth is, we just don't know.[36] Therefore, a wise policy would dictate that we make some modest preparations today, setting aside judiciously selected resources in special bunkers to aid our (hypothetical) great-grandchildren as they seek to build a Postnucleocene life for themselves. Seeds, tools, medicines, basic survival handbooks, and designs for simple machines might help them get through the first few hard years. And for the period that came after, we might offer samplings of world art, literature, and science, so that the countless miracles of creativity that dot the human past are not erased.[37]

Short of this extreme scenario, the main possibilities for a lower-level disaster are twofold: accidental release of a few missiles; and small-scale war between two nuclear nations. The first of these poses an ever-present danger. A malfunctioning computer, a flight of geese triggering an early warning radar, a malicious hacker, an incompetent group of officers in a command-and-control center – any combination of such factors could trigger the launch of a limited number of missiles. We have come close enough in various hair-raising instances over the past decades to know that this is a real ongoing risk.[38] If the mistake were caught in time – moments after launch – it's possible that the persons on the receiving end of the missiles could be warned, and perhaps persuaded not to launch a massive counterstrike. ("I'm really, really sorry, Vladimir, but. . . ").

In the second case, we have an all-out war, but it takes place between two nations whose supply of nukes is relatively limited – say, Pakistan (140 warheads) versus India (130 warheads). If most of the warheads were successfully launched, such an exchange might be expected to kill hundreds of millions of persons within the first few years after the attacks – not only within the targeted territories themselves, but also around the world as the nuclear winter effects spread across the atmosphere.[39] The 1986 meltdown at Chernobyl – releasing the equivalent radiation of a single large warhead – caused toxic materials to circumnavigate the globe many times over.[40] An India–Pakistan war would increase that global impact a hundredfold, coupled with a 20 percent reduction in the Earth's protective ozone layer. The worst effect of all would be the severe climate disturbances caused by the five million tons of smoke and dense particulate matter projected into the atmosphere by the blasts and burning cities.[41] Experts estimate that global agriculture would fail in major ways for at least a few years. Far more people would probably die from starvation and disease in the aftermath than from the direct impact of the atomic attacks themselves.

Even within today's self-help system of international relations, nations can still take collective steps of risk reduction that are clearly in their mutual self-interest.[42] An accidental launch of missiles could be rendered less catastrophic by the following kinds of measures:

- Drastically reduce the overall number of warheads everywhere. Fewer warheads means simpler command and control systems, and fewer places where things can go wrong. This should be one of our highest priorities over the coming years.

- Avoid delivery systems such as hypersonic missiles that shorten the warning time for attacks. Use arms control treaties to work out arrangements for ongoing inspection of delivery systems to ensure compliance by all players.

- Reduce automation in missile launch systems, taking care to include failsafe mechanisms for human intervention and judgement before actual launch takes place.

- Set up a global system of emergency top-level communications among *all* the nuclear powers, similar to the White House–Kremlin hotline.

- Install advanced missile defense systems in all nuclear nations, capable of intercepting a small volley of incoming warheads. This would not be a comprehensive nuclear shield for all-out war, but a partial shield designed to minimize the damage from a limited accidental launch. Such a shield would need to be built up via a carefully orchestrated, multilateral process that included all the major players, so as not to destabilize the balance of nuclear deterrence.

- Encourage all nuclear nations to sign a treaty committing themselves to "no first use" of nuclear weapons. This would be a largely symbolic gesture, since any nation finding itself in a dire military predicament might still opt to use its nuclear arsenal as a last resort. But it would help to draw a clear line between these weapons and all other offensive systems, affirming the principle that nukes only exist to deter the use of nukes by other powers. In a crisis, such a principle might exert a crucial stabilizing effect, discouraging leaders from considering a "tactical" or "limited" first use of these weapons.

- Prepare civilian populations for a limited nuclear strike. Educate the public about what to do if their vicinity is hit. Set up a system of shelters, emergency health procedures, and first responders to deal with a limited strike. Such a program would have the important side effect of vividly reminding the public about the ever-present danger under which they live – which might in turn lead voters to support leaders who seek reductions in warheads and other risk-mitigation measures.

A "small-scale" nuclear war like the India–Pakistan conflict described above could be rendered less horrific (relatively speaking) by the following kinds of steps:

- Vigorously continue to pursue nonproliferation, limiting both the number of nuclear powers and the size of their arsenals.
- Provide strong incentives for mortal nuclear enemies (like India and Pakistan, or Israel and Iran) to gradually shift their relationships toward stabler forms of peace. Both carrots and sticks could be applied in this international effort: if Great Powers like the United States, China, Germany, Russia, and Japan were to offer major financial and commercial benefits for peacebuilding measures, coupled with sanctions and penalties for warlike actions, the chances of stabilization would go up.
- Put in place measures for feeding the world's most impoverished people in the aftermath of a limited nuclear war, for they would be the ones most harshly stricken by famine. This would probably have to be an international program aimed at staving off starvation for hundreds of millions of people, sustained over as much as ten to fifteen years while the partial nuclear winter gradually subsided. Researchers could work today to develop new strains of crops that can flourish under conditions of limited sunlight, lowered temperatures, higher ultraviolet exposure, and drought. Having such preparations in place, ready to go, could save countless lives.

PANDEMICS

When it comes to naturally arising viral threats like COVID-19, experts point to four sensible (and affordable) measures we should adopt today that would greatly mitigate the damage.[43]

1. Change the Way People Interact with Susceptible Animals

Most of the deadly outbreaks of the past have occurred when crossover happens between various animal species and humans. A virus endemic among chickens, pigs, bats, or monkeys suddenly mutates and makes the leap into the human world; our immune systems are vulnerable, and people get sick and die. If we're lucky, the virus mutates in a way that does not allow it to spread directly between one person and another. If we're unlucky, we get something like the 1919 influenza pandemic (which killed 50 million people) or the relatively milder COVID-19. Unlike the 1919 virus, which killed young and old alike, the SARS-Cov-2 virus afflicted the elderly more severely than the young – which helps explain why it killed far fewer human beings worldwide. But if a fierce new pathogen similar to the 1919 influenza were to emerge in today's world – with global air travel, a world population that is four times greater, and twice as many people concentrated in cities – public health officials warn that the contagion's toll could prove far worse than even the horrific toll of 1919.[44]

A logical first step is to change the way people handle animals. When humans live in close quarters with livestock under conditions of low hygiene, the chance for viruses to make the leap into human bodies is much greater. Simple sanitary regulations could make a big difference here, at ground zero where the first spark of pandemics gets ignited. Of course, this is easier said than done. In a world wracked by poverty and illiteracy, it's hard to get people to comply with high standards of hygiene. In a self-help world, it's difficult to persuade the rich countries to provide the cash and resources needed to assist the poor countries in raising their standards.

This puts global development aid in a new light. When rich countries help the poor countries, they are partly acting from compassion and a moral imperative to succor those in need; but they are also acting in their own long-term self-interest. Poverty and illiteracy are the breeding grounds where the virus is spawned that is going to threaten your children someday – maybe tomorrow, maybe 20 years out. We need to ramp up our international aid efforts massively for both kinds of reasons – if we want to be good, and if we know what's good for us.

2. Create an Effective Early Warning System

Already today, public health authorities have put in place the beginnings of a surveillance system in the hot spots – particularly Southeast Asia and Africa – where animal-to-human crossovers typically occur. This is an excellent start, but the researchers are unanimous in calling for greater resources to be allocated so that they can do their work more effectively. "To establish a worldwide safety net," writes the Stanford biologist Nathan Wolfe, "we would need to monitor thousands of people exposed to animals in dozens of sites throughout the world – not only hunters but also people working on farms and in animal markets."[45] In 2009, the US Agency for

International Development created the PREDICT program, partnering with 30 other nations in an effort to build precisely such an advanced monitoring network, equipped with state-of-the-art technology and highly trained staff.[46] Unfortunately, the US federal budgets for 2018 and 2019 cut funding for such programs by roughly one-third.[47] We should be doing the exact opposite.

3. Develop Measures for Rapid Containment

In Vignette #1, the single most important factor in rendering Jim and Evelyn's engineered virus horrifically deadly was the bug's relatively long incubation period. During the ten days in which infected people were contagious but symptom-free, they were able to travel around the world and unwittingly spread the disease beyond any hope of containment. A similarly long incubation period characterized the SARS-Cov-2 virus of 2019 (but the low lethality of the COVID-19 disease kept the overall death toll relatively modest compared to other pandemics).

How to avoid such a dismal outcome in the future? Imagine if a simple breathalyzer machine existed that allowed for a ten-second test to be performed, detecting a broad range of potential infections in a person's body before they became symptomatic. Such devices are under development today, and their efficacy is likely to improve rapidly over the coming decades.[48] Now imagine that, when you pass through security at your local airport before boarding a flight, you not only get your body and baggage scanned, but also have to take a quick breathalyzer test to determine whether you are unknowingly carrying an infectious disease. This simple measure – preventing infected persons from traveling far and wide – would go a long way toward rendering an outbreak more manageable.

Of course, it would also amount to a dramatic expansion of governmental surveillance over the bodies of citizens and would no doubt face significant objections from civil libertarians. In the tug-of-war between privacy and security, it would amount to an important shift away from privacy. But in the aftermath of the COVID-19 pandemic and the havoc it has wreaked on countless lives, perhaps a majority of the world's citizenry will accept the need for such routine breathalyzer tests as a worthwhile trade-off. (A compromise solution might be for the breathalyzers to be required only in those specific areas where a pandemic outbreak is showing signs of breaking out.) This is a policy debate that we are likely to see happening in the coming years.

Some of the news from the antivirus frontlines is actually quite encouraging. Researchers today are making progress on developing a flu vaccine that works for all strains of the disease, not just for a small subset of the bugs.[49] They are also working on ingenious ways to mass-produce new vaccines much more swiftly than in the past, building on the remarkable progress triggered by COVID-19. In 2018, an international group of scientists launched the Global Virome Project, with $1.2 billion in funding: their goal was to identify up to 70 percent of all the viruses on the planet, zeroing in on those that could serve as crossover vehicles for a future pandemic.[50] Powerful new machines for genomic sequencing allow fieldworkers and doctors to identify novel viruses in mere hours (compared with the months or years that such genetic sleuthwork used to take). Computer modeling and analytic tools allow epidemiologists to make accurate predictions in real time, mapping the key spots for intervention by emergency teams.[51] National governments should strongly support all these kinds of monitoring and research; when one compares the modest costs of funding such measures with the colossal economic toll of a pandemic like COVID-19, the policy choice becomes particularly clear.

4. Reduce Reliance on Market Mechanisms and Private Funding

"When the last Ebola outbreak exploded in 2014, eventually killing more than 11,000 people," writes a journalist for *Time* magazine,

> the virus wasn't a mystery to scientists: it was discovered in 1976. But even though it had been killing people on and off for decades, there were no drugs or vaccines approved to fight it – and there still aren't today, chiefly because there's little incentive for pharmaceutical companies to bring them to market.[52]

The Gates Foundation, recognizing the lack of governmental initiatives to prepare for pandemics, allocated $100 million in 2017 to create the Coalition for Epidemic Preparedness Innovations (CEPI), a public–private partnership for building capacity for emergency interventions in public health.[53]

But this is ridiculous. We shouldn't have to rely on privately owned drug companies and far-sighted private citizens like Bill and Melinda Gates to safeguard our future, based on their own initiative and assessment of the dangers. This is a key reason why governments exist in the first place: to serve the public interest by preparing in advance for long-term threats that private citizens and corporations have insufficient incentives or resources to address. Our federal government today should be hiring the experts, assessing the most serious threats, and working proactively to build capacity for dealing with those threats.

ARTIFICIAL INTELLIGENCE

An indication of the impressive number of researchers who are concerned about the long-term safety and security of AI emerged from a 2017 conference at Asilomar, California, in which a set of 23 ethical principles were adopted as the voluntary guidelines for the field to follow – a sort of Hippocratic Oath for the AI enterprise. The 22nd principle read:

> AI systems designed to recursively self-improve or self-replicate in a manner that could lead to rapidly increasing quality or quantity must be subject to strict safety and control measures.[54]

Among the document's 1,273 signatories one finds a veritable Who's Who of the world's leading AI scientists in both academia and industry. Allan Dafoe, an Oxford researcher who writes about the long-term governance of AI, observed in 2018: "You can now talk about the risks of AI without seeming like you are lost in science fiction."[55]

Since improperly designed AGI machines could someday pose a serious safety risk to human society – perhaps even an existential danger – it behooves us to start actively monitoring developments in the AI field. What's the best way to do this, while minimizing red tape and interference with the roboticists and computer science researchers? The answer depends on how close we are at any given moment to witnessing the creation of a full-fledged AGI. Expert opinion is divided about how long this will take: estimates range from ten years to a whole century.[56] (Stuart Russell's estimate is about 80 years.)[57] If we take the average of these expert predictions and settle on a timeframe of 30 to 80 years, this still leaves our society some breathing room.

We could start today by creating an independent federal oversight agency tasked with simply keeping tabs on the progress of the field and submitting annual reports for policymakers and the public. As the technology develops over the coming years, this agency could be endowed with special investigative authority that required all governmental, corporate, or university-based AI projects to report on their progress (under confidentiality rules that would protect the trade secrets of their research while still allowing for expert oversight). If at some point certain projects started to approach AGI-level capabilities, the oversight agency could assign panels of experts to make sure that appropriate safety and security procedures were being followed. Projects that failed to meet these standards could be de-funded, or, if necessary, legally compelled to shut down.

One obvious target for such government oversight would be those projects that explicitly pursue the goal of pushing beyond narrow AI. Consider for example OpenAI, an organization launched in 2015 by Elon Musk. The billionaire creator of Tesla and SpaceX was one of the signatories of the 2015 Open Letter on Artificial Intelligence, calling for intensified research into pathways for controlling advanced AI.[58] But his solution to the challenge was a startling one: he was seeking up to $1 billion in funding for OpenAI, whose mission was to build a powerful form of artificial super-intelligence as soon as possible. Musk reasoned that the greatest danger of superintelligence lay in the wrong people being the first ones to get their hands on this game-changing technology and then dictating terms to the rest of the world from a position of unassailable strength. Musk's solution: his team would be the ones to win this race, and they would share their discovery equally with all humankind. "If everyone has AI powers," he argued, "then there's not any one person or a small set of individuals who can have AI superpower."[59]

Musk's initiative may have been launched with the best of intentions, but it could also put humankind at risk if it succeeds at creating a true AGI or ASI before such machines can be guaranteed to be safe and secure. We have laws on the books that prevent ordinary folks like you and me from building nukes of our own or conducting experiments with the water supply: surely these considerations of public safety apply with equal force to organizations like OpenAI that have launched potentially dangerous lines of AI research. Over the coming decades, such projects should be required to report regularly on the methods they are using, as well as on the safety and security procedures under which they are operating. (Unfortunately, none of these precautionary measures will apply to secret AI research conducted by military cyberwarfare labs. I'll take up this thorny matter in Chapter 11.)

A second pressing challenge posed by advanced AI has to do with the rapid rise of automation. The robots are coming for you, but it won't be like the *Terminator* movies: they have no interest in killing you. They just want your job.

Some people dismiss the threat of rising automation, saying that new kinds of jobs will always emerge after the humdrum tasks have been taken over by smart machines.[60] "Just look at agriculture," they argue. "In the early nineteenth century more than 80 percent of the population worked on the land, and today the mechanization of farming means that only 2 percent of the population are employed that way – yet all those farm workers who were replaced by machines eventually found jobs in new economic sectors like industry or service work."

This kind of reasoning has made sense – until now. What's different today is the sheer potency and versatility of the machines, and the rapidly broadening scope of the tasks they are capable of performing. As AI and robotics converge over the coming two or three decades, our increasingly brilliant machines will be able to outperform humans in so many kinds of jobs that there won't be much left for humans to do.[61]

To be sure, some forms of work will be hard to automate. If you're a poet, musician, or novelist, no machine will be able to replace you. The same goes for priests, eldercare givers, or masseurs. Entrepreneurs in the business world who use their creativity to generate new products and start new companies will probably do just fine. All these jobs require a special human touch that machines will probably be unable to offer for a very long time (if ever).[62] But how many of the Earth's eight billion people are poets, priests, entrepreneurs, or masseurs? What will happen to the billions of human beings who toil today in the majority of other professions?

The first wave to lose their jobs will be the truck drivers, Uber and Lyft drivers, mail carriers, secretaries, factory workers, receptionists, customer service assistants, accountants, clerks, advertising reps, and retail sales-persons. These professions are already being automated today to varying degrees. Plumbers, handymen, waiters, construction workers, and garden-ers will be harder to replace because it will take a few more decades for the robots to acquire the high level of situational awareness and versatility that such jobs require.[63] But if you visit the websites of robot-design labs and companies like Boston Dynamics, you will see the automated future taking shape before your eyes.[64] A six-foot tall machine that looks like a giant chicken swoops and swirls on a warehouse floor, balancing exquisitely, grabbing cardboard boxes from a shelf, wheeling about and zooming to a nearby conveyor belt, placing the box there, patting it smartly into place. A swarm of small drones hovers in formation, then starts maneuvering in a swiftly flowing figure eight: you can picture the myriad tasks such coordin-ated flyers will be able to perform once they are equipped with actuators and grabbers.[65] These kinds of machines will form part of a second wave of advanced automation within the next two or three decades.[66]

Many forms of automation will not necessarily take shape as a full *replacement* of human workers. Instead, the brilliant machines will work alongside a small number of humans who supervise their functioning –

and ten people will be able to do the work formerly done by a hundred or a thousand. This is precisely what took place in agriculture over the past hundred years, and it will probably happen over the coming decades for the myriad manual jobs described above, as well as for highly skilled professionals such as doctors, lawyers, journalists, engineers, architects, scientists, and teachers. The machines will work together with humans, tremendously multiplying their efficiency and thereby reducing the need to hire more human workers.[67]

The implications are alarming. Growing numbers of economists who study this phenomenon have concluded that mass unemployment on a staggering scale is coming our way – probably within a few decades' time. Forty or fifty years from now, as much as half the working-age population could find itself chronically out of a job.[68] This wrenching disruption of our economic system will generate severe political upheaval, as both leaders and citizens struggle to figure out how to respond. (Just look at what happened when unemployment hit 25 percent during the 1930s: one direct result was the rapid growth of Fascist and Communist parties in many countries, and a global war.) This is a problem that cuts to the core of how we run our modern civilization.

The solution? Today's mantra among politicians is to provide retraining programs and reeducation for workers so they can shift to new lines of work. But this assumes that those new lines of work will exist. What happens when you try to switch jobs and discover a robot placidly performing your intended new profession, working 24/7 without complaint? Some emerging sectors of tomorrow's economy may indeed offer novel labor opportunities that are uniquely keyed to the special capabilities of humans. But most new jobs probably won't work that way. For an employer struggling to make ends meet, automation is almost always cheaper and more efficient in the long run than going with human labor; most of the newly created positions will be filled by the ever more brilliant machines.[69]

One radical approach to this conundrum would be to follow the advice of Mohandas K. Gandhi: simply melt down the brilliant machines for scrap and go back to doing things by hand, such as spinning your own cotton cloth. But this approach is unlikely to persuade most denizens of modernity, who prefer to buy their loincloths readymade from Target.

This leaves only one other solution that's even more radical than Gandhi's: Basic Income. It comes in two versions: full-strength or lite.[70] The full-strength version is known as Universal Basic Income (UBI). The government sends a monthly check to every individual in the nation, providing an ample amount for food, housing, healthcare, education, and other essential needs. Everyone gets the same amount, regardless of whether they're rich or poor, young or old, employed or unemployed. If you are ambitious and want more than the monthly allowance, you are welcome to do whatever you want to earn more. The lite version is known as Guaranteed Minimum Income (GMI), and it would be similar to UBI except that the checks would only be sent to people at the lower echelons of the income spectrum, and the cash amounts would decline proportionately as your income level goes up. People above a certain threshold would get no check at all. I suspect that most such programs in the future will take the GMI route rather than the UBI route, because it will be hard to justify sending monthly checks for several thousand dollars to people like Jeff Bezos and Bill Gates.

This idea boasts a long pedigree and an astonishingly broad array of supporters.[71] Thomas Paine, Charles Fourier, John Stuart Mill, Edward Bellamy, and Bertrand Russell all endorsed it. The presidential candidate George McGovern proposed a version of it in the 1970s, and the economist John Kenneth Galbraith championed it to the end of his days. Richard Nixon tried and failed to implement a GMI program for American working-class families in 1969. Even more surprising was the strong support the concept received from two paragons of free-market thought, the Nobel-prizewinning economists Milton Friedman and Friedrich Hayek. Friedman called for all persons whose income fell below a certain threshold to receive an annual supplementary payment from the government – a negative income tax. "We have a maze of detailed governmental programs that have been justified on welfare grounds," he wrote. "The negative income tax would be vastly superior to this collection of welfare measures. It would concentrate public funds on supplementing the incomes of the poor – not distribute funds broadside in the hope that some will trickle down to the poor."[72]

Small-scale experiments with the GMI concept have been attempted here and there. In the 1970s, for example, the state of Alaska started sending annual dividend checks to each and every resident, based on the tax revenue earned from the Prudhoe Bay oil field. The amounts vary from year to year, ranging between $400 and $2,000 depending on the broader economy.[73] The city of Stockton, California also launched a small pilot project of GMI supplements in 2019 – handing out no-strings-attached checks for $500 to a subset of its residents.[74]

Objections to GMI fall into three main categories. First, the argument goes, it will be expensive to implement, and will require raising new taxes. In response to this criticism, supporters of GMI point out that today's society is already spending vast sums on social welfare programs, which would no longer be needed once a GMI goes into effect. But there is no denying that it would amount to an ongoing redistribution of wealth from the elite sectors of society to all the others – and this is precisely what rendered it appealing to various socialist thinkers of the past two centuries. It would not result in the radical equalization envisioned by Marxists, but it would significantly reduce the inequality between rich and poor.[75]

Second, some people consider it both unfair and unwise to simply give money to people who have done nothing to earn it. A GMI would break the age-old link between labor and self-esteem: it would rob people of the feeling that they make a valuable contribution to society and are being justly compensated for it. Some citizens might become chronically lazy and shift-less, playing endless video games or the like: what would this do to their sense of dignity and their solidarity with other members of society? The AI researcher Kai-Fu Lee and the high-tech entrepreneur Martin Ford, both of whom believe that some form of GMI will be unavoidable down the line, have given considerable thought to this problem. Ford concludes that the dollar amount of the monthly payment will need to be carefully calibrated: it needs to provide a measure of basic security, but should still be low enough to incentivize people to go out into the world and supplement their income through useful work.[76] For Lee, the deepest challenge of the GMI system will be a moral one: creating a new social order in which people feel an intrinsic sense of social solidarity, so that they will *want* to go out and contribute to the welfare of their fellow citizens regardless of the compensation.[77]

The most challenging problem with GMI is how to extend the concept to the global level.[78] Automation will be ramping up throughout the world over the coming decades, eliminating millions of jobs in many different countries at roughly the same time. If rich nations set up a GMI system for their own citizens, the demand for immigration into those countries will skyrocket. Immigration controls would have to be ratcheted to even higher levels than today, and the division between the world's haves and have-nots would grow harsher than ever: plush gated community up here, wretched slum down there. Creating a truly global system of GMI would require unprecedented levels of international solidarity among the world's peoples, as well as strong supranational institutions to administer the wealth redistribution process. We remain far today from such a world, to put it mildly. (I'll return to this topic in Chapter 19.)

Still, what's the alternative? Economists who study this phenomenon seem just as flummoxed by their own projections as anyone else. The syllogism appears inescapable: automation rises and spreads; new jobs fail to keep pace; unemployment hits crisis levels and stays that way; people demand an effective solution. Some form of GMI appears to be the only viable answer. Or not. There is always the option of Gated Community and Wretched Slum – but that is hardly a sustainable model for the long term. Sooner or later the wretched billions will probably find a way to get their needs met, and that pathway is likely to be a violent one – just as it was when humankind "resolved" the Great Depression crisis at the end of the 1930s.

I can picture Karl Marx here, laughing heartily. Granted, his prediction that capitalism would succumb to its own internal contradictions has proved incorrect. Capitalism has been ingeniously tweaked and adjusted over the years since his death, and continues to structure most economic transactions throughout the globe; it has even seeped into Communist China. But now the capitalist system faces a deep challenge from an unexpected quarter: science, technology, and smart machines. As we look to the coming decades, it appears that the dream of many socialists may come partly true, taking form as a new hybrid of capitalism and socialism in which wealth is more-or-less redistributed and everyone is guaranteed a decent living.

The sci-fi writer Arthur C. Clarke saw this possibility coming a long time ago and cheerfully embraced it: "The goal of the future," he said, "is full unemployment, so we can play."[79] In other words, let the machines take care of feeding and clothing us, building our houses, cooking us meals, making our cars and phones and other devices, driving us around town, handling our medical, legal, and administrative needs. We humans can then spend all our time on creative pursuits, leisure, play, scientific research, travel, entertainment, new business ventures, taking care of the sick, or helping each other out with various ideas and projects. In such a world, we would become like the eighteenth-century aristocrats, living off the labor of others and having a grand time doing whatever we please – except that this time around the leisure class would include all humans everywhere, and it is the machines that would be doing the work.

Over the coming two or three decades, the deep automation problem will start to present itself ever more vividly and concretely in our world, as it starts to leach away more and more jobs from people we know. We would be well advised to put this on the action agenda for today, before the level of unemployment becomes too severe, and societal and political dislocation start taking a toll. The 2020 presidential candidate Andrew Yang did the nation a service by putting the Basic Income idea on the table for widespread discussion – helping people to see the relevance of this seemingly weird and radical concept.[80] We need to go beyond the experiments somewhat gingerly attempted in Alaska and Stockton, and start figuring out how to make this thing work at a much larger scale.

CAN A FEDERAL BUREAUCRACY BE NIMBLE? NEW FORMS OF OVERSIGHT AND REGULATION

The foregoing discussion suggests that we're going to need better tools for monitoring and regulating newly emerging technologies like synthetic biology and AI. At first glance, it might seem as though this would require a totalitarian surveillance apparatus worthy of Orwell's *1984*. Wouldn't we have to monitor every molecular biology lab (including corporate, university, and garage labs in private homes), as well as every organization engaged in advanced computer science and robotic research? The answer, fortunately, is No. The vast majority of scientists and engineers who toil in these domains are not engaged in research activities that are closely related to building apocalyptic technological capabilities: only a small minority in each field actually works on the ultra-dangerous stuff. This means that regulatory agencies could adopt a calibrated approach to surveillance, focusing the brunt of their efforts on those specific scientific specialty areas that posed the highest potential danger.

Synthetic biology presents the toughest challenge. As we saw in Chapter 7, the current patchwork system of regulation for biotech in the United States is clearly inadequate because it leaves glaring gaps in oversight. The wisest move, therefore, is to create a new field-specific agency – let's call it the Office for Emerging Biotechnology (OEB) – that would take over the regulatory functions for cutting-edge biotech that are currently spread out in ill-coordinated fashion among the EPA, FDA, and USDA. An urgent first step for the OEB would be to require all DIY biologists to undergo basic levels of certification, coupled with a licensing requirement for all machines that are essential to advanced genetic manipulation.[81] Companies that sell materials for genetic manipulation should be closely regulated, ensuring that they screen all orders and submit periodic reports to the OEB detailing the orders filled. All synthetic biology researchers who work on hazardous pathogens should be required to report on the safety measures followed by their labs. This could be implemented via regular self-reporting by these laboratories, coupled with random inspections by OEB experts to make sure the self-reporting was being done accurately.

Particularly high-risk research could be subjected to commensurately higher levels of scrutiny. This kind of surveillance would no doubt be greeted with exasperation by researchers, but – like the TSA system for airline travel – it could presumably be implemented in a way that minimized red tape and allowed researchers to get on with their work. The trade-off would be worth it: a modest increase of hassle for the scientists, in exchange for a more comprehensive oversight system to protect the public.

Fortunately, today's state-of-the-art in AI remains far from the advanced levels of performance that set off alarm bells. For the time being, therefore, the federal government can focus primarily on providing funding and other incentives for those researchers in the field who work on AI safety and security. As the work advances, and the machines' performance starts to show signs of pushing beyond narrow AI, the monitoring could incrementally become more fine-grained. At that point, all the leading AI development projects could be required to report regularly on their achievements, as well as on the safety and security procedures they were following.[82]

Some of this surveillance activity could be rendered more effective through the use of AI itself. When you travel out of state and purchase something with your credit card, for example, a simple AI machine at your credit card company flags the anomalous purchase, compares it to your past travel and purchase patterns, and (in some cases) alerts a human specialist who contacts you to make sure your card hasn't been stolen. In recent years, even this last stage has come to be automated: the AI itself calls you on the phone, issues screening questions to make sure you are really who you say you are, and decides whether to proceed with authorizing the transaction.

One can readily imagine an array of more advanced AI machines operating on behalf of governmental surveillance teams. In each domain – synthetic biology, AI, or other hazardous fields of emerging technology – the monitoring machines would continuously scour the relevant databases, looking for patterns or anomalies that raise red flags. They would evaluate such factors as the purchases of machines and materials, licensing and certification records, personnel dossiers and employment histories, waiver requests, publications, internal Institutional Review Board documents, grant applications, newspaper articles, private investment funding, and principal investigators' self-reporting files. On those occasions when a deeper search seemed warranted, the AI would alert a human monitoring official, who could then seek judicial authorization to extend further scrutiny into emails, Web-based activities, and other private communications. An impromptu onsite inspection might then follow up on these background surveillance operations. The bulk of day-to-day monitoring would be handled by the AI machines, leaving the most sensitive and tricky interventions to authorized human officials.

Implicit in the regulatory system I've been describing is a fundamental shift from hard law to soft law, and from "governing over" to "governing with."[83] According to this approach, federal oversight bodies like the proposed OEB would no longer rely exclusively on a rigid set of top-down rules; instead, they would operate in ongoing partnership with the organizations they were overseeing, implementing a more provisional set of guidelines that could be amended through mutual negotiation as time went by. The underlying assumption here is that both regulators and those they regulate share a common goal of advancing innovation while avoiding risky practices that endanger the public.

Under this hybrid system, a combination of top-down and bottom-up approaches could be tailored to meet the specific needs of a particular field, and governance could be expedited because it would be approached on both sides as a more experimental and open-ended undertaking than before. Corporate or university researchers could engage in voluntary forms of self-reporting that worked most efficiently for their particular fields, thereby avoiding the cumbersome restrictions to which they had been answerable in the past. Such self-regulation could follow looser codes of conduct that aimed at a broadly defined goal, leaving the specifics of implementation to the particular lab and its staff to design in the most streamlined manner possible.

All too often, moreover, science and technology tend to advance more rapidly than the legal mechanisms that are supposed to regulate them. This phenomenon – known as "the pacing problem" – results in laws that are obsolete soon after they come into effect.[84] One way to get around this is to create specialized courts whose purview is confined to a narrow range of scientific matters. The states of Michigan and Maryland are experimenting with such courts, hoping that they will lead to swifter and better-informed legal decisions regarding rapidly changing technologies.[85] Another good idea in this regard is to include a sunset clause in legislation covering science and technology: incorporating an expiration date into the law itself forces legislators to revisit the law periodically and reassess its relevance.

A federal oversight body for AI or synthetic biology would function most effectively if it worked in tandem with field-specific teams of experts. The scholars Gary Marchant and Wendell Wallach have devised an innovative proposal in this regard:

> We recommend the creation of issue managers for the comprehensive oversight of each field of research. We call these issue managers

Governance Coordinating Committees (GCCs). These committees, led by accomplished elders who have already achieved wide respect, are meant to work together with all the interested stakeholders to monitor technological development and formulate solutions to perceived problems. .... [They] would serve as "orchestra conductors," [and] would neither replicate nor usurp the tasks fulfilled by other institutions such as regulatory agencies. They would, however, search for gaps, overlaps, conflicts, inconsistencies, and synergistic opportunities among the various public and private entities already involved in shaping the course of an emerging field.[86]

The underlying idea would be to establish a flexible, layered structure of governance, with the federal regulators at the pinnacle, the field-specific coordinating committees at the middle level, and the researchers and labs operating at the ground level of innovation. This layered structure would help keep the national regulatory apparatus from becoming a huge, sprawling bureaucracy, since many of its ongoing oversight functions could be devolved to the intermediary level of the GCCs.

Unfortunately, creating new federal oversight bodies for AI and synthetic biology will no doubt prove politically difficult. Some business constituencies might look askance at any federal agency like the proposed OEB that promised to wield so much power over cutting-edge domains of research and invention. Here the story of a similar governmental body, the Office of Technology Assessment (OTA), is instructive. This pioneering organization, housed in the US Congress from 1972 to 1995, was charged with providing legislators, journalists, and the public with concise reports about the societal implications of new technologies. As one scientist recalled:

An OTA study was balanced, including both pros and cons of policy options, and members on opposite sides of an issue often cited the same OTA report to make their case ... A 1984 study questioning the reliability of polygraph tests led Congress to enact limits on their use by employers. Another report from 1994 helped lawmakers assess the Social Security Administration's computer procurement plan, and ended up saving the government $368 million. OTA reports in 1987 and 1990, which concluded that Pap smears and mammograms for older women could save thousands of lives, were instrumental in extending Medicare reimbursement for these tests.[87]

Here, in other words, was a government body that helped lawmakers make smarter decisions about technology policy – precisely the sorts of well-informed decisions that are so urgently needed today regarding dangerous emerging technologies. During the OTA's 23 years of activity, its scientists issued more than 700 studies on issues ranging from health care to climate change. Yet it was shut down in 1995 by Newt Gingrich and other congressional Republicans – resulting in annual savings of $20 million (about one-hundredth of 1 percent of the $1.5 trillion federal budget).[88] Why? Despite strenuous efforts by OTA scientists to present their technical findings in nonpartisan language, some of their reports had recommended policies for reining in polluting industries or restricting certain kinds of hazardous medical technologies. This was enough for influential congressional right-wingers to tar the agency with the label of "anti-business." And down it went.[89] Reversing this mistake – reinstating the OTA with strong funding and support – should be a high priority for the policymakers of today.

Last but not least, we come to the thorny problem of uncertainty. How to regulate cutting-edge technologies when no one is entirely sure how dangerous they'll turn out to be a few decades hence? For example, consider the idea I discussed earlier about combatting global warming by imitating volcanic eruptions – deliberately spewing chemical particles into the stratosphere to partially shield the planet from the Sun's energy.[90] Will this work well? What might be the unintended effects? How will plants and plankton and bees react to the reduced sunlight? No one knows for sure. If you were the EPA official in charge of regulating such an operation, what kind of evidence would you need before giving the green light?

Dealing with these kinds of uncertainty falls under the purview of a field known as risk management – a multidisciplinary endeavor whose practitioners continually find themselves facing difficult trade-offs.[91] If they err too far on the side of caution, blocking the implementation of new technologies, they can end up stifling innovation and undermining economic growth. But if they err too far in the other direction, they can end up subjecting society to significant harms.

Here an ingenious idea known as the precautionary principle comes into play. First articulated by the German philosopher Hans Jonas in the 1970s, this principle has now come into widespread use in crafting regulatory legislation in the European Union and elsewhere.[92] It can be summarized as follows: when the suspected risks are very great, it is better to err on the side of caution, even if the state of our present knowledge is imperfect.[93] Implicit here lie three interlocking elements:

1. Cost–benefit logic. If a new technology is suspected of posing a risk to society, then it should not be adopted unless its projected benefits outweigh its projected drawbacks.

2. Burden of proof. If no scientific consensus exists about the level of risk involved, then the burden of proof lies with the promoters of the technology to show that its projected benefits outweigh its drawbacks.

3. Proportionality. The greater the level of potential harm associated with a technology, the higher the bar should be set for scientific consensus about its net benefits before the technology is adopted.

Consider for example global warming. Even though most climate scientists agree today that this is a real phenomenon, and that it is caused by human technological activities, they still don't have absolute certainty about how rapidly it will progress and how drastic its effects will be. Our scientific models are simply not sophisticated enough yet to offer full clarity in this domain. Nevertheless, the precautionary principle does offer helpful guidance. In the majority of plausible scenarios, the projected harms caused by global warming are catastrophic in nature; therefore, we should take vigorous action today to dial back greenhouse gas emissions. It's reasonable for humankind to make a big effort in the present in order to avoid disastrous consequences in the future – even though we cannot be sure precisely what those dire consequences will turn out to look like.[94]

* * *

11

Constructive Moves on the International Front for the Next 25 Years

NEW TREATIES

During the Cold War, some of the worst excesses of the arms race were reined in by multilateral or bilateral treaties on arms control. Since the collapse of the Soviet Union, however, this system has gradually frayed at the edges, and today the Russians and Americans are racing once again to build faster, deadlier, scarier weapons systems to aim at each other.[1] What's more, the Chinese have now vaulted past the Russians in economic clout, and are equipping themselves with cutting-edge military technologies for the oceans, land, skies, and space.[2] We are gradually slipping into a new geopolitical era that could become even more volatile and dangerous than the Cold War – for a military deterrence system with three dance partners is much harder to manage than one with two. Tripolar arms races are notoriously unstable.[3]

Since the UN is too weak at present to do much about this, we need to fall back on treaties and other old-fashioned diplomatic arrangements among groups of nation-states as the vehicles for reining in these escalating arms races. Three main areas urgently need attention. In the age of CRISPR and other powerful biotech innovations, the danger of modern bioweapons becomes more alarming than ever. The 1972 Biological Weapons Convention remains in force today, binding 183 nations to refrain from developing biological and toxin weaponry. Unfortunately, the treaty has lost a great deal of credibility, because we now know that one of the key players (the USSR) cheated systematically on its treaty obligations over many years. A straightforward solution would be to convene a global conference for revisiting the treaty, with the additional goal this time around of creating a rigorous system for verification and mutual inspections. This will no doubt prove politically difficult to accomplish, but a significant precedent already exists. Under the 1987 Intermediate-Range Nuclear Forces (INF) Treaty, signed by Ronald Reagan and Mikhail Gorbachev, Russian experts were allowed to visit US weapons sites on short notice, gaining access to the records they needed to ensure that the Americans were in full compliance – and American experts were granted the same right at Russian sites.[4] The aim here would be to set up a similar verification system for bioweapons, applicable to all the treaty signatories with equal rigor.

A separate treaty will also be needed for AI and cyberwarfare. This is in some respects even more important than the bioweapons treaty, because (as far as we know) few nations if any are actively pursuing bioweapons today, whereas most leading industrial powers are already racing with each other for dominance in AI. It's the Wild West out there, when it comes to cyberwarfare. (Witness the ease with which shady players "probably somewhere in Eastern Europe" were able to shut down one of the major gasoline pipelines supplying the entire US East Coast in May 2021.)[5] One can envision two valuable international accords in this regard: one for peacetime, the other for military rivalries or confrontations.[6] A peacetime cyberspace treaty was proposed in 2017 by Microsoft's president, Brad Smith, who referred to it as a 'digital Geneva Convention.' "What we need," he told an audience of UN diplomats,

> is an approach that governments will adopt that says they will not attack civilians in times of peace. They will not attack hospitals. They will not attack the electrical grid. They will not attack the political processes of other countries ... We simply cannot live in a safe and secure world unless there are new rules for the world.[7]

Such new rules for AI and cyberweaponry are even more urgently needed when it comes to the ongoing military rivalries among the world's Great Powers. When a nation finds its core security systems or military installations under large-scale cyberattack, it may not always be clear who the attacking party is – and this could lead to extremely volatile confrontations, with the ever present possibility of escalation to a full-on shooting war. A comprehensive military treaty for AI could offer some of the same key benefits that nuclear agreements provided during the Cold War: it could help manage the frantic pace of development for AI technologies themselves, while also providing the Great Powers with well-understood rules of engagement that would limit the chances of runaway escalation.[8] Even a partial treaty of this sort would be a major step forward.

Finally, of course, we must not neglect the newly emerging domains of warfare in the depths of the oceans and outer space. The submarine-detection technology I described in Chapter 7 – coupling next-generation satellite sensors with undersea attack drones – illustrates just how dangerous these kinds of innovations can become. The whole edifice of submarine-based deterrence and mutually assured destruction could be fatally undermined.[9] Here, too, a comprehensive treaty would bring badly needed stability and procedural ground rules, averting an uncontrolled slide into a new global arms race.

Some might object that these treaties may sound attractive in principle, but would be impossible to implement given current domestic and international political realities. After all, can one really imagine American, Russian, and Chinese leaders shaking hands on such a deal, given the ongoing rancor and skullduggery that characterize today's superpower relations? This is a valid objection, but it can be met with a simple counterquestion: was there not plenty of rancor and skullduggery afoot in the world when the United States and USSR signed the partial atmospheric test ban treaty in 1963, or when Nixon and Brezhnev signed the SALT I agreement in 1972? Of course there was. The underlying point is that those arms-control accords were overwhelmingly in the interest of all the nations involved – just as it is overwhelmingly in the interest of today's Great Powers to avoid the three arms races I've just described. The goal of strengthening national security via any of these weapons systems is a dangerous mirage: no one will ever attain lasting dominance in any of these technologies. All they will get, instead, is endless cycles of fear, instability, and frightfully expensive weaponry – rolling the dice of Armageddon day after day. That is no rational way to run any country's security system. It's time to sit down at the negotiating table and see these treaties through.

NEW INTERNATIONAL REGULATORY NETWORKS

Imagine for a moment that a coalition of US legislators, nongovernmental organizations, and citizen activists managed to overcome the various political obstacles, and succeeded in bringing about the creation of an Office for Emerging Biotechnology (OEB) along the lines I sketched in Chapter 10. From this point on, the nation's synthetic biology labs – from university to corporation to garage workshop – are being proactively overseen by an agency that operates with a light touch but also wields all the instruments it needs for enforcing its decisions. Now imagine that other leading nations, impressed by this development in the United States, and alarmed at the dangers they recognize within their own biotech research system, create similar bodies of their own. Such agencies could start working together across borders, exchanging information and "best practices," conducting joint training programs, and perhaps even collaborating on enforcement operations when the need arose. (I'll describe this idea more fully in Part IV.) Where once there had been a fairly anarchic arena of biological experimentation, now a new layer of ordered governance would emerge – not just domestically, but internationally as well. Here we can revisit the harrowing story of our high school biologists from Vignette 1, replaying it against this backdrop of global regulation.

Vignette 4: How Jim and Evelyn Were Prevented from Killing Half the World (2051)

Jim and Evelyn sit sprawled on the beat-up couch in the corner of their garage lab, sipping Coke, avoiding eye contact, their movements brittle with nervousness. Today is the day when the email from the Stanford admissions office is scheduled to arrive. Today is when they find out whether all their hard work has paid off.

Certainly, their series of experiments over the past eighteen months has been an impressive success. The supplemental materials they submitted with their admissions applications included a thick dossier documenting the procedures they followed, along with a letter from their case officer at the OEB in Bethesda. At every step of the way, they've followed the protocols for advanced biotech research in a home laboratory.

- *The DNA fragments they bought online were registered in a series of transaction reports filed with the OEB.*
- *The machines they bought on eBay for manipulating DNA have been registered with the OEB.*
- *They've taken all the required certification courses in lab safety and biohazard management.*
- *Their high school biology teacher, Ms. Woods, who supervises their research, has submitted the required quarterly reports on their aims and methods.*
- *Their garage lab has been inspected and certified as compliant by an inspector from the OEB. When the earthquake struck six months ago, it did quite a bit of structural damage, but the extensive retrofit they had done to the wall shelving and refrigeration units was enough to keep everything in place. The inspector gave them a solid rating of "pass."*
- *When they registered as participants in the annual competitions of iGEM in Boston, they also signed a legal release allowing heightened scrutiny of their emails and other correspondence by the surveillance AI of the OEB.*

Vignette 4: (cont.)

- *The experimental virus they created was approved by their OEB case officer because it was robustly "escape-resistant." It was engineered to self-destruct after three reproductive cycles, and (most importantly) was also dependent on artificial chemical supplements that could only be provided within the lab environment. If it ever did manage somehow to escape, it would be incapable of infecting anyone and would die within minutes.*
- *Although the experimental virus they created was based on DNA, they also conducted preliminary experiments with a similar virus based on XNA. This new XNA-based virus would add a further layer of safety to any future experiments they carried out.*

Jim's cell phone pings, indicating an incoming email. He and Evelyn glance at each other. But it's not from Stanford, it's from their friend Xiaoyu, whom they met at iGEM last year. She too is applying to Stanford, and like them, she and three of her friends have set up a lab of their own at her parents' home in Qingdao. She's done some amazing work this past year with E. coli bacteria. Though he won't admit it, Jim has a bit of a crush on her.

Xiaoyu's home lab is subject to the same multilayered scrutiny as Jim and Evelyn's. The Chinese OEB, based in Shenzhen, has twice inspected her equipment and safety protocols, making sure she's stayed in compliance throughout her research. Both the US and Chinese governments are members of the international OEB network, coordinated via the United Nations Biotech Directorate in Geneva. All 189 member-states in the network operate under common guidelines and best practices. Compliance with these common rules is required before major annual grants can be released to each nation from the UN Biotech Research Fund.

Jim is typing quickly with his thumbs, replying to Xiaoyu's message. Just then his phone pings again. Another email.

It's from Stanford. He and Evelyn look at each other. Jim's finger hovers over the email link. He takes a deep breath.

"Ready?" he asks. Evelyn grins, then nods.

Jim opens the link.

REFORMING THE UN

The United Nations grew out of the military alliance that won World War II, and was designed from the start to have teeth. Its creators were determined not to repeat the mistake that had fatally undermined the League of Nations: allowing all member nations equal voting power was a noble Wilsonian gesture, but it flew in the face of great-power realities. Tiny Luxembourg or Haiti could not be allowed to override the will of China, Russia, or the United States – or else the UN would become an irrelevant debating society like its predecessor.[10] As a result, the UN still operates today as a forthrightly hierarchical organization, with two levels of power: the General Assembly houses all 193 member nations, and here every country has one vote; but executive decisions concerning peace and war are made by fifteen nations in the Security Council. Within the Security Council, five nations have permanent seats (China, France, Russia, the United Kingdom, and the United States) while the ten remaining seats rotate among other nations that serve a two-year term. Most importantly, the five permanent members of the Security Council (known as the P5) have veto power over all Security Council resolutions and actions.[11]

The UN fields a small military force to enforce its decisions; it currently has about 90,000 uniformed personnel and an annual military budget of $8 billion. Here too, the founders of the UN were pragmatic: they knew that the Great Powers on the Security Council would be calling the shots in world politics, and that UN forces would never be able to accomplish much on their own if one or more leading nations opposed them. Therefore, provision was made in the UN Charter for all nations to supply manpower for enforcement actions on an ad hoc basis, whenever the Security Council authorized armed intervention to keep the peace.[12]

This system has actually worked well on a few occasions. In 1950, the Security Council approved UN action to reverse the aggression of North Korea against South Korea, and the result was an intensive three-year war that eventually restored the status quo.[13] In 1956, when Israel, France, and the United Kingdom abruptly invaded the Suez Canal zone in Egypt, the UN General Assembly (in a rare display of near-unanimity) ordered them out; finding both the Russian and American superpowers aligned against them, they retreated ignominiously, and a UN military force moved in to keep the peace in the canal territory.[14] In 1991, after Iraq invaded Kuwait, a powerful UN force moved in, trounced the Iraqis, and freed Kuwait.[15]

All these success stories shared a common feature: for reasons particular to each crisis, the bitter rivalry between the superpowers did not block UN action.[16] Alas, they were rare exceptions. Throughout the Cold War, the far more common experience was deadlock on the Security Council, as one crisis after another met with a *Nyet* from the Russians (especially during the 1950s and 1960s) or a *Nope* from the Americans (especially after the 1970s). Hopes therefore ran high with the collapse of the Soviet empire in 1989–91, leading observers as pragmatic as President George H. W. Bush to speak of a "new world order" in which the Great Powers and small nations would work together through the UN in unprecedented ways. That optimistic vision has yet to materialize. The multipolar world that replaced the Cold War has turned out to be an unstable arena in which the UN leadership finds it difficult to forge common policies and take decisive action. The tragic cases of Yugoslavia, Rwanda, and Syria, in which the UN proved useless as an instrument of pacification, starkly revealed how much work remains to be done.[17]

The historian Paul Kennedy, in his book *The Parliament of Man*, makes a compelling case that the UN has become outdated in ways that undermine its legitimacy and threaten to render it irrelevant.[18] He surveys a wide range of reforms that have been proposed, ranging from small tweaks to full-scale dismantling and reconstruction from the ground up. In the end, he argues, the more radical proposals stand little political chance of success, while the more easily feasible changes will not make a sufficient difference. Instead, he recommends five moderately deep reforms that could be undertaken today.

First and foremost among these is expanding the core membership of the Security Council to include new Great Powers that have emerged since 1945 – nations such as Germany, Japan, India, Brazil, Italy, and Canada, whose exclusion from the inner circle flies in the face of common sense as well as geopolitical reality. It's absurd that nations like Japan and Germany, which contribute huge sums annually in UN dues, should be denied a proportionate voice in the governance of that body. But adding five or six newcomers with veto power risks further paralyzing the UN through deadlocks and delays. Therefore, Kennedy argues, a second reform would need to be adopted concurrently with this expansion: changing the veto rule so that two veto votes in the Security Council would be required to stop UN action from going forward, rather than the current absolute single veto.

Both these measures would be resisted ferociously by hardcore nationalists within each of the P5 (veto-wielding) countries, who would balk at seeing their nation's power diluted in this manner. The challenge here is therefore straightforward: a two-pronged pressure campaign will be required, aimed at wearing down the resistance of the P5 to these vitally important reforms. At the international level, the non-P5 nations should start complaining loud and long about the ludicrously anachronistic structure of the Security Council. This could add up to a significant form of pressure, because it would comprise 188 nations (give or take) speaking with rare unanimity on a matter of great importance to all of them. Imagine for example if the national leaders of Argentina, Australia, Brazil, Canada,

Germany, India, Indonesia, Italy, Japan, Mexico, Saudi Arabia, South Africa, South Korea, and Turkey all spoke with one voice on this matter. These are the G20 countries not represented within the P5 group; taken together, their share of global GDP is roughly the same as that of the P5. Presumably a strong and sustained appeal by such a bloc of nations would get the attention of the P5 leaders.

The other prong of the pressure campaign would need to come from within the P5 nations themselves. Fortunately, not all the citizens of those five nations are knee-jerk nationalists; some are committed internationalists who clearly see the need to bolster the effectiveness of the UN. Many others are neither nationalist nor internationalist in ideological bent: they are pragmatists who are willing to support international institutions if those institutions deliver good results. A new political constituency will therefore have to be gradually built within the P5 nations – an influential group of citizens and leaders who see the urgent need for updating the UN, and who are willing to trade away their nation's P5 advantage in exchange for the major benefits that would flow from having a more effective Security Council. Consolidating such "pro-UN" constituencies may take a great deal of time and effort, but it is a prerequisite for launching the reforms that the Security Council so badly requires.[19]

Concurrent with this process, according to Kennedy, momentum must also be built for a third reform: cultivating an ethos of restraint among Security Council members when it comes to using the veto. From 1946 to 2016, vetoes have been issued on 258 occasions. The leader here is Russia/ USSR with 122 cases of *Nyet!*, followed by the United States with 79 cases of *Nope!* Many of these vetoes have concerned urgent military matters, such as the invasion of one country by another; but others have concerned events that were far less pressing in nature, such as the election of a particular person as the UN Secretary-General.[20] In 2017, for example, the United States vetoed a resolution calling on countries to avoid establishing embassies in Jerusalem; and in 2008, China and Russia vetoed a resolution regarding the legitimacy of the Zimbabwean general election. These latter issues are undoubtedly weighty ones from the perspective of the nations involved, but they clearly don't rate as high in importance as a military attack or the acquisition of weapons of mass destruction by a nation that previously hadn't possessed them. Kennedy argues that vetoes should be reserved for the most truly egregious kinds of cases.[21]

The fourth and fifth reforms on Kennedy's list are designed to mitigate one of the fundamental problems in today's UN, namely, the hierarchical relationship between the Security Council (where all the most consequential decisions are taken) and the General Assembly (where very little executive power is vested).[22] Kennedy argues that two reform measures could render the UN much more democratically responsive. First, certain rotating members of the Security Council should be allowed to serve multiple terms consecutively, and perhaps even be considered for gradual elevation in status within that body:

> If a nation such as Singapore or Germany has done great service over the preceding two years on the Security Council and is supported for prolongation by its friends and neighbors, why make that impossible? . . . If, say, South Africa was reelected for a second or third time, the notion that it might become a permanent member, and then one with a veto, would seem less and less strange to the P5 and others.[23]

Second, a Peacebuilding Commission could be created, deliberately designed to blur the boundary between the Security Council (whose role centers around questions of war and security) and the General Assembly (whose role centers around civilian and peacetime endeavors). This new body would oversee the arduous processes of reconstruction and healing that are required *after* a military conflict has been successfully resolved. The hybrid nature of its assignment – somewhere in between war and peace – would bring members of the General Assembly into more active and ongoing partnership with the most powerful members of the Security Council.[24]

Taken together, Kennedy's five "moderate" reforms would render the UN far more effective than it is today, allowing it to intervene more boldly and proactively to keep or restore the peace. Over time, if more Great Powers are encouraged to play key roles in the UN's ongoing operations, their populations will tend to perceive themselves as direct stakeholders in its actions. The legitimacy of the institution will grow. Decade by decade, the UN will have a chance to build up a track record of impressive achievements, casting off its image as a marginal player in world politics.

* * *

12

Breaking the Political Logjam

THREE CORE IDEAS IN THIS BOOK WILL SLAM into the brick wall of political partisanship: the climate change issue, the role of government regulation, and the need for strong global institutions and collective military security beyond the nation-state. (It's probably more than just these three, but they are the most salient ones.) Major political constituencies both within the United States and abroad hold the diametric opposite view to the one espoused in these pages. And if we cannot agree on diagnosing the problem, how are we ever going to forge consensus about solutions, let alone take effective action?

Part of the problem stems from a form of political tribalism that's become much worse over the past quarter century.[1] Whereas the legislators of previous generations were generally able to work out pragmatic compromise solutions across the aisle, today's political landscape has become so toxically polarized that even modest measures fail to garner the necessary votes. The only point everyone seems to agree on these days is that our system is broken.[2] This isn't solely an American affliction: one sees worrisome signs of the same type of phenomenon in most of the major industrial democracies throughout the world.[3]

Some of the issues that divide Left and Right are inherently polarizing ones that cannot be easily adjudicated. Abortion is a prime example. If you believe that a fetus becomes a human person at conception, then you may conclude that abortion is morally wrong and should be prohibited by law. If you believe that a fetus becomes a human person at some murkier point down the developmental line, then you may conclude that a woman's right to decide what happens inside her body outweighs considerations about the rights of this not-yet-person. There is not much room for compromise here, and national policy is simply a question of how many voters feel one way or the other at a given time.[4]

Most of the other issues that divide Left from Right are not nearly as stark, however: there is plenty of room for nuances and gradations of belief, and hence for pragmatic compromise. Politicians of past generations knew that they could find space within the gray areas, and learned how to make deals and swaps that allowed the republic to address pressing issues and to function relatively smoothly. But over the past three decades, a form of tribal mentality has emerged that leads citizens to sort themselves into black-and-white ideological camps, squaring off against each other like rival football teams on a field. Only one side can triumph in this new political game, and since the stakes are high, it becomes acceptable to do whatever it takes to win. Both sides distort the facts, sling mud, paint their opponent as holding extreme views that they know many of those folks don't really hold, and generally do all they can to make the other side look scary and evil. After a while, as both sides escalate this nasty round of underhanded tricks, trust breaks down, and people really do come to believe the worst of their opponents. Compromise becomes a dirty word, because citizens on one side no longer believe that those on the other side share the same fundamental values: you don't compromise with evil people. Demonization takes the place of dialogue and reasoned debate: pragmatic deals become well-nigh impossible.[5]

When politics divides like this into hardened camps, one unfortunate consequence is the linkage of totally unrelated issues into ideological clusters.[6] For example, if I'm a right-wing gun-rights advocate and you come to me with scientific evidence that the planet is warming, I'll assume these days that you are a Democrat. This means that you voted for Obama and Biden, whose policies I detest; you are probably pro-abortion; you want to take away the rifles and pistols I inherited from my grandfather; you want to raise my taxes to pay for wasteful government programs; you get your news by reading the *New York Times* or watching MSNBC; you don't believe in the kind of God I've been brought up to believe in and worship. In short, you're one of *Them.* So I look at your alarming statistics about global warming and respond with visceral distrust. Where did you get these climate numbers? What hidden agenda are you trying to promote? If I go online and look up the debates over climate change, I'll find plenty of persuasive-sounding evidence from people within my own camp that confirms my worst suspicions. This climate change thing is a hoax, and you are promoting it because you want a bigger role for government in regulating every aspect of our lives. If you insist on showing me a lot more scientific evidence, it won't convince me at this point: it only proves how passionate you are about your hidden socialist/liberal agenda.[7] Even though I realize that global warming has nothing to do with guns or abortion, I now lump it together with those issues when it comes to how I weigh the evidence and cast my vote.

We can repeat the example from the other side too. If I am a left-wing green activist and you come to me with scientific evidence that nuclear technology could play a major role in the battle against global warming, I'll assume these days that you have been duped by the pro-nuclear lobby. You've aligned yourself with people who uncritically embrace the pro-growth economic models of modern capitalism – those who want abundant cheap energy so our society can continue with unrestrained business expansion. You are willfully ignoring the long and deep connection between nuclear reactors and Cold War militarism. You're a believer in large-scale techno-fixes and centralized systems of technology, linked to big corporations and the financial markets that bankroll them; you probably read the *Wall Street Journal* or watch Fox News, and you no doubt scoff at the decentralized, grass-roots nature of solar and wind energy, considering them a quaint distraction from the demands of a modern economy. In short, you're one of *Them*. So I look at your description of Generation IV reactors and respond with visceral distrust. Where did you get these statistics? What hidden agenda are you trying to promote? If I go online and look up the debates over nuclear energy, I'll find plenty of persuasive-sounding evidence from people within my own camp that confirms my worst suspicions. Safe, cheap, plentiful nuclear energy is a dangerous myth, and you are promoting it because you've bought into the dominant ideology of modern capitalism, predicated on the principle of endless growth. If you insist on showing me engineering designs for small, modular LFTR reactors that can be flexibly deployed in a decentralized grid, it won't convince me at this point: it only proves how passionate you are about your techno-optimist agenda. At a visceral level, I associate nuclear technology with those who have stood on the opposite side of the barricades from people like me over the past 40 years, and I lump it together with their consumerist worldview when it comes to how I weigh the evidence and cast my vote.

Obviously these two examples, drawn from Right and Left, are based on caricatures that would be wide of the mark in characterizing a great many individuals in either camp. I nonetheless sketched them here in order to illustrate the widespread tendency to link disparate issues into broad clusters – a quick sort of shorthand by which people tend to organize their moral worldviews and political alignments: if you believe X then you must also believe Y and Z and support policies A, B, and C. This doesn't leave much room for constructive conversation and exchange of views, and it leads people to distrust even the most rigorous scientific evidence if that evidence has been marshalled by folks in the other camp.

The politicization of science has been the subject of much journalistic writing and academic research over the past few decades.[8] At one level, it should not surprise us that people squabble over the implications of scientific studies, because science and technology generate vast economic and military power – and power usually means fighting. Scholars and journalists have documented how citizens of both Left and Right have distorted major scientific and technological questions in ways that serve their own ideological ends – from antivaccination campaigns on the Left to creationist jihads on the Right.[9] The demise of the Office of Technology Assessment (described in Chapter 10) was a classic exemplar of this kind of politicization, since it ran afoul of powerful business interests represented by congressional Republicans during the 1990s.[10]

Clearly, this kind of politicization – no matter who does it – runs against the national interest. No modern society can flourish if it bases its policies on distorted scientific facts and ideologically filtered half-truths. Although it is true, as many scholars have noted, that the practice of science is unavoidably shaped by the society and culture in which it is embedded, this does not mean that "truth" and "facts" no longer apply to it.[11] On the contrary, the immense predictive power unleashed by science derives precisely from its reliance on rules of evidence and logic that minimize the bias of the observer. The whole point of scientific research is to test predictions and hypotheses in empirical experiments, accepting the verdict of experience regardless of whether it meshes with our expectations and hopes. This is what objectivity in science means.[12] Scientists ask questions about the world, and when the world replies with answers that the scientist didn't want or expect, it's the scientist's model that gets changed. The facts and theories that result from such research – while still being subject to the inherent limitations of all human knowledge – fall into a special category. They are not subjective, in the sense that you can interpret them any way you wish: they offer precise and reliable predictions about how the world works. If you ignore them, and try to go ahead with your plans in defiance of them, things will not go well for you.[13]

This concept of objectivity underpins my discussion of climate change. Twenty or thirty years ago, it was still possible to entertain reasonable doubts about how serious the threat of climate change was, and how swiftly its effects would be felt. The scientists themselves were proceeding with characteristic caution in making their assessment.[14] They traveled to Antarctica to bore holes in the deep ice layers, probing the trapped gases for a glimpse into the state of the Earth over thousands of years. They devised clever new methods for tracing the sources of atmospheric CO_2, and closely monitored the Earth's ecosystems, from coral reefs to glaciers to insect populations. They debated with each other about the computer models they were using, and about the possible causes of the troubling data that emerged, seeking to take into account every possible factor. But eventually the accumulating evidence began speaking with such clarity that the overwhelming majority of climate scientists converged on a trenchant conclusion: climate change was happening; it was caused primarily by human economic practices; and it posed an unprecedented threat to the welfare of all life forms. Fossil fuels were the main culprit, and humankind needed to make a swift transition to a carbon-free economic system.[15]

Quite understandably, the fossil fuel industry and its political supporters were not pleased. They responded with a cunning and well-funded campaign to blunt the impact of the scientific consensus, taking their playbook directly from the disinformation methods used by the tobacco industry 30 years earlier as it sought to keep people smoking cigarettes as long as possible.[16] They found a few climate scientists who dissented from the majority consensus, and widely publicized their skeptical arguments; they paid professional lobbyists to travel around the country organizing political resistance to climate-friendly regulation; and they created a petition allegedly signed by 31,000 experts claiming that global warming posed no real threat (the petition was subsequently debunked as a disinformation ploy, and the allegedly "expert" signatories were found to include very few credentialed climate scientists).[17] Above all, they succeeded in linking the battle against climate change to a broader cluster of left-wing ideas that conservatives detested. One of the two major political parties in the United States thus came to identify itself as "climate skeptical" and began blocking or weakening all legislative action to rein in greenhouse gas emissions. The result has been political gridlock on one of the most urgent and consequential challenges of our time.[18]

In this book I take the overwhelming consensus of the climate scientists as an established fact. At bottom, this issue hinges on whether we trust the expertise of professionals or not.[19] For example, if you were to develop strange medical symptoms and consulted 100 doctors for a diagnosis, how would you respond if 97 physicians said you were in danger and required urgent surgery, while three said you were going to be fine and should do nothing? The "debate" over climate change is that lopsided.[20] I see no point in seeking to persuade hardened ideologues that climate change is real, for as I noted above, those people have developed a self-reinforcing logical framework that paints all new evidence as just another part of the elaborate hoax. My assumption is that they will gradually be persuaded to alter their views over the coming years as the escalating storms, droughts, fires, floods, and other climate disasters become an increasingly undeniable reality. Mother Nature doesn't care a whit about partisan ideologies.

UNDOING POLITICAL GRIDLOCK

At the heart of pragmatism lies a willingness to take seriously any idea that works well, regardless of its provenance in one camp or another. Every one of us can make a better contribution if we are willing to dissolve the partisan issue-clusters described above, considering each problem and each solution on its own merits. Pragmatists enjoy the advantage of being able to take the best ideas from both sides, integrating them into a new package that delivers results.

The best compromise solutions rarely emerge from straightforwardly splitting the difference between two extremes. Some ideas and policies are simply awful in nature, and incorporating them into your solution accomplishes nothing but a wishy-washy mess. But if one proceeds critically and with a measure of impartiality, one can often find ways to harness the tension between two opposed solutions and generate a hybrid that works even better than the original ideas in isolation.[21] Consider for example the question of government regulation. Leftist policies tend to push for more government intervention, whereas Rightist policies pull in the opposite direction, clamoring for deregulation and untrammeled market mechanisms. The smart compromise is not to simply split the difference between the two; it rests on the recognition that governmental action is a necessary component of a society's functioning, but a component that easily falls prey to sclerosis, bureaucracy, turf battles, intrusiveness, and entrenched special interests. Therefore, the pragmatist's goal is to create the minimum amount of government intervention that's essential, while making sure that plenty of checks and balances are put in place to keep that intervention as nimble and accountable as possible. By embracing the Left's insistence on government action, a society can equip itself to address problems like corporate monopolies, extreme inequality, racism, environmental degradation, or rapacious business practices. By embracing the Right's suspicion of government, a society can keep a healthy vigilance over the laws and their implementation, set up potent vehicles for transparency and accountability, avoid bloated bureaucracies, and end up with policies that work relatively efficiently. The best results emerge when ideas drawn from Left and Right are judiciously integrated into a common system.[22]

When speaking of "the Left" and "the Right," moreover, it's essential to remember that these political camps are not internally homogeneous. Each camp may vote with a common voice in US presidential elections, for example, but when it comes to the nitty-gritty of specific laws and policies, one finds a broad range of views within each grouping – from people like Alexandria Ocasio-Cortez to Nancy Pelosi on the Left, from figures like Mitt Romney to Donald Trump on the Right (along with all the myriad gradations and combinations in between). This broad diversity is a good thing, because it opens up spaces for moderates and open-minded pragmatists on both sides to find specific issues on which they see eye to eye.[23] For example, if a moderate Democrat Senator and a moderate Republican Senator both agree that fighting climate change is important, they can craft legislative solutions that appeal to both their constituencies – such as using flexible market mechanisms like a carbon tax to reduce greenhouse gas emissions, rather than imposing rigid regulations and red tape on businesses. In promoting such a policy, sensible voters on both sides would find something to approve of and support.[24]

To be sure, in today's hyperpolarized political arena, such a pragmatic compromise remains rare. But that's precisely the point. This polarization itself needs to be recognized as one of the most grievous threats to the viability of our republic. If more citizens on the Left or Right come to see hyper-partisanship as the primary problem, then the reflex of automatic and passionate alignment with one camp or the other can perhaps be diminished over time. There is nothing wrong with people weighing the issues and taking sides, but hyper-partisanship is in no one's interest because it paralyzes our government and renders our society incapable of addressing its many challenges. Whichever side you are on, your most dangerous enemy is not the folks in the rival political party: it's our incapacity to work together as citizens of a common nation.

Rebuilding trust will play a key role here. One of the best ways to do this is for citizens from both camps to participate side-by-side in common endeavors that they regard as inherently valuable.[25] Nine years ago, for example, I started volunteering at a homeless shelter in Nashville where I live. One night a week during the winter months, I drive down there and spend three hours getting homeless men and women boarded on small buses sent by local churches to come fetch them for a warm meal and a safe night's sleep. I am still astonished at the changes this simple practice has wrought in my life and worldview. For one thing, it's a surprisingly nice feeling to make oneself tangibly useful to other people in need (even if only for a few hours a week). Second, I came to know who the homeless people in my city were, appreciating them for the first time as remarkable individuals whose courage, resilience, and humor elicited my awe and respect. And finally, I reveled in working alongside my fellow volunteers, getting to know them better each week, until we became a circle of friends. Within that circle you can find young and old people, black and white and Hispanic people, left-wingers and right-wingers, churchgoers and atheists, farmers and professors and office workers. I am sure we vote differently from each other in local and national elections, but I like and admire all these people, including those who I know are casting votes that counterbalance my own. As I have gotten to know them better, I see that we share deep common values: kindness to strangers, love of family, affection for our city, a belief in the inherent dignity of every person, a concern for the future welfare of our country. It's impossible to hate somebody when you know them in this way; on the contrary, you become curious about how they see the world, eager to learn more about why they have reached the convictions they hold about politics, justice, and what it means to live a good life. I know that if I sat down with these people, tasked with finding practical solutions to some of our city's worst problems, we would be able to work well together in devising reasonable policies that a majority of us could support. Yet in the portrayal of the news media, or seen through the lens of the political parties, this circle of friendly volunteers is simplified down into the abstraction of Left and Right, implacable enemies.

Scholars and activists who offer remedies for political polarization point to this sort of shared activity as a powerful resource in getting beyond the prejudices that divide citizens from each other.[26] Among the precepts they recommend: stop demonizing one another, and learn to catch yourself in the act when the reflex of political labeling arises in your mind. Keep coming back to the wholeness of the person in front of you: not just a Republican or a Democrat, but a three-dimensional individual who confronts life each day out of the same kind of richly complex story, worldview, and identity that you possess yourself. Resist the impulse of abstraction: seek out the full humanity of the people you encounter – especially if your interaction with them is happening via email or social media. Assume good intentions and basic decency in other people, just as you would want them to acknowledge the good intentions you recognize within yourself. And above all, when discussing political matters, seek out the fundamental values you hold in common with your interlocutor. If you are trying to work together with someone on a civic project or political endeavor, try to agree first on the deeper shared goals that animate both of you. Only then, after this common ground has been established, should you move on to finding specific solutions and tangible actions to propose.[27]

It's also helpful to realize you are not alone in seeking to build bridges across the political divide. The news media and political parties thrive on bitter division, actively fomenting it because it riles people up and thereby generates revenue, influence, volunteers, website clicks, and donations. Hate pays off well for some institutions and groups, and they have become quite skilled at stoking its fires. But if you feel revulsion at what this is doing to your country, you aren't alone. A visit to my local bookstore yields dozens of titles like these: *The Reunited States of America: How We Can Bridge the Partisan Divide*; *Talking Together: Getting Beyond Polarization Through Civil Dialogue*; *Them: Why We Hate Each Other, and How to Heal*; *Solutions to Political Polarization in America*; *Ending Our Uncivil War: A Path to Political Recovery and Spiritual Renewal*; *The Parties Versus the People: How to Turn Republicans and Democrats into Americans*.[28] "What voters want, and what America needs," writes the political mediator Mark Gerzon, "are leaders who will seek relationship with their adversaries rather than control over them. Since we are not going to have one-party rule, we need politicians who will work together."[29]

Citizens' groups for nonpartisan action have formed across the land, at all levels from neighborhoods to cities to states to the nation as a whole. A quick survey online shows dozens of such organizations with names like these: Public Conversations Project; Bipartisan Congressional Retreats; National Coalition for Dialogue and Deliberation; Breakthrough Institute; Living Room Conversations; Village Square; More in Common; Everyday Democracy; No Labels; #Cut50; Voice of the People; Future 500; Convergence Center for Policy Resolution.[30] Despite their kaleidoscopic differences, these groups spring from a growing wave of alarm at the hate that divides Americans; and they share a common passion for breaking the political logjam, finding pragmatic solutions to the pressing problems that beset our country.

Recent public opinion surveys give some grounds for (cautious) hope. One 2014 survey by the University of Maryland carried out a meta-analysis of ten nationwide polls conducted by Pew Research, ABC News, CBS News, *Time*, and *Newsweek*. It found that Americans were far less divided on most issues than one might be led to believe by reading the daily political news. Only 4 percent of the poll questions revealed deep division, and these had to do with hot-button issues like same-sex marriage, gun control, or abortion. But on 69 percent of the topics (266 questions out of 388), the polls showed no statistically significant division between red districts and blue districts.

The issues on which a majority or plurality agreed ranged from health care reform to immigration, from foreign aid to climate change.[31]

Another large-scale survey conducted in 2018 by the nonpartisan group More in Common found equally intriguing results. About 14 percent of Americans fit the categories of Far Left (8 percent) or Far Right (6 percent) activists – the angry people who turn up for demonstrations and voice strident opposition to each other's views on TV. But 56 percent fell into a category dubbed the "Exhausted Majority" – center-left or center-right moderates, or politically disengaged individuals, who did not conform to clear partisan ideology. "They share a sense of fatigue with our polarized national conversation," wrote the report's authors, "a willingness to be flexible in their political viewpoints, and a lack of voice in the national conversation." Fully 65 percent of this group endorsed the statement, "The people I agree with politically need to be willing to listen to others and compromise."[32]

One should not underestimate how hard it will be to dial back polarization: the institutions and groups that thrive on division are well funded and deeply entrenched in our news media, political parties, and mental habits. As evolutionary psychologists remind us, the impulse of tribalism runs deep in the emotional and cognitive wiring of our species.[33] But it's nonetheless helpful to be reminded that the hyper-partisan ideologues are actually a marginal group in American life. The angry ones at the fringes exert disproportionate influence over our public governance because they are well organized and strongly motivated. They make noise and grab our attention. But if passionately pragmatic moderates can join together over the coming years, forming organized coalitions of their own, they can easily outvote the strident hardliners, electing a new type of leader who seeks sensible compromise rather than division.

DELIBERATIVE DEMOCRACY: A PROMISING NEW TOOL FOR COMBATTING THE FAKE NEWS EPIDEMIC

When you approach a traffic light in your car, it's important for you and the other drivers to agree about which color signal is flashing. This is why the red, yellow, and green colors are arranged vertically, so that even a color-blind person can know when to go and when to stop. Without this system of understanding – this shared perception of a common reality – everyone would crash into everyone else.

Over the past couple decades, a truly dreadful thing has been happening: we can no longer take for granted that the most basic facts about our world are shared by our fellow citizens. I say that Joe Biden clearly won the 2020 election; you say with equal conviction that he stole it. I say that COVID-19 is dangerous and we should all get vaccinated; you say it's the vaccine that's dangerous because it contains microchips that will allow the government to track your movements. I say the escalating seasons of West Coast wildfires are early signs of global warming; you say they're caused by space lasers operated by Jewish conspiracies. Both of us can point to all kinds of news sources and websites that we have come to trust and that support our views; both of us have plenty of friends and family who share and corroborate our understanding of how the world works. Both of us have Twitter and Facebook feeds that further reinforce our interpretations of events every morning; both of us consider ourselves upstanding, responsible persons who are knowledgeable and well-informed. How can we possibly live peaceably side-by-side as fellow citizens if our basic perceptions of reality diverge this profoundly?[34]

Since this problem threatens the very foundations of any democracy, scholars and public officials have worked hard to find new approaches for bringing people back into a common space of civic information and action. One of the most promising such innovations, developed over the past 30 years, is known as deliberative democracy.[35] The underlying idea is straightforward: in today's society, most people are unfortunately casting their votes on the basis of fairly rudimentary or incomplete knowledge about the issues they are voting on – and this undermines the effectiveness and legitimacy of democratic electoral processes. Elections tend to become more about getting your party to win by any means necessary, even if it means distorting the positions of the rival party and having your politicians make vague and inflated promises they know they can't keep. It's an exercise in mass manipulation rather than a chance for citizens to make their actual policy views and preferences known.

The solution, according to advocates of deliberative democracy, lies in a practice that was pioneered 2,500 years ago in ancient Athens.[36] You take a randomly selected subgroup of citizens, carefully chosen to include a representative microcosm of the broader electorate. This means selecting appropriate numbers of males and females, rich and poor, educated and illiterate, left-wing and right-wing citizens (and so on) in the same proportion that they occupy within the broader society; the sample size also needs to be large enough to be statistically significant – on the order of several hundred individuals. Then you give these people a chance to acquire all the information they need about the issues being voted on. They hear presentations by experts on the issues, offering the full range of opinions and arguments. Every relevant ideological perspective is brought to the table and given a chance to make its case. Over a two-day period, these citizens meet in small and large groups and discuss together the pros and cons of the various options, taking care to address the complexities and indirect consequences of each proposal. Trained facilitators oversee the discussions, making sure that all voices are heard and everyone gets a fair chance to air their views. At the end of this structured deliberation process, the citizens cast their votes. The results are then shared with the broader voting public, along with detailed written explanations by the participants of their reasons for voting the way they did. If the sample of citizens was properly selected – including the right proportion of representatives from all walks of life – then you can say with confidence that you have given the citizenry a chance to make a truly well-informed decision about the policies that matter to their lives. By following this procedure, the larger voting public can learn much from the rationales articulated by the deliberative subgroup, and cast its vote on the basis of much better information than it would otherwise have done.

Variants of this approach have been adopted over recent years in many countries and at many levels of government, from municipal elections to national referendums. They have racked up an impressive track record in a wide variety of contexts, from local ballots in rural Uganda to statewide polls in California, from national plebiscites in Australia to supranational policymaking in the European Union.[37] Critics have argued that the deliberative polls can still be manipulated by some participants who are better educated or more stridently opinionated than others, but proponents of the polls have made a persuasive case that such distortions can be successfully minimized if the process is sufficiently well-structured.[38]

Overall, this approach offers a promising way to bring an element of accurate information, reasoned discussion, and common ground into the electoral environment of modern democracies. It will prove particularly helpful in setting public policy for managing our four mega-dangers, for these all require voters to acquire a fairly sophisticated background of scientific and technological knowledge. When coupled with the contribution made by nongovernmental organizations and citizens' advocacy groups, deliberative polls can add a significant element of democratic input and participation to the sometimes insular and top-heavy processes by which experts and government insiders regulate scientific and technological innovation. They can also help to counteract the phenomenon known as regulatory capture, which refers to the sometimes excessively cozy relationships that build up over time between government agencies and the industries they are supposed to oversee.[39]

LOCAL ACTION

Scholars who study public perceptions of risk have observed that people tend to be quite bad at calibrating the right level of concern for various kinds of threats: they grossly overreact to certain minor dangers while casually ignoring much more serious problems and risks.[40] For example, I may be afraid to fly in an airplane, but have no problem with driving around town in my car – despite statistics showing the latter to be far more likely to kill me than the former. Mega-dangers like climate change, nuclear war, pandemics, or runaway AI can seem rather abstract and remote to most people, compared with the vivid horror of the latest terrorist attack. Psychological studies have shown that people experience strong visceral reactions when they envision harm to someone they know or to individuals with whom they can identify; but this concern for others does not scale up in proportion to the number of people harmed, as one might expect it to do. Vast calamities with high casualties – among masses of faceless strangers – elicit responses that are surprisingly blasé or downright indifferent.[41]

When it comes to future mega-dangers, moreover, many people tend to believe that these are matters over which they personally have very little control. They may indeed hear reports about such dangers in the news, but assume that other people – the experts, the government, the activist groups – are out there making sure everything will turn out alright. Surely, they think to themselves, if the danger is so serious, there must be plenty of smart folks with their hands on the steering wheel and foot on the brakes. (Wrong.)

This is where each of us, as a citizen, can make an important contribution to controlling mega-dangerous technologies: we can help spread the word. Many of the people around us remain unaware of these threats or tend to underestimate how seriously they loom in our future. To the extent that they can be made aware of the problem, new pathways of effective action will open up. If you talk about this subject with your family members, friends, and coworkers – stirring things up, fomenting discussion and debate – you are already taking a tangible step toward making the world safer.

When you bring up these existential dangers, some folks will no doubt respond with skepticism, and snicker that you sound like Chicken Little. Your reply can go something like this: "That may be, but if so I'm in good company. For climate change, I'm in the company of leaders like Pope

Francis and Ban Ki-Moon, climate experts like James Hansen and Katharine Hayhoe, activists like Arnold Schwarzenegger and Emma Thompson, or politicians like Al Gore and Michael Bloomberg. For nukes, I'm in the company of statesmen like George Schultz, Sam Nunn, William Perry, and Henry Kissinger. For synthetic biology, I'm in the company of Harvard's George Church, Stanford's Drew Endy, and Berkeley's Jennifer Doudna. For AI, I'm in the company of Bill Gates, Elon Musk, Stuart Russell, and Stephen Hawking. Are all of them Chicken Littles as well?"

You also don't need to wait for your government to take action: individual citizens can adopt a wide variety of helpful measures in their daily lives. This is particularly true for climate change. You can't do much directly about nukes, AI, or pandemics (other than wearing a face mask when asked by public officials to do so), but when it comes to global warming you can make changes in your daily habits that start immediately taking our society down the right path. How you run the energy systems in your home, how you get to and from work, what you do on vacations, what foods you choose to eat – in all these areas the influence of a single individual can seem trifling, but when you aggregate it across millions of households it adds up to a tremendous impact.[42] One also shouldn't underestimate the power of setting an example: when you implement tangible changes in your daily activities, others who know and respect you will take notice, and will in turn become more likely to adopt similar measures in their own lives. This propagation effect is not just wishful thinking: scholars have studied and documented its impact.[43]

You can get together with like-minded people in advocacy groups that grab the attention of politicians and policymakers. Here for example are some of the wide-ranging possibilities available in the US. For climate change, you have a veritable panoply of options: if you're a leftist you can join an activist group like Greenpeace; if you're a passionate centrist you can join the World Wide Fund for Nature (formerly known as the World Wildlife Fund); and if you're a Christian conservative you can join one of the many church groups that focus on environmental stewardship.[44] At Vanderbilt University where I teach, a group of undergraduate students circulated a petition in 2019, and as a direct result of the 3,400 signatures it garnered, the university committed itself to 100 percent renewable energy and becoming a carbon-neutral institution by the year 2050.[45] For nuclear weapons, you can support think-tanks like the Carnegie Endowment for International Peace, or join activist coalitions such as Global Zero or the International Campaign to Abolish Nuclear Weapons.[46] (Even if you deem it impossible for humankind to get all the way down to zero nukes, such organizations lobby vigorously for phased reductions in nuclear arsenals.) For synthetic biology, you can write letters to your congressional representatives advocating better funding for the CDC (Centers for Disease Control) and WHO (World Health Organization), or support the work of smaller private groups such as the Hastings Center, the ETC Group, or Synbiosafe.[47] For AI, you can support the important work of organizations such as the Future of Life Institute, OpenAI, the Machine Intelligence Research Institute (MIRI), the Center for Human-Compatible Artificial Intelligence at U.C. Berkeley, the Center for the Study of Existential Risk at Cambridge University, or Oxford University's Future of Humanity Institute.[48]

Many universities throughout the world have programs dedicated to science studies and technology policy, with faculty who specialize in thinking about technological risk management, governance regimes, and long-term forecasting. You can reach out to those scholars and see if they can use your help: if you are wealthy, you may be able to endow a professorship or provide research funding, and if you are retired, they may be able to use your time and effort in conducting research. The underlying point here is that with the stakes as high as they are, each of us can be creative and proactive in seeking to make a tangible contribution.

At a more personal level, we can also cultivate a new kind of ethics when it comes to our own relationship with technology, measuring every technological innovation against the yardstick of human values and flourishing.[49] This may seem obvious, but in practice it's hard to do because our whole culture in today's industrial civilization is viscerally tuned to words like "new," "faster," and "more." Wisdom, in this context, requires the ability to pause for a moment before clicking the "Get It Now" button, and asking ourselves a few basic questions. Do I really need this? If I do acquire it, what new capabilities – and constraints – will this bring into my life? How will this change the way I relate to other people, to the natural world, to myself? What might be the unintended side-effects of my using this new technology – both for myself and for the broader social order when millions of people start using it as I do? When all these pros and cons are taken into account, will this technology contribute to the qualities that make my life meaningful and worth living?[50]

This kind of critical, selective approach can be fruitfully applied to all forms of technology, from our everyday gadgets to massive systems like the electrical grid, the healthcare network, or social media. By evaluating our machines and practices against the yardstick of human flourishing, we bring a greater measure of choice and flexibility into our relationship with technology. Restraint, in this context, becomes much more than just giving something up: it means *prioritizing certain values over others.* Progress means choosing which pathways seem most likely to nurture the life-qualities we hold dear. In this way, we are not turning away from modernity, but rather channeling it to make it align more closely with our ideals and beliefs.[51]

* * *

13

Lessons from the Green Movement:
How to Build Lasting Change in the Absence of Full
Consensus

THE LAST THREE CHAPTERS LAID OUT A NUMBER of action-items for our national and international "to do" list. But how do we generate the political will for making these things happen? This question is a tough one, because it not only opens up the Pandora's Box of political partisanship within nations, but also runs up against the myriad dimensions of economic, societal, and cultural division among the world's peoples. It's a daunting prospect.

Nevertheless, we do have one story to which we can turn for inspiration in this regard: the impressive cumulative impact of the global environmental movement. What's particularly instructive about this story, for our present purposes, is the fact that the world's green activists have mostly operated as fringe minorities and outsiders. This was especially true in the early days of their movement during the 1950s and 1960s, but it remains true to some extent today. Large, wealthy, and politically well-connected segments of modern society have fiercely opposed their efforts, using every instrument available, from derision to disinformation to legal challenges. *There has never been, over the past seven decades, a clear societal consensus around any unified or comprehensive environmentalist vision.* The issue has remained fraught with controversy throughout its long history. And yet the world is a very different place than it would have been in the absence of the green movement. The original vision of a wholly sustainable civilization remains far from fulfillment, but every sector of modern society now shows tinges and striations of green ideas. To adopt a meteorological metaphor: one way to get sopping wet is to stand outside for five minutes during a monsoon downpour. The other is to walk for several hours through dense fog. The history of the green movement fits the latter model: it's a story of countless small, seemingly insignificant changes gradually accumulating into something deep and pervasive.

The environmentalists of the 1960s tackled a breathtakingly complex challenge: how to turn modern civilization away from its mantra of "faster–bigger–more;" how to persuade their fellow citizens to make the transition into an ecologically sustainable way of life.[1] In the years immediately following World War II, almost no one was thinking in terms of ecology or the environment. Humankind's attention focused on getting economies moving again and dealing with the hair-raising tensions of the emerging Cold War. Then, in the late 1950s and early 1960s, a few isolated voices began to speak out: figures like Rachel Carson in the United States, Roger Heim in France, and E. F. Schumacher in Britain, began sounding the alarm. At first no one took them seriously, but over time their persuasive arguments began to win over larger numbers of people. New thinkers joined the movement and took up the cause, adding their own ideas to the mix: the fragile balance of nature, the contradictions of endless economic growth, the finitude of spaceship Earth. Throughout the 1960s and early 1970s, they agitated for the defense of national parks, protested against oil spills, air pollution, and overpopulation, and forced the larger public to grapple with troubling questions about the overall trajectory of modern civilization.[2]

All this did not happen smoothly or easily: it's a story fraught with conflict, missteps, and confusion. Government officials remained skeptical about the new green ideas, and business leaders regarded their proposals as a misguided form of idealism that would undermine prosperity. Nevertheless, the green ideas made inroads, taking concrete form as small, incremental victories, many of them more symbolic than substantial: a new national park, a law banning certain kinds of pesticides, a local recycling program, a new set of organic foods and eco-friendly products in the neighborhood supermarket. Some environmentalists began forming political parties or lobbying groups, aiming to influence the political process more directly. Some industrial firms decided that cultivating a green image could be good for business and established new products and procedures that touted their eco-friendly credentials. Politicians recognized the growing popularity of green initiatives and began the slow process of institutionalizing ecological principles in the ponderous mechanisms of government. The United States created the Environmental Protection Agency; France created the Ministry of the Environment; the UN organized Earth Day and began convening regular international conferences on sustainability. These new institutions, in turn, further solidified the credibility of green ideas, moving them into the mainstream and strengthening citizens' perceptions of their importance. Elementary school textbooks began teaching children about ecologically responsible citizenship; law schools offered courses on environmental torts. Specialized businesses sprang up, addressing the needs of environmental testing, pollution abatement, water treatment, and clean processing of garbage: green ideas were now making money for ambitious entrepreneurs.[3]

As the 1980s and 1990s went by, this process continued, embodied in new laws and oversight agencies, industrial practices, consumer habits, research projects in the universities, and pragmatic ideas among the citizenry – all influencing each other in a complex web of reciprocal cause and effect over time. By the first decades of the new millennium, you would be hard pressed to find a single aspect of a modern industrial economy that remained untouched at some level by green innovations. From cars to cosmetics, from education to business, everything now had an ecological footprint, and everything was subject in some form or other to considerations of sustainability.

A triumph for the Sixties greens? Far from it. Industrial civilization today has a long road yet to travel if it is to achieve the sort of sustainable balance that those activists advocated.[4] Their dream of "back to nature" and "Small is Beautiful" seems almost quaint compared to the frenetically advancing information society that has come into being. And yet, we should not underestimate the shift that has occurred. What has taken place is not the drastic change-of-course that the original protestors had hoped for – a 90-degree turn in a wholly new direction. Instead, what we have lived through is a more modest *deflection* of history, down a significantly different path. The green militants failed to achieve everything they wanted, but they catalyzed a broader historical process that refined the original environmentalist goals over time, gradually rendering them more sophisticated and effective. Our economic system today is certainly not as green as the activists of the 1960s hoped; but it is far greener than it would have been if they had thrown up their hands in resignation.

Here, then, is a rather encouraging story – a case study of partial success in tackling one of the most daunting planet-scale challenges humankind has ever faced. It strikingly illustrates the space that humans have for shaping their own history.[5] Each of the choices we make as individuals can only exert a limited impact on the vast processes that structure our social institutions and determine global economic developments. And yet, those large-scale systems are nothing more than aggregations of billions of ongoing human choices, assumptions, and habits.[6] If a creative individual can find a way to modify the underlying assumptions that shape the expectations of other individuals – and if this modification propagates through the minds and habits of still other individuals – the possibility opens up for an exponential multiplication of influence. A single idea can light up entire continents, profoundly altering large-scale institutions and practices.

The key to the green activists' achievement lay in the eclectic nature of the strategies they pursued. It was a multidimensional endeavor, loosely coordinated yet decentralized in nature, open to ongoing revision as the process unfolded. It aimed at bringing gradual changes at all levels of modern society: institutions, jobs, market transactions, laws, habits, and underlying assumptions. Most importantly, it operated from a new conception of "Us" that was deeply inclusive and compelling: Spaceship Earth, Gaia, our shared home. A tie-dyed hippie woman from Berkeley could find some common ground here with a pin-striped industrialist, a soccer mom, or a fundamentalist preacher from Alabama: "conservation" and "stewardship for our grandchildren" resonated well across the worldviews of these diverse constituencies. Such people might not all identify with the "green" label, but this became a strength of the movement rather than a weakness: each group could come up with its own distinctive ideas, strategies, and solutions; each could press for the kinds of societal change that they deemed most ethical and effective. This breadth of reach became a major advantage, for in most cases the diverse pro-environment actions they undertook proved synergistic in their ultimate effect. Techies could focus on building better solar panels; business leaders could carve out new niches of sustainable products and jobs; spiritual folks could invent new visions of common purpose that helped vitalize the movement, grounding it in an ethical horizon beyond the welter of competing ideologies of the present day.

This kind of incremental transformation is probably the most we can reasonably hope for when it comes to shaping the development of mega-dangerous technologies over the coming century.[7] Just as the green movement brought about a reassessment of the human relationship with nature, this new movement will flow from a critical reassessment of the relation between humankind and technology. Environmental activism rests on the premise that our economic activities are endangering the planet's ecosystems. This new phase of activism will rest on the dawning realization that humans have now become powerful enough – through at least four technological pathways – to unleash catastrophic events that threaten modern civilization. While the watchword of the greens was about saving animals and ecosystems, the watchword for the coming era will be about safeguarding the human future itself. (I call to mind here a bumper sticker of the 1980s: a grinning whale holding a placard that reads, "Save the Humans.")

The new movement for global technological governance will stand its best chance of success if it operates as the green movement has done – at many levels simultaneously. At the cultural level, citizens and policymakers will need to educate themselves about the basic science underpinning these powerful technologies, paying particular attention to the unintended consequences of the machines and inventions they use over the long haul. At the institutional level, we will need effective instruments for regulation, surveillance, and enforcement of compliance – achieved simultaneously at home and abroad. At the political level, we will need leaders who see beyond short-term solutions, and who are committed to building a strong global framework of cooperation and collective security – for it is only on that globe-spanning basis that such mega-dangerous technologies can ultimately be controlled.

All this will take time – just as it did with the partial success of the green movement, which required decades to make a major impact and remains an unfinished project today. We need to buy ourselves as much time as we can: time to build a resilient global governance regime; time for our scientists and engineers to work on new solutions for improved safety; time for our politicians and diplomats to work out new societal practices for enhanced security.

Most of us are not technical experts, so we can't expect to sit down with a scratch pad and sketch out some new design breakthrough that renders AI reliably stable and friendly, or that reins in the reproductive zeal of synthetic microbes. What we *can* do, however, is help build a social and political system that strongly supports the scientists and technologists as they work on these kinds of fundamental safety problems – a system that shifts the incentive structure away from the mindless mantra of More, More, More. How do we do that? By getting involved.

Science and technology are powerfully shaped by the socioeconomic and cultural systems in which they are embedded. Scientists have to get grants in order to do their research; corporations have to make products that people want to buy; engineers and inventors must comply with the national and international regulations their legislators have put in place. At all these levels, we citizens can become activists who press for certain values to be emphasized: safety prioritized over profits; deliberation and appropriate restraint instead of blind competition and haste; taking the long view instead of seeking short-term gains; ethical responsibility, public transparency, and accountability. Each of us is not only a voter and a consumer, but also a potential carrier of ideas, an informal organizer who can mobilize public interest in these issues and press for wise policies to be adopted.

UNITED BY A MAJOR THREAT

In my college course on World War II, I ask students to find someone who was at least 15 years old in 1945 and interview them about their wartime experiences, whether on the home front or out on the beaches of Normandy or Guadalcanal. The students often return with a sense of awe at what those people accomplished, and one of the impressions that strikes them most vividly is the deep unity that pervaded Americans during that period. "We pulled together." "We cast aside our differences." "It was one of the best times of my life, because I felt such a strong bond with my fellow citizens as we sacrificed side-by-side and prevailed together."

That historical moment is intriguing, because the American citizenry was actually quite bitterly divided in the years running up to wartime. How should the nation respond to the calamity of the Great Depression? Was the New Deal a great idea or a socialist deviation? Should we join Britain in fighting the Germans? On all these questions, Americans simply could not reach agreement.[8] Then came Pearl Harbor, followed by Hitler's (idiotic) decision to declare war on us. Within a few days' time, the spirit of the country changed dramatically. Young people rushed to enlist, old people bought war bonds, and everyone turned to the task at hand. Together. Even large numbers of African Americans and Japanese-Americans, who had been appallingly treated in the prewar years and the aftermath of Pearl Harbor, willingly joined in.[9]

There were still dissenters, of course. Conscientious objectors declined to enlist and sought roles as medics or nonmilitary volunteers. Some isolationists persisted in their belief that we should stay out of the European war. Many were anguished to see their sons, husbands, or fathers ship off into deadly peril. (We tend to forget today that World War II was a draft war: young men could not say No if Uncle Sam called them to fight.) But the majority of the citizenry came on board and participated in any way they could. For many of them, the feeling of pitching in to a common cause became one of the defining experiences of their lives.[10]

My point here is that people can put aside their deep divisions and disagreements if they perceive a sufficiently serious common threat. Could something similar happen with the four mega-dangers described in this book, mustering a gradual mobilization of effort on a scale commensurate with a world war? One hopes that it won't take a disaster like Pearl Harbor to wake us up this time around – flooded cities, collapsing agriculture, mass migrations, nuclear crises, pandemics, or AI accidents. The awakening to the common threat will probably unfold haltingly over the coming decades, propelled by a gradual accumulation of alarming evidence that we are headed for big trouble unless we take concerted action. But to the extent that this awakening does happen, we may yet prove capable of overcoming our differences and pull together as we have so effectively done in the past.

Some might object, however, that this unification around a common threat can only take place *within* nations. "It worked for America in World War II," they may argue, "but it will never work at the level of the whole planet." Yet there is plenty of evidence that this isn't true. Achievements like the 1987 Montreal Protocol that addressed the fraying ozone layer demonstrate that extremely diverse human groups can work effectively together across the globe when they are sufficiently motivated and ably led.[11]

This treaty, ratified by 197 nations, stands as one of the great success stories of international cooperation: in the three decades since it went into force, it has effectively addressed the problem of atmospheric ozone holes created by the release of chlorofluorocarbons (CFCs) in aerosols and refrigeration systems. Once it became clear to scientists in the 1970s that CFCs were harming the Earth's protective ozone layer, they sounded the alarm: unless urgent action was taken, rising ultraviolet radiation would cause skin cancers, degraded agriculture, and the devastation of phytoplankton in the oceans. The stakes were high, and in this instance humankind swiftly rose to the occasion. The rich nations not only phased out CFCs within their own borders, but also set up a fund to assist the poor nations in doing the same thing as well. Britain's Margaret Thatcher (not known for soft-heartedness toward the poor) took the lead in pushing the assistance fund through: she recognized that the danger was great, and that developing countries simply lacked the wherewithal to convert their economies away from CFCs without outside help.

It's also important to remember that humankind does not require total unanimity among its citizens in order to press ahead with sensible and urgently needed measures. After the 9/11 attacks, for example, quite a few people thought that setting up passenger-screening checkpoints in all the world's airports was a quixotic idea: it would be too expensive, too bureaucratic, and much too hard to realize effectively across the entire network of planetary air travel. Yet a sufficient number of people around the world did come to see the pragmatic need, and the screening system came into being. It has actually worked fairly well.[12]

A GLOBAL UNIFYING FORCE?

The challenge of climate change differs in three important respects from the other mega-dangers in this book: it is not subject to the logic of arms races; it threatens to bring tangible harms that affect all human beings; and its disasters will escalate gradually over the coming decades, giving people a chance to wake up and respond constructively. This adds up to a promising set of factors because it means that the campaign to reverse global warming could plausibly unite humankind in ways that other dire threats have failed to do. It could help pave the way for the more cooperative global governance framework that the planet so badly needs. Let us examine these three factors one at a time.

The insidious logic of arms races makes it very hard to restrain the development of nukes, biotechnology, and AI. Nations and corporations vie with each other to achieve the greatest potency with these technologies, and the result is a spiral of competition that is difficult to break. You get more power and influence in the self-help world if you have more nukes, better biotech, or faster AI. But climate change is different. If your country is the top contributor to global warming, this does not *in itself* make you more powerful than other nations: it just means you're burning more fossil fuels than everyone else. Consider for example the case of France. This mid-sized nation ranks #19 in the world in CO_2 emissions: it contributes much less to global warming than Japan, Germany, Canada, Saudi Arabia, Brazil, Mexico, Indonesia, South Africa, Australia, Italy, or Turkey.[13] Why? Because it gets about 75 percent of its electricity from nuclear reactors. Yet France is a military Great Power with its own nuclear-missile triad, a permanent member of the UN Security Council, a leading member of the EU, and the sixth-ranked economy in the world. It arguably wields more global influence than most of those other nations even though its contribution to the planet's warming is relatively low. My point here is that the logic of arms races does not apply to fossil fuels: increasing your fossil fuel consumption does not necessarily correlate with greater global status and power.

Over the coming decades, in fact, the exact opposite will probably be true. The leading powers of the year 2050 or 2070 are likely to be the same nations that have mastered the technologies of clean energy and carbon removal, and are selling them at great profit throughout the world. China is poised to take the lead in this beneficial race for advanced renewable and nuclear energy technologies, and other nations will struggle to catch up with it.[14] The countries that stubbornly hang on to fossil-fuel-based systems will be left in the dust. You will not get more power or influence in the world by being the top consumer of fossil fuels: all you will get is a (well-deserved) reputation for selfishness, short-sightedness, and technological backwardness.

The second factor that sets climate change apart from other mega-dangers lies in the way its harms will be distributed. For the next couple decades, rich people will find themselves less grievously affected by global warming than poor people, because they will be able to pay whatever it costs to buy themselves protections from the disasters of a hotter planet. The same goes for rich nations compared with poor nations. But over time, this distinction will start to blur. By the second half of the century, no human being anywhere will remain unscathed by the ravages of a hot planet, and no amount of money will buy you full protection. Rich people and rich nations will have to massively readjust their lives and suffer awful consequences, just as the paupers of the world will already have had to do.[15]

This could potentially exert a powerful unifying effect on humankind, giving people an incentive to overcome their differences of class, race, religion, or nationality and pull together to save themselves. Whereas, in the short term, climate change will probably exacerbate the divisions between rich and poor, over time the common nature of the escalating climate disasters may perhaps come to serve as a kind of equalizer. An intriguing historical parallel lies in the experience of Great Britain during the 1930s and 1940s. The Great Depression sharply accentuated class divisions in British society because wealthy Britons were able to insulate themselves from economic hardship much more effectively than the poor.[16] But all this changed in World War II. Hitler's Germany posed so dire a threat that it clearly affected every Briton, rich or poor. With their backs against the wall, the Brits closed ranks in a manner not seen before in their long history: rich and poor, aristocrats and commoners, sacrificed together at home and fought side-by-side abroad. At war's end, after prevailing in the military contest, they enacted a sweeping package of social and economic reforms that guaranteed decent education, housing, and healthcare to all citizens "from cradle to grave." To be sure, significant class distinctions and fractures still existed in postwar Britain, but the wartime ethos of pulling together, coupled with the important new institutions of the welfare state, ensured that British society would not return to the status quo of the 1930s.[17] In a similar way, at the global level, the threat of climate change – and the shared experience of suffering on a hotter planet – could bring the world's far-flung peoples together in new ways, giving them powerful reasons to work alongside one another in concerted action for a common cause.

This brings me to the third factor that sets climate change apart. Nuclear conflict, a pandemic that kills billions, a bioweapons attack that spreads uncontrollably, a Great Power war escalating out of cyberwarfare, an intelligence explosion among AI machines – these are all-or-nothing sorts of events. Until they happen, life goes on pretty much as usual; and after they happen, they threaten to tear the fabric of history right apart. It's hard for humankind to "learn a lesson" from such cataclysmic events because (in many plausible scenarios) they will so thoroughly disrupt our civilization that entirely new socioeconomic rules may have to be invented in their aftermath. But climate change will probably not work that way: it is unlikely to hit us overnight like a sudden thunderclap.[18] Rather, its harms will gradually escalate over the coming years and decades, exerting incremental pressure on human civilization in ways that cannot be ignored – and this may afford people a precious interval of time in which to learn the lesson. It will not be possible for life to go on as usual, as this pressure inexorably mounts. More and more people will eventually wake up to the danger, and this will give humankind a chance to get organized around the threat and craft a sensible planet-level response.

Here a skeptic might reply that the climate crisis could equally plausibly have the *opposite* effect: it could lead people to circle the wagons, closing in on their local, regional, or national communities, just as they instinctively did in the Great Depression.[19] The rising climate calamities could impel people to build walls, erect tariff barriers, husband their dwindling resources, eject foreigners, and seek to insulate themselves from the tumult beyond their borders. We can already see signs of this go-it-alone mentality today: few nations are stepping forward with the expensive and draconian measures that are needed to combat global warming effectively. In a self-help world, it's in every nation's interest to be a free rider on the efforts of others, letting one's neighbors pay the price and then reaping the collective benefits.

But here too, climate change is different. Its escalating harms will harshly punish all nations, including the free riders; and eventually it will become clear to more and more people that effective action can only come about if everyone contributes their fair share. Even the most hardened nationalists will be forced to recognize this fact: their coastal cities will be underwater, their agriculture will be failing, their homes will be ravaged by an onslaught of natural disasters. No nation can beat climate change by going it alone; this is a problem that cannot be dealt with effectively in an international system that operates through self-help logic.

One of the first steps that nations will probably take as they coordinate their actions on climate change will be to set up strong incentives for countries to chip in, and equally strong penalties for free-rider countries that opt out.[20] As the harms of climate change accumulate, more and more nations will rise to the challenge, ramping up their transition to a carbon-free economy, allocating precious resources to create expensive carbon-removal technologies. They will not look kindly on the countries that persist in free riding, and will no doubt hit those recalcitrant players with punitive economic sanctions. The free riders will hear the same message from their neighbors all around: "If we can't persuade you to stop wrecking our planetary home, we can definitely make you pay a high economic price for your antisocial behavior." Here too, as in military matters, the logic of collective security can forcefully rein in rogue behaviors that threaten the common good.

For all these reasons, then, the mobilization against climate change could provide a uniquely powerful impetus that unites humankind around a common threat. Somewhat paradoxically, we have here a triple stroke of good luck: the struggle to reverse global warming eludes the arms race trap; it compels us to get creative in moving beyond the national self-help system; and it will do these things via a gradual escalation of pressure, giving us a precious space of time to make the necessary transition in our hearts, minds, habits, and institutions. It could end up playing a lead role in the long, arduous process of building a global framework for cooperative technological governance.

PART IV

THE MIDDLE-TERM GOAL:

NEW INTERNATIONAL TOOLS FOR THE LATE TWENTY-FIRST CENTURY

14

A Promising Track Record:
The Dramatic Growth of International Institutions
and Networks Since 1900

I N OCTOBER 1945, GEORGE C. MARSHALL was invited by the New York Herald Tribune Forum to offer his assessment of the world situation. General Marshall enjoyed high credibility in this regard, because he had just presided over victory in World War II. He had been a central player among those who organized the globe-spanning Allied military machine that crushed Fascism. In typical fashion, he got right to the point:

> For centuries man has been seeking, I believe, to extend [political order] to the level of the entire planet . . . Time and space have been so shrunken that the world must, I believe, establish definite global rules. Community and national rules no longer suffice. They by themselves are no longer realistic . . .
>
> We and our Allies have recently advanced the structure of the United Nations organization as a vehicle to promote the cooperative idea of global order.[1]

Already in 1945, Marshall saw clearly that the old order of nation-states was gradually coming to an end. Humankind was transitioning into a new epoch in which globe-spanning technologies presented unprecedented opportunities – and vulnerabilities. Citizens and leaders would have to adapt, making deep adjustments in their thinking. Just as the advent of the nation-state had brought stability and peace to large chunks of territory in which people had previously been at each other's throats, now the rule of law would need to extend one step further, to the planetary level. Building this edifice of global cooperation, while still preserving the liberties for which past generations had fought so hard – this, in Marshall's judgement, was the core challenge of the century to come. His words are worth repeating: "Community and national rules no longer suffice. They by themselves are no longer realistic."

The trends that Marshall discerned in 1945 have accelerated in the ensuing decades, and the world has kept getting smaller and more tightly interconnected, bound together by new technologies and by economic shifts that even he could scarcely have imagined. Flows of capital, people, goods, and information have intensified, directly linking far-flung regions in a web of daily undertakings. Entire industries have arisen and passed away in this frenetic cycle of innovation, and in one domain after another, established ways of doing things have been relentlessly swept aside. World economic output has increased swiftly, impressively – and unevenly. The patterns of wealth have shifted, and the total number of people worldwide living in extreme poverty has declined – but billions of human beings still struggle daily with penury, illiteracy, oppression, and disease.

Amid all this globe-spanning creativity and upheaval, a whole new class of borderless problems has emerged. Infectious diseases like the 1919 Spanish flu or the 2019 coronavirus spread swiftly around the planet despite frantic efforts to rein them in. Chemicals released by an old refrigerator in Alabama waft up to fray the atmospheric ozone layer, bringing skin cancers to the children of Australia. A reactor meltdown in Soviet Ukraine bathes Western Europe in a radioactive cloud. A bank failure in Rio de Janeiro rocks the London financial district and sends the Hong Kong stock market into free fall – causing mutual funds in New York to lose value. A failed state in the Middle East disgorges hundreds of thousands of refugees, upsetting the political equilibrium of Germany. Islamic terrorists loosely connected through the Web strike targets in Florida, Bali, and Moscow. Cybercriminals attack computers on six continents simultaneously, infecting them with ransomware.

Two common threads run through these diverse events: growing interdependence and shared vulnerability.[2] When it comes to such borderless hazards as these, citizens of the strongest nations find themselves in some ways equally as exposed as the citizens of the world's poorest countries. The mere fact of living in a wealthy superpower, protected by the world's most formidable military, does not greatly alter the odds of suffering grievously if such events materialize. Radioactive clouds, acid rain, and pandemics do not stop at borders; terrorists and cybercriminals cannot be blocked by military action alone; financial crises reverberate across the global commercial networks in milliseconds. Globalization has put all humans increasingly into the same boat, and our fates are bound together across the oceans – even more tightly than they were in 1945 when Marshall gave his speech.

Humankind thus finds itself standing awkwardly astride two very different kinds of order: the old nation-state system, which still provides the underlying structure of world politics; and the emerging reality at the planet scale, beyond borders, imposing its challenges on us with increasing pressure every year. In the economic and technological spheres, the transition to globalism is already well advanced; but in the political, legal, and cultural spheres our institutions and habits of mind lag far behind. This is the great historical drama to which we are all first-hand witnesses.

AMERICAN TRADITIONS OF NATIONALISM
AND INTERNATIONALISM

Most people today probably have a vague sense that a variety of international institutions are out there doing their thing – the UN, NATO, the World Health Organization, and so on – but they actually have no grasp of just how dense and vibrant the networks of global governance have become. Nor do they appreciate what a vital role these bodies are playing every day in keeping the wheels of global commerce, public health, security, and communication turning smoothly.[3] Starting with the Hague Conferences of the early twentieth century, humankind has gradually put together a multilayered mesh of organizations for coordinating the cross-border activities of the planet's peoples. Some of these organizations are intergovernmental, like the UN; others are nongovernmental, like Greenpeace or Human Rights Watch. Some are global, like the World Trade Organization; others are regional, like ASEAN (the Association of Southeast Asian Nations). Some are all-purpose coordinating bodies, like the Organization of American States; others serve a specialized function, like Interpol or the International Criminal Court. Some, like the International Labour Organization, orchestrate the relationships among fully sovereign countries; others, like the European Union, operate as supranational entities to which member states have voluntarily surrendered a portion of their sovereignty.[4]

More than any other country, the United States has taken the lead over the past century in building this global institutional network – and this is not entirely surprising, since this period also coincides with the "American Century," the rise of the United States to preeminence as a world power. It was American statesmen who helped organize the Hague Conferences of 1899 and 1907; the League of Nations after World War I; the United Nations and its affiliated bodies after World War II; and the myriad organizations that sprang into existence during the 1940s, 1950s, and 1960s, ranging from military alliances like NATO to development agencies like the Food and Agriculture Organization.[5]

But the United States has also shown a deep ambivalence toward its own creations. Two powerful constituencies gradually emerged among American voters and leaders: those who advocated swift adaptation to the globalizing trend, and those who took a more skeptical view, insisting on the continued primacy of national sovereignty. These two loose groupings, whom we can label as internationalists versus nationalists, spanned political parties and ideological backgrounds: one can find prominent figures from both the Republicans and the Democrats in both camps. Depending on which group happened to be ascendant in domestic politics at any given moment, the role of the United States as a leader in international institution-building has periodically waxed and waned.[6]

Thus, it was President Wilson who created the League of Nations; but his vision was famously rebuffed by isolationists in the Senate who refused to ratify American membership. The United Nations was ardently promoted by Franklin Roosevelt, but a significant contingent of American politicians and business leaders viewed this new body with suspicion. Later in the century, President Nixon pushed through the Biological Weapons Convention, but subsequent US administrations have balked at the inspections required for giving this treaty full credibility. During the 1990s, President Clinton's team at the UN strongly supported the creation of the International Criminal Court – an independent tribunal empowered to try individual statesmen and military leaders for particularly heinous crimes such as genocide. But President George W. Bush announced in 2002 that the United States would not be joining the 124 other nations that were full members of the court.

There are plenty of good reasons for this ambivalence. In too many cases, international organizations have failed to live up to the hopes of their creators.[7] The 1907 Hague Convention sought to create a world court whose verdicts would possess binding authority over all its member-states. Andrew Carnegie provided the cash for the court's brand-new building, the imposing Peace Palace at The Hague, which first opened its doors in August 1913. It became one of history's most striking cases of bad timing: the new court had not even gotten a chance to convene when the conflagration of the First World War engulfed Europe.[8]

Wilson's League of Nations, created a few years later, ultimately fared no better: it possessed weak and clumsy instruments for enforcing its decisions, and devolved into a powerless debating society that stood helplessly by while Hitler, Mussolini, and the Japanese launched escalating campaigns of aggression during the 1930s.[9] The United Nations, created in San Francisco in 1945, soon found itself hamstrung by the Cold War rivalry that blocked effective action in the Security Council. The International Court of Justice that was also created in 1945 (not to be confused with the more recent International Criminal Court) required the *consent* of the accused transgressor nation before it could initiate judicial proceedings. ("Dear Saddam Hussein, could you please sign here ... ")[10]

Precisely because the world is in the midst of a transitional phase, both these schools of thought – the nationalists as well as the internationalists – have valid points to make. Nationalists emphasize the self-help arrangements that have worked fairly well in the long past and that still operate potently in the present; internationalists emphasize the planet-level challenges that have been emerging over the past century, requiring innovative cross-border arrangements to address them. To omit either dimension – national or global – is to lose sight of a crucial aspect of our contemporary reality.

FOUR LEVELS OF COOPERATION

The crux of the matter lies in national sovereignty, and the degree to which states are willing to surrender it as they work with other states in pursuit of common goals. As a UN staffer once wryly remarked: "Everyone is for coordination but nobody wants to be coordinated."[11] This will be one of the central questions facing humankind over the coming century: to what extent are we willing to relinquish a degree of our national autonomy, in the name of finding common ground with other peoples in tackling the toughest global challenges? Or, to put it differently: *When is it in our self-interest to play by rules that we have worked out in compromise with other peoples?*

The following examples illustrate four models of international cooperation, arranged along a rising gradient of shared governance: the Organisation for Economic Co-operation and Development (OECD), United Nations (UN), North Atlantic Treaty Organization (NATO), and European Union (EU). All four of these institutions emerged out of the trauma of World War II. They were founded under the banner of lofty ideals – but their real roots lay in pragmatic self-interest. Without exception, these innovations in governance were created because national leaders believed that their populations would fare better in the long run as members of these international clubs rather than onlookers.

The OECD is a bit like Diet Coke: it captures the flavor of shared governance without imposing the caloric burden of binding national commitments. Founded in 1948 as an instrument for allocating funds sent to European nations under the Marshall Plan, its role gradually evolved after the late 1950s into a consultative body that allowed the world's richest democracies to streamline key areas of economic policy.[12] Today it boasts a membership of 38 countries, greasing the wheels of global capitalism by setting common standards for businesses – reducing corruption, combating money laundering and spam on the Internet, coordinating tax policy for cross-border transactions, and providing reliable statistics on key economic indicators. The OECD operates via soft law: it relies on shared norms and peer pressure among its member nations, and when a nation transgresses those norms, the furthest the OECD can go is to add the nation's name to a published blacklist. This naming and shaming does exert a certain leverage – for having the world's 38 richest democracies officially frowning on you will probably result in poor economic outcomes for your country over the long run. But beyond this mild form of moral/economic pressure, the OECD has no means of more tangibly enforcing its will.[13]

The United Nations raises the bar one small step higher. Participating in UN organizations like the World Health Organization means subordinating your own country's practices to a set of common rules established together with all the other member-nations. For example, if your country joins with others in a UN-led enforcement action, this can require you to place some of your military personnel under the control of officers from other nations. But at root, all this remains purely voluntary. If a nation's leaders decide that the costs of such cooperation are not worth the benefits, they can always opt out. In this sense, the UN regularly provides *opportunities* for international cooperation, but the choice of participating remains firmly in the hands of each country.[14] (I'll return to the role played by national sovereignty in the UN in the coming chapters.)

NATO, my third example, goes one significant step further: it is a military alliance in which the 30 member nations have bound themselves to come to each other's aid in the event that any of them is attacked by another country. The pact was created in 1949 to deter Soviet aggression against Western Europe. It did so by placing American soldiers among the defensive units stationed along the eastern borders of Western Europe – making it clear than any Soviet attack would be killing US personnel and triggering a full-scale war with the United States.[15] This was a revolutionary act in the history of American foreign policy, which had always rested on the bedrock principle of avoiding entangling alliances at all costs.[16] President Truman and his Secretary of State George Marshall had become convinced that Soviet hegemony over Western Europe would gravely threaten the security of the United States, and that this danger justified a departure from the long tradition of American standoffishness. The US Senate agreed, ratifying the NATO treaty by a vote of 82 to 13. American national sovereignty was now blurred somewhat, because the nation's leaders had opted for collective security in cooperation with other nations, rather than following the traditional path of "every man for himself."[17] Nevertheless, the sheer dominance of the United States within NATO – both economically and militarily – ensures that this alliance remains firmly within the orbit of American decision-making.

Finally we have the European Union, which has gradually created the highest level of shared governance ever undertaken by independent nations.[18] The process has been slow and halting, extending over more than half a century of incremental steps, punctuated by frequent setbacks and crises, then doggedly plodding forward once again. One historian has likened the building of the EU to the annual procession held in the village of Echternach in Luxembourg, where pilgrims make their way through the streets to the tomb of St. Willibrord, accompanied by brass bands and moving in a swaying rhythm, five steps forward, three steps back, five steps forward, three steps back.[19]

The cumulative progress, nonetheless, has been impressive. The EU today comprises the second-largest economic bloc in the world, nearly equal to the United States in total GDP, and considerably larger than China. More importantly, the daily operation of this union has rendered war unthinkable among the peoples of Western Europe – a territory whose history of bloodshed extended back for centuries before reaching its culminating spasms with World Wars I and II. Youths from these countries now engage in cross-border educational exchanges, then go to work freely in one country or another. They speak each other's languages, learn each other's cultures, use the same currency, and intermarry with growing frequency. Factories and farms in the EU follow environmental rules that are as binding in Greece as they are in Denmark. Manufactured goods and agricultural products flow freely across the rivers and mountain passes, unhindered by tariffs and other restrictions. Labor laws protect the rights of workers with equal rigor in all the member nations; social programs, retirement benefits, and educational standards follow common guidelines. When disagreements arise, the litigants can take their case before a European high court that enforces European laws. Though the EU remains a far from perfect instrument, the plain fact remains: European integration has coincided with 70 years of stability, peace, and unprecedented prosperity – coupled with high levels of freedom and democratic rights.[20]

HOW HUMANS ROSE TO DOMINANCE

All four of these institutions – OECD, UN, NATO, EU – embody the same basic principle: *humans coordinating their efforts, giving away a degree of autonomy in exchange for greater security and prosperity.* Social science research over the past few decades has amply documented this phenomenon: humans have emerged as the preeminent species on planet Earth primarily because of their unique ability to work flexibly together in groups. To be sure, other social species such as bees, ants, or apes have also achieved impressive dominance over their own biological niches; but humans also possessed the ability to deliberately modify their patterns of cooperation over time, adapting swiftly to new needs and opportunities as they arose. This combination – teamwork and flexibility – has allowed the power of humans to grow exponentially, granting them sway over all other creatures.[21]

The trade-off implicit here is always the same: you surrender a bit of the freedom to do whatever you please, and agree to realign your actions in accordance with the will of the larger group (whose aims you have had a partial say in shaping). In exchange, you get the protection of the collectivity, and share in the amplified gains that become possible through concerted action. Everybody wins.

The four institutions I have just described illustrate this trade-off at work, with each level yielding a correspondingly higher dividend of augmented security and power. The OECD exemplifies what might be called *loose concertation*: an agreement to consult with partners on modestly important matters and to abide by certain common ground rules – with little or no penalty for noncompliance. The United Nations embodies *voluntary coordination*: a system of shared institutions through which nations harmonize their efforts on vital common interests – but once again, with only weak penalties for those who opt out. NATO is an exemplar of *binding coordination*: each member of this alliance is pledged to the defense of the others, and noncompliance would result in expulsion from the pact. The European Union embodies what might be termed *partial integration*, with many areas of socioeconomic and civic life operating under a common legal system, and a few key domains such as military and diplomatic affairs left to individual member-states. The final step, of course, would be *full integration*, which does not yet exist for any group of countries. One can easily picture it, though, if one imagines a European Union in which all functional areas including military defense and foreign policy fall under a single legal and political structure, so that it becomes a unitary actor in world politics alongside other Great Powers like the United States or China.

THE GROWING ROLE OF INGOs

The planet, the biosphere, the billions of humans – in the end these concepts are all mere abstractions, vague constructs through which each of us as an individual struggles to grapple with the immensities of the world around us. A great chasm separates us from the global dimension of our daily reality, imperfectly mediated through such instruments as the Internet, Skype, news media, casual tourism, UN conferences, or the Olympic Games. Over the past half century, however, and especially since the end of the Cold War, new bridges across this chasm have begun to take shape. Cross-border relations are no longer the exclusive purview of diplomats representing nation-states, or of large and imposing bodies like the UN or NATO. Instead, people have invented new vehicles for connecting with each other directly and working side-by-side across borders: international nongovernmental organizations (INGOs).

The number of INGOs has grown dramatically in recent years, with current estimates standing at about 40,000 distinct organizations.[22] Some are small, local, and chronically underfunded – a group of clinics in rural West Africa, for example – while others like Greenpeace, Doctors Without Borders, Amnesty International, or Human Rights Watch are globally linked and relatively well heeled. Some are new and experimental in nature, others have been operating for decades and have long histories of ups and downs behind them. Some, like the International Campaign to Ban Landmines, focus on advocacy, seeking to influence the policies of governments; others, like Oxfam, are on-the-ground operational bodies that directly provide services. This smorgasbord of organizations offers individual citizens myriad options for reaching beyond their tiny sphere of daily life and lending a hand in concrete projects throughout the planet. You can write a check, send packages of clothes or educational materials, mail letters on behalf of political prisoners, or volunteer to travel overseas and help heal the sick.[23]

I was in graduate school in 1984 when I encountered the following news item casually mentioned in a magazine article about famine in the horn of Africa: "In the Northwest territories of Canada, two Eskimo villages raised $7,000 for Ethiopian relief."[24] Eskimos coming to the aid of Ethiopians. This is the other side of globalization: a gossamer thread of human solidarity strung across the hemispheres. The 40,000 INGOs operating today, with their millions of members and volunteers, blanket the Earth with countless lines of direct connection like these. Over the years, such encounters have gradually built an important new layer of impactful human activity at the global level – well beyond the abstraction of "international relations."

Improbable friendships and cohorts have emerged, linking countless individuals who would otherwise never have known each other; these in turn have often matured into stable, long-term partnerships devoted to solving thorny practical problems that stumped international bodies like the World Bank or Food and Agriculture Organization. In the process, some of the old schemas of international charity-based giving have been unsettled and even reversed: it's no longer automatically a matter of educated, rich Northerners going to aid illiterate, starving villagers in the rural areas of the global South. The innovative Grameen Bank, for example, founded in Bangladesh to provide micro-loans and banking services to the rural poor there, now operates 20 branches in 13 cities in the United States, helping America's most impoverished citizens create new businesses of their own.[25] The Kenyan environmentalist Wangari Maathai started out as a local forestry activist before founding the influential Green Belt Movement, which has been emulated in dozens of other countries.[26] Many of Maathai's key ideas in later life were derived in turn from the Japanese waste-reduction philosophy of *mottainai*, a Buddhist approach that she learned about during her travels to promote sustainable forestry.[27] In such ways, the myriad cross-border connections have enriched each other via unforeseeable and creative exchanges, even as they proliferated among themselves.

A NEW LAYER OF INTERNATIONAL POWER: DIRECT QUASI-GOVERNMENTAL NETWORKS

Perhaps not surprisingly, the world's kinder, gentler folks have not been the only ones to get creative with cross-border teamwork; plenty of people with nastier intentions have done so as well, creating what might be described as criminal INGOs. Terrorists, human traffickers, drug cartels, money-launderers, tax evaders, child pornographers, smugglers, and cybercriminals have all taken advantage of opportunities for planet-level action.[28] This rapid rise of sophisticated international criminality has in turn elicited increasingly innovative responses by a wide variety of state-level officials, ranging from law enforcement agents to regulatory commissioners, judges, lawyers, and legislators.[29] Tracking down money-launderers for the drug cartels, for example, might require a Drug Enforcement Administration (DEA) agent to reach out and work closely with police officers, tax officials, bank officers, undercover agents, judges, military leaders, and politicians in several foreign lands at the same time. All these officials still get their salaries paid by local or national governments: their primary job description remains anchored to state-level goals. But in the process of doing their daily work, they have discovered that certain kinds of challenges invariably spill over national boundaries, requiring them to make connection with their counterparts in other countries.

At first, such contacts and collaborations might take shape in a casual or ad hoc manner, but over time, as these people have worked together on project after project, they have gradually bound together their agencies and staffs into increasingly stable cross-border partnerships.[30] Their informal partnerships (let's call them *quasi-governmental* networks) operate in the interstices of global politics, below the level of state diplomacy; yet they are also quite distinct from the INGOs because they bring together actual employees of local and national governments. These officials remain answerable to their home governments (and hence indirectly to voters) in ways that the leaders of INGOs are not; and they also carry a different kind of clout than most INGO workers, because they regularly rely on the enforcement powers of national agencies like the FBI, CIA, DEA, or local police.

According to the political theorist Anne-Marie Slaughter, the emergence of these quasi-governmental networks over recent decades adds up to an important new layer of international power.

> Stop imagining the international system as a system of states – unitary entities like billiard balls or black boxes – subject to rules created by international institutions that are apart from, "above" these states. Start thinking about a world of governments, with all the different institutions that perform the basic functions of governments – legislation, adjudication, implementation – interacting both with each other domestically and also with their foreign and supranational counterparts. States still exist in this world; indeed, they are crucial actors. But they are "disaggregated." They relate to each other not only through the Foreign Office but also through regulatory, judicial, and legislative channels.[31]

Slaughter shows how the day-to-day impact of these quasi-governmental networks extends well beyond "policing" functions, into such domains as environmental regulation, public health, human rights, and international commerce. Such informal cross-border partnerships allow national officials not only to share information with each other, but also to assist each other with training and expertise; to harmonize national policies so that they enhance each other's effectiveness instead of working at cross-purposes; to shape legislation in ways that work smoothly across borders; and to collaborate in major enforcement operations.[32] The great advantage of these loose networks is that – unlike the ponderous apparatus of nation-states working through treaties and diplomacy – they can respond quickly and effectively to the rapidly shifting challenges of the contemporary world. They are nimble, adaptable, and decentralized, while still being tied to the central authority of the nations they serve. Taken as a whole, they have gradually come to constitute an important new tier in the layer-cake of global governance.

RESPONSIBILITY TO PROTECT

One indirect effect of all this pullulating cross-border activity has been an ethical and legal reframing of the idea of sovereignty itself. In the vicious civil wars that ravaged Rwanda and the former Yugoslavia during the 1990s, the blue-helmeted soldiers of the UN were prohibited by international law from blocking the massacres that unfolded right before their eyes. The ironclad principle of national sovereignty meant that no outsiders could legally interfere with events unfolding within the borders of another country. In the aftermath of these horrors, the UN Secretary-General Kofi Annan tasked an international commission of jurists to find ways to address this glaring problem.[33]

Their report, issued in 2001, asserted a new principle of international law: the Responsibility to Protect (R2P, in the UN's acronym-rich lingo). When genocides or massive violations of human rights were occurring, the primary responsibility for putting a swift end to the butchery would continue to reside with the local nation-state. But whenever a national government proved unwilling or unable to quell the violence (or when that government itself was the perpetrator of the butchery), the international community had not only a right, but an actual *duty*, to intervene forcefully. This new doctrine was formally adopted by the world's nations at the 2005 UN summit meeting: the sovereignty of the nation-state, which had until this point been sacrosanct, had now been rendered conditional rather than absolute.[34] In the eyes of the British historian Martin Gilbert, it amounted to "the most significant adjustment to sovereignty in 360 years."[35] Henceforth, if a vicious national leader like Yugoslavia's Slobodan Milošević or Rwanda's Juvénal Habyarimana launched genocidal policies, their government would forfeit the right to do whatever it pleased within its territory; and other nations had a positive responsibility to send in whatever troops were needed to halt the bloodshed. In the new world of R2P, the international community would no longer accept the role of passive spectator to genocide; there would be no more gut-wrenching images of blue-helmeted soldiers standing by in helpless anguish while a slaughter of civilians took place a few streets away.

To be sure, this R2P mandate was limited in scope: it could not be used to force regime change in the target country, but only to stop the ongoing carnage. This issue came to a head in 2011, when the Libyan dictator

Muammar Gaddafi started massacring his opponents, and his army advanced with murderous intent on the rebel stronghold of Benghazi. The UN swiftly invoked the R2P doctrine and dispatched NATO airstrikes against Gaddafi's forces; but the fierce NATO intervention wreaked such havoc among Gaddafi's tanks and troops that the rebels were able to advance from Benghazi, capturing and killing Gaddafi shortly afterwards. This outcome clearly exceeded the R2P mandate and prompted protests at the UN by Russia and China. Nevertheless, the R2P principle still stands today as a new factor of international law – one of the first cracks in the armor of absolute national sovereignty.

* * *

15

How to Escape the Sovereignty Trap: Lessons and Limitations of the European Union Model

BENEFITS OF NATIONHOOD

There was a time, not all that long ago, when the nation-state did not yet enjoy full legitimacy in the eyes of the people living in its territory. The consolidation of nation-states as political, economic, and cultural units unfolded over many centuries: people had to learn to think in new ways about who their enemies were, and where their flag allegiances lay. This process only seems natural and inevitable in retrospect, as citizens of each nation look back on what they now take to be their obvious common heritage, language, and ancestry.[1] In actual fact, the process was messy, confused, and conflictual, as various peoples groped their way forward into something that eventually came to be called distinct nationhood. It was also impressively violent and cruel in many cases, as large groups swallowed their weaker neighbors and forced them to accept integration into the new polity.[2]

National sovereignty offered many important benefits. Precisely because it asserted the absolute right of populations to run their own internal affairs, sovereignty prevented the sorts of endless cross-border raids, massacres, and counter-massacres that had ravaged Europe before the Peace of Westphalia in 1648. As the modern state-system emerged, it stabilized the territorial spaces of the world, and outbursts of violence among local groups and factions dramatically declined.[3] These stabilized spaces were also much larger than the counties, city-states, bishoprics, and duchies they replaced, so they allowed people to harness more efficient and impactful economic forces, marshalling their collective resources in impressive new ways. Entire new professions and economic opportunities emerged. Disputes among the citizens of these states could now be adjudicated not by force of arms but by courts operating under a system of common laws, backed up by the reliable enforcement capabilities of a central government. The military leverage conferred by these expanded territorial units not only deterred outsiders from invading and pillaging the local cities and farms, but also made possible the projection of power into uncharted regions in other parts of the world. And last but not least, the nation-state eventually came to offer its members a deep sense of shared cultural belonging.

The historian Benedict Anderson argues that any human community on the scale of a modern nation is perforce an *imagined community*. Every nation comes into being as a construct of the mind, a creation of convention and artifice, an emerging pattern of shared belonging, practice, and law. In this sense, the feeling of being "an American" or "a Brazilian" may exert tremendous psychological and moral force, but it has to be recognized for what it is: a learned cultural habit that displaced older cultural habits of attachment to village, clan, county, bishop, or chieftain. National identity was not one of nature's givens, like the law of gravity or the succession of day and night: it was a cultural creation, a distinctive new layer of shared allegiances particular to its own epoch.[4]

This historical fact has important implications for the coming century of global governance. There is no reason why nation-states have to provide the ultimate stage of human political identity for the next thousand years. Cultures evolve, economies shift, technologies emerge, migrations and intermarriages blur the lines – and as these processes unfold, people are brought together in new patterns. Trying to hold them in place is like trying with your bare hands to hold back the incoming tide.

Let us imagine for a moment what such a future world might look like – gradually edging beyond the unitary nation-state. The UN, in this scenario, has by this point established a proven track record of successful conflict resolution, including a variety of interventions ranging from warnings and sanctions to direct military action. Most nations still possess standing armies of their own, but these have come to play increasingly sporadic roles, since most of the policing of international affairs is now being conducted by coalitions of blue-helmeted soldiers flying the UN flag. Some countries have opted to go the route of Costa Rica, which enjoys a much higher standard of living than its neighbors, partly through the savings it reaps by having no national army at all.[5] As a political institution, the UN has remained faithful to the principle of subsidiarity – minimizing its interference in the regional and local self-government of peoples, and only intervening when global peace and security come under direct threat. Although it remains a two-tiered structure, reflecting the lingering disparities among Great Powers and lesser powers, it has evolved into a relatively responsive institution in which the lesser powers can often have a say in shaping important global policies and decisions.

If all this were to happen – and it's of course a very big if – then there will perhaps come a time when most of the world's citizens no longer view the UN in the way they do today: as a somewhat strange, abstract, and weak layer of activity hovering above the national level where the real power lies.[6] Over the coming century, in this scenario, the UN gradually comes to take on new authority in the eyes of many people, for it is now regularly doing things that directly affect them in their daily lives: streamlining global commerce, safeguarding the environment, nipping epidemics in the bud, protecting the rights of women, neutralizing terrorist networks, shielding religious and ethnic minorities from abuse. While many of these functions are still being implemented via national and local governments, it's the UN that now plays the coordinating role, setting broad goals and ensuring that all peoples do their share in furthering those goals. When serious conflicts arise between nations (or groups of nations), the UN offers arbitration through its own specialized court, which is staffed by jurists from all over the world. The benefits of submitting to arbitration under international law are now widely perceived as outweighing the short-term gains of unilateral action – for every nation, large and small, participates so intensively in the dense global web of commerce and interdependence that the cost of defecting from that system would be prohibitively high.

What I am describing here, of course, is the same *E Pluribus Unum* process ("many into one") that gradually built the nation-state. It mirrors, on a global scale, the trade-off that took place within a given slice of territory when various regional communities and groups transferred allegiance to the Leviathan of the new central government. The psychologist Steven Pinker cites this trade-off as the principal factor behind the striking decline of violence that has characterized the past few centuries:

> A state that uses a monopoly on force to protect its citizens from one another may be the most consistent violence-reducer that we have encountered ... When bands, tribes, and chiefdoms came under the control of the first states, the suppression of raiding and feuding reduced their rates of violent death fivefold. And when the fiefs of Europe coalesced into kingdoms and sovereign states, the consolidation of law enforcement eventually brought down the homicide rate another *thirtyfold.*[7]

To be sure, this drastic reduction in daily, face-to-face violence was replaced by large-scale wars that happened less frequently but still resulted in major carnage. What's worse, they also carried the escalation of weaponry to the threshold of apocalypse. My argument here is that a final planetary consolidation may be underway over the coming century or two, as nations gradually cede the function of enforcing the peace to a higher Leviathan above them all – a Leviathan constituted through their citizens' own voluntary choice.

This is a terribly scary prospect to some people. "We'd be controlled by other people whom we don't know or trust," they exclaim. "We'd lose our autonomy. We'd be forced to share our wealth and resources with strangers who mean nothing to us."

If we look at the history of nation-states, these were precisely the sorts of laments that were stridently raised by members of small communities, clans, or fiefdoms when it came to the new national center of power.[8] Yet in time, these fears gradually dissipated. The broader territorial space brought new flows of commerce and new opportunities for social and cultural interaction – all under the umbrella of a state that kept the domestic peace. Those unknown outsiders who had once been viewed as threatening came to be interwoven into a new, broader "Us." What had once been frighteningly alien eventually became familiar.

Today, in a nation like the United States, it's hard to imagine a situation in which the people who live in Oregon, Kansas, and Florida were to regard each other as mutually foreign competitors – strangers to be treated with deep distrust. We have gotten beyond that stage, and those far-removed individuals, most of whom will never know each other personally, have become part of a viscerally felt "Us." (Political polarization of Left and Right cuts across these territorial boundaries, despite the mythology of "red states" and "blue states." All 50 states are actually colored in various tints of purple.)[9] This feeling of common belonging is particularly striking when one considers the sheer scale of a country like the United States, and the deeply diverse types of people – urban and rural, rich and poor, white and black and brown, with ancestors hailing from cultures around the globe – who nonetheless consider themselves fellow citizens of a shared homeland. Is it really so hard to envision a situation (a century or two hence) when the gradual integration of global cultures will lead us to feel similar forms of direct kinship with people on other continents? Certainly this seems like one plausible trajectory toward which the history of the past centuries is pointing.[10]

BEYOND HEGEMONY: TWO CASES OF PRAGMATIC PARTNERSHIP ON THE SHARED WORLD STAGE

The rise of China as an economic and military superpower in recent decades has brought a major new player into the game of world politics, potentially upsetting the international status quo. Throughout history, the arrival of such newcomers has often been accompanied by war – whether because the newcomer used war to assert its presence, or because the balance among existing powers was thrown off kilter by the newcomer's arrival, and a major conflict resulted.[11] These upheavals might be described as "wars of adjustment" or "wars of rebalancing" – though this bland terminology obscures the fact that such conflicts have often been devastating, protracted, blood-drenched affairs. In a nuclear-armed world, with the advent of China as a brash new Great Power, how might such a war be averted?

Two historical examples offer encouraging possibilities for the political leaders and diplomats of the twenty-first century to emulate: the way the rise of Germany was accommodated within the map of Europe, and the way the rise of the European Union was accommodated within global affairs. The German case is particularly instructive, because it took several "tries" to get it to work, but eventually resulted in remarkable success.

One of the longstanding goals of French foreign policy after the Middle Ages was to keep the German states and principalities to the north squabbling and competing among themselves. As long as Prussians were bickering with Bavarians and Hessians, these militarily formidable neighbors would pose no big threat to France. But all this changed dramatically in the 1860s, when Otto von Bismarck became chief minister of Prussia. Within the space of eight years, Bismarck engineered a series of short intra-German wars that consolidated Prussia's dominance, and in 1870 he fomented a larger war with France. The Germans trounced the French, lopped off two of their northeastern provinces (Alsace and Lorraine), and in 1871 announced the creation of a new unitary state, Imperial Germany, in the Hall of Mirrors at Versailles.[12]

Over the next four decades the French seethed with rage, vowing revenge – but they couldn't do much on their own because Germany swiftly became the leading land power in Europe, surpassing Great Britain as an industrial nation around 1900. When World War I came, the French were finally able to achieve their goal by working in partnership with the British, Russians, and Americans: after the German surrender in 1918 they grabbed back their "lost provinces" of Alsace and Lorraine, and tried to persuade their wartime allies to break up the German nation into a smattering of smaller states. The British and Americans scoffed at this unworkable proposal, and instead argued that German power would henceforth be "contained" within the international vessel of the League of Nations.[13]

It didn't work. Now it was the Germans who raged and hungered for revenge, and Adolf Hitler adroitly used these sentiments to help propel his Nazi party to absolute power in 1933. The French spent huge sums on building the Maginot Line during the 1930s, hoping that a network of massive fortifications along their northern border would keep their formidable neighbor at bay. That didn't work either: in 1940 the Germans plunged into France, forcing French capitulation and a precipitous British retreat across the Channel. Once again, it took a formidable team of major nations working together over four years of bloody fighting to crush Germany's remarkable military power.[14]

This time around, however, the trauma had cut so deeply that it opened up radical new possibilities. West Germany was now a pariah nation and much of its territory lay in ruins; France had endured the existential dread of total helplessness under enemy occupation; and the specter of the victorious Red Army loomed just over the horizon. The citizens of both countries were ripe for transformative change, and fortunately, visionary leaders emerged on both sides of the Rhine, eager to deliver that change. French leaders came to grips with the fact that West Germany's immense economic and military power could not be wished away, so they said to themselves, in effect: "We will seize this opportunity to embed German power within a broader network of shared relationships: a supranational web of institutions and ongoing transactions that are based on close partnership rather than rivalry." This bold idea worked well because it also offered an appealing pathway for the West Germans: they would be allowed to resume a "normal" role in European affairs, growing strong again and playing a lead role on the continent. The United States eagerly supported this nascent Franco-German partnership, moreover, because it would make the Russians think twice about asserting their superpower status to bully the West Europeans.[15]

It was a classic win–win strategy, and it continued to bear fruit, decade after decade, because all the major players saw it as clearly serving their long-term interests. The multilateral relationship that emerged was so robust by the early 1990s that it even provided a framework for the peaceful reunification of East and West Germany after the collapse of the Soviet empire.[16] Germany today is unquestionably the most powerful nation on the continent – its economy is number 4 in the world, 2.5 times greater than Russia's and half again as large as France's – but German leaders follow a restrained foreign policy and play by rules that are negotiated collectively with the other key partners in the EU. German power, in other words, has been turned into an engine of prosperity and stability for its neighbors in Western Europe – *an asset rather than a threat.*[17]

In this ingenious system, the relentless struggle for national hegemony has been set aside. To be sure, leading nations like France and Germany continue to be disproportionately powerful in European affairs (compared to Czechia, Holland, or Belgium), but their preponderant power is now embedded within a system that compensates them with many advantages for accepting to have their freedom of action somewhat constrained. Europe's largest nations reap major rewards – stability, peace, security – for playing by collective rules that everyone has helped to shape over time, and that everyone is following.

A second "newcomer story" along these lines is the rise of the EU itself – for things could have gone very differently as this unique player on the world stage gradually consolidated its power. Today, even after the setback of Brexit, the EU economy remains larger than China's. What if the Europeans had leveraged this economic might to build a "Third Superpower" during the Cold War years – equipped with its own potent military and itching for independent action alongside the Americans and Russians? This may seem like a far-fetched idea, but it was vigorously espoused by right-wing thinkers and politicians in nearly every member country (and it still resonates broadly in some European conservative circles today).[18] In France, such persons referred to themselves as "Euro-Gaullists" – by which they meant that Europe should assert its power far more boldly than in the recent past, cutting itself loose from American leadership and charting its own course.[19] Many such thinkers openly sang the praises of the colonial era, in which Europeans had taken forceful control over swaths of the global South. They spoke of a "natural" European hegemony over Africa – a renewed and modernized form of paternalism in which the Europeans would provide scientific and technological expertise, while the Africans would provide raw materials, manpower, and expanded markets for European manufactured goods. Armed with nukes of its own, this vigorous new Europe could "matter" once again, returning to the dominant role in world affairs that it had enjoyed in the nineteenth century.[20]

Fortunately, this aggressive vision remained a far-right fantasy. The majority of European citizens were quite content with the bland prosperity and security of their continental union – and had no taste for projecting military power into other parts of the world. To be sure, they chafed and grumbled under the military and diplomatic leadership of the Americans, but most of them never seriously considered opting out of NATO or the transatlantic partnership. (Even Charles de Gaulle, a chafer if ever there was one, made sure to keep the fundamentals of transatlantic comity firmly in place.)[21]

American leaders, for their part, recognized the vital importance of keeping Western Europe strong, independent, democratic – and firmly aligned with the United States. They acknowledged that as Europe recovered from the war, its industrial firms would begin competing fiercely with their

American counterparts – Airbus sapping away some of Boeing's aircraft sales, for example – but they regarded this as an encouraging sign of a vibrant transatlantic market economy at work. When businessmen on one side or the other voiced grievances about the practices on the far shores, these disputes were regularly submitted for arbitration to the World Trade Organization, and both sides continued to play by the agreed rules. At the diplomatic level, too, there were plenty of occasions when European and American policies diverged, but the two sides nearly always took pains to smooth over their differences and to avoid open confrontation whenever possible.[22]

It's important to realize that transatlantic relations could have gone very differently after 1945, with the United States withdrawing once again into aloof isolationism. But the Cold War, and the fear of Russia among American and European leaders, helped to motivate this strong and enduring partnership. And while the United States did play the lead role, its statespersons and diplomats also had to learn how to listen to what the Europeans wanted at various key moments, modifying American policies to fit European interests and keep the Europeans fully committed to the ongoing relationship. Compromise and negotiation have helped the two players on either side of the Atlantic to work together rather than at cross-purposes, even after the Russian threat receded somewhat in the 1990s.[23]

Here lies a second historical example, then, of an international Great Power system that moves beyond the temptation of one-sided hegemony. The postwar rise of the EU in world affairs was accommodated via a network of institutions – Marshall Plan, NATO, UN, WHO, the International Monetary Fund (IMF) – that brokered compromises and collective rules for the key players to follow. This arrangement has held firm over the ups and downs of seven decades, bringing stability, peace, and security across the Atlantic. Though it suffered serious blows during the presidency of Donald Trump, it still endures today.

A TRULY RADICAL EXPERIMENT

One of the father-figures of the European Union was the French businessman Jean Monnet. Born in 1888 in the village of Cognac, into a prosperous family of brandy merchants, Monnet's international travels for the family business convinced him early on that the best hope for peace and prosperity in Europe lay in creating a continent-spanning federation explicitly modeled on the United States.[24] Many other European thinkers and leaders eventually came to share this view, and in the years after 1945 they posed a bold series of questions to their fellow citizens: Does the historical consolidation into ever larger political units necessarily have to stop with the nation-state, or can it be pushed even further, into the supranational level? Does it have to "just happen" on its own, or can it be deliberately fostered and encouraged by the people who are experiencing it? Can the integration of Western Europe be pushed along and sped up?

What set Monnet apart, however, was his vision of how to make this dream a reality. Most European federalist thinkers in the late 1940s proposed creating a new political union of European states, but Monnet thought this approach was like putting the cart before the horse.[25] People were still too attached to their nationalist modes of thinking. How appealing would it be, five years after World War II, for an Italian communist auto worker to be governed from Strasbourg, France, by a conservative German Minister of the Interior?

In Monnet's view, political and military union could only come about as the end-result of a decades-long process of small, incremental changes.[26] The place to start was with modest forms of integration in the economic sphere, giving people a chance to get used to working together across national boundaries. With time, as they focused on technical cooperation aimed at concrete goals, they would experience the tangible benefits that cross-border teamwork would yield. These joint economic projects would provide the basic foundation, but they would also need to be complemented by concurrent efforts in the social, cultural, and legal spheres. Only after several generations had grown up working side-by-side, residing in each other's countries, studying in each other's universities, using a common currency, intermarrying across borders, learning each other's languages, literatures, and regional traditions, voting for European political representatives, obeying European laws, arguing about how to solve European-level problems – only then could the United States of Europe become a plausible goal.[27]

Monnet's idea worked. The endeavor began in 1951 with the creation of the European Coal and Steel Community (ECSC), which placed the coal and steel industries of France, Germany, Italy, and the Benelux countries under a single supranational authority. Here began the halting, frustrating, inspiring process – five steps forward, three steps back – that gradually built the intricate institutional structure of today's European Union. Monnet died in 1979, having lived long enough to see his idea start bearing fruit: though the United States of Europe still lay far over the horizon, the number of member-states had by that point grown to nine (adding Denmark, the United Kingdom, and Ireland); a single currency was being actively prepared; economic and legal integration proceeded apace;

agricultural, environmental, and educational systems were moving into alignment with each other across borders; and although periodic disagreements and tensions continued to rankle, armed conflict among the community's nations was by that point about as likely as a war between the United States and Canada.[28]

A key factor in this process was the principle of subsidiarity, which eventually emerged as one of the philosophical pillars of the EU.[29] The idea was simple: decisions should be made and implemented at the lowest, most local level possible, by the people most directly concerned. How to run a neighborhood school, in other words, should be decided by the school's personnel and the students' parents, and not by bureaucrats in a far-off capital. Consider for example the regulation of wetlands in the lush *marais poitevin* of western France.[30] This natural habitat is affected by laws emanating from no fewer than six layers of political organization: town, county (*département* in French), regional government, nation, EU, and United Nations. Each level in this administrative layer-cake has its own rules, which the park rangers have to take into account as they oversee the place. But as long as they respect those broad policy guidelines, the most important decisions about how to manage the wetlands and protect them over time is left up to them. In the federal structure of the United States, this principle is echoed in the concept of states' rights, which affects such issues as school curricula, the death penalty, gun control, and the legalization of marijuana.[31]

In the eyes of the European federalists, subsidiarity played a key role for two kinds of reasons: it was intrinsically valuable as an ethical principle, and it was also pragmatically essential to the success of the European project. Over time, they realized, the European peoples might perhaps be willing to engage in new forms of teamwork across national borders, if they saw the benefits that such teamwork brought. But they would resist this process tooth-and-nail if they perceived it as a threat to local identity and cherished customs and practices. Continent-spanning allegiances had to be perceived as a *complement* to existing local, regional, and national identities – not as a replacement for them.[32] This is why the creators of the EU have continually sought to reinforce the power of local decision-making bodies, encouraging the teaching of linguistic dialects in schools, while fostering regional cultural traditions and festivals.[33] A "Europe of regions" is more than just a slogan: it offers a guarantee to the populations of localities such as Lombardy, Brittany, or Bavaria that building this supranational entity will not result in the erasure of important local and national traditions.

To be sure, the EU has not been without its critics – as the Brexit vote of 2016 made abundantly clear.[34] Among the chief complaints against this supranational organization, the following four stand out. When European citizens cast their ballots regarding EU matters, they are only voting for the representatives who will serve at the European Parliament in Strasbourg, not for the executive officers who will actually call the shots at the EU headquarters in Brussels. This has come to be known as the "democratic deficit" of the organization – a lack of accountability that has allowed a large and increasingly powerful bureaucracy to build up over the decades, staffed by people who are appointed by national governments but never directly answerable to voters.[35]

Second, the common currency of the euro has created serious problems for those member nations like Greece, Spain, or Italy whose economies are weaker and more debt-ridden than those of, say, Germany or Denmark. Monetary and fiscal policies that work well for an economy like Germany's do not necessarily fit the bill for Greece – and this has led to financial turmoil, job losses, and political tensions within the Eurozone.[36]

Third, the EU has made great strides toward full integration in matters of economic and social policy, but it does not have a single foreign policy or a common military. Some of the prosperity enjoyed by European nations can be attributed to the fact that they spend far less per capita on defense than the United States does, and tacitly rely on the US security umbrella – a fact that increasingly rankles among American conservatives. When it comes to foreign policy, EU nations have adopted sharply divergent approaches in handling such crises as the OPEC oil embargo of the 1970s, the Yugoslavian civil war in the 1990s, or the Iraq war of 2003. As the US Secretary of State Henry Kissinger is reputed to have once asked, "When I want to phone Europe, whom do I call?"[37]

A fourth criticism is that the EU has simply grown too large, too fast – prematurely admitting to membership a variety of countries that fit poorly with the economic system and political culture of the six core nations that launched the integration project in the early 1950s.[38] Poland and Hungary, for example, have been veering away from democratic government in recent years, and their populist, xenophobic, and authoritarian policies cause headaches for the other European leaders. This unwelcome and intractable form of "diversity" within the union may someday reach a breaking point.

All these problems stem from the fact that the EU is very much a work in progress. Many of the bureaucratic and legal mechanisms by which it functions have never been used before, and a certain amount of trial and error is required before they can work smoothly. In this sense, the history of the EU is a story of innovation, tinkering, partial failures, and going back to the drawing board. On the other hand, the very fact that the EU has proved amenable to deep structural reforms, again and again over the past seven decades, suggests that this institution may possess the internal flexibility and resilience required to endure over the long haul.[39]

LIMITATIONS OF THE EUROPEAN MODEL AT THE GLOBAL LEVEL

Some proponents of world federalism have held up the EU as a model that could perhaps be emulated in setting up a better system of planet-level governance. But while the EU experience offers many valuable lessons, it's unlikely that the "European template" would fit smoothly at the global level. Here are some key reasons why.

1. Scale and Scope of Diversity

The economic, cultural, and political differences among the world's nations are much greater than they are within Europe.[40] At the global level, one sees political institutions that include parliamentary democracy, strongman dictatorship, one-party oligarchy, and many hybrids in between. Some economies are based on relatively free markets while others are heavily regulated and centralized in nature; some are avid producers of sophisticated industrial goods while others are predominantly agricultural systems operating with methods that haven't changed much in centuries. Though most of the great religions do share certain basic moral precepts, they comprise a wide range of mutually incompatible beliefs ranging from nontheistic Buddhism to polytheistic Hinduism to monotheisms like Christianity, Islam, and Judaism. Some cultures, like those in the Middle East, harbor deeply conservative values that clash with many aspects of cosmopolitan modernity; others have flung themselves into modernity with zest and enthusiasm. These deep differences among the world's peoples present a dauntingly complex set of challenges to anyone seeking to build greater cooperation among them.

2. Haves and Have-nots

The world's 42 richest persons hold the same amount of wealth today as the world's 3.7 billion least wealthy persons; the richest three Americans hold the same wealth as the bottom half of the country's population.[41] This kind of radical (and growing) inequality, which also divides the planet's hemispheres into a relatively prosperous North and a relatively poor South, poses a major obstacle to global cooperation. In a region where clean water is a luxury, where women are oppressed and children starve, where malaria and dysentery are daily scourges, the threat of mega-dangerous technologies will hardly seem like an urgent priority. To the billions who struggle under such conditions, the real concern is simply making it through alive into next week.

When representatives of these countries come to the United Nations and other forums of global governance, they understandably put their main emphasis on procuring basic food, shelter, hygiene, and education for their people. Those have-not nations, which comprise half of humankind, cannot reasonably be expected to get on board with the global regulation of mega-dangerous technologies until their more pressing needs have been met. Indeed, a strong moral argument can be made that the plight of those regions – where immense suffering and millions of preventable deaths are a present-day reality – should constitute the single highest priority of humankind.[42] The suffering caused by poverty is terrible right now.

3. The Ugly Side of Globalization

Suppose I own a California-based shoe factory that has been making footwear in Sacramento for the past hundred years. It's a family owned business that has grown rapidly in recent decades and now employs 200 people locally. One day I learn that I can save 60 percent on labor costs by shifting my main factory operations overseas to Southeast Asia. Even though I have to pay for transporting the shoes back across the ocean for sale in the US market, the net savings are still huge. I face stiff competition from domestic and foreign shoe manufacturers who produce their shoes for much less than I do: they have been increasingly undercutting my sales over recent years. I am also having to deal with the hassle and expense of complying with California's myriad environmental and labor laws, which add to my operating costs and force me to raise the price of my product. In Southeast Asia my new factory would face far fewer restrictions: I can run my business pretty much as I please. Reluctantly, I make my announcement: we are laying off 140 employees next year and shifting our operations overseas. I feel bad about doing this to my employees, some of whose families have been working for my family for three generations. But the hard logic of the situation leaves me no choice: I have to do this or face the probable failure of my company a few years down the line.

This is the ugly face of globalization.[43] It is based on a conception of capitalism that focuses primarily on efficiency and net profits. At one level, it's true that my globalized company will make shoes more efficiently than it currently does, and will be able to offer a high-quality product to American consumers at a lower price. But the hidden costs of this system are steep: unemployment and upheaval in the lives of the workers at home; people overseas who work long hours under tough factory conditions for one-tenth the wage of American workers, with no pension plans or trade unions to protect their interests; environmental harms off-loaded onto a far-off part of the world where few regulations exist.

In England during the time of Charles Dickens, the factory system exploited workers in a similar fashion; but over time those English workers organized themselves with trade unions and a Labour Party, launching waves of strikes and agitation that resulted in gradual reform of the entire manufacturing system. Today's global capitalism operates a similarly Dickensian system of harsh exploitation, but its effects are harder to discern because they are displaced onto distant sites where consumers don't have to witness at first hand the ravaging costs that this system is imposing on human beings at home and abroad. When I buy a pair of shoes at a Walmart in Illinois, I don't see the unemployed shoe workers of Sacramento, the dirt-poor sweatshop employees in Southeast Asia who can barely feed their families, the toxic pollution being dumped into rivers of a far-off land. I just see a shiny pair of shoes available for a low price.

We ignore this ugliness at our peril. The global economic system can perhaps continue functioning in this lopsided, slash-and-burn fashion for a few more decades' time, but in the long run it constitutes an unsustainable way to make and sell things. People at home and abroad will probably rebel against being treated this way: they will organize themselves, just as the English workers in the nineteenth century did, and demand a more decent arrangement. Just as national laws were gradually passed in Britain to protect the working classes from the most rapacious excesses of capitalism, so the working classes of the rich and poor countries will need to get organized over the coming decades and demand regulations that protect them at the global level.[44]

Unfortunately, some workers' organizations have adopted a misguided approach to dealing with this challenge: they react today as they did during the Great Depression, calling for tariff barriers and seeking to seal themselves off from the unregulated capitalism that prevails in other parts of the world.[45] Most economic historians agree that those kinds of autarkic moves in the 1930s made things even worse, rendering the Depression longer and

more damaging than it would have been. The reflex of defensive retrench-
ment behind national walls is an understandable one, perhaps, but in the
modern global economy with its cross-border flows of people, capital, and
goods, it has been shown again and again to be self-defeating.[46]

Globalization is not something we can hide from or avoid: the best
strategy is to move forward with it while actively regulating its development,
with all the international participants working together to restrain its excesses
and mitigate its imbalances. Humankind has already built significant infrastructure for precisely this purpose – powerful institutions like the IMF, World
Trade Organization, World Bank, and United Nations Economic and Social
Council. In some respects, however, these institutions have perpetuated or
even exacerbated the harsh inequalities that plague the world's economies:
the World Bank, for example, required for many years that recipient nations
cleave to austerity measures and fiscal discipline that took a heavy toll among
the local populations, applying rigid neoliberal economic principles whose
full enactment would never have been tolerated if they had been imposed on
the donor nations themselves.[47] The challenge over the coming decades will
be to further ramp up and refine this global regulatory infrastructure, building instruments of international economic governance that allow humankind
to reap the benefits of globalization while avoiding its ugliest excesses.[48]

4. Global Instruments of Cultural Integration Remain Relatively Weak

Just as Jean Monnet predicted, economic cooperation provided a good
starting point for the European integration movement – but it was not in
itself sufficient. The process only moved toward full fruition after it had
spilled over from the economic sphere into the social and cultural domains.
In France and Germany, for example, two visionary leaders, Charles de
Gaulle and Konrad Adenauer, signed a formal accord in 1963 (the Elysée
Treaty) that sought to completely reinvent the relationship between their
two peoples. They established regular consultation with each other at the
highest levels of government, and set up a lavishly funded program to
sponsor face-to-face encounters between French and German citizens.
Over the decades that followed, youth groups spent months at a time visiting
similar groups across the border; hundreds of twin-town relationships fostered contacts among municipal and business leaders; church groups and
civic organizations began working together across the Rhine; trade unions
adopted convergent policies for regulating labor conditions. The result,
a half-century later, was breathtaking: these two bitter enemies had gradually transformed themselves into close partners.[49]

At the global level, one of the instruments designed to push forward this kind of cross-border cultural integration is UNESCO (the United Nations Educational, Scientific, and Cultural Organization). Some people enjoy poking fun at UNESCO: they dismiss its goals as overly idealistic; they complain about particular projects or declarations that the organization has made. Japan, for example, suspended funding in 2016, after UNESCO included documents related to the 1937 Rape of Nanking in its "Memory of the World" program. The United States has twice broken off relations with UNESCO, citing alleged bias against Israel in its programs. (Since the 1970s, a majority of the UN's 193 member states have consistently sided against the United States and Israel over the fraught Palestinian question).[50]

But if we look more closely at UNESCO's achievements over the years, their range and depth are actually remarkable.[51] The organization launched programs for basic education in dozens of countries, markedly increasing literacy rates, especially for women. It mounted a vigorous campaign against racist ideas and practices over many decades, undermining the legitimacy of racist regimes like the one in South Africa (which angrily withdrew from membership in 1956). Throughout the world, it intervened directly to protect dozens of cultural sites from degradation or destruction – the most famous of which was the relocation of Egypt's Abu Simbel temple to keep it from being swamped by the Nile after the construction of the Aswan dam. The organization strongly supported the dissemination of environmentalist ideas through such high-profile efforts as the Man and the Biosphere Program.

UNESCO's annual budget for 2020 was a paltry $535 million – about the same as the cost of making two or three Hollywood blockbuster movies. The United States withdrew its funding for the organization in 2011, after Palestine was admitted as a member. But if we want to get serious about building bridges of cultural understanding across the continents, then organizations like UNESCO will need to receive much more serious financial and political support over the coming decades. Precisely because the cultural chasms separating the world's peoples at the global level are deeper and wider than those within Europe, such a long-term effort would offer a badly needed complement to the economic and technological processes of globalization that are already underway.

5. Migration and Xenophobia

A wave of nationalist fervor has swept through many countries in the past decade, bringing new prominence to hardline politicians like Donald

Trump in the United States, Jair Bolsonaro in Brazil, Narendra Modi in India, Recep Erdoğan in Turkey, Marine Le Pen in France, Viktor Orbán in Hungary, Matteo Salvini in Italy, Sebastian Kurz in Austria, and the Brexit advocates in Britain. One thing that all these politicians have in common is their success in tapping voter anxieties about foreigners, foreign powers, and foreign influence. The particulars of the story vary significantly from one country to another – from fear of Mexican laborers or Islamic terrorists in the United States, to anxieties about African migrants in Italy, to resentment of East European immigrants in Britain. All these politicians have proved deft at stoking fears of an external "Other" who is going to swamp the native-born people demographically, take away jobs, import foreign cultural practices, and bring unwanted forms of economic and social transformation.[52]

This nationalist fervor often rests on racist prejudice or nativist xenophobia, and it has been exacerbated by recent waves of migrants seeking to escape the failed states and wretched poverty of their home regions in the Middle East, Africa, or Latin America. Global warming will further increase the number of such desperate migrants from tropical regions seeking survival for their families in prosperous countries of the temperate zones. Under these circumstances, opening up the borders would yield mass migration on a scale that even the richest nations would find hard to manage. Migration can be a tremendous boon to both the migrants themselves and to the country that receives them, as long as it is conducted in an orderly fashion, with proper institutional supports to help the newcomers adapt and flourish in their new home. But chaotic and unregulated mass migration is in no one's interest.

The proper solution lies – once again – at the planet level: the best way to control migration is to remove the incentive for vast numbers of desperate people to leave their homelands in the first place. Alongside efforts to mitigate climate change, the rich countries will need to massively ramp up their aid programs to assist the poor nations with economic development and genuine democratization over the coming years, for this will be the most effective long-term solution to the challenge of mass migration. As long as prosperous democracies coexist on the planet alongside dirt-poor and strife-ridden autocracies, this problem will not subside.[53]

For all these reasons, then, the "EU model" cannot be straightforwardly scaled up to the global level. Although some of its institutional innovations suggest promising possibilities upon which to build, it would be a mistake to think that its structures and rules could provide a direct template for an expanded UN. Effective planetary governance will almost certainly require different frameworks and novel arrangements, commensurate with the daunting scope of global divergences and challenges. (I'll sketch some possibilities along these lines in Chapters 18, 19, and 20.)

Nevertheless, the historical precedent set by the EU is an impressive and encouraging one. It provides a "proof of concept" that democratic nations *can* meld their economies and legal systems, creating higher-level institutions that deliver tangible benefits. It demonstrates that national sovereignty *can* be incrementally dismantled, yielding new forms of institutionalized cooperation among formerly separate peoples. Before the EU came into being, one might reasonably have voiced skepticism over whether such a path-breaking experiment could ever succeed – particularly within a continent that had just witnessed a devastating war. But now that the EU has been operating successfully for many decades, we can adopt the cheeky observation of the economist Kenneth Boulding: "If it exists, it must be possible!"[54]

BEYOND THE FALSE DICHOTOMY OF "REALISM" AND "IDEALISM"

Some readers may be thinking at this point: the ideal of heightened global cooperation sounds nice enough, but in practice it will never work. History is littered with the wreckage of ambitious proposals like the ones laid out in the preceding chapters – calls for greater cross-border concertation, compromise, and global integration. The actual track record of humankind, such readers might observe, is a fairly dismal chronicle that suggests a very different set of conclusions. People are selfish, and their allegiances tend to be narrow and rigid; competition is ever present (even during periods of relative peace); and it's naïve to think that humankind can escape from this entrenched pattern. As one looks to the coming century, therefore, one is better off assuming continued struggles for dominance among the Great Powers – and preparing to navigate the challenges that present themselves according to the time-tested rules of power politics and self-help.

Those who subscribe to this view of history usually call themselves "realists" – and that is how their tradition of thought is also described in the terminology of political science.[55] Among the proponents of this view we find some impressive names: Thucydides, Machiavelli, Otto von Bismarck, Camillo Cavour, Hans Morgenthau, Henry Kissinger. Such thinkers usually acknowledge that their vision is pessimistic, but argue that it is ultimately wiser to operate on the basis of an accurate assessment of the limits of human potential, rather than launching high-minded projects that are rooted in an excessively rosy portrayal of human nature. It was the ardent idealists, they maintain, who gave us disasters like the French Revolution when it turned into Terror, the Russian Revolution when it veered into Stalinism, or the Chinese revolution when it degenerated into Maoism. In the end, according to them, "realism" is a morally superior vision, because its hard-nosed approach addresses the facts of power and competition forthrightly, whereas idealism unleashes grandiose but false hopes that ultimately bring disaster.

My argument here is not that the "realist" position is wrong, but merely that it is incomplete and tendentious. It arises from a selective reading of history that picks out the most salient bad traits of humans and treats these traits as essential qualities that can never be altered. Traditional "realism," in short, oversimplifies human nature in two basic ways. First, it makes us out to be worse than we really are: even though competition and cooperation have played equally important roles in shaping history, "realism" skews the balance toward competition. Second, it ignores the fundamental ways in which humans have changed over the centuries: adaptability and malleability have played key roles in the human story, and "realism" turns a blind eye to that dimension.

If you read the headlines of the daily newspaper, you can easily see where the "realist" bias comes from: most of what counts as news is actually *bad* news. Conflicts, betrayals, wars, disasters, violence, winners and losers – these are what people are interested in. "Bread successfully delivered to supermarket" does not make the cut; neither does "Doctor repairs grandma's knee" or "Teacher shows first graders how to read." Like the submerged portion of an iceberg, the dense web of cooperative acts through which people make society work, day-to-day, can slip past our attention, precisely because it is so all-pervasive that we tend to take it for granted. And yet, as a factor in shaping history, this web of cooperation is actually the most primordial fact of all: it built empires out of scattered tribes and allowed humans to dominate all other species.[56] Even when groups of humans compete violently against each other, they do so far more effectively when they know how to work well with fellow team members. Cooperation is everywhere – even in conflict itself – and it plays at least as important a role as competition does in shaping our lives. "Realist" thinkers tend to miss this basic fact, and as a result, they underestimate the potential for new forms of organized cooperation that lie latent in our species.

This brings me to my second point: "realist" thinkers paint an excessively static portrait of humankind. We are not the same today as we were during the time of Thucydides, and we will not be the same in the year 2200 as we are today. History is a tapestry woven from two elements – continuities and change – and both are fundamental to the flow of events. Change is constant, cumulative, and sometimes profound. Consider for example the following aspects of the human life-world, and how they have shifted over the past centuries. Our relationship with the natural environment has been fundamentally altered many times over: hunter-gathering, agriculture, industrial factories, cyberspace. Belief in supernatural forces no longer plays the same role for a majority of people that it once did, and our cosmologies reflect that transformation. The role of women in society has undergone a radical transformation. The principle of democratic rule by all members of a polity marked a major innovation, and the concept of universal human rights would have made little sense to the inhabitants of most premodern societies. Daily violence among individuals has declined steadily and dramatically since the time of the hunter-gathering tribes. The tools we have invented have changed us profoundly: from sticks and fire to steam engines to the telephone to the Internet. Today's pace of change itself would confound a visitor transported from ancient Greece or medieval Italy, as we reinvent our culture and behavior over and over, decade by decade.

To be sure, these transformations have taken place against an equally significant backdrop of basic continuities. People still live in family units, build cities, practice agriculture, war with each other, and write poetry – just as they did 2,000 years ago. But the broader context in which these activities unfold has changed profoundly: the words "father" and "mother" do not carry the same meaning nowadays as they once did; cities operate very differently today; agriculture is practiced in ways that would seem unrecognizable to a premodern person; war is not the same when it is conducted via cruise missiles as opposed to spears; a poem by Sappho or Virgil operates differently than a rap song or a spoken-word performance. The continuities are undeniable, but so is the change – and it is precisely the interplay between these two that renders history so interesting to study.

This is where the "realists" fall short. In their eagerness to identify the underlying rules of human behavior, they have tended to think of human nature as a set of immutable, essential qualities, rather than as a set of patterns that gradually shift over time.[57] This makes it hard for them to explain many important historical developments that fall outside the parameters of their vision. Their rigid emphasis on competitive power politics, for example, leaves them unable to explain certain transformative historical processes like the post-1945 Franco-German reconciliation.

What this suggests is that the political scientists' label of "realism" is itself misleading. It's a bit like the Russian word "Bolshevik," which means "larger

231

faction" – a term that Lenin shrewdly chose for his party even though he knew full well that he and his comrades were actually a rather small minority group. If you call yourself "the larger faction," people will take you more seriously. In a similar way, the word "realism" implies a privileged view into the inner workings of the world: if you call yourself a realist, then those who criticize you will appear (by definition) as "nonrealists" – clueless folks who indulge in wishful thinking. But in actual fact, "realism" is nothing more than one particular school of historical interpretation alongside many others, with distinctive strengths and weaknesses of its own. And when it comes to explaining certain important developments like the Franco-German reconciliation, "realism" turns out to be disappointingly unrealistic.

If we adopt an alternative explanatory framework, in which both competition and cooperation are taken equally seriously, and in which gradual transformative processes are allowed for, we stand a better chance of accurately analyzing the full range of historical events. I will call this framework "dynamic pragmatism." The advantage of this approach is that it gets us out of the vicious circle that "realism" imposes on us: for pessimism in human affairs tends to become a self-fulfilling prophecy. If you expect people to behave nastily toward you in the future, this will incline you to prepare for the worst – which will lead you to take strong defensive measures. But those measures will probably appear to your neighbors as an aggressive move on your part. Your neighbors will then respond with countermeasures of their own – which will in turn appear to you as precisely the aggressive moves that you feared they would make – thereby justifying your initial distrust of them. This vicious circle of expectations and actions is the psychological linchpin of all arms races: each side perceives its own actions as defensive moves against the aggressive moves of the other side, and the escalation spirals ever onward.

Dynamic pragmatism gets us out of this trap. Precisely because it is neither pessimistic nor optimistic, it does not predispose you to see your neighbors' actions as a threat. You gain a certain freedom of movement, allowing you to wait and see how things work out. The chain of escalation is broken, and both you and your neighbors can begin experimenting with more constructive modes of interaction. Precisely because you acknowledge that people can change over time (and sometimes cooperate very effectively with each other), the track record of the past no longer locks you into a spiral of tit-for-tat actions. You gain the ability to do what the French and Germans did after 1945, namely, try something really new.

* * *

16

Taking the United Nations Up a Notch:
Planet-Level Solutions for the Year 2100

E VEN IF THE FIVE UN REFORMS DESCRIBED in Chapter 11 were carried out successfully, this would still leave the international self-help system firmly in place. As long as that system holds sway, no nation can compel any other to rein in its consumption of fossil fuels. No international body controls what is done with nuclear weaponry. No clear or binding regulation exists at the planetary level for advanced biotech and AI. Here we might therefore ask: what strategies would allow us to start addressing this weakness of global governance – gradually, sensibly, but also tangibly, in ways that go beyond symbolism and yield actual norms and guidelines that can be enforced? Since the international self-help system isn't likely to go away anytime soon, how can new rules emerge in the interstices of this system, putting stronger safeguards in place that mitigate the dangers of these four technologies?

In this chapter, I describe a "second wave" of modifications to the UN system that would further beef up its capabilities during the latter half of the twenty-first century. In order to keep the discussion concretely grounded, I'll focus on two major challenges that the UN will be facing during the coming decades: the international regulation of biotechnology, and the global effort to remove excess CO_2 from the Earth's atmosphere.

MANAGING CRISPR

In 2012 two brilliant biochemists, Jennifer Doudna and Emmanuelle Charpentier, developed a powerful new technique for editing genomes.[1] It was known as CRISPR-Cas9, and it used an enzyme borrowed from bacteria to insert new genes into strands of DNA. The invention allowed scientists to rewrite the genome of any DNA-based organism at will – with great precision and reliability, and for a relatively low cost. With this discovery, the promise of the 2003 Human Genome Project finally came to fruition: what had once been science fiction now became straightforwardly feasible. If people wanted to create designer babies, a technique now existed for making that happen.[2]

Doudna, for one, expressed deep ambivalence about her discovery – a combination of excitement at the possibilities now opening up for curing awful genetic diseases, coupled with a gnawing fear that she and Charpentier had unleashed a Frankenstein. One night in the spring of 2014 she had a revelatory nightmare.

> In this particular dream, a colleague approached me and asked if I would be willing to teach somebody how the gene-editing technology worked. I followed my colleague into a room to meet this person and was shocked to see Adolf Hitler, in the flesh, seated in front of me. . . . Fixing his eyes on me with keen interest, he said, "I want to understand the uses and implications of this amazing technology you've developed." His terrifying appearance and sinister request were enough to jolt me awake. As I lay in the dark, my heart racing, I couldn't escape the awful premonition with which the dream had left me. The ability to refashion the human genome was a truly incredible power, one that could be devastating if it fell into the wrong hands . . . The technique was simple enough, and academic experiments with animal genomes had become so routine, that it wasn't hard to imagine biohackers messing with more complex genetic systems – up to and including our own.[3]

Sure enough, it didn't take long for a rogue scientist to carry out precisely the sort of reckless hacking that Doudna had feared. In November 2018 a Chinese biophysicist named He Jiankui announced that he had successfully used CRISPR to edit the genomes of twin girls, Lulu and Nana – the world's first true designer babies whose modified genes would be passed on to all their descendants.[4] Jiankui had tweaked a gene called *CCR5* in the girls, thereby reducing their susceptibility to the AIDS virus. Somewhat naively, he expected accolades and world renown to follow his creation, but what he got instead was a global chorus of opprobrium. Scientists pointed out that the modification was medically unnecessary, because an effective technique already existed for allowing people with AIDS to have babies who would be free from the disease. Worse still, by altering germline cells that would be transmitted to the girls' descendants, Jiankui had ignored fundamental guidelines of self-imposed restraint that scientists had established at an international meeting on CRISPR in 2015. The Chinese government, whose news media initially crowed about this "milestone accomplishment," soon found itself acutely embarrassed by the growing scandal.[5] Hastily reversing course, it launched an official investigation of Jiankui, and in December 2019 he was fined $430,000 and thrown in jail for a three-year term.[6]

Scientists and bioethicists have been divided about the best path forward in the wake of this scandal. Some have called for an international moratorium to be enacted on all experiments in human germline editing; others (including Doudna herself) have argued that the potential medical benefits of CRISPR are simply too powerful to be put indefinitely on hold. In September 2020, a report by an international science commission argued that research on the technique should definitely go forward, as long as it was conducted in responsible ways, with full transparency and rigorous ethical oversight.[7]

One would be naïve, however, to think that the story of He Jiankui will be the last of the rogue episodes involving CRISPR. We live in a world in which regulation of biotech experiments (and enforcement of those regulations) is still carried out exclusively by national agencies and governments – and if you map out the policies of those governments in this regard, the implications are sobering (see Figure 16.1).

What jumps out from this map is not just the wide array of regulatory norms adopted by various nations – ranging from restrictive to permissive. An even more striking feature is how many countries with advanced scientific establishments, such as Russia, Spain, and Italy, show up in the bland color that implies "no restriction" or "status unknown." In many ways, at the global level, this is yet another case of a regulatory Wild West. A 2019 article in *Nature* about the He Jiankui scandal painted a sobering picture of the situation.

> There are many places with lax policies governing new biomedical technologies … Perhaps a researcher or physician from a more developed and tightly regulated country will travel somewhere to produce a gene-edited baby. That happened with mitochondrial replacement therapy, when a doctor from New York travelled to Mexico to help a couple interested in using the technology.[8]

He Jiankui violated a variety of ethical and legal norms with his reckless experiment, and it's possible that the tweaks he introduced into the genomes of little Lulu and Nana will result in poor health outcomes for the girls. (The current status of the twins has not been made public, out of respect for the privacy of their families.) Yet the broader implications of his deed suggest even more troubling possibilities for the coming decades – along the lines of Jennifer Doudna's nightmare. In some countries, where lax regulations on gene editing are in place, it's not hard to imagine a scenario in which ambitious and irresponsible scientists begin to undertake far more radical experiments. Since no enforceable global regulations exist, who can be sure that the proper safety and containment measures will be followed, and that the experiments do not pose a grievous danger to the broader human population?

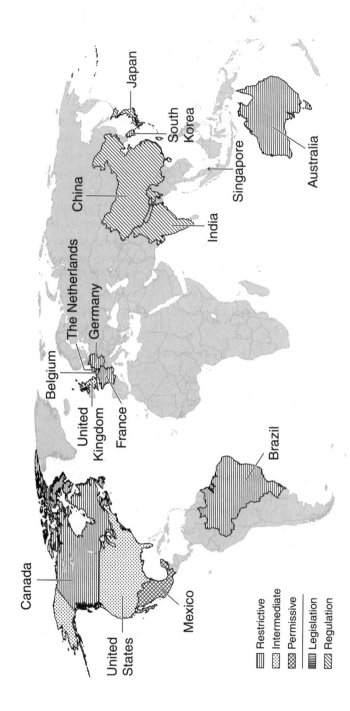

Figure 16.1 Widely varying degrees of restrictions on gene editing technologies characterize the world's nations. **Restrictive:** Canada, Brazil, France, Germany, the Netherlands, Belgium, South Korea, India, Japan, and Australia. **Intermediate:** United States, United Kingdom. **Permissive:** China, Mexico.[9]

Vignette 5: New Biological Frontiers in a Caribbean Republic (2079)

Liarra Ondo, the UN Secretary-General, leaned toward the airplane's window so she could get a better view of the beaches and plantations below. At that moment the pilot banked sharply to the right, which tilted the plane so she could see the island's whole coastline, shrouded in light blue haze on the far horizon. Jacones Cay was 15 kilometers long from north to south, and 8 kilometers wide from the Atlantic side to the Gulf side. It stood alone in the ocean, its volcanic center rising up to 700 meters above the tropical jungle on its steep flanks.

It was the island's stark isolation that had rendered it so attractive to the Croatian billionaire Roche Mogol. He and his followers could do anything they wanted here. The place was theirs.

Ondo felt a slight twinge of nausea as she looked down at the graceful plantation buildings below, their white columns and dark blue swimming pools and fountains surrounded by straight rows of lush experimental crops extending east to west. They reminded her of the wealthier coastal plantations in her native Gabon. Men in yellow hazmat suits were pulling long tubes that extended into the main research buildings. Not 50 meters to the west, along the Gulf shore, she could see the white beaches with waves lapping, and clear water down to 30 meters of depth beyond the artificial reef. Mogol's geneticists had used bioengineering on the coral itself, tuning it to thrive in the warming and acidified ocean waters.

Even the coral, Ondo thought to herself. They even transmogrified that.

She ran her hand unconsciously through the short curls of her graying hair, shifting her lanky body uncomfortably in the seat as she glanced back toward the hazmat vehicles. For years now the scientists from top universities had been warning that something like this was going to happen. They'd been practically begging the political leaders to build global bioengineering safeguards.

And now this. They'd come within a hairsbreadth of catastrophe. Pure blind luck.

The pilot straightened the plane and commenced his final approach to the private airport's long runway. Ondo could see several huge UN cargo planes parked to one side, along with a bevy of trucks and tractors and emergency vehicles. Just over the cane fields, as the plane glided down, she saw the excavation site where the mass graves had been dug.

News of the outbreak had emerged a week earlier, when emergency distress messages had been broadcast from the island in a frantic twelve-hour crescendo that ended abruptly in silence. Biohazard specialists from the WHO had flown in as quickly as possible, but it was already over. In the space of 24 hours the island's human population had succumbed. One frantic group of inhabitants

Vignette 5: (cont.)

had tried to escape by plane, but the pilot had sickened rapidly in flight and the plane had plunged into the Gulf waters and sunk 120 miles to the north. Pure blind luck.

Mogol's Experiment, as he called it, had begun nine years earlier. In a New York Times *interview he'd described it with characteristic bluntness. "We're tired of these bland bioenhancements people are doing these days. We're sick of the bioethics people telling us what we can and can't do. I've bought a beautiful island and invited 3,000 of my fellow transhumanists to join me there, where we're creating our own small nation-state. The Republic of Jacones Cay. Now no one can interfere with us: it's our jurisdiction, our sovereignty. Our own laws, our own morals, will guide what we do. And for us, the ultimate morality is transcendence. We will remake ourselves, leaving behind the chrysalis of our birth bodies. Using the most advanced tools, we will take evolution into our own hands and guide it where we want to go – beyond five senses, beyond disease, beyond death, beyond the fixed limits that natural selection has imposed on our minds. Our aim is to join the Higher Intelligence that rules the Universe – but no longer as mere supplicants. We will join it as equals."*

The plane landed with a soft bump, and Ondo heard the hydrogen engines reverse. She looked to her left at her assistant, Minot, who had insisted on accompanying her on this grim journey. Some of her advisors had warned Ondo against making the trip, saying it might not be safe yet. But the WHO scientists had been clear. The engineered virus was present everywhere on the island, but the hazmat suit and decontamination protocols would protect her, just as they protected the hundreds of UN and WHO workers who were tasked with decontamination and disposal of human remains. Intelligence officers and military scientists from China, the United States, India, the EU, and Russia had also been among the first to arrive. They were keenly interested in the secret research that Mogol's teams of scientists had been doing in the island's ultramodern labs.

Minot put his hand on Ondo's forearm. His large Thai eyes fluttered slightly. "I'm scared," he said, with a slight smile. Ondo nodded. "Me too. Not so much about infection. More for the things we're about to see."

The plane taxied to a stop and ground crew in hazmat suits began setting up the biofilm over the plane's forward door. After ten minutes the chief scientist came aboard and signaled to Ondo with his hand, beckoning her forward. Together she and Minot came down the aisle, holding hands. Since the tabloids had broken the story about their affair, six months earlier, Ondo and Minot had become more relaxed about appearances. Her divorce was already underway in Libreville.

Vignette 5: (cont.)

They emerged from the plane's folding stairs into a biofilm tent where they donned hazmat gear. Ondo was vaguely familiar with the procedure, since she'd visited the H7N5 outbreak sites in Bolivia and Burma several times during her early years as Deputy Secretary. This was part of her job: showing up to establish a personal presence wherever the UN was doing its most important work.

Serge Trygve, the chief scientist, had been on the island since Day 3. He gave them one final looking over, making sure their suits were properly sealed, then led the way out the biofilm pressure door onto the tarmac. They got into an SUV, speaking to each other via radio like astronauts on a foreign planet. Ondo could immediately feel the tropical heat on her suit and was grateful for the air conditioning in the car.

After a short drive through tall cane fields and palm groves, the SUV turned into the entrance of the main research facility, next door to Mogol's enormous mansion. All the island's inhabitants had enjoyed lavish housing in villas along the western coast: Mogol had wanted his co-Experimenters to feel a strong attachment to their new island lives and their citizenship as Jaconesians.

After they'd pulled up near the large, glass-paneled building, Trygve led the way down the pathway under the swaying palms toward the doorway. He paused by the door before opening it and turned to face them.

"Prepare yourselves," he said.

He'd explained it to them during the teleconference briefing. Animal experiments were the foundation of the whole system of modern medicine. Without animal trials, no human medications, no new surgical methods, could be adopted. And this also applied to the experiments the transhumanist scientists had been conducting on Jacones Cay. Animals first, then humans.

Ondo gestured for Trygve to lead the way, and they went in. The foyer was brightly lit, with two long hallways extending from the back. "The dead have been removed for autopsy and burial," noted Trygve as he strode past the empty reception desk. As far as the scientists could tell, the island's non-human animals had been completely unaffected by the engineered virus. Only the humans had succumbed.

Trygve took the left-hand corridor, which led into a long building lit by skylights. Down the corridor, he stopped at the third side door and opened it, beckoning them in. "These are the space ferrets," he said.

Ondo and Minot approached the low stall fence, where a dozen or so white ferrets sat on a layer of hay. Suddenly one of them gagged, retched violently, shook itself, then staggered a few feet away and sat down listlessly. Then another ferret: heaving, trying to vomit, nothing coming out.

Vignette 5: (cont.)

They looked at Trygve.

"They've been engineered to develop modified vestibular systems in their ears, as a preparation for protracted space travel and zero gravity. Mogol wanted to start a transhumanist colony on a giant space station. The genetic edits seem to have worked well, but down here on the Earth, the ferrets are constantly nauseous. We feed them parahistamines to try to control it. Eventually we'll have to put them down."

They followed Trygve a little farther down the hall into a wider space divided into two long compartments. On the left side, four large pigs sat close together in a bed of clean straw. Their eyes were closed but they didn't appear to be sleeping. They had a strange expression on their features – placid yet focused, in an ethereal sort of way. Ondo glanced at Minot. He grinned back at her. "They look happy," he said.

Trygve nodded. "They are."

"What's been done to them?" asked Ondo.

Trygve gestured with his hand. "It's a combination of pharmaceuticals and strong epigenetic modifications. The researchers wanted to see how much bliss they could induce."

Ondo frowned as she looked down at them, studying their expressions. Limitless bliss. Engineered.

She shook her head in disgust as she strode over to the other stall. Trygve and Minot walked along behind her.

A small gray macaque sat before a holographic computer screen, rapt with concentration, furiously manipulating a pair of hand controls. On the screen a series of complex geometric shapes flashed quickly by, changing color and orientation in seemingly random patterns. The monkey paid no heed to the human visitors, its attention fixed on the screen.

After a moment the intricate movement on the screen abruptly stopped, and a bell chimed once. On a table to the monkey's left a small red pellet rolled down a metal chute and landed in a waiting tray. Without taking its eyes off the screen, the monkey grabbed the pellet with its left hand and popped it into its mouth, chewing it quickly.

The screen lit up again, filling with a new stream of geometric shapes that looked even more complex than before. The monkey began once again frenziedly maneuvering the hand controls.

"Well?" asked Ondo – glancing at Trygve and speaking softly, not wanting to distract the monkey from its task.

"Memory augmentation," said Trygve in a flat voice. "Combo of drugs, brain implants, and genetic engineering."

Vignette 5: (cont.)

"Those are memory exercises?" asked Minot.

Trygve nodded. "Spatial memory." A pause. "No human could come close to doing that – no unmodified human, at any rate."

"What else can it do?" Ondo asked.

Trygve shrugged. "This is all it ever wants to do." He turned before she could say anything and went over and waited for them by the door.

Next stall. A small white terrier, sleeping. "This is one of the first experiments they did, eight years ago when the lab was just opened. The dog is eight years old chronologically but only one year old in terms of its telomeres and cellular ageing. They were running a lot of experiments here on radical rejuvenation. This is one of the first attempts, and it appears to have been successful." Trygve looked down at the sleeping creature. "At least, from what we can tell."

Next stall. Five rhesus monkeys with a thin mesh of fine blue filaments surrounding their skulls. "They have induction brain–machine interfaces," explained Trygve.

Ondo frowned. "Neurologists have been doing this for years, for paralyzed patients."

"Yes, but these interfaces are at a whole new level. Trillion-point connection between brain and machine. The scientists here were trying to establish full-scale brain-to-brain communication between these creatures."

Ondo shook her head. "I think I've seen enough."

Trygve nodded. "There's one more at the end of the hall that you really need to see."

They followed him down the hallway toward the far end. Trygve stopped at a larger door and gestured for them to be quiet. Then he led them in.

The space was broad, the size of half a tennis court, with a ceiling of skylights about ten meters above. Ondo could see woven nets of thick rope dangling down from several banana trees. A row of tall steel bars separated the entryway from the rest of the space. There was a greenish canvas tent standing in the far back corner, about three meters tall.

Must be some kind of ape, she thought to herself as they approached the bars.

Trygve pressed a series of buttons on the wall console, linking his hazmat suit radio to a speaker on the wall.

"Milton," he called out.

Nothing. No movement in there.

"Milton," he repeated, more loudly this time.

241

Vignette 5: (cont.)

Still nothing.

"I've got a piece of candy for you," said Trygve.

A video screen on the wall lit up briefly, then darkened, then lit up again.

"Come on out, Milton," urged Trygve.

Words began forming on the video screen.

WHERE LUCY.

"Come on out," Trygve said in a cajoling voice.

BLU.

"OK, a grape candy. Now will you come out?"

GRAP.

"Yes, I said grape. One grape candy. I promise."

The tent flaps parted, and he came out. Ondo found herself involuntarily taking a step back. It was a gorilla. A large one, with dense black fur.

"Come on over and get your candy," said Trygve.

The ape advanced abruptly, holding a meter-long keyboard in its right hand. With surprising swiftness it approached the steel bars and sat on the floor, crossing its legs and laying the keyboard across them.

Paying no attention to Ondo and Minot, its eyes intent on Trygve, it tapped roughly on the keyboard's large keys with its thick index fingers.

WHERE LUCY.

"I told you, Milton. Lucy is no longer here. She... went away."

Tap tap tap tap tap.

WHY FREND GO WAY.

"I know she was your friend. She didn't want to go away. But she had to."

NO FREND NOW.

"I know it's hard, Milton. I told you, I want to be your new friend now, if you'll let me."

LUCY FREND.

Trygve looked over at Ondo and Minot. He reached over to the shelf and took down a wrapped hard candy from the box there.

"Here is your grape candy, as I promised."

The huge brown fingers came up between the bars and took the candy, deftly unwrapping it. He put it into his mouth and even through her suit Ondo could hear it crunching under his teeth.

"You see, Milton. I can be your friend."

Tap tap tap tap tap.

Vignette 5: (cont.)

NO FREND NOW.

Trygve looked down at the ground. "OK. I understand." He turned toward Ondo and Minot. "We'd better move on."

Ondo turned to leave, then stopped. She looked back at Milton and gave a little wave with her hand. The gorilla stared intently at her for a moment, then stood up with his keyboard and shuffled back into the tent.

They went into the hall. Ondo and Minot followed Trygve back toward the foyer.

"What did we just see, Serge?" asked Ondo.

Trygve kept walking. "Twenty percent human genes. They called it Uplift," he said.

They went on in silence. Uplift. Ondo repeated the word to herself.

As they reached the end of the corridor Trygve wheeled about and looked piercingly at them. "This is what happens – "

His face reddened with emotion, and he seemed unable to find the right words. Finally he shook his head and turned, continuing down the brightly lit hall.

The foregoing vignette is science fiction, of course. But the CRISPR revolution, along with other developments in cutting-edge bioelectronics and pharmaceuticals, opens up a doorway through which the sorts of radical experiments just described could realistically become feasible – perhaps sooner than most people realize. (A sizeable philosophical literature exists today, seriously debating the ethics of making profound modifications to animals and humans.)[10] It's likely that the majority of citizens of the late twenty-first century will find these sorts of extreme modifications abhorrent, and support national legislation banning or restricting them. But given the wide range of rigor with which such regulations are applied and enforced – from restrictive to permissive to nonexistent – what is to prevent fringe groups of scientists and entrepreneurs from pushing the boundaries of experimentation into radical new territory? If we are to emerge from the regulatory Wild West that currently prevails in the world, we'll need to build new international arrangements over the coming century – instruments considerably more potent than those operating today.

MAKING THE UN A MORE EFFECTIVE INSTRUMENT

To illustrate this last point, let's consider the example of a single tangible project: managing the removal of large amounts of excess CO_2 from the

Earth's atmosphere. Over the coming decades, this will emerge as one of the clear priorities for humankind – but who will coordinate this gargantuan and expensive undertaking, in which the active participation of so many countries will be required? Here are some of the main questions we'll face when it comes to scrubbing the skies. Who foots the bill for this endeavor, and how will the cost be apportioned? Which technologies should be prioritized for doing the actual carbon removal? Will lots of advanced nuclear reactors be required as an energy source? Where should these giant air-scrubbing machines be installed? Who will build the machines, and how will they be compensated for their work? Which technologies will we decide *not* to use, as we seek to cool the planet, and how will this decision be made? How fast should humankind proceed with this collective project?

These are not just technological or scientific questions: they are inherently political in nature. (In academic lingo, they are fraught with "technopolitics.")[11] If the UN is the most likely forum for making these tough political choices – for where else would we turn, if not there? – then it will need to possess a new set of capabilities that it manifestly lacks today. It will need a far better institutional mechanism for making decisions, beyond the fickle dynamics of the weirdly structured Security Council. It will need greater democratic responsiveness and moral legitimacy, offering the world's peoples a sense that their voices are having a real impact in shaping global policies. And it will need effective enforcement tools for nudging recalcitrant players to comply with majority decisions. Let's look at each of these areas in turn.

In Chapter 11 I suggested that the world's leaders should start pressuring the P5 nations on the UN Security Council to accept an expansion of the Council's permanent membership to include Great Powers like Japan, Germany, India, Italy, Brazil, and Canada. It's ridiculous for these major nations to be spectators when the Council makes key decisions: three of them have economies bigger than France's, and all of them except Brazil have economies bigger than Russia's. An update is clearly overdue. But if all these nations acquire a veto, then the Council risks deadlock even more frequently than today. The veto rule would therefore need to be amended, so that two vetoes by permanent members would be required to block UN action. If the pressure campaign for these twin reforms were to start mounting today, then perhaps it would have acquired enough momentum a few decades hence to push through these badly needed changes.

Second, the UN General Assembly (where each nation gets one vote) should be complemented by the creation of a new World Parliament – a body whose representatives would be directly elected by all the billions of human beings on the planet.[12] This was precisely the sort of measure that gave tremendous momentum and legitimacy to the movement for European unification, when a new European Parliament opened its doors in Strasbourg in 1979.[13] Like its European counterpart, this new world body would start off its operations with very limited, "consultative" powers. In its early days it would not be able to pass new laws or regulations, but would confine its work to debating and voting on resolutions regarding key issues in world affairs; these resolutions would be nonbinding, but would inform and guide the executive decisions being made by the enlarged Security Council. Then, as time went by, the powers of this new body could be incrementally expanded – as was gradually done with the European Parliament – and it would eventually begin to pass new "world laws" with broader scope and reach.[14]

Presumably, the creation of such a World Parliament would not be politically feasible until later in this century, but here too the important thing would be to get the process started today, so that people around the planet can become acquainted with the idea and start debating the pros and cons of it among themselves. The fact that the new deliberative body would possess only symbolic powers in its early years of operation would probably render its creation easier to swallow for those who were skeptical or apprehensive about it. But even symbolic powers can play a significant role. For the first time, the world's peoples would be able to vote directly for representatives who could give their views and priorities a voice in a truly global forum.

The key problem here, of course, is that many of the world's nations are not democracies – so how would their citizens be expected to cast votes for a World Parliament when they can't even cast meaningful votes for their own local and national leaders? According to the "democracy index" compiled by the British magazine *The Economist*, about 49 percent of the world's population lives in democratic polities, while about 51 percent lives in authoritarian or dictatorial polities.[15] Freedom House, a US-based watchdog group, classifies 82 countries as free, 59 as partly free, and 54 as unfree, and notes a troubling decline in the number of free countries over the past couple decades. (Its website also notes that the United States itself has faced alarming challenges to the integrity of its democratic system during the presidency of Donald Trump and its aftermath.)[16] This is a dilemma that bedevils proponents of global governance: should representation in world bodies be open to all countries, regardless of their form of government, or should dictatorships be denied participation? Persuasive arguments can be made on both sides: excluding some nations contradicts the ideal of universal participation, but including dictatorships risks skewing the votes and decisions made by such bodies, and can be seen as rewarding the bad behavior of tyrants.[17]

From its inception in 1945, the UN has taken the inclusive route, because shutting out Joseph Stalin's USSR would have undermined the rationale for the whole endeavor. The future World Parliament would probably need to go this inclusive route as well, in the interest of directly engaging as many of the planet's peoples as possible. One can expect that participating dictatorial regimes would no doubt conduct sham elections for the global deliberative body, putting forward hand-picked candidates under rigged voting systems. This would tend to undermine the World Parliament's democratic legitimacy, since a sizeable number of its delegates would be mere puppets obeying the will of tyrants or oligarchs who held sway in their home nations. I see no way around this basic problem: it's the price that we have to pay for a UN that actively engages despotic regimes like those of Russia and China. The alternative – pretending those countries didn't exist, and excluding them from participation in global decisions – would be far worse: many of the world's dictatorial countries are economically and militarily powerful, and their voice definitely needs to be heard, no matter how unpalatable their political system may be.[18] (I'll discuss the nuts and bolts of voting procedures and seat allocations within such a parliament in Chapter 18.)

To be sure, authoritarian leaders could also opt out of participating in such global elections in the first place – but this would mean forgoing membership in the World Parliament, and missing out on the valuable economic and political connections associated with it. This motivating factor would tend to become increasingly significant over time, as the influence of the new parliament grew incrementally in scope. Opting out of participation would mean, in effect, sidelining one's nation in regard to key economic and political processes shaping the contemporary world. Dictatorial governments would pay a steep price for this sort of isolation.

A third way to take the UN up a notch would be to endow it with better enforcement tools. While still working within the established system of sovereign nation-states, its operations would now begin to incrementally modify the self-help rules through which that system has been functioning over recent centuries. If the UN standing army were boosted in size from its current 90,000 troops to, say, 400,000 – along with a commensurately increased budget and appropriate modern weaponry – then such an army could be used as a "first responder" in dealing with a greater number of world crises and conflicts.[19] (By comparison, the United States has about 1.4 million men and women in arms; China has two million and Russia has one million.)[20] Equipped with this enlarged military force, the UN would potentially accumulate a track record over time of successful peacekeeping interventions, which would boost its credibility as an actor on the world stage; and the United States would benefit from not having to act periodically as a self-appointed "world policeman." Other leading nations such as Russia and China would have a say in all such UN military actions, which would help to mitigate their complaints about American unilateralism.

A mid-sized army of 400,000 UN troops would steer between the twin dangers of being perceived by others as either too weak or too strong: it would wield enough clout to make a real difference in a serious crisis but would remain small enough to allay fears of its straying beyond its assigned missions. Since it would operate under a UN flag, moreover, it would be poised to act relatively quickly, without having to wait for the cumbersome machinery of mustering an international "coalition of the willing." In this scenario, the international self-help system of today would still remain in operation – but a new kind of actor would have come on stage, ready to intervene decisively on behalf of collective mandates from the enlarged Security Council. In cases of Security Council deadlock (under the two-veto rule), the UN army would stay in its barracks, and other military forces would need to be brought into play, just as they are today. But even if only a fraction of the world's periodic violent crises – civil wars, massacres, cross-border incursions – were addressed by this newly beefed-up international army, this would significantly alter perceptions of the UN in the eyes of the world's citizens.

Vignette 6: The First True "World Law" (2081)

The Palais des Nations in Geneva had first been built in the 1930s to serve as the headquarters of the League of Nations. Its classical white marble structure had gone up over the same years in which the League itself had been going down into craven uselessness. Construction was completed with a grand flourish in 1938, just as Hitler made the first moves toward dismembering Czechoslovakia.

Then, after 1945, the majestic building had been substantially enlarged so it could accommodate key offices of the newly created UN. Now it had undergone its third major renovation, with the erection of a sprawling complex to house the new World Parliament. Its name had been changed from "Palais des Nations" to "Palais des Peuples" – the "Palace of Peoples."

Mary Kerkorian climbed, panting slightly, up the paved pathway to the top of the wooded hillock. Her graying hair pulled back in a fashionable ponytail, she looked younger than her 67 years. She laid her briefcase on a nearby park bench and surveyed the broad panorama. From this vantage point across the boulevard from the construction site, she had an unencumbered view of the entire Palais des

Vignette 6: (cont.)

Peuples and its terraced surroundings. For several minutes she stood in silence, surveying the busy activity over there, where the final touches of landscaping were being hastily put in, alongside the enormous white domed hall where the parliament's 800 members would convene for the first time just two hours from now. Today was the first full session with an important vote scheduled, and she would serve as a representative of the United States.

The World Parliament was going to be a compromise, a hybrid of defeat and hope, like most major advances in history. She turned the other way and gazed across the brilliant blue lake waters at the arc of the Alps still covered with snow, the towering plume of water of the Jet d'Eau, the orderly facades of stately old buildings along the far lakeshore. Then she turned back to the white dome and marble columns. So much talk had passed through that succession of buildings over the years, so many words, and so few results to come from them.

It wasn't going to be much different this time, either. The deal that the world's leaders had made was straightforward. We'll go ahead and create this path-breaking international body, whose delegates will be directly elected by the nine billion citizens of planet Earth. And we will make sure it has no real power at all. It will possess nothing more than "consultative authority" – a euphemism for talk, talk, talk. The real power would still lie with the enlarged Security Council.

But the way Mary saw it, this new building was still cause for celebration. When the EU had created its own parliament in Strasbourg in 1979, it too had been nothing but a powerless talk shop. Yet over the years, bit by bit, the peoples of Europe had started taking their continent-wide elections more seriously; they'd started debating with each other in terms of Europe-level problems and Europe-level solutions. Elected delegates had gotten used to working together across traditional boundaries of language and custom, forming continental coalitions of like-minded thinkers and decision-makers. Conservatives, progressives, greens – each had their own cross-national groupings.

Mary turned and walked briskly back down the winding path, crossing the bustling boulevard where she could see other delegates now approaching across the far lawns and causeways. She felt a measure of excitement and nervousness as she went through the security screening and made her way up the esplanade and into the immense domed hall.

Arrayed in concentric semicircles around the central stage, the 800 seats were assigned for national delegations, but the actual voting was clearly not going to run that way. The delegates here in Geneva would most likely be voting only

Vignette 6: (cont.)

rarely in national blocs: following the example of the European Parliament, they were each affiliated with loose political clusters along the left–right spectrum. Mary had joined the center-left coalition of Social Democrats, whose platform ran along the lines of the British Labour party, US Democratic party, and Scandinavian moderate left. She'd briefly considered the Global Greens, but their adamant opposition to nuclear energy had turned her off.

She took her seat, the first of her group to arrive, and tried out her headset, fiddling with its soft earpieces. The US group had 61 delegates, based on the formula that factored population size, economic weight, and other attributes; China had 68. Since this meant that China could outvote the United States whenever it wanted, some right-wingers back home were screaming bloody murder; but the President and US congressional leaders knew that broad coalitions of delegates from all over the world would be shaping the parliament's resolutions – and they felt secure in the knowledge that even if things went against American wishes on one resolution or another, the real executive decisions would always be made by the Security Council.

The planet-wide election two years earlier had astonished her. Her name as founding CEO of SunFern had turned out to be recognizable well beyond US borders, particularly in financial and environmentalist circles, so she'd gotten a smattering of votes from Europe, and even a few from Asia and the global South. The majority, of course, had come from other American progressives like herself. Her campaign staff had cast her as a centrist and pragmatist, and the strategy had worked. Despite complaints from some quarters about electing yet another billionaire, she'd ended up garnering the third-highest tally among the entire US delegation. The UN electoral commission had certified that even in some dictatorships like Hungary and the Philippines, and authoritarian states like China and Russia, sufficiently free and fair elections for the World Parliament had been successfully conducted. Granted, the criteria had been deliberately kept quite lax, so that only the truly wacko regimes like North Korea and Venezuela would be banned from participation.

She reviewed her policy notes over the next half hour as the other delegates filed in and the 800 seats gradually filled. Finally the moment came. Mary watched the UN Secretary-General, Liarra Ondo, stride solemnly to the podium. The hall became hushed. Ondo gave a brief speech, officially calling the session to order, then handed the gavel to one of the delegates from Fiji, Laura Bainivalu, who'd been elected to serve as chairperson.

Vignette 6: (cont.)

The main item on the agenda today was a global treaty to restrict bioenhancement technologies. The photos from Jacones Cay had shocked people out of their complacency. Modest bioenhancements had become relatively commonplace in the past few decades among the world's wealthier families. For $225,000 you could tweak your kid's genes during gestation, boosting the likelihood of disease resistance. For $60,000 per year, you could epigenetically modify your kids after they were born, slightly increasing the chances they'd turn out smarter as their development progressed. Bioelectronic implants under the scalp were allowing simple forms of direct connection to the Web, for as little as $38,000. All manner of expensive designer drugs were available, some of them legal and some on the black market, allowing heightened attention, memory, and mood control. Rejuvenation clinics claimed they could partially reverse the effects of ageing, offering treatment packages that ranged from $385,000 to $20 million; the top-rated clinics in Switzerland and Japan were already booked solid for the next two years. "For the price of a sports car," the ads went, "you'll not only look ten years younger. You'll _feel_ ten years younger."

All these enhancements had met with little controversy thus far, apart from hand-wringing in bioethics journals and predictable complaints from left-wing media and conservative religious groups. Then came Jacones Cay. There was the immediate horror of the mass graves and grotesque animal experiments, but beneath these images lay an even more troubling realization. Here was a near future in which some humans would not merely be tweaked a couple notches above their fellows: they would soar to superhuman levels. Smarter, healthier, living longer lives in youthfulness – they would effortlessly dominate the world. And over time, as they redesigned themselves and their children, taking on ever greater powers and ever stranger shapes, they would also fragment the species. Within half a century, or maybe even sooner, novel strains of humans would be walking the planet, each biologically distinct from the others.

Mary looked on as speaker after speaker came to the podium and vowed that this must never be allowed to happen. Modest enhancements and rejuvenation were acceptable, but all forms of radical modification would be banned outright, with harsh penalties for violators. The consensus was striking: conservatives and liberals, radicals and moderates, Christians and Muslims and Buddhists, North and South – nearly everyone supported the treaty. When a representative of the United Transhumanists came forward, stridently repudiating the Mogol

Vignette 6: (cont.)

experiments but also advocating a milder set of restrictions, the howls from the chamber drowned her out. At the end of the session, the roll call vote tallied 761 to 13, with 26 abstentions.

From here, Mary thought to herself, the resolution would go up to the Security Council, where it would no doubt be swiftly approved. And from there it would be passed back down to the national governments, where the enforcement power still lay.

Mary's cell phone on the leather desktop flashed a new message. She leaned forward and checked it, then turned the phone face down. Leaning back in her chair, she surveyed the vast space under its elegant white dome, where 800 men and women had come to Geneva to speak for their portion of humankind.

* * *

17

The Other Path to 2100:
Ruthless Competition, Fingers Crossed

To a hard-nosed 'realist' reader, the preceding chapter will no doubt have come across as an idealistic fantasy. A reformed Security Council, a nascent World Parliament, the first true "world laws" – how far removed these all are from the harsh realities of today's world! In the eyes of such a reader, we are likely to see a very different sort of future unfold in the second half of the twenty-first century – a geopolitics based on continued rivalry, arms races, and frantic competition for dominance among China, the United States, and Russia, alongside the restless jockeying of new powers like India, Brazil, Japan, and perhaps a more tightly consolidated EU.

Walking down the aisle of my excellent local bookstore, I come to the section on international topics, and the titles jump forth aggressively from the shelf: China rising! Russia on a rampage! American decline![1]

Today's geopolitical situation fully justifies these alarmist titles. Things are not going well in world politics, unless you happen to be a Russian oligarch, a kleptocrat in a developing country, or an investor in China-based industries. When the Soviet Union collapsed in 1991, it looked for a while as though the "new world order" heralded by President George H. W. Bush might actually be taking form. The liberal international system, created after World War II under US leadership, was adapting nicely to post-Cold War challenges. NATO admitted new members from Eastern Europe; German reunification made far fewer waves than it might have; Russia staggered toward democratic normalcy; the EU pressed forward with its integration project; international bodies like the UN, World Bank, WHO, and IMF plodded ahead with their cross-border work; and China, recovering from the Tiananmen upheavals, consolidated its rising prosperity under a stable, authoritarian regime. When Yugoslavia descended into an orgy of ethnic cleansing, murder, and rape in the early 1990s, NATO and UN forces eventually intervened to quell the violence, and some of the most vicious Yugoslavian leaders were brought to trial before a UN criminal court at The Hague. President Bush could be forgiven for concluding – alongside many diplomats, journalists, and scholars at the time – that the American-led international system was in pretty good shape.

Thirty years on, it's clear that the optimism of that historical moment was premature. Russia under Putin has become a potent disruptive force in world affairs, eagerly fomenting conflict among and within the world's democratic nations, which it regards with unconcealed rancor. Russian nationalists have not taken kindly to their country's sudden demotion as a geopolitical player: they viewed the expansion of NATO into Eastern Europe as an intolerable affront to their regional dominance.

The United States, meanwhile, has fallen prey to crippling levels of left–right polarization, wealth disparity, and racial tensions, leading many Americans to lose faith in their country's democratic system. Under President Trump, the United States actively undermined many of the core institutions and principles of the liberal world order it had once championed: he and his emissaries not only scorned international bodies like the UN and WHO, but openly questioned the NATO alliance itself, as well as the long-standing partnership with the EU.[2] After Trump's defeat in 2020, the Republican Party closed ranks around both Trump himself and the aggressively nationalist ideology he had espoused; this development clearly signaled to America's allies that the Trump foreign policy had been no mere aberration, and that powerful constituencies in US politics would continue to pursue those chauvinist policies for the foreseeable future.[3] Despite frantic efforts by President Biden to repair the damage, America's credibility as a reliable partner and responsible world power was not likely to recover anytime soon.[4]

The real question mark, however, lay with China. Buoyed by decades of heady economic growth, China stood poised to surpass America's GDP by 2032. Under the leadership of Xi Jinping, the nation launched an ambitious program of military buildup and diplomatic outreach, asserting its ascendant role as the leading power in Asian affairs. The 2013 Belt and Road Initiative applied the leverage of China's immense economy to development projects in dozens of countries throughout Southeast Asia, Africa, and the Middle East, openly calling on them to shift their allegiance and diplomatic orientation toward Beijing. At the same time, China's leaders vigorously promoted the authoritarian political system of the Chinese Communist Party as a model for other nations to emulate, using diplomatic and economic cudgels to stifle criticism of its government.[5]

When foreign policy experts look ahead at the coming century, therefore, many of them express deep skepticism about the continued viability of the liberal international order.[6] It's clear to most observers that the "American Century" – the period of overwhelming US dominance in world affairs – is coming to an end. But what sort of global order will replace it?

Two prominent scholars of international relations, Alexander Cooley of Columbia University and Daniel Nexon of Georgetown University, conclude in a recent book that the three likeliest outcomes for the coming century are all fairly grim.[7] As the American-led system unravels, they argue, the US–China rivalry could plausibly assume two starkly different forms: a traditional great-power competition, or a far more hostile and volatile relationship reminiscent of the worst periods of the Cold War. Much will depend on the ideology and ethos of the leadership that emerges in these two nations over the coming decades. Strong undercurrents of nostalgia for the Han Dynasty "golden age" run through some constituencies in the Chinese political and military leadership, and if this group prevails in setting policy over the coming years, then the nation will likely see authoritarian rule on the domestic front and increasingly aggressive moves in Asia and beyond.[8] If it's a matter of "Make China Great Again" vs. "Make America Great Again," then the two superpowers could end up maneuvering around each other in increasingly tight circles of nasty intrigue and openly hostile acts. The danger of a shooting war in such a scenario would be far from negligible.

On the other hand, it's also possible that wiser leadership will prevail in both nations, aimed at managing the US–China relationship according to the principle of "competitive interdependence." This is the term coined by the Brookings Institution scholar Ryan Hass as he describes the deep tensions between these two peoples who are nonetheless tightly bound together by major economic forces.[9] China today is America's number one source of foreign goods, and the third-largest market for American exports; America is China's number one trading partner, with US consumers purchasing $452 billion in Chinese products per year – a fifth of China's total exports.[10] Each year, America's largest industrial and commercial companies receive from one-third to one-half of their profits from trade with China.[11] The resultant relationship is inherently paradoxical, Hass argues.

> Competition is the principal feature, and the costs of breaking free of interdependence are prohibitive. Neither country is capable of imposing its will on the other at acceptable cost or risk, and yet both countries hold preferences and priorities that place them at sharp odds with each other on

fundamental issues, ranging from the balance between social stability versus individual liberties to the role of the state in the economy and the distribution of power in the international system.[12]

Smart management of this fraught relationship would require that both sides respect each other's most vital interests, avoiding direct confrontation wherever possible, while seeking mutual accommodation and pragmatic compromise in all those secondary instances when core principles or essential interests were not in play. Few China scholars express confidence that this bilateral relationship will go easily or smoothly over the coming decades, but in this scenario the two superpowers will at least have avoided a head-on clash that would risk disaster for both of them (and most likely for the rest of the world as well).[13]

A third possibility for twenty-first-century geopolitics, according to Cooley and Nexon, would be a multipolar world in which formal international institutions like the UN and WHO play ever smaller roles, and the five or six leading nations relate to each other through direct transactions and ad hoc arrangements in much the same manner that the European Great Powers did in the nineteenth century.[14] Such loosely governed systems can be notoriously unstable, of course, but over time this process might result in a return to regional spheres of influence, with Great Powers unabashedly exerting dominance over their immediate neighbors. The fate of liberal democracies, in such an order, would depend on which hegemonic Great Power had managed to grab control over a particular global neighborhood.

In all three of these scenarios, unfortunately, the planet-level instruments for managing our four mega-dangers would be distressingly weak. Whether it's a strident China–America Cold War, a more traditional bipolar rivalry, or an international free-for-all among Great Powers, the opportunities for large coalitions of nations to come together successfully in coordinated, long-range projects will be rare. Leading countries are far more likely to keep scrambling for one-sided advantage at each other's expense, and to cast blame on each other for unresolved crises. When they do manage to work together on matters of clear common interest, their ad hoc partnerships will tend to be narrowly transactional arrangements between small numbers of players, and their cooperative actions will likely be temporary in duration and restricted in scope. As soon as the narrow goal is attained, it will be back to business as usual: rivalry, skulduggery, and distrust.

Vignette 7: Going to War over Sunlight? (2076)

The Xi'an Y-70 leveled off as it reached 51,000 feet, its massive wings fully extended to maximize lift at this altitude, which was 10 percent beyond its normal flight ceiling. Its pilot, commander Biyu Fang, closely monitored the readout on her AI monitor, as the nav system made constant infinitesimal adjustments to keep it perfectly in formation with the other 250 planes in the group.

"Get ready," she said into the intercom to the other eight crew members. "Release point approaching in five minutes."

Far below, she could make out the broad curving shape of the Qinghai Lake, surrounded by the arid Hainan foothills to the south. The giant plane was quivering slightly as it cut through the turbulence of the high jet stream, but its weight kept it relatively steady. Its payload, 161,000 kilograms of sulfate aerosols and calcium carbonate, would be sprayed out through an array of 30 nozzles mounted under the rear fuselage. Charting a northeastward course, the fleet of cargo aircraft would release a swath of microscopic particles along the entire western portions of the nation. Then the steady current of the jet stream would carry them eastward, blanketing the heavily populated provinces along the Pacific coast. Keeping the sunlight at bay. The residents of Shanghai, Beijing, Chongqing, Tianjin, and Shenzhen would be protected.

Glancing to her left and right, she could see the other planes in the advancing fleet, spaced 500 meters apart along a 100-kilometer diagonal gradient across the sky.

"Sixty seconds," she said into the intercom. Then her nav system monitor went haywire. Static and flashes filled the screen, and her instrument panel lit up with error warnings. An emergency klaxon began to squawk, and she silenced it.

Her years of training kicked in. "Nav failure," she said crisply into the intercom. "Going to manual controls and VFR." The plane shuddered as she took the yoke and began flying it herself.

"Cancel aerosol release," she said. She glanced at her radio operator, who was frantically adjusting dials and flipping switches, seeking to restore the nav system. Finally he looked over at her and shook his head. "It's not internal. We're being jammed from outside."

She spoke her call sign into the radio. "Nav system jammed from external source. Maintaining course. Permission to reduce altitude."

Liarra Ondo, the UN Secretary-General, glanced at the silent TV screen on the corner wall opposite her desk. CNN: an anchorwoman speaking somberly; a banner scrolling at the bottom with the words, Breaking News.

Vignette 7: (cont.)

Everything these days was always Breaking News.

Something about the anchorwoman's expression made her pause. On the split screen she was speaking with a reporter outside the UN building.

She picked up the remote and turned on the volume. Without realizing it she stood up from her chair. China had just launched a first wave of Solar Radiation Management planes in defiance of the UN Security Council draft resolution that was coming up for a vote this afternoon. The United States had warned yesterday that launching those planes would be considered a hostile act. The Chinese had gone ahead anyway, preempting the Security Council vote. President Sledge had just placed the US military on higher alert.

Jesus, she thought. Were they actually going to go to war over this?

The hard thing was when both sides had equally valid arguments. And their leaders were equally arrogant and unpleasant to deal with. And their fingers on the nuclear button were equally twitchy.

No, actually, it wasn't just those things. It was when you agreed more with one side than the other but had to maintain impartiality at all costs.

She ran her hand through her short-cropped hair, staring absently out the broad window at the skyline of New York before her. From up here in her corner office she had a sweeping view of Manhattan to the north and across the East River at Roosevelt Island and the Queensboro Bridge. She looked back down at her desk where the Sketch of the Problem lay splayed across the large electronic display, with knots of tiny words and phrases in French linked by dotted lines and arrows. She'd been using this mapping technique since her days in architecture school to visualize a thorny situation in all its complexity, and it had never let her down. Somewhere in this mess a path to a solution lay waiting.

The Chinese-led bloc wanted both types of Solar Radiation Management to start immediately on a massive scale. Short-term SRM would blanket the skies with fine particulates spewed from fleets of cargo planes, mimicking the effect of volcanic eruptions that cooled the planet rapidly for several years. And long-term SRM would build a solar shield at the Lagrange Point between the Earth and the Sun, blocking 2 percent of the Sun's rays from reaching the Earth. The pro-SRM camp had dozens of nations behind it: China, India, Pakistan, Bangladesh, Indonesia, Brazil, the African Union, Australia, South Korea, the Organization of Latin American States, the Arab League, Israel, and the Alliance of Small Island States. These were the territories where climate change had been hitting the hardest. Their

Vignette 7: (cont.)

leaders claimed that together they represented a far larger portion of humankind, and that their will should therefore hold sway.

The American-led bloc was more compact and comprised territories where climate change had not yet reached such catastrophic levels: the United States, Russia, the EU, the Scandinavian countries, Switzerland, Japan, Canada, Argentina, Chile, and South Africa. This camp argued that both types of SRM were far too risky and stood a good chance of wrecking the world's ecological and agricultural systems. These nations claimed that even though the pro-SRM group was a majority, this did not justify their taking actions that would endanger the entire planet.

The arrows on Ondo's sketch traced the weird dynamics of the crisis: Israel alongside Iran, the United States in bed with the Russians, Australia split off from its European allies. Climate politics had temporarily thrown the old alignments into disarray. Which made the situation all the more unstable and hard to manage.

The phone on the desk buzzed, and Ondo answered it. "Dr. Ondo, you have President Zhui from Beijing on line 3."

Ondo took a deep breath, then pressed the button. "My dear Mr. President, thank you for calling me back."

The massive Y-70 responded sluggishly as commander Fang made small adjustments to the control yoke.

Again she spoke her call sign into the radio. "Nav system jammed. Permission to reduce altitude."

Static filled her headset, getting so loud she had to pull it off. She glanced instinctively to left and right, and saw the flight formation breaking up, the long line of huge planes angling slowly downward in disarray.

Two planes far off to the right were drifting toward each other. Just as they were about to collide, the nearer plane veered violently away and down, averting disaster.

She tried her headset again. Loud static. "Emergency channel," she said into the intercom.

"Not functional," replied the radio operator.

47,000 feet. They were slowly losing altitude, maintaining course in a controlled descent. To her left and right she could see dozens of giant aircraft on a similar gentle incline. No more near misses. The pilots were back in control.

Vignette 7: (cont.)

42,000. 36,000. At 31,000 the nav screen suddenly cleared and the static disappeared from her headset. With her free hand she slipped it back on and spoke her call sign. "Nav system restored and functional. Jamming has stopped. Maintaining course. Request instructions."

President Sledge glanced at his national security staff standing in a taut semicircle around the Oval Office. He brought his gaze down toward the surface of his desk as he spoke into the phone, concentrating on saying the words calmly and firmly so Zhui would understand. "Yes, we did it, President Zhui. Of course we did it. And we'll do it again if you send those planes on another illegal mission."

He heard Zhui speaking fast harsh words in Chinese to one side. Then the Chinese leader came back to the call. "This is an extreme provocation. Very dangerous."

"You are the ones doing the provocation. You're in violation of a UN Security Council resolution."

"Very dangerous. Two planes were nearly in collision."

"We saw that too, Mr. President. Now maybe you'll think twice about pulling this kind of stunt again."

The line went dead. Sledge looked over at his defense secretary and national security advisor.

"Take the alert level up another notch," he said.

* * *

PART V

THE LONG-TERM GOAL:
ENVISIONING A MATURE SYSTEM OF GLOBAL GOVERNANCE FOR THE TWENTY-SECOND CENTURY

These final chapters are entirely speculative in nature: I haven't the faintest idea what the world is going to be like in 2150. Nevertheless, when you're heading out on a long journey, it's best to start with some notion of where you're wanting to go. If humankind wishes to head in the general direction of a more peaceful and just world, it makes sense to give some thought to how such a world might work in concrete practice, day to day.

The proposals I sketch below may strike you as unworkable or undesirable, for any number of reasons. But it's nonetheless helpful to open up a conversation about this topic among ourselves sooner rather than later – weighing the options, trading ideas, gradually giving the subject greater substance in our minds. In ways that might surprise us, such future-oriented thought experiments may subtly influence the solutions we bring forward to handle the more pressing problems of the present day.

* * *

18

Global Government in a World of Democracies and Dictatorships: What It Might Look Like in 2150

A QUESTION OF POLITICAL WILL

In this chapter, I sketch a potential architecture of global federal government, drawing on the work of several generations of scholars, diplomats, and statespersons who have thought long and hard about this topic. For the most part, the ideas I'll explore are not my own: I have borrowed and adapted them from the writings of historians like Paul Kennedy and Mark Mazower, international relations theorists like Anne-Marie Slaughter, Robert Keohane, and Joseph Nye, peace activists like Kenneth Boulding and Mary Kaldor, proponents of realpolitik like Hans Morgenthau and Thomas Schelling, world federalists like Thomas Weiss, Andreas Bummel, and Joseph Schwartzberg, as well as UN officials such as Brian Urquhart, Dag Hammarskjold, and Kofi Annan (to name just a few).[1]

Every idea I present below rests on a common premise: if a global federation comes into being someday, it will only be possible because a majority of the world's peoples have come to actively *want* such a system to exist. When the Germans and the French overcame their enmity in the decades after 1945, this only became possible because the goal of reconciliation made sense to large swaths of the population on both sides of the Rhine. When the United States and EU created their vibrant and resilient transatlantic relationship – rejecting the struggle for one-sided advantage and opting instead for a partnership of mutual accommodation and compromise – this only became a reality when voters on both sides clearly saw the benefits of working together.

In both these success stories, fear definitely played just as important a role as idealism. Stalin's Red Army, along with the Orwellian dictatorships behind the Iron Curtain and in China, loomed large in the minds of citizens in Western Europe and the United States, impelling them to get creative in overcoming their myriad practical and ideological disagreements. The external threat of the Russian tanks and missiles – a clear and present danger – served as a potent motivator of cooperative efforts in the West. But at the planet level, no such external threat exists. Who is the common enemy of humankind?

The answer is obvious. The unifying threat at the planet level is the danger of technological self-destruction – a catastrophe unleashed upon our world through our own ignorant or malevolent actions. Consider for example the three pathways for twenty-first-century geopolitics described in Chapter 17: a harsh China–America Cold War, a more traditional bipolar rivalry, or an international free-for-all among Great Powers. All of these scenarios rest on the assumption that "business as usual" will continue through the coming decades, with the world's largest nations competing fiercely against each other, seeking dominance within an international system of self-help. Under these conditions, here's what we can expect:

- concerted action against climate change will tend to be weak, uncoordinated, and sporadic, and will fail to make a decisive difference in the trajectory of global warming;
- escalating climate disasters will propel new waves of desperate migrants to seek admission to the world's richer countries (whether legally or illicitly), likely spurring xenophobia and harsher immigration battles;
- nations will keep modernizing their nuclear arsenals and aiming fearsome weaponry at each other;
- arms races will continue to operate, bringing novel weapons of mass destruction into play, with new theaters of conflict in the oceans, cyberspace, and outer space;
- biotechnologies will not be well managed at the global level, leaving some nations as "regulation havens" where lax rules allow dangerous experiments and innovations to go forward;
- pandemic preparedness will be left up to individual nations to work out for themselves, with the world's poorer regions providing entry points to crossover viruses from the animal world;
- and the Wild West in cyberwarfare and advanced AI will continue to hold sway, with some nations or corporations free to experiment with powerful and perhaps disastrously unsafe AI machines.

Will all this add up to a "clear and present danger" in the eyes of the world's peoples? Will it prove sufficient to motivate the kinds of constructive change I've been describing in the foregoing chapters? I don't know. Ultimately, the choice will come down to each of us, as citizens, as voters, as parents of children who we hope will live on into the twenty-second century.

THE ASTONISHING POWER OF SMALL GAINS

The economist Kenneth Boulding once argued that peace is best thought of by analogy with a beachside house that is buffeted by periodic storms.[2] If the house has been weakly built, then a minor squall may bring it down, but if it was strongly built, then even hurricanes will leave it relatively unscathed. This analogy is helpful because it gets us away from thinking of peace and war as all-or-nothing states of affairs: they are actually relative qualities that vary in degree along a broad spectrum of relationships among peoples and polities. Canada and the United States are not at war with each other, and neither are India and Pakistan – but their relationships are profoundly different. Canada and the United States are in a state of stable peace, built on a solid foundation of trust, commerce, common values, institutionalized cooperation, and convergent interests; whereas India and Pakistan share very few of these qualities, and hover perpetually on the brink of armed conflict. Peace is an edifice that can be significantly weakened or strengthened over time.[3]

Cooperating with other people is relatively easy when the benefits are clear and the ground rules already agreed upon. The real test lies in the tough cases when one side sees a chance for unilateral gain at the expense of the others, or when the ground rules are hazy and the parties are riven by deep disagreement. In such cases, the temptation to defect from cooperation is strong, and it's then that one hears questions like the following: "Why should we keep compromising with those other guys, when their demands seem unreasonable to us, and we can gain so much just by taking the spoils for ourselves?"

Here lies the difference between stable peace and unstable peace. In stable peace, the parties have established a history of working through these kinds of tough cases, because they recognize that they are all going to be much better off in the long run by sticking with cooperation. As long as their mutual relationships over time are perceived as fair – with each party making concessions in roughly equal measure at various moments – then the overall benefits of the system still outweigh the costs. Each participant has to be willing to compromise in good faith, to accept unpalatable trade-offs, in the interest of keeping the overall system in place. In unstable peace, by contrast, the parties reject this logic. They regard competition as the fundamental reality and are only willing to cooperate with other players as a temporary means to an opportunistic end.[4]

The crucial factor in both these cases is the track record that builds up over time. Every instance of successful cooperation, yielding tangible benefits for all, strengthens the case for further efforts at cooperation in the future. Conversely, every time the parties slide back into the self-help mode, the chances of future cooperation diminish. Each mode of interaction – cooperation or self-help – operates as a kind of self-fulfilling prophecy, paving the way for more of the same down the line.

Implicit here lies an encouraging observation about the way history unfolds: even seemingly small gains can make a lasting difference. You don't have to wait until you get all the way to full global transformation in order to start reaping significant rewards. It's helpful to keep this in mind, as we think about strategies for dealing with these looming mega-dangers. One can easily get discouraged if one assumes that reining in our four horsemen requires a planet-level metamorphosis, based on dramatic, all-or-nothing solutions. A more fruitful way to approach this challenge is to picture it in the way Boulding did, as a broad spectrum: at one pole lies a free-for-all of self-interested forces furiously vying with each other, while at the other pole lies a highly integrated global framework of democratic and cooperative governance. We find ourselves in today's world at some point between these two extremes. Our goal should be to move the world toward the cooperative pole, bearing in mind that every small advance in that direction helps improve our safety and security immediately, in tangible ways. Our society may never get all the way "there" – but we can boost our odds of survival even by traveling part of the way down that road.

HOW MIGHT IT WORK IN PRACTICE?

The international framework I'm about to describe may strike the reader as Byzantine in complexity and extremely unlikely to ever see the light of day. Here it's good to remember two points. If you sit down and try to diagram the functioning of the American federal government, you might be surprised at how Byzantine your drawing quickly becomes: nested layers of boxes and arrows would soon fill your page. Modern societies like the United States are complicated structures, and the mechanisms and rules we create for governing their behavior are inevitably also complex in nature. The same goes for global society and governance, *a fortiori*: no matter how hard we try to keep things simple and manageable, a certain degree of layered intricacy is unavoidable.

The second point to remember is that the system I'm describing would not spring into existence overnight: rather, it would evolve, like a house being remodeled by successive owners with the passing of time. Going back to Boulding's analogy of the beachside dwelling: one owner builds a new foundation, jacking the house up 20 feet and putting it on concrete pillars so the storm surge can flow harmlessly underneath; a few decades later, a new family moves in and installs storm-resistant windows; scroll forward a bit more, and yet another owner arrives, adding a different kind of roof and walls with improved shear strength. All this accumulates over time into something significant: where once this quaint old house would have been flattened by a middling storm, it now laughs at passing hurricanes. This is hopefully what will happen to the UN over the coming century or two. What I'm describing below is one possible end-result of the haggling and tinkering of successive generations.

I'm also not assuming a major change in human nature: twenty-second-century people will most likely still behave toward each other in much the same ways (both kind and nasty) that they do today. What I *am* hypothesizing, however, is that more and more citizens of countries throughout the planet may eventually come to see the advantages of strong partnerships across borders and a world system governed by common laws. Their grasp of planet-level problems, and receptiveness to global solutions, could gradually deepen in significant ways. People, in other words, can learn.

Here's a brief summary of what I envision; I'll unpack each of these elements more fully afterwards. A world federal government would center on a revamped United Nations, comprising a bicameral legislature, an executive council, a World Constitution and World Court, and a mid-sized army for enforcing the peace. The system would emulate the ingenious division of powers of the US federal government, but unlike the United States it would not have a strong presidency; rather, it would follow the example of the EU with its plural executive body, designed to equitably accommodate multiple kinds and sizes of nation-states.[5] In this federal structure, existing national governments would continue to do most of the day-to-day running of people's affairs; only the truly global matters such as climate change, military security, pandemics, or the regulation of dangerous new technologies would be assigned to the UN and its affiliated bodies. The global federation would be open to the voluntary participation of all the world's nations, and any nation could opt out if it wished. Dictatorships and democracies (and everything in between) would be encouraged to participate, but the functioning of the federation itself would adhere to strict democratic principles of accountability, transparency, and civil rights. When the UN faced major decisions affecting world peace or other such weighty matters, strong majority or supermajority votes would be required before the executive council could take action.

In its day-to-day functioning, this world federation would operate on the core principle of subsidiarity: it would serve as a *coordinator* of planet-level actions by its national members, and would leave the management of people's daily business to the downward chain of existing national, provincial, or municipal governments already in place. In order to keep this system accountable to the world's citizens and independent in its operation, it would be based on strong internal checks and balances designed to prevent would-be tyrants from seizing control. The distribution of power within this federal system would be intentionally structured so as to prevent any single region, bloc, or nation from exerting unilateral sway over the management of world affairs; all key decisions would require the collective assent of broad majorities of humankind. In cases of intractable disagreement on pressing matters, the system would possess robust mechanisms for bringing forward negotiated solutions that reflected compromise among the major stakeholders.

LEGISLATURE

Many of the world's existing nations use federal systems of political organization, dividing the powers of domestic government between two or more levels. This arrangement allows a collection of lower-level units – states, provinces, cantons – to work constructively together on matters of common interest, while preserving their own jealously guarded traditions and local self-rule. Examples of federal rule include seven of the eight largest countries in the world – Russia, Canada, the United States, Brazil, Australia, India, and Argentina, as well as nations comprising mixed linguistic or ethnic groups within their territories, such as Belgium, Nigeria, and Switzerland. (China is the prominent exception among the large nations, with its centralized and unitary system.) Two of the world's longest-running governments, the United States and Switzerland, operate on federal principles: indeed, the Swiss actually emulated certain American institutional innovations when they drew up their federal constitution in 1848.[6]

The federal idea clearly makes the most sense for any planet-level government, since it would allow the hard-bitten nationalists in each participating country to feel that their local prerogatives of self-determination were being rigorously protected, even as many large-scale actions were now being managed via coordination (and compromise) with other peoples. Every federation works out its own unique way of balancing the two levels of power, with some putting most of the important action in the central core, and others insisting on keeping key decisions anchored to locally elected bodies.[7] The US constitution, for example, features a dominant central government, allocating only relatively minor prerogatives to the states and cities (such as whether you can legally smoke pot, for example, or what textbooks should be used in the elementary schools). Other systems, like the one in Switzerland, go the opposite route: they keep most of the power at the cantonal level, and use the central government only for narrowly defined common functions such as military defense.[8]

Many federal systems have set up bicameral legislatures for themselves: one house for the provinces, states, or cantons, the other for direct popular suffrage. This division (exemplified by the Senate and House of Representatives in the United States) allows the provinces or states to have a distinct voice of their own in collective decisions, via the Chamber of States, while the citizenry as a whole can speak its mind in selecting representatives for the people's chamber. The existence of a Chamber of States helps reassure the residents of smaller or weaker provinces that they can have a meaningful say in setting national policy: in the United States, for example, diminutive Wyoming and Delaware exert the same power with their two seats in the Senate as do the behemoths like California and New York.

A global legislature would work best if it too adopted the bicameral principle: a Chamber of States would allow each nation to speak with its own unitary voice in the halls of world power, while a World Parliament would give the nine or ten billion individuals from all countries a chance to vote directly for global representatives of their choice. (See Chapter 16 for a discussion of the challenges of conducting legitimate elections for the World Parliament in dictatorial countries.) Representatives in the Chamber of States would be appointed by each national government, and each nation would get one seat, for a total of 193. The World Parliament would need to be considerably larger in order to accommodate representative slices of the world's population – but it should not be so huge as to become unwieldy. Perhaps something on the order of 800 seats would work well; today's European Parliament, by way of comparison, has 705 seats.

WEIGHTED VOTING AND THE ALLOCATION OF SEATS

Animated no doubt by sincere democratic impulses, the founders of the UN in 1945 decided to give each national member of the General Assembly one equal vote. The result, however, has been exactly the opposite of what the founders wanted: the General Assembly quickly became a talk shop like the League of Nations. It provided a valuable forum for weak or impoverished nations to voice their grievances but offered little in the way of concrete decisions that could actually be implemented and enforced. Most of the real action has happened in the Security Council and in the various specialized agencies like the WHO or Food and Agriculture Organization.[9]

The reason is simple. "One nation one vote" reliably leads to preposterous results that fly in the face of the realities of world politics. The tiny island nation of Nauru, with a population of 10,800, has the same voting power as China, whose population is 1.4 billion (and where the heck is Nauru, anyway?). In this system, a group of 129 nations comprising only 8 percent of the world's population could get together a two-thirds majority in the General Assembly and block substantive action. Throughout the past decades, coalitions of smaller or poorer nations like the Non-Aligned Movement and G77 have joined forces in hopes of making their voices heard: the results have been disappointing, as the leading economic and military powers often ignored the steady stream of ardent proclamations from the General Assembly, and blithely went on with business as usual.[10]

In order to address this problem, some form of weighted voting is clearly needed – a system that allocates decision-making power in the UN in proportion to each nation's actual influence in the world arena. Some UN delegates from smaller countries endorsed this idea from the very start. The UN ambassador of the Philippines, Carlos Romulo, stated in 1946: "My nation would be very happy indeed to trade the fiction of equality in a powerless Assembly for the reality of a vote equal to our actual position in the world in an Assembly endowed with real power."[11] The British ambassador to the UN, Hartley Shawcross (one of the prosecutors at the Nuremberg Trials), agreed: "Someday it might be necessary to devise a weighted form of voting which gave each member State a voting strength in the Assembly consonant with its real influence in world affairs."[12]

At the 1944 Bretton Woods Conference, when the future World Bank and IMF were being designed, this kind of realistic thinking prompted the delegates to adopt a weighted voting system for the IMF: each member nation would have a say in direct proportion to its financial contributions to the system (and this principle still remains in force at the IMF today).[13] Clearly, after seven decades of fruitless posturing and powerless flailing in the General Assembly, the experiment with "one nation one vote" needs to come to an end. If we want the UN to work well someday and actually do the jobs assigned to it, we'll need a better way to allocate power among its far-flung and highly diverse participants.

But how? Here I turn to the work of the late Joseph Schwartzberg, a professor of geography at the University of Minnesota and a long-standing advocate of world federalism. In his 2013 book, *Transforming the*

United Nations System: Designs for a Workable World, Schwartzberg offered a comprehensive blueprint for a future global government organized along federal lines. (Adding a touch of piquancy, this was the last book published by the United Nations University Press before it was shuttered after drastic funding cuts in the UN budget.)[14]

Schwartzberg understood all too well the fraught politics involved in the selection of weighting factors. Going with a factor based on population size would please China and India but become an instant deal breaker for the United States and other rich and powerful nations. A factor of economic clout would raise a hue and cry among the developing countries of the global South. Using military power as a benchmark would have the undesirable side effect of encouraging arms races. In the end, therefore, he crafted a hybrid of three factors: the democratic principle (P), which rests on population size; the economic principle (C), determined by a nation's Gross National Product and its proportionate contribution to UN coffers; and a "sovereign equality" principle (M), designed to mitigate the chasm of power between UN members like Nauru and China.[15] This latter factor M would be the same for all nations, and was calculated as the country's unit share of the total UN membership, or $1/193$ (0.051) in 2020. The formula for computing a nation's voting weight (W) then became:

$$W = (P+C+M)/3.$$

Under this scheme, for example, the voting weight for the United States using 2020 statistics would be determined as follows:

P = 4.24 (US population as a percentage of the global total)

C = 22.17 (US GNP and proportional UN contribution as a percentage of total UN contributions)

M = 0.51 (the country's unit share of the total UN membership, or 1/193 in 2020)

Applying the formula, one sums these three factors and then divides by three, yielding a voting weight for the United States of 10.50.

For China, the calculation for 2020 would run like this:

P = 18.12
C = 14.13
M = 0.51
W = 12.45

For Nauru and other diminutive microstates, the calculation would run approximately like this:

P = 0.00005
C = 0.00005
M = 0.51
W = 0.17

Here below is a table adapted from Schwartzberg's book, showing the resultant voting weights of leading nations using this three-factor formula under 2020 statistics (Table 18.1).

We can readily make a number of observations. Since the voting weights are tied to historically fluid factors such as relative economic might and population size, they would need to be recalibrated every so often to keep them updated with shifting distributions of world power. Thus, for example, the weights for China and the United States when Schwartzberg first calculated them using 2009 statistics were about equal: 9.64 (China) and 9.93

Table 18.1 Voting weights for leading nations using Schwartzberg's three-factor formula and 2020 statistics

The calculated voting weight is highlighted under "W" in the second column from right. The far right column shows how many seats each nation would receive using these proportions in a hypothetical 800-member World Parliament. P stands for the population factor; C stands for the economic contribution factor, derived from GNP; and M stands for the sovereign equality factor, or 1/193. Adapted from J. Schwartzberg, *Transforming the United Nations System.*[16]

Nation	GNP ($Tr)	Pop (million)	GNP (%)	Pop (%)	Sov equ	Formula	Wgt (%)	WP seats
			C	P	M	(P+C+M)/3	W	x/800
China	13	1,412	0.141304	0.181258	0.051	0.124521	12.45208	100
USA	20.4	331	0.221739	0.04249	0.051	0.105077	10.50765	84
India	2.7	1,380	0.029348	0.17715	0.051	0.085833	8.583267	69
Japan	5	125	0.054348	0.016046	0.051	0.040465	4.046468	32
Germany	4	83	0.043478	0.010655	0.051	0.035044	3.504432	28
Brazil	1.9	212	0.020652	0.027214	0.051	0.032956	3.295552	26
Indonesia	1.2	270	0.013043	0.03466	0.051	0.032901	3.29011	26
UK	2.8	67	0.030435	0.008601	0.051	0.030012	3.001185	24
France	2.8	65	0.030435	0.008344	0.051	0.029926	2.992627	24
Russia	1.7	145	0.018478	0.018614	0.051	0.029364	2.936396	23
Nigeria	0.4	206	0.004348	0.026444	0.051	0.027264	2.7264	22
Mexico	1.3	128	0.01413	0.016431	0.051	0.027187	2.718725	22
Pakistan	0.3	208	0.003261	0.026701	0.051	0.026987	2.698726	22
Italy	2	60	0.021739	0.007702	0.051	0.026814	2.681377	21
Canada	1.8	38	0.019565	0.004878	0.051	0.025148	2.514776	20
Bangladesh	0.3	164	0.003261	0.021053	0.051	0.025105	2.51045	20
Spain	1.5	46	0.016304	0.005905	0.051	0.024403	2.440312	20

(United States). But given China's remarkable economic growth during the 2010s – its GNP nearly tripled from $5.1 trillion to $13 trillion – its calculated weight for 2020 surpassed that of the US for the first time (12.4 vs. 10.5). What's more, this disparity between the two superpowers would probably keep on widening over the coming decade or two, since China's GNP is projected by many economists to surpass that of the United States around 2032. Cue the howls of indignation from nationalist circles in the United States, for whom this development would explicitly mark the end of the "American Century."

But these raw numbers need to be put back into their geopolitical context. More often than not, the United States and its allies tend to align their votes in the UN, forming broad coalitions of like-minded actors on the world stage. In a future crisis over the fate of Taiwan or the Senkaku Islands, for example, one can imagine a large number of nations siding with the United States in a key vote, adding up to a collective voting weight that greatly outstrips the impact of China. If the United States voted with Japan, Germany, the UK, France, Mexico, Italy, Canada, and Spain, for example, the total weight would add up to 37.6. It's worth remembering here that China's relationship with its great-power neighbors is far from close: India and Japan are regional rivals of China, and Russia has shown itself to be something of a wild card. In a bid to outvote the US bloc just described, China would need to bring on board India, Russia, Indonesia, Nigeria, Pakistan, and Bangladesh – and this would still not suffice, for it would only add up to a weight of 34.9. If one compares these two hypothetical voting blocs, moreover, the United States enjoys a clear advantage, for its grouping is comprised of reliable, long-standing allies, whereas China's grouping is far more tenuous in nature.

The underlying point here is that both superpowers would need to work assiduously to court allies around the world, using diplomatic, economic, and military incentives to build strong and stable working coalitions – just as the Americans and Russians found themselves compelled to do during the Cold War. Diplomacy, in such a world, would continue to play an essential role in relations between the Great Powers and the lesser powers of the planet. Most important of all, the rise of China would no longer be quite so likely to destabilize the global balance of power: it could be contained and managed via skillful maneuvering in the UN by the United States and its allies over the long haul.

The islanders of Nauru would no doubt be displeased at all this, for their voting power would decline more than fivefold, from 1.0 in the present

273

General Assembly to 0.17 in the new World Parliament. But in the end, they might be persuaded to accept the compensatory benefits of the new system: as the Philippine ambassador once pointed out, it's better to have a small say in a potent body that actually gets things done, rather than a larger say in a weak body that never accomplishes anything of lasting importance. Schwartzberg's formula, moreover, still amplifies the voting clout of Nauru's citizens well beyond their actual influence in world affairs: the third weighting factor, M, is deliberately designed to mitigate the gross disparities in economic, demographic, and military power that characterize the world's nations. The real-world ratio of power between China and Nauru is on the order of 140,000 to 1 (population) or 118,000 to 1 (economy); but the ratio between their weighted votes would be 73 to 1. The underlying principle of the three-factor formula is to strike a delicate balance – paying due respect to the very real differences in clout among nations, while still giving the smaller countries a meaningful say in collective policymaking. In this scenario, politics in the UN legislative body would no longer unfold in a weird, ethereal space of fictional equality, totally separate from the actual landscape of economic or military might. The UN legislature would become a place of real politics – the forum where coalitions of Great Powers, middling powers, and lesser powers transacted the major deals and compromises required to manage global affairs.

Such a bicameral legislature would be highly unlikely to come into being at one fell swoop; rather, it would evolve by degrees over long spans of time.[17] The process could start with the creation of a "purely consultative" but symbolically important World Parliament in today's UN system – an 800-seat assembly directly elected by all the world's citizens, and operating according to the weighted seating system set forth in the far right column of Table 18.1 above. Then, after a few decades had gone by and people had become accustomed to the operation of this new body (and duly noticed that the world did not come to an end with its creation), they could gradually expand its powers beyond the purely consultative role. They might allow it to pass binding legislation in low-stakes domains where little controversy prevailed (the regulation of air travel, for example, or the harmonization of national telecommunication systems). These would be the first true "world laws" to be passed by the UN – moving a qualitative step beyond the old system of nation-to-nation treaties. As a few more decades went by, the scope of the binding laws passed by this body could be extended into more important areas of global governance, such as labor regulation, environmental management, or the restriction of offshore tax havens. At some point in this process, the old General Assembly could be converted into a Chamber of States using weighted voting, and from that point on a majority vote in both chambers of the UN legislature could be required before any binding world laws would take effect. And in tandem with this process, of course, the other principal organs of the UN would also need to undergo incremental reforms.

THREE OPTIONS FOR A REVAMPED UN EXECUTIVE

Since the Security Council is where the main action happens at the UN, this would most likely be the toughest nut to crack when it came to deep reforms. Option One would therefore be to keep the existing format in place, but to at least open up the number of permanent, veto-wielding seats so that all the Great Powers of today's world were represented. In such a system, the question of the veto could be handled in one of two ways. Switching to a two-veto requirement would render it harder for any single obstreperous nation to block UN action; but this would still keep the Council weak and unreliable, since it wouldn't be all that hard for two nations to team up in vetoing important decisions that were unpalatable to one or both of them. A three-veto requirement for Option One might therefore be even better over the long haul.

Joseph Schwartzberg, however, puts forward an entirely different and novel proposal in his book: to get rid of the Security Council altogether, and replace it with a more universal executive system based on twelve world regions.[18] Let's call this Option Two. Every nation would be invited to join one region or another, and each region would send one delegate to the new, twelve-member UN Executive Council. The principle of weighted voting would apply here, with each regional delegate wielding a vote share commensurate with his or her region's actual weight in world affairs. Three of the regions (China, the United States, and India) would be comprised by single large and powerful nations; the other nine would be composed of groupings of countries that were based on territorial, cultural, political, or historical affinities. Here in Figure 18.1 is Schwartzberg's map of his proposed system, showing the regional groupings and their relative voting weight using his three-factor formula and 2009 demographic and economic statistics.

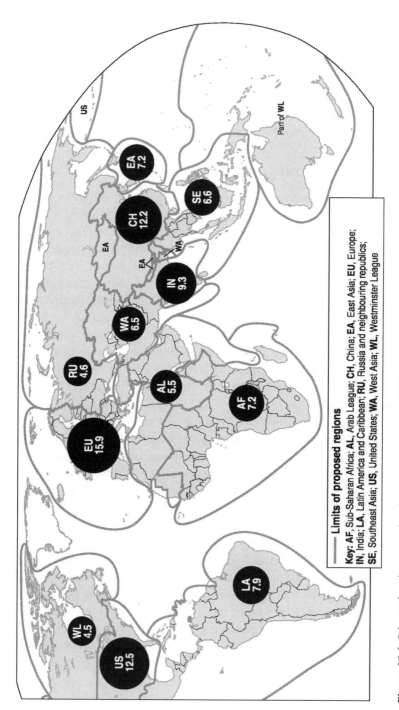

Figure 18.1 Schwartzberg's proposed twelve-region system for a UN Executive Council using 2009 statistics; numbers and circle sizes denote each region's weighted vote as a percentage of the global total.[19]

Key: **AF**, Sub-Saharan Africa; **AL**, Arab League; **CH**, China; **EA**, East Asia; **EU**, Europe; **IN**, India; **LA**, Latin America and Caribbean; **RU**, Russia and neighbouring republics; **SE**, Southeast Asia; **US**, United States; **WA**, West Asia; **WL**, Westminster League

— Limits of proposed regions

Schwartzberg readily acknowledges the many quirks and obvious drawbacks of this proposed system. Canada would form part of a newly minted construct known as the Westminster League, which would also include Australia, New Zealand, and the island statelets of the western Pacific. Israel would be separated from its Middle East neighborhood and grouped together with the EU. Japan would form part of the same East Asia region as South Korea *and* North Korea(!).[20] Some regions, like the Russian and East Asian ones, would be dominated by single nations (Russia and Japan, respectively) wielding preponderant economic and military power over their fellow regional members. In a post-Brexit world, moreover, the United Kingdom might well wish to join its Commonwealth partners in the Westminster League, adding a third continent to that region's rather bizarre territorial boundaries; and if this happened, it would reduce the dominant weight of the EU. The weighting numbers, once updated for current statistics, would also need to allocate considerably greater power to China.

For all these reasons, then, Schwartzberg's twelve-region proposal is unlikely to become a reality. Nevertheless, I've included it here because its advantages are also quite compelling and provide constructive food for thought. In many cases, these twelve regions align neatly with existing regional organizations (the EU, Organization of American States, Arab League, African Union, Association of Southeast Asian Nations, etc.) through which the world's nations have already organized themselves. The current North–South imbalance in the Security Council, and the gross over-representation of Europe, would be effectively addressed. Most important of all, every country in the world, large or small, would be given an ongoing say in the executive decisions of the UN – not just lip service as in today's system, but actual voting power. Despite these impressive advantages, however, the fatal flaw of the twelve-region idea lies in the politically fraught nature of the regional boundaries, which require too many bizarre territorial contortions and diplomatic realignments, and would probably render the concept a no-go.

Option Three, therefore, would be to combine the best elements of the first two ideas: keep the Security Council, but enlarge it significantly; abolish the veto altogether; and switch the decision-making mechanism to a weighted voting system. Today's G20 group comprises the world's leading economic powers, which have been holding annual meetings since 1999 to keep the global economy running smoothly. If the revamped Security Council included the top fifteen G20 nations plus one seat for the African Union, the following countries would be given seats there: the United States, China, Japan, Germany, India, United Kingdom, France, Italy, Brazil, Canada, Russia, South Korea, Australia, Spain, Mexico, and the

African Union. (The seat for the African Union, which comprises 55 member nations, would give a voice to that continent, where no single nation wields sufficient economic clout to make the top fifteen in the G20 list.) Not only are these the world's largest economic players, accounting for more than 90 percent of Gross World Product, but they constitute about 70 percent of the global population and three-quarters of the world's land area. Such a sixteen-member executive would greatly strengthen the UN's legitimacy as a representative governing body: its inclusion of China, India, the African Union, Brazil, Australia, and Mexico would provide substantial representation of the global South.

How would the voting weights for the Security Council be calculated? Among the many possibilities, the following method might work best. We can adopt the same weights for individual nations as those calculated via Schwartzberg's three-factor formula for the World Parliament (the resulting percentages would be slightly higher because the Security Council would only comprise 16 members rather than 193). For the African Union, however, an adjustment would need to be made, because its large collective population and low economic output would distort its voting power within the Security Council. (Its unmodified voting weight would be 11.2, putting it on a par with the world's most powerful countries – an unreasonable allotment, given the realities of world politics, and one that would definitely be a deal breaker for the G20 nations.) One sensible compromise would be to allot the African Union a weight equal to the *average* of all the other fifteen nations' voting weights. This method would yield the table of voting weights shown in Table 18.2.[21]

Some readers might object that it's a mistake, both practically and morally, to treat the African Union as a special case in this way. But what are the alternatives? If the number of Security Council members is limited to the top fifteen G20 nations, so as to keep the system manageable, then no African countries would be represented there at all. If the number were expanded so as to include on the Council the African nation with the highest GDP (Nigeria, the 27th ranked economy in the world), the Council would need to operate with an unwieldy total of 27 members. The solution proposed here – treating the African Union as a single entity on the Council, with a voting weight of 6.21 – is admittedly an imperfect one, because its combined GDP and population are about equal to those of India, which enjoys a voting weight of 12.46. Why not calculate the voting weight for the African Union using the same formula – which would yield a weight of 11.2? The answer is simple: India is a unitary nation, whereas the African Union is not. India,

Table 18.2 Security Council voting weights for top fifteen G20 nations plus African Union using Schwartzberg's three-factor formula and 2020 statistics

The calculated voting weight is highlighted in the far right column. The weight for the African Union is the average of all the other nations' voting weights. Adapted from J. Schwartzberg, *Transforming the United Nations System.*[22]

| | Security Council Fifteen plus African Union | | | |
Nation	GNP ($Tr)	Pop. (million)	World Parliament voting weight	Security Council weight w/Afr U
China	13	1,412	12.45207903	18.28
USA	20.4	331	10.50765009	15.36
India	2.7	1,380	8.583267288	12.46
Japan	5	125	4.046467973	5.64
Germany	4	83	3.504431545	4.83
Brazil	1.9	212	3.295551711	4.51
UK	2.8	67	3.001185094	4.07
France	2.8	65	2.992627114	4.06
Russia	1.7	145	2.936395602	3.97
Mexico	1.3	128	2.718725233	3.64
Italy	2	60	2.681377091	3.59
Canada	1.8	38	2.514775539	3.34
S. Korea	1.6	51	2.497938643	3.31
Spain	1.5	46	2.440311808	3.23
Australia	1.3	26	2.282268237	2.99
African U	2.2	1,250		6.21

moreover, is the world's largest democracy, whereas the African Union comprises many despotic or authoritarian countries. This compromise solution would give a substantial voice to the African continent in Security Council decisions, while keeping its representation more closely proportional to the continent's actual sway in world political and economic affairs. It is an imperfect solution, but arguably better than all the other politically feasible alternatives.

In order to "veto" a motion or decision in this system, one of these sixteen members would need to cobble together an ad hoc coalition of like-minded Security Council members, mustering a sufficient percentage of voting weights to block (or push through) a given resolution. In this scenario, the politics within the Council would fairly accurately reflect the actual ongoing relationships among the world's leading nations, ideological groupings, or regional blocs.[23] (I'll discuss the practical workings of this political system in greater detail in the next two chapters.) Although 123 smaller countries would still remain spectators to Security Council action, every continent would be represented by two or more nations, and the vast majority of the world's population would be represented in the Council's decisions.[24]

WORLD CONSTITUTION AND WORLD COURT

For the sake of argument, then, let's imagine that what I've sketched so far has become a reality at some point in the coming hundred years or so. The UN now operates via a bicameral world legislature and a sixteen-member Security Council, both of which use the three-factor formulas for weighted voting described above. What's clearly missing in this picture is the crucial element of law. Such a world will need a constitution to lay out the basic rules and principles through which the system will operate, as well as a high court to interpret those rules and principles, and to adjudicate disputes among the players.

Here, too, the process will likely be slow and incremental in nature. In our present world, national sovereignty rules the day: even entangling military alliances like NATO are based on nation-to-nation treaties that can be revoked at any time, and even the partially supranational EU still relies on national leaders to frame its key executive decisions.[25] But ever since 1919, humankind has been experimenting with ways to extend the rule of law to a higher sphere above the nation-state, and the process has gained new momentum in recent decades. In 1952, as the six founding members of the EU got the ball rolling for the European integration process, one of their first acts was to create a European Court of Justice empowered to provide binding arbitration for disputes among the participants; it currently has 27 member nations, and comprises a basic element in the day-to-day operations of the EU.[26] The World Trade Organization, created in 1995, provides an independent judicial organ for resolving trade disputes, and its 164 member states have bound themselves to accept the verdicts rendered and to promptly rectify any violations.[27] The International Criminal Court, which opened its doors in 2002, is charged with prosecuting genocidal acts or other crimes against humanity. Since that time the court's membership has grown to 123 nations, each of which has agreed to grant the court full jurisdiction over its own citizens in cases when those citizens have engaged in genocidal activities.[28]

These halting, tentative steps still leave us a very long way from a full-fledged World Constitution and World Court. But the logic behind these path-breaking judicial innovations is unambiguous: if nations wish to work peacefully together over the long haul, they need agreed-upon rules to guide them and a formal institution above them to adjudicate their inevitable disputes. If the UN comes to be incrementally transformed over the next century, therefore, a core component of this process will necessarily entail a constitutional convention at some point in the future – a major conference that not only replaces the old UN Charter with a different foundational document, but also creates an effective World Court.[29] The existing UN court – the International Court of Justice created in 1945 – is a pathetically weak instrument because it relies on the *voluntary* submission of nations to its authority. Over time, in gradual increments, this situation will have to change: just as the legislative reach of the World Parliament would progressively broaden in scope with the passing decades, so the authority of the World Court would also need to grow in tandem with the other UN bodies. In the end, the value of a court only extends as far as its ability to hand down enforceable decisions on those who are brought before it.

MANAGING THE GLOBAL ECONOMY

The Nobel-prizewinning economist Joseph Stiglitz has made a persuasive argument that the Europeans committed a major mistake when they launched their common currency, the euro, in 1999.[30] In fact, he maintains, it was two mistakes wrapped into one. The European Union was not yet ready to have a common currency, in his view; and worse still, the way the euro itself was set up was far too rigid and constraining, robbing the member-nations' central banks of key instruments for managing the ups and downs of their national economies. Although economic and political integration had indeed come far since the 1950s, the fundamental disparities among EU countries were still far too pronounced. National banks and political leaders in northern and southern Europe were still playing by very different sets of rules when it came to matters like deficit spending, taxation, or providing a generous cushion of welfare guarantees to their populations. A country like Germany, with its abhorrence of inflation and its strictly disciplined limits on budgetary deficits, was fundamentally ill-suited to work in enforced lockstep with nations like Greece, Italy, Spain, or Portugal, in which far looser constraints were the norm.

For Stiglitz, binding all these disparate countries to a common currency under the authority of a single central bank was practically guaranteed to produce a crisis sooner or later, because it removed essential tools (such as interest rates, monetary liquidity, or currency devaluation) that states could use in responding proactively to local challenges or instability in their individual economic cycles. To make matters worse, the euro system tended to keep interest rates artificially low year after year, thereby incentivizing runaway borrowing by the EU's weaker economies – which in turn left them particularly vulnerable to sudden fluctuations in the global markets.[31]

When the crisis finally hit after the American financial meltdown of 2008, the Eurozone plunged into a serious downturn from which it had still not fully recovered a dozen years later. Weak growth rates, chronically high unemployment, and harsh austerity measures provoked deep discontent among the European populations, fueling the rise of right-wing populist demagogues who called for nationalist economic remedies that (so they claimed) would bring swift relief. The Brexit calamity was one direct result of this crisis, and in Stiglitz's view, the EU was headed for even worse instability in the coming years unless drastic reforms were undertaken.

The Eurozone monetary system, in short, had been launched much too soon; and its rules of operation had been far too inflexibly designed. Proponents of a united Europe had wagered that a common currency would greatly accelerate the economic, political, and social integration among the member countries; but it ended up having the opposite effect. Precisely because it had been established prematurely, when its members were still insufficiently aligned in their budgetary, fiscal, and market systems, it had precipitated a chronic crisis that threatened the long-term viability of the union itself.

For proponents of a global federal government, the implicit lesson here is straightforward: when it comes to economic and financial governance, don't try to jump the gun. A single currency, a central bank, a unified set of economic and fiscal rules – these should be seen as the crowning results of a long process of social, economic, and political integration that has finally reached its mature and culminating stages of development. They should definitely not be regarded as tools for pushing forward the alignment of national economies during the earlier phases of the global integration process.

It's likely, therefore, that the coming century will not see the emergence of a single global bank and common currency – even if the UN system does manage to gradually advance toward a more integrated form of political federalism. According to the economists Barry Eichengreen, Arnaud Mehl, and Livia Chitu, it's quite possible for several major currencies to function effectively alongside each other as the anchoring benchmarks for global economic transactions.[32] In their book, *How Global Currencies Work: Past, Present, and Future,* they argue that the American dollar and Chinese renminbi will probably come to coexist as central factors in global affairs over the coming decades – and that they may even be joined in this role by other alternatives based on Brazilian, Indian, or EU financial instruments (or perhaps, one might add, by even newer cryptocurrency instruments like Bitcoin).[33] Precisely because global economic disparities are even more extreme and wide-ranging than the disparities within the EU, the integration of the world's financial systems will probably advance slowly over the coming century or so. Today's core institutions such as the IMF, World Bank, and WTO will no doubt need to be periodically modified or even perhaps revamped as the decades go by, but we are unlikely to witness anything comparable at the global level to what happened with the advent of the euro in 1999 – not, at least, unless the world's political unification has in the meantime progressed to far higher levels.

KEY AGENCIES

The newly invigorated UN will need a broad array of subsidiary agencies to carry out its expanded coordinating roles on the world stage. I'll only list three of the most important action-areas here (a vast scholarly literature exists for each of them). The core issues of accountability, economic development, and enforcement are discussed in Chapters 19 and 20.

UN Office for Emerging Technologies. Alongside such fields as AI, nanotechnology, and biotech, who knows what new powers the scientists and engineers of the coming century will deliver into the hands of humankind? Most of these new inventions (if not all of them) will inevitably be Janus-faced in nature, serving as potential vehicles of great benefit *or* harm. It will fall to national governments to regulate these new technological domains, making sure that proper safeguards are in place to protect the public. But without strong global coordination, these national efforts will remain weak, uneven, and ultimately ineffective. The UN's role here will be fourfold: to serve as the central clearing house for accurate information on these cutting-edge domains; to coordinate national regulatory efforts, setting basic standards, benchmarks, and "best practices;" to channel UN funding and assistance to poorer nations, so that they don't become weak spots in the global chain of protections; and to enforce the basic rules that have been established, applying economic sanctions and other pressures to ensure that all researchers and labs in every nation are in compliance.

World Health Organization. This UN agency is already doing invaluable work today: among its achievements so far are the eradication of smallpox, near-eradication of polio, creation of an Ebola vaccine, and major reductions in HIV/AIDs, malaria, and tuberculosis worldwide. During the COVID-19 pandemic, however, the vulnerability of the WHO to political pressures from leading nations became apparent: the Chinese successfully lobbied the agency to play down the severity of the outbreak in its early weeks, while the Americans under President Trump reviled the agency and threatened to reduce its funding.[34] Over the coming century, this global agency will need to be more rigorously insulated from such political pressures, and armed with sufficient budgetary and human resources to do its vitally important job.

UN Office for Climate Change Mitigation. From an institutional point of view, it may prove helpful to separate climate change from the other challenges of ecological management and sustainable development: coordinating the decarbonization of the world's economies, coupled with the gargantuan technological project of removing excess CO_2 from the atmosphere, are more likely to be handled successfully by a single-focus agency with its own experts, diplomats, and budget. Ultimately, though, the sheer scale and financial cost of this endeavor will no doubt require the ongoing involvement of both the UN legislature and the Security Council. The fraught global politics of climate change will probably dominate the headlines for at least the next hundred years. Here is a fictional sketch of how the process might unfold.

Vignette 8: Cooling a Planet (2133)

My brother Samuel was born in the Bad Year. 2039. The year the mare, Nessie, gave birth to a stillborn foal.

Samuel died three years ago at the age of 91. The malaria finally got him. God willed it to be so. We buried him the way he would have wanted, Amish style, in a pine casket, and laid him to rest in our community cemetery overlooking the view to the west, the gentle hills of our Ohio home. We placed a wooden gravestone, marked only with his first name, to remind us that our presence here is transient like wood, and that our names are known intimately by God.

I'm still wearing black though the other women in the family have gone back to their customary clothes. "Hannah," my friend Sarah asked me, "you just had your 94th birthday last week. Don't you think it's time to let him go?"

I told her, "Samuel was dear to me, and I miss him."

"We all miss him," she said.

Vignette 8: (cont.)

I nodded. Wearing black makes me feel closer to him. It doesn't hurt anybody, and I intend to keep doing it.

They called it the Bad Year because out in the broader world many calamities befell humankind. The great storm struck the East Coast cities, Washington, New York, and Boston, leaving them under six feet of water for three days. Even here in Ohio, the rains were terrible that summer. Scientists said the Great Barrier Reef had completely died that year in the warming ocean. Six F5 tornadoes hit the country that season, along with fires throughout the Pacific Northwest. Many died.

I know these things because I've been serving as the chronicler for our community these past decades, the person charged with recording what happens. Eli Troyer and the other elders asked me to perform this service, saying I was gifted by the Lord with the skills for it. I didn't want to do it. I wanted to tend to my husband Levi and my daughter Rebecca and our farm. But they insisted, so I eventually said Yes. They asked me to begin reading a national newspaper regularly so that I could relate to the elders the important things that were happening in the outside world, the world of the English. Once again I was reluctant to do this, but they said our community needed to understand what was happening out there if it was to succeed at perpetuating its ways through these times of turbulence. So I said Yes to that as well. I chose the Christian Science Monitor, *which everyone said was a reliable source of information, and read its news summary once a week, relaying it to the elders as best I could.*

The English responded to the Bad Year by making many changes. A new political group formed, known as the BP, or Beyond Polarization movement. It didn't succeed as a party, but its groundswell of support among the citizenry made a big impact on the Republicans and Democrats. They stopped bickering so much and elected new leaders who promised to seek compromise solutions. From what I can tell, the gridlock really did decline somewhat after that.

The new carbon tax didn't affect us here in Sweetwater, of course, because we scarcely relied on fossil fuels at all. We stopped using kerosene in our lamps, and built a solar installation along the ridge facing south by the Yoder and Hershberger farms. We used the electricity to charge batteries for our new LED lamps, and life went on as before. But out in the English world, big change was afoot. They had to redesign their cars, their homes, their food, their cities. It took many years, but eventually they did it.

Also the robots came. We laughed, some of us, when we saw them. Eli Troyer called them the Devil's Handiwork, but my husband Levi said they were

Vignette 8: (cont.)

hilarious to watch. They acted just like humans – English humans. But unlike the English they were always polite.

The Guaranteed Minimum Income began in 2066, the same year Aaron Stoltzfus died after his plough horse kicked him in the head. This new law didn't affect us Amish either, because we didn't have unemployment. On the contrary! We had to work harder than ever, what with the climate getting hotter, the dust and droughts. Down in Coshocton they even had a wildfire in the forest by the old Erie Canal. For the English it meant another big change when the GMI began. But they had no choice. All those polite robots.

I turned 31 in 2070. My daughter Rebecca was six. In the Christian Science Monitor *that year a huge headline read: NET ZERO. It seems the English and the other peoples of the world had succeeded in reducing their greenhouse gas emissions to nearly nothing. There was still some methane coming from farms, and some carbon dioxide coming from agriculture, but these could be offset by the new carbon-removal machines that were being built here and there.*

But the planet kept warming. The science of it was complicated, but it seems there were vast areas in northern Canada and Siberia where permafrost was melting, and this was releasing a lot of methane. Also the polar ice was melting, which was making things worse. So even though they'd reached Net Zero, global warming kept on getting worse.

Here on our farms we could clearly see it. Every year a little hotter than the last. Water was becoming hard to come by on some of the hilltop farms. Dust filled the air when the horses dragged the reaper machinery through the fields. New kinds of bugs and birds appeared. Old kinds dwindled and vanished. I began seeing armadillos trundling down the dirt road by the creek.

And then malaria came, along with other tropical diseases. We were unprepared for that, and poor Samuel got bitten by a new kind of mosquito from the Gulf Coast and became so ill he almost died. We managed to save him but it was a close thing, and the doctors down at the university hospital in Columbus never did succeed in getting that parasite completely out of his system.

So when they put in the giant carbon removal machines in Sandusky, I was gladdened. I explained it to the elders. The machine takes carbon dioxide from the air and pumps it deep underground for permanent storage. It's powered by a nuclear plant that generates millions of watts of electricity without affecting the climate. Eli Troyer said nuclear plants were the Devil's Handiwork, but I explained that these were a new kind of nuclear plant that couldn't melt down

Vignette 8: (cont.)

and didn't produce materials for nuclear weapons. He said it was the Devil's Handiwork nonetheless. I told him this kind of nuclear plant actually consumed the spent fuel from old warheads, making it easier to get rid of the weapons. He stroked his gray beard a moment, then said the Devil was cunning and sometimes concealed his schemes in the appearance of good. I told him the nuclear plant was necessary to power the gigantic machine that was removing huge amounts of carbon dioxide from the atmosphere 24 hours a day. He shook his head and said the whole thing was Devil's work from start to finish.

Then the English started with the artificial clouds. Solar Radiation Management, it was called. I tried to explain this to the elders as well. Eli Troyer had died the year before – it was 2086. The elders said it sounded like an especially clear case of Devil's Handiwork. Interfering with the sunlight itself. They stroked their beards and shook their heads. They asked why the English were doing this strange thing. I explained that it was an emergency measure to try to cool the Earth before the planet's warming cycle got totally out of control. They shook their heads.

They were right. It didn't go well. Insects stopped being able to find their way back to their nests and hives, particularly the bees. So they died in great numbers, and could no longer pollinate the plants. You could see their tiny bodies gathered in piles here and there where the wind currents collected them. The English tried using genetic methods to develop new bee species that could navigate better with the altered sunlight. But it didn't work. They also tried to pollinate the plants using billions of tiny microdrones that could fly from one flower to another. That failed too.

So the English stopped making artificial clouds. And gradually over several years the bees came back and the plants were pollinated once more. The English kept frantically building more of the nuclear-powered carbon removal machines, installing them all over the planet. It was very expensive, but at this point there was no longer any choice. The newspaper headline read: TIPPING POINT.

It was a close thing, from what I can gather.

The summer of 2097 was the hottest on record, with temperatures of 127 over several days in our part of Ohio. We didn't have air conditioning so we suffered a great deal. The old people and the sick ones had to be temporarily moved up to air-conditioned housing in Akron to keep them from dying in the heat. Many animals didn't make it through that summer.

Vignette 8: (cont.)

All over the world the English and the other peoples ended up building 35,000 of the enormous carbon removal machines, powered by 3,000 new reactors. It was a race against time, the editorials said. And it felt that way. Every country was slashing its military budgets and pouring money into carbon removal technologies. When I told this to the elders, they stood in a circle and gave a prayer of thanks. Then they quietly broke out a bottle of elderberry wine and we all sipped it together, clinking our glasses. Even me.

The tide turned in 2110. I remember it well because my granddaughter, Mary, gave birth to her first son that December, a baby boy whom we christened Amos. That was the first year the scientists reported that average global temperatures had apparently leveled off. For several years we all held our breaths as the scientific teams reported the yearly averages. They were holding steady.

In 2114, on Christmas day, the front page headline in the Christian Science Monitor *was not about Christmas. It read: COOLING! The scientists' verdict had come in, and the year 2114 had been slightly less hot than the average for the preceding decade. Celebrations for New Year's that December 31 were the most hope-filled ones in many years. The next year was a hot one again, but the following two were both cooler. And the trend went on, with the carbon removal machines frantically sucking carbon dioxide from the atmosphere, gradually outstripping the natural sources of greenhouse gases.*

And once the cooling got started, the climate cycle turned the other way. The ice at the polar regions began slowly re-forming, reflecting more of the Sun's light back into space; the permafrost stayed colder each year and released less methane; the reforestation programs started making an impact. From one year to another it was hard to see a difference, but over time it was unmistakable.

This year, 2133, the average temperature is back down to where it was in the year 2050. The scientists are confident that if we keep going like this over the next 30 years we'll be able to bring it back down to where it was in the year 1800. Then we can gradually turn off the carbon removal machines and let the planet start taking care of its own balance once again.

I won't be here to see it, of course. By that time I will have joined Samuel and the others up on the cemetery hill with its view over the Ohio valleys.

It's nice to think of it, though. Our people will be able to keep living the way we've done for the past three centuries. We are the real conservatives. That's why no one pays much attention to us. And we like it that way.

* * *

19

Keeping the System Accountable and Fair

ACCOUNTABILITY AND INDEPENDENCE

The world's federal government will be a mighty instrument – and lots of power-hungry leaders and groups from around the planet will vie with each other to manipulate it to their parochial ends. Some will no doubt attempt to seize outright control over it. They'll try every Machiavellian trick in the book, and we therefore need to anticipate their moves and equip the system to thwart them effectively and reliably. This is something every democratic government has always needed to do, in order to remain genuinely democratic over time, and the principle will apply just as strongly at the global level. Vigilance will always be the price of freedom, at all levels of government.

The founding fathers of the United States voiced precisely such worries about their nascent federal system, and devised a rigorous separation of powers that served the nation well in keeping the government accountable to the citizenry and in protecting basic freedoms. In the revamped UN I've just sketched, this principle of checks and balances has not only been emulated, but also ratcheted up even further. Four features of this proposed design would work together to "preserve, protect, and defend" the independence and accountability of the global body: strong subsidiarity, the separation of powers, an executive branch with plural leadership, and a high bar of supermajority voting before major action can occur in the legislature. Let's look at each of these features in turn.

In the centralized American system, the states are relatively weak in comparison with the power of the feds, whereas in the EU the opposite is the case: the key executive bodies in Brussels (European Council and European Commission) rely on high-level officials appointed by each member nation to make key decisions and initiate major new policies.[1] The revamped UN would follow the EU's more decentralized example. Strong subsidiarity would be the system's core principle, and most of the key decisions affecting people's lives would continue to be handled exactly as they are today, as the sovereign purview of existing national, provincial, and municipal governments. The World Constitution would strictly limit the role of the UN to handling only those specific planet-level challenges that cannot be dealt with effectively except via global coordination. These would include, for example: climate change, peace and war, global health, and dangerous emerging technologies. Even here, moreover, the principal role of the UN would be to serve as a forum for negotiation and coordination: only those policies that were supported by clear majorities of delegates in both houses of the global legislature would become world laws, binding upon all humankind.

Enforcement of world laws, moreover, would not be carried out directly by the UN: it would take place through the downward chain of command of national, provincial, and municipal governments. (The sole exception would be the UN's mid-sized military force, which would give the Security Council a rapid-response instrument for halting genocides and other crimes against humanity; but such interventions would be strictly limited in duration and scope. I'll return to this topic in the next chapter.) This system of rigorous subsidiarity is precisely how the EU has been handling its affairs over the past seven decades, in a supranational entity that comprises small and large nations, relatively richer and poorer nations, and 24 distinct ethno-linguistic groups of citizens.[2] The EU federal system operates with a light touch, and this has been one of the key factors in its long-term resilience and success; the revamped UN would closely emulate this basic principle.

Second, the separation of powers in the UN would mirror that of leading democratic nations. Its constitutional division between legislative, executive, and judicial branches of government would render it hard for any one group to wield disproportionate control over global decisions. Most importantly, the system of weighted voting would project the dynamics of a global balance of power into the daily operations of the UN: any nation or ideological group that sought to dominate the world body would soon find itself confronted by strong coalitions of opponents pulling resolutely in the opposite direction. Only decisions supported by a broad majority of the world's peoples could be successfully enacted in such a system.

Third, the revamped UN would also emulate the EU's design for its executive branch. Unlike the United States, where a strong presidency allows a single person to wield extraordinary influence, the UN would operate under a plural executive comprised of the sixteen members of the Security Council. To be sure, the UN would have a figurehead leader in the

Secretary-General, but this person's role would be to oversee the smooth functioning of the UN bureaucracy, not to propose legislation or make major executive decisions. In the Security Council and legislature, chairpersons would be elected to serve for short terms that rotated among the member states, and those individuals would act as formal conveners of meetings and sessions, wielding no more power than the other delegates.[3]

Finally, the procedural rules governing the Chamber of States and World Parliament would also be designed to thwart attempts at seizing undue influence. Apart from the system of weighted voting, a series of rising legislative thresholds could set precise limits on the kinds of laws passed and how they could be enacted.[4] Thus, for relatively low-stakes governance matters (such as setting the boundaries for ocean fishing rights, for example), a simple majority of 51 percent in both houses of the bicameral legislature might work well. For more contentious matters (such as regulating advanced AI), a 67 percent majority in both houses might be required. For still more controversial questions (such as imposing economic sanctions on a rule-breaking nation), a 75 percent supermajority in both houses might be needed. And finally, in the presumably rare cases when the Security Council and legislature were at loggerheads, or if a significant amendment to the World Constitution were proposed, an even higher supermajority of 80 percent might be required. These escalating thresholds would ensure that major substantive changes in UN policy were always in tune with the will of strong majorities of humankind.

Diplomats and scholars of global governance have also proposed a variety of other sensible ideas for keeping the UN system responsive to its citizens. With the rapid rise of thousands of new international nongovernmental organizations over recent decades, it would behoove the UN to have a mechanism for giving those myriad lobbying bodies a formal voice in ongoing deliberations over global laws and policies. Joseph Schwartzberg has suggested that the INGOs be divided into five thematic groups – one each for human rights, environment, economic development, peace and security, and democratic governance. According to his proposal, each of these groups would convene regularly in a UN-based Civil Society Coordination Council (CSCC), with voting power allotted to participating organizations on the basis of a weighted formula that reflected their membership numbers, funding, and regional provenance.[5] These five CSCCs would deliberate among themselves and then make formal recommendations to the members of the UN bicameral legislature, helping to advise the delegates as they shaped legislation. Although the role of the CSCCs would be purely advisory (since the INGOs themselves are not elected bodies), their on-the-ground expertise would tend to enhance the efficacy and legitimacy of the resulting policies. This system would give ordinary citizens and volunteers from around the world a chance to participate more directly in the UN decision-making process.

Funding the UN's daily operations has been a constant source of acrimony and frustration over recent decades. When a leading nation like the United States or China or Japan dislikes a certain decision made in the Security Council or General Assembly, it can simply withhold its share of funding in subsequent years. The UN, with its basic budget thus reduced, then faces an unpleasant choice: either submit to the economic blackmail and modify its policies (thereby losing credibility as an independent world body), or suffer a major impairment in its ability to function normally.[6] This vulnerability of the UN's budget to political manipulation clearly needs to come to an end – and the introduction of weighted voting would provide an excellent means for solving the problem. Since a key factor in the weighting formula is based on a nation's contributions to the UN budget, the rules could stipulate that this applies to contributions *actually paid* by member states. Delinquent members would see their voting weights swiftly reduced, and this would provide a strong incentive to keep paying up.

How much should each nation pay? The UN budget for 2020 was about $3 billion – roughly 37 cents per human being on Earth.[7] (By comparison, the US federal budget was $4.8 trillion in 2020 – $14,545 for each American citizen.) If UN funding were increased tenfold – to $3.70 per person – the range and scope of UN operations could be completely overhauled. Granted, this is politically impossible in today's world. But if we want to get serious with boosting the efficacy of global governance over the coming century, we'll need to change the way we think of the money we send to the UN. The revamped UN of the year 2150 would be a crucial vehicle for dealing with planet-level dangers, and today's UN, for all its flaws, is a first major step in that direction. Surely that's worth $3.70?

Two other features for keeping the future UN accountable would be a UN Administrative Academy and a board of auditors. In January 2021, President Donald Trump sought to subvert the electoral process in one of the key states he had lost, asking the Georgia Secretary of State Brad Raffensperger in a conference call to "find 11,780 votes" with which to throw the election back to Trump. Raffensperger, a Republican official, refused: he told the President that the Georgia election had been fair and honest. Trump then responded with a thinly veiled threat, telling Raffensperger that if he didn't obey, "that's a criminal offence. And you know, you can't let that happen. That's a big risk to you."[8] Still

Raffensperger stuck to his guns. The presence of a courageous official like Raffensperger – willing to go against his own party and his own president in defense of basic democratic principles – was a testament to the integrity of the administrative apparatus in the United States electoral system.

If such an egregious thing can happen in the United States, it can happen anywhere – including at the revamped UN of the future. This is where a UN Administrative Academy could make a substantial difference. Schwartzberg notes in his book that in today's UN system, the educational background and professional preparation of UN staffers and officials are notoriously uneven. In a great many cases, the people who work at the UN are highly motivated and extremely effective at what they do; but in too many other cases, the national provenance and narrow political loyalties of a given official outweigh the merit-based criteria required for staffing UN offices according to basic principles of good governance. Newspaper headlines about UN management practices resound from time to time with stories of junkets, nepotism, incompetence, or outright corruption.[9]

But what if all UN staffers and officials were required to go through a rigorous training process at a dedicated UN administrative academy before serving their terms? What if the funding for such training were to come from the UN itself, so that worthy candidates from even the poorest countries could have a chance to attend? In this scenario, Schwartzberg argues, a combination of thorough training and merit-based examinations would raise the performance bar much higher.[10] The UN would come to be known for the high capability of its staff, and in times of crisis it could reliably turn to administrative professionals who (like Georgia's Brad Raffensperger) would be better prepared to resist political pressures and to stand fast in defense of ethics and the rule of law. If one added to this mix an independent board of auditors, amply staffed and empowered to examine all the official records and transactions of the UN, the institution's reputation (and its actual practices) would undoubtedly improve in significant ways.[11]

FAIRNESS

A world in which poverty, disease, and illiteracy afflict billions of people will never be a peaceful or stable world – not to mention a just one. Dealing with this age-old problem will pose an especially daunting challenge over the coming decades, because the spread of advanced automation means that the disparity between rich and poor is likely to get even worse as the years go by. Many nations will probably be forced to start setting up a variety of

Guaranteed Minimum Income (GMI) schemes for their citizens, as the rising pressure from chronic mass unemployment becomes irresistible. (See the discussion in Chapters 5 and 10.) This in itself will create a major planet-level problem, because such nations will become targets of greatly increased legal and illicit immigration. The potential for heightened nativism, xenophobia, and outright conflict will grow swiftly; borders will become even nastier places than they are today.

Reducing world poverty has been on the international agenda for decades – with mixed results. Extreme forms of poverty – outright starvation – have declined significantly, but billions of people still languish in terrible living conditions. Poverty is known to development experts as a "wicked problem" because, while its symptoms are stark and relatively simple to observe, its underlying causes tend to be extremely complex in nature. Fighting poverty requires sophisticated, multipronged interventions that attack the problem simultaneously at multiple levels; economy, finance, healthcare, laws, education, culture, and environment are all entangled with each other in mutually reinforcing webs of interaction. No single solution in itself provides the key.[12]

Having said this, however, it's worth asking a few simple questions. Could a system of GMI ever be made to work well at the global level? According to the World Bank, a quarter of the world's population in 2020 lived on less than $1,160 per year.[13] What if, every year, the UN were to send a check for, say, $500 to every one of those two billion persons? The result would be an average 43 percent increase in the disposable income of those individuals – and even more in the millions of extreme low-income households where the annual total falls below this average figure. Presumably, this would dramatically change the lives of those people for the better. (Since such a measure might indirectly incentivize poor families to have more children so as to qualify for more $500 payments, the policy could limit the benefits to two children per family.) One of the great advantages of this scheme, moreover, is that it would bypass the thickets of corrupt officials and kleptocrats who regularly skim off for themselves a portion of foreign aid payments to national governments; global GMI would put all the money directly into the hands of the intended recipients.

How much would it cost to do this? About $1 trillion per year.[14] Just for the sake of argument, how might this amount be raised? There are currently about 295,000 persons worldwide who are classified as "ultra-high net worth individuals" because their wealth is greater than $30 million.[15] Together they own 8.3 percent of global wealth, or about $36 trillion.[16]

Historical statistics over the past three decades suggest that the average annual wealth gain for these ultra-wealthy people, via their investment portfolios, is on the order of 6.7 percent, or $2.4 trillion.[17] Now suppose that a flat annual wealth tax of 42 percent were levied on the annual gain in those persons' portfolios. This tax would yield the required total of $1 trillion per year, leaving the remaining $1.4 trillion to go into the pockets of the ultra-wealthy persons. In this scenario, as the $500 UN checks were transforming the lives of the poorest quarter of humankind, the millionaires and billionaires would continue enjoying an average annual 3.9 percent increase in their wealth. The "poorest" members of this wealthy group – owning just $30 million – would still see their portfolio grow by $1.2 million each year. The 2,700 billionaires in this group, with a collective net worth of $13 trillion, would still reap an average income of $187 million per person.[18] The rich would keep getting richer, but a bit more slowly, as a portion of their annual income was being redirected to the world's poorest households.

Needless to say, such a thing isn't likely to happen anytime soon, for any number of complicated (and simple) reasons. But this thought experiment does illustrate an intriguing point. Making a huge positive impact on the lives of one-quarter of humankind today would be relatively easy to do, *without tangibly altering the daily lifestyle of the rest of humankind in the slightest way*. It's a question of will and organization, not of available resources. The French economist Thomas Piketty, in his influential 2014 book *Capital in the Twenty-First Century*, has laid out a comprehensive scenario for precisely this sort of progressive global wealth tax, in great detail and with full discussion of the many practical challenges such a measure would entail. He concludes that such a tax would be eminently feasible, provided that sufficient levels of global political cooperation have been attained – and he makes a persuasive argument that the benefits of this taxation system would be tremendous and far-reaching in their impact.[19]

The conclusion I draw from this is that global GMI may indeed become feasible someday, but only in a more integrated world where a revamped UN provides a trustworthy instrument for the equitable collection and redistribution of funds. The millionaires and billionaires might not vote for it, but the billions of impoverished humans probably would – and in the UN I've been envisioning, the voice of those billions of humans would stand a good chance of being heard. (I suspect we might even be astonished at how many of the millionaires and billionaires might themselves support such a policy, if they knew their money was actually going to end up in the hands of those who needed it.)

Vignette 9: A Satisfying View: Guaranteed Minimum Income at the Global Level (2113)

Morne Boeuf was "only" 1,684 meters tall. So said the map. Javier still found himself panting hard as he and Soledad came up the steep winding trail through the scraggly growth of thorn bushes, cacti, and palmettos. All the big trees had been felled and hauled away centuries ago, so there was a good view over the surrounding Haitian valleys and villages as they climbed. René, their guide, was waiting where the trail turned to the left 50 yards ahead, smiling broadly as he gestured at the panorama.

Twenty minutes later they'd reached their destination, the tip of the promontory where a sweeping view to the north and west spread before them. The blue haze over the Golfe de la Gonâve filled the far horizon. Closer in, it was rolling hilltops with lush planted fields along the valleys and slopes.

"I don't care what you say, there was plenty of room up here to land the helicopter," said Javier, panting, as he caught up with Soledad and René.

Soledad turned to him and smiled. "Wimp."

She took off her backpack and pulled out her water bottle, taking several long swigs. Then she pointed down to the west. "See, over there? Those are the eleven villages we've been working with most closely."

Javier shielded his eyes with his hand and squinted, surveying the tiny knots of bright-colored houses amid the terraced fields. Over to the right was the shimmering water of the Lac de la Créplaine, behind the huge earthen dam that had been financed entirely by their Foundation. He could see the irrigation canals radiating along the hillsides toward the villages. Hard to believe that a land, a people, could accumulate so many centuries of unspeakable injustices and wretchedness and yet, somehow. . .

"The whole economy is coming round," she said. "We did our bit, but the real clincher was the GMI checks from the UN."

He nodded. They were getting similar reports from various parts of Asia, Africa, and Latin America about the swift impact of the global Guaranteed Minimum Income program. The exodus from the rural areas to the megacities had stopped. People were staying put, because there was work now. Towns that had emptied out were slowly repopulating. Long abandoned fields were tended once again. New resorts and hotels were being built along the coastlines. But also roads, schools, markets, hospitals. Once you got out of the vicious circle, things took off on their own.

Vignette 9: (cont.)

René pulled the small cooler from his backpack and brought out the sand-wiches and beer. The three of them sat on low rounded boulders near the edge of the steep incline and munched their sandwiches in silence. Javier could dimly hear the whine of an electric truck on a far-off road somewhere below. A seagull glided along the contours of the ridgeline before them, passing close enough that he could hear the air rushing through its wings.

* * *

DEMOCRATIZATION AND HUMAN RIGHTS

The US-based watchdog organization Freedom House compiles an annual list of all the world's nations, assigning them a score from 100 to 1 based on their civil liberties, democratic institutions, and protection of human rights. Sweden, Norway, and Finland top the list, with a score of 100; Syria, South Sudan, and North Korea languish at the bottom, with scores between 1 and 3. The current US score is 83. In recent years, the news from Freedom House has been alarming, for the average global score, which used to be slowly creeping upwards, has started gradually declining.[20] The autocrats, kleptocrats, and tyrants have had some good years.

Over the coming century, however, it's possible that a revamped UN could become a potent instrument for the spread of genuine democracy and human rights around the world. While all nations, from democracies to tyrannies, would be represented in the global legislature and Security Council, the daily business of the UN would be conducted according to rigorously democratic principles. Let's imagine a scenario in which the UN's three-factor weighted voting system (described in Chapter 18) has been introduced at some point in the coming century and is working reason-ably well. One day, the world's democratic nations come together as a bloc and introduce a "Freedom Initiative" at the UN. Under this initiative, a new, *four*-factor weighting formula for the UN's bicameral legislature will be intro-duced, in which a nation's score on the global democracy index will be added to the mix: the stronger your country's democratic institutions and protec-tions of human rights, the greater this factor will be. The formula could work exactly as described in Chapter 18, but with this modification:

$$W = ((P+C+M)/3) + F$$

The new "Freedom" factor F here is computed as 2 percent of the nation's score on the 100-point global list created by Freedom House. For example: Sweden, Norway, and Finland would have a factor score of 2, while Syria, South Sudan, and North Korea would have a factor score around 0.04.

Under this scheme, the voting weight for the United States would be determined as follows, using 2020 statistics:

P = 4.24 (US <u>population</u> as a percentage of the global total)

C = 22.17 (US GNP and proportional UN <u>contribution</u> as a percentage of total UN contributions)

M = 0.51 (this would be the same for all nations: the country's unit share of the total UN <u>membership</u>, or 1/193 in 2020)

F = 1.66 (2 percent of the US score of 83 on the Freedom House list)

W = 12.16 (applying the formula, one arrives at a voting weight (W) for the United States)

For China, the calculation for 2020 would run like this:

P = 18.12

C = 14.13

M = 0.51

F = 0.18 (2 percent of China's score of 9 on the Freedom House list; this is roughly nine times lower than the US score, in direct proportion to China's low ranking on the list)

W = 12.63

Table 19.1 shows the resultant voting weights of leading nations using this new four-factor formula under 2020 statistics. We can readily see what the "freedom factor" would accomplish. China and the United States would now carry about equal weight in the UN legislature, and India and Brazil would be rewarded for their partially democratic systems. The big relative winners would be the genuine democracies like the United States, Japan, Germany, the United Kingdom, France, Italy, Canada, and Spain, while the autocracies like China, Russia, Pakistan, Bangladesh, and Nigeria would find their relative voting power reduced.

Could such a reform realistically be pushed through? It would depend on the ability of the democratic nations to form a cohesive bloc, while offering tangible incentives to the "partly democratic" nations to join their coalition. When one considers that Freedom House classifies 82 countries as free, 59 as partly free, and 54 as unfree, the plausibility of such a scenario is clear: the 136 free and partly free nations greatly

Table 19.1 Voting weights for leading nations in World Parliament using Schwartzberg's three-factor formula and 2020 statistics, plus fourth factor F

F is calculated as Freedom House score ×0.02. The new voting weight that includes the F factor is in the second column from right. The "sovereign equality" principle (M) is designed to mitigate the chasm of power between the largest and smallest UN member-nations; it is calculated as the country's unit share of the total UN membership, and is the same number (1/193) for all nations. Adapted from Schwartzberg, *Transforming the United Nations System.*[21]

Voting weights with "freedom factor" F

Nation	GNP ($Tr)	Pop (million)	GNP (%) C	Pop (%) P	Sov equ M	Freedom factor F	Old weight	New weight with F	Difference from old score
China	13	1,412	0.141304	0.181258	0.051	9	12.45	12.63	0.18
US	20.4	331	0.221739	0.04249	0.051	83	10.5	12.16	1.66
India	2.7	1,380	0.029348	0.17715	0.051	67	8.58	9.92	1.34
Japan	5	125	0.054348	0.016046	0.051	96	4.04	5.96	1.92
Germany	4	83	0.043478	0.010655	0.051	94	3.5	5.38	1.88
UK	2.8	67	0.030435	0.008601	0.051	93	3	4.86	1.86
France	2.8	65	0.030435	0.008344	0.051	90	2.99	4.79	1.8
Brazil	1.9	212	0.020652	0.027214	0.051	74	3.29	4.77	1.48
Italy	2	60	0.021739	0.007702	0.051	90	2.68	4.48	1.8
Indonesia	1.2	270	0.013043	0.03466	0.051	59	3.29	4.47	1.18
Canada	1.8	38	0.019565	0.004878	0.051	98	2.51	4.47	1.96
Spain	1.5	46	0.016304	0.005905	0.051	90	2.44	4.24	1.8
Mexico	1.3	128	0.01413	0.016431	0.051	61	2.71	3.93	1.22
Nigeria	0.4	206	0.004348	0.026444	0.051	45	2.72	3.62	0.9
Pakistan	0.3	208	0.003261	0.026701	0.051	37	2.69	3.43	0.74
Russia	1.7	145	0.018478	0.018614	0.051	20	2.93	3.33	0.4
Bangladesh	0.3	164	0.003261	0.021053	0.051	39	2.51	3.29	0.78

outweigh the unfree ones. In the sixteen-member Security Council described earlier, only three players (China, Russia, and the African Union) qualify as unfree, while a whopping 71 percent of the voting weights are controlled by free countries (the United States, Japan, Germany, the United Kingdom, France, Italy, Canada, South Korea, Spain, and Australia) or partially free countries (India, Brazil, Mexico). It's entirely possible that the unfree countries, even acting in concert with each other, would fail to block the passage of this sort of Freedom Initiative.

Over time, the effects of such a reform might well prove dramatic: free countries would wield even greater influence than before in the day-to-day running of global affairs; partially free nations would receive strong incentives for strengthening the democratic features and human rights records of their political systems; and unfree nations would find themselves paying a significant ongoing price for their autocratic ways.

* * *

20

Collective Military Security and Economic Sanctions: How to Handle Rogues, Cheaters, and Fanatics

A NY GOVERNMENT THAT WANTS TO BE TAKEN seriously needs teeth. Throughout history, as city-states, principalities, and national units have jostled on the map, they have wielded a broad range of tools to influence each other's behavior – from diplomacy and economic favors at one end of the spectrum, to threats, hard sanctions, and military action at the other. The revamped UN of the twenty-second century will need access to the full range of these tools. What I sketch in this chapter is a world in which national governments will still play a key role, but in which they have also worked together to create a stable system of collective security.

In the discussion that follows I'll make a distinction between two basic kinds of military confrontation: clashes among lesser powers, as opposed to conflicts involving Great Powers and the possibility of nuclear escalation. In the former category we can count such wars as the Iraqi invasion of Kuwait in 1990, the civil wars in Yugoslavia and Rwanda, or even the 1956 invasion of Egypt by the combined forces of Israel, France, and the United Kingdom. In all these cases, no nuclear weapons were directly in play, and the scale of the clashing forces remained well below the superpower threshold.[1] Examples of the latter group would include the Korean War, the Taiwan Strait crisis of 1954, the Cuban Missile Crisis, or the 2014 Russian annexation of Crimea. Here the direct involvement of nuclear-armed nations (Russia, China, the United States) wielding huge military resources raised the calculus of catastrophic risk to a qualitatively higher level.

Civil wars, which have resulted in some of the bloodiest and most intractable conflicts since 1945, can also be categorized along these lines: when nuclear-armed Great Powers are directly involved in such conflicts, the stakes change dramatically. The civil wars of the 1990s in Yugoslavia and Rwanda, for example, grew out of long-standing internal ethnic and political rivalries; none of the warring parties were acting as direct proxies for an external superpower. By contrast, the Korean and Vietnam wars played into the broader Cold War confrontation between capitalism and communism; major Great Powers perceived these conflicts as directly affecting their national security interests, and therefore threw their own military forces into the fray.

CONFLICTS AMONG LESSER POWERS

In Chapter 16 I suggested that a good step toward more effective forms of collective security would be to endow the UN with a larger army than the one it commands today – a well-equipped force of 400,000 soldiers, standing at the ready to act as a first responder in times of civil war, genocide, or other major unrest. Here's an example of how such a force might be put to good use.

Vignette 10: The UN Army Neutralizes a Genocide (2077)

Unlike the other times, when the sound of gunshots had given enough warning to run out the back door into the jungle, this time they came silently in the middle of the night. This time it was not by chance that they came, on a last-minute whim.

Ngabo Mbabazi hid with his little sister Lolo in the storage space above the rafters while the soldiers raped his mother in the room below. They were taking turns. He heard them laughing as they watched each other do it. They had killed his father when they first arrived. Men and boys first. Now it was the women's turn.

His sister's hand was trembling. He squeezed it in the darkness and tried not to listen to his mother's cries. They seemed to be dying down now. At last.

He felt the soft pressure of his sister's tiny hand. In the darkness it was the only solid thing, amid this churning maze of terror. Keep quiet, Lolo, keep quiet. Suddenly there was a warm wetness on his bare feet where he crouched next to her. What was it? What was it? Then he knew. It was urine from Lolo.

The terror was passing now. He could feel it turning into something else, something that burned on his face like flames coming off his skin.

A bitter voice spoke inside his mind. It was his father's voice: he recognized it. You can be the quivering child in the rafters hoping your body's fluids released in uncontrollable fear won't leak down through the ceiling and drip onto the soldiers and give you away.

Or you can be the soldier. No other possibility exists.

At dawn on the third day of the nationwide rampage, as the death toll neared 40,000, the sky over Kigali filled with planes – huge white transport craft, escorted by jet fighters and helicopter gunships. The transport planes circled

Vignette 10: (cont.)

lazily over the airport, then opened their freight doors and released clouds of assault drones that fanned out rapidly across the runways and buildings below. Within minutes the local police and military forces had been pinned down and the airport was secured. The transport planes swung round and landed, one after another, until the tarmac was filled. On each plane the blue UN logo could be plainly seen.

Similar scenes were playing out simultaneously across the nation's other towns and cities – Ngoma, Kinazi, Kigarama, Ruhondo, and Nyagatare. A massive invasion of white planes from the skies.

Troops in blue helmets emerged from the planes and formed up in phalanxes that marched from the airport, fanning out among the capital's streets. Armored personnel carriers and small robotic tanks rolled down from the planes' giant freight doors and headed toward the city center. Jeeps and armored pickup trucks, all bearing the same UN logo, carried other troops swiftly into the suburbs.

Fierce battles broke out as the UN troops encountered roving gangs of Hutu and Tutsi militiamen. But the locals were no match for the technology deployed against them. Blue-helmeted soldiers released swarms of intelligent microdrones that flew into the midst of the militiamen, injecting them with somnistat. Each dronelet was three centimeters long, powered by miniaturized hydrogen fuel cells. After the soldiers opened the canisters and let them fly, the shriek of their thrust nozzles filled the air. They had tiny stingers under their wings, like the ultimate wasp – and there was no escaping them. While a frantic militiaman was wildly waving his arms and gun to fend off one of them, three other dronelets would come hissing in from all sides and inject him.

Soon the forests and fields surrounding the city were filled with fleeing men. Assault drones flew rapidly ahead of them, circling and delivering short machine gun bursts that brought the fleeing soldiers to a halt. A loudspeaker on one of the drones bellowed a harsh command, repeating it every 20 seconds. "Drop your weapons and lie on the ground with your hands in front of you. If you comply you will not be harmed." The militiamen obeyed. UN soldiers moved in, guns at the ready, and began handcuffing them.

From the city center the sound of gunfire and muffled explosions resounded for the next two hours, as UN forces seized control of the major arteries and buildings. A large group of heavily armed militiamen holed up in the Defense Ministry complex, spraying bullets from the windows into the surrounding

Vignette 10: (cont.)

streets. Microdrone swarms enveloped the building and found their way in through chimneys and ventilation grates. The UN soldiers waited at nearby street corners, listening to the shouts and cries of alarm from inside the building. Within ten minutes all the defenders lay slumped along the building's corridors, asleep.

A hush fell over the capital city, its population held now under an implacable grip of curfew and martial law. By nightfall the other major towns and roadways throughout the country had fallen in line. Casualties among the UN Peace Force numbered 117, with nine dead. The tally of Hutu and Tutsi militiamen killed stood at 94. All the other rampaging militiamen, numbering in the tens of thousands, were either in a forced sleep or in handcuffs.

Liarra Ondo, the UN Secretary-General, issued a broadcast from New York, calling for calm among the population. Rwanda, she explained, was now under a UN antigenocide protectorate, governed by international law. A representative of the African Union, the Nigerian diplomat Kimathi Adebayo, had been installed as the interim leader of the entire country. Adebayo's charge was to ensure that order was maintained and to preside over the gradual restoration of normalcy. The economy, Ondo emphasized, would soon be working properly again, with strong UN support. Now that the bloodletting had been brought to a halt, officials of the UN Peacebuilding Agency were already on their way, and would provide the resources to launch a robust process for truth, justice, and reconciliation. The goal, she assured the Rwandan people, was to ensure a smooth transition into prosperity and full democratic self-rule.

* * *

CONFLICTS INVOLVING GREAT POWERS

In the foregoing vignette, a decisive UN military intervention was possible because the clashing militias in Rwanda were no match for the weaponry and soldiers available to the broader international community. Such was also the case when Iraq invaded Kuwait in 1990: the UN-authorized military force, under American leadership, was able to dispatch Saddam Hussein's forces in short order and send them scurrying back into Iraq. The Suez Crisis of 1956 was somewhat different in one important respect, because the attacking forces included France and Great Britain, both of them Great Powers (the Brits already had nuclear weapons, but France did not acquire nukes until 1960). In the end, though, the UN was able to intervene successfully in this conflict as well, because both the Americans and Russians strongly opposed the surprise attack on Egypt, and issued peremptory orders for the attackers to cease and desist. The Anglo–French–Israeli leaders knew that their forces were no match for the two Cold War superpowers acting in concert: they immediately understood that they had badly miscalculated the politics of the situation, and called their soldiers home.[2]

But what happens when the transgressor nation is itself a nuclear-armed superpower? How can the UN enforce its will against a country whose military capabilities greatly outmatch the soldiers of the international army? (Not to mention the transgressor's nuclear missiles silently poised in their silos.) How can the world community respond effectively in a case like the 2014 Russian annexation of Crimea, which violated at least four major treaties as well as the rules of international law? What if a country like China, Russia, or the United States were to simply thumb its nose at an unfavorable verdict from the World Court?

The traditional response in such cases has been for the community of nations to impose economic sanctions against the aggressor/transgressor state. Scholars and diplomats have engaged in a passionate debate in recent decades over whether such sanctions actually work.[3] Some have claimed that they rarely succeed at compelling a transgressor to back down, and in some cases actually make things worse by triggering a "rally round the flag" response in the targeted nation.[4] Among the classic historical cases that are often cited, the following ones stand out.[5]

- The sanctions imposed against Mussolini's Italy by the League of Nations after the 1935 invasion of Ethiopia failed to undo the Italian aggression and may have actually helped drive Mussolini into the arms of Hitler.
- The harsh sanctions and oil embargo that the United States and other nations imposed on Japan in 1940–41, after the Japanese conquest of French Indochina, not only failed to get the Japanese to back down, but also convinced many Japanese leaders that war with the United States was justified and unavoidable.
- The US economic blockade against Cuba after Castro's accession to power in 1959 failed to bring the Communist leader to heel, and consolidated support for him among portions of the Cuban population.
- The economic boycott of Rhodesia by many nations, after the 1965 creation of a white supremacist regime there, failed to convince the

white minority to relent in their harsh policies, and the regime continued its rule until it was overturned via a guerilla war in 1979.

Arguing for the other side, however, the political scientist David Baldwin makes a compelling case in his book, *Economic Statecraft,* that these cases – far from proving that "economic sanctions never work" – actually deserve careful reconsideration.[6]

- The sanctions imposed against Italy in 1935 were mild and half-hearted in nature, reflecting the deep reluctance of France and Britain to antagonize Mussolini; these sanctions failed because they were far too weak to "bite."
- Most historians now concur that war between the United States and Japan had become nearly unavoidable by 1940, because Japan's leaders were hell-bent on a campaign of violent expansion and imperial conquest; the oil embargo merely precipitated a war that was going to come one way or another. What's more, the embargo did succeed in depriving Japan of badly needed oil supplies, which put the United States in a more favorable military position from which to conduct that war.
- Within a year of the US economic blockade against Cuba, Castro was able to secure major economic and diplomatic support from the Soviet Union; the sanctions failed because they were undermined by massive infusions of Russian goods.
- Sanctions against the Rhodesian white supremacists were weakened by systematic economic aid from neighboring South Africa; but these sanctions, coupled with ongoing global denunciation of the white supremacist system, did help lend legitimacy to the guerrilla insurgency that ultimately toppled the regime.[7]

What we have here, therefore, is something of a mixed bag. Economic sanctions are unlikely to succeed in achieving their maximal aims if they are weak or half-hearted in nature, or if they are "broken" by third parties who provide the targeted nation with an alternate source of economic goods. But even in such difficult cases, sanctions can still impose hard penalties on nations for their transgressive acts, thereby weakening their influence in the international arena. They also send an important signal to other potential transgressor nations, helping to deter them from similar forms of bad behavior.[8]

Here, once again, the revamped UN of the future could play an important and innovative role. In the global framework I've been sketching, opportunities for broad concertation in applying economic sanctions against a transgressor would tend to arise more often than they do today.

The bicameral world legislature, the enlarged and more representative Security Council, the World Constitution and World Court – all these institutions would provide a valuable forum for coordinating national policies to a degree that lies beyond reach in today's system.

Just to be clear: I am not postulating here a Pollyanna world where everybody gets along. Human nature being what it is, I am sure that ruthless games of power will still be played, and that competition, intrigue, deception, and greed will still characterize many of the interactions among nations. But if the system works the way it's supposed to, a new set of possibilities will also have opened up for the statespersons of that era: in at least *some* crises and confrontations, they will see that it's in their self-interest to work together through the potent coordinating instruments of the UN system.

This could have a transformative impact on the effectiveness of economic sanctions. If a nuclear-armed Great Power engages in egregious misbehavior, it could now find itself isolated on the world stage, confronted by a broad, grim coalition of tightly coordinated opponents. The bite of economic sanctions in such a situation could become far more serious.

Vignette 11: How Collective Security Blocked Rogue Action by a Great Power (2139)

Viktor Kromenko hadn't intended to betray his country. He'd always been a Russian patriot and had thrown his prodigious mathematical talent into the top-secret bioengineering project from the start, convinced that this was necessary to preserve his country's status as a Great Power for the twenty-second century. But two new factors had gradually emerged. First, the project had taken on heavier military overtones over the past few years, as the convergence of CRISPR and nanotech methods made new phyla of synthetic life forms possible. The Russian biotech team was coming close to creating an entirely new kind of pathogen – in flagrant violation of several UN treaties to which Russia was a signatory.

Second, Russia's oligarchical leadership had grown increasingly strident and dictatorial under the leadership of Oleg Dzerzhinsky. The secret police had recently arrested three of the most prominent pro-democracy intellectuals, including Vladimir Arbatov, the broadly popular leader of Democratic Motherland, the largest opposition party. After the arrests, five other activists who organized big protest rallies in Moscow and Saint Petersburg had

Vignette 11: (Cont.)

"disappeared" – but everyone knew what had happened to them: Dzerzhinsky's thugs had kidnapped them, and it was only a matter of time before their decayed bodies turned up in a ditch somewhere. This was how the government operated these days. In fact, it was no longer a real government: it was a mafia.

Gradually, with the passing months, Kromenko had fallen into deep despondency, and finally he'd come to his decision. The greatest danger to his country was now the leadership itself, not the foreigners whom they blamed for all the nation's woes. A true patriot had to know when to draw this line.

Things went quickly after that. Through a friend in the pro-democracy movement, Kromenko contacted a man who put him in touch with an undercover agent from UNIS, the United Nations Intelligence Service. They met in a hotel bar in Moscow, not far from the Kremlin itself. Kromenko told the agent about the information he wanted to share, and the agent said he would need incontrovertible proof. Kromenko said the security around the biotech project was impenetrable. The agent offered a large sum of money, along with various schemes for getting Kromenko out of the country, but Kromenko indignantly refused. "This is not about me, and what I can get out of it. I am doing this because I love my country. I am prepared to face the consequences." The agent nodded, then suggested a clever way to get the evidence out of the top-secret research complex where the pathogen was being developed.

Three days later, the two of them met again at the same hotel bar. They spoke briefly, and then each of them took off his tweed jacket, laying it on the empty chair beside them. They ordered drinks and sipped at them. Then the agent got up, put on Kromenko's tweed, and shook hands with him. Kromenko stayed on, sipping the remains of his drink, watching the agent go out through the revolving door. Ten minutes later he put on the agent's jacket, placed a tip on the table, and left.

The agent went through the heavy security at Moscow's Sheremetyevo airport late that evening. A battery of sophisticated scanners analyzed his suitcase, briefcase, and clothes. No alarms sounded. The tweed was made of smart wool fibers, with microprocessors and sensors embedded at the nanoscale, to allow the jacket to adapt to changing weather. Most clothes nowadays had some such smart feature, and the security scanners were calibrated to take them into account. Each of the 2,000 microprocessors in this tweed jacket had been packed with compressed digital files. Kromenko had uploaded in there all the data and evidence he could fit. It painted a comprehensive portrait of the illicit Russian bioweapon program.

Vignette 11: (cont.)

The agent walked calmly out of security, went down the long corridor to his gate, and boarded his flight. Five hours later the plane landed in New York. He went straight to the UN security building and handed the jacket over to the intelligence analysts.

The UN Secretary-General, Juan Antonio de Riberas-Mont, was awakened at 4:20 a.m. by a phone call from his chief of staff, Jordan Watkins. Watkins explained the situation. Riberas-Mont was silent for a moment. Finally he spoke: "Set an emergency Security Council meeting for 11 this morning."

At the meeting, the Russian delegate denied everything. He denounced the allegations as baseless slander against his country. Red-faced, he promised that there would be an accounting for such disgraceful trumped-up accusations. The Security Council drafted a formal statement condemning the covert Russian bioweapons project as a major violation of several treaties. By seeking to create this new pathogen, the Russian government was putting the rest of humankind at existential risk. This mortal threat would not be tolerated, the Security Council statement said. It demanded prompt remedial action from the Russian government, showing proof that the project had been suspended, and allowing UN teams to inspect all Russian research facilities – as the 2073 New Delhi Treaty on Advanced Biotechnologies had stipulated. Failure to comply, the statement warned, would result in severe consequences.

The Russian delegate was outvoted, fifteen to one, with a weighted tally of 95.9 vs. 3.9. The Security Council statement was made public on April 3, 2139.

President Dzerzhinsky went on Russian television that night, denouncing the UN resolution, and calling on all Russian patriots to rally behind him. The streets of Moscow, St. Petersburg, and half a dozen other Russian cities filled with clashing demonstrators – some bearing placards in support of Dzerzhinsky, others calling for his resignation. Police swarmed over the demonstrations, brutally restoring order.

Over the coming week, the Security Council met daily, frantically seeking a peaceful resolution to the crisis. It published a redacted summary of the intelligence findings, sharing the overwhelming proof of the Russian violations for all the world to see. Newspaper headlines responded accordingly. Even the stodgy Financial Times *of London ran an editorial that asked: "Shall we allow the Russians to endanger us all?" The New York* Daily Tabloid *was more blunt: "Crush Them Now!"*

Vignette 11: (cont.)

The Security Council issued two more resolutions on April 7 and 9, calling on the Russian government to respond immediately to the allegations – or suffer the consequences. But Dzerzhinsky and his fellow oligarchs only deepened their defiance. They acknowledged that advanced synthetic life forms were being developed in their labs, but insisted that all such research lay well within New Delhi Treaty stipulations. No bioweapon was being sought.

At the UN, the Russian delegate accused the Americans and Chinese of wanting to gain access to the Russian research data for their own nefarious purposes. He claimed that the principle of subsidiarity was being violated, and that his country's honor had been affronted. On April 11, President Dzerzhinsky declared a state of emergency. He allowed pro-government street demonstrations to continue in major Russian cities and clamped down harder than ever on all forms of dissidence.

On April 12, UN Secretary-General Riberas-Mont conferred by phone with the leaders of the world's most powerful nations. All were saying the same thing: this requires action. If the UN can't take care of it, we will.

Military forces around the world stood on high alert. In Moscow, Dzerzhinsky and his closest allies in the oligarchy hunkered down in the command center under the Kremlin.

Riberas-Mont went on television on April 13, flanked by statesmen representing the EU, the African Union, and the Latin American Confederation, as well as the United States, China, the United Kingdom, Germany, France, Japan, and Korea. Behind them in three rows stood the high officials of two dozen other major nations. It was an unprecedented show of global unanimity, and billions of persons around the world watched the Secretary-General's speech.

In his lightly accented English, Riberas-Mont laid out a set of crippling economic sanctions against Russia – a meshwork of phased restrictions. Every two days over the coming month, the sanctions would go up a notch, growing tighter and broader in scope. Within 30 days, if the Russians did not comply, their nation would be entirely cut off from the world economy. Any country or corporation that violated the sanctions and traded with Russia would also be placed under the ban. Phase One of the sanctions was going into effect immediately: a freezing of Russian assets in foreign banks and a prohibition on Russian nationals traveling abroad. Phase Two, a suspension of trade in foodstuffs, would go into effect two days later. The middle increments of sanctions would block all imports and exports completely, and the final steps

Vignette 11: (cont.)

would shut down the electric transmission lines from the network of advanced fusion reactors in Germany and France – a vital source of supplementary energy for the fragile Russian economy.

"Make no mistake about it," said Riberas-Mont, looking directly into the camera. "We will not relent, we will not bargain or negotiate. We are ready to make whatever sacrifices are needed to safeguard the world from the criminal actions of the Russian government."

The Secretary-General paused. "But the Russian people must also understand: as soon as their leaders comply with their treaty obligations, the response will be prompt and positive. The sanctions can be lifted at any moment. The choice is up to the Russian leadership, and more broadly to the Russian people."

Behind closed doors, the Secretary-General and the world's leaders entertained no illusions about the ability of the Russians to withstand the sanctions for a long time. Russia was a large country with plentiful domestic resources, and the Russian people were known for their hardiness. The real pressure would be political, not economic. No regime in history had ever endured such draconian sanctions without facing severe destabilization. The real goal of the sanctions was to drive an ever-greater wedge between the regime and the Russian people.

In the weeks that followed, the Russian government remained defiant. Dzerzhinsky declared martial law, issuing increasingly strident statements with each turn of the sanctions screw. "We are facing nothing less than all-out economic warfare," he said. "Just as we held firm against the Fascist invaders in the Great Patriotic War, so we will hold firm against this criminal assault on our country."

The world economy reacted immediately to the crisis, going into a steady slide. Stock markets declined everywhere, and joblessness ticked upward on all the continents as factories and businesses laid off workers. International travel declined noticeably. Governments scrambled to meet the needs of the newly unemployed. In some cities here and there – Paris, Seattle, Buenos Aires – street demonstrations called for an end to the Russian boycott and a return to the precrisis status quo. But these were exceptions. For the most part, the world's peoples rallied behind the UN and supported the sanctions. Fear of bioweaponry proved to be a powerful uniting force.

In Russia the situation swiftly degenerated. Within two weeks there were serious food shortages, and mandatory rationing was initiated. Within four

Vignette 11: (cont.)

weeks hospitals were announcing that they could no longer adequately care for their patients. At six weeks, assembly lines in key factories ground to a halt, as supplies of raw materials ran out. Inflation ravaged the value of the currency despite all measures the government took. The black market flourished. Some factories had to be shuttered to preserve electricity. Electric vehicles were being abandoned along the roads as the recharging stations shut down. Criminal gangs began openly roaming the streets, and army units had to be rushed in to restore order. Cholera broke out in Volgograd after the sewer treatment system failed.

On June 1 in St. Petersburg the first major antigovernment demonstration took place, in defiance of martial law. The protestors sang patriotic songs and chanted religious hymns, calling for Dzerzhinsky's resignation and free elections. They were mowed down by phalanxes of riot police, with thousands killed or injured.

News of the massacre spread quickly, abetted by UN satellites that bypassed the jamming technologies deployed by the government. A nationwide resistance movement swiftly formed, communicating from city to city via a revived Samizdat network that relied on paper copies distributed by hand. On June 3, demonstrations took place in Moscow, Novosibirsk, Yekaterinburg, Nizhny Novgorod, and other large cities. Each was harshly put down by riot police and special FSB troops, but the photos of the violence spread rapidly by Samizdat and stoked even more dissent. On June 4, antigovernment demonstrations broke out in more than 20 cities and towns, some of them becoming pitched battles as protestors armed themselves to fight back against the riot police. That night Dzerzhinsky went on national television, appealing for the population's support against what he described as a foreign-sponsored wave of subversive acts by malcontents and fringe elements.

The next day, June 5, huge crowds gathered simultaneously in three of Moscow's largest public squares, compelling the riot police to divide their forces as they sought to quell the demonstrations. Waving patriotic flags, the protestors converged on Lubyanka Maximum Security Prison, where Vladimir Arbatov, the head of the Democratic Motherland opposition party, was being held. Overwhelming the guards posted at the entrance, they forced their way into the prison and emerged triumphantly 20 minutes later with Arbatov in their midst. The crowd surged down the street to the nearby building of the central television station, where once again they overpowered the building's defenders

Vignette 11: (cont.)

and took control of the cameras. Arbatov, looking gaunt and disheveled, addressed the nation. "The criminal behavior of the previous regime," he stated in his low voice, "has brought our beloved country to the brink of catastrophe: we commit ourselves today to reestablishing genuine civil rights and rule of law." He called on his fellow citizens to stay calm, to reject violence, and to come to the support of the new democratic order that was being born.

Widespread clashes broke out in Moscow and other major cities. One regiment of soldiers at a barracks outside Moscow mobilized their tanks and began marching on the Kremlin, aiming to encircle the building and defend Dzerzhinsky and his regime. Alerted to this through the UN satellite feed, the prodemocracy rebels enlisted the aid of a much larger artillery regiment, which intercepted the oncoming tanks and blocked them from advancing. Meanwhile, prodemocracy soldiers were also mobilizing, taking up position at strategic buildings and crossroads throughout the capital. Other prodemocracy leaders were already on planes to other key cities, seeking to ignite the revolution in the provinces as well.

The consolidation process went on for several days, with demonstrations and counterdemonstrations in the streets, and frequent flare-ups of violence. But by June 9 it was clear that the new government had taken hold. Dzerzhinsky was caught trying to escape the encircled Kremlin compound via underground tunnels on the night of June 9, and arrested. Arbatov took care to include all the opposition parties across the key posts of power as he formed a provisional government. He replaced several dozen generals and admirals who had opposed the new order, and purged the secret police of individuals placed there by Dzerzhinsky.

Although UN officials requested that Dzerzhinsky and his associates be handed over for prosecution by the International Criminal Court at The Hague, Arbatov rebuffed this move. "These are our citizens," he insisted, "and we must try them here on Russian soil." He did, however, solemnly reaffirm Russia's commitment to abide by the New Delhi Treaty and ordered full cooperation with the UN inspection teams that flew into the country on June 23. "The illegal attempt by the Dzerzhinsky regime to create a novel bioweapon," he said, "is a blight on our nation's history. It will never happen again."

Two years later, at the culmination of an elaborate trial in the Russian High Court, Dzerzhinsky and his associates were found guilty of treason, crimes

Vignette 11: (cont.)

against humanity, and a variety of other violations. Dzerzhinsky stood and read aloud an impassioned statement:

"I am proud of my actions, which were always aimed at building the glory and strength of my beloved Mother Russia."

Since the death penalty had been abolished in Russia, Dzerzhinsky was imprisoned under eleven separate sentences of life without parole. He is currently held in the Lubyanka Prison in Moscow.

* * *

THE FINAL STEP... WHICH WILL NEVER BE TRULY FINAL

Zero Nukes... the words beckon like a mirage shimmering along the distant horizon. The geopolitical strategist Thomas Schelling saw it all too clearly when he reasoned his way through the contours of this compelling idea: abolishing nuclear weaponry in today's international system might actually render the world a *more* dangerous place.[9] Nations today are engaged in a ruthless zero-sum game of competition for dominance, and in this system, fear of nuclear catastrophe exerts an important stabilizing effect because the Great Powers know they have to avoid full-scale war with each other at all costs. The ominous presence of the nukes forces them to tread lightly around each other and displaces their bitter rivalries onto proxy wars and frenzied competition in the economic and technological spheres.

Remove the nuclear weapons from this equation, and suddenly you have a world in which the Great Powers might be more willing than before to risk direct confrontation. Any one of these conflicts could escalate into a major conventional war, and if such a war were going badly for one side, the temptation to rapidly rebuild as many nukes as possible and fire them at the enemy would be great. Knowing this, all the Great Powers would have contingency plans in place for rebuilding and launching their nuclear arsenals on short notice. It would be a nominally nuclear-free planet, but in some ways an even more precarious and perilous situation than the one that holds today.

It's only in a very particular kind of future that the complete abolition of nuclear weapons would make sense – a world in which the current self-help system has been gradually replaced by a stable, positive-sum game of collective security. This would have to be a planetary order akin to today's EU, in which all the national leaders (and a majority of the citizenry) recognize that the long-term benefits of working within the system vastly outweigh the short-term rewards of defecting back to self-help. Instead of automatically scrambling for unilateral advantage at the expense of other players, the nations in such a system have become conditioned to take each other's vital interests carefully into account – and they of course expect similar consideration from their counterparts in other countries. Only after a cooperative global framework like this had stabilized and proven its resilience over many years would it make sense to draw the nukes down to zero.

And even then, Schelling pointed out, this would always remain a strictly conditional state of affairs. The nukes can perhaps be dismantled someday, but the possibility will always remain of their being rebuilt by a new generation of leaders hungering after dominance or animated by fear of their fellow humans. The best that our species can hope for when it comes to these kinds of weapons is a relatively stable world system in which all the players clearly see the benefits of continuing to play by the common rules. As long as this advanced form of collective security holds sway, our species can enjoy a *provisional* reprieve from the instruments of our planetary suicide.

Despite these important caveats, however, Zero Nukes is still an excellent vision to pursue – for even a partial realization of this goal would greatly improve the long-term chances of human survival. Here's a sketch of how the process might unfold. The first step would be to beef up the UN army in the manner described earlier. Presumably, after several decades have passed, this enlarged UN force will have had a chance to log an impressive series of successful military operations, proving its ability to keep the peace (or restore the peace) in a wide variety of small-scale and even medium-scale conflicts. I depicted an example of this kind of decisive UN peacekeeping in Vignette 10.

At this point the world's nations could undertake a negotiated process of reducing their standing armies – slowly, incrementally, and in a balanced fashion that kept existing proportions of national military strength unchanged.[10] In the initial phase, for example, the world's defense forces could be reduced 10 percent across the board, in every country. UN inspection teams could monitor the process to ensure that everyone was making the same comparable set of reductions and no one was cheating.[11] If this went smoothly, another increment of military reductions could follow a decade or so later, bringing down the world's forces another 10 percent, with the partial disarmament process targeting every sector of offensive weaponry – land, oceans, skies, outer space, cyberspace. Russia and the

United States, whose 6,000 nuclear warheads apiece comprise 90 percent of the world's total, would reduce their respective arsenals down to 2,000 warheads; all other nuclear powers would simultaneously dismantle 20 percent of their warheads. The global total would go down by two-thirds, from 14,000 to 5,000 warheads, with proportionate reductions in nuclear missile and drone delivery-systems. Defensive technologies such as spy satellites and cyber firewalls would, of course, be left in place.

These two waves of reductions would save a lot of money. If the resulting funds amounted to 20 percent of global military spending, then in today's dollars it would add up to $400 billion (the world's nations currently spend about $2 trillion each year for military purposes).[12] Among the many excellent uses for this sum, perhaps the most symbolically impactful would be a treaty-based agreement to direct the savings of $400 billion per year toward paying for the CO_2-removal machines that were actively scrubbing the world's skies. Swords into ploughshares – or in this case, swords into a cooling planet.

Having witnessed the beneficial effects of this colossal peace dividend, the world's peoples might then be motivated at some point to undertake another round of military reductions: a further 20 percent drawdown in conventional forces, coupled with a second drastic dismantling of nuclear warheads. The Russians and Americans could come down to 200 warheads apiece, and the other powers could have 50 apiece, for a new global total of 750 warheads. This would still be enough firepower to severely degrade modern civilization, but with 95 percent fewer nukes in play than today's world, the risks of a war resulting in planetary ecocide would decline substantially. Meanwhile, of course, the gradual modification of the UN system I've been describing would also be taking place, and the political instruments of a global federal government would be emerging.

Some nations may prove refractory, and stubbornly refuse to go along with this process. But if the global federal institutions work properly, they will allow the other nations to act in concert together much more effectively than they do today. A majority of nations working in unison can put escalating economic pressure on recalcitrant members of the human community, in the manner illustrated in Vignette 11. Even a nuclear-armed Great Power can only endure so long in the face of such isolation and sustained sanctions: in the tightly integrated global economy of the twenty-first and twenty-second centuries, no country can long afford to go it alone. It's likely that any government seeking to pursue such aggressive or atavistic policies would eventually be overthrown from within, by its own citizens.[13]

Scroll forward another century or so from that point, and who knows? One possibility would be that a hundred years of living under a mature system of democratic global governance would eventually make an impact on the mentalities of the world's peoples, in a similar way to the wondrous transformation that the West Europeans have experienced since World War II. Imagine it for a moment.

It's 2250 now. The Chinese, Russians, and Americans view each other in roughly the same way as do the French and Germans today: as active partners who have managed to climb out of a rocky past and build something better for themselves. The global political mechanisms are running relatively smoothly, giving the nations potent tools for managing the conflicts and disagreements that arise from time to time. Climate change is going in reverse, and the planet is cooling back toward nineteenth-century levels. Pandemics are under preemptive control, via a global monitoring system and advanced medical and antimicrobial technologies. AI machines are everywhere, but they are subject to strict design specifications that keep them humble, stable, and tuned to fulfilling human needs. Military reductions have freed up significant funds for new spending on pressing domestic priorities, and global GMI has put an end to the worst disparities in human opportunities to thrive.

Over the years, science and engineering have continued their rapid advance. The resulting machines and biological constructs have become radically more powerful than they are today – yielding technologies that put Promethean possibilities into the hands of humankind. If they wish, the people of that era can cure diseases, explore other planets, invent new art forms and modes of communication, or plumb the subtle intellectual mysteries of the cosmos. Also, if they wish, they can craft ingenious new instruments of ravaging violence and harm.

But they choose not to build those deadly instruments, because there's no plausible reason for such weaponry to exist anymore. The harsh self-help world, the games of intrigue and zero-sum competition, have been gradually left behind, and the global federation provides a stable forum for working out international conflicts in constructive ways. The old rivals have become familiar and active partners, and the gnawing fear of Other People from Other Nations has faded into memory.

Now, at long last, the nukes can indeed come down to zero. Weapons of mass destruction are regarded by the people of this era in the same way as slavery, leeching, child labor, and cannibalism: they are part of the remarkable contortions of the human past. The knowledge of how to build such weapons will never go away, of course. But as long as the new framework that the humans have created for themselves can endure, the terrible weapons can stay safely dismantled.

* * *

21

What Could Go Wrong?

B UILDING AND MAINTAINING A GLOBAL federal government won't be easy: plenty of things could go awry along the way, and plenty more could go sour even after the government was up and running. Among the many grim possibilities, here are four salient ones.

- It's entirely possible that humans will fail to control the global warming process, and that we will cross a fateful tipping point in the coming century, beyond which no human actions will suffice to stop runaway climate change. Under these increasingly harsh conditions, one plausible reaction by the world's peoples will be to retrench back into regional or local enclaves, building walls of concrete and hate to keep out the desperate people beyond their borders.

- The global legislature and executive council could divide internally into hostile blocs of roughly equal voting power and military/economic clout. If this were to happen, the revamped UN would become just as thoroughly hamstrung as its predecessor was during the Cold War years. Global federal institutions would become little more than empty facades behind which the old logics of distrust, intrigue, and competition would still be running the show.

- Someone like today's Vladimir Putin – a cunning and cold-blooded leader hungry for domination – could perhaps find a way someday to subvert the checks-and-balances and other protective mechanisms that keep the UN accountable and democratic in its functioning. This is the long-standing nightmare of those who fear "world government" – the emergence of a global autocracy and police state. In this Orwellian scenario, it's likely that at some point in the decades after this dictatorship seizes power, a series of global resistance movements would rise up, seeking to wrest control back from the tyrannical regime. The result would be a planet-level civil war, unleashing bloodshed and misery on an unimaginable scale.

- A fanatical or dictatorial government along the lines of today's North Korea could perhaps manage to build a secret arsenal of advanced weapons of mass destruction, and use them to blackmail the rest of the world into compliance with its wishes.

In all these cases, what we are envisioning is really one and the same thing: a resurgence of the zero-sum system of "Us vs. Them" that prevails among the world's peoples today. There is no overarching, reassuring answer to such grim scenarios: their underlying logic has characterized the games of power and domination that have often prevailed here and there since the earliest civilizations. They form a perfectly real and plausible possibility for our collective future – and we'll need to be ever-vigilant in our efforts to prevent them.

CAN DICTATORSHIPS AND DEMOCRACIES REALLY COEXIST?

Without a doubt, one of the hardest challenges facing proponents of world government will lie in persuading autocratic and democratic states to play by a common set of rules. One can easily imagine, for example, a dictator seeking to game the UN system of weighted voting – giving inflated figures for population size and economic heft in order to boost the potency of their votes in UN bodies. In a democratic polity, this would be much harder to do, because the internal checks and balances of the system would allow whistle-blowers in the press or even in the government itself to come forward and denounce the false numbers being reported to the UN. A tyrant would presumably have a much easier time suppressing or deterring such whistle-blowers.

The underlying problem here lies in the qualitatively different sets of ethical and legal principles undergirding autocratic and democratic polities. In a genuinely democratic state, everything is deliberately geared toward protecting the transparency of the system's operation, as well as the citizens' freedom of action. The people who drafted the constitutions of democratic systems understood that it is deeply ingrained within human nature for humans to compete with each other for power and influence, forming groups and organizations to further their own interests. Therefore, the key to good governance lies in balancing these groups against each other, letting them serve as checks to each other's power, so that no single constituency can come to dominate all the others. Maintaining this delicate balance in an open and free civic space is one of the founding principles of the laws in all democracies. In autocratic polities, by contrast, the dominance of one group over all the others becomes the founding premise – whether this dominance is simply asserted by brute force (after a military coup, for example) or elaborately justified via a pyramid-like structure of laws and ideological principles (as in Communist China or Fascist Italy).

How can a world government work properly, when its member-states are so radically different from each other at this most elemental level of their civic and political functioning? This will no doubt prove to be one of the toughest challenges facing humankind over the coming century. Nevertheless, the *possibility* of a constructive answer lies in making a distinction between the domestic rules of operation that apply within a nation-state, as opposed to the external rules by which separate states conduct their business with each other. While it's generally true that democracies and dictatorships have a hard time getting along, there are still plenty of historical examples of their developing stable, nondestructive relationships that serve their mutual interests.

The most salient recent example is the Cold War relationship between the United States and Soviet Union – a particularly challenging case because their rivalry was both geopolitical and ideological at the same time. A traditional great-power competition (similar to the eighteenth-century rivalry between France and Britain, for example) was overlaid with an intense ideological competition between two rival political systems vying for the hearts and minds of the world's peoples. And yet, these two arch-enemies did not go to war. To be sure, they came hair-raisingly close in the Cuban Missile Crisis, but as the decades went by after that, they were eventually able to set up a tacitly agreed playbook of rules for dealing with each other. By the time of the INF treaty in the 1980s, they had even accepted limited mutual inspections of each other's military installations, in the interest of maintaining a stabilized condition of symmetrical arms control.[1]

My hypothesis here is that something analogous could perhaps emerge one day as a basic principle for nations coexisting under a world federal government. Many of them will not like each other. Many will be profoundly different from each other in the ways they run their societies back at home. Some of them will have long histories of mutual rivalry and even enmity. But the question remains: if they perceive it to be clearly in their national interest to do so, can they not learn over time to play by a well-defined set of rules that the UN has established as the baseline for active membership?

The UN framework will not work well unless the majority of its members – democracies and autocracies alike – come to see the special value of this global institution and actively *want* it to work well. The key here will lie with the planet-level solutions that the UN will be uniquely equipped to offer for the mega-dangers facing humankind. Over time, if the UN proves to be a relatively effective instrument in this regard, and the solutions it delivers are impactful and enduring, then most nations will probably be willing to override their misgivings and play by the basic UN rules. The trade-off will be worth the price.

The US–Soviet example suggests that this is not an unrealistic hypothesis. In order to build a constructive relationship, these two rival nations did not need to undergo the remarkable and extreme form of reconciliation that took place between the French and Germans after World War II; instead, all that the Russians and Americans needed to do was to identify precise areas of common interest, and then proceed rationally with implementing mutually aligned policies that served both of them effectively. In this respect, it did not matter that the Soviet Union was a totalitarian dictatorship and the United States was a democracy: their clear self-interest as nations lay in establishing simple forms of cooperation in key areas of foreign policy and military security. As long as it remained in their perceived interest to do so – as long as the benefits of the arrangement outweighed the costs – the system held firm.

If the world federal government is going to function effectively, certain core principles will need to be accepted by all major nations participating in the UN system. These will include, at a minimum:

- willingness to follow the common rules that govern the day-to-day operations of core UN institutions;
- willingness to obey decisions handed down by the World Court;
- transparency and accuracy in key statistics reported to the UN regarding population size, economic performance, and other factors related to voting weights;
- willingness to submit to ongoing UN inspections for verifying the accuracy of official records and statistics about voting-weight factors.

More broadly, what all this implies is a willingness to accept certain well-defined constraints on national sovereignty, in exchange for the benefits conferred by participating in the UN governance system. Nations will only accept these constraints if they believe that the overall trade-off redounds to their clear benefit; but if they do see such a benefit, then it will be strongly in their self-interest to play by the common rules that all the other member-nations are also following.

To be sure, this by no means implies that the functioning of such a world government would be peaches and cream. Human nature being what it is, and given the fraught history of international relations, one can expect that individual nations will be constantly jockeying for special advantages within such a system, engaging in all manner of power-plays, intrigue, cabals, and subterfuge – just as they have always done. After all, one sees these sorts of power games being routinely played by rival constituencies *within* our national governmental systems today, and there is no reason to believe such underhanded competitive practices would go away simply because the new framework had become global in scope.

But what a different world it would still be, compared with the semi-anarchic international system of today! Just as the nation-state brought a higher degree of order to the wide-ranging human behaviors within its territory, so the global federation would usher in a qualitatively new era in relations among peoples and states. There would be clear rules for everyone to follow – commonly agreed rules voluntarily accepted by member-states because of the advantages they delivered in terms of stability and security. Violators of these rules would face swift penalties for their misdeeds, in the same way that law-breakers face punishment in today's nation-states. The power-plays and intrigue among human groups would certainly continue to occur, but they would now be operating within a regulated space that placed clear limits on how far the skulduggery could go. Competitive gambits would only very rarely extend all the way into overt military threats; instead, they would now routinely take form as conventional games of politics, within a domesticated (global) sphere of tactics and strategies. This was precisely the "pacification effect" delivered by the advent of nation-state governance several hundred years ago – and to the extent that a planetary federation could be made to operate effectively, it too would deliver a whole new level of global civil order.

Here we come to the nub of the matter. What if certain large and powerful nations simply refuse to participate? One can readily imagine such a thing happening, for example, with harsh autocracies like Putin's Russia or Xi Jinping's China, or even with democratic countries in which populist and stridently nationalist leaders have won election. What then?

The answer is straightforward. As long as large numbers of the world's peoples still think of themselves according to the old mentalities of "Me First Always" and "Beware of the Nasty Others," the idea of a planetary federation will remain nothing but a pipe dream. This has been the premise of my argument all along. The mentalities of humankind began to change somewhat gingerly a hundred years ago, as the horrors of World War I impressed themselves on thoughtful people here and there. They changed even more drastically with the trauma of World War II and the grim prospect of nuclear holocaust. Now, with pandemics and climate change vividly on our minds, still more people are beginning to see the need for planet-level instruments of governance. My hypothesis is that as these planet-level pressures continue to escalate over the coming decades, more and more people will start to question the narrow, constricted nationalisms of the past. Whether they like it or not, they will be compelled to seek ways to work constructively with total strangers on other continents – and this will require them to create new institutional tools that bridge the gaps between them. Still more importantly, this process will demand new mental frameworks for thinking about who we are and how we draw boundaries around ourselves. Strong incentives will come into play, pushing the world's peoples toward a more cooperative ethos that makes such cross-border partnerships possible.

Still, all this remains nothing but a hypothesis: it's far from clear whether we'll be able to make this transition. Tribalism runs deep in the traditions of all human cultures, and who knows if we'll prove capable of moving beyond those primeval ways of seeing each other, gradually coming to envision ourselves within a new planetary tribe that includes us all? But here I take heart from the richness of the historical track record. In some respects, human nature has not changed much since ancient times, but this is definitely not the case with the arrangements through which humans have related to each other and conducted their daily business with each other. How we organize our societies, how we feed ourselves, how we use tools and exchange goods – these systems *have* changed many times over, sometimes quite profoundly, with the passing centuries. Perhaps there is room here for the eventual emergence of yet another set of arrangements – new patterns of expectation, reward, motivation, and exchange that bind us together more seamlessly across ancient borders. Today we remain far indeed from where we'll ultimately need to be, but it's possible that incremental changes – generation by generation, under the rising pressures of planetary dangers – will nudge a sufficient number of us gradually into a different frame of mind.

It comes down in the end to ongoing choices that we will make, and that our descendants will make. But it's very important to realize that these are indeed *choices*, not fixed or preordained pathways lying ahead of us. The future is more open than many people tend to think.

* * *

323

22

Conclusion

I WAS ACTUALLY A BIT SURPRISED BY THE way this book turned out. When I first started working on it, I was convinced that humankind was headed into a truly awful century of wrenching upheaval – and I saw very few reasons for hope. Climate change was progressing more rapidly than expected, and we were failing to take effective action. America and Russia were both moving back toward an aggressive arms race, and China was brashly entering the game of superpower rivalries. No one was doing much of anything about regulating synthetic biology and bioweapons. The slow and uneven response to the COVID-19 pandemic starkly exposed the weakness of international health systems; only the remarkable self-sacrifice of the nurses, doctors, and other essential workers kept the horrific toll from being even higher. A perilous race for AI dominance was already underway, and weekly headlines about successful cyberattacks presaged a grim future of insecurity in the digital sphere. The EU was dealing with the Brexit calamity, and many countries (including my own) were indulging in an atavistic nationalism that ran in the exact opposite direction from the international cooperation that we so urgently need. My motivation for undertaking this project went something like this: "Well, things look really bad, but if I at least chart the contours of the problem, maybe this will help someone else to figure out a set of solutions that I can't presently see."

But researching and writing this book changed my perspective. Strange as it may seem, I am more optimistic than when I started this project – for several reasons. Looking beyond today's discouraging events, I can now discern a broader horizon of cumulative developments that give grounds for hope. A hundred years ago, all we had was the vague rhetoric of the Hague conferences and the pathetically weak instruments of the League of Nations. Today we have a densely woven, multilayered meshwork of institutions coordinating (or at least seeking actively to coordinate) the myriad interactions of the world's peoples: from the UN and International Criminal Court to regional bodies like the EU or ASEAN; from the Universal Declaration of Human Rights to UNESCO; from business networks like the OECD and IMF to regulatory bodies like the World Health Organization; from antiterrorist organizations like Interpol to military alliances like NATO; from grass-roots groups like Greenpeace or Amnesty International to volunteer bodies like Doctors Without Borders and Oxfam. If you were to make a fast-forward movie of these endeavors as they emerged and spread their influence over the past half century, it would look like the self-organization of a young life form – a new kind of creature assembling its sinews, nerves, and vital organs around the planet's spherical core.

HISTORY IS A NONLINEAR PROCESS

Scientists who study complex systems point out that such systems come in two flavors: linear and nonlinear.[1] In a linear system, the dynamics are machinelike: examples would include a lawn mower or a spring-powered clock. Causal relations here tend to be simple, direct, fully predictable, and finely controllable. Parts interact with other parts in ways that can be well-characterized and understood. If you put together two or more of these processes, their interaction remains aggregative: it yields nothing more than the sum of the factors involved.

Nonlinear systems are a whole different kettle of fish. Here, the dynamics are fluid and often astonishing. We encounter such systems and processes scattered throughout the natural world: a large-scale weather pattern, a colony of ants operating via a sophisticated division of labor, a flock of birds shifting its aerial formation as one, an animal's immune system responding to a virus, or the firing of neurons within the human brain.[2] In these cases, causal relations tend to be reciprocally interactive and adaptive, hard or impossible to predict, and resistant to straightforward control. Parts interact with other parts in ways that are influenced by the larger whole of which they form elements; this often renders their behavior difficult to characterize and understand. Feedback loops come into play, reverberating back through the system and subtly altering the initial points of departure. If you put together two or more of these processes, their interaction is not always aggregative: it sometimes yields entirely new phenomena that exhibit a higher-order pattern of activity, not reducible to the mere sum of the factors involved. The soaring emotional tone of a Bach cantata emerges out of the sparking synapses inside a person's head.

Human civilization is a good example of an open-ended, nonlinear process operating through time. Our history books are full of stories in which relatively small changes at one point in the past ended up exerting an unexpectedly strong influence on the shape of the decades or even centuries that followed.[3] The French medieval historian Marc Bloch, writing in the summer of 1940 after the defeat of France, sought to think of ways that he and his friends might someday rebuild a new society in the wake of the terrible war that raged all around them. He articulated it this way:

> But of what is the general mind composed if not of a multitude of individual minds which continually act and react upon one another? For a man to form a clear idea of the needs of society and to make an effort to spread his views widely is *to introduce a grain of leaven into the general mentality.* By so doing he gives himself a chance to modify it to some small extent, and, consequently, to bring some influence to bear upon the course of events which, in the last analysis, are dictated by human psychology.[4]

Bloch joined the anti-Nazi Resistance not long afterwards; he was arrested and shot by the Germans outside of Lyon in June 1944 (just as the Allies were establishing their bridgeheads on the beaches of Normandy). But his hope-filled words captured the essential paradox of human agency. Our range of action as an individual person is always dwarfed by the collective patterns that govern our epoch: at any given moment, our power as individuals is heavily limited by the prevailing structures and rules. At the same time, when we exchange ideas with other people, and they in turn exchange those slightly altered ideas with still others, a single individual's impact can end up being multiplied tremendously, thereby modifying the broader societal structures and rules in significant ways.

As a concrete example, consider the way the Revolutions of 1989 spread across Eastern Europe and the Soviet empire. It's fair to say that most people who lived through the events of that year – including academic experts, journalists, diplomats, and statespersons –were *quadruply* astonished by the events that rippled so swiftly across the region.[5] We were astonished by how earnestly Mikhail Gorbachev and his team pursued their democratizing reforms; how pervasively the Soviet system had lost legitimacy and support – not just among the peoples of Eastern Europe but also among the republics of the Soviet Union; how rapidly the totalitarian political system, which had seemed so solid and impregnable for decades, imploded on itself; and how easily one of the most formidable military empires in history just fell apart. At one level, it seemed like a fairy tale: in one country after another, the people came out into the streets, chanting their slogans and waving their placards that demanded basic freedoms; the police beat them back; on the following days the crowds grew even larger; the politicians frantically made concessions in a bid to slow the hemorrhaging of their power; the crowds swelled into millions; and the regimes fell.

Historians can now look back with hindsight and discern in the preceding decades some of the deeper causal factors – the "grains of leaven" – that made this strange series of revolutions possible. There was the Prague Spring of 1968, which discredited the Soviet brand of communism by graphically showing its tyrannical nature – in ways that dispirited even some circles of Soviet intellectuals themselves. There was the image of German Chancellor Willy Brandt with his policy of *Ostpolitik*, seeking friendship with the peoples behind the Iron Curtain, kneeling and weeping before the Warsaw Ghetto in 1970. There was the Czech writer Václav Havel doggedly writing his dissident plays in jail, satirizing the government's double-speak and asserting the value of simply telling the truth. There was the Solidarity movement in Poland, exerting "people power" over more than a year before being crushed under martial law in 1981. And finally, there was the image of Gorbachev's reforms – of *glasnost* and *perestroika* transforming the political culture at the heart of the Soviet system itself. To an outside observer, all these developments seemed at the time like brave but futile events, compared with the immense, static structures of Soviet power. It carried a sense of sad hopelessness, like watching desperate civilians throwing rocks at the massive steel carapace of an unmovable Russian tank. But it turns out in retrospect that these seeming defeats, and the ferment of ideas and hopes that animated them, were quietly adding up to something profound. They were robbing the system of its legitimacy in the eyes of its own people, and eventually in the eyes of some of its own key leaders.[6]

Implicit here lies a significant piece of good news: small events can quietly accumulate influence far beyond the scope of their immediate impact. Precisely because history is a dynamic, nonlinear process, ideas matter – and by communicating them with each other and debating them among ourselves, we can tangibly alter the range of possibilities for what may happen far down the road. Seemingly minor decisions and deeds can gently bend the sequence of events down new trajectories. When Eskimo villagers take up a collection among themselves and send money to starving Ethiopians, the fabric of world governance toughens ever so slightly.[7] People who learn of the Eskimos' choice start to think of borders and oceans and strangers in a more open light. When the leaders of Great Powers find ways to work together through the ponderous mechanisms of the UN, rather than taking unilateral action, they are invisibly strengthening the credibility of global institutions in the eyes of the world's citizens.[8] As such events occur, whether we can see it or not, something shifts far down the line – at some point beyond the horizon – and new possibilities for global coordination spring into existence. Those distant possibilities become a little less far-fetched, and inch a small way closer to becoming a reality.

It's important here not to make the same mistake that Karl Marx made – thinking of history as an inexorable progression toward a predetermined end point. This was where his zealous Hegelianism let him down. Marx hoped that his confident analysis in *Das Kapital* would embolden the working class, since it framed their class struggle as a process that would inevitably lead to a triumphant result down the line. Taking up arms to hasten the process along, he believed, was justified by the glorious new social order that awaited humankind at the culmination of the long struggle. But in the end this teleological conception of history, along with its legitimation of violence, shunted the working-class movement down a path that led to Stalinism, Maoism, and other nightmares.[9]

We should learn the lesson from Marx's arrogance and take a more humble approach. Globalization proceeds apace, but there is no guarantee that it will lead humankind to invent the right solutions down the line. We are brilliant at creating new technological powers for ourselves, but then wind up using them all too readily in infantile struggles for dominance. Democratic forms of planet-level governance are badly needed for navigating the coming century, but our species may falter in its efforts to create them. The chances of a spectacular failure are as real as they can be.

But so are the chances of success. This is one of the key takeaways I draw from researching the present book. Looking toward the year 2100, I am sometimes tempted to think of the way ahead as a narrow and precarious path through a gauntlet of deadly traps – like a tiny ledge across a high cliff, surrounded by chasms on all sides. Yet this is probably a misguided way to frame the future for ourselves. Among the trillions of plausible pathways, there are a billion good ones to choose from, as our ideas and hopes and actions bifurcate forward through the ever broadening branches of decision-points. We may never get all the way to Peace and Justice, but we definitely have what it takes to gradually put in place a less dangerous, less violent, and more equitable world system. If we survey the landscape of the past century, tallying up the innovations humankind has made in creating instruments of global cooperation, the achievements are impressive ones. We have every reason to work together in carrying that process further, knowing that our efforts are building toward something of deep and lasting impact.

* * *

Endnotes

1 INTRODUCTION

1. John Horgan, "Bethe, Teller, Trinity, and the end of the Earth," *Scientific American* online (August 4, 2015). https://blogs.scientificamerican.com/cross-check/bethe-teller-trinity-and-the-end-of-earth/.
2. Horgan, "Bethe, Teller, Trinity."
3. Rhodes, *The Making of the Atomic Bomb*, 670.
4. James Conant, quoted in Hershberg, *James B. Conant*, 759.
5. The literature on this topic is of course immense. The following two books are a good place to start: Sewell, *Logics of History*; and Sunstein, *How Change Happens*.
6. Image courtesy of Our World in Data: https://ourworldindata.org/grapher/global-primary-energy. Source of statistics is Vaclav Smil, *Energy and Civilization*, and BP Statistical Review of World Energy: https://www.bp.com/en/global/corporate/energy-economics/statistical-review-of-world-energy.html.
7. Smil, *Energy and Civilization*; Yergin, *The New Map*; Landes, *The Unbound Prometheus*.
8. Image courtesy of Wikimedia Commons: "Nuclear fission chain reaction:" MikeRun modified by Michael Bess. https://commons.wikimedia.org/wiki/File:Nuclear_fission_chain_reaction.svg.
9. Image courtesy of Wikimedia Commons: "Cell proliferation:" https://commons.wikimedia.org/wiki/File:Cell_proliferation.jpg.
10. Christof Koch, "AI software teaches itself video games," *Scientific American Mind* (July 1, 2015), at: https://www.scientificamerican.com/article/ai-software-teaches-itself-video-games/; Elizabeth Gibney, "Self-taught AI is best yet at strategy game Go," *Nature* (October 18, 2017), at: https://www.nature.com/news/self-taught-ai-is-best-yet-at-strategy-game-go-1.22858; Ian Sample, "'It's able to create knowledge itself': Google unveils AI that learns on its own," *The Guardian* (October 18, 2017), at: https://www.theguardian.com/science/2017/oct/18/its-able-to-create-knowledge-itself-google-unveils-ai-learns-all-on-its-own.
11. Image courtesy of Google's AI project, DeepMind. See John Hessler, "Computing Space VIII: Games cartographers play: AlphaGo, neural networks, and Tobler's First Law," (April 12, 2016): Library of Congress website: https://blogs.loc.gov/maps/2016/04/alphago-neural-networks-and-toblers-first-law/.

12. George Musser, "Artificial imagination: how machines could learn creativity and common sense, among other human qualities," *Scientific American* 320:5 (May 2019), 58–63.

13. Sanger, *The Perfect Weapon*; Buchanan, *The Hacker and the State*; Singer and Friedman, *Cybersecurity and Cyberwar*; Perlroth, *This Is How They Tell Me the World Ends*; Chertoff, *Homeland Security*; Bernstein, Buchmann, and Dahmen, eds., *Post-quantum Cryptography*.

14. Ord, *The Precipice*; McKibben, *Falter*; Bostrom and Cirkovic, eds., *Global Catastrophic Risks*; Wuthnow, *Be Very Afraid*; Wallach, *A Dangerous Master*; Posner, *Catastrophe*; Dennis Overbye, "Government seeks dismissal of end-of-world suit against collider," *New York Times* (June 27, 2008). https://www.nytimes.com/2008/06/27/science/27collider.html. Accessed May 20, 2018.

15. Sunstein, *Laws of Fear*; Beck, *Risk Society*.

16. See the discussion of the epistemological dimension of climate science in Chapter 12.

17. Archer, *Global Warming*, 122–31; Romm, *Climate Change*; Nordhaus, *Climate Casino*; Dryzek, Norgaard, and Schlosberg, eds., *The Oxford Handbook of Climate Change and Society*; Intergovernmental Panel on Climate Change (IPCC), *AR6 Synthesis Report: Climate Change 2022*, at: https://www.ipcc.ch/report/sixth-assessment-report-cycle/ ; David King, et al., "Climate change: a risk assessment," Centre for Science and Policy, Cambridge University (2015), at: file:///E:/Mike/Wisdom%20at%20the%20Brink/Images/climate-change–a-risk-assessment-v9-spreads.pdf; Hansen, *Storms of My Grandchildren*; Vandenbergh and Gilligan, *Beyond Politics*.

18. Church and Regis, *Regenesis*, 231–32.

19. Church and Regis, *Regenesis*; Gronvall, *Synthetic Biology*; Schmidt, ed., *Synthetic Biology*; Carlson, *Biology Is Technology*.

20. Italics added. Stephen Hawking, Stuart Russell, Max Tegmark, Frank Wilczek, "Stephen Hawking: 'Transcendence' looks at the implications of artificial intelligence – but are we taking AI seriously enough?" *The Independent* (May 1, 2014), available at: http://www.independent.co.uk/news/science/stephen-hawking-transcendence-looks-at-the-implications-of-artificial-intelligence-but-are-we-taking-9313474.html.

21. Estimates of the size of the asteroid or comet range from 7 to 50 miles in diameter. The crater it left is about 100 miles wide. Shonting and Ezrailson, *Chicxulub*.

22. Nugent, *Asteroid Hunters*.

23. Breining, *Super Volcano*; see also Ord, *The Precipice*, 74–77.

24. Ethan Siegel, "Could the Large Hadron Collider make an Earth-killing black hole?" *Forbes* (March 11, 2016); Eric Johnson, "The black hole case: the injunction against the end of the world," *Tennessee Law Review* 76:4, 819–908; Lincoln, *The Large Hadron Collider*.

25. Rudy Baum, "Nanotechnology: Drexler and Smalley make the case for and against 'molecular assemblers,'" *Chemical Engineering News* 81:48 (December 1, 2003), available at: http://pubs.acs.org/cen/coverstory/8148/8148counterpoint.html.

26. Kurzweil, *The Singularity Is Near*, 403.
27. Ibid, 419–20.
28. Mumford and Winner, *Technics and Civilization*; Ellul, *The Technological Society*; Illich, *Tools for Conviviality*; McKibben, *Enough*; Berry, *A Place on Earth*; Berry, *It All Turns on Affection*; Berry, *Life Is a Miracle*; Bonzo and Stevens, *Wendell Berry and the Cultivation of Life*.
29. Nye, *Technology Matters*, 47; see also Pool, *Beyond Engineering*.
30. Seidensticker, *Future Hype*, 68–69.

2 FOSSIL FUELS AND CLIMATE CHANGE

1. Archer, *Global Warming*; Motoaki Sato, "Thermochemistry of the formation of fossil fuels," *The Geochemical Society, Special Publication* No. 2 (1990), at: https://www.geochemsoc.org/files/6214/1261/1770/SP-2_271-284_Sato.pdf.
2. Image courtesy of Gail Tverberg, OurFiniteWorld.com. "Per capita world energy consumption, calculated by dividing world energy consumption by population estimates, based on Angus Maddison data" at: https://ourfinite world.com/2012/03/12/world-energy-consumption-since-1820-in-charts/.
3. Image courtesy of Our World in Data, "World GDP over the last two millennia," at: https://ourworldindata.org/grapher/world-gdp-over-the-last-two-millennia?time=1.2015.
4. Pinker, *Enlightenment Now*.
5. Smil, *Energy and Civilization*.
6. Archer, *Global Warming*, 122–31; Romm, *Climate Change*; Nordhaus, *Climate Casino*; Dryzek, Norgaard, and Schlosberg, eds., *The Oxford Handbook of Climate Change and Society*; Intergovernmental Panel on Climate Change (IPCC), *AR6 Synthesis Report*; King, et al., "Climate change;" Hansen, *Storms of My Grandchildren*; Vandenbergh and Gilligan, *Beyond Politics*.
7. Image courtesy of Scripps Institution of Oceanography: https://keelingcurve.ucsd.edu/.
8. Archer, *Global Warming*, 120–22
9. Archer, *Global Warming*, 120–22; Intergovernmental Panel on Climate Change (IPCC), *AR6 Synthesis Report*; King, et al., "Climate change;" Hansen, *Storms of My Grandchildren*.
10. Tim Lenton, et al., "Climate tipping points – too risky to bet against," *Nature* 575:592–95 (2019); Daniel Rothman, "Thresholds of catastrophe in the Earth system," *Science Advances* 3:1–12 (2017); Lenton, *Earth System Science*.
11. Image courtesy of John Englander, "Chart of 420,000 year history: temperature, CO_2, sea level." See John Englander, *Moving to Higher Ground: Rising Sea Level and the Path Forward* (Science Bookshelf, 2021); JohnEnglander.net, at: https://johnenglander.net/chart-of-420000-year-history-temperature-co2-sea-level/.

12. Romm, *Climate Change*; Lynas, *Six Degrees*; Wallace-Wells, *The Uninhabitable Earth*; Dryzek, Norgaard, and Schlosberg, eds., *The Oxford Handbook of Climate Change and Society*; Hansen, *Storms of My Grandchildren*.

13. Bess, *The Light-Green Society*.

14. Romm, *Climate Change*; Lynas, *Six Degrees*; Wallace-Wells, *The Uninhabitable Earth*; Archer, *Global Warming*; Dryzek, Norgaard, and Schlosberg, eds., *The Oxford Handbook of Climate Change and Society*; Intergovernmental Panel on Climate Change (IPCC), *AR6 Synthesis Report*; King, et al., "Climate Change;" Hansen, *Storms of My Grandchildren*.

15. Sander van der Linden, Anthony Leiserowitz, Seth Rosenthal, and Edward Maibach, "Inoculating the public against misinformation about climate change," *Global Challenges* 1:2 (2017), 1600008; Naomi Oreskes, "The scientific consensus on climate change," *Science* 306:5702 (December 2004), 1686; Hulme, *Why We Disagree About Climate Change*; Oreskes and Conway, *Merchants of Doubt*; Marshall, *Don't Even Think About It*; Kolbert, *The Sixth Extinction*; Deese, ed., *Climate Change and the Future of Democracy*.

16. Gates, *How to Avoid a Climate Disaster*; Romm, *Climate Change*; Lynas, *Six Degrees*; Wallace-Wells, *The Uninhabitable Earth*; Archer, *Global Warming*; Dryzek, Norgaard, and Schlosberg, eds., *The Oxford Handbook of Climate Change and Society*; Intergovernmental Panel on Climate Change (IPCC), *AR6 Synthesis Report*; King, et al., "Climate change;" Hansen, *Storms of My Grandchildren*.

17. Under this midrange scenario, the new normal around the year 2100 would be on track to look something like this:

- Greenhouse gas emissions continue to rise until the 2040s, then gradually stabilize and decline to zero by 2070.

- Global average temperature in 2100 is 3 degrees Celsius higher than preindustrial times, and the climate is still warming because feedback mechanisms from factors such as melting permafrost, ice loss, water vapor, and wildfires are propelling new rises in temperature.

- Frantic attempts to remove accumulated greenhouse gases from the atmosphere via new technologies deployed in the latter decades of the century are struggling to keep up with the new greenhouse gases released naturally by a warmer planet.

- Oceans have risen by 3 feet and are still rising by as much as a foot per decade after 2100, forcing most coastal cities to be evacuated and relocated. About 40 percent of the planet's human population is directly affected.

- Droughts are much more frequent and severe than today, and agriculture has become impossible in many regions where it used to be practiced.

- Extreme weather events such as floods, superstorms, heat waves, and wildfires have become much more common and deadly than today.

- Ocean acidification and warmer waters have decimated the world's fisheries, and portions of the world's oceans are becoming dead zones.

- Many forms of wildlife and insects are going extinct.
- Tropical diseases have become endemic in most northern and southern regions nearer the poles.
- Forced migrations have become so severe that draconian measures of immigration control have been adopted by many nations, leaving millions to perish in the increasingly uninhabitable portions of the equatorial planet.
- Local wars and widespread civil strife are spreading as desperate populations in large swaths of the planet compete violently for dwindling resources of water and food.
- The global economy has slowed significantly as a result of the rising costs and burdens imposed by the challenges of working and living in a hotter climate.

18. Romm, *Climate Change*; Lynas, *Six Degrees*; Wallace-Wells, *The Uninhabitable Earth*; Archer, *Global Warming*; Dryzek, Norgaard, and Schlosberg, eds., *The Oxford Handbook of Climate Change and Society*; Intergovernmental Panel on Climate Change (IPCC), *AR6 Synthesis Report*; King, et al., "Climate change;" Hansen, *Storms of My Grandchildren*.

3 NUKES FOR WAR AND PEACETIME

1. Rachel Dobbs, "What was at stake in 1962?" *Foreign Affairs* (July 10, 2012), available at http://foreignpolicy.com/2012/07/10/what-was-at-stake-in-1962/.
2. Michael Dobbs, *One Minute to Midnight*.
3. Dobbs, *One Minute to Midnight*, 303.
4. Svetlana Savranskaya, "New sources on the role of Soviet submarines in the Cuban Missile Crisis," *Journal of Strategic Studies*, 28:2 (2005), 233–59.
5. Robert S. McNamara, interviewed by Errol Morris in *The Fog of War* (Academy Award-winning documentary film), Columbia Tristar DVD, 2004.
6. Thomas Blanton, "The Cuban Missile Crisis: 40 years later," Washingtonpost.com (October 16, 2002), available at https://web.archive.org/web/20080830221337/http://discuss.washingtonpost.com/zforum/02/sp_world_blanton101602.htm.
7. Image courtesy of Errol Morris. Still image of Robert McNamara taken from *The Fog of War*.
8. Image courtesy of Wikimedia Commons. Photo taken on February 17, 1955 by Olga Arkhipova: https://commons.wikimedia.org/wiki/File:Vasili_Arkhipov_young.jpg.
9. Olga Arkhipova, interviewed in "The Man Who Saved the World," PBS documentary (October 23, 2012). Available at: https://www.youtube.com/watch?v=qr_WkfOMx4c.
10. Ibid.
11. Ambinder, *The Brink*; Downing, *1983*.
12. Downing, *1983*, 198.
13. Image courtesy of Associated Press. Photo of Stanislav Petrov taken August 27, 2015 by Pavel Golovkin; see also Greg Myre, "Stanislav Petrov, 'The Man Who

' Saved The World,' dies at 77," *National Public Radio* (September 18, 2017), at: https://www.npr.org/sections/thetwo-way/2017/09/18/551792129/stanislav-petrov-the-man-who-saved-the-world-dies-at-77.

14. Henry Stimson, quoted in Rhodes, *The Making of the Atomic Bomb*, 642.

15. Michael Lennick, "We knew that if we succeeded, we could at one blow destroy a city," Interview with Edward Teller, *American Heritage* 56:3 (June/July 2005).

16. Four more such subs carry long-range cruise missiles rather than ballistic missiles, bringing the US total to eighteen. See the website of the Federation of American Scientists for an overview: https://fas.org/nuke/guide/usa/slbm/ssbn-726.htm.

17. Bess, *The Light-Green Society*, ch. 1.

18. See the more detailed discussion in Chapter 6.

19. Henry Fountain, "Compact nuclear fusion reactor is 'very likely to work,' studies suggest," *New York Times* (September 29, 2020). https://www.nytimes.com/2020/09/29/climate/nuclear-fusion-reactor.html?action=click&module=News&pgtype=Homepage.

20. Stanley Reed and Jack Ewing, "Hydrogen is one answer to climate change. Getting it is the hard part," *New York Times* (July 13, 2021).

4 PANDEMICS, NATURAL OR BIOENGINEERED

1. Drexler, *Engines of Creation*, 58.

2. Stephenson, *The Diamond Age*; Crichton, *Prey*.

3. Kurzweil, *The Singularity Is Near*, 399–400.

4. Drexler, *Radical Abundance*; Gordijn and Cutter, eds., *In Pursuit of Nanoethics*; O'Mathuna, *Nanoethics*; Allhof, et al., eds., *Nanoethics*; Bennett-Woods, ed., *Nanotechnology*; Foster, *Nanotechnology*; Jotterrand, ed., *Emerging Conceptual, Ethical, and Policy Issues in Bionanotechnology*; Berube, *Nano-Hype*; Hall, *Nanofuture*; Milburn, *Nanovision*.

5. Richard Smalley, "Of chemistry, love, and nanobots," *Scientific American* (September 2001), 76–77.

6. Rudy Baum, "Nanotechnology."

7. Adam Keiper, "Nanoethics as a discipline?" *The New Atlantis* (Spring 2007), 55–67; Chris Phoenix and Mike Treder, "Nanotechnology as a global catastrophic risk," in Bostrom and Cirkovic, eds., *Global Catastrophic Risks*, ch. 21; Robert Freitas, "Some limits to global ecophagy by biovorous nanoreplicators, with public policy recommendations," Foresight Institute (April 2000); online at: http://www.foresight.org/nano/Ecophagy.html.

8. Drexler, *Radical Abundance*.

9. Church and Regis, *Regenesis*; Baldwin, et al., *Synthetic Biology*; Bray, *Wetware*; Carlson, *Biology Is Technology*; ETC Group, *Extreme Genetic Engineering*; Schmidt, ed., *Synthetic Biology*; Solomon, *Synthetic Biology*; Wohlsen, *Biopunk*.

10. Drew Endy, quoted in Markus Schmidt and Camillo Meinhart, "Synbiosafe," documentary film (ISBN: 978-3-200-01623-1), (2009); trailer online at: http://www.synbiosafe.eu/DVD/Synbiosafe.html.

11. Robert Service, "Synthetic microbe lives with fewer than 500 genes," *Science* (March 24, 2016), available at: http://www.sciencemag.org/news/2016/03/synthetic-microbe-lives-fewer-500-genes.

12. Wil Hylton, "Craig Venter's bugs might save the world," *New York Times* (May 30, 2012).

13. Kevin Kelleher, "Here's why nobody's talking about nanotech anymore," *Time* (October 9, 2015).

14. Church and Regis, *Regenesis*, 232–33.

15. Porcar and Pereto, *Synthetic Biology*.

16. See the iGEM website for results from past annual competitions: https://igem.org/.

17. See the Parts Registry on the iGEM website at https://igem.org/Registry.

18. Ann Trafton, "Rewiring cells: how a handful of MIT electrical engineers pioneered synthetic biology," *MIT Technology Review* (April 19, 2011), online at: http://www.technologyreview.com/article/423703/rewiring-cells/.

19. Quoted in Loren Grush, "SXSW 2015: I reprogrammed a lifeform in someone's kitchen while drinking a beer," *Popular Science* (March 14, 2015); Joi Ito, "Kitchen counter biohacking," personal blog, available at: https://joi.ito.com/weblog/2014/09/01/kitchen-counter.html.

20. Jennifer Couzin-Frankel, "Poliovirus baked from scratch," *Science* (July 11, 2002), available at: http://www.sciencemag.org/news/2002/07/poliovirus-baked-scratch.

21. Church and Regis, *Regenesis*; Wohlsen, *Biopunk*; Gronvall, *Synthetic Biology*; Schmidt, ed., *Synthetic Biology*; Baldwin, et al., *Synthetic Biology*; Carlson, *Biology Is Technology*; Sutton, *Biosecurity Law and Policy*.

22. Terence M. Tumpey, et al., "Characterization of the reconstructed 1918 Spanish influenza pandemic virus," *Science* 310:5745 (October 7, 2005), 77–80.

23. Wohlsen, *Biopunk*.

24. Gronvall, *Synthetic Biology*; Emily Baumgaertner, "As D.I.Y. gene editing gains popularity, 'someone is going to get hurt,'" *New York Times* (May 14, 2018), https://www.nytimes.com/2018/05/14/science/biohackers-gene-editing-virus.html?hp&action=click&pgtype=Homepage&clickSource=story-heading&module=second-column-region&region=top-news&WT.nav=top-news. Accessed May 20, 2018.

25. Burnette, ed., *Biosecurity*, ch. 15.

26. James Randerson, "Revealed: the lax laws that could allow assembly of deadly virus DNA," *The Guardian* (June 14, 2006); https://www.theguardian.com/world/2006/jun/14/terrorism.topstories3.

27. Ryan S. Noyce, Seth Lederman, David H. Evans, "Construction of an infectious horsepox virus vaccine from chemically synthesized DNA fragments," *PLoS One*

(January 19, 2018): http://journals.plos.org/plosone/article?id=10.1371/jour nal.pone.0188453.

28. Emily Baumgaertner, "As D.I.Y. gene editing gains popularity, 'someone is going to get hurt.'"

29. Catherine Jefferson, Filippa Lentzos, and Claire Marris, "Synthetic biology and biosecurity: challenging the "myths," *Frontiers in Public Health* 2:115 (August 21, 2014); Ben Ouagrham-Gormley, *Barriers to Bioweapons*.

30. Drew Endy, quoted in ETC Group, *Extreme Genetic Engineering*, 23.

31. Church and Regis, *Regenesis;* Baldwin, et al., *Synthetic Biology;* Carlson, *Biology Is Technology;* ETC Group, *Extreme Genetic Engineering;* Schmidt, ed., *Synthetic Biology;* Solomon, *Synthetic Biology*.

32. Donald Frederickson, "The first twenty-five years after Asilomar," *Perspectives in Biology and Medicine* 44:2 (Spring 2001), 170–82; Marcia Barinaga, "Asilomar revisited: lessons for today?" *Science* 287:5458 (March 3, 2000), 1584–85; Donald Frederickson, "Asilomar and recombinant DNA: the end of the beginning," in Kathi Hanna, ed., *Biomedical Politics* (National Academy Press, 1991), 258–324; Paul Berg, et al., "Summary statement of the Asilomar conference on recombinant DNA molecules," *Proceedings of the National Academy of Sciences* 1975:72, 1981–84.

33. Frederickson, "The first twenty-five years after Asilomar;" Barinaga, "Asilomar revisited: lessons for today?"

34. Nicholas Wade, "Scientists seek ban on method of editing the human genome," *New York Times* (March 19, 2015), available at: https://www.nytimes.com/2015/03/20/science/biologists-call-for-halt-to-gene-editing-technique-in-humans.html.

35. Church and Regis, *Regenesis*, 231–32.

5 ARTIFICIAL INTELLIGENCE: EXTREME REWARD AND RISK

1. Russell, *Human Compatible;* Christian, *The Alignment Problem;* Mitchell, *Artificial Intelligence;* Hawkins, *A Thousand Brains;* Kanaan, *T-Minus AI;* Bostrom, *Superintelligence;* Tegmark, *Life 3.0;* David Chalmers, "The singularity: a philosophical analysis," *Journal of Consciousness Studies* 17 (2010), 7–65; Barratt, *Our Final Invention;* Nilsson, *The Quest for Artificial Intelligence;* Chace, *Surviving AI;* Goertzel, *The AGI Revolution;* Pfeiffer and Scheier, eds., *Understanding Intelligence;* Rychlak, *Artificial Intelligence and Human Reason;* Wallach and Allen, *Moral Machines;* McCorduck, *Machines Who Think;* Breazeal, *Designing Sociable Robots;* Arkin, *Governing Lethal Behavior in Autonomous Robots;* Brooks, *Flesh and Machines;* Dreyfus and Dreyfus, *Mind over Machine;* Minsky, *The Emotion Machine;* Moravec, *Mind Children;* Moravec, *Robot;* Eden, Moor, Soraker, and Steinhart, eds., *Singularity Hypotheses*.

2. Here for example is a recent effort at song lyrics by a Google machine-learning system:

come on, uh
you remember the voice of the widow
i love the girl of the age
i have a regard for the whole
i have no doubt of the kind
i am sitting in the corner of the mantelpiece.

Karen Hao, "These awful AI song lyrics show us how hard language is for machines," *Technology Review* (November 13, 2018), online at: https://www.techno logyreview.com/the-download/612412/these-awful-ai-song-lyrics-show-us-how-hard-language-is-for-machines/.

3. Tad Friend, "How frightened should we be of AI?" *The New Yorker* (May 14, 2018); Raffi Khatchadourian, "The Doomsday Invention: will artificial intelligence bring us utopia or destruction?" *The New Yorker* (November 23, 2015); Alex Hern, "Experts including Elon Musk call for research to avoid AI pitfalls," *The Guardian* (January 12, 2015); Michael Sainato, "Stephen Hawking, Elon Musk, and Bill Gates warn about Artificial Intelligence," *The Observer* (August 19, 2015). Gates is quoted in the *Observer* article as having stated in 2015: "I am in the camp that is concerned about super intelligence. First the machines will do a lot of jobs for us and not be super intelligent. That should be positive if we manage it well. A few decades after that though the intelligence is strong enough to be a concern. I agree with Elon Musk and some others on this and don't understand why some people are not concerned."

4. Goodfellow, Bengio, and Courville, *Deep Learning*; Russell, *Neural Networks*; Russell and Norvig, *Artificial Intelligence*.

5. Alison Gopnik, "Making AI more human," *Scientific American* 316:6 (June 2017), 60–65; George Musser, "Artificial imagination" ; Gary Marcus, "Am I human? Researchers need new ways to distinguish artificial intelligence from the natural kind," *Scientific American* 316:3 (March 2017), 59–63; Gary Marcus, Francesca Rossi, and Manuela Veloso, "Beyond the Turing Test," Special Issue of *AI Magazine*, 37:1 (Spring 2016); Sam Adams, Guruduth Banavar, and Murray Campbell, "I-Athlon: toward a multidimensional Turing Test," *AI Magazine* (Spring 2016), 78–85.

6. The San Francisco-based AI research group, OpenAI, has a language model program known as Generative Pre-trained Transformer 3 which can perform remarkably well on certain classes of SAT problems. "When asked to complete SAT analogy problems, the model correctly answered 14 percent more problems than an average college applicant." Scott Huston, "GPT-3 Primer: Understanding OpenAI's cutting-edge language model," Towards Data Science website (August 20, 2020): https://towardsdatascience.com/gpt-3-primer-67bc2d821a00.

7. Scientists are actually teaching robots to carry out precisely these kinds of tasks today. Matt Simon, "Why scientists love making robots build IKEA furniture," *Wired* (July 9, 2021): https://www.wired.com/story/why-scientists-love-making-robots-build-ikea-furniture/.

8. Hector Levesque, *Common Sense, the Turing Test, and the Quest for Real AI.*
9. Musser, "Artificial imagination."
10. Tegmark, *Life 3.0*; Gunkel, *The Machine Question*; Brynjolfsson and McAfee, *The Second Machine Age*; Lee, *AI Superpowers*; Ford, *Rise of the Robots*; Ross, *The Industries of the Future*; Institute of Electrical and Electronics Engineers, *Ethically Aligned Design.*
11. Goodfellow, Bengio, and Courville, *Deep Learning*; Russell, *Neural Networks*; Russell and Norvig, *Artificial Intelligence.*
12. Gerrish, *How Smart Machines Think*; Sejnowski, *The Deep Learning Revolution*; Ford, *Architects of Intelligence.*
13. David Silver, et al., "A general reinforcement learning algorithm that masters chess, shogi, and Go through self-play," *Science* 362:6419 (December 7, 2018), 1140–44.
14. Steven Strogatz, "One giant step for a chess-playing machine," *New York Times* (December 26, 2018).
15. David Silver, "Discovering new knowledge," video interview (Google DeepMind, 2017), at: https://www.youtube.com/watch?v=WXHFqTvfFSw.
16. Gibney, "Self-taught AI is best yet at strategy game Go".
17. Here I'm drawing broadly on a wide range of forecasts within the AI literature, in particular: Bostrom, *Superintelligence*; Tegmark, *Life 3.0*; Chalmers, "The singularity;" Moravec, *Mind Children*; Barratt, *Our Final Invention*; Minsky, *The Emotion Machine*; Brynjolfsson and McAfee, *The Second Machine Age*; Lee, *AI Superpowers*; Ford, *Rise of the Robots*; Ross, *The Industries of the Future.*
18. Russell, *Human Compatible*, 93.
19. Russell, *Human Compatible*, 94–95.
20. Francois Chollet, "The implausibility of intelligence explosion," Medium/Artificial Intelligence (November 27, 2017): https://medium.com/@francois.chollet/the-impossibility-of-intelligence-explosion-5be4a9eda6ec; Eliezer Yudkowsky, "A reply to Francois Chollet on intelligence explosion," Machine Intelligence Research Institute (December 6, 2017): https://intelligence.org/2017/12/06/chollet/; Drew McDermott, "Response to 'The singularity: a philosophical analysis' by David Chalmers," *Journal of Consciousness Studies* 19: 1–2 (2012), 167–172: http://cs-www.cs.yale.edu/homes/dvm/papers/chalmers-singularity-response.pdf.
21. Haslam, Smillie, and Song, *An Introduction to Personality, Individual Differences, and Intelligence.*
22. Chollet, "The impossibility of intelligence explosion;" McDermott, "Response to 'the singularity'; Robin Hanson and Eliezer Yudkowsky, "The AI-Foom debate," Machine Intelligence Research Institute (2013): http://intelligence.org/files/AIFoomDebate.pdf.
23. Haslam, Smillie, and Song, *An Introduction to Personality*; Goldstein, *Cognitive Psychology*; Ciccarelli and White, *Psychology.*
24. See the extended discussion by Yudkowsky in Hanson and Yudkowsky, "The AI-Foom debate"; Stephen Omohundro, "The nature of self-improving artificial intelligence" (Self-Aware Systems, 2008), available at: http://citeseerx.ist.psu.e

du/viewdoc/download?doi=10.1.1.137.1199&rep=rep1&type=pdf; Bostrom, *Superintelligence*, ch. 2; Tegmark, *Life 3.0*; Chalmers, "The singularity."

25. Bostrom, *Superintelligence*, 19. (The polls asked respondents to assume that "human scientific activity continues without major negative disruption" – i.e., that we haven't blown ourselves up in the intervening years.)

26. Tegmark, *Life 3.0*, 157.

27. Steven Pinker, "What do you think about machines that think?" Edge.org (2015) https://www.edge.org/response-detail/26243.

28. Cade Metz, "Mark Zuckerberg, Elon Musk, and the feud over killer robots," *New York Times* (June 9, 2018).

29. Catherine Clifford, "This favorite saying of Mark Zuckerberg reveals the way the Facebook billionaire thinks about life," CNBC.com (November 30, 2017), available at: https://www.cnbc.com/2017/11/30/why-facebook-ceo-mark-zuckerberg-thin ks-the-optimists-are-successful.html.

30. Metz, "Mark Zuckerberg, Elon Musk, and the feud over killer robots."

31. Anders Sandberg and Nick Bostrom, "Whole brain emulation: a roadmap," Technical Report #2008-3, Future of Humanity Institute, Oxford University (2008); Hanson, *The Age of Em*; Yampolskiy, *Artificial Superintelligence*; Bostrom, *Superintelligence*, ch. 2; Tegmark, *Life 3.0*; Chalmers, "The singularity."

32. Hawkins, *A Thousand Brains*; Tononi, *Phi*; Damasio, *The Feeling of What Happens*; Koch, *The Quest for Consciousness*; LeDoux, *Synaptic Self*; Bear, et al., *Neuroscience*; Brendan Koerner, "Philip Kennedy: Melding man and machine to free the paralyzed," *US News and World Report* (January 3, 2000), 65.

33. Goodfellow, Bengio, and Courville, *Deep Learning*; Russell, *Neural Networks*; Gerrish, *How Smart Machines Think*; Sejnowski, *The Deep Learning Revolution*.

34. Brooks, *Flesh and Machines*, chs. 4–6.

35. Omohundro, "The nature of self-improving artificial intelligence"; Bostrom, *Superintelligence*, ch. 2; Hanson and Yudkowsky, "The AI-Foom debate"; Chalmers, "The singularity."

36. Yudkowsky, "A reply to Francois Chollet."

37. Mullaney, Peters, Hicks, and Philip, eds., *Your Computer Is On Fire*, especially Part II; Christian, *The Alignment Problem*, 25ff.

38. Mullaney, et al., eds., *Your Computer Is On Fire*, Part II; Christian, *The Alignment Problem*, 61–63; Bess, *Our Grandchildren Redesigned*, 165–68.

39. Holtzman, *Privacy Lost*, chs. 12, 13; Lessig, *Code, Version 2.0*, ch. 11; Igo, *The Known Citizen*.

40. McGonigal, *Reality Is Broken*; Castronova, *Exodus to the Virtual World*; Castronova, *Synthetic Worlds*; Boellstorff, *Coming of Age in Second Life*; Nardi, *My Life as a Night Elf Priest*; Taylor, *Play Between Worlds*.

41. Blascovich and Bailenson, *Infinite Reality*.

42. Brynjolfsson and McAfee, *The Second Machine Age*; Lee, *AI Superpowers*; Ford, *Rise of the Robots*; Ross, *The Industries of the Future*; Institute of Electrical and Electronics Engineers, *Ethically Aligned Design*.

43. Levesque, *Common Sense, the Turing Test, and the Quest for Real AI.*
44. Lenat and Guha, *Building Large Knowledge-Based Systems*; Barratt, *Our Final Invention*, 167.
45. Asimov, *I, Robot.*
46. Ernest Davis, "Ethical guidelines for a superintelligence," *Artificial Intelligence* 220 (2015), 121–24, available at: https://cs.nyu.edu/davise/papers/Bostrom.pdf; Eliezer Yudkowsky, "Complex value systems are required to realize valuable futures," Machine Intelligence Research Institute, 2011; Eliezer Yudkowsky, "Artificial intelligence as a positive and negative factor in global risk," in Bostrom and Cirkovic, eds., *Global Catastrophic Risks*; Nate Soares, "The value learning problem," presented at 25th International Joint Conference on Artificial Intelligence (New York, 2016), available at: http://intelligence.org/files/ValueL earningProblem.pdf ; Steve Omohundro, "The basic AI drives," available online at: https://selfawaresystems.files.wordpress.com/2008/01/ai_drives_final.pdf; Carl Shulman, "Omohundro's 'basic AI drives' and catastrophic risks" (The Singularity Institute, 2010); Steve Omohundro, "Autonomous technology and the greater human good," *Journal of Experimental and Theoretical Artificial Intelligence* 26:3 (2014), 303–15; Nate Soares and Benya Fallenstein, "Agent foundations for aligning machine intelligence with human interests: a technical research agenda," Machine Intelligence Research Institute, Report 2014-8 (2014); Bostrom, *Superintelligence*, chs. 9 and 12; Eden, Moor, Soraker, and Steinhart, eds., *Singularity Hypotheses*, chs. 6–10; Anderson and Anderson, eds., *Machine Ethics*, chs. 14–27.
47. This is an adaptation of an example given by Bostrom in *Superintelligence*, 120.
48. Bostrom, *Superintelligence*, 122–25; Omohundro, "The nature of self-improving artificial intelligence."
49. The most wide-ranging, detailed, and persuasive discussion of this topic is Russell, *Human Compatible*. See also Nick Bostrom, Allan Dafoe, and Carrick Flynn, "Policy desiderata in the development of machine superintelligence," Working Paper (2016), at https://nickbostrom.com/papers/aipolicy.pdf.
50. Russell, *Human Compatible*; Kanaan, *T-Minus AI*; Bostrom, *Superintelligence*; Tegmark, *Life 3.0*; Chalmers, "The singularity;" Barratt, *Our Final Invention*; Chace, *Surviving AI*; Moravec, *Mind Children*; Moravec, *Robot*; Eden, Moor, Soraker, and Steinhart, eds., *Singularity Hypotheses.*
51. It is even possible that the consequences would radiate outward from our planet, affecting the rest of the Solar System and perhaps the Galaxy. See Ord, *The Precipice*, Bostrom, *Superintelligence*, and Tegmark, *Life 3.0.*
52. Sanger, *The Perfect Weapon.*
53. Sanger, *The Perfect Weapon*; Buchanan, *The Hacker and the State*; Singer and Friedman, *Cybersecurity and Cyberwar*; Perlroth, *This Is How They Tell Me the World Ends*; Chertoff, *Homeland Security*; Bernstein, Buchmann, and Dahmen, eds., *Post-quantum Cryptography.*
54. Putin in CNN: https://www.cnn.com/2017/09/01/world/putin-artificial-intelligence-will-rule-world.

55. Sanger, *The Perfect Weapon*; Buchanan, *The Hacker and the State*; Perlroth, *This Is How They Tell Me the World Ends*.

56. Sanger, *The Perfect Weapon*, ch. 13.

6 HOW TO BEAT CLIMATE CHANGE

1. Nordhaus, *Climate Casino*; Wagner and Weitzman, *Climate Shock*; Dryzek, Norgaard, and Schlosberg, eds., *The Oxford Handbook of Climate Change and Society*; Hansen, *Storms of My Grandchildren*; Vandenbergh and Gilligan, *Beyond Politics*.

2. Nordhaus, *Climate Casino*, ch. 19.

3. Dryzek, Norgaard, and Schlosberg, eds., *The Oxford Handbook of Climate Change and Society*, chs. 20–23.

4. The literature is clear and nearly unanimous on this point, with the only dissenting publications coming from sources linked to organized climate denial or the coal industry itself. Archer, *Global Warming*; Romm, *Climate Change*; Nordhaus, *Climate Casino*; Dryzek, Norgaard, and Schlosberg, eds., *The Oxford Handbook of Climate Change and Society*; Intergovernmental Panel on Climate Change (IPCC), *AR6 Synthesis Report*; King, et al., "Climate change;" Hansen, *Storms of My Grandchildren*; Vandenbergh and Gilligan, *Beyond Politics*; Oreskes and Conway, *Merchants of Doubt*.

5. Romm, *Climate Change*, 202; Vandenbergh and Gilligan, *Beyond Politics*.

6. Brand, *Whole Earth Discipline*.

7. Wikipedia article: Wind power in Denmark: https://en.wikipedia.org/wiki/Wind_power_in_Denmark#cite_ref-en2014_3-0.

8. Wikipedia article: Renewable energy in China: https://en.wikipedia.org/wiki/Renewable_energy_in_China.

9. Source: Our World in Data; energy production: https://ourworldindata.org/energy-production-and-changing-energy-sources.

10. Wikipedia article: World energy consumption: https://en.wikipedia.org/wiki/World_energy_consumption.

11. Mark Jacobson and Mark Delucchi, "A path to sustainable energy," *Scientific American* (November 2009), 58–65; for a systematic critique of the approach advocated by Jacobson and Delucchi, see Christopher Clack, et al., "Evaluation of a proposal for reliable low-cost grid power with 100% wind, water, solar," *Proceedings of the National Academy of Sciences* 114:26 (June 27, 2017), 6722–27; Mark Jacobson and Mark Delucchi, "Providing all global energy with wind, water, and solar power, Part I: Technologies, energy resources, quantities and areas of infrastructure, and materials," *Energy Policy* 39 (2011), 1154–69; Mark Jacobson, et al., "100% clean and renewable wind, water, and sunlight all-sector energy roadmaps for 139 countries of the world," *Joule* 1 (September 6, 2017), 108–21.

12. Jacobson and Delucchi, "A path to sustainable energy," 61; Jessica Lovering, Alex Trembath, Marian Swain, and Luke Lavin, "Renewables and nuclear at

a glance," Breakthrough Institute: https://thebreakthrough.org/issues/energ y/renewables-and-nuclear-at-a-glance.

13. Let's say you could quadruple this amount by including all 6 million American commercial buildings and installing solar panels over every garage and parking lot: you still have to find about 1.4 *billion* other rooftops elsewhere. Benjamin Sigrin and Meghan Mooney, "Rooftop solar technical potential for low-to-moderate income households in the United States," National Renewable Energy Laboratory, Technical Report NREL/TP-6A20-70901 (April 2018). The article by Sigrin and Mooney includes statistics on total available residential potential as well as the potential for low to middle income households. US Energy Information Administration, "A look at the US commercial building stock" (March 4, 2015); Mark Jacobson, et al.,"100% clean and renewable wind, water, and sunlight (WWS) all-sector energy roadmaps for the 50 United States," *Energy and Environmental Science* 8 (2015), 2093; Jacobson and Delucchi, "A path to sustainable energy," 61.

14. Jesse Ausubel, "Renewable and nuclear heresies," *International Journal of Nuclear Governance, Economy, and Ecology*, 1:3 (2007), 229–43; Williams, Haley, and Jones, *Policy Implications of Deep Decarbonization in the United States*; Duane, Koomey, Belyeu, and Hausker, *From Risk to Return*; Jacobson, *100% Clean and Renewable Wind, Water, and Sunlight All-Sector Energy Roadmaps*.

15. Another obstacle to renewable energy stems from the sheer inertia of the fossil fuel-based system that's already in place. Once an electric utility has built a coal-fired power plant, it takes decades of operation to pay off the loans that financed its construction. Once auto dealerships have invested in equip-ment to repair gasoline-powered vehicles, it costs money to retool their shops for servicing electric vehicles. The physical and economic infrastructure con-nected with fossil-fuel-based energy is massive and pervasive: shifting over to a new system is a bit like executing a 90-degree turn with a giant supertanker. It takes time. Mark Diesendorf, "Redesigning energy systems," in Dryzek, Norgaard, and Schlosberg, eds., *The Oxford Handbook of Climate Change and Society*, ch. 38.

16. I'm including here the cancer deaths from the 1957 Windscale fire in Britain. See Wikipedia article: List of nuclear and radiation accidents by death toll: https://en.wikipedia.org/wiki/List_of_nuclear_and_radiation_accidents_by_ death_toll#Windscale_fire (accessed December 7, 2021); Hannah Ritchie, "What are the safest and cleanest sources of energy?" *Our World in Data* article: https://ourworldindata.org/safest-sources-of-energy.

17. Brand, *Whole Earth Discipline*, 92. The higher estimate of 9,000 cancer deaths is the more plausible one, based as it is on an exhaustive UN report published in 2006: see Mark Peplow, "Special Report: counting the dead," *Nature* 440 (April 1, 2006), 982–83.

18. Wikipedia article: Chernobyl disaster: https://en.wikipedia.org/wiki/Chernobyl_ disaster#Experiment_and_explosion.

19. Wikipedia article: Aviation accidents and incidents: https://en.wikipedia.org/wiki/Aviation_accidents_and_incidents#Statistics.
20. World Health Organization, Road Traffic Deaths: https://www.who.int/gho/road_safety/mortality/en/.
21. Image courtesy of Hannah Ritchie, "What are the safest and cleanest sources of energy?" *Our World in Data* article: https://ourworldindata.org/safest-sources-of-energy.
22. Wikipedia article: List of coal mining accidents in China: https://en.wikipedia.org/wiki/List_of_coal_mining_accidents_in_China.
23. World Health Organization: Ambient (outdoor) air quality and health: https://www.who.int/en/news-room/fact-sheets/detail/ambient-(outdoor)-air-quality-and-health.
24. Ritchie, "What are the safest and cleanest sources of energy?"
25. Brand, *Whole Earth Discipline*, 91–92.
26. Image courtesy of Wikimedia Commons, "Global public support for energy sources:" https://commons.wikimedia.org/wiki/File:Global_public_support_for_energy_sources_(Ipsos_2011).png; see also Ipsos MORI, "Strong global opposition towards nuclear power" (June 23, 2011): https://www.ipsos.com/ipsos-mori/en-uk/strong-global-opposition-towards-nuclear-power.
27. Montgomery and Graham, Jr., *Seeing the Light*; Martin, *Super Fuel*; Ferguson, *Nuclear Energy*; Cravens, *Power to Save the World*; Mahaffey, *Atomic Awakening*; Lynas, *Nuclear 2.0*; Hargraves, *Thorium*; Nordhaus and Shellenberger, *Break Through*; Brand, *Whole Earth Discipline*; Pinker, *Enlightenment Now*; Hore-Lacy, *Nuclear Energy in the 21st Century*. For a dissenting view see Sovacool, *Contesting the Future of Nuclear Power*; I find Sovacool's argument unpersuasive because it focuses primarily on the drawbacks of Generation II reactors and doesn't sufficiently take into account the innovations of Generation IV machines. See also the website of the Breakthrough Institute: https://thebreakthrough.org/energy/advanced-nuclear.
28. Montgomery and Graham, *Seeing the Light*, 90–94; Martin, *Super Fuel*, 70–80; Ferguson, *Nuclear Energy*, 48–50.
29. Montgomery and Graham, *Seeing the Light*, 90–94; Martin, *Super Fuel*, 70–80.
30. Montgomery and Graham, *Seeing the Light*, 90–94; Martin, *Super Fuel*, 70–80.
31. Kletz and Amyotte, *Process Plants*; Montgomery and Graham, *Seeing the Light*; Martin, *Super Fuel*; Ferguson, *Nuclear Energy*; Hore-Lacy, *Nuclear Energy in the 21st Century*.
32. Image courtesy of US Department of Energy Nuclear Energy Research Advisory Committee and Wikimedia Commons: https://commons.wikimedia.org/wiki/File:Molten_Salt_Reactor.svg.
33. Montgomery and Graham, *Seeing the Light*, 90–94; Martin, *Super Fuel*, 70–80.
34. Montgomery and Graham, *Seeing the Light*, 90–94; Martin, *Super Fuel*, 70–80.
35. Montgomery and Graham, *Seeing the Light*, ch. 9; Martin, *Super Fuel*, ch. 8.
36. Bess, *The Light-Green Society*, 92–103; Brand, *Whole Earth Discipline*, 111–12.
37. Martin, *Super Fuel*, ch. 8.
38. Lovering, Trembath, Swain, and Lavin, "Renewables and nuclear at a glance."

39. Edwin Lyman, "'Advanced' Isn't Always Better: Assessing the Safety, Security, and Environmental Impacts of Non-Light-Water Nuclear Reactors" (Cambridge, MA: Union of Concerned Scientists, 2021), at: https://doi.org/10.47923/2021.14000

40. Bess, *The Light-Green Society*, 107–09.

41. Cravens, *Power to Save the World*, ch. 18; Ferguson, *Nuclear Energy*, chs. 5 and 7; Montgomery and Graham, *Seeing the Light*, ch. 8.

42. Nordhaus, *Climate Casino*, 176–81; William Nordhaus, "Integrated assessment models of climate change," National Bureau of Economic Research, NBER Reporter 2017, no. 3, at: https://www.nber.org/reporter/2017number3/nord haus.html; Wagner and Weitzman, *Climate Shock*; *Nature* editorial, "Curbing global warming could save US$20 trillion," *Nature* 557 (May 23, 2018), 467–68: https://www.nature.com/articles/d41586-018-05219-5; Marshall Burke, W. Matthew Davis & Noah S. Diffenbaugh, "Large potential reduction in economic damages under UN mitigation targets" *Nature* 557 (May 23, 2018), 549–53.

43. Wagner and Weitzman, *Climate Shock*; Nordhaus, *Climate Casino*; Romm, *Climate Change*; Lynas, *Six Degrees*; Wallace-Wells, *The Uninhabitable Earth*; Hansen, *Storms of My Grandchildren*; Dryzek, Norgaard, and Schlosberg, eds., *The Oxford Handbook of Climate Change and Society*.

44. Mike Collins, "The big bank bailout," *Forbes* (July 14, 2015); Daniel Trotta, "Iraq war costs US more than $2 trillion," *Reuters* (March 14, 2013); on the COVID-19 measures see https://www.usaspending.gov/disaster/covid-19.

45. Archer, *Global Warming*, 122–31; Intergovernmental Panel on Climate Change (IPCC), *AR6 Synthesis Report*; King, et al., "Climate change;" Hansen, *Storms of My Grandchildren*.

46. Anne Nielsen, Andrew Plantinga, and Ralph Alig, "New cost estimates for carbon sequestration through afforestation in the US," USDA Forest Service General Technical Report PNW-GTR-888 (March 2014); OneTreePlanted.org: https://onetreeplanted.org/blogs/news/14245701-how-planting-trees-can-help-reduce-yo ur-carbon-footprint.

47. T. W. Crowther, H. B. Glick, M. A. Bradford, et al., "Mapping tree density at a global scale," *Nature* 525 (September 10, 2015), 201–05.

48. Archer, *Global Warming*, 123–24; Dryzek, Norgaard, and Schlosberg, eds., *The Oxford Handbook of Climate Change and Society*, chs. 2 and 3; King, et al., "Climate change"; Romm, *Climate Change*, 21–22.

49. National Academies of Science, Engineering, and Medicine, *Negative Emissions Technologies and Reliable Sequestration: A Research Agenda*, chs. 3 and 7, at: https://doi.org/10.17226/25259.

50. The math is straightforward: 10 billion trees yield 10 billion tons of carbon dioxide removed, divided by the 40 years required for the tree to grow. This comes out to 250 million tons per year. For a more detailed analysis see National Academies, *Negative Emissions Technologies*, chs. 3, 7.

51. University of Georgia, Center for Invasive Species and Ecosystem Health, "Forest tree planting," at: https://www.bugwood.org/intensive/forest_tree_planting.html.

52. This is merely my own illustrative calculation. For a more scientific estimate see Sten Nilsson and Wolfgang Schopfhauser, "The carbon sequestration potential of a global afforestation program," *Climatic Change* 30:3 (July 1995), 267–93; National Academies, *Negative Emissions Technologies*, chs. 3, 7.

53. Diana Urge-Vorsatz, et al.,"Measuring the co-benefits of climate change mitigation," *Annual Review of Environment and Resources* 39 (2014), 549–82; Jan Mayrhofer and Joyeeta Gupta, "The science and politics of co-benefits in climate policy," *Environmental Science and Policy*, 57 (2016), 22–30.

54. Steven Chu, et al.,"Carbon capture and sequestration," *Science* 325:5948 (September 2009), 1599; Archer, *Global Warming*, ch. 9; Dryzek, Norgaard, and Schlosberg, eds., *The Oxford Handbook of Climate Change and Society*, ch. 38; King, et al., "Climate change"; Romm, *Climate Change*, 218–24.

55. Alessandro Franco and Ana Diaz, "The future challenges for 'clean coal technologies': joining efficiency increase and pollutant emission control," *Energy* 34:3 (March 2009), 348–54; Richard Heinberg and David Fridley, "The end of cheap coal," *Nature* 468:7322 (2010), 367; Romm, *Climate Change*, 218–24.

56. Douglas Fox, "The carbon rocks of Oman: could an unusual outcropping of Earth's interior solve the world's climate problem?" *Scientific American* 325:1 (July 2021), 44–53; Richard Conniff, "The last resort: can we remove enough CO_2 from the atmosphere to slow or even reverse climate change?" *Scientific American* 320:1 (January 2019), 52–59; National Academies, *Negative Emissions Technologies*, ch. 5; David Keith, et al., "A process for capturing CO_2 from the atmosphere," *Joule* 2 (August 15, 2018), 1573–94; James Mulligan, et al., "Technological carbon removal in the United States," World Resources Institute Working Paper (September 2018); Sabine Fuss, et al., "Betting on negative emissions," *Nature Climate Change* 4 (October, 2014), 850–53; Robbie Gonzalez, "The potential pitfalls of sucking carbon from the atmosphere," *Wired* (June 13, 2018); Klaus Lackner, "A guide to CO_2 sequestration," *Science* (June 13, 2003), 1677–78; Elizabeth Kolbert, "Can carbon dioxide removal save the world?" *The New Yorker* (November 20, 2017).

57. Gates, *How to Avoid a Climate Disaster*, 95.

58. Conniff, "The last resort," 52–59; Climeworks, "The world's largest climate-positive direct air capture plant: Orca!" on Climeworks web page at: https://cl imeworks.com/orca.

59. National Academies, *Negative Emissions Technologies*, ch. 5.

60. Conniff, "The last resort," 54–59; National Academies, *Negative Emissions Technologies*, ch. 5.

61. Christian Breyer, Mahdi Fasihi, and Arman Aghahosseini, "Carbon dioxide direct air capture for effective climate change mitigation based on renewable electricity: a new type of energy system sector coupling," *Mitigation and Adaptation Strategies for Global Change* 25 (2020), 43–65.

62. As the authors of the National Academies report on negative emissions technologies put it: "Gigaton-scale direct air capture necessitates an enormous

increase in low- or zero-carbon energy to meet energy demands." (National Academies, *Negative Emissions Technologies*, 10–11.) In my opinion, this is precisely what makes the combination of nuclear power and direct air capture technology so appealing. But it's worth noting that none of the scientific articles on direct air capture explicitly mention nuclear energy as a potential power source for this energy-intensive technology: they merely state that the power source should ideally be carbon neutral or renewable in nature.

63. See for example Duncan McLaren, "Quantifying the potential scale of mitigation deterrence from greenhouse gas removal techniques," *Climatic Change* 162 (2020), 2411–28; Kevin Anderson and Glen Peters, "The trouble with negative emissions," *Science* 354:6309 (October 14, 2016), 182–83. For a persuasive rebuttal see Klaus Lackner, et al., "The promise of negative emissions," *Science* 354:6313 (November 11, 2016).

64. Image courtesy of Carbon Engineering and 1PointFive. See also Robert Service, "Cost plunges for capturing carbon dioxide from the air," *Science* (June 7, 2018): https://www.sciencemag.org/news/2018/06/cost-plunges-capturing-carbon-dioxide-air.

65. I calculate it this way: researchers today are speaking of building direct air capture CO_2 removal machines that can sequester one million tons per year each. This means it would take 20,000 such machines to make a 20-billion-ton impact. According to Richard Conniff and others, each such machine would require a power plant capable of supplying between 300 and 500 megawatts. Since one of today's nuclear plants can generate about eight to ten times this much (4 gigawatts), I calculated that one nuclear plant could power ten such machines for carbon sequestration. This adds up to 2,000 reactors. My sources for these statistics: Carbon Engineering, "Engineering begins on UK's first large-scale facility that captures carbon dioxide out of the atmosphere" (June 23, 2021): https://carbonengineering.com/news-updates/uks-first-large-scale-dac-facility/; Conniff, "The last resort," 54–59; National Academies, *Negative Emissions Technologies*, ch. 5; David Keith, et al.,"A process for capturing CO_2"; June Sekera and Andreas Lichtenberger, "Assessing carbon capture: public policy, science, and societal need," *Biophysical Economics and Sustainability* 5:14 (2020); James Mulligan, et al., "Technological carbon removal"; Sabine Fuss, et al., "Betting on negative emissions."

66. Jeff Tollefson, "Sucking carbon dioxide from air is cheaper than scientists thought," *Nature* 558 (2018), 173; Giulia Realmonte, et al., "An inter-model assessment of the role of direct air capture in deep mitigation pathways," *Nature Communications* 10 (2019), 3277; Noah McQueen, et al.,"Cost analysis of direct air capture and sequestration coupled to low-carbon thermal energy in the United States," *Environmental Science and Technology* 54:7542–51 (2020); Ryan Hanna, et al.,"Emergency deployment of direct air capture as a response to the climate

crisis," *Nature Communications* 12 (2021), 368; David Keith, et al., "A process for capturing CO_2"; National Academies, *Negative Emissions Technologies*, ch. 5.

67. National Academies, *Negative Emissions Technologies*, 224; I am using a figure of $87 trillion for 2018 global GDP: http://statisticstimes.com/economy/pro jected-world-gdp-ranking.php.

68. Some versions of direct air capture could be used to turn atmospheric CO_2 into usable fuel for vehicles. But this would be a net-neutral emissions technology, not a negative emissions technology, because that CO_2 would return to the air as it was burned in the vehicles' engines. Carbon Engineering, a company based in Squamish, Canada, is pioneering both aspects of this direct air capture technology – the fuel option and the deep underground storage option: https://carbonengineering.com/. See Kolbert, "Can carbon dioxide removal save the world?"

69. *Nature* editorial, "Curbing global warming could save US$20 trillion": https://www.nature.com/articles/d41586-018-05219-5; Marshall Burke, W. Matthew Davis & Noah S. Diffenbaugh, "Large potential reduction in economic damages," 549–53. See also Nordhaus, *Climate Casino*; Wagner and Weitzman, *Climate Shock*.

70. Archer, *Global Warming*; Romm, *Climate Change*; Intergovernmental Panel on Climate Change (IPCC), *AR6 Synthesis Report*; King, et al., "Climate change;" Nordhaus, *Climate Casino*; Dryzek, Norgaard, and Schlosberg, eds., *The Oxford Handbook of Climate Change and Society*; Hansen, *Storms of My Grandchildren*.

71. National Academies, *Negative Emissions Technologies*, ch. 5; David Keith, et al., "A process for capturing CO_2"; James Mulligan, et al., "Technological carbon removal"; Sabine Fuss, et al., "Betting on negative emissions."

72. Dana Ehlert and Kirsten Zickfeld, "Irreversible ocean thermal expansion under carbon dioxide removal," *Earth System Dynamics* 9 (2018), 197–210; Katarzyna Tokarska and Kirsten Zickfeld, "The effectiveness of net negative carbon emissions in reversing anthropogenic climate change," *Environmental Research Letters* 10 (2015), 094013; David Keller, et al., "The effects of carbon dioxide removal on the carbon cycle," *Current Climate Change Reports* 4 (2018), 250–65.

73. Jerome Hilaire, et al.,"Negative emissions and international climate goals – learning from and about mitigation scenarios," *Climatic Change* 157 (2019), 189–219; Massimo Tavoni and Robert Socolow, "Modeling meets science and technology: an introduction to a special issue on negative emissions," *Climatic Change* 118 (2013), 1–14.

74. Nordhaus, *Climate Casino*, 239–41.

75. Michael Grunwald, "The trouble with the Green New Deal," *Politico* (January 15, 2019): https://www.politico.com/magazine/story/2019/01/15/the-trouble-with-the-green-new-deal-223977; The White House, "The Recovery Act made the largest single investment in clean energy in history, driving the deployment of clean energy, promoting energy efficiency, and supporting manufacturing,"

(February 25, 2016): https://obamawhitehouse.archives.gov/the-press-office/201 6/02/25/fact-sheet-recovery-act-made-largest-single-investment-clean-energy.

76. Vandenbergh and Gilligan, *Beyond Politics*.

77. Vandenbergh and Gilligan, *Beyond Politics*, 120.

78. Stine Jacobsen, "World's largest container shipper Maersk aims to be CO_2 neutral by 2050," *Reuters* (December 5, 2018).

79. Neal Boudette and Coral Davenport, "G.M. announcement shakes up US automakers' transition to electric cars," *New York Times* (January 29, 2021).

80. Vandenbergh and Gilligan, *Beyond Politics*, 123.

81. Vandenbergh and Gilligan, *Beyond Politics*, 249–59.

82. Vandenbergh and Gilligan, *Beyond Politics*, 256.

83. Vandenbergh and Gilligan, *Beyond Politics*, 413.

84. Hawken, ed., *Drawdown*, 42–43.

85. SixDegrees.org, "The carbon footprint of a cheeseburger," at: https://www .sixdegreesnews.org/archives/10261/the-carbon-footprint-of-a-cheeseburger. See also Jamais Cascio, "The cheeseburger footprint," Open The Future, at: http:// www.openthefuture.com/cheeseburger_CF.html.

86. Hawken, ed., *Drawdown*, 39.

87. Image courtesy of United Nations Environment Programme (UNEP), "Emissions Gap Report," November 2017: https://www.unep.org/resources/e missions-gap-report-2017.

7 WISE GOVERNANCE FOR NUKES AND PANDEMICS: WHERE TO GO FASTER AND WHERE TO SLOW DOWN

1. Clark, *The Emerging Era in Undersea Warfare*; Sebastian Brixey-Williams, "Prospects for game-changers in submarine-detection technology," *The Strategist* (Australian Strategic Policy Institute, August 22, 2020), at: https://www.aspistrategist.org.au/ prospects-for-game-changers-in-submarine-detection-technology/.

2. Ambrose, *The Control Agenda*; Hoffmann, *The Dead Hand*; Williams and Viotti, *Arms Control*.

3. Sagan and Waltz, *The Spread of Nuclear Weapons*; Waltz, *Man, the State, and War*.

4. Keohane and Nye, Jr., *Power and Interdependence*.

5. Sanger, *The Perfect Weapon*.

6. World Institute for Nuclear Security, "The journey beyond 2016: WINS strategy and goals," online pamphlet at: file:///D:/Dropbox/Beacon/Downloads/2017 0328_wins_strategy_2020_l10_web_1.pdf.

7. Ben Ouagrham-Gormley, *Barriers to Bioweapons*, 156–60; Richard Lugar, "Cooperative Threat Reduction and nuclear security," *Georgetown Journal of International Affairs* 10 (2009), 183–89; see also the description on the website of the Center for Arms Control and Non-Proliferation: https://armscontrolcenter .org/fact-sheet-the-nunn-lugar-cooperative-threat-reduction-program/.

8. Carlson, *Biology Is Technology*, ch. 9; Hodge, Bowman, and Maynard, eds., *International Handbook on Regulating Nanotechnologies*; Stock, *Redesigning Humans*, ch. 7; Wohlsen, *Biopunk*; Allhof, et al., eds., *Nanoethics*, chs. 15–18.

9. Carlson, *Biology Is Technology*, 127.

10. Joi Ito, quoted in Grush, "SXSW 2015."

11. Jefferson, Lentzos, and Marris, "Synthetic biology and biosecurity"; Ben Ouagrham-Gormley, *Barriers to Bioweapons*.

12. Ben Ouagrham-Gormley, *Barriers to Bioweapons*.

13. Ibid.

14. Parens, Johnston, and Moses, *Ethical Issues in Synthetic Biology*; Kaebnick and Murray, eds., *Synthetic Biology and Morality*; Robert Tucker and Raymond Zilinskas, "The promise and peril of synthetic biology," *The New Atlantis* 12 (Spring 2006), 25–45; Gurumurthy Ramachandran, et al., "Recommendations for oversight of nanobiotechnology", *Journal of Nanoparticle Research* 13:4 (2011), doi: 10.1007/s11 051-011-0233-2; Heather Lowrie and Joyce Tait, *Guidelines for the Appropriate Risk Governance of Synthetic Biology* (International Risk Governance Council, 2010); Church and Regis, *Regenesis*; Wohlsen, *Biopunk*; Porcar and Pereto, *Synthetic Biology: From iGEM to the Artificial Cell*; ETC Group, *Extreme Genetic Engineering*.

15. Church and Regis, *Regenesis*, 201.

16. According to a primer on synthetic biology published by the Woodrow Wilson International Center for Scholars, "In the absence of a national regulatory structure dedicated to Do-It-Yourself projects, the [synthetic biology] community has proactively begun to devise its own codes." Daniel Grushkin, Todd Kuiken, and Piers Millet, "Seven myths and realities about Do-It-Yourself biology," Woodrow Wilson International Center for Scholars, Synthetic Biology Project (November 2013), 14. See also Sutton, *Biosecurity Law and Policy*, 572.

17. Starting in 2004, the US Department of Health and Human Services established a new category of biological research, designated under the acronym of DURC (Dual-Use Research of Concern). Recognizing that new genetic modification techniques could yield major benefits as well as significant harms, the agency mandated that all federally funded research on certain dangerous pathogens would henceforth be submitted to review before being allowed to proceed: scientists working on such pathogens would have to adopt a risk mitigation plan for their laboratories and demonstrate that the projected benefits of their work would outweigh the risks. Gronvall, *Synthetic Biology*, 49ff.

18. Here is the language in the framework document itself: "The working group sought to achieve a balance between regulation adequate to ensure health and environmental safety while maintaining sufficient regulatory flexibility to avoid impeding the growth of an infant industry. Upon examination of the existing laws available for the regulation of products developed by traditional genetic manipulation techniques, the working group concluded that, for the most part, these laws as currently implemented would address regulatory needs adequately." Executive Office of the President, Office of Science and

Technology Policy, "Coordinated Framework for Regulation of Biotechnology," 51 FR 23302 (June 26, 1986), 3.

19. Presidential Commission for the Study of Bioethical Issues, *New Directions: The Ethics of Synthetic Biology and Emerging Technologies*, 82–83.

20. Here are examples of the oversight gaps noted in the Presidential Commission's report:

- The Department of Health and Human Services has weighed in with "guidance" to DNA synthesis companies about screening customers' orders, but "compliance with the guidance is voluntary." (Ibid., 88)
- The National Institutes of Health has similarly issued guidelines for conducting lab research in synthetic biology, but it has devolved the administration and enforcement of these guidelines to Institutional Biosafety Committees (IBC) housed in each university or corporation sponsoring the research; there is no federal-level mechanism for ensuring that these committees do their work equally rigorously at every participating institution. (See the NIH document laying out the function of IBCs: http://osp.od.nih.gov/sites/default/fi les/IBC_FAQs.pdf). Needless to say, DIY biologists working in home labs or other nonregulated sites are not required to submit to any such IBC oversight.
- The Centers for Disease Control and NIH have established clear protocols governing biosafety in microbiological labs (BMBL), but, according to the presidential commission report, "there is no federal law that requires compliance for all researchers regardless of funding." (Ibid., 91)
- The EPA regulates biological products that are intended for the market or for importation, but has no jurisdiction over noncommercial activities such as lab research. Moreover, according to the report, "manufacturers need not test new chemicals for toxicity, pathogenicity, or other harmful effects before they submit a notification to EPA. Therefore, EPA may have limited information on which to base its risk assessment." (Ibid., 93) The report concludes: "The reach of the law is limited to commercial or commercial R&D activities. It is unclear that all potential users or developers of synthetic biology products, for example, noncommercial research efforts by DIY users, are covered." (Ibid., 94).

21. Presidential Commission for the Study of Bioethical Issues, 8.

22. Markus Schmidt, "Xenobiology: a new form of life as the ultimate biosafety tool," *BioEssays* 32 (2010), 322–31.

23. George Church, "A synthetic biohazard non-proliferation proposal" (Harvard University, 2004); Church and Regis, *Regenesis*, 236.

24. Parens, Johnston, and Moses, *Ethical Issues in Synthetic Biology*.

25. Garfinkel, Endy, Epstein, and Friedman, *Synthetic Genomics*; Carter, Rodemeyer, Garfinkel, and Friedman, *Synthetic Biology and the U.S. Biotechnology Regulatory System*; Grushkin, Kuiken, and Millet, "Seven myths and realities."

26. Gronvall, *Synthetic Biology*, 57.

27. Presidential Commission for the Study of Bioethical Issues, *New Directions: The Ethics of Synthetic Biology and Emerging Technologies* (Washington, D.C., 2010), 115, 122, 127.
28. See the description at the OSTP website: https://obamawhitehouse.archives.gov/administration/eop/ostp/about.

8 CONTROLLING THINGS VERSUS CONTROLLING AGENTS: THE CHALLENGE OF HIGH-LEVEL AI

1. Humphreys, *Emergence*; Murphy, Ellis, and O'Connor, eds., *Downward Causation and the Neurobiology of Free Will*; Laughlin, *A Different Universe*; Sawyer, ed., *Social Emergence*; Bedau and Humphreys, eds., *Emergence*; Holland, *Emergence*; Clayton and Davies, *The Re-emergence of Emergence*; Johnson, *Emergence*; Licata and Sakaji, eds., *Physics of Emergence and Organization*; Mitchell, *Complexity*; Juarrero, *Dynamics in Action*; Miller and Page, *Complex Adaptive Systems*; Dupuy, *On the Origins of Cognitive Science*.
2. Eckard Wimmer, quoted in ETC Group, *Extreme Genetic Engineering*, 42.
3. Anderson and Anderson, eds., *Machine Ethics*; Hibbard, *Superintelligent Machines*; Williams, *Arguing AI*.
4. I draw heavily in the discussion that follows on the analysis in Bostrom, *Superintelligence*, ch. 9.
5. See for example Yorick Wilks, "Will There Be Superintelligence and Would It Hate Us?" *AI Magazine* 38:4 (Winter 2017), 66; Pedro Domingos, "AI Will Serve Our Species, Not Control It," *Scientific American* 319:3 (September 2018), 90–93.
6. Chalmers, "The singularity."
7. Will Knight, "The dark secret at the heart of AI," *Technology Review* (April 11, 2017).
8. Russell and Norvig, *Artificial Intelligence*.
9. Russell, *Human Compatible*.
10. Russell, *Human Compatible*, 173.
11. Russell, *Human Compatible*, 175.
12. Russell, *Human Compatible*, ch. 7.
13. Kahneman, *Thinking, Fast and Slow*.
14. Russell, *Human Compatible*, ch. 8.
15. The most prominent sites for such safety research are Russell's Center for Human-Compatible AI at U.C. Berkeley, the Machine Intelligence Research Institute (also in Berkeley), the Future of Life Institute in Cambridge, Massachusetts, OpenAI in San Francisco, and Oxford University's Future of Humanity Institute. All of these have relatively small staffs and budgets. There are also specialized AI safety researchers at various universities and in some corporations, sharing their findings via professional bodies like the IEEE (Institute of Electrical and Electronics Engineers) and AAAI (Association for the Advancement of Artificial Intelligence).

16. Russell, *Human Compatible*, 159–60.
17. Institute of Electrical and Electronics Engineers, *Ethically Aligned Design*.
18. Jonathan Vanian, "Four big takeaways from Satya Nadella's talk at Microsoft Build," Fortune (May 7, 2018), available at: http://fortune.com/2018/05/07/microsoft-satya-nadella-build/.
19. Program of the Thirty-Second AAAI Conference on Artificial Intelligence, New Orleans (February 2–7, 2018), available at: https://aaai.org/Conferences/AAAI-18/; Program of the AAAI/ACM Conference on "Artificial Intelligence, Ethics, and Society," New Orleans (February 2–7, 2018), available at: http://www.aies-conference.com/sessions/.

9 THE INTERNATIONAL DIMENSION: WHERE EVERY SOLUTION STUMBLES

1. Elinor Ostrom, *Governing the Commons*.
2. Nordhaus, *Climate Casino*, 254–57.
3. Victor, *Global Warming Gridlock*, ch. 2.
4. Robinson, *Climate Justice*; Kanbur and Shue, eds., *Climate Justice*; Vandenbergh and Gilligan, *Beyond Politics*, 394–401.
5. Climate scientists refer to this distinction with the words "flows" (for greenhouses gases emitted today) versus "stocks" (greenhouse gases emitted in the past and currently "stored" in the atmosphere).
6. Sweet, *Climate Diplomacy from Rio to Paris*; Hoffmann, *Climate Governance at the Crossroads*; Victor, *Global Warming Gridlock*.
7. I rely heavily in my account here on James Chace, "Sharing the atom bomb," *Foreign Affairs* 75:1 (January/February 1996), 129–44.
8. Office of the Historian, United States Department of State, "The Acheson–Lilienthal and Baruch Plans, 1946" at: https://history.state.gov/milestones/1945-1952/baruch-plans.
9. Harry Truman, quoted in Chace, "Sharing the atom bomb," 142.
10. Mazower, *Governing the World*, chs. 7–10.
11. Ronald Reagan, "Address to the Nation on Defense and National Security" (March 23, 1983), reprinted on the website Atomicarchive.com: http://www.atomicarchive.com/Docs/Missile/Starwars.shtml.
12. Reiss, *The Strategic Defense Initiative*; FitzGerald, *Way Out There in the Blue*; York and Lakoff, *A Shield in Space?*
13. Service, *The End of the Cold War*; Sebestyen, *Revolution 1989*; Sarotte, *1989*; Grachev, *Gorbachev's Gamble*; Remnick, *Lenin's Tomb*.
14. Stockholm International Peace Research Institute, *SIPRI Yearbook 2020: Armaments, Disarmament, and International Security* (SIPRI, 2020): https://www.sipri.org/sites/default/files/YB20%2010%20WNF.pdf.
15. Bess, *Realism, Utopia, and the Mushroom Cloud*.

16. Bess, *Realism, Utopia, and the Mushroom Cloud*; Cortright, *Peace*; Wittner, *Confronting the Bomb*; Moorehead, *Troublesome People*.

17. Taubman, *The Partnership*.

18. Schell, *The Fate of the Earth* and *The Abolition*; Cortright, *Peace*; Wittner, *Confronting the Bomb*; Moorehead, *Troublesome People*.

19. Thomas Schelling, "A world without nuclear weapons?" *Daedalus* (Fall 2009), at: https://www.amacad.org/content/publications/pubContent.aspx?d=945; see also Schelling, *Arms and Influence*.

20. Bryan Walsh, "The world is not ready for the next pandemic," *Time* (May 4, 2017).

21. Garrett, *The Coming Plague*; Piot, *No Time to Lose*; Quammen, *Spillover*; Wolfe, *The Viral Storm*.

22. Price-Smith, *Contagion and Chaos*, 219.

23. Koblentz, *Living Weapons*.

24. Raymond Zilinskas, "The Soviet biological weapons program and its legacy in today's Russia," Occasional Paper 11, Center for the Study of Weapons of Mass Destruction (Washington, D.C.: National Defense University Press, 2016); Guillemin, *Biological Weapons*; Tucker, *War of Nerves*; Miller, Engelberg, and Broad, *Germs*; Burnette, ed., *Biosecurity*; Price-Smith, *Contagion and Chaos*; Gerstein, *National Security and Arms Control in the Age of Biotechnology*; Gerstein, *Bioterror in the 21st Century*; Vogel, *Phantom Menace or Looming Danger?*; National Biosurveillance Advisory Committee, *Improving the Nation's Ability to Detect and Respond to 21st Century Urgent Health Threats*; National Academy of Sciences Committee on Advances in Technology and the Prevention of Their Application to Next Generation Biowarfare Threats, *Globalization, Biosecurity, and the Future of the Life Sciences*.

25. Alibek and Handelman, *Biohazard*.

26. Putin falsely claimed that the Soviet era experiments were purely for defensive or peaceful purposes, and were therefore allowable under the treaty rules. Lukas Trakimavicius, "Is Russia violating the Biological Weapons Convention?" website of the Atlantic Council (May 23, 2018), at: https://www.atlanticcouncil.org/blo gs/new-atlanticist/is-russia-violating-the-biological-weapons-convention; Zilinskas, "The Soviet biological weapons program and its legacy," 3.

27. Paul Mozur, "Beijing wants AI to be made in China by 2030," *New York Times* (July 20, 2017).

28. Bess, *Realism, Utopia, and the Mushroom Cloud*; Ambrose, *The Control Agenda*; Hoffmann, *The Dead Hand*; Williams and Viotti, *Arms Control*.

29. Furcht and Hoffman, *The Stem Cell Dilemma*, ch. 3.

30. Ladikas, Chaturvedi, Zhao, and Stemerding, eds., *Science and Technology Governance and Ethics*; Toke, *The Politics of GM Food*; Gottweis, *Governing Molecules*; D. R. J. Macer, J. Azariah, and P. Srinives, "Attitudes to biotechnology in Asia," *International Journal of Biotechnology* (January 2000); R. Pardo, C. Midden, and J. D. Miller, "Attitudes toward biotechnology in the European Union," *Journal of Biotechnology* 98:1 (September 11, 2002), 9–24.

PROLOGUE TO PARTS III, IV, AND V

1. Hegel, *The Phenomenology of Spirit.*
2. Smith, *The Wealth of Nations.*
3. Darwin, *The Origin of Species.*
4. Sagan, *Pale Blue Dot,* 305–06.

10 DO IT NOW: FIVE POINTS OF LEVERAGE

1. Dryzek, Norgaard, and Schlosberg, eds., *The Oxford Handbook of Climate Change and Society,* chs. 29–38.
2. Hawken, *Drawdown,* 40. The calculation includes 26 gigatons of reduced emissions from the dietary change itself, plus another 39 gigatons from avoided deforestation (all the forested land that wouldn't be slashed and burned to make way for cattle ranching). The total would be 66 gigatons by the year 2050, which averages out over 31 years to about 2 gigatons per year. See also the similar calculations reported in J. Poore and T. Nemecek, "Reducing food's environmental impacts through producers and consumers," Science 360:6392 (June 1, 2018), 987–92. http://science.sciencemag.org/content/360/6392/987.
3. Gates, *How to Avoid a Climate Disaster;* see the 2019 Netflix video, "Inside Bill's Brain" for an account of his work with Generation IV reactors. David Guggenheim, "Inside Bill's Brain," *Netflix* (2019).
4. Buck, *After Geoengineering,* ch. 9; Kostigen, *Hacking Planet Earth;* Philip Rasch, et al., "An overview of geoengineering of climate using stratospheric sulphate aerosols," *Philosophical Transactions of the Royal Society* (August 29, 2008), https://doi.org/10.1098/rsta.2008.0131; Morton, *The Planet Remade;* Goodell, *How to Cool the Planet.*
5. Romm, *Climate Change;* Lynas, *Six Degrees;* Wallace-Wells, *The Uninhabitable Earth;* Dryzek, Norgaard, and Schlosberg, eds., *The Oxford Handbook of Climate Change and Society;* Hansen, *Storms of My Grandchildren.*
6. Buck, *After Geoengineering;* Rasch, et al., "An overview of geoengineering;" Morton, *The Planet Remade;* Goodell, *How to Cool the Planet.*
7. Joan-Pau Sanchez and Colin McInnes, "Optimal sunshade configurations for space-based geoengineering near the Sun–Earth L1 point," *PLoS One* (August 26, 2015), at: https://journals.plos.org/plosone/article?id=10.1371/journal.pone.0136648; Roger Angel, "Feasibility of cooling the Earth with a cloud of small spacecraft near the inner Lagrange point (L1)," *Proceedings of the National Academy of Sciences* 103:46 (November 14, 2006), 17184–89.
8. Angel, "Feasibility of cooling the Earth."
9. Morton, *The Planet Remade;* Goodell, *How to Cool the Planet.*
10. Victor, *Global Warming Gridlock,* 176–78.

11. Bowman, et al., *Ecology*; Urry, et al., *Campbell Biology*; Purves, et al., *Life*.
12. Buck, *After Geoengineering*, ch. 9.
13. Victor, *Global Warming Gridlock*, ch. 1.
14. Victor, *Global Warming Gridlock*, ch. 8.
15. Victor, *Global Warming Gridlock*, ch. 9.
16. "World population projected to reach 9.8 billion in 2050 and 11.2 billion in 2100," United Nations Department of Economic and Social Affairs (June 21, 2017): https://www.un.org/development/desa/en/news/population/world-population-prospects-2017.html.
17. Bess, *The Light-Green Society*, 180–81.
18. Ibid.
19. I am not asserting here that the 627 million tons of trash produced in 1996 were entirely unproblematic or benign in impact. They resulted from a steady expansion of consumerism that entailed all manner of complex environmental costs, and they formed part of an overall system of production and consumption that remained fundamentally unsustainable. See Bess, *The Light-Green Society*, ch. 11.
20. Four main factors influence the rate of a nation's population growth: the relative prosperity of the citizenry; their level of education; their average life-expectancy; and their fertility rates. Historians and demographers have observed that in nearly all cases, as prosperity and education increase, life-expectancy also goes up – and fertility rates go down. As people become better educated and feel more secure about their life prospects, they tend voluntarily to have fewer children. Overall, global fertility rates have been going steadily down over the past century: they currently stand at 2.55 children per woman and are projected by the UN to continue declining to about 2.02 children per woman by the year 2050 – roughly the same fertility level that characterizes the United States today. Cohen, *How Many People Can the Earth Support?*; Angus and Butler, *Too Many People?*; Kenny, *Getting Better*; Banerjee and Duflo, *Poor Economics*; Sachs, *The End of Poverty*; Diamandis and Kotler, *Abundance*; Bess, *The Light-Green Society*, 180–81.
21. Bess, *The Light-Green Society*, Part IV.
22. Bradley Hope and Nicole Friedman, "Climate change is forcing the insurance industry to recalculate," *Wall Street Journal* (October 28, 2018); Englander, *Moving to Higher Ground*.
23. Richard Klein, et al., "Technological options for adaptation to climate change in coastal zones," *Journal of Coastal Research*, 17:3 (Summer 2001).
24. Randeep Ramesh, "Paradise almost lost; Maldives seek to buy a new homeland," *The Guardian* (November 9, 2008); Jon Shenk, *The Island President*, documentary film (ITVS films, March 2012).
25. Victor, *Global Warming Gridlock*, 179.
26. Cahill, *Tropical Diseases in Temperate Climates*; Rahman and Kamruzzaman, *Impact of Climate Change on the Outbreak of Infectious Diseases*.

27. Craig Welch, "Climate change pushing tropical diseases toward Arctic," *National Geographic* (June 14, 2017).

28. Victor, *Global Warming Gridlock*, 176–78.

29. Jeannie Sowers, et al.,"Climate change, water resources, and the politics of adaptation in the Middle East and North Africa," *Climatic Change* 104 (2011), 599–627.

30. Don Wall, "National Building Code to include climate change obligations," *Daily Commercial News* (December 20, 2018).

31. Terry Hughes, et al., "Global warming transforms coral reef assemblages," *Nature* 556 (2018), 492–96.

32. Wallace-Wells, *The Uninhabitable Earth*, 94–100.

33. Global Genome Biodiversity Network website: https://wiki.ggbn.org/ggbn/About_GGBN.

34. Dryzek, Norgaard, and Schlosberg, eds., *The Oxford Handbook of Climate Change and Society*, chs. 12–19; Intergovernmental Panel on Climate Change (IPCC), *AR6 Synthesis Report*; David King, et al., "Climate change."

35. Dryzek, Norgaard, and Schlosberg, eds., *The Oxford Handbook of Climate Change and Society*, ch. 19; for a novel depicting such a world see Lanchester, *The Wall*.

36. Solomon and Marston, eds., *The Medical Implications of Nuclear War*; Peterson, *The Aftermath*; Wade, *A World Beyond Healing*.

37. A novel that brilliantly depicts this cyclical reemergence of civilization after a nuclear holocaust is Miller, *A Canticle for Leibowitz*.

38. Patricia Lewis, Heather Williams, Benoit Pelopidas, and Sasan Aghlani, "Too close for comfort: cases of near nuclear use and options for policy," Chatham House Report (The Royal Institute of International Affairs, April 2014); Union of Concerned Scientists, "Close calls with nuclear weapons," Fact Sheet (January 2015), at: https://www.ucsusa.org/sites/default/files/attach/2015/0 4/Close%20Calls%20with%20Nuclear%20Weapons.pdf.

39. Davis, ed., *The India–Pakistan Military Standoff*; Solomon and Marston, eds., *The Medical Implications of Nuclear War*; Peterson, *The Aftermath*; Wade, *A World Beyond Healing*; see also the website of NuclearDarkness.org for a detailed analysis and description of such a scenario: http://www.nucleardarkness.org/warconse quences/fivemilliontonsofsmoke/.

40. Plokhy, *Chernobyl*.

41. NuclearDarkness.org: http://www.nucleardarkness.org/warconsequences/five milliontonsofsmoke/.

42. See the many valuable studies published in partnership between Oxford University Press and the Stockholm International Peace Research Institute, listed at: https://global.oup.com/academic/content/series/s/sipri-monographs-siprimo/?cc=us&lang=en&; Doyle, *Nuclear Safeguards, Security, and Nonproliferation*; Schelling and Halperin, *Strategy and Arms Control*; Larsen and Wirtz, eds., *Arms Control and Cooperative Security*; Larsen, *Arms Control*; Williams and Viotti, *Arms Control*.

43. I rely heavily in the discussion that follows on the following sources: World Health Organization, "WHO Strategic Action Plan for Pandemic Influenza" (WHO, 2007), at: http://www.who.int/csr/resources/publications/influenza/Str egPlanEPR_GIP_2006_2.pdf; Garrett, *The Coming Plague*; Piot, *No Time to Lose*; Quammen, *Spillover*; Wolfe, *The Viral Storm*; Davies, Kamradt-Scott, and Rushton, *Disease Diplomacy*; Price-Smith, *Contagion and Chaos*; Lemon, Hamburg, Sparling, Choffnes, and Mack, *Ethical and Legal Considerations in Mitigating Pandemic Disease*; Walsh, "The world is not ready."

44. Garrett, *The Coming Plague*; Piot, *No Time to Lose*; Quammen, *Spillover*; Wolfe, *The Viral Storm*.

45. Nathan Wolfe, "How to prevent a pandemic," Edge (April 30, 2009) at: https://www.edge.org/conversation/nathan_wolfe-how-to-prevent-a-pandemic.

46. See the PREDICT website at: http://www.vetmed.ucdavis.edu/ohi/predict/.

47. Carol Morello, "Foreign aid cuts proposed, but 'friends' might be protected," *Washington Post* (February 12, 2017); Michael Igoe and Adva Saldinger, "What Trump's budget request says about US aid," *Devex* (May 23, 2017).

48. Suzanne Hodsden, "Breathalyzer diagnoses 17 different diseases using a single breath," *Med Device Online* (January 3, 2017); R. McNerney, et al., "Field test of a novel detection device for *Mycobacterium tuberculosis* antigen in cough," *BMC Infectious Diseases* 10:161 (2010); Freya Preimesberger, "Researchers design flu virus breathalyzer," *The Daily Texan* (February 16, 2017); Jill Sakai, "Metabolic breathalyzer reveals early signs of disease," *University of Wisconsin-Madison News* (February 6, 2012).

49. National Institute of Allergy and Infectious Diseases, "Universal influenza vaccine research" (May 2018), at: https://www.niaid.nih.gov/diseases-conditions/universal-influenza-vaccine-research.

50. Dennis Carroll, et al., "The Global Virome Project," *Bulletin of the World Health Organization* (March 5, 2018); Kat Kerlin, "Ambitious Global Virome Project could mark the end of pandemic era," University of California Davis News (February 22, 2018); see the website of the Global Virome Project at: http://www.globalviromeproject.org/.

51. Garrett, *The Coming Plague*; Piot, *No Time to Lose*; Quammen, *Spillover*; Wolfe, *The Viral Storm*.

52. Walsh, "The world is not ready."

53. Jean Song, "Bill Gates on how to outsmart global epidemics," *CBS News online* (January 18, 2017); Catherine Cheney, "CEPI, a year in: how can we get ready for the next pandemic?" *Devex* (February 5, 2018); Coalition for Epidemic Preparedness Innovations website: http://cepi.net/mission.

54. Future of Life Institute, "Asilomar AI principles" (2017), available at: https://futureoflife.org/ai-principles/; Katja Grace, "The Asilomar Conference: a case study in risk mitigation" (Machine Intelligence Research Institute, Technical Report 2015-9, 2015).

55. Metz, "Mark Zuckerberg, Elon Musk, and the feud over killer robots."

56. See the discussion in Chapters 6 and 9. For a broader discussion of the hype that sometimes surrounds high technology forecasts, see Seidensticker, *Future Hype.*

57. Russell, *Human Compatible,* 77.

58. Hern, "Experts including Elon Musk call for research"; Sainato, "Stephen Hawking, Elon Musk, and Bill Gates warn about artificial intelligence."

59. Musk, quoted in Theo Priestley, "Does Elon Musk and OpenAI want to democratise or sanitise artificial intelligence?" *Forbes* (December 13, 2015), online at: http://www.forbes.com/sites/theopriestley/2015/12/13/does-elon-musk-and-openai-want-to-democratise-or-sanitise-artificial-intelligence/#39f48fd489a4.

60. Ford, *Rise of the Robots,* ch. 2; Levy and Murnane, *The New Division of Labor.*

61. Brynjolfsson and McAfee, *The Second Machine Age;* Ford, *Rise of the Robots;* Lee, *AI Superpowers;* Rifkin, *The Zero Marginal Cost Society;* Kaplan, *Humans Need Not Apply;* Nourbakhsh, *Robot Futures;* Husain, *The Sentient Machine;* Tegmark, *Life 3.0.*

62. Brynjolfsson and McAfee, *The Second Machine Age,* ch. 12; Lee, *AI Superpowers,* ch. 8; Ford, *Rise of the Robots,* ch. 7.

63. Ford, *Rise of the Robots,* chs. 1, 3, 7.

64. See the display videos on the Boston Dynamics website: https://www.bostondynamics.com/.

65. Scharre, *Army of None;* David Hambling, "What are drone swarms and why does every military suddenly want one?" *Forbes* (March 1, 2021): https://www.forbes.com/sites/davidhambling/2021/03/01/what-are-drone-swarms-and-why-does-everyone-suddenly-want-one/.

66. Brynjolfsson and McAfee, *The Second Machine Age;* Ford, *Rise of the Robots;* Lee, *AI Superpowers;* Tegmark, *Life 3.0.*

67. Brynjolfsson and McAfee, *The Second Machine Age,* ch. 12; Ford, *Rise of the Robots.*

68. Brynjolfsson and McAfee, *The Second Machine Age;* Ford, *Rise of the Robots;* Lee, *AI Superpowers;* Tegmark, *Life 3.0.*

69. Brynjolfsson and McAfee, *The Second Machine Age;* Ford, *Rise of the Robots;* Lee, *AI Superpowers;* Tegmark, *Life 3.0.*

70. Van Parijs and Vanderborght, *Basic Income;* Brynjolfsson and McAfee, *The Second Machine Age,* chs. 13, 14; Ford, *Rise of the Robots,* ch. 10; Lee, *AI Superpowers,* ch. 8; Tegmark, *Life 3.0,* ch. 3.

71. Van Parijs and Vanderborght, *Basic Income,* chs. 2–4.

72. Milton Friedman, quoted in Van Parijs and Vanderborght, *Basic Income,* 85.

73. Ford, *Rise of the Robots,* 268; Dylan Matthews, "The amazing true socialist miracle of the Alaska Permanent Fund," *Vox* (February 13, 2018).

74. Rachel Treisman, "California program giving $500 no-string-attached stipends pays off, study finds," *National Public Radio* (March 4, 2021), at: https://www.npr.org/2021/03/04/973653719/california-program-giving-500-no-strings-attached-stipends-pays-off-study-finds.

75. Parijs and Vanderborght, *Basic Income,* ch. 5.

76. Ford, *Rise of the Robots,* ch. 10.

77. Lee, *AI Superpowers*, chs. 7–9.
78. Parijs and Vanderborght, *Basic Income*, ch. 8.
79. Arthur C. Clarke, interviewed by Gene Youngblood in the *Los Angeles Free Press* (April 25, 1969), 42–43, 47. The interview was reprinted in Stephanie Schwam, ed., *The Making of 2001: A Space Odyssey* (Modern Library, 2000), 258–69.
80. Yang, *The War on Normal People*; Adams and Kreiss, *Power in Ideas*.
81. Church and Regis, *Regenesis*.
82. Conducting random inspections of high-risk research labs would constitute a vital element in any credible surveillance system, particularly if heavy emphasis is placed on those labs self-reporting about their work. This raises the question of protecting trade secrets: if outside inspectors are given access to the cutting-edge methods and unpublished discoveries of leading researchers, what would prevent them from divulging this information to outsiders? Fortunately, this problem has already been addressed through two kinds of existing arrangements. When inspectors from a government body such as OSHA (Occupational Safety and Health Administration) pay a visit to a lab, they can be required by the lab's administrators to sign a nondisclosure agreement before being granted access to the researchers' confidential work. As an additional protection, those inspectors can be subject to legal penalties if they disclose trade secrets gleaned during the course of their work. Singer and Upton, *Guidelines for Laboratory Quality Auditing*, 176. Protecting the secrecy of military research, while subjecting it to rigorous oversight, presents an even more daunting challenge. Here the traditional solution has been to delegate authority to an independent governmental body, such as the Office of the Inspector General of the Department of Defense, tasked with ensuring that proper safety and security procedures are being followed. See the website of the Department of Defense Office of Inspector General at http://www.dodig.mil/; Defense Science Board Task Force, "Department of Defense Biological Safety and Security Program" (Office of the Under Secretary of Defense For Acquisition, Technology, and Logistics, 2009), at: https://fas.org/irp/agen cy/dod/dsb/biosafety.pdf; see also United States Government General Accounting Office, *Inspectors General: Department of Defense IG Peer Reviews* (US GAO, 2011).
83. Sunstein, *Simpler*; Robin Craig and J. B. Ruhl, "Designing administrative law for adaptive management," *Vanderbilt Law Review* 67:1 (2014); Marchant, Abbott, and Allenby, eds., *Innovative Governance Models for Emerging Technologies*; Tucker, ed., *Innovation, Dual Use, and Security*; Wallach, *A Dangerous Master*; Marchant, Allenby, and Herkert, eds., *The Growing Gap Between Emerging Technologies and Legal-Ethical Oversight*; Guston and Sarewitz, eds., *Shaping Science and Technology Policy*; Konrad, Coenen, Dijkstra, Milburn, and van Lente, eds., *Shaping Emerging Technologies*.

84. Marchant, Allenby, and Herkert, eds., *The Growing Gap Between Emerging Technologies and Legal-Ethical Oversight.*

85. David Rejeski, "Public policy on the technological frontier," in Marchant, Allenby, and Herkert, eds., *The Growing Gap Between Emerging Technologies and Legal-Ethical Oversight,* ch. 4.

86. Wendell Wallach and Gary Marchant, "Governing the governance of emerging technologies," in Marchant, Abbott, and Allenby, eds., *Innovative Governance Models for Emerging Technologies.*

87. Celia Wexler, "Bring back the OTA," *New York Times* (May 28, 2015).

88. Sclove, *Reinventing Technology Assessment;* Volti, *Society and Technological Change,* 345–46; Bruce Bimber and David Guston, "Politics by the same means: government and science in the United States," in Jasanoff, et al., eds., *Handbook of Science and Technology Studies,* ch. 24; Jathan Sadowski, "The much-needed and sane congressional office that Gingrich killed off and we need back," *The Atlantic* (October 26, 2012), online at: http://www.theatlantic.com/technology/archive/2012/10/the-much-needed-and-sane-congressional-office-that-gingrich-killed-off-and-we-need-b ack/264160/#.

89. Sadowski, "The much-needed and sane congressional office."

90. Rasch, et al., "An overview of geoengineering"; Morton, *The Planet Remade;* Goodell, *How to Cool the Planet.*

91. Beck, *Risk Society;* Callon, Lascoumes, and Barthe, *Acting in an Uncertain World;* Whiteside, *Precautionary Politics;* Sunstein, *Laws of Fear;* Coleman, *A Practical Guide to Risk Management;* Morris, *Rethinking Risk and the Precautionary Principle;* Tucker, ed., *Innovation, Dual Use, and Security.*

92. Jonas, *The Imperative of Responsibility.*

93. The precautionary principle has been defined in a wide variety of ways, which makes it rather hard to pin down. There is a weak version that basically says, "Be careful," and a very strong version that basically says, "Don't proceed unless you're really sure what you're doing is completely safe." And there is a broad spectrum of variants in between these two poles. The three-pronged articulation of the principle that I present here is my own preferred formulation – one that incorporates certain commonsense principles from risk–benefit analysis. See Bess, *The Light-Green Society,* 228–29.

94. Sunstein, *Laws of Fear,* ch. 5.

11 CONSTRUCTIVE MOVES ON THE INTERNATIONAL FRONT FOR THE NEXT 25 YEARS

1. See for example the 2016 debate over President Obama's proposed trillion-dollar nuclear modernization program in the *New York Times:* "A nuclear weapons upgrade," at: https://www.nytimes.com/roomfordebate/2016/10/26/a-nuclear-arsenal-upgrade. Not surprisingly, the Trump Administration pushed these policies

even further. Jonathan Swan, "Trump's budget calls for major boost to nukes," *Axios* (February 9, 2020): https://www.axios.com/trump-budget-nuclear-weapons-da635f80-0161-4eda-bdc5-f4acdaa6855b.html.

2. Hass, *Stronger*, Friend and Thayer, *How China Sees the World*; Dollar, Huang, and Yang Yao, eds., *China 2049*; Cooley and Nexon, *Exit from Hegemony*; Spalding, *Stealth War*; Haass, *A World in Disarray*; Koenig, *The Return of Great Power Rivalry*.

3. Waltz, *Theory of International Politics*, chs. 6, 9.

4. Downing, *1983*; Talbott, *Endgame*; Harahan, *On-Site Inspections under the INF Treaty*, chs. 3, 4.

5. David Sanger and Pranshu Verma, "The F.B.I. confirms that DarkSide, a ransomware group, was behind the hack of a major US pipeline," *New York Times* (May 10, 2021): https://www.nytimes.com/2021/05/10/us/politics/dark-side-hack.html.

6. Sanger, *The Perfect Weapon*; Buchanan, *The Hacker and the State*; Singer and Friedman, *Cybersecurity and Cyberwar*; Perlroth, *This Is How They Tell Me the World Ends*.

7. Brad Smith, quoted in Perlroth, *This Is How They Tell Me the World Ends*, 344.

8. Alexi Franklin, "An international cyber warfare treaty: historical analogies and future prospects," *Journal of Law and Cyber Warfare* 7:1 (Fall 2018), 149–64; Sanger, *The Perfect Weapon*; Buchanan, *The Hacker and the State*; Singer and Friedman, *Cybersecurity and Cyberwar*; Perlroth, *This Is How They Tell Me the World Ends*.

9. Clark, *The Emerging Era in Undersea Warfare*; Brixey-Williams, "Prospects for game-changers in submarine-detection technology."

10. Kennedy, *The Parliament of Man*; Mazower, *Governing the World*; Weiss and Daws, eds., *The Oxford Handbook of the United Nations*.

11. Fasulo, *An Insider's Guide to the UN.*

12. Kennedy, *The Parliament of Man*; Fasulo, *An Insider's Guide to the UN.*

13. Hastings, *The Korean War*; Cumings, *The Korean War*; Halberstam, *The Coldest Winter.*

14. Nichols, *Eisenhower 1956*; Louis and Owen, *Suez 1956*; Turner, *Suez 1956.*

15. Finlan, *The Gulf War 1991*; Allison, *The Gulf War, 1990–91*; Atkinson, *Crusade.*

16. The Korean case was the result of an anomaly: the Russians were boycotting the Security Council to protest the fact that the Chinese seat was being held by tiny Taiwan rather than the new Communist government on the mainland. This happened to be the moment when the North Koreans launched their attack, and in the absence of a Russian veto the Security Council swiftly approved military intervention. A strong US-led coalition force, flying the UN flag, landed in Korea and pushed back the North Korean aggressor. In the case of the 1956 Suez Crisis, the surprise attack by Anglo–French–Israeli forces caught American leaders off guard; President Eisenhower, furious at having been blindsided by these three close allies, joined with the Soviet Union in condemning the attack. This rare alignment of superpower views allowed the Security Council to take

forceful action; the Soviets threatened to use long-range missiles in support of Egypt, and the Americans refused to intervene. Anglo–French–Israeli leaders, realizing how badly they had miscalculated, were forced to retreat with their tails between their legs. It was a triumphant moment for the cause of collective security and peacekeeping during the Cold War, earning high praise for the skillful leadership of UN Secretary-General Dag Hammarskjöld. A similar miscalculation appears to have animated Iraqi leader Saddam Hussein when he invaded Kuwait in 1990: he failed to grasp the implications of the Cold War's ending, and evidently believed he could count on the customary paralysis at the UN. When the Russians and Americans joined other nations in strongly condemning his attack on a neighboring country, this paved the way once again for a potent UN coalition force (under US leadership) to reverse the act of aggression and restore the status quo. Kennedy, *The Parliament of Man*; Mazower, *Governing the World*.

17. Haass, *A World in Disarray*; Kennedy, *The Parliament of Man*; Mazower, *Governing the World*.
18. Kennedy, *The Parliament of Man*.
19. Sluga, *Internationalism in the Age of Nationalism*; Mazower, *Governing the World*; Kaldor, *Global Civil Society*; Keohane and Nye, *Power and Interdependence*; Baratta, *The Politics of World Federation*; Hauss, *Security 2.0*.
20. Roberts and Kingsbury, eds., *United Nations, Divided World*.
21. Kennedy, *The Parliament of Man*, 253. Kennedy's list of moderate reforms meshes well with those advocated by another expert on the UN, Weiss, *What's Wrong with the United Nations and How to Fix It*. See also Weiss and Daws, eds., *The Oxford Handbook of the United Nations*.
22. Mazower, *Governing the World*, 254–72.
23. Kennedy, *The Parliament of Man*, 252.
24. Kennedy, *The Parliament of Man*, 264.

12 BREAKING THE POLITICAL LOGJAM

1. Sunstein, *#Republic: Divided Democracy in the Age of Social Media*; Gerzon, *The Reunited States of America*; Tomasky, *If We Can Keep It*; Hetherington and Rudolph, *Why Washington Won't Work*; McCarty, Poole, and Rosenthal, *Polarized America*; Thurber and Yoshinaka, eds., *American Gridlock*; Springs, *Healthy Conflict in Contemporary American Society*; Persily, ed., *Solutions to Political Polarization in America*; Hopkins and Sides, eds., *Political Polarization in American Politics*; Whelan, *The Centrist Manifesto*.
2. Snowe, *Fighting for Common Ground*; Altmire, *Dead Center*; Sasse, *Them*; Brown, *Ending Our Uncivil War*; Edwards, *The Parties versus the People*; Lott and Daschle, *Crisis Point*.
3. Ugarriza and Caluwaerts, eds., *Democratic Deliberation in Deeply Divided Societies*.

4. Camosy, *Beyond the Abortion Wars*; Kaczor, *The Ethics of Abortion*; Manninen, *Pro-Life, Pro-Choice*; Sterrett, *Aborting Aristotle*; Talisse, *Democracy and Moral Conflict*; Moreno, *The Body Politic*; Kitcher, *Science in a Democratic Society*.

5. Gerzon, *The Reunited States of America*; Hetherington and Rudolph, *Why Washington Won't Work*; McCarty, Poole, and Rosenthal, *Polarized America*; Thurber and Yoshinaka, eds., *American Gridlock*.

6. Dan Kahan, Hank Jenkins-Smith, and Donald Braman, "Cultural cognition of scientific consensus," *Journal of Risk Research* 14:2 (February 2011), 147–74.

7. Kathleen Hall Jamieson, "How to debunk misinformation about COVID, vaccines, and masks," *Scientific American* 324:4 (April 2021), 44–51; Cook, *Cranky Uncle vs. Climate Change*.

8. Felt, Fouché, Miller, and Smith-Doerr, eds., *The Handbook of Science and Technology Studies*; Gordon Gauchat, "Politicization of science in the public sphere: a study of public trust in the United States, 1974 to 2010," *American Sociological Review* 77:2 (April 2012); Otto, *The War on Science*; Kitcher, *Science in a Democratic Society*; Steel, ed., *Science and Politics*; Kahan, et al., "Cultural cognition of scientific consensus."

9. Berezow and Campbell, *Science Left Behind*; Mooney, *The Republican Brain*.

10. Sadowski, "The much-needed and sane congressional office."

11. Felt, Fouché, Miller, and Smith-Doerr, eds., *The Handbook of Science and Technology Studies*, section I; Biagioli, ed., *The Science Studies Reader*; Harding, *Objectivity and Diversity*; Daston and Galison, *Objectivity*; Latour and Woolgar, *Laboratory Life*; Shapin and Schaffer, *Leviathan and the Air-Pump*; MacKenzie and Wajcman, eds., *The Social Shaping of Technology*.

12. Humphreys, ed., *The Oxford Handbook of Philosophy of Science*; Barker and Kitcher, *Philosophy of Science*; Cover, Pincock, and Curd, *Philosophy of Science*; Godfrey-Smith, *Theory and Reality*.

13. I am aware that using this language will seem quaintly outdated, or epistemologically naïve, to some readers who have been trained in the complexities of science studies. I readily acknowledge the importance of new and sophisticated approaches to showing the inherent biases and limitations of all forms of scientific research, but I still believe that an important distinction can be made – and must be made – between overtly politicized research and other forms of research that are based on even-handed and methodologically rigorous experimental design and methods. The concept of objectivity is a vitally important one, and while it is helpful to be cognizant of hidden assumptions that constrain or color our research, our society still needs a reliable way to distinguish legitimate science from hack science. Most philosophers of science, and most scientists, accept the need for such a core distinction. Sheila Jasanoff, "Cosmopolitan knowledge: climate science and global civic epistemology," in Dryzek, Norgaard, and Schlosberg, eds., *The Oxford Handbook of Climate Change and Society*, ch. 9; Myanna Lahsen, "Technocracy, democracy, and US climate politics: the need for demarcations," *Science, Technology, and Human Values* 30:1 (Winter 2005), 138–

39. See also Haskell, *Objectivity Is Not Neutrality*; Humphreys, ed., *The Oxford Handbook of Philosophy of Science*; Barker and Kitcher, *Philosophy of Science*; Cover, Pincock, and Curd, *Philosophy of Science*; Godfrey-Smith, *Theory and Reality*.

14. Jasanoff, "Cosmopolitan knowledge," in Dryzek, Norgaard, and Schlosberg, eds., *The Oxford Handbook of Climate Change and Society*, ch. 9.

15. Archer, *Global Warming*, 122–31; Romm, *Climate Change*; Nordhaus, *Climate Casino*; Dryzek, Norgaard, and Schlosberg, eds., *The Oxford Handbook of Climate Change and Society*; Intergovernmental Panel on Climate Change (IPCC), *AR6 Synthesis Report*; King, et al., "Climate change;" Hansen, *Storms of My Grandchildren*; Vandenbergh and Gilligan, *Beyond Politics*.

16. Oreskes and Conway, *Merchants of Doubt*; Riley Dunlap and Aaron McCright, "Organized Climate Change Denial," in Dryzek, Norgaard, and Schlosberg, eds., *The Oxford Handbook of Climate Change and Society*, ch. 10.

17. Lahsen, "Technocracy, democracy, and US climate politics"; van der Linden, et al., "Inoculating the public."

18. Dryzek, Norgaard, and Schlosberg, eds., *The Oxford Handbook of Climate Change and Society*, chs. 8–11; Hulme, *Why We Disagree About Climate Change*; Oreskes and Conway, *Merchants of Doubt*; Marshall, *Don't Even Think About It*. For a dissenting view see Lomborg, *Cool It*.

19. Dryzek, Norgaard, and Schlosberg, eds., *The Oxford Handbook of Climate Change and Society*, chs. 8–11.

20. Van der Linden, et al., "Inoculating the public;" Oreskes, "The scientific consensus on climate change."

21. Fisher, Ury, and Patton, *Getting to Yes*.

22. Gerzon, *The Reunited States of America*; Tomasky, *If We Can Keep It*; Hetherington and Rudolph, *Why Washington Won't Work*; McCarty, Poole, and Rosenthal, *Polarized America*; Thurber and Yoshinaka, eds., *American Gridlock*.

23. Snowe, *Fighting for Common Ground*; Altmire, *Dead Center*; Sasse, *Them*; Edwards, *The Parties versus the People*; Lott and Daschle, *Crisis Point*.

24. Nordhaus, *Climate Casino*, chs. 19, 20.

25. Sasse, *Them*, ch. 7; Persily, ed., *Solutions to Political Polarization in America*, chs. 14–20; Meacham, *Talking Sense About Politics*.

26. Berners-Lee, *There Is No Planet B*, chs. 8, 9.

27. Hayhoe, *Saving Us*; Gerzon, *The Reunited States of America*; Tomasky, *If We Can Keep It*; Hetherington and Rudolph, *Why Washington Won't Work*; McCarty, Poole, and Rosenthal, *Polarized America*; Thurber and Yoshinaka, eds., *American Gridlock*.

28. Gerzon, *The Reunited States of America*; McClaughlin, *Talking Together*; Sasse, *Them*; Persily, ed., *Solutions to Political Polarization in America*; Brown, *Ending Our Uncivil War*; Edwards, *The Parties Versus the People*.

29. Gerzon, *The Reunited States of America*, 52.

30. Public Conversations Project: http://civicactivism.buildingchangetrust.org/tools-directory/Public-Conversations-Project-Dialogue; Bipartisan Congressional Retreats: http://mediatorsfoundation.org/gallery/bipartisan-congressional-re

treats/; National Coalition for Dialogue and Deliberation: http://ncdd.org/; Breakthrough Institute: https://thebreakthrough.org/; Living Room Conversations: https://www.livingroomconversations.org/; Village Square: https://tlh.villagesquare.us/blog/about/; More in Common: https://www.mor eincommon.com/; Everyday Democracy: https://www.everyday-democracy.org/; No Labels: https://www.nolabels.org/; #Cut50: https://www.cut50.org/; Voice of the People: http://vop.org/; Future 500: https://www.future500.org/; Convergence Center for Policy Resolution: https://www.convergencepolicy.org/.

31. Program for Public Consultation, University of Maryland, and Voice of the People, "A not so divided America" (2014): http://publicconsultation.org/wp-content/uploads/reports/Red_Blue_Report_Jul2014.pdf.

32. Stephen Hawkins, et al., "Hidden tribes: a study of America's polarized land-scape," More in Common (2018): https://www.moreincommon.com/hidden-tribes.

33. Buss, *Evolutionary Psychology*; Gaulin and McBurney, *Evolutionary Psychology*, 2nd ed.; Sapolsky, *Behave*.

34. Zimdars and McLeod, eds., *Fake News*; O'Connor and Weatherall, *The Misinformation Age;* Lee McIntyre, *Post-Truth*.

35. Fishkin, *Democracy When the People Are Thinking*; Bohman and Rehg, eds., *Deliberative Democracy*; Dryzek, *Foundations and Frontiers of Deliberative Governance*; Elster, ed., *Deliberative Democracy*; Baber and Bartlett, *Consensus and Global Environmental Governance*.

36. The description in this paragraph is based primarily on the ideas and practices described in Fishkin, *Democracy When the People Are Thinking*.

37. Fishkin, *Democracy When the People Are Thinking*, Part III.

38. Sunstein, *Going to Extremes*; for a rebuttal see Fishkin, *Democracy When the People Are Thinking*, Part III.

39. Carpenter and Moss, *Preventing Regulatory Capture*.

40. Jonathan Gilligan, "Flexibility, clarity, and legitimacy: considerations for managing nanotechnology risks," *Environmental Law Reporter* 36:12 (2006), 10924; Sunstein, *Laws of Fear*; Kahneman, Slovic, and Tversky, eds., *Judgment Under Uncertainty*; Beck, *Risk Society*; Callon, Lascoumes, and Barthe, *Acting in an Uncertain World*; Whiteside, *Precautionary Politics*; Coleman, *A Practical Guide to Risk Management*; Morris, *Rethinking Risk and the Precautionary Principle*; Tucker, ed., *Innovation, Dual Use, and Security*.

41. Jonathan Wiener, "The Tragedy of the Uncommons: on the politics of apocalypse," *Global Policy* 7:1 (May 2016), 67–80; Balleisen, Bennear, Krawiec, and Wiener, eds., *Policy Shock*; Shafir, ed., *The Behavioral Foundations of Public Policy*; Posner, *Catastrophe*; S. Baum and B. Tonn, "Introduction: confronting future catastrophic threats to humanity," *Futures* 72 (2015), 1–3.

42. Vandenbergh and Gilligan, *Beyond Politics*.

43. Green, *Rethinking Private Authority*; Morgenstern and Pizer, *Reality Check*; Paul Harland, Henk Staats, and Henk Wilke, "Situational and personality factors as

direct or personal norm mediated predictors of pro-environmental behavior," *Basic and Applied Social Psychology* 29:4 (2007), 323–34; Paul Stern, et al., "A value-belief-norm theory of support for social movements: the case of environmentalism," *Human Ecology Review* 6:2 (Winter 1999), 81–97; Michael Vandenbergh, "Order without social norms: how personal norm activation can protect the environment," *Northwestern University Law Review* 99:3 (2004–2005), 1101–65; Alex Geisinger, "A belief change theory of expressive law," *Iowa Law Review* 35 (2002–2003), 37–63.

44. For a listing of such organizations see the START website: http://www .startguide.org/orgs/orgs08.html; for a listing by nation see the Wikipedia page on environmental organizations: https://en.wikipedia.org/wiki/ List_of_environmental_organizations.

45. Rachel Friedman, "Students petition to transition Vanderbilt to renewable energy by 2050," *Vanderbilt Hustler* (February 4, 2019): https://vanderbilthustler .com/21150/featured/students-petition-to-transition-vanderbilt-to-renewable-energy-by-2050/ ; Ann Marie Owens, "Vanderbilt announces new collaboration to accelerate efforts to address its carbon footprint and tackle climate change," *Vanderbilt News* (May 24, 2021): https://news.vanderbilt.edu/2021/05/24/van derbilt-announces-new-collaboration-to-accelerate-efforts-to-address-its-carbon-footprint-and-tackle-climate-change/?utm_source=myvupreview&utm_me dium=myvu_email&utm_campaign=myvupreview-2021-05-24.

46. Carnegie Endowment for International Peace: https://carnegieendowment .org/; Global Zero: https://www.globalzero.org/; International Campaign to Abolish Nuclear Weapons: http://www.icanw.org/.

47. Centers for Disease Control and Prevention: https://www.cdc.gov/; World Health Organization: http://www.who.int/; Hastings Center: https://www .thehastingscenter.org/; the ETC Group: http://www.etcgroup.org/; Synbiosafe: http://synbiosafe.eu/.

48. IEEE (Institute of Electrical and Electronics Engineers): https://www.ieee.org/; AAAI (Association for the Advancement of Artificial Intelligence): http://www .aaai.org/; Future of Life Institute: https://futureoflife.org/; OpenAI: https:// openai.com/; the Machine Intelligence Research Institute (MIRI): https://intel ligence.org/; Future of Humanity Institute: https://www.fhi.ox.ac.uk/.

49. One can draw here on a broad academic literature on positive psychology and developmental economics. Peterson and Seligman, *Character Strengths and Virtues*, ch. 1; Haidt, *The Happiness Hypothesis*; Csikszentmihalyi, *Flow*; Peterson, *A Primer in Positive Psychology*; Kahneman, Diener, and Schwarz, *Well-Being*; Lyubomirsky, *The How of Happiness*; Sen, *The Idea of Justice*; Nussbaum, *Creating Capabilities*.

50. Allenby and Sarewitz, *The Techno-Human Condition*; Lanier, *You Are Not a Gadget*; Berry, *It All Turns on Affection*; Wallach, *A Dangerous Master*; McKibben, *Enough*; Turkle, *Alone Together*; Bess, *Our Grandchildren Redesigned*, ch. 6; Bess, *The Light-Green Society*.

51. Among the myriad writers who address this topic, the philosopher/farmer/poet Wendell Berry stands out as one of the most persuasive. See "Pray without ceasing," first published in 1992, and available in Berry, *Fidelity*. Other key works: Berry, *A Place on Earth; Citizenship Papers; It All Turns on Affection; Life Is a Miracle; The Selected Poems of Wendell Berry.* Three fine books on Berry are: Bonzo and Stevens, *Wendell Berry and the Cultivation of Life;* Mitchell and Schueter, eds., *The Humane Vision of Wendell Berry;* Oehlschlaeger, *The Achievement of Wendell Berry.*

13 LESSONS FROM THE GREEN MOVEMENT: HOW TO BUILD LASTING CHANGE IN THE ABSENCE OF FULL CONSENSUS

1. I draw heavily in the argument that follows on Bess, *The Light-Green Society.* For a wide range of up-to-date resources on the topic see the website of the American Society for Environmental History: http://aseh.net/teaching-research/environ mental-history-bibliographies.
2. Bess, *The Light-Green Society,* chs. 1–5.
3. Ibid., chs. 7–10.
4. Ibid., ch. 11.
5. Thompson, *The Poverty of Theory and Other Essays;* Sunstein, *How Change Happens;* Sewell, *Logics of History;* Sawyer, *Social Emergence;* Smith, *What Is a Person?,* especially chs. 4–6.
6. Human agency, in this picture, is both asymmetrical and reflexive in nature. It is *asymmetrical* because one's range of action as an individual person is always dwarfed by the collective patterns that govern the dominant practices of one's epoch: at any given moment, our power as individuals is heavily limited by the prevailing structures and rules. At the same time, through the exponential vehicle of cultural influence, a single individual's impact can be multiplied tremendously, thereby altering those broader structures and rules in significant ways. At this point the causal power of our deeds becomes *reflexive,* because those modified structures and rules then constitute the new societal context within which each of us will henceforth operate. The British historian E. P. Thompson described this circular interplay of "micro" and "macro" as "the crucial ambivalence of our human presence in our own history, part-subjects, part-objects." Thompson, *The Poverty of Theory,* 88.
7. Wallach, *A Dangerous Master;* Tucker, ed., *Innovation, Dual Use, and Security;* Konrad, Coenen, Dijkstra, Milburn, and van Lente, eds., *Shaping Emerging Technologies;* Guston and Sarewitz, eds., *Shaping Science and Technology Policy;* Marchant, Allenby, and Herkert, eds., *The Growing Gap Between Emerging Technologies and Legal-Ethical Oversight;* Marchant, Abbott, and Allenby, eds., *Innovative Governance Models for Emerging Technologies;* Owen, Bessant, and Heintz, eds., *Responsible Innovation;* Sandler, ed., *Ethics and Emerging Technologies.*

8. Kennedy, *Freedom from Fear*.
9. Bess, *Choices Under Fire*. African Americans flocked to new jobs and opportunities in the war factories, and served with distinction in the Army, Navy, and Army Air Force. Japanese-Americans were more limited in their options, because most of them were confined in detention camps against their will; but a significant number of young Japanese-American men did volunteer as soldiers for their country, eventually forming one of the most decorated American fighting units in the European theater. Clayborne Carson, "African Americans at war," in Dear and Foot, eds., *The Oxford Companion to World War II*; Asahina, *Just Americans: How Japanese Americans Won a War at Home and Abroad*.
10. Terkel, *'The Good War'*.
11. Benedick, *Ozone Diplomacy*.
12. Price, *Practical Aviation Security*.
13. It's worth mentioning here that, although France's current emission flows are lower than those of eighteen other nations, its *cumulative* contribution to atmospheric stocks of greenhouse gases no doubt ranks higher, because it was among the first nations to undergo industrialization, and therefore started emitting greenhouse gases sooner than many other nations. The ranking listed here is taken from Union of Concerned Scientists, "Each country's share of CO_2 emissions" at: https://www.ucsusa.org/global-warming/science-and-impacts/science/each-countrys-share-of-co2.html.
14. Dominic Dudley, "China is set to become the world's renewable energy superpower, according to new report," *Forbes* (January 11, 2019); Alice Shen, "How China hopes to play a leading role in developing next-generation nuclear reactors," *South China Morning Post* (January 10, 2019); World Nuclear Association, "Nuclear power in China" (April 2019) at: http://www.world-nuclear.org/information-library/country-profiles/countries-a-f/china-nuclear-power.aspx.
15. Dryzek, Norgaard, and Schlosberg, eds., *The Oxford Handbook of Climate Change and Society*, chs. 14, 19, 21, 22, 26, 34; Romm, *Climate Change*; Archer, *Global Warming*; Lynas, *Six Degrees*; Wallace-Wells, *The Uninhabitable Earth*; Hansen, *Storms of My Grandchildren*; Intergovernmental Panel on Climate Change (IPCC), *AR6 Synthesis Report*; King, et al., "Climate change."
16. Overy, *The Twilight Years*; Constantine, *Social Conditions in Britain, 1918–1939*; Taylor, *English History, 1914–1945*, chs. 8–10; Orwell, *The Road to Wigan Pier*.
17. Field, *Blood, Sweat, and Toil*; Rose, *Which People's War?*; Marwick, *War and Social Change in the Twentieth Century*; Calder, *The People's War*; Hobsbawm, *The Age of Extremes*, 161–62; Addison, *The Road to 1945*; Fraser, *The Evolution of the British Welfare State*, 222–23; Mike Savage, "Changing social class identities in post-war Britain: perspectives from mass-observation," *Sociological Research Online* 12:3 (May 2007), 6.
18. There is, to be sure, a possibility of a sudden shift in ocean currents once a climatic tipping point has been crossed, potentially leading to rapid and very dramatic changes such as the onset of a major ice age within a few years' time.

This possibility cannot be discounted a priori, but most climate scientists consider it unlikely unless the warming passes the 4-degree threshold or higher. Lynas, *Six Degrees*, 46, 88, 228, 270; Romm, *Climate Change*, 140–50; Anthony Barnosky, et al., "Approaching a state shift in Earth's biosphere," *Nature* 486 (June 7, 2012), 52–58; Dave Levitan, "Quick-change planet: do global climate tipping points exist?" *Scientific American* (March 25, 2013).

19. Kindleberger and Aliber, *Manias, Panics, and Crashes*; Bernstein, *The Great Depression*; Morris, *A Rabble of Dead Money*; Parker, ed., *The Economics of the Great Depression*.

20. Victor, *Global Warming Gridlock*, chs. 8, 9.

14 A PROMISING TRACK RECORD: THE DRAMATIC GROWTH OF INTERNATIONAL INSTITUTIONS AND NETWORKS SINCE 1900

1. George C. Marshall, "Speech to the New York Herald Tribune Forum," October 29, 1945, in Larry Bland, ed., *The Papers of George Catlett Marshall*, vol. 5, 337–38.

2. Keohane and Nye, *Power and Interdependence*.

3. Slaughter, *A New World Order*; Karns, Mingst, and Stiles, *International Organizations*; Frederking and Diehl, eds., *The Politics of Global Governance*; Weiss and Wilkinson, eds., *International Organization and Global Governance*; Barnett and Finnemore, *Rules for the World*; Sinclair, *Global Governance*; Fasulo, *An Insider's Guide to the UN*.

4. Mazower, *Governing the World*; Sluga, *Internationalism in the Age of Nationalism*; Leinen and Bummel, *A World Parliament*; Kaldor, *Global Civil Society*; Osterhammel and Petersson, *Globalization*; Hathaway and Shapiro, *The Internationalists*.

5. Sluga, *Internationalism in the Age of Nationalism*; Combs, *The History of American Foreign Policy from 1895*; Kaufman, *A Concise History of US Foreign Policy*; Peterson, *American Foreign Policy*.

6. Bacevich, ed., *Ideas and American Foreign Policy*; Peterson, *American Foreign Policy*; Papp, Johnson, and Endicott, *American Foreign Policy*.

7. Art and Jervis, eds., *International Politics*; Falk, *Reframing the International*; Galtung, *Searching for Peace*; Hoffmann, *Duties Beyond Borders*; McNamara, *Wilson's Ghost*; Puchala, *Theory and History in International Relations*; Rosenau and Czempiel, eds., *Governance Without Government*; Schell, *The Unconquerable World*; Bess, *Realism, Utopia, and the Mushroom Cloud*; Sluga, *Internationalism in the Age of Nationalism*; Kaldor, *Global Civil Society*; Mazower, *Governing the World*; Osterhammel and Petersson, *Globalization*; Keohane and Nye, *Power and Interdependence*.

8. David Bettez, "Unfulfilled initiative: disarmament negotiations and the Hague Peace Conferences of 1899 and 1907," *Royal United Services Institute for Defence Studies* 133:3 (June 1988), 57–62.

9. The League has also been criticized, with justification, as an explicitly neocolonialist instrument, since its "mandate system" perpetuated prewar colonial empires, and indeed expanded them considerably. Pedersen, *The Guardians*.

10. Kolb, *The International Court of Justice.*
11. Karns, Mingst, and Stiles, *International Organizations,* 586.
12. When the OECD was first created as part of the Marshall Plan, its name was slightly different: Organization for European Economic Cooperation. The name was changed, and the mission rendered more global, in the early 1960s.
13. Karns, Mingst, and Stiles, *International Organizations;* Frederking and Diehl, eds., *The Politics of Global Governance;* Barnett and Finnemore, *Rules for the World;* Weiss and Wilkinson, eds., *International Organization and Global Governance.*
14. Kennedy, *The Parliament of Man;* Fasulo, *An Insider's Guide to the UN.*
15. Kaplan, *NATO Divided, NATO United;* Johnston, *How NATO Adapts.*
16. Combs, *The History of American Foreign Policy from 1895;* Kaufman, *A Concise History of US Foreign Policy;* Peterson, *American Foreign Policy.*
17. Stanley Sloan, *Defense of the West.*
18. Dinan, *Origins and Evolution of the European Union,* 2nd ed.; McCormick, *Understanding the European Union.*
19. Mayne, *The Community of Europe.*
20. Olsen and McCormick, *The European Union: Politics and Policies;* Nelsen and Stubb, *The European Union;* Leonard, *The Routledge Guide to the European Union;* Tiersky and Jones, eds., *Europe Today;* Hancock, et al., *Politics in Europe.*
21. Fry, *Beyond War;* Buss, *Evolutionary Psychology;* Gaulin and McBurney, *Evolutionary Psychology;* Sapolsky, *Behave;* West, *Scale;* Diamond, *Guns, Germs, and Steel.*
22. Slaughter, *A New World Order;* Keck and Sikkink, *Activists Beyond Borders;* Sikkink, *Evidence for Hope;* Cole, *Engines of Liberty;* Sluga, *Internationalism in the Age of Nationalism.* For more pessimistic analyses see Moyn, *Not Enough;* Posner, *The Twilight of Human Rights Law;* Hopgood, *The Endtimes of Human Rights.*
23. For a directory of INGO groups see the World Association of Non-Governmental Organizations: https://www.wango.org/resources.aspx?section=ngodir.
24. *Newsweek* (November 26, 1984), 56.
25. Bornstein, *The Price of a Dream;* Grameen America website: https://www.grameenamerica.org/.
26. Maathai, *The Green Belt Movement;* see also: http://www.greenbeltmovement.org/.
27. Wangari Maathai, "Statement by Prof. W. Maathai, Nobel Peace Laureate, on behalf of Civil Society," United Nations Summit on Climate Change (September 22, 2009), at: https://web.archive.org/web/20110601034605/http://www.un.org/wcm/webdav/site/climatechange/shared/Documents/SpeechMaathai.pdf.
28. Hesterman, *The Terrorist-Criminal Nexus;* Kaldor, *Global Civil Society.*
29. I draw heavily on Slaughter, *A New World Order,* in the paragraphs that follow.
30. Slaughter, *A New World Order,* chs. 4, 5.
31. Slaughter, *A New World Order,* 5.
32. Slaughter, *A New World Order,* chs. 4, 5.

33. Bellamy and Dunne, eds., *The Oxford Handbook of the Responsibility to Protect*; Bellamy and Luck, *The Responsibility to Protect*.
34. Fasulo, *An Insider's Guide to the UN*; Singer, *One World Now*.
35. Martin Gilbert, quoted in Singer, *One World Now*, 150.

15 HOW TO ESCAPE THE SOVEREIGNTY TRAP: LESSONS AND LIMITATIONS OF THE EUROPEAN UNION MODEL

1. Anderson, *Imagined Communities*.
2. Maier, *Leviathan 2.0*; Elias, *The Civilizing Process*; Scott, *Against the Grain*.
3. Pinker, *The Better Angels of Our Nature*, chs. 2, 3.
4. Anderson, *Imagined Communities*; Hobsbawm, *Nations and Nationalism Since 1780*; Gellner, *Nations and Nationalism*; Smith, *Nationalism*.
5. Molina and Palmer, *The History of Costa Rica*.
6. Cabrera, *The Practice of Global Citizenship*; Frankman, *World Democratic Federalism*.
7. Pinker, *The Better Angels of Our Nature*, 680–81. Emphasis added.
8. For examples of this phenomenon from the case of France, see Weber, *Peasants into Frenchmen*; Hélias, *The Horse of Pride*.
9. John Sides, "Most Americans live in Purple America, not Red or Blue America," *Washington Post* (November 12, 2013): https://www.washingtonpost.com/new s/monkey-cage/wp/2013/11/12/most-americans-live-in-purple-america-not-r ed-or-blue-america/.
10. Cabrera, *The Practice of Global Citizenship*; Frankman, *World Democratic Federalism*.
11. Kennedy, *The Rise and Fall of the Great Powers*; Reus-Smit and Snidal, eds., *The Oxford Handbook of International Relations*; Morgenthau, *Politics Among Nations*; Bull, *The Anarchical Society*; Stoessinger, *Why Nations Go to War*.
12. Taylor, *The Struggle for Mastery in Europe, 1848–1918*.
13. McDougall, *France's Rhineland Policy, 1914–1924*.
14. Overy, *The Origins of the Second World War*.
15. Krotz and Schild, *Shaping Europe*; Sheehan, *Where Have All the Soldiers Gone?*; Adamthwaite, *Britain, France, and Europe, 1945–1975*; Haas, *The Uniting of Europe*.
16. Bozo, Rodder, and Sarotte, eds., *German Reunification*.
17. Haftendorn, *Coming of Age: German Foreign Policy Since 1945*; Sheehan, *Where Have All the Soldiers Gone?*
18. Von Mering and McCarty, *Right-Wing Radicalism Today*; Betz, *Radical Right-Wing Populism in Europe*; Akkerman, de Lange, and Rooduijn, eds., *Radical Right-Wing Populist Parties in Western Europe*; Weinberg, *Right-Wing Violence in the Western World Since World War II*.
19. Bess, *Realism, Utopia, and the Mushroom Cloud*, ch. 1.
20. Consider for instance the following excerpt from a 1985 pamphlet by Jean-Marc Brissaud, the secretary-general of the European Parliament's extreme right wing grouping at the time, and a prominent member of Jean-Marie Le Pen's National

Front: "Europe – a united and independent Europe capable of defending itself – must understand that its future and its expansion lie to the south. Eurafrica (*sic*) must become the master word of tomorrow. The European states allowed their first chance to go by when they lost their colonial empires; they must not miss this second opportunity. In the hour of the great empires – America on one side, Soviet Russia on the other – in the hour of the rising political power of China and economic power of Japan – in the hour of the renewal of Islam and the danger of demographic invasion – Europe, only Europe possesses the scale required to meet the economic, technological, political, and military challenges of the 21st century." Jean-Marc Brissaud, *Éléments pour une nouvelle politique étrangère* [My translation].

21. Even though de Gaulle withdrew France from formal membership in NATO's command structure, for example, he kept the French closely connected to NATO operational systems, and French nuclear missile submarines continued to rely on NATO satellites for their ballistic guidance. The French returned to full participation in NATO in 2009.

22. McGuire and Smith, *The European Union and the United States*.

23. McGuire and Smith, *The European Union and the United States*.

24. Duchene, *Jean Monnet*.

25. Gilbert, *European Integration*; Bickerton, *European Integration*; Wiener, Borzel, and Risse, eds., *European Integration Theory*.

26. Monnet, *Memoirs*; Duchene, *Jean Monnet*.

27. Haas, *The Uniting of Europe*.

28. Gilbert, *European Integration*; Bickerton, *European Integration*.

29. McCormick, *Understanding the European Union*; Olsen and McCormick, *The European Union*; Nelsen and Stubb, *The European Union: Readings on the Theory and Practice of European Integration*; Leonard, *The Routledge Guide to the European Union*; Tiersky and Jones, eds., *Europe Today*; Hancock, et al., *Politics in Europe*.

30. Bess, *The Light-Green Society*, 205–06, 263–64.

31. McDonald, *States' Rights and the Union*; Hueglin and Fenna, *Comparative Federalism*, chs. 2–5.

32. Baratta, *The Politics of World Federation*; Mazower, *Governing the World*.

33. Gráinne de Búrca, "Reappraising subsidiarity's significance after Amsterdam," Harvard Jean Monnet Working Paper 7/99, Harvard Law School (1999), at: https://www.jeanmonnetprogram.org/archive/papers/99/990701.rtf . See also the text of the 1997 Treaty of Amsterdam, one of the key constitutive documents of the union, under the section, "Protocol on the application of the principles of subsidiarity and proportionality," in European Union, "Treaty of Amsterdam" (Luxembourg, 1997), 105.

34. Clarke, Goodwin, and Whiteley, *Brexit*; Dinan, Nugent, and Paterson, eds., *The European Union in Crisis*; Soros and Schmitz, *The Tragedy of the European Union*.

35. McCormick, *Understanding the European Union*, ch. 5.

36. Soros and Schmitz, *The Tragedy of the European Union*, 55–92.

37. McCormick, *Understanding the European Union*, ch. 9.

38. Dinan, Nugent, and Paterson, eds., *The European Union in Crisis*, chs. 12–14, 17.

39. Dinan, *Origins and Evolution of the European Union*; Olsen and McCormick, *The European Union: Politics and Policies*; Nelsen and Stubb, *The European Union: Readings on the Theory and Practice of European Integration*; Tiersky and Jones, eds., *Europe Today*.

40. Although it's probably true that the diversity among the world's regions is qualitatively greater than the diversity within each of those regions, it's also possible to take this assumption too far. Is the difference between, say, Germany and Hungary, or Denmark and Greece, much less significant than the difference between Japan and Burma, Rwanda and South Africa, Chile and Venezuela? Was the hatred between the French and German populations in 1945 any less ferocious than the enmity between Indians and Pakistanis, or Israelis and Palestinians? Might there not be an implicit form of racism hidden within the idea that Europeans are relatively homogeneous within their continent, compared with the alleged non-homogeneity of the other world's regions? I merely mention these questions here, as a cautionary note. For the purposes of my present argument, the overriding reality is the stark and deep set of divergences that one sees among the world's nations and peoples. See Cabrera, *The Practice of Global Citizenship*.

41. Diego Pimentel, Iñigo Aymar and Max Lawson, "Reward work, not wealth," Oxfam Briefing Paper (January 2018), at: https://oi-files-d8-prod.s3.eu-west-2.amazonaws.com/s3fs-public/file_attachments/bp-reward-work-not-wealth-220118-en.pdf.

42. Singer, *One World Now*; Sachs, *The End of Poverty*; Sachs, *A New Foreign Policy*; Piketty, *Capital in the Twenty-First Century*.

43. Moyn, *Not Enough*; Sachs, *The End of Poverty*; Osterhammel and Petersson, *Globalization*; Rodrik, *The Globalization Paradox*.

44. Moyn, *Not Enough*; Sachs, *The End of Poverty*; Sachs, *A New Foreign Policy*.

45. Edward Mansfield, Diana Mutz, and Devon Brackbill, "Effects of the Great Recession on American attitudes toward trade," *British Journal of Political Science* 49:1 (November 2016), 37–58; Heydon and Woolcock, eds., *The Ashgate Research Companion to International Trade Policy*; Jonathan Hopkin, "When Polanyi met Farage: market fundamentalism, economic nationalism, and Britain's exit from the European Union," *The British Journal of Politics and International Relations* 19:3 (June 2017), 465–78;

46. Kindleberger and Aliber, *Manias, Panics, and Crashes*; Bernstein, *The Great Depression*; Morris, *A Rabble of Dead Money*; Parker, ed., *The Economics of the Great Depression*.

47. Crouch, *The Globalization Backlash*; Pogge, *World Poverty and Human Rights*, 2nd ed.; Kennedy, *The Parliament of Man*, ch. 4; Mazower, *Governing the World*, ch. 12; Singer, *One World Now*, ch. 3.

48. Giridharadas, *Winners Take All.*
49. Krotz and Schild, *Shaping Europe*; Sheehan, *Where Have All the Soldiers Gone?*; Bocquet, Deubner, and Peel, *The Future of the Franco-German Relationship*; Cole, *Franco-German Relations*; Farquharson and Holt, *Europe from Below*; Laird, ed., *Strangers and Friends*; McCarthy, ed., *France-Germany, 1983–1993*; McCarthy, ed., *France-Germany in the Twenty-First Century.*
50. Kennedy, *The Parliament of Man*, 73ff.
51. Duedahl, ed., *A History of UNESCO.*
52. FitzGerald, *Refuge Beyond Reach*; Collier and Betts, *Refuge*; Fiddian-Qasmiyeh, Loescher, Long, and Sigona, eds., *The Oxford Handbook of Refugee and Forced Migration Studies*; Miliband, *Rescue.*
53. Sachs, *A New Foreign Policy*, ch. 17; Collier, *Refuge*, chs. 6–8; Miliband, *Rescue*, ch. 4; Fiddian-Qasmiyeh, Loescher, Long, and Sigona, eds., *The Oxford Handbook of Refugee and Forced Migration Studies*, chs. 37–41.
54. Boulding, *Stable Peace*, 93.
55. Goodin, *The Oxford Handbook of Political Science*; Morgenthau, *Politics Among Nations*; Art and Jervis, eds., *International Politics*; Falk, *Reframing the International*; Hoffmann, *Duties Beyond Borders*; Puchala, *Theory and History in International Relations*; Keohane and Nye, *Power and Interdependence.*
56. Christakis, *Blueprint*; Bregman, *Humankind*; Fry, *Beyond War*; Pinker, *The Better Angels of Our Nature*; Buss, *Evolutionary Psychology*; Gaulin and McBurney, *Evolutionary Psychology*; Sapolsky, *Behave*; Diamond, *Guns, Germs, and Steel.*
57. Pinker, *The Blank Slate*; Nietzsche, *Basic Writings of Nietzsche.*

16 TAKING THE UNITED NATIONS UP A NOTCH: PLANET-LEVEL SOLUTIONS FOR THE YEAR 2100

1. Doudna and Sternberg, *A Crack in Creation*; Isaacson, *The Code Breaker.*
2. The literature on this topic is immense. See the bibliography in Bess, *Our Grandchildren Redesigned.*
3. Doudna and Sternberg, *A Crack in Creation*, 199.
4. The scientist's family name is He and given name is Jiankui: since 'He' can be confusing in an English sentence, I'll refer to him henceforth as Jiankui. The names of the genome-edited baby girls, Lulu and Nana, were pseudonyms assigned to protect their privacy. I draw heavily on Isaacson, *The Code Breaker*, in the description that follows.
5. Isaacson, *The Code Breaker*, 318.
6. David Cyranoski, "The CRISPR-baby scandal: what's next for human gene-editing," *Nature* 566 (February 26, 2019), 440–42: https://www.nature.com/art icles/d41586-019-00673-1.
7. Isaacson, *The Code Breaker*, chs. 38–39. See also "Heritable genome editing," in International Society for Stem Cell Research, *"ISSCR Guidelines,"* updated

2021: https://www.isscr.org/policy/guidelines-for-stem-cell-research-and-clinical-translation/key-topics/heritable-genome-editing.

8. Cyranoski, "The CRISPR-baby scandal."

9. Adapted from image courtesy of Springer Nature and Giorgia Guglielmi. See Cyranoski, "The CRISPR-baby scandal"; this article in turn draws upon R. Isasi, E. Kleiderman, and B. M. Knoppers, "Editing policy to fit the genome?" *Science* 351: 6271 (January 22, 2016), 337–39: https://science.sciencemag.org/content/351/6271/337.

10. See the bibliography in Bess, *Our Grandchildren Redesigned.*

11. Johnson and Wetmore, eds., *Technology and Society*; Nye, *Technology Matters.*

12. Leinen and Bummel, *A World Parliament*; Schwartzberg, *Transforming the United Nations System*, ch. 3; Held, *Democracy and the Global Order*; Keohane, *Power and Governance in a Partially Globalized World*; Karns, Mingst, and Stiles, *International Organizations*; Frederking and Diehl, eds., *The Politics of Global Governance*; Weiss and Wilkinson, eds., *International Organization and Global Governance.*

13. Dinan, *Origins and Evolution of the European Union*; McCormick, *Understanding the European Union.*

14. Leinen and Bummel, *A World Parliament*, ch. 26.

15. Economist Intelligence Unit, "Democracy Index 2020: In sickness and in health?": https://www.eiu.com/n/campaigns/democracy-index-2020/#mktoForm_anchor.

16. Sarah Repucci and Amy Slipowicz, "Democracy under siege: Freedom in the World, 2021" (Freedom House, 2021): https://freedomhouse.org/report/free dom-world/2021/democracy-under-siege.

17. Kennedy, *The Parliament of Man*, ch. 1; Leinen and Bummel, *A World Parliament*, ch. 6; Fasulo, *An Insider's Guide to the UN*, chs. 1–4; Singer, *One World Now*, ch. 4; Schwartzberg, *Transforming the United Nations System*, ch. 3.

18. Leinen and Bummel, *A World Parliament*, ch. 6; Schwartzberg, *Transforming the United Nations System*, ch. 3.

19. I choose the figure of 400,000 because it is 25 percent above the average size of the military forces of the world's nations (296,000 troops). A military force this size would render the UN army the tenth-largest military force on the planet. Such a force would of course be incapable of forcing its will on large nations or on coalitions of smaller nations, but – provided it enjoyed broad support from the Great Powers – it would possess sufficient clout for significant pacification operations in a broad range of circumstances.

20. Kimberly Amadeo, "US military budget, its components, challenges, and growth," *The Balance* (September 3, 2020): https://www.thebalance.com/u-s-mi litary-budget-components-challenges-growth-3306320; see also the Wikipedia article on the topic: https://en.wikipedia.org/wiki/List_of_countries_by_number_of_military_and_paramilitary_personnel.

17 THE OTHER PATH TO 2100: RUTHLESS COMPETITION, FINGERS CROSSED

1. For insightful recent overviews see Cooley and Nexon, *Exit from Hegemony;* Haass, *A World in Disarray;* Kagan, *The Jungle Grows Back;* Koenig, *The Return of Great Power Rivalry;* Lissner and Rapp-Hooper, *An Open World.*
2. Cooley and Nexon, *Exit from Hegemony;* Haass, *A World in Disarray.*
3. Steven Erlanger, "Europe lauds Biden but wonders: what will he want? How long will he stay?" *New York Times* (January 7, 2021).
4. David Sanger and Eric Schmitt, "Biden signals break with Trump foreign policy in a wide-ranging State Dept. speech," *New York Times* (February 4, 2021).
5. Hass, *Stronger;* Friend and Thayer, *How China Sees the World;* Dollar, Huang, and Yao, eds., *China 2049;* Cooley and Nexon, *Exit from Hegemony;* Spalding, *Stealth War;* Haass, *A World in Disarray;* Koenig, *The Return of Great Power Rivalry.*
6. Cooley and Nexon, *Exit from Hegemony;* Haass, *A World in Disarray;* Kagan, *The Jungle Grows Back;* Koenig, *The Return of Great Power Rivalry;* Lissner and Rapp-Hooper, *An Open World.*
7. Cooley and Nexon, *Exit from Hegemony.*
8. Friend and Thayer, *How China Sees the World.*
9. Hass, *Stronger.*
10. Dollar, Huang, and Yao, eds., *China 2049.*
11. Hass, *Stronger,* 2.
12. Hass, *Stronger,* 4–5.
13. Hass, *Stronger;* Friend and Thayer, *How China Sees the World;* Cooley and Nexon, *Exit from Hegemony;* Haass, *A World in Disarray;* Kagan, *The Jungle Grows Back;* Koenig, *The Return of Great Power Rivalry.*
14. Cooley and Nexon, *Exit from Hegemony.*

18 GLOBAL GOVERNMENT IN A WORLD OF DEMOCRACIES AND DICTATORSHIPS: WHAT IT MIGHT LOOK LIKE IN 2150

1. Not surprisingly, the literature on this topic is vast. A good place to start is Kennedy, *The Parliament of Man;* Fasulo, *An Insider's Guide to the UN;* Singer, *One World Now;* and Leinen and Bummel, *A World Parliament.* See also Clark and Sohn, *World Peace Through World Law;* Keohane and Nye, *Power and Interdependence;* Mazower, *Governing the World;* Boulding, *Stable Peace;* Falk, Kim, and Mendlovitz, eds., *Toward a Just World Order;* Morgenthau, *Politics Among Nations;* Schelling, *Arms and Influence;* Power, *A Problem from Hell;* Weiss, *What's Wrong with the United Nations and How to Fix It;* Baratta, *The Politics of World Federation;* Schwartzberg, *Transforming the United Nations System;* Urquhart, *A Life in Peace and War;* Urquhart, *Hammarskjold;* Annan, *We the Peoples.* Good background sources are: Held, *Democracy and the Global Order;* Keohane, *Power and Governance in a Partially Globalized World;* Karns, Mingst, and Stiles, *International Organizations;*

Frederking and Diehl, eds., *The Politics of Global Governance*; Weiss and Wilkinson, eds., *International Organization and Global Governance*.

2. Boulding, *Stable Peace*.
3. Davenport, Melander, and Regan, *The Peace Continuum*; Wood, *Current Debates in Peace and Conflict Studies*; Cooper and Finley, *Peace and Conflict Studies Research*; Galtung, *Peace by Peaceful Means*; Jeong, *Peace and Conflict Studies*; Barash, *Approaches to Peace*.
4. Boulding, *Stable Peace*.
5. McCormick, *Understanding the European Union*, 76–79.
6. Hueglin and Fenna, *Comparative Federalism*; Rozell and Wilcox, *Federalism*; Linder, *Swiss Democracy*.
7. Hueglin and Fenna, *Comparative Federalism*.
8. Linder, *Swiss Democracy*.
9. Kennedy, *The Parliament of Man*; Fasulo, *An Insider's Guide to the UN*; Mazower, *Governing the World*.
10. Schwartzberg, *Transforming the United Nations System*, ch. 2.
11. Carlos Romulo, quoted in Leinen and Bummel, *A World Parliament*, 61.
12. Hartley Shawcross, quoted in Leinen and Bummel, *A World Parliament*, 61.
13. Kennedy, *The Parliament of Man*, 30; see also the IMF web page at: https://www.imf.org/en/About.
14. I draw heavily in the discussion that follows on two excellent books: Schwartzberg, *Transforming the United Nations System*; and Leinen and Bummel, *A World Parliament*.
15. Schwartzberg, *Transforming the United Nations System*, chs. 2–4.
16. Adapted from Schwartzberg, *Transforming the United Nations System* (Table 2.3) © United Nations University. Adapted with the permission of the United Nations University. See Schwartzberg, *Transforming the United Nations System*, 25.
17. The idea that a World Parliament could only be created through a gradual, incremental process is shared by Schwartzberg, *Transforming the United Nations System*; and Leinen and Bummel, *A World Parliament*.
18. Schwartzberg, *Transforming the United Nations System*, ch. 4.
19. Image courtesy of Joseph Schwartzberg and United Nations University Press. Schwartzberg, *Transforming the United Nations System* (Figure 4.3) © United Nations University. Reproduced with the permission of the United Nations University. See Schwartzberg, *Transforming the United Nations System*, 76.
20. Putting the two Koreas together in the same regional group sounds like a recipe for trouble, so it might be better to reassign North Korea to the China region. Since North Korea's economic clout and population are small, this wouldn't alter China's overall weight very much.
21. An alternate approach would be to simply go with the average of each nation's raw economic and population numbers as shown in Table E.1, making the same adjustment for the African Union as before.

Table E.1 Security Council voting weights for fifteen largest G20 nations plus African Union using the average of each nation's population and economic output as a percentage of global totals. The weight for the African Union is the average of all the other nations' voting weights.

Nation	GNP ($Tr)	Pop (million)	GNP (%)	Pop (%)	Formula	Wgt (%)
			C	P	(C+P)/2	
China	13	1,412	0.19697	0.260565	0.228767	23.34272
US	20.4	331	0.309091	0.061081	0.185086	18.97461
India	2.7	1,380	0.040909	0.25466	0.147784	15.24443
Japan	5	125	0.075758	0.023067	0.049412	5.407228
Germany	4	83	0.060606	0.015316	0.037961	4.262127
Brazil	1.9	212	0.028788	0.039122	0.033955	3.861474
UK	2.8	67	0.042424	0.012364	0.027394	3.205407
France	2.8	65	0.042424	0.011995	0.02721	3.186954
Russia	1.7	145	0.025758	0.026758	0.026258	3.091764
Mexico	1.3	128	0.019697	0.023621	0.021659	2.631878
Italy	2	60	0.030303	0.011072	0.020688	2.534759
Canada	1.8	38	0.027273	0.007012	0.017143	2.180255
South Korea	1.6	51	0.024242	0.009411	0.016827	2.148688
Spain	1.5	46	0.022727	0.008489	0.015608	2.026796
Australia	1.3	26	0.019697	0.004798	0.012247	1.690745
African Union	2.2	1250				6.25

This latter approach has the advantage of being simpler, but the absence of the "disparity-reducing" factor of M (the third factor in Schwartzberg's formula) results in a significant increase of weights at the top of the list and a concomitant diminution of weights for the bottom nations. In this scenario, the reduced weight of the twelve smaller members would render it much harder for coalitions of those nations to counterbalance the decisions made by one of the Big Three at the top. In order to counterbalance China, for example, a coalition comprising the United Kingdom, France, Russia, Mexico, Italy, Canada, South Korea, Spain, and Australia (combined weight of 22.7) would still not suffice to outweigh China's weight of 23.3. Such a top-heavy weighting system would no doubt prove unacceptable to a majority of G20 nations. Here we see the importance of the third factor in Schwartzberg's formula, which helps to mitigate the great inequalities of world power.

An even simpler approach, of course, would be to use economic clout as the sole weighting factor. This is the system that has long been favored by the US in its UN diplomacy, for reasons that become obvious when one looks at the resultant array of weights in Table E.2.

Table E.2 Security Council voting weights for fifteen largest G20 nations plus African Union using each nation's economic output (GNP) as the weighting factor, with 2020 statistics.

Nation	GNP ($Tr)	Security Council Weight
US	20.4	20.4
China	13	13
Japan	5	5
Germany	4	4
UK	2.8	2.8
France	2.8	2.8
India	2.7	2.7
African Union	2.2	2.2
Italy	2	2
Brazil	1.9	1.9
Canada	1.8	1.8
Russia	1.7	1.7
South Korea	1.6	1.6
Spain	1.5	1.5
Mexico	1.3	1.3
Australia	1.3	1.3

Here the disparity among nations is even more pronounced, and the system is clearly a nonstarter from a geopolitical point of view: nearly everyone except the Americans would reject it.

22. Adapted from Schwartzberg, Joseph E., *Transforming the United Nations System* (Table 2.3) © United Nations University. Adapted with the permission of the United Nations University. See Schwartzberg, *Transforming the United Nations System*, 25.

23. Switzerland has been governed since 1848 by a plural executive of this sort, with seven members on its executive council. The key to the success of the Swiss plural executive system has lain in the fact that the seven members of the executive council are elected by the representatives in the Federal Assembly, who are themselves directly elected via the country's major political parties. Both the Federal Assembly and the executive council therefore closely reflect the nation's political landscape, with power allocated in strict proportion to the cantonal, linguistic, and ideological groupings among the population. The sixteen-member UN Security Council being proposed here would loosely emulate the Swiss principle of governance, via the weighted voting system which allocates power in proportion to the national groupings of the member states. See Linder, *Swiss Democracy*, chs. 1, 2.

24. The African Union, with its 55 member states, would only have one weighted vote in the Security Council, to be sure, but since it is a collective body representing all the nations in the continent, it is reasonable to claim that all of those nations would thereby acquire a partial but significant say in key UN decisions.
25. McCormick, *Understanding the European Union*, 76–79.
26. McCormick, *Understanding the European Union*, 91–93.
27. Van den Bossche and Zdouc, *The Law and Policy of the World Trade Organization*.
28. Schabas, *An Introduction to the International Criminal Court*; Bosco, *Rough Justice*.
29. Schwartzberg, *Transforming the United Nations System*, chs. 5–7.
30. Stiglitz, *The Euro*; see also Nordvig, *The Fall of the Euro*.
31. Jeffry Frieden and Stefanie Walter, "Understanding the political economy of the Eurozone crisis," *Annual Review of Political Science* 20 (2017), 371–90.
32. Eichengreen, Mehl, and Chitu, *How Global Currencies Work*.
33. Eichengreen, Mehl, and Chitu, *How Global Currencies Work*; see also Cohen, *The Future of Global Currency*.
34. Kathy Gilsinan, "How China Deceived the WHO," *The Atlantic* (April 12, 2020); David Fidler, "The World Health Organization and Politics," *Think Global Health* (April 10, 2020); Spencer Bokat-Lindell, "Is the coronavirus killing the World Health Organization?" *New York Times* (July 7, 2020).

19 KEEPING THE SYSTEM ACCOUNTABLE AND FAIR

1 Hueglin and Fenna, *Comparative Federalism*; McCormick, *Understanding the European Union*.
2 McCormick, *Understanding the European Union*.
3 Schwartzberg, *Transforming the United Nations System*, chs. 4, 8, 9.
4 This idea is described in detail in Schwartzberg, *Transforming the United Nations System*, ch. 14.
5 Schwartzberg, *Transforming the United Nations System*, ch. 10.
6 Kennedy, *The Parliament of Man*; Fasulo, *An Insider's Guide to the UN*.
7 UN News, "General Assembly approves $3 billion UN budget for 2020," *United Nations* (December 27, 2019): https://news.un.org/en/story/2019/12/1054431
8 Michael Shear and Stephanie Saul, "Trump, in taped call, pressured Georgia official to 'find' votes to overturn election," *New York Times* (January 3, 2021); Cameron McWhirter and Lindsay Wise, "Trump pressured Georgia Secretary of State to 'find' votes," *Wall Street Journal* (January 4, 2021); Wall Street Journal Staff, "Trump's Georgia call: listen to the audio and read a full transcript: President urged Georgia Secretary of State Brad Raffensperger to overturn the state's victory for President-elect Joe Biden," *Wall Street Journal* (January 3, 2021).
9 Schwartzberg, *Transforming the United Nations System*, ch. 9; Fasulo, *An Insider's Guide to the UN*, ch. 18. For a listing of specific scandals see the section on scandals

in the Wikipedia article on "Criticisms of the United Nations:" https://en
.wikipedia.org/wiki/Criticism_of_the_United_Nations#Criticisms_of_scandals.

10 Schwartzberg, *Transforming the United Nations System*, ch. 9.

11 Schwartzberg, *Transforming the United Nations System*, 203, 303.

12 Kenny, *Getting Better*; Banerjee and Duflo, *Poor Economics*; Sachs, *The End of Poverty*; Munk, *The Idealist*; see the World Bank data on this topic at: https://data .worldbank.org/topic/poverty.

13 Andres Castaneda, et al., "Global poverty update from the World Bank: New annual poverty estimates using the revised 2011 PPPs," *World Bank Blogs* (September 2020) at: https://blogs.worldbank.org/opendata/september-2020-global-poverty-update-world-bank-new-annual-poverty-estimates-using-revised.

14 Two billion individuals at $500 apiece is $1 trillion.

15 Reliable statistics on privately held wealth are notoriously hard to verify, but the most respected and widely-cited source available is compiled by an organization named Wealth-X. Wealth-X, "New report reveals global UHNW population grew 1.7% in 2020 despite Covid-19 disruption," at: http://go.wealthx.com/world-ultra-wealth-report-2021; see also Piketty, *Capital in the Twenty-First Century*, chs. 7–12.

16 Wealth-X, "New report reveals global UHNW population grew 1.7%"; see also Inequality.Org, "Global inequality," Institute for Policy Studies (April 2021): http s://inequality.org/facts/global-inequality/#global-wealth-inequality; and Boston Consulting Group, "When clients take the lead: global wealth 2021," at: https:// web-assets.bcg.com/d4/47/64895c544486a7411b06ba4099f2/bcg-global-wealth-2021-jun-2021.pdf.

17 Piketty, *Capital in the Twenty-First Century*, ch. 12. See also the Wikipedia page "Ultra high net worth individual," which cites historical statistics on portfolio growth from the World Ultra Wealth Report and Boston Consulting Group Global Wealth Report: https://en.wikipedia.org/wiki/Ultra_high-net-worth_individual#cite_note-10.

18 My math here is simple: the total wealth of the billionaires is $13 trillion. Divide this by 2,700 and you get an average of $4.8 billion per billionaire. If this $4.8 billion grows by an annual average of 6.7 percent, it yields $321 million per year in wealth gain. Tax this amount at 42 percent, and the remaining 58 percent that goes into the pockets of the billionaires is an average of $187 million for each of the 2,700 persons. Kerry Dolan, "Forbes' 35th Annual World's Billionaires List: Facts and Figures 2021," *Forbes* (April 6, 2021): https://www.forbes.com/sites/kerryado lan/2021/04/06/forbes-35th-annual-worlds-billionaires-list-facts-and-figures-2021/ ?sh=1f2837845e58.

19 Piketty, *Capital in the Twenty-First Century*, ch. 15, "A global tax on capital."

20 See the Freedom House website at: https://freedomhouse.org/countries/free dom-world/scores.

21 Adapted from Schwartzberg, *Transforming the United Nations System* (Table 2.3) © United Nations University. Adapted with the permission of the United Nations

University. See Schwartzberg, *Transforming the United Nations System*, 25. The Freedom House national scores are available at: https://freedomhouse.org/co untries/freedom-world/scores.

20 COLLECTIVE MILITARY SECURITY AND ECONOMIC SANCTIONS: HOW TO HANDLE ROGUES, CHEATERS, AND FANATICS

1. To be sure, the Russians did issue a veiled threat in 1956 to use missiles in defense of Egypt if the Anglo–French–Israeli forces failed to comply with the UN's order to withdraw; but this was never a serious threat because the US was actively siding with the Russians in this crisis, and it was fairly clear to all the players that the Russian threat was not going to materialize, and would remain primarily at the level of rhetoric.

2. Smith, ed., *Reassessing Suez 1956.*

3. Baldwin, *Economic Statecraft*; Early, *Busted Sanctions*; Dörfler, *Security Council Sanctions Governance*; Blackwill and Harris, *War by Other Means*; Happold and Eden, eds., *Economic Sanctions and International Law*; Hufbauer, et al., *Economic Sanctions Reconsidered.*

4. See for example Robert Pape, "Why economic sanctions do not work," *International Security* 22:2 (1997), 90–136; and Stephanie Lenway, "Between war and commerce: economic sanctions as a tool of statecraft," *International Organization* 42:2 (1988), 397–426.

5. I derive these cases directly from Baldwin, *Economic Statecraft*, ch. 8.

6. Baldwin, *Economic Statecraft*, ch. 8.

7. Baldwin, *Economic Statecraft*, ch. 8.

8. Hufbauer, et al., *Economic Sanctions Reconsidered*, ch. 6.

9. Thomas Schelling, "A world without nuclear weapons?" *Daedalus* (Fall 2009), at: https://www.amacad.org/content/publications/pubContent.aspx?d=945; see also Schelling, *Arms and Influence.*

10. A partial precedent for this sort of treaty can be found in the 1922 Washington Naval Treaty, which set fixed limits on the naval forces of Britain, the United States, France, Italy, and Japan.

11. Plesch, Miletic, and Rauf, eds., *Reintroducing Disarmament and Cooperative Security to the Toolbox of 21st Century Leaders*; Dunworth and Hood, eds., *Disarmament Law*; Garcia, *Disarmament Diplomacy and Human Security.*

12. Stockholm International Peace Research Institute, *SIPRI Yearbook 2020*: https://www.sipri.org/sites/default/files/YB20%2010%20WNF.pdf.

13. Baldwin, *Economic Statecraft*; Early, *Busted Sanctions*; Blackwill and Harris, *War by Other Means*; Happold and Eden, eds., *Economic Sanctions and International Law*; Hufbauer, et al., *Economic Sanctions Reconsidered.*

21 WHAT COULD GO WRONG?

1. Downing, *1983*; Talbott, *Endgame*; Harahan, *On-Site Inspections under the INF Treaty*, chs. 3, 4.

22 CONCLUSION

1. Mitchell, *Complexity*.
2. Laughlin, *A Different Universe*; Juarrero, *Dynamics in Action*; Miller and Page, *Complex Adaptive Systems*; Bedau and Humphreys, eds., *Emergence*; Holland, *Emergence*; Mitchell, *Complexity*.
3. Thompson, *The Poverty of Theory*; Sunstein, *How Change Happens*; Sewell, *Logics of History*, especially chs. 4 and 88; Smith, *What Is a Person?*, especially chs. 4–6; Taleb, *The Black Swan*.
4. Bloch, *Strange Defeat*, 173.
5. Service, *The End of the Cold War*; Sebestyen, *Revolution 1989*; Sarotte, *1989*; Grachev, *Gorbachev's Gamble*; Remnick, *Lenin's Tomb*.
6. Gorbachev, *Memoirs*; Zantovsky, *Havel*; Palazchenko, *My Years with Gorbachev and Shevardnadze*.
7. *Newsweek* (November 26, 1984), 56.
8. Two good examples of these divergent approaches are the way George H. W. Bush handled the first Iraq war, compared with how Margaret Thatcher handled the 1982 Falkland Islands crisis. When Saddam Hussein's Iraq invaded Kuwait in 1990, American and Russian leaders joined together in condemning the attack; they moved a swift resolution through the Security Council, and a powerful UN coalition force defeated the Iraqis and sent them running back home. This was exactly the sort of bold collective action that the architects of the UN had envisioned back in 1945. Although the intervention was led by American generals and dominated by American troops and materiel, the Gulf War coalition was a credibly international force that comprised military units from 34 nations and whose $60 billion cost was borne by an even larger number of countries. It provided an impressive example of how effective the UN could be as a peace enforcer when its key members spoke with one voice. President George H. W. Bush could certainly have opted to disregard the UN and dispatch an exclusively American force to rebuff Hussein's act of aggression; but, to his credit, he chose the more cumbersome route of moving through the UN – allowing the officials of that body to apply sanctions, issue warnings, and build a multinational coalition. By relinquishing the cowboy image of America as the world's police-man, and handing over this role to the UN, he significantly strengthened the reputation of that institution, and bolstered its prospects as a future focal point of global governance.

Britain's Margaret Thatcher, by contrast, chose the cowboy option in 1982, when Argentine generals launched an invasion of the Falkland Islands in the

South Atlantic. She was no big fan of the UN and saw the rash action of the Argentine dictatorship as a perfect opportunity to flex some British muscle. "The Empire Strikes Back," read the cover of *Newsweek* magazine: she dispatched British warships to the South Atlantic, where they swiftly defeated the Argentines and restored the islands to British control. Cue the raucous jingoist songs and triumphant parades back in London: Thatcher's popularity, which had been sagging, now soared to new heights. But a precious opportunity had been lost. The Falklands invasion would have offered an excellent chance for effective action by the UN, for it fell outside the standard political alignments that so often blocked decisions by that body. Neither China nor Russia had explicit interests in the conflict, and although many developing nations sided with Argentina because of anticolonialist sentiment, their reaction was muted in this case because the war had started through unprovoked aggression by a nasty dictatorial regime. The US and the EU both condemned the attack, as did the UN Security Council. Under these unusual circumstances, it would have been quite feasible for a UN military coalition to confront the Argentines in the South Atlantic and force them to retreat. The world would have been presented with another impressive example of UN collective security at work, and the track record of international cooperation would have been further strengthened. What the world got, instead, was a brief pageant of old-fashioned, flag-waving nationalism doing its all-too-familiar thing.

If we compare the military actions taken by Thatcher and Bush, it is Bush who arguably made the greater long-term contribution to world peace. He was pioneering an innovative form of collective intervention that will prove increasingly important during the twenty-first century and beyond – whereas all she did was play another round of the old game by the old rules. World leaders who understand the urgent need to move beyond the self-help system can look to statesmen like Bush as their model, as they face the military crises of their own time in office. Finlan, *The Gulf War 1991*; Allison, *The Gulf War, 1990–91*; Atkinson, *Crusade*; "The Empire Strikes Back," cover story, *Newsweek* (April 19, 1982); Middlebrook, *The Falklands War*; Hastings and Jenkins, *Battle for the Falklands*.

9. Fortunately, one branch of the movement split off in the late 1800s, insisting on nonviolent means in pursuit of their class aims, and this movement matured into the trade unions and modern democratic-socialist parties that wield power constructively in many countries today. One of the classic instances of this debate took place within the European Left in the late nineteenth and early twentieth centuries, pitting advocates of reform such as Eduard Bernstein and Jean Jaurès against militants such as V. I. Lenin and Rosa Luxemburg. For an overview see Kolakowski, *Main Currents of Marxism*.

Bibliography

Adams, Kirsten, and Daniel Kreiss, *Power in Ideas: A Case-Based Argument for Taking Ideas Seriously in Political Communication* (Cambridge University Press, 2021).

Adams, Sam, Guruduth Banavar, and Murray Campbell, "I-Athlon: toward a multidimensional Turing Test," *AI Magazine* (Spring 2016).

Adamthwaite, Anthony, *Britain, France, and Europe, 1945–1975: The Elusive Alliance* (Bloomsbury, 2020).

Addison, Paul, *The Road to 1945: British Politics and the Second World War* (Jonathan Cape, 1975).

Akkerman, Tjitske, Sarah de Lange, and Matthijs Rooduijn, eds., *Radical Right-Wing Populist Parties in Western Europe: Into the Mainstream?* (Routledge, 2016).

Alibek, Ken, and Stephen Handelman, *Biohazard: The Chilling True Story of the Largest Covert Biological Weapons Program in the World – Told from the Inside by the Man Who Ran It* (Delta, 1999).

Allenby, Braden, and Daniel Sarewitz, *The Techno-Human Condition* (MIT Press, 2013).

Allhof, Fritz, Patrick Lin, James H. Moor, John Weckert, and Mihail C. Roco, eds., *Nanoethics: The Ethical and Social Implications of Nanotechnology* (Wiley, 2007).

Allison, William, *The Gulf War, 1990–91* (Palgrave Macmillan, 2012).

Altmire, Jason, *Dead Center: How Political Polarization Divided America and What We Can Do About It* (Sunbury, 2017).

Ambinder, Marc, *The Brink: President Reagan and the Nuclear War Scare of 1983* (Simon & Schuster, 2018).

Ambrose, Matthew, *The Control Agenda: A History of the Strategic Arms Limitation Talks* (Cornell University Press, 2018).

Anderson, Benedict, *Imagined Communities: Reflections on the Origin and Spread of Nationalism* (Verso, 2016).

Anderson, Kevin, and Glen Peters, "The trouble with negative emissions," *Science* 354:6309 (October 14, 2016).

Anderson, Michael, and Susan Leigh Anderson, eds., *Machine Ethics* (Cambridge University Press, 2011).

385

Angel, Roger, "Feasibility of cooling the Earth with a cloud of small spacecraft near the inner Lagrange point (L1)," *Proceedings of the National Academy of Sciences* 103:46 (November 14, 2006).

Angus, Ian, and Simon Butler, *Too Many People? Population, Immigration, and the Environmental Crisis* (Haymarket, 2011).

Annan, Kofi, *We the Peoples: A UN for the Twenty-First Century* (Routledge, 2014).

Archer, David, *Global Warming: Understanding the Forecast*, 2nd ed. (Wiley, 2012).

Arendt, Hanna, *The Origins of Totalitarianism* (Harcourt, Brace, Jovanovich, 1973).

Arkin, Ronald, *Governing Lethal Behavior in Autonomous Robots* (CRC Press, 2009).

Art, Robert J., and Robert Jervis, eds., *International Politics: Enduring Concepts and Contemporary Issues* (HarperCollins, 1996).

Asahina, Robert, *Just Americans: How Japanese Americans Won a War at Home and Abroad* (Gotham, 2006).

Asimov, Isaac, *I, Robot* (Doubleday, 1950).

Atkinson, Rick, *Crusade: The Untold Story of the Persian Gulf War* (Mariner, 1994).

Ausubel, Jesse, "Renewable and nuclear heresies", *International Journal of Nuclear Governance, Economy, and Ecology*, 1:3 (2007).

Baber, Walter, and Robert Bartlett, *Consensus and Global Environmental Governance: Deliberative Democracy in Nature's Regime* (MIT Press, 2015).

Bacevich, Andrew, ed., *Ideas and American Foreign Policy: A Reader* (Oxford University Press, 2018).

Baldwin, David, *Economic Statecraft* (Princeton University Press, 2020).

Baldwin, Geoff, Travis Bayer, Robert Dickinson, et al., *Synthetic Biology: A Primer* (Imperial College Press, 2012).

Balleisen, Edward, Lori Bennear, Kimberly Krawiec, and Jonathan Wiener, eds., *Policy Shock: Recalibrating Risk and Regulation after Oil Spills, Nuclear Accidents, and Financial Crises* (Cambridge University Press, 2017).

Banerjee, Abhijit, and Esther Duflo, *Poor Economics: A Radical Rethinking of the Way to Fight Global Poverty* (Public Affairs, 2012).

Barash, David, *Approaches to Peace: A Reader in Peace Studies* (Oxford University Press, 2013).

Baratta, Joseph, *The Politics of World Federation: From World Federalism to Global Governance* (Praeger, 2004).

Barinaga, Marcia, "Asilomar revisited: lessons for today?" *Science* 287:5458 (March 3, 2000).

Barker, Gillian, and Philip Kitcher, *Philosophy of Science: A New Introduction* (Oxford University Press, 2013).

Barnett, Michael, and Martha Finnemore, *Rules for the World: International Organizations in Global Politics* (Cornell University Press, 2004).

Barnett, Victoria J., *Bystanders: Conscience and Complicity During the Holocaust* (Praeger, 2000).

Barnosky, Anthony, Elizabeth A. Hadly, Jordi Bascompte, et al., "Approaching a state shift in Earth's biosphere," *Nature* 486 (June 7, 2012).

BIBLIOGRAPHY

Barr, Niall, *Eisenhower's Armies: The American-British Alliance During World War II* (Pegasus, 2015).

Barratt, James, *Our Final Invention: Artificial Intelligence and the End of the Human Era* (Thomas Dunne Books, 2013).

Baum, Rudy, "Nanotechnology: Drexler and Smalley make the case for and against 'molecular assemblers,'" *Chemical Engineering News* 81:48 (December 1, 2003).

Baum, S., and B. Tonn, "Introduction: Confronting future catastrophic threats to humanity,' *Futures* 72 (2015).

Baumgaertner, Emily, "As D.I.Y. gene editing gains popularity, 'someone is going to get hurt,'" *New York Times* (May 14, 2018).

Bear, Mark, Barry W. Connors, and Michael A. Paradiso, *Neuroscience: Exploring the Brain*, 3rd ed. (Lippincott, Williams & Wilkins, 2006).

Beck, Ulrich, *Risk Society: Towards a New Modernity*, trans. by Mark Ritter (Sage, 1986, 2013).

Bedau, Mark, and Paul Humphreys, eds., *Emergence: Contemporary Readings in Philosophy and Science* (MIT Press, 2008).

Beinart, Peter, *The Icarus Syndrome: A History of American Hubris* (Harper, 2011).

Bellamy, Alex, and Edward Luck, *The Responsibility to Protect: From Promise to Practice* (Polity, 2018).

Bellamy, Alex, and Tim Dunne, eds., *The Oxford Handbook of the Responsibility to Protect* (Oxford University Press, 2016).

Benedick, Richard, *Ozone Diplomacy: New Directions in Safeguarding the Planet* (Harvard University Press, 1998).

Bennett-Woods, Deb, ed., *Nanotechnology: Ethics and Society* (CRC Press, 2008).

Ben Ouagrham-Gormley, Sonia, *Barriers to Bioweapons: The Challenges of Expertise and Organization for Weapons Development* (Cornell University Press, 2014).

Berezow, Alex, and Hank Campbell, *Science Left Behind: Feel-Good Fallacies and the Rise of the Anti-Scientific Left* (PublicAffairs, 2012).

Berg, Paul, "Summary statement of the Asilomar Conference on Recombinant DNA Molecules," *Proceedings of the National Academy of Sciences* 72:6 (1975).

Berners-Lee, Mike, *There Is No Planet B: A Handbook for the Make or Break Years* (Cambridge University Press, 2021).

Bernstein, Daniel, Johannes Buchmann, and Erik Dahmen, eds., *Post-quantum Cryptography* (Springer, 2009).

Bernstein, Michael, *The Great Depression: Delayed Recovery and Economic Change in America, 1929–1939* (Cambridge University Press, 1989).

Berry, Wendell, *A Place on Earth* (Counterpoint, 1983).

Fidelity: Five Stories (Pantheon, 1992).

The Selected Poems of Wendell Berry (Counterpoint, 1998).

Life Is a Miracle: An Essay Against Modern Superstition (Counterpoint, 2000).

Citizenship Papers (Shoemaker and Hoard, 2003).

It All Turns on Affection (Counterpoint, 2012).

Berube, David, *Nano-Hype: The Truth Behind the Nanotechnology Buzz* (Prometheus Books, 2006).

Bess, Michael, *Realism, Utopia, and the Mushroom Cloud: Four Activist Intellectuals and Their Strategies for Peace* (University of Chicago Press, 1993).

The Light-Green Society: Ecology and Technological Modernity in France, 1960–2000 (University of Chicago Press, 2003).

Choices Under Fire: Moral Dimensions of World War II (Knopf, 2006).

Our Grandchildren Redesigned: Life in the Bioengineered Society of the Near Future (Beacon, 2015).

Bettez, David, "Unfulfilled initiative: disarmament negotiations and the Hague Peace Conferences of 1899 and 1907," *Royal United Services Institute for Defence Studies* 133:3 (June 1988).

Betz, Hans-Georg, *Radical Right-Wing Populism in Europe* (Palgrave, 1994).

Biagioli, Mario, ed., *The Science Studies Reader* (Routledge, 1999).

Bickerton, Chris, *European Integration: From Nation-States to Member-States* (Oxford University Press, 2013).

Blackwill, Robert, and Jennifer Harris, *War by Other Means: Geoeconomics and Statecraft* (Harvard University Press, 2016).

Bland, Larry, ed., *The Papers of George Catlett Marshall*, vol. 5 (Johns Hopkins University Press, 2003).

Blanton, Thomas, "The Cuban Missile Crisis: 40 years later," Washingtonpost.com (October 16, 2002).

Blascovich, Jim, and Jeremy Bailenson, *Infinite Reality: The Hidden Blueprint of our Virtual Lives* (Morrow, 2011).

Bloch, Marc, *Strange Defeat*, trans. by Gerard Hopkins (Norton, 1999).

Blustein, Paul, "Laid low: the IMF, the Euro Zone, and the first rescue of Greece," CIGI Paper no. 61 (Center for International Governance Innovation, April 2015).

Bocquet, Dominique, Christian Deubner, and Quentin Peel, *The Future of the Franco-German Relationship: Three Views* (Royal Institute of International Affairs, 1997).

Boellstorff, Tom, *Coming of Age in Second Life: An Anthropologist Explores the Virtually Human* (Princeton, 2008).

Bohman, James, and William Rehg, eds., *Deliberative Democracy: Essays on Reason and Politics* (MIT Press, 1997).

Bokat-Lindell, Spencer, "Is the coronavirus killing the World Health Organization?" *New York Times* (July 7, 2020).

Bonzo, Matthew, and Michael Stevens, *Wendell Berry and the Cultivation of Life* (Brazos Press, 2008).

Bornstein, David, *The Price of a Dream: The Story of the Grameen Bank* (University of Chicago Press, 1997).

Bosco, David, *Rough Justice: The International Criminal Court in a World of Power Politics* (Oxford University Press, 2013).

Bostrom, Nick, *Superintelligence: Paths, Dangers, Strategies* (Oxford University Press, 2014).

Bostrom, Nick, Allan Dafoe, and Carrick Flynn, "Policy desiderata in the development of machine superintelligence," Future of Humanity Institute Working Paper (Oxford University, 2016).

Bostrom, Nick, and Milan Cirkovic, eds., *Global Catastrophic Risks* (Oxford University Press, 2008).

Boudette, Neal, and Coral Davenport, "G.M. announcement shakes up U.S. automakers' transition to electric cars," *New York Times* (January 29, 2021).

Boulding, Kenneth, *Stable Peace* (University of Texas Press, 1978).

Bowman, William, et al., *Ecology*, 4th ed. (Sinauer/Oxford, 2017).

Bozo, Frédéric, Andreas Rodder, and Mary Elise Sarotte, eds., *German Reunification: A Multinational History* (Routledge, 2016).

Brand, Stewart, *Whole Earth Discipline: Why Dense Cities, Nuclear Power, Transgenic Crops, Restored Wildlands, and Geoengineering Are Necessary* (Penguin, 2009).

Bray, Dennis, *Wetware: A Computer in Every Living Cell* (Yale, 2009).

Breazeal, Cynthia, *Designing Sociable Robots* (MIT Press, 2002).

Bregman, Rutger, *Humankind: A Hopeful History*, trans. by Elizabeth Manton and Erica Moore (Little, Brown, 2020).

Breining, Greg, *Super Volcano: The Ticking Time Bomb Beneath Yellowstone National Park* (Voyageur, 2007).

Breyer, Christian, Mahdi Fasihi, and Arman Aghahosseini, "Carbon dioxide direct air capture for effective climate change mitigation based on renewable electricity: a new type of energy system sector coupling," *Mitigation and Adaptation Strategies for Global Change* 25:1 (2020).

Brissaud, Jean-Marc, *Éléments pour une nouvelle politique étrangère* (Front National, Université d'Été, September 1985).

Brixey-Williams, Sebastian, "Prospects for game-changers in submarine-detection technology," *The Strategist* (Australian Strategic Policy Institute, August 22, 2020).

Brooks, Rodney, *Flesh and Machines: How Robots Will Change Us* (Pantheon, 2002).

Brown, Archie, *Seven Years That Changed the World: Perestroika in Perspective* (Oxford University Press, 2009).

Brown, James, *Ending Our Uncivil War: A Path to Political Recovery and Spiritual Renewal* (Agape, 2017).

Brown, Jeremy, and Matthew Johnson, *Maoism at the Grassroots: Everyday Life in China's Era of High Socialism* (Harvard University Press, 2015).

Browning, Christopher, *Ordinary Men: Reserve Police Battalion 101 and the Final Solution in Poland* (Harper, 2017).

Brynjolfsson, Erik, and Andrew McAfee, *The Second Machine Age: Work, Progress, and Prosperity in a Time of Brilliant Technologies* (Norton, 2016).

Buchanan, Ben, *The Hacker and the State: Cyber Attacks and the New Normal of Geopolitics* (Harvard University Press, 2020).

Buck, Holly, *After Geoengineering: Climate Tragedy, Repair, and Restoration* (Verso, 2019).

Bull, Hedley, *The Anarchical Society: A Study of Order in World Politics*, 4th ed. (Red Globe, 2012).

Burke, Marshall, W. Matthew Davis, and Noah S. Diffenbaugh, "Large potential reduction in economic damages under UN mitigation targets" *Nature* 557 (May 23, 2018).

Burnette, Ryan, ed., *Biosecurity: Understanding, Assessing, and Preventing the Threat* (Wiley, 2013).

Buss, David, *Evolutionary Psychology: The New Science of the Mind*, 5th ed. (Psychology Press, 2014).

Cabrera, Luis, *The Practice of Global Citizenship* (Cambridge University Press, 2010).

Cahill, Kevin, *Tropical Diseases in Temperate Climates* (J. B. Lippincott, 1965).

Calder, Angus, *The People's War: Britain, 1939–1945* (Pimlico, 1992).

Callon, Michel, Pierre Lascoumes, and Yannick Barthe, *Acting in an Uncertain World: An Essay on Technical Democracy*, trans. by Graham Burchell (MIT Press, 2011).

Camosy, Charles, *Beyond the Abortion Wars: A Way Forward for a New Generation* (Eerdmans, 2015).

Carlson, Robert, *Biology Is Technology: The Promise, Peril, and New Business of Engineering Life* (Harvard University Press, 2010).

Carpenter, Daniel, and David Moss, *Preventing Regulatory Capture: Special Interest Influence and How to Limit it* (Cambridge University Press, 2013).

Carroll, Dennis, Brooke Watson, Eri Togami, et al., "The Global Virome Project," *Bulletin of the World Health Organization* (March 5, 2018).

Carson, Clayborne, "African Americans at war," in I.C.B. Dear and M.R.D. Foot, eds., *The Oxford Companion to World War II* (Oxford University Press, 1995).

Carter, April, *Peace Movements: International Protest and World Politics Since 1945* (Routledge, 1992).

Carter, Sarah, Michael Rodemeyer, Michele Garfinkel, and Robert Friedman, *Synthetic Biology and the U.S. Biotechnology Regulatory System: Challenges and Options* (J. Craig Venter Institute, May 2014).

Castaneda, Andres, et al., "Global poverty update from the World Bank: New annual poverty estimates using the revised 2011 PPPs," *World Bank Blogs* (September 2020), at: https://blogs.worldbank.org/opendata/september-2020-global-poverty-update-world-bank-new-annual-poverty-estimates-using-revised.

Castronova, Edward, *Synthetic Worlds: The Business and Culture of Online Games* (University of Chicago Press, 2005).

Exodus to the Virtual World: How Online Fun Is Changing Reality (Palgrave, 2007).

Chace, Callum, *Surviving AI: The Promise and Peril of Artificial Intelligence* (Three C's Press, 2015).

Chace, James, "Sharing the atom bomb," *Foreign Affairs* 75:1 (January/February 1996).

Chalmers, David, "The singularity: a philosophical analysis," *Journal of Consciousness Studies* 17, 7–65 (2010).

Cheney, Catherine, "CEPI, a year in: how can we get ready for the next pandemic?" *Devex* (February 5, 2018).

Cherny, Andrei, *The Candy Bombers: The Untold Story of the Berlin Airlift and America's Finest Hour* (Dutton Caliber, 2009).

Chertoff, Michael, *Homeland Security: Assessing the First Five Years* (University of Pennsylvania Press, 2009).

Christian, Brian, *The Alignment Problem: Machine Learning and Human Values* (Norton, 2020).

Chollet, François, "The implausibility of intelligence explosion," *Medium/Artificial Intelligence* (November 27, 2017).

Christakis, Nicholas, *Blueprint: The Evolutionary Origins of a Good Society* (Little, Brown Spark, 2019).

Chu, Steven, "Carbon capture and sequestration," *Science* 325:5948 (September 2009).

Church, George, *A Synthetic Biohazard Non-Proliferation Proposal* (Harvard University, 2004); https://arep.med.harvard.edu/SBP/Church_Biohazard04c.htm.

Church, George, and Ed Regis, *Regenesis: How Synthetic Biology Will Reinvent Nature and Ourselves* (Basic Books, 2012).

Ciccarelli, Saundra, and J. Noland White, *Psychology*, 5th ed. (Pearson, 2017).

Clack, Christopher, Staffan A. Qvist, Jay Apt, et al., "Evaluation of a proposal for reliable low-cost grid power with 100% wind, water, solar," *Proceedings of the National Academy of Sciences* 114:26 (June 27, 2017).

Clark, Bryan, *The Emerging Era in Undersea Warfare* (Center for Strategic and Budgetary Assessments, 2015).

Clark, Grenville, and Louis Sohn, *World Peace Through World Law: Two Alternative Plans*, 3rd ed. (Harvard University Press, 1966).

Clark, Ronald, *The Life of Bertrand Russell* (Bloomsbury, 2012).

Clarke, Harold, Matthew Goodwin, and Paul Whiteley, *Brexit: Why Britain Voted to Leave the European Union* (Cambridge University Press, 2017).

Claude, Inis, *Swords into Ploughshares*, 3rd ed. (Random House, 1964).

Clayton, Philip, and Paul Davies, *The Re-emergence of Emergence: The Emergentist Hypothesis from Science to Religion* (Oxford University Press, 2006).

Clendinnen, Inga, *Reading the Holocaust* (Cambridge University Press, 1999).

Clifford, Catherine, "This favorite saying of Mark Zuckerberg reveals the way the Facebook billionaire thinks about life," CNBC.com (November 30, 2017).

Cohen, Benjamin, *The Future of Global Currency: The Euro versus the Dollar* (Routledge, 2011).

Cohen, Joel, *How Many People Can the Earth Support?* (Norton, 1995).

Coldewey, Devin, "OpenAI shifts from nonprofit to 'capped-profit' to attract capital," *Techcrunch* (March 11, 2019).

Cole, Alistair, *Franco-German Relations* (Longman, 2001).

Cole, David, *Engines of Liberty: The Power of Citizen Activists to Make Constitutional Law* (Basic Books, 2016).

Coleman, Thomas, *A Practical Guide to Risk Management* (CFA Institute, 2011).

Collier, Ellen, *Bipartisanship and the Making of Foreign Policy: A Historical Survey* (XLibris, 2011).

Collier, Paul, and Alexander Betts, *Refuge: Rethinking Refugee Policy in a Changing World* (Oxford University Press, 2017).

Collina, Tom, "Russia, U.S. working on joint launch notification," *Arms Control Association* (July 2, 2010).

Collins, Mike, "The big bank bailout," *Forbes* (July 14, 2015).

Combs, Cynthia, *Terrorism in the 21st Century*, 7th ed. (Pearson, 2012).

Combs, Jerald, *The History of American Foreign Policy from 1895* (Routledge, 2012).

Conant, James, *Harvard to Hiroshima and the Making of the Nuclear Age* (Stanford University Press, 1995).

Conniff, Richard, "The last resort: can we remove enough CO_2 from the atmosphere to slow or even reverse climate change?" *Scientific American* 320:1 (January 2019).

Constantine, Stephen, *Social Conditions in Britain 1918–1939* (Routledge, 2006).

Cook, John, *Cranky Uncle vs. Climate Change: How to Understand and Respond to Climate Science Deniers* (Citadel, 2020).

Cooley, Alexander, and Daniel Nexon, *Exit from Hegemony: The Unraveling of the American Global Order* (Oxford University Press, 2020).

Cooper, Robin, and Laura Finley, *Peace and Conflict Studies Research: A Qualitative Perspective* (Information Age, 2014).

Cortright, David, *Peace: A History of Movements and Ideas* (Cambridge University Press, 2008).

Cotton, Matthew, *Ethics and Technology Assessment: A Participatory Approach* (Springer, 2014).

Couzin-Frankel, Jennifer, "Poliovirus baked from scratch," *Science* (July 11, 2002).

Cover, J.A., Christopher Pincock, and Martin Curd, *Philosophy of Science: The Central Issues* (Norton, 2012).

Craig, Robin, and J.B. Ruhl, "Designing administrative law for adaptive management," *Vanderbilt Law Review* 67:1 (2014).

Cravens, Gwyneth, *Power to Save the World: The Truth About Nuclear Energy* (Vintage, 2007).

Crichton, Michael, *Prey* (Harper, 2002).

Cronon, William, ed., *Uncommon Ground: Rethinking the Human Place in Nature* (Norton, 1996).

Crouch, Colin, *The Globalization Backlash* (Polity, 2019).

Crowther, T. W., H. B. Glick, M. A. Bradford, et al., "Mapping tree density at a global scale," *Nature* 525 (September 10, 2015).

Csikszentmihalyi, Mihaly, *Flow: The Psychology of Optimal Experience* (Harper, 2008).

Cumings, Bruce, *The Korean War: A History* (Modern Library, 2011).

Cyranoski, David, "The CRISPR-baby scandal: what's next for human gene-editing," *Nature* 566 (February 26, 2019).

Damasio, António, *The Feeling of What Happens: Body and Emotion in the Making of Consciousness* (Harcourt, 1999).

Darwin, Charles, *The Origin of Species* (Signet, 2003 [first published 1859]).

Daston, Lorraine, and Peter Galison, *Objectivity* (Zone Books, 2010).

Davenport, Christian, Erik Melander, and Patrick Regan, *The Peace Continuum: What It Is and How to Study It* (Oxford University Press, 2018).

Davies, Sara, Adam Kamradt-Scott, and Simon Rushton, *Disease Diplomacy: International Norms and Global Health Security* (Johns Hopkins University Press, 2015).

Davis, Ernest, "Ethical guidelines for a superintelligence," *Artificial Intelligence* 220 (2015).

Davis, Zachary, ed., *The India–Pakistan Military Standoff: Crisis and Escalation in South Asia* (Palgrave MacMillan, 2011).

De Búrca, Gráinne, "Reappraising subsidiarity's significance after Amsterdam," Harvard Jean Monnet Working Paper 7/99 (Harvard Law School, 1999).

Deese, R.S., ed., *Climate Change and the Future of Democracy* (Springer, 2019).

Defense Science Board Task Force, "Department of Defense Biological Safety and Security Program" (Office of the Under Secretary of Defense for Acquisition, Technology, and Logistics, 2009).

Diamandis, Peter, and Steven Kotler, *Abundance: The Future is Better Than You Think* (Free Press, 2012).

Diamond, Jared, *Guns, Germs, and Steel: The Fates of Human Societies* (Norton, 2017).

DiGiovanna, Sean, and Ann Markusen, *From Defense to Development? International Perspectives on Realizing the Peace Dividend* (Routledge, 2003).

Dinan, Desmond, *Origins and Evolution of the European Union*, 2nd ed. (Oxford University Press, 2014).

Dinan, Desmond, Neill Nugent, and William Paterson, eds., *The European Union in Crisis* (Palgrave, 2016).

Dobbs, Michael, *One Minute to Midnight: Kennedy, Khrushchev, and Castro on the Brink of Nuclear War* (Vintage, 2009).

Dobbs, Rachel, "What was at stake in 1962?" *Foreign Affairs* (July 10, 2012).

Dolan, Kerry, "Forbes' 35th Annual World's Billionaires List: facts and figures 2021," *Forbes* (April 6, 2021), at: https://www.forbes.com/sites/kerryadolan/2021/04/06/forbes-35th-annual-worlds-billionaires-list-facts-and-figures-2021/?sh=1f2837845e58.

Dollar, David, Yiping Huang, and Yang Yao, eds., *China 2049: Economic Challenges of a Rising Global Power* (Brookings Institution Press, 2020).

Domingos, Pedro, "AI will serve our species, not control it," *Scientific American* 319:3 (September 2018).

Dörfler, Thomas, *Security Council Sanctions Governance* (Routledge, 2019).

Doudna, Jennifer, and Samuel Sternberg, *A Crack in Creation: Gene Editing and the Unthinkable Power to Control Evolution* (Mariner, 2018).

Downing, Taylor, *1983: Reagan, Andropov, and a World on the Brink* (Da Capo Press, 2018).

Doyle, James, *Nuclear Safeguards, Security, and Nonproliferation: Achieving Security with Technology and Policy* (Butterworth-Heinemann, 2008).

Drexler, K. Eric, *Engines of Creation: The Coming Era of Nanotechnology* (Anchor Doubleday, 1986).

Radical Abundance: How a Revolution in Nanotechnology Will Change Civilization (Public Affairs, 2013).

Dreyfus, Hubert, and Stuart Dreyfus, *Mind over Machine* (Simon & Schuster, 2000).

Dryzek, John, *Foundations and Frontiers of Deliberative Governance* (Oxford University Press, 2011).

Dryzek, John, Richard Norgaard, and David Schlosberg, eds., *The Oxford Handbook of Climate Change and Society* (Oxford University Press, 2011).

Duane, Tim, Jonathan Koomey, Kathy Belyeu, and Karl Hausker, *From Risk to Return: Investing in a Clean Energy Economy* (Risky Business Project, 2016).

Duchene, Francois, *Jean Monnet: The First Statesman of Interdependence* (Norton, 1980).

Dudley, Dominic, "China is set to become the world's renewable energy superpower, according to new report," *Forbes* (January 11, 2019).

Duedahl, Poul, ed., *A History of UNESCO: Global Actions and Impacts* (Palgrave Macmillan, 2016).

Dunworth, Treasa, and Anna Hood, eds., *Disarmament Law: Reviving the Field* (Routledge, 2020).

Dupuy, Jean-Pierre, *On the Origins of Cognitive Science: The Mechanization of the Mind,* trans. by M. B. DeBevoise (MIT, 2009).

Early, Bryan, *Busted Sanctions: Explaining Why Economic Sanctions Fail* (Stanford University Press, 2015).

Eden, Amnon, James Moor, Johnny Soraker, and Eric Steinhart, eds., *Singularity Hypotheses: A Scientific and Philosophical Assessment* (Springer, 2012).

Edwards, Mickey, *The Parties versus the People: How to Turn Republicans and Democrats into Americans* (Yale University Press, 2012).

Ehlert, Dana, and Kirsten Zickfeld, "Irreversible ocean thermal expansion under carbon dioxide removal," *Earth System Dynamics* 9 (2018).

Eichengreen, Barry, Arnaud Mehl, and Livia Chitu, *How Global Currencies Work: Past, Present, and Future* (Princeton University Press, 2018).

Elias, Norbert, *The Civilizing Process: Sociogenetic and Psychogenetic Investigations* (Blackwell, 2000).

Ellul, Jacques, *The Technological Society,* trans. by John Wilkinson (Vintage, 1964).

Elster, Jon, ed., *Deliberative Democracy* (Cambridge University Press, 1998).

Englander, John, *Moving to Higher Ground: Rising Sea Level and the Path Forward* (Science Bookshelf, 2021).

Enthoven, Alain, and Wayne Smith, *How Much is Enough? Shaping the Defense Program, 1961–1969* (Harper & Row, 1971).

Erlanger, Steven, "Europe lauds Biden but wonders: what will he want? How long will he stay?" *New York Times* (January 7, 2021).

ETC Group, *Extreme Genetic Engineering: An Introduction to Synthetic Biology* (ETC Group, January 2007).

Executive Office of the President, Office of Science and Technology Policy, "Coordinated framework for regulation of biotechnology," 51 FR 23302 (Executive Office of the President, June 26, 1986).

Falk, Richard, *Reframing the International: Law, Culture, Politics* (Routledge, 2002).

Falk, Richard, and Andrew Strauss, *A Global Parliament: Essays and Articles* (Committee for a Democratic UN, 2011).

Falk, Richard, Samuel Kim, and Saul Mendlovitz, eds., *Toward a Just World Order* (Routledge, 2018).

Farquharson, John E., and Stephen C. Holt, *Europe from Below: An Assessment of Franco-German Popular Contacts* (Allen & Unwin, 1975).

Fasulo, Linda, *An Insider's Guide to the UN*, 3rd ed. (Yale University Press, 2015).

Felt, Ulrike, Rayvon Fouché, Clark Miller, and Laurel Smith-Doerr, eds., *The Handbook of Science and Technology Studies*, 4th ed. (MIT, 2017).

Ferguson, Charles, *Nuclear Energy: What Everyone Needs to Know* (Oxford University Press, 2011).

Fiddian-Qasmiyeh, Elena, Gil Loescher, Katy Long, and Nando Sigona, eds., *The Oxford Handbook of Refugee and Forced Migration Studies* (Oxford University Press, 2016).

Fidler, David, "The World Health Organization and politics," *Think Global Health* (April 10, 2020).

Field, Geoffrey, *Blood, Sweat, and Toil: Remaking the British Working Class, 1939–1945* (Oxford University Press, 2011).

Figes, Orlando, *Revolutionary Russia, 1891–1991: A History* (Metropolitan, 2014).

Finlan, Alastair, *The Gulf War 1991* (Osprey, 2003).

Fish, M. Steven, *Democracy Derailed in Russia: The Failure of Open Politics* (Cambridge University Press, 2005).

Fisher, Roger, William Ury, and Bruce Patton, *Getting to Yes: Negotiating Agreement Without Giving In* (Penguin, 2011).

Fishkin, James, *Democracy When the People Are Thinking: Revitalizing Our Politics Through Public Deliberation* (Oxford University Press, 2018).

FitzGerald, David, *Refuge Beyond Reach: How Rich Democracies Repel Asylum Seekers* (Oxford University Press, 2019).

FitzGerald, Frances, *Way Out There in the Blue: Reagan, Star Wars and the End of the Cold War* (Simon & Schuster, 2000).

Flam, Faye, "Americans are a little too relaxed about nukes," *Bloomberg Opinion* (August 30, 2017).

Flynn, Michael E., "The international and domestic sources of bipartisanship in U.S. foreign policy," *Political Research Quarterly* 67:2 (February 2014).

Ford, Martin, *Rise of the Robots: Technology and the Threat of a Jobless Future* (Basic, 2016).

Architects of Intelligence: The Truth about AI from the People Building It (Packt Publishing, 2018).

Foster, Lynn, *Nanotechnology: Science, Innovation, and Opportunity* (Prentice Hall, 2006).

Fountain, Henry, "Compact nuclear fusion reactor is 'very likely to work,' studies suggest," *New York Times* (September 29, 2020).

Fox, Douglas, "The carbon rocks of Oman: could an unusual outcropping of Earth's interior solve the world's climate problem?" *Scientific American* 325:1 (July 2021).

Franco, Alessandro, and Ana Diaz, "The future challenges for 'clean coal technologies': joining efficiency increase and pollutant emission control," *Energy* 34:3 (March 2009).

Franklin, Alexi, "An international cyber warfare treaty: historical analogies and future prospects," *Journal of Law and Cyber Warfare* 7:1 (Fall 2018).

Frankman, Myron, *World Democratic Federalism: Peace and Justice Indivisible* (Palgrave Macmillan, 2004).

Fraser, Derek, *The Evolution of the British Welfare State*, 5th ed. (Red Globe Press, 2017).

Frederickson, Donald, "Asilomar and recombinant DNA: the end of the beginning," in Kathi Hanna, ed., *Biomedical Politics* (National Academy Press, 1991).

"The first twenty-five years after Asilomar," *Perspectives in Biology and Medicine* 44:2 (Spring, 2001).

Frederking, Brian, and Paul Diehl, eds., *The Politics of Global Governance: International Organizations in an Interdependent World*, 5th ed. (Rienner, 2015).

Freitas, Robert, "Some limits to global ecophagy by biovorous nanoreplicators, with public policy recommendations," *Foresight Institute* (April 2000).

Fried, Charles, and Gregory Fried, *Because It Is Wrong: Torture, Privacy, and Presidential Power in the Age of Terror* (Norton, 2010).

Frieden, Jeffry, and Stefanie Walter, "Understanding the political economy of the Eurozone crisis," *Annual Review of Political Science* 20 (2017).

Friend, John, and Bradley Thayer, *How China Sees the World: Han-Centrism and the Balance of Power in International Politics* (Potomac Books, 2018).

Friend, Tad, "How frightened should we be of AI?" *The New Yorker* (May 14, 2018).

Fry, Douglas, *Beyond War: The Human Potential for Peace* (Oxford University Press, 2007).

Fukuyama, Francis, *Our Posthuman Future: Consequences of the Biotechnology Revolution* (Farrar Straus Giroux, 2002).

Furcht, Leo, and William Hoffman, *The Stem Cell Dilemma*, 2nd ed. (Arcade, 2011).

Fuss, Sabine, Josep G. Canadell, Glen P. Peters, et al., "Betting on negative emissions," *Nature Climate Change* 4 (October 2014).

Future of Life Institute, "*Asilomar AI Principles*" (Future of Life Institute, 2017).

Gaddis, John Lewis, *The Cold War: A New History* (Penguin, 2006).

Galtung, Johan, *Peace by Peaceful Means: Peace and Conflict, Development and Civilization* (Sage, 1996).

Searching for Peace: The Road to Transcend (Pluto, 2002).

Grachev, Andrei, *Gorbachev's Gamble: Soviet Foreign Policy and the End of the Cold War* (Polity, 2008).

Garcia, Denise, *Disarmament Diplomacy and Human Security: Regimes, Norms and Moral Progress in International Relations* (Routledge, 2011).

Garfinkel, Michele, Drew Endy, Gerald Epstein, and Robert Friedman, *Synthetic Genomics: Options for Governance* (J. Craig Venter Institute/CSIS/MIT, 2007).

Garrett, Laurie, *The Coming Plague: Newly Emerging Diseases in a World Out of Balance* (Penguin, 1994).

Gates, Bill, *How to Avoid a Climate Disaster: The Solutions We Have and the Breakthroughs We Need* (Knopf, 2021).

Gauchat, Gordon, "Politicization of science in the public sphere: a study of public trust in the United States, 1974 to 2010," *American Sociological Review* 77:2 (April 2012).

Gaulin, Steven, and Donald McBurney, *Evolutionary Psychology*, 2nd ed. (Pearson, 2004).

Geisinger, Alex, "A belief change theory of expressive law," *Iowa Law Review* 35 (2002–2003).

Gellner, Ernest, *Nations and Nationalism*, 2nd ed. (Cornell University Press, 2009).

Gelman, Vladimir, *Authoritarian Russia: Analyzing Post-Soviet Regime Changes* (University of Pittsburgh Press, 2015).

Gerrish, Sean, *How Smart Machines Think* (MIT, 2019).

Gerstein, Daniel, *Bioterror in the 21st Century* (Naval Institute Press, 2009).

National Security and Arms Control in the Age of Biotechnology (Rowman and Littlefield, 2013).

Gerzon, Mark, *The Reunited States of America: How We Can Bridge the Partisan Divide* (Berrett-Koehler, 2016).

Gessen, Masha, *The Man Without a Face: The Unlikely Rise of Vladimir Putin* (Riverhead, 2013).

Gibney, Elizabeth, "Self-taught AI is best yet at strategy game Go," *Nature* (October 18, 2017).

Gilbert, Mark, *European Integration: A Concise History* (Rowman & Littlefield, 2011).

Gilligan, Jonathan, "Flexibility, clarity, and legitimacy: considerations for managing nanotechnology risks," *Environmental Law Reporter* 36:12 (2006).

Gilsinan, Kathy, "How China deceived the WHO," *The Atlantic* (April 12, 2020).

Giridharadas, Anand, *Winners Take All: The Elite Charade of Changing the World* (Vintage, 2019).

Gleditsch, Nils, Olav Bjerkholt, Ron Smith, and Paul Dunne, eds., *The Peace Dividend* (Emerald, 1996).

Godfrey-Smith, Peter, *Theory and Reality: An Introduction to the Philosophy of Science* (University of Chicago Press, 2003).

Goertzel, Ben, *The AGI Revolution* (Humanity+ Press, 2016).

Goldstein, E. Bruce, *Cognitive Psychology: Connecting Mind, Research, and Everyday Experience*, 3rd ed. (Wadsworth, 2011).

Gomatos, Leonidas, *Global Economic Crisis: The Case of Greece* (Lambert, 2016).

Gonzalez, Robbie, "The potential pitfalls of sucking carbon from the atmosphere," *Wired* (June 13, 2018).

Goodell, Jeff, *How to Cool the Planet: Geoengineering and the Audacious Quest to Fix Earth's Climate* (Mariner, 2010).

Goodfellow, Ian, Yoshua Bengio, and Aaron Courville, *Deep Learning* (MIT Press, 2016).

Goodin, Robert, *The Oxford Handbook of Political Science* (Oxford University Press, 2011).

Gopnik, Alison, "Making AI more human," *Scientific American* 316:6 (June 2017).

Gorbachev, Mikhail, *Memoirs* (Doubleday, 1995).

Gordijn, Bert, and Anthony Cutter, eds., *In Pursuit of Nanoethics* (Springer, 2014).

Gore, Al, *An Inconvenient Truth: The Crisis of Global Warming* (Viking, 2007).

An Inconvenient Sequel: Truth to Power (Rodale, 2017).

Gottweis, Herbert, *Governing Molecules: The Discursive Politics of Genetic Engineering in Europe and the United States* (MIT, 1998).

Gourevitch, Philip, *We Wish to Inform You That Tomorrow We Will Be Killed with Our Families: Stories From Rwanda* (Picador, 1999).

Grace, Katja, "The Asilomar Conference: a case study in risk mitigation," Technical Report 2015–9 (Machine Intelligence Research Institute, 2015).

Grachev, Andrei, *Gorbachev's Gamble: Soviet Foreign Policy and the End of the Cold War* (Polity, 2008).

Green, Jessica, *Rethinking Private Authority: Agents and Entrepreneurs in Global Environmental Governance* (Princeton University Press, 2013).

Gronvall, Gigi, *Synthetic Biology: Safety, Security, and Promise* (Health Security Press, 2016).

Grunwald, Michael, "The trouble with the Green New Deal," *Politico* (January 15, 2019).

Grush, Loren, "SXSW 2015: I reprogrammed a lifeform in someone's kitchen while drinking a beer," *Popular Science* (March 14, 2015).

Grushkin, Daniel, Todd Kuiken, and Piers Millet, *Seven Myths and Realities about Do-It-Yourself Biology* (Woodrow Wilson International Center for Scholars, Synthetic Biology Project, November 2013).

Guillemin, Jeanne, *Biological Weapons: From the Invention of State-Sponsored Programs to Contemporary Bioterrorism* (Columbia University Press, 2005).

Gunkel, David, *The Machine Question: Critical Perspectives on AI, Robots, and Ethics* (MIT, 2012).

Guston, David, and Daniel Sarewitz, "Real-time technology assessment," *Technology in Society* 24:1–2 (January 2002).

Guston, David, and Daniel Sarewitz, eds., *Shaping Science and Technology Policy: The Next Generation of Research* (University of Wisconsin Press, 2006).

Haas, Ernst B., *The Uniting of Europe: Political, Social, and Economic Forces, 1950–1957* (University of Notre Dame Press, 2004).

Haas, Peter, *Morality After Auschwitz: The Radical Challenge of the Nazi Ethic* (Fortress Press, 1988).

Haass, Richard, *A World in Disarray: American Foreign Policy and the Crisis of the Old Order* (Penguin, 2017).

Haftendorn, Helga, *Coming of Age: German Foreign Policy Since 1945* (Rowman & Littlefield, 2006).

Happold, Matthew, and Paul Eden, eds., *Economic Sanctions and International Law* (Hart, 2019).

Haidt, Jonathan, *The Happiness Hypothesis: Finding Modern Truth in Ancient Wisdom* (Basic Books, 2006).

Halberstam, David, *The Coldest Winter: America and the Korean War* (Hachette, 2008).

Hall, J. Storrs, *Nanofuture: What's Next for Nanotechnology* (Prometheus, 2005).

Hamer, Christopher, *A Global Parliament: Principles of World Federation* (Self-published, 1998).

Hancock, M. Donald, Christopher J. Carman, Marjorie Castle, et al., *Politics in Europe*, 6th ed. (CQ Press, 2014).

Hanna, Ryan, et al., "Emergency deployment of direct air capture as a response to the climate crisis," *Nature Communications* 12:368 (2021).

Hansen, James, *Storms of My Grandchildren: The Truth About the Coming Climate Catastrophe and Our Last Chance to Save Humanity* (Bloomsbury, 2009).

Hanson, Robin, *The Age of Em: Work, Love, and Life When Robots Rule the Earth* (Oxford University Press, 2015).

Hanson, Robin, and Eliezer Yudkowsky, "The AI-Foom debate" (Machine Intelligence Research Institute, 2013).

Hao, Karen, "These awful AI song lyrics show us how hard language is for machines," *Technology Review* (November 13, 2018).

Harahan, Joseph P., *On-Site Inspections under the INF Treaty* (US Department of Defense, 1993).

Harari, Yuval, *Sapiens: A Brief History of Humankind* (Harper, 2018).

Harding, Sandra, *Objectivity and Diversity: Another Logic of Scientific Research* (University of Chicago Press, 2015).

Hargraves, Robert, *Thorium: Energy Cheaper Than Coal* (Self-published, 2012).

Harland, Paul, Henk Staats, and Henk Wilke, "Situational and personality factors as direct or personal norm mediated predictors of pro-environmental behavior," *Basic and Applied Social Psychology* 29:4 (2007).

Harris, Sam, *The Moral Landscape: How Science Can Determine Human Values* (Free Press, 2011).

Haskell, Thomas, *Objectivity Is Not Neutrality: Explanatory Schemes in History* (Johns Hopkins University Press, 1998).

Haslam, Nick, Luke Smillie, and John Song, *An Introduction to Personality, Individual Differences, and Intelligence*, 2nd ed. (Sage, 2017).

Hass, Ryan, *Stronger: Adapting America's China Strategy in an Age of Competitive Interdependence* (Yale University Press, 2021).

Hastings, Max, *The Korean War* (Simon & Schuster, 1988).

Hastings, Max, and Simon Jenkins, *The Battle for the Falklands* (Norton, 1983).

Hathaway, Oona, and Scott Shapiro, *The Internationalists: How a Radical Plan to Outlaw War Remade the World* (Simon & Schuster, 2017).

Hauss, Charles, *Security 2.0: Dealing with Wicked Global Problems* (Rowman & Littlefield, 2015).

Hawken, Paul, ed., *Drawdown: The Most Comprehensive Plan Ever Proposed to Reverse Global Warming* (Penguin, 2017).

Hawking, Stephen, Stuart Russell, Max Tegmark, and Frank Wilczek, "Stephen Hawking: 'Transcendence' looks at the implications of artificial intelligence – but are we taking AI seriously enough?" *The Independent* (May 1, 2014).

Hawkins, Jeff, *A Thousand Brains: A New Theory of Intelligence* (Basic, 2021).

Hawkins, Stephen, et al., "Hidden tribes: a study of America's polarized landscape," *More in Common* (2018).

Hayhoe, Katharine, *Saving Us: A Climate Scientist's Case for Hope and Healing in a Divided World* (One Signal Publishers/Atria, 2021).

Hedgpeth, Dana, "Congress says DHS oversaw $15 billion in failed contracts," *Washington Post* (September 17, 2008).

Hegel, G.W.F., *The Phenomenology of Spirit*, trans. by Terry Pinkard (Cambridge University Press, 2019).

Heinberg, Richard, and David Fridley, "The end of cheap coal," *Nature* 468:7322 (2010).

Held, David, *Democracy and the Global Order: From the Modern State to Cosmopolitan Governance* (Stanford University Press, 1995).

Hélias, Pierre-Jakez, *The Horse of Pride: Life in a Breton Village*, trans. by June Guicharnaud (Yale University Press, 1980).

Hennigan, W.J., "Donald Trump is playing a dangerous game of nuclear poker," *Time* (February 1, 2018).

Hern, Alex, "Experts including Elon Musk call for research to avoid AI pitfalls," *The Guardian* (January 12, 2015).

Hershberg, J.G., *James B. Conant: Harvard to Hiroshima and the Making of the Nuclear Age* (Stanford University Press, 1995).

Hesterman, Jennifer, *The Terrorist-Criminal Nexus: An Alliance of International Drug Cartels, Organized Crime, and Terror Groups* (CRC Press, 2013).

Hetherington, Marc, and Thomas Rudolph, *Why Washington Won't Work: Polarization, Political Trust, and the Governing Crisis* (University of Chicago Press, 2015).

Heydon, Kenneth, and Stephen Woolcock, eds., *The Ashgate Research Companion to International Trade Policy* (Ashgate, 2012).

Hibbard, Bill, *Superintelligent Machines* (Kluwer, 2002).

Hilaire, Jerome, Jan C. Minx, Max W. Callaghan et al., "Negative emissions and international climate goals – learning from and about mitigation scenarios," *Climatic Change* 157 (2019).

Hilberg, Raul, *Perpetrators, Victims, Bystanders: The Jewish Catastrophe, 1933–1945* (HarperCollins, 1992).

Hilley, John, *The Challenge of Legislation: Bipartisanship in a Partisan World* (Brookings, 2007).

Hobsbawm, Eric, *The Age of Extremes: A History of the World, 1914–1991* (Vintage, 1996). *Nations and Nationalism Since 1780: Programme, Myth, Reality*, 2nd ed. (Cambridge University Press, 2012).

Hodge, Graeme, Diana Bowman, and Andrew Maynard, eds., *International Handbook on Regulating Nanotechnologies* (Edward Elgar, 2010).

Hodsden, Suzanne, "Breathalyzer diagnoses 17 different diseases using a single breath," *Med Device Online* (January 3, 2017).

Hoffmann, David, *The Dead Hand: The Untold Story of the Cold War Arms Race and Its Dangerous Legacy* (Anchor, 2010).

Hoffmann, Matthew, *Climate Governance at the Crossroads: Experimenting with a Global Response after Kyoto* (Oxford University Press, 2012).

Hoffmann, Stanley, *Duties Beyond Borders: On the Limits and Possibilities of Ethical International Relations* (Syracuse University Press, 1981).

Hogan, Michael, *A Cross of Iron: Harry S. Truman and the Origins of the National Security State, 1945–1954* (Cambridge University Press, 2000).

Holland, John, *Emergence: From Chaos to Order* (Basic, 1998).

Holtzman, David, *Privacy Lost: How Technology Is Endangering Your Privacy* (Jossey-Bass, 2006).

Hope, Bradley, and Nicole Friedman, "Climate change is forcing the insurance industry to recalculate," *Wall Street Journal* (October 28, 2018).

Hopgood, Stephen, *The Endtimes of Human Rights* (Cornell University Press, 2014).

Hopkin, Jonathan, "When Polanyi met Farage: market fundamentalism, economic nationalism, and Britain's exit from the European Union," *The British Journal of Politics and International Relations* 19:3 (June 2017).

Hopkins, Daniel, and John Sides, eds., *Political Polarization in American Politics* (Bloomsbury, 2015).

Hore-Lacy, Ian, *Nuclear Energy in the 21st Century*, 4th ed. (World Nuclear Association, 2018).

Horgan, John, "Bethe, Teller, Trinity, and the end of the Earth," *Scientific American online* (August 4, 2015).

Horvath, Robert, *The Legacy of Soviet Dissent: Dissidents, Democratization, and Radical Nationalism in Russia* (Routledge, 2012).

Hueglin, Thomas, and Alan Fenna, *Comparative Federalism: A Systematic Inquiry*, 2nd ed. (University of Toronto Press, 2015).

Hufbauer, Gary, Jeffrey J. Schott, Kimberly Ann Elliott, and Barbara Oegg, *Economic Sanctions Reconsidered*, 3rd ed. (Peterson Institute for International Economics, 2009).

Hughes, Terry, James T. Kerry, Andrew H. Baird et al., "Global warming transforms coral reef assemblages," *Nature* 556 (April 18, 2018).

Hulme, Mike, *Why We Disagree about Climate Change: Understanding Controversy, Inaction and Opportunity* (Cambridge University Press, 2009).

Humphreys, Paul, *Emergence: A Philosophical Account* (Oxford University Press, 2016).

———, ed., *The Oxford Handbook of Philosophy of Science* (Oxford University Press, 2016).

Husain, Amir, *The Sentient Machine: The Coming Age of Artificial Intelligence* (Scriber, 2017).

Huston, Scott, "GPT-3 primer: understanding OpenAI's cutting-edge language model," *Towards Data Science* website (August 20, 2020).

Huxley, Aldous, *Brave New World* (Harper, 2006).

Hylton, Wil, "Craig Venter's bugs might save the world," *New York Times* (May 30, 2012).

Igo, Sarah, *The Known Citizen: A History of Privacy in Modern America* (Harvard University Press, 2018).

Igoe, Michael, and Adva Saldinger, "What Trump's budget request says about US aid," *Devex* (May 23, 2017).

Illich, Ivan, *Tools for Conviviality* (Marion Boyars Press, 2001).

Institute for Policy Studies, "Global inequality," Inequality.org (April 2021), at: https://inequality.org/facts/global-inequality/#global-wealth-inequality.

Institute of Electrical and Electronics Engineers, *Ethically Aligned Design: A Vision for Prioritizing Human Well-Being with Autonomous and Intelligent Systems* (IEEE, New York, 2017).

Intergovernmental Panel on Climate Change (IPCC), *AR6 Synthesis Report: Climate Change 2022*.

Isaacson, Walter, *The Code Breaker: Jennifer Doudna, Gene Editing, and the Future of the Human Race* (Simon & Schuster, 2021).

Isasi, R., E. Kleiderman, and B.M. Knoppers, "Editing policy to fit the genome?" *Science* 351:6271 (January 22, 2016).

Ito, Joi, "Kitchen counter biohacking," Online personal blog, available at: https://joi.ito.com/weblog/2014/09/01/kitchen-counter.html.

Jacobsen, Stine, "World's largest container shipper Maersk aims to be CO_2 neutral by 2050," *Reuters* (December 5, 2018).

Jacobson, Mark, and Mark Delucchi, "A path to sustainable energy," *Scientific American* (November 2009).

——— "Providing all global energy with wind, water, and solar power, Part I: Technologies, energy resources, quantities and areas of infrastructure, and materials," *Energy Policy* 39 (2011).

Jacobson, Mark, Mark A. Delucchi, Zack A. F. Bauer, et al., "100% clean and renewable wind, water, and sunlight all-sector energy roadmaps for 139 countries of the world," *Joule* 1:1 (2017).

Jacobson, Mark, Mark A. Delucchi, Gillaume Bazaouin, et al., "100% clean and renewable wind, water, and sunlight (WWS) all-sector energy roadmaps for the 50 United States," *Energy and Environmental Science* 8 (May 27, 2015).

Jamieson, Kathleen, "How to debunk misinformation about COVID, vaccines, and masks," *Scientific American* 324:4 (April 2021).

Jarausch, Konrad, *Broken Lives: How Ordinary Germans Experienced the Twentieth Century* (Princeton University Press, 2018).

Jasanoff, Sheila, Gerald E. Markle, James C. Peterson, and Trevor Pinch, eds., *Handbook of Science and Technology Studies* (Sage Publications, 2001).

Jefferson, Catherine, Filippa Lentzos, and Claire Marris, "Synthetic biology and biosecurity: challenging the "myths," *Frontiers in Public Health* 2:115 (August 21, 2014).

Jeong, Ho-Won, *Peace and Conflict Studies: An Introduction* (Routledge, 2000).

Johnson, Deborah, and Jameson Wetmore, eds., *Technology and Society: Building Our Sociotechnical Future* (MIT Press, 2009).

Johnson, Eric, "The black hole case: the injunction against the end of the world," *Tennessee Law Review* 76:4 (2009).

Johnson, Steven, *Emergence: The Connected Lives of Ants, Brains, Cities, and Software* (Scribner, 2001).

Johnston, Seth, *How NATO Adapts: Strategy and Organization in the Atlantic Alliance Since 1950* (Johns Hopkins, 2017).

Jonas, Hans, *The Imperative of Responsibility: In Search of an Ethics for the Technological Age* (University of Chicago Press, 1985).

Jotterrand, Fabrice, ed., *Emerging Conceptual, Ethical, and Policy Issues in Bionanotechnology* (Springer, 2008).

Juarrero, Alicia, *Dynamics in Action: Intentional Behavior as a Complex System* (MIT, 1999).

Kaczor, Christopher, *The Ethics of Abortion: Women's Rights, Human Life, and the Question of Justice*, 2nd ed. (Routledge, 2014).

Kaebnick, Gregory, and Thomas Murray, eds., *Synthetic Biology and Morality: Artificial Life and the Bounds of Nature* (MIT, 2013).

Kagan, Robert, *The Jungle Grows Back: America and Our Imperiled World* (Vintage, 2018).

Kahan, Dan, Hank Jenkins-Smith, and Donald Braman, "Cultural cognition of scientific consensus," *Journal of Risk Research* 14:2 (February 2011).

Kahneman, Daniel, *Thinking, Fast and Slow* (Farrar, Straus, and Giroux, 2013).

Kahneman, Daniel, Ed Diener and Norbert Schwarz, *Well-Being: The Foundations of Hedonic Psychology* (Russell Sage, 2003).

Kahneman, Daniel, Paul Slovic, and Amos Tversky, eds., *Judgment Under Uncertainty: Heuristics and Biases* (Cambridge University Press, 1982).

Kaldor, Mary, *Global Civil Society: An Answer to War* (Polity, 2003).

Kanaan, Michael, *T-Minus AI: Humanity's Countdown to Artificial Intelligence and the New Pursuit of Global Power* (BenBella, 2020).

Kanbur, Ravi, and Henry Shue, eds., *Climate Justice: Integrating Economics and Philosophy* (Oxford University Press, 2018).

Kaplan, Jerry, *Humans Need Not Apply: A Guide to Wealth and Work in the Age of Artificial Intelligence* (Yale University Press, 2015).

Kaplan, Lawrence, *NATO Divided, NATO United: The Evolution of an Alliance* (Praeger, 2004).

Karns, Margaret, Karen Mingst, and Kendall Stiles, *International Organizations: The Politics and Process of Global Governance*, 3rd ed. (Rienner, 2015).

Kaufman, Joyce, *A Concise History of U.S. Foreign Policy*, 4th ed. (Rowman & Littlefield, 2017).

Keck, Margaret, and Kathryn Sikkink, *Activists Beyond Borders: Advocacy Networks in International Politics* (Cornell University Press, 1998).

Keiper, Adam, "Nanoethics as a discipline?" *The New Atlantis* (Spring 2007).

Keith, David, Geoffrey Holmes, David St. Angelo, and Kenton Heidel, "A process for capturing CO_2 from the atmosphere," *Joule* 2:8 (August 15, 2018).

Kelleher, Kevin, "Here's why nobody's talking about nanotech anymore," *Time* (October 9, 2015).

Keller, David, et al., "The effects of carbon dioxide removal on the carbon cycle," *Current Climate Change Reports* 4 (2018).

Kelly, Kevin, *What Technology Wants* (Penguin, 2011).

Kennedy, David, *Freedom from Fear: The American People in Depression and War, 1929–1945* (Oxford University Press, 1999).

Kennedy, Paul, *The Rise and Fall of the Great Powers: Economic Change and Military Conflict from 1500 to 2000* (Vintage, 1989).

The Parliament of Man: The Past, Present, and Future of the United Nations (Vintage, 2007).

Kenny, Charles, *Getting Better: Why Global Development Is Succeeding – and How We Can Improve the World Even More* (Basic, 2011).

Keohane, Robert, *Power and Governance in a Partially Globalized World* (Routledge, 2002).

Keohane, Robert, and Joseph Nye, Jr., *Power and Interdependence*, 4th ed. (Longman/Pearson, 2011).

Kerlin, Kat, "Ambitious Global Virome Project could mark the end of pandemic era," *University of California Davis News* (February 22, 2018).

Kettl, Donald, *Politics of the Administrative Process*, 6th ed. (CQ Press, 2014).

Khatchadourian, Raffi, "The Doomsday Invention: will artificial intelligence bring us utopia or destruction?" *The New Yorker* (November 23, 2015).

Kindleberger, Charles, and Robert Aliber, *Manias, Panics, and Crashes; A History of Financial Crises*, 7th ed. (Palgrave Macmillan, 2015).

King, David, Daniel Schrag, Zhou Dadi, Qi Ye, and Arunabha Ghosh, "Climate change: a risk assessment," *Centre for Science and Policy*, Cambridge University (2015).

Kitcher, Philip, *Science in a Democratic Society* (Prometheus, 2011).

Klein, Richard, Robert J. Nicholls, Sachooda Ragoonaden, and Michele Capobianco, "Technological options for adaptation to climate change in coastal zones," *Journal of Coastal Research* 17:3 (Summer 2001).

Kletz, Trevor, and Paul Amyotte, *Process Plants: A Handbook for Inherently Safer Design* (CRC Press, 1998).

Knight, Will, "The dark secret at the heart of AI," *Technology Review* (April 11, 2017).

Koblentz, Gregory, *Living Weapons: Biological Warfare and International Security* (Cornell University Press, 2009).

Koch, Christof, *The Quest for Consciousness: A Neurobiological Approach* (Roberts, 2004).

"AI software teaches itself video games," *Scientific American Mind* (July 1, 2015).

Koerner, Brendan, "Philip Kennedy: melding man and machine to free the paralyzed," *US News and World Report* (January 3, 2000).

Koenig, Matthew, *The Return of Great Power Rivalry: Democracy versus Autocracy from the Ancient World to the U.S. and China* (Oxford University Press, 2020).

Kolakowski, Leszek, *Main Currents of Marxism (3 volumes)*, trans. by P. S. Falla (Norton, 2008).

Kolb, Robert, *The International Court of Justice* (Hart Publishing, 2013).

Kolbert, Elizabeth, *The Sixth Extinction: An Unnatural History* (Picador, 2014).

"Can carbon dioxide removal save the world?" *The New Yorker* (November 20, 2017).

Konrad, Kornelia, Christopher Coenen, Anne Dijkstra, Colin Milburn, and Harro van Lente, eds., *Shaping Emerging Technologies: Governance, Innovation, Discourse* (IOS Press, 2013).

Kostigen, Thomas, *Hacking Planet Earth: How Geoengineering Can Help Us Reimagine the Future* (Tarcher, 2020).

Krepon, Michael, and Dan Caldwell, *The Politics of Arms Control Treaty Ratification* (Palgrave Macmillan, 1992).

Krotz, Ulrich, and Joachim Schild, *Shaping Europe: France, Germany, and Embedded Bilateralism from the Elysée Treaty to Twenty-First Century Politics* (Oxford University Press, 2013).

Krugman, Paul, *The Return of Depression Economics and the Crisis of 2008* (Norton, 2009).

Kurzweil, Ray, *The Singularity Is Near: When Humans Transcend Biology* (Viking, 2005).

Lackner, Klaus, "A guide to CO_2 sequestration," *Science* 300:5626 (June 13, 2003).

Lackner, Klaus, et al., "The promise of negative emissions," *Science* 354:6313 (November 11, 2016).

Ladikas, Miltos, Sachin Chaturvedi, Yandong Zhao, and Dirk Stemerding, eds., *Science and Technology Governance and Ethics: A Global Perspective from Europe, India, and China* (Springer, 2015).

Lahsen, Myanna, "Technocracy, democracy, and U.S. climate politics: the need for demarcations," *Science, Technology, and Human Values* 30:1 (Winter 2005).

Laird, Robin F., ed., *Strangers and Friends: The Franco-German Security Relationship* (St. Martin's, 1989).

Lanchester, John, *The Wall: A Novel* (Norton, 2019).

Landes, David, *The Unbound Prometheus: Technological Change and Industrial Development in Western Europe from 1750 to the Present* (Cambridge University Press, 2003).

Lanier, Jaron, *You Are Not a Gadget* (Vintage, 2011).

Laqueur, Walter, *A History of Terrorism* (Transaction, 2001).

Larsen, Jeffrey, *Arms Control: Cooperative Security in a Changing Environment* (Rienner, 2002).

Larsen, Jeffrey, and James Wirtz, eds., *Arms Control and Cooperative Security* (Rienner, 2009).

Latour, Bruno, and Steve Woolgar, *Laboratory Life: The Construction of Scientific Facts* (Princeton University Press, 1986).

Laughlin, Robert, *A Different Universe: Reinventing Physics from the Bottom Down* (Basic, 2005).

Law, Randall, *Terrorism: A History* (Polity, 2016).

LeDoux, Joseph, *Synaptic Self: How Our Brains Become Who We Are* (Viking, 2002).

Lee, Kai-Fu, *AI Superpowers: China, Silicon Valley, and the New World Order* (Houghton Mifflin Harcourt, 2018).

Leinen, Jo, and Andreas Bummel, *A World Parliament: Governance and Democracy in the 21st Century*, trans. by Ray Cunningham (Democracy Without Borders, 2018).

Lemon, Stanley, Margaret Hamburg, P. Frederick Sparling, Eileen Choffnes, and Alison Mack, *Ethical and Legal Considerations in Mitigating Pandemic Disease* (National Academies Press, 2007).

Lenat, Douglas, and R.V. Guha, *Building Large Knowledge-Based Systems: Representation and Inference in the Cyc Project* (Addison-Wesley, 1990).

Lennick, Michael, "We knew that if we succeeded, we could at one blow destroy a city," Interview with Edward Teller, *American Heritage* 56:3 (June/July 2005).

Lenton, Tim, *Earth System Science: A Very Short Introduction* (Oxford University Press, 2016).

Lenton, Tim, Johan Rockström, Owen Gaffney, et al., "Climate tipping points – too risky to bet against," *Nature* 575 (November 27, 2019).

Leonard, Dick, *The Routledge Guide to the European Union* (Routledge, 2016).

Lessig, Lawrence, *Code, Version 2.0* (Basic Books, 2006).

Levesque, Hector, *Common Sense, the Turing Test, and the Quest for Real AI* (MIT Press, 2017).

Levitan, Dave, "Quick-change planet: do global climate tipping points exist?" *Scientific American* (March 25, 2013).

Levy, Frank, and Richard Murnane, *The New Division of Labor: How Computers Are Creating the Next Job Market* (Princeton, 2012).

Lewin, Moshe, *The Making of the Soviet System* (Pantheon, 1985).

Lewin, Moshe, and Gregory Elliott, *The Soviet Century* (Verso, 2016).

Lewis, Patricia, Heather Williams, Benoit Pelopidas, and Sasan Aghlani, "Too close for comfort: cases of near nuclear use and options for policy," Chatham House Report (The Royal Institute of International Affairs, April 2014).

Licata, Ignazio, and Ammar Sakaji, eds., *Physics of Emergence and Organization* (World Scientific Publishing, 2008).

Lifton, Robert J., "Beyond nuclear numbing," *Teachers College Record* 84:1 (1982).

Lincoln, Don, *The Large Hadron Collider: The Extraordinary Story of the Higgs Boson and Other Stuff That Will Blow Your Mind* (Johns Hopkins University Press, 2014).

Linder, Wolf, *Swiss Democracy: Possible Solutions to Conflict in Multicultural Societies*, 2nd ed. (Palgrave, 1998).

Lissner, Rebecca, and Mira Rapp-Hooper, *An Open World: How America Can Win the Contest for Twenty-First Century Order* (Yale University Press, 2020).

Lomborg, Bjorn, *Cool It: The Skeptical Environmentalist's Guide to Global Warming* (Vintage, 2010).

Lott, Trent, and Tom Daschle, *Crisis Point: Why We Must – and How We Can – Overcome Our Broken Politics in Washington and Across America* (Bloomsbury, 2016).

Louis, William Roger, and Roger Owen, *Suez 1956: The Crisis and its Consequences* (Clarendon, 1991).

Lovering, Jessica, Alex Trembath, Marian Swain, and Luke Lavin, "Renewables and nuclear at a glance" (Breakthrough Institute, 2014), at: https://thebreak through.org/issues/energy/renewables-and-nuclear-at-a-glance.

Lowrey, Annie, "Are states really more efficient than the federal government?" *The Atlantic* (October 2, 2017).

Lowrie, Heather, and Joyce Tait, *Guidelines for the Appropriate Risk Governance of Synthetic Biology* (International Risk Governance Council, 2010).

Lugar, Richard, "Cooperative threat reduction and nuclear security," *Georgetown Journal of International Affairs* 10 (2009).

Lyman, Edwin, "'Advanced' isn't always better: assessing the safety, security, and environmental impacts of non-light-water nuclear reactors" (Union of Concerned Scientists, 2021), at: https://doi.org/10.47923/2021.14000.

Lynas, Mark, *Six Degrees: Our Future on a Hotter Planet* (National Geographic, 2008).

Nuclear 2.0: Why a Green Future Needs Nuclear Power (UIT Cambridge, 2013).

Lyubomirsky, Sonja, *The How of Happiness: A New Approach to Getting the Life You Want* (Penguin, 2008).

Maathai, Wangari, *The Green Belt Movement: Sharing the Approach and the Experience* (Lantern Publishing, 2003).

Macer, D. R. J., J. Azariah, and P. Srinives, "Attitudes to biotechnology in Asia," *International Journal of Biotechnology* (January 2000).

MacKenzie, Donald, and Judy Wajcman, eds., *The Social Shaping of Technology* (Open University Press, 1999).

Maddison, Angus, *Contours of the World Economy 1–2030 AD* (Oxford University Press, 2007).

Mahaffey, James, *Atomic Awakening: A New Look at the History and Future of Nuclear Power* (Pegasus, 2009).

Maier, Charles, *Leviathan 2.0: Inventing Modern Statehood* (Belknap, 2012).

Mann, Michael, *The New Climate War: The Fight to Take Back Our Planet* (PublicAffairs, 2021).

Manninen, Bertha, *Pro-Life, Pro-Choice: Shared Values in the Abortion Debate* (Vanderbilt University Press, 2014).

Mannix, Daniel, *The History of Torture* (Sutton/The History Press, 2003).

Mansfield, Edward, Diana Mutz, and Devon Brackbill, "Effects of the Great Recession on American attitudes toward trade," *British Journal of Political Science* 49:1 (November 2016).

Marchant, Gary, Braden Allenby, and Joseph Herkert, eds., *The Growing Gap Between Emerging Technologies and Legal-Ethical Oversight* (Springer, 2011).

Marchant, Gary, Kenneth Abbott, and Braden Allenby, eds., *Innovative Governance Models for Emerging Technologies* (Edward Elgar Publications, 2014).

Marcus, Gary, "Am I human? Researchers need new ways to distinguish artificial intelligence from the natural kind," *Scientific American* 316:3 (March 2017).

Marcus, Gary, Francesca Rossi, and Manuela Veloso, "Beyond the Turing Test," *Special Issue of AI Magazine*, 37:1 (Spring 2016).

Markandya, A. and P. Wilkinson, "Electricity generation and health," *The Lancet*, 370:9591 (2007).

Marrus, Michael, *The Holocaust in History* (University Press of New England, 1987).

Marshall, George, *Don't Even Think About It: Why Our Brains Are Wired to Ignore Climate Change* (Bloomsbury, 2014).

Martin, Lisa, "Institutions and cooperation: sanctions during the Falkland Islands conflict," *International Security* 16:4 (Spring 1992).

Martin, Richard, *Super Fuel: Thorium, The Green Energy Source for the Future* (St. Martin's Griffin, 2012).

Marwick, Arthur, *War and Social Change in the Twentieth Century: A Comparative Study of Britain, France, Germany, Russia, and the United States* (Macmillan, 1974).

Matthews, Dylan, "The amazing true socialist miracle of the Alaska Permanent Fund," *Vox* (February 13, 2018).

Mayer, Milton, *They Thought They Were Free: The Germans, 1933–45* (University of Chicago Press, 2017).

Mayne, Richard, *The Community of Europe: Past, Present, and Future* (Norton, 1963).

Mayrhofer, Jan, and Joyeeta Gupta, "The science and politics of co-benefits in climate policy," *Environmental Science and Policy* 57 (March 2016).

Mazower, Mark, *Governing the World: The History of an Idea, 1815 to the Present* (Penguin, 2013).

McCarthy, Patrick, ed., *France-Germany, 1983-1993: the Struggle to Cooperate* (St. Martin's, 1993).

———, ed., *France-Germany in the Twenty-First Century* (Palgrave, 2001).

McCarty, Nolan, Keith Poole, and Howard Rosenthal, *Polarized America: The Dance of Ideology and Unequal Riches*, 2nd ed. (MIT Press, 2016).

McClaughlin, Kay, *Talking Together: Getting Beyond Polarization Through Civil Dialogue* (Lifeforce, 2017).

McCorduck, Pamela, *Machines Who Think* (A.K. Peters, 2004).

McCormick, John, *Understanding the European Union: A Concise Introduction*, 6th ed. (Palgrave, 2014).

McCray, Matthew, "Rapid reaction capability of the European Union: taking that last big step," *Connections* 13:4 (Fall, 2014).

McDermott, Drew, "Response to 'The singularity: a philosophical analysis' by David Chalmers," *Journal of Consciousness Studies* 19:1–2 (2012).

McDonald, Forrest, *States' Rights and the Union: Imperium in Imperio, 1776–1876* (University Press of Kansas, 2000).

McDougall, Walter, *France's Rhineland Policy, 1914-1924: The Last Bid for a Balance of Power in Europe* (Princeton University Press, 2016).

McGonigal, Jane, *Reality is Broken: Why Games Make Us Better and How They Can Change the World* (Penguin, 2011).

McGuire, Steven, and Michael Smith, *The European Union and the United States: Competition and Convergence in the Global Arena* (Red Globe Press, 2008).

McIntyre, Lee, *Post-Truth* (MIT Press, 2018).

McKibben, Bill, *Enough: Staying Human in an Engineered Age* (Times Books, 2003).

Falter: Has the Human Game Begun to Play Itself Out? (Holt, 2019).

McLaren, Duncan, "Quantifying the potential scale of mitigation deterrence from greenhouse gas removal techniques," *Climatic Change* 162 (2020).

McNamara, Robert S., *Wilson's Ghost: Reducing the Risk of Conflict, Killing, and Catastrophe in the 21st Century* (Public Affairs, 2003).

McNerney, Ruth, Beyene A. Wondafrash, Kebede Amena et al., "Field test of a novel detection device for *Mycobacterium tuberculosis* antigen in cough," *BMC Infectious Diseases* 10:161 (2010).

McQueen, Noah, Peter C. Psarras, Hélène Pilorgé, and Simona Liguori, "Cost analysis of direct air capture and sequestration coupled to low-carbon thermal energy in the United States," *Environmental Science and Technology* 54:12 (2020).

McWhirter, Cameron, and Lindsay Wise, "Trump pressured Georgia Secretary of State to 'find' votes," *Wall Street Journal* (January 4, 2021).

Meacham, Jack, *Talking Sense About Politics: How to Overcome Political Polarization In Your Next Conversation* (Quaerere, 2017).

Metz, Cade, "Inside OpenAI, Elon Musk's wild plan to set artificial intelligence free," *Wired* (April 27, 2016).

"Mark Zuckerberg, Elon Musk, and the feud over killer robots," *New York Times* (June 9, 2018).

Middlebrook, Martin, *The Falklands War* (Pen and Sword, 2012).

Milburn, Colin, *Nanovision: Engineering the Future* (Duke, 2008).

Milgram, Stanley, *Obedience to Authority: An Experimental View* (Harper & Row, 1974).

Miller, John, and Scott Page, *Complex Adaptive Systems: An Introduction to Computational Models of Social Life* (Princeton, 2007).

Miller, Judith, Stephen Engelberg, and William Broad, *Germs: Biological Weapons and America's Secret War* (Simon & Schuster, 2002).

Miller, Melanie, and Scott Page, *Complex Adaptive Systems: An Introduction to Computational Models of Social Life* (Princeton, 2007).

Miller, Walter, *A Canticle for Leibowitz* (Bantam, 1984).

Miliband, David, *Rescue: Refugees and the Political Crisis of Our Time* (TED, 2017).

Minsky, Marvin, *The Emotion Machine: Commonsense Thinking, Artificial Intelligence, and the Future of the Human Mind* (Simon & Schuster, 2006).

Mitchel, Mark, and Nathan Schueter, eds., *The Humane Vision of Wendell Berry* (ISI, 2011).

Mitchell, Melanie, *Complexity: A Guided Tour* (Oxford, 2009).

Artificial Intelligence: A Guide for Thinking Humans (Farrar, Straus, and Giroux, 2019).

Molina, Ivan, and Steven Palmer, *The History of Costa Rica*, 2nd ed. (UCR, 2007).

Monnet, Jean, *Memoirs*, trans. by Richard Mayne (Doubleday, 1978).

Montgomery, Scott, and Thomas Graham, Jr., *Seeing the Light: The Case for Nuclear Power in the 21st Century* (Cambridge University Press, 2017).

Mooney, Chris, *The Republican Brain: The Science of Why They Deny Science – and Reality* (Wiley, 2012).

Moorehead, Caroline, *Troublesome People: The Warriors of Pacifism* (Adler & Adler, 1987).

Moravec, Hans, *Mind Children: The Future of Robot and Human Intelligence* (Harvard, 1988).

Robot: Mere Machine to Transcendent Mind (Oxford, 1999).

Morello, Carol, "Foreign aid cuts proposed, but 'friends' might be protected," *Washington Post* (February 12, 2017).

Moreno, Jonathan, *The Body Politic: The Battle Over Science in America* (Bellevue, 2011).

Morgenstern, Richard, and William Pizer, *Reality Check: The Nature and Performance of Voluntary Environmental Programs in the United States, Europe, and Japan* (Resources for the Future, 2007).

Morgenthau, Hans, *Politics Among Nations: The Struggle for Power and Peace*, 7th ed. (McGraw-Hill, 2005).

Morris, Charles, *A Rabble of Dead Money: The Great Crash and the Global Depression: 1929-1939* (Public Affairs, 2017).

Morris, Julian, *Rethinking Risk and the Precautionary Principle* (Butterworth/ Heinemann, 2000).

Morton, Oliver, *The Planet Remade: How Geoengineering Could Change the World* (Princeton University Press, 2016).

Moyn, Samuel, *Not Enough: Human Rights in an Unequal World* (Belknap, 2018).

Mozur, Paul, "Beijing wants AI to be made in China by 2030," *New York Times* (July 20, 2017).

Mullaney, Thomas, Benjamin Peters, Mar Hicks, and Kavita Philip, eds., *Your Computer Is On Fire* (MIT Press, 2021).

Mulligan, James, Gretchen Ellison, Kelly Levin, and Colin McCormick, "Technological carbon removal in the United States," Working Paper (World Resources Institute, September 2018).

Mumford, Lewis, and Langdon Winner, *Technics and Civilization* (University of Chicago Press, 2010).

Munk, Nina, *The Idealist: Jeffrey Sachs and the Quest to End World Poverty* (Anchor, 2013).

Murphy, Nancey, George Ellis, and Timothy O'Connor, eds., *Downward Causation and the Neurobiology of Free Will* (Springer, 2009).

Musser, George, "Artificial imagination: how machines could learn creativity and common sense, among other human qualities," *Scientific American* 320:5 (May 2019).

Myers, Steven, *The New Tsar: The Rise and Reign of Vladimir Putin* (Vintage, 2016).

Naimark, Norman, *Genocide: A World History* (Oxford University Press, 2016).

Nardi, Bonnie, *My Life as a Night Elf Priest: An Anthropological Account of World of Warcraft* (Digital Culture Books, 2010).

National Academies of Science, Engineering, and Medicine, *Negative Emissions Technologies and Reliable Sequestration: A Research Agenda* (National Academies Press, 2019).

National Academy of Sciences Committee on Advances in Technology and the Prevention of Their Application to Next Generation Biowarfare Threats, *Globalization, Biosecurity, and the Future of the Life Sciences* (National Academies Press, 2006).

National Biosurveillance Advisory Committee, *Improving the Nation's Ability to Detect and Respond to 21st Century Urgent Health Threats* (Createspace, 2014).

National Institute of Allergy and Infectious Diseases, "Universal influenza vaccine research" (May 2018), at: https://www.niaid.nih.gov/diseases-conditions/uni versal-influenza-vaccine-research.

Nature editorial board, "Curbing global warming could save US$20 trillion," *Nature* online (May 23, 2018).

Nelsen, Brent, and Alexander Stubb, *The European Union: Readings on the Theory and Practice of European Integration*, 4th ed. (Rienner, 2014).

New York Times, "Russell on preventive war" (December 3, 1961).

Nichols, David, *Eisenhower 1956: The President's Year of Crisis – Suez and the Brink of War* (Simon & Schuster, 2012).

Nielsen, Anne, Andrew Plantinga, and Ralph Alig, "New cost estimates for carbon sequestration through afforestation in the U.S.," General Technical Report PNW-GTR-888 (USDA Forest Service, March 2014).

Nietzsche, Friedrich, *Basic Writings of Nietzsche* (Modern Library, 2000).

Nilsson, Nils, *The Quest for Artificial Intelligence* (Cambridge, 2010).

Nilsson, Sten, and Wolfgang Schopfhauser, "The carbon sequestration potential of a global afforestation program," *Climatic Change* 30:3 (July 1995).

Nordhaus, Ted, and Michael Shellenberger, *Break Through: Why We Can't Leave Saving the Planet to Environmentalists* (Mariner, 2009).

Nordhaus, William, *Climate Casino: Risk, Uncertainty, and Economics for a Warming World* (Yale University Press, 2013).

"Integrated assessment models of climate change," *National Bureau of Economic Research, NBER Reporter* 2017, no. 3.

Nordvig, Jens, *The Fall of the Euro: Reinventing the Eurozone and the Future of Global Investing* (McGraw Hill, 2014).

Nourbakhsh, Illah, *Humans Need Not Apply: A Guide to Wealth and Work in the Age of Artificial Intelligence* (Yale University Press, 2015).

Noyce, Ryan S., Seth Lederman, and David H. Evans, "Construction of an infectious horsepox virus vaccine from chemically synthesized DNA fragments," *PLOS One* (January 19, 2018).

Nugent, Carrie, *Asteroid Hunters* (Ted Books / Simon & Schuster, 2017).

Nussbaum, Martha, *Creating Capabilities: The Human Development Approach* (Harvard, 2011).

Nye, David, *Technology Matters: Questions to Live With* (MIT, 2006).

O'Connor, Cailin, and James Weatherall, *The Misinformation Age: How False Beliefs Spread* (Yale University Press, 2020).

Oehlschlaeger, Fritz, *The Achievement of Wendell Berry: The Hard History of Love* (University of Kentucky, 2011).

Olsen, Jonathan, and John McCormick, *The European Union: Politics and Policies*, 6th ed. (Westview, 2016).

O'Mathuna, Donal, *Nanoethics: Big Ethical Issues with Small Technology* (Continuum, 2009).

Omohundro, Stephen, *"The Nature of Self-Improving Artificial Intelligence"* (Self-Aware Systems, 2008).

"The basic AI drives," at: https://selfawaresystems.files.wordpress.com/2008/0 1/ai_drives_final.pdf.

"Autonomous technology and the greater human good," *Journal of Experimental and Theoretical Artificial Intelligence* 26:3 (2014).

Ord, Toby, *The Precipice: Existential Risk and the Future of Humanity* (Hachette, 2020).

Oreskes, Naomi, "The scientific consensus on climate change," *Science* 306:5702 (December 2004).

Oreskes, Naomi, and Erik Conway, *Merchants of Doubt: How a Handful of Scientists Obscured the Truth on Issues from Tobacco Smoke to Global Warming* (Bloomsbury, 2010).

Organization for Economic Cooperation and Development, "Statistics on resource flows to developing countries" (OECD, updated December 22, 2017).

Orwell, George, *The Road to Wigan Pier* (Gollancz, 1937).

1984 (Signet, 1950).

Osterhammel, Jurgen, and Niels Petersson, *Globalization: A Short History* (Princeton University Press, 2009).

Ostrom, Elinor, *Governing the Commons: The Evolution of Institutions for Collective Action* (Cambridge University Press, 2015).

Otto, Shawn, *The War on Science* (Milkweed, 2016).

Overbye, Dennis, "Government seeks dismissal of end-of-world suit against collider," *New York Times* (June 27, 2008).

Overy, Richard, *Why the Allies Won* (Norton, 1997).

The Twilight Years: The Paradox of Britain Between the Wars (Penguin, 2009).

The Origins of the Second World War (Routledge, 2016).

Owen, Richard, John Bessant, and Maggy Heintz, eds., *Responsible Innovation: Managing the Responsible Emergence of Science and Innovation in Society* (Wiley, 2013).

Palazchenko, Pavel, *My Years with Gorbachev and Shevardnadze: The Memoir of a Soviet Interpreter* (Pennsylvania State University Press, 1997).

Page, Scott, *Complex Adaptive Systems: An Introduction to Computational Models of Social Life* (Princeton, 2007).

Panda, Ankit, "The uncertain future of the INF Treaty" (Council on Foreign Relations, February 21, 2018), at: www.cfr.org/backgrounder/uncertain-future-inf-treaty.

Papp, Daniel, Loch Johnson, and John Endicott, *American Foreign Policy: History, Politics, and Policy* (Pearson, 2004).

Pardo, R., C. Midden, and J. D. Miller, "Attitudes toward biotechnology in the European Union," *Journal of Biotechnology* 98:1 (September 11, 2002).

Parens, Erik, Josephine Johnston, and Jacob Moses, *Ethical Issues in Synthetic Biology: An Overview of the Debates* (Woodrow Wilson International Center for Scholars and Hastings Center, 2009).

Paris, Celia, "Breaking down bipartisanship: when and why citizens react to cooperation across party lines," *Public Opinion Quarterly* 81:2 (May 2017).

Parker, Randall, ed., *The Economics of the Great Depression: A Twenty-First Century Look Back at the Economics of the Interwar Era* (Edward Elgar, 2007).

Pedersen, Susan, *The Guardians: The League of Nations and the Crisis of Empire* (Oxford University Press, 2017).

Peplow, Mark, "Special Report: counting the dead," *Nature* 440 (April 1, 2006).

Perlroth, Nicole, *This Is How They Tell Me the World Ends: The Cyber-Weapons Arms Race* (Bloomsbury, 2021).

Persily, Nathaniel, ed., *Solutions to Political Polarization in America* (Cambridge University Press, 2015).

Peterson, Christopher, *A Primer in Positive Psychology* (Oxford, 2006).

Peterson, Christopher, and Martin Seligman, *Character Strengths and Virtues: A Handbook and Classification* (Oxford, 2004).

Peterson, James, *American Foreign Policy: Alliance Politics in a Century of War, 1914-2014* (Bloomsbury, 2014).

Peterson, Jeannie, *The Aftermath: The Human and Ecological Consequences of Nuclear War* (Pantheon, 1983).

Pfeiffer, Rolf, and Christian Scheier, eds., *Understanding Intelligence* (MIT, 1999).

Piketty, Thomas, *Capital in the Twenty-First Century*, trans. Arthur Goldhammer (Belknap, 2014).

Pimentel, Diego, Iñigo Aymar, and Max Lawson, "Reward work, not wealth," Oxfam Briefing Paper (Oxfam, January 2018).

Pincus, Walter, "New agreement on missile monitoring facility has elements of old plan," *Washington Post* (July 13, 2009).

Pinker, Steven, *The Blank Slate: The Modern Denial of Human Nature* (Penguin, 2003). *The Better Angels of Our Nature: Why Violence Has Declined* (Viking, 2011). "What do you think about machines that think?" *Edge.org* (2015). *Enlightenment Now: The Case for Reason, Science, Humanism, and Progress* (Viking, 2018).

Piot, Peter, *No Time to Lose: A Life in Pursuit of Deadly Viruses* (Norton, 2012).

Plesch, Dan, Kevin Miletic, and Tariq Rauf, eds., *Reintroducing Disarmament and Cooperative Security to the Toolbox of 21st Century Leaders* (Stockholm International Peace Research Institute, 2017).

Plokhy, Serhii, *Chernobyl: The History of a Nuclear Catastrophe* (Basic, 2018).

Pogge, Thomas, *World Poverty and Human Rights*, 2nd ed. (Polity, 2008).

Pool, Robert, *Beyond Engineering: How Society Shapes Technology* (Oxford University Press, 1997).

Poore, J., and T. Nemecek, "Reducing food's environmental impacts through producers and consumers," *Science* 360:6392 (June 1, 2018).

Porcar, Manuel, and Juli Pereto, *Synthetic Biology: From iGEM to the Artificial Cell* (Springer, 2014).

Posner, Eric, *The Twilight of Human Rights Law* (Oxford University Press, 2014).

Posner, Richard, *Catastrophe: Risk and Response* (Oxford University Press, 2004). "The 9/11 report: a dissent," *New York Times* (August 29, 2004).

Power, Samantha, *A Problem from Hell: America and the Age of Genocide* (Basic Books, 2002).

Preimesberger, Freya, "Researchers design flu virus breathalyzer," *The Daily Texan* (February 16, 2017).

Presidential Commission for the Study of Bioethical Issues, *New Directions: The Ethics of Synthetic Biology and Emerging Technologies* (Washington, D.C., 2010).

Price, Jeffrey, *Practical Aviation Security: Predicting and Preventing Future Threats*, 2nd ed. (Butterworth-Heinemann, 2013).

Price-Smith, Andrew, *Contagion and Chaos: Disease, Ecology, and National Security in the Era of Globalization* (MIT, 2009).

Priestley, Theo, "Does Elon Musk and OpenAI want to democratise or sanitise artificial intelligence?" *Forbes* (December 13, 2015).

Program for Public Consultation, University of Maryland, and Voice of the People, "A not so divided America" (2014), at: https://publicconsultation.org/wp-content/uploads/reports/Red_Blue_Report_Jul2014.pdf.

Puchala, Donald, *Theory and History in International Relations* (Routledge, 2003).

Purves, William, Gordon H. Orians, H. Craig Heller, and David E. Sadava, *Life: The Science of Biology*, 5th ed. (Freeman/Sinauer, 1998).

Quammen, David, *Spillover: Animal Infections and the Next Human Pandemic* (Norton, 2012).

Rahman, Redwanur and A. K. M. Kamruzzaman, *Impact of Climate Change on the Outbreak of Infectious Diseases* (Lap Lambert Academic Publishing, 2015).

Ramachandran, Gurumurthy, Susan M. Wolf, Jordan Paradise, et al., "Recommendations for oversight of nanotechnobiology," *Journal of Nanoparticle Research* 13:4 (2011).

Ramesh, Randeep, "Paradise almost lost; Maldives seek to buy a new homeland," *The Guardian* (November 9, 2008).

Randerson, James, "Revealed: the lax laws that could allow assembly of deadly virus DNA," *The Guardian* (June 14, 2006).

Rasch, Philip, Simone Tilmes, Richard P. Turco et al., "An overview of geoengineering of climate using stratospheric sulphate aerosols," *Philosophical Transactions of the Royal Society* (August 29, 2008).

Realmonte, Giulia, Laurent Drouet, Ajay Gambhir et al., "An inter-model assessment of the role of direct air capture in deep mitigation pathways," *Nature Communications* 10 (2019).

Reed, Stanley, and Jack Ewing, "Hydrogen is one answer to climate change. Getting it is the hard part," *New York Times* (July 13, 2021).

Reiss, Edward, *The Strategic Defense Initiative* (Cambridge University Press, 1992).

Remnick, David, *Lenin's Tomb: The Last Days of the Soviet Empire* (Vintage, 1994).

Reus-Smit, Christian, and Duncan Snidal, eds., *The Oxford Handbook of International Relations* (Oxford University Press, 2011).

Rhodes, Richard, *The Making of the Atomic Bomb* (Simon & Schuster, 1987).

Rifkin, Jeremy, *The Zero Marginal Cost Society: The Internet of Things, the Collaborative Commons, and the Eclipse of Capitalism* (Palgrave/Macmillan, 2014).

Ritchie, Hannah, "What are the safest and cleanest sources of energy?" *Our World in Data* (May 5, 2021), at: https://ourworldindata.org/safest-sources -of-energy.

Roberts, Adam, and Benedict Kingsbury, eds., *United Nations, Divided World: The UN's Role in International Relations*, 2nd ed. (Clarendon, 1994).

Roberts, J. M., and O. A. Westad, *The History of the World*, 6th ed. (Oxford, 2013).

Robinson, Kim Stanley, *The Ministry for the Future* (Orbit, 2020).

Robinson, Mary, *Climate Justice: Hope, Resilience, and the Fight for a Sustainable Future* (Bloomsbury, 2018).

Rodrik, Dani, *The Globalization Paradox: Democracy and the Future of the World Economy* (Norton, 2012).

Romm, Joseph, *Climate Change: What Everyone Needs to Know*, 2nd ed. (Oxford University Press, 2018).

Rose, Sonya, *Which People's War? National Identity and Citizenship in Wartime Britain, 1939–1945* (Oxford University Press, 2003).

Rosenau, James N., and Ernst-Otto Czempiel, eds., *Governance Without Government: Order and Change in World Politics* (Cambridge University Press, 1992).

Ross, Alec, *The Industries of the Future* (Simon & Schuster, 2017).

Rothman, Daniel, "Thresholds of catastrophe in the Earth system," *Science Advances* 3 (2017).

Rozell, Mark R., and Clyde Wilcox, *Federalism: A Very Short Introduction* (Oxford University Press, 2019).

Ruffini, Pierre-Bruno, *Science and Diplomacy: A New Dimension of International Relations* (Springer, 2017).

Russell, Rudolph, *Neural Networks: Easy Guide to Artificial Neural Networks* (CreateSpace, 2018).

Russell, Stuart, *Human Compatible: Artificial Intelligence and the Problem of Control* (Penguin, 2019).

Russell, Stuart, and Peter Norvig, *Artificial Intelligence: A Modern Approach*, 3rd ed. (Prentice Hall, 2010).

Rychlak, Joseph, *Artificial Intelligence and Human Reason: A Teleological Critique* (Columbia University Press, 1991).

Rychlak, Joseph, and Christian Scheier, eds., *Understanding Intelligence* (MIT, 1999).

Sachs, Jeffrey, *The End of Poverty: How We Can Make It Happen in Our Lifetime* (Penguin, 2005).

A New Foreign Policy: Beyond American Exceptionalism (Columbia University Press, 2018).

Sadowski, Jathan, "The much-needed and sane congressional office that Gingrich killed off and we need back," *The Atlantic* (October 26, 2012).

Sagan, Carl, *Pale Blue Dot* (Ballantine, 1997).

Sagan, Scott, and Kenneth Waltz, *The Spread of Nuclear Weapons: An Enduring Debate* (Norton, 2013).

Sainato, Michael, "Stephen Hawking, Elon Musk, and Bill Gates warn about artificial intelligence," *The Observer* (August 19, 2015).

Sakai, Jill, "Metabolic breathalyzer reveals early signs of disease," *University of Wisconsin-Madison News* (February 6, 2012).

Sakharov, Andrei, *Memoirs* (Knopf, 1990).

Sample, Ian, "'It's able to create knowledge itself': 'Google unveils AI that learns on its own," *The Guardian* (October 18, 2017).

Sanchez, Joan-Pau, and Colin McInnes, "Optimal sunshade configurations for space-based geoengineering near the Sun–Earth L1 point," *PLOS One* (August 26, 2015).

Sandberg, Anders, and Nick Bostrom, "Whole brain emulation: a roadmap," Technical Report #2008-3 (Future of Humanity Institute, Oxford University, 2008).

Sandler, Ronald, ed., *Ethics and Emerging Technologies* (Palgrave Macmillan, 2013).

Sanger, David, *The Perfect Weapon: War, Sabotage, and Fear in the Cyber Age* (Crown, 2018).

Sanger, David, and Eric Schmitt, "Biden signals break with Trump foreign policy in a wide-ranging State Dept. speech," *New York Times* (February 4, 2021).

Sanger, David, and Pranshu Verma, "The F.B.I. confirms that DarkSide, a ransomware group, was behind the hack of a major U.S. pipeline," *New York Times* (May 10, 2021).

Sanger, David, and William Broad, "To counter Russia, U.S. signals nuclear arms are back in a big way," *New York Times* (February 4, 2018).

Sapolsky, Robert, *Behave: The Biology of Humans at Our Best and Worst* (Penguin, 2018).

Sarotte, Elise, *1989: The Struggle to Create Post-Cold War Europe* (Princeton University Press, 2009).

Sasse, Ben, *Them: Why We Hate Each Other – and How to Heal* (St. Martin's, 2018).

Sato, Motoaki, "Thermochemistry of the formation of fossil fuels," *Geochemical Society Special Publication* No. 2 (1990).

Savage, Mike, "Changing social class identities in post-war Britain: perspectives from mass-observation," *Sociological Research Online* 12:3 (May 2007).

Sawyer, R. Keith, ed., *Social Emergence: Societies as Complex Systems* (Cambridge University Press, 2005).

Schabas, William, *An Introduction to the International Criminal Court*, 6th ed. (Cambridge University Press, 2020).

Scharre, Paul, *Army of None: Autonomous Weapons and the Future of War* (Norton, 2018).

Schell, Jonathan, *The Fate of the Earth* and *The Abolition* [combined volume] (Stanford University Press, 2000).

   The Unconquerable World: Power, Nonviolence, and the Will of the People (Metropolitan Books, 2003).

Schelling, Thomas, *Arms and Influence* (Yale University Press, 2008 [first published 1966]).

"A world without nuclear weapons?" *Daedalus* (Fall 2009).

Schelling, Thomas, and Morton Halperin, *Strategy and Arms Control* (Martino Fine, 2014).

Schmidt, Markus, "Xenobiology: a new form of life as the ultimate biosafety tool," *BioEssays* 32 (2010).

Schmidt, Markus, ed., *Synthetic Biology: Industrial and Environmental Applications* (Wiley-Blackwell, 2012).

Schnirring, Lisa, "Experts propose $2 billion global vaccine fund," *Center for Infectious Disease Research and Policy* (July 23, 2015).

Schwam, Stephanie, ed., *The Making of 2001: A Space Odyssey* (Modern Library, 2000).

Schwartzberg, Joseph, *Transforming the United Nations System: Designs for a Workable World* (United Nations University Press, 2013).

Sclove, Richard, *Reinventing Technology Assessment: A 21st Century Model* (W. Wilson International Center for Scholars, 2010).

Scott, James, *Against the Grain: A Deep History of the Earliest States* (Yale University Press, 2018).

Sebestyen, Victor, *Revolution 1989: The Fall of the Soviet Empire* (Vintage, 2009).

Seidensticker, Bob, *Future Hype: The Myths of Technology Change* (Berrett-Koehler, 2006).

Sejnowski, Terrence, *The Deep Learning Revolution* (MIT, 2018).

Sekera, June, and Andreas Lichtenberger, "Assessing carbon capture: public policy, science, and societal need," *Biophysical Economics and Sustainability* 5:14 (2020).

Sen, Amartya, *The Idea of Justice* (Belknap, 2009).

Service, Robert F., "Synthetic microbe lives with fewer than 500 genes," *Science* (March 24, 2016).

"Cost plunges for capturing carbon dioxide from the air," *Science* (June 7, 2018).

Service, Robert J., *The End of the Cold War: 1985–1991* (Public Affairs, 2015).

Sewell, William, *Logics of History: Social Theory and Social Transformation* (University of Chicago Press, 2005).

Shafir, Eldar, ed., *The Behavioral Foundations of Public Policy* (Princeton University Press, 2012).

Shafritz, Jay, and Albert Hyde, *Classics of Public Administration* (Cengage, 2016).

Shapin, Steven, and Simon Schaffer, *Leviathan and the Air-Pump: Hobbes, Boyle, and the Experimental Life* (Princeton University Press, 2017).

Shear, Michael, and Stephanie Saul, "Trump, in taped call, pressured Georgia official to 'find' votes to overturn election," *New York Times* (January 3, 2021).

Sheehan, James, *Where Have All the Soldiers Gone? The Transformation of Modern Europe* (Houghton Mifflin, 2008).

Shen, Alice, "How China hopes to play a leading role in developing next-generation nuclear reactors," *South China Morning Post* (January 10, 2019).

Shonting, David, and Cathy Ezrailson, *Chicxulub: The Impact and Tsunami* (Springer, 2017).

Shulman, Carl, *"Omohundro's 'Basic AI Drives' and Catastrophic Risks"* (The Singularity Institute, 2010).

Sides, John, "Most Americans live in Purple America, not Red or Blue America," *Washington Post* (November 12, 2013).

Siegel, Ethan, "Could the Large Hadron Collider make an Earth-killing black hole?" *Forbes* (March 11, 2016).

Sigrin, Benjamin, and Meghan Mooney, "Rooftop solar technical potential for low-to -moderate income households in the United States," Technical Report NREL/TP-6A20-70901 (National Renewable Energy Laboratory, April 2018).

Sikkink, Kathryn, *Evidence for Hope: Making Human Rights Work in the 21st Century* (Princeton University Press, 2017).

Silver, David, Thomas Hubert, Julian Schrittwieser, et al., "A general reinforcement learning algorithm that masters chess, shogi, and Go through self-play," *Science* 362:6419 (December 7, 2018).

Sinclair, Timothy, *Global Governance* (Polity, 2012).

Singer, Donald, and Ronald Upton, *Guidelines for Laboratory Quality Auditing* (CRC Press, 1992).

Singer, Peter, *One World Now: The Ethics of Globalization* (Yale University Press, 2016).

Singer, P. W., *Wired for War: The Robotics Revolution and Conflict in the 21st Century* (Penguin, 2009).

Singer, P. W., and Allan Friedman, *Cybersecurity and Cyberwar: What Everyone Needs to Know* (Oxford University Press, 2014).

Slaughter, Ann-Marie, *A New World Order* (Princeton University Press, 2004).

Sloan, Stanley, *Defense of the West: NATO, The European Union, and the Transatlantic Bargain* (Manchester University Press, 2016).

Sluga, Glenda, *Internationalism in the Age of Nationalism* (University of Pennsylvania Press, 2015).

Smalley, Richard, "Of chemistry, love, and nanobots," *Scientific American* (September 2001).

Smil, Vaclav, *Energy and Civilization: A History* (MIT, 2017).

Smith, Adam, *The Wealth of Nations* (Simon and Brown, 2012 [first published 1776]).

Smith, Anthony, *Nationalism: Theory, Ideology, History* (Polity, 2010).

Smith, Christian, *What Is a Person? Rethinking Humanity, Social Life, and the Moral Good from the Person Up* (University of Chicago Press, 2010).

Smith, Simon, ed., *Reassessing Suez 1956: New Perspectives on the Crisis and Its Aftermath* (Routledge, 2016).

Snowe, Olympia, *Fighting for Common Ground: How We Can Fix the Stalemate in Congress* (Weinstein Books, 2013).

Soares, Nate, "The value learning problem," presented at 25th International Joint Conference on Artificial Intelligence (New York, 2016), at: https://intelli gence.org/files/ValueLearningProblem.pdf.

Soares, Nate, and Benya Fallenstein, "Agent foundations for aligning machine intelligence with human interests: a technical research agenda," Report 2014–8 (Machine Intelligence Research Institute, 2014).

Solomon, Fred, and Robert Marston, eds., *The Medical Implications of Nuclear War* (National Academies Press, 1986).

Solomon, Lewis, *Synthetic Biology: Science, Business, and Policy* (Transaction, 2012).

Song, Jean, "Bill Gates on how to outsmart global epidemics," *CBS News online* (January 18, 2017).

Soros, George, and Gregor Schmitz, *The Tragedy of the European Union: Disintegration or Revival?* (Public Affairs, 2014).

Sotala, Kaj, and Roman Yampolskiy, "Responses to catastrophic AGI risk: a survey," Technical Report 2013–2 (Machine Intelligence Research Institute, 2015).

Sovacool, Benjamin, *Contesting the Future of Nuclear Power: A Critical Global Assessment of Atomic Energy* (World Scientific, 2011).

Sowers, Jeannie, Avner Vengosh, and Erika Weinthal, "Climate change, water resources, and the politics of adaptation in the Middle East and North Africa," *Climatic Change* 104 (2011).

Spalding, Robert, *Stealth War* (Penguin Random House, 2019).

Spindlove, Jeremy, and Clifford Simonsen, *Terrorism Today: The Past, the Players, the Future*, 5th ed. (Pearson, 2013).

Springs, Jason, *Healthy Conflict in Contemporary American Society: From Enemy to Adversary* (Cambridge University Press, 2018).

Staub, Ervin, *The Roots of Evil: The Origins of Genocide and Other Group Violence* (Cambridge University Press, 1989).

Steel, Brent, ed., *Science and Politics: An A-to-Z Guide to Issues and Controversies* (CQ Press, 2014).

Stephenson, Neal, *The Diamond Age* (Bantam, 2000).

Stern, Paul, Thomas Dietz, Troy Abel, Gregory A. Guagnano and Linda Kalof, "A value-belief-norm theory of support for social movements: the case of environmentalism," *Human Ecology Review* 6:2 (Winter 1999).

Sterrett, Dave, *Aborting Aristotle: Examining the Fatal Fallacies in the Abortion Debate* (St. Augustine's Press, 2015).

Stiglitz, Joseph, *The Euro: How a Common Currency Threatens the Future of Europe* (Norton, 2016).

Stock, Gregory, *Redesigning Humans: Choosing Our Genes, Changing Our Future* (Mariner, 2003).

Stockholm International Peace Research Institute, *SIPRI Yearbook 2017: Armaments, Disarmament, and International Security* (SIPRI, 2017), at: https://www.sipri.org /sites/default/files/2017-09/yb17-summary-eng.pdf.

Stockholm International Peace Research Institute, *SIPRI Yearbook 2020: Armaments, Disarmament, and International Security* (SIPRI, 2020), at: https://www.sipri.org /sites/default/files/YB20%2010%20WNF.pdf.

Stoessinger, John, *Why Nations Go to War*, 11th ed. (Wadsworth, 2010).

Stoler, Mark, *Allies and Adversaries: The Joint Chiefs of Staff, the Grand Alliance, and U.S. Strategy in World War II* (University of North Carolina Press, 2003).

Strogatz, Steven, "One giant step for a chess-playing machine," *New York Times* (December 26, 2018).

Sunstein, Cass, *Laws of Fear: Beyond the Precautionary Principle* (Cambridge University Press, 2005).

Going to Extremes: How Like Minds Unite and Divide (Oxford University Press, 2009).

Simpler: The Future of Government (Simon & Schuster, 2013).

#Republic: Divided Democracy in the Age of Social Media (Princeton University Press, 2018).

How Change Happens (MIT Press, 2019).

Sutton, Victoria, *Biosecurity Law and Policy* (Vargas, 2014).

Svetlana, Savranskaya, "New sources on the role of Soviet submarines in the Cuban Missile Crisis," *Journal of Strategic Studies*, 28:2 (2005).

Swan, Jonathan, "Trump's budget calls for major boost to nukes," *Axios* (February 9, 2020).

Sweet, William, *Climate Diplomacy from Rio to Paris: The Effort to Contain Global Warming* (Yale University Press, 2016).

Talbott, Strobe, *Endgame: The Inside Story of SALT II* (HarperCollins, 1980).

Taleb, Nassim, *The Black Swan: The Impact of the Highly Improbable* (Random House, 2007).

Talisse, Robert, *Democracy and Moral Conflict* (Cambridge University Press, 2009).

Taubman, Philip, *The Partnership: Five Cold Warriors and Their Quest to Ban the Bomb* (Harper, 2012).

Tavoni, Massimo, and Robert Socolow, "Modeling meets science and technology: an introduction to a special issue on negative emissions," *Climatic Change* 118 (2013).

Taylor, A .J. P., *English History, 1914–1945* (Oxford University Press, 1965).

The Struggle for Mastery in Europe, 1848-1918 (Oxford University Press, 1980).

Taylor, T. L., *Play Between Worlds: Exploring Online Game Culture* (MIT, 2009).

Tegmark, Max, *Life 3.0: Being Human in the Age of Artificial Intelligence* (Knopf, 2017).

Terkel, Stud, *'The Good War:' An Oral History of World War II* (Pantheon, 1984).

"The Empire Strikes Back," cover story, *Newsweek* (April 19, 1982).

Thompson, Edward, *The Poverty of Theory and Other Essays* (Monthly Review Press, 1978).

The Heavy Dancers (Merlin Press, 1985).

Thornton, Chuck, "US–Russia proposed joint data exchange center: a historical compilation," *Scribd* (September 2009).

Thucydides, *The Peloponnesian War* (Oxford University Press, 2009).

Thurber, James, and Antoine Yoshinaka, eds., *American Gridlock: The Sources, Character and Impact of Political Polarization* (Cambridge University Press, 2015).

Tiersky, Ronald, and Erik Jones, eds., *Europe Today: A Twenty-First Century Introduction*, 5th ed. (Rowman & Littlefield, 2014).

Tollefson, Jeff, "Sucking carbon dioxide from air is cheaper than scientists thought," *Nature* 558 (June 7, 2018).

Tokarska, Katarzyna, and Kirsten Zickfeld, "The effectiveness of net negative carbon emissions in reversing anthropogenic climate change," *Environmental Research Letters* 10 (September 10, 2015).

Toke, Dave, *The Politics of GM Food* (Routledge, 2004).

Tomasky, Michael, *If We Can Keep It: How the Republic Collapsed and How It Might Be Saved* (Liveright, 2019).

Tononi, Giulio, *Phi: A Voyage from the Brain to the Soul* (Pantheon, 2012).

Townsend, Charles, *Terrorism: A Very Short Introduction* (Oxford University Press, 2018).

Trafton, Ann, "Rewiring cells: how a handful of MIT electrical engineers pioneered synthetic biology," *MIT Technology Review* (April 19, 2011).

Trakimavicius, Lukas, "Is Russia violating the biological weapons convention?" *Atlantic Council website* (May 23, 2018).

Treisman, Rachel, "California program giving $500 no-string-attached stipends pays off, study finds," *National Public Radio* (March 4, 2021).

Trotta, Daniel, "Iraq war costs US more than $2 trillion," *Reuters* (March 14, 2013).

Tucker, Jonathan, *War of Nerves: Chemical Warfare from World War I to Al-Qaeda* (Anchor, 2006).

Tucker, Jonathan, ed., *Innovation, Dual Use, and Security* (MIT, 2012).

Tucker, Robert, and Raymond Zilinskas, "The promise and peril of synthetic biology," *The New Atlantis* 12 (Spring 2006).

Tumpey, Terrence M., Christopher F. Basler, Patricia V. Aguilar, et al., "Characterization of the reconstructed 1918 Spanish influenza pandemic virus," *Science* 310:5745 (October 7, 2005).

Turkle, Sherry, *Alone Together: Why We Expect More from Technology and Less From Each Other* (Basic, 2011).

Turner, Barry, *Suez 1956: The Inside Story of the First Oil War* (Hodder & Stoughton, 2007).

The Berlin Airlift: A New History of the Cold War's Decisive Relief Operation (Icon, 2017).

Ugarriza, Juan, and Didier Caluwaerts, eds., *Democratic Deliberation in Deeply Divided Societies: From Conflict to Common Ground* (Palgrave Macmillan, 2014).

United Nations, "General Assembly approves $3 billion UN budget for 2020," *UN News* (December 27, 2019), at: https://news.un.org/en/story/2019/12/1054431.

United Nations Department of Economic and Social Affairs, "World population projected to reach 9.8 billion in 2050 and 11.2 billion in 2100" (June 21, 2017).

Union of Concerned Scientists, "Close calls with nuclear weapons," Fact Sheet (January 2015), at: https://www.ucsusa.org/sites/default/files/attach/2015/04/Close%20Calls%20with%20Nuclear%20Weapons.pdf.

"Each country's share of CO_2 emissions," at: https://www.ucsusa.org/global-warming/science-and-impacts/science/each-countrys-share-of-co2.html.

United States Government General Accounting Office, *Inspectors General: Department of Defense IG Peer Reviews* (US GAO, 2011).

Urge-Vorsatz, Diana, et al., "Measuring the co-benefits of climate change mitigation," *Annual Review of Environment and Resources* 39 (2014).

Urquhart, Brian, *A Life in Peace and War* (Norton, 1991).

Hammarskjold (Norton, 1994).

Urry, Lisa, Michael Cain, Steven Wasserman, Peter Minorsky, and Jane Reece, *Campbell Biology*, 11th ed. (Pearson, 2016).

US Energy Information Administration, "A look at the U.S. commercial building stock," (March 4, 2015), at: https://www.eia.gov/consumption/commercial/reports/2012/buildstock/.

Vandenbergh, Michael, "Order without social norms: how personal norm activation can protect the environment," *Northwestern University Law Review* 99:3 (2004–2005).

Vandenbergh, Michael, and Jonathan Gilligan, *Beyond Politics: The Private Governance Response to Climate Change* (Cambridge University Press, 2017).

Van den Bossche, Peter, and Werner Zdouc, *The Law and Policy of the World Trade Organization: Text, Cases, and Materials*, 4th ed. (Cambridge University Press, 2017).

Van der Linden, Sander, Anthony Leiserowitz, Seth Rosenthal, and Edward Maibach, "Inoculating the public against misinformation about climate change," *Global Challenges* 1:2 (2017).

Van Eijndhoven, Josée, "Technology assessment: product or process?" *Technological Forecasting and Social Change* 54:2–3 (1997).

Vanian, Jonathan, "Four big takeaways from Satya Nadella's talk at Microsoft Build," *Fortune* (May 7, 2018).

Van Parijs, Philippe, and Yannick Vanderborght, *Basic Income: A Radical Proposal for a Free Society and a Sane Economy* (Harvard University Press, 2017).

Victor, David, *Global Warming Gridlock: Creating More Effective Strategies for Protecting the Planet* (Cambridge University Press, 2011).

Volti, Rudi, *Society and Technological Change*, 8th ed. (Worth Publishers, 2017).

Vogel, Kathleen, *Phantom Menace or Looming Danger? A New Framework for Assessing Bioweapons Threats* (Johns Hopkins University Press, 2013).

Von Mering, Sabine, and Timothy McCarty, *Right-Wing Radicalism Today: Perspectives from Europe and the US* (Routledge, 2013).

Wade, Nicholas, *A World Beyond Healing: The Prologue and Aftermath of Nuclear War* (Norton, 1987).

"Scientists seek ban on method of editing the human genome," *New York Times* (March 19, 2015).

Wagner, Gernot, and Martin Weitzman, *Climate Shock: The Economic Consequences of a Hotter Planet* (Princeton University Press, 2015).

Wall Street Journal Staff, "Trump's Georgia call: listen to the audio and read a full transcript: President urged Georgia Secretary of State Brad Raffensperger to overturn the state's victory for President-elect Joe Biden," *Wall Street Journal* (January 3, 2021).

Wall, Don, "National Building Code to include climate change obligations," *Daily Commercial News* (December 20, 2018).

Wallace-Wells, David, *The Uninhabitable Earth: Life After Warming* (Tim Duggan Books, 2019).

Wallach, Wendell, *A Dangerous Master: How to Keep Technology from Slipping Beyond Our Control* (Basic, 2015).

Wallach, Wendell, and Colin Allen, *Moral Machines: Teaching Robots Right from Wrong* (Oxford University Press Scholarship Online, 2009).

Walsh, Bryan, "The world is not ready for the next pandemic," *Time* (May 4, 2017).

Waltz, Kenneth, *Man, the State, and War* (Columbia University Press, 2001).

Theory of International Politics (Waveland Press, 2010).

Weart, Spencer, *The Discovery of Global Warming*, 2nd ed. (Harvard University Press, 2008).

Weber, Eugen, *Peasants into Frenchmen: The Modernization of Rural France, 1870–1914* (Stanford University Press, 1976).

Weinberg, Leonard, *Right-Wing Violence in the Western World Since World War II* (World Scientific Publishing, 2021).

Weinberg, Leonard, and Susanne Martin, *The Role of Terrorism in Twenty-First Century Warfare* (Manchester University Press, 2016).

Weiss, Thomas, *What's Wrong with the United Nations and How to Fix It*, 3rd ed. (Polity, 2016).

Weiss, Thomas, and Rorden Wilkinson, eds., *International Organization and Global Governance* (Routledge, 2014).

Weiss, Thomas, and Sam Daws, eds., *The Oxford Handbook of the United Nations*, 2nd ed. (Oxford University Press, 2018).

Welch, Craig, "Climate change pushing tropical diseases toward Arctic," *National Geographic* (June 14, 2017).

West, Geoffrey, *Scale: The Universal Laws of Life, Growth, and Death in Organisms, Cities, and Companies* (Penguin, 2018).

Westad, Odd, *The Cold War: A World History* (Basic, 2017).

Wexler, Celia, "Bring back the OTA," *New York Times* (May 28, 2015).

Whelan, Charles, *The Centrist Manifesto* (Norton, 2013).

White House, "The Recovery Act made the largest single investment in clean energy in history, driving the deployment of clean energy, promoting energy efficiency, and supporting manufacturing," Fact Sheet (The White House, Office of the Press Secretary, February 25, 2016).

Whiteside, Kerry, *Precautionary Politics: Principle and Practice in Confronting Environmental Risk* (MIT, 2006).

Wiener, Antje, Tanja Borzel, and Thomas Risse, eds., *European Integration Theory*, 3rd ed. (Oxford University Press, 2009).

Wiener, Jonathan, "The Tragedy of the Uncommons: on the politics of apocalypse," *Global Policy* 7:1 (May 2016).

Wilks, Yorick, "Will there be superintelligence and would it hate us?" *AI Magazine* 38:4 (Winter 2017).

Williams, James, Benjamin Haley, Ryan Jones, *Policy Implications of Deep Decarbonization in the United States* (Energy and Environmental Economics, Institute for Sustainable Development and International Relations, and Deep Decarbonization Pathways Project, 2015).

Williams, Robert, and Paul Viotti, *Arms Control: History, Theory, and Policy* (Praeger, 2012).

Williams, Sam, *Arguing AI: The Battle for 21st Century Science* (AtRandom Books, 2002).

Wilson, James, *Bureaucracy: What Government Agencies Do and Why They Do It* (Basic, 1991).

Wittner, Lawrence, *Confronting the Bomb: A Short History of the World Nuclear Disarmament Movement* (Stanford University Press, 2009).

Toward Nuclear Abolition: A History of the World Nuclear Disarmament Movement (Stanford University Press, 2003).

Wohlsen, Marcus, *Biopunk: DIY Scientists Hack the Software of Life* (Current, 2011).

Wolfe, Nathan, "How to prevent a pandemic," *Edge* (April 30, 2009).

The Viral Storm: The Dawn of a New Pandemic Age (Times Books, 2011).

Wood, David, *Deep Time, Dark Times: On Being Geologically Human* (Fordham University Press, 2019).

Wood, Houston, *Current Debates in Peace and Conflict Studies* (Oxford University Press, 2017).

World Health Organization, "WHO Strategic Action Plan for pandemic influenza" (WHO, 2007) at: http://www.who.int/csr/resources/publications/influ enza/StregPlanEPR_GIP_2006_2.pdf.

World Institute for Nuclear Security, "The journey beyond 2016: WINS strategy and goals" (2015).

World Nuclear Association, "Nuclear power in China" (April 2019).

Wuthnow, Robert, *Be Very Afraid: The Cultural Response to Terror, Pandemics, Environmental Devastation, Nuclear Annihilation, and Other Threats* (Oxford University Press, 2010).

Yampolskiy, Roman, *Artificial Superintelligence: A Futuristic Approach* (CRC Press, 2016).

Yang, Andrew, *The War on Normal People: The Truth About America's Disappearing Jobs and Why Universal Basic Income Is Our Future* (Hachette, 2018).

Yergin, Daniel, *The New Map: Energy, Climate, and the Clash of Nations* (Penguin, 2020).

York, Herbert, and Sanford Lakoff, *A Shield in Space? Technology, Politics, and the Strategic Defense Initiative* (University of California Press, 1989).

Young, Robert, *Postcolonialism: A Very Short Introduction* (Oxford University Press, 2003).

Yudkowsky, Eliezer, "A reply to Francois Chollet on intelligence explosion" (Machine Intelligence Research Institute, 2017), at: https://intelligence.org /2017/12/06/chollet/.

"Complex value systems are required to realize valuable futures" (Machine Intelligence Research Institute, 2011), at: http://intelligence.org/files/Com plexValues.pdf.

Zantovsky, Michael, *Havel: A Life* (Grove, 2014).

Zilinskas, Raymond, "The Soviet biological weapons program and its legacy in today's Russia," Center for the Study of Weapons of Mass Destruction, Occasional Paper 11 (National Defense University Press, 2016).

Zimdars, Melissa, and Kembrew McLeod, eds., *Fake News: Understanding Media and Misinformation in the Digital Age* (MIT Press, 2020).

Index